'Of the thousands of historians who h  and its
abolition, only a handful have ever gi̶ on that
vast subject ... Robin Blackburn is ̶ among
those few ... *The American Crucible* ̶ ̶ture as
well as a bold reappraisal of the historicaı pası.

Stephen Howe, *Independent*

'Blackburn describes emancipation in all its vexed, indeterminate grandeur,
propelled by violent clashes, public debate, harrowing exposés, and the consolidation of new notions of freedom and equality.'

Greg Grandin, *Guardian*

'The book is an outstanding example of a major trend in recent historical writing: looking beyond national boundaries in favor of Atlantic or transnational
history.'

Eric Foner, *Nation*

'The best treatment of slavery in the western hemisphere I know of. I think it
should establish itself as a permanent pillar of the literature.'

Eric Hobsbawm

'Robin Blackburn has already secured his position as Britain's pre-eminent
historian of slavery. This new volume confirms that position. It is an important
contribution to our understanding of the shaping of the modern western world.'

James Walvin, *BBC History Magazine*

'Blackburn writes authoritatively across centuries and continents.'

Joseph P. Reidy, *Journal of American History*

'Blackburn describes and stakes a position on a number of the most contested
issues in the history of slavery.'

Alan Singer, *Encounter*

'A marvellous book – insightful and stimulating.'

Stanley Engerman, University of Rochester

'A magisterial history of transatlantic slavery.'

Ian Thomson, *Times Literary Supplement*

ROBIN BLACKBURN is the author of *The Making of New World Slavery: From the Baroque to the Modern, 1492–1800* and *The Overthrow of Colonial Slavery, 1776–1848*. He teaches at the University of Essex in the United Kingdom, where he holds a Leverhulme research award, and was Visiting Distinguished Professor at the New School for Social Research in New York from 2001 to 2010. He is a contributor to *New Left Review* and a member of its editorial committee.

The American Crucible

SLAVERY, EMANCIPATION AND HUMAN RIGHTS

Robin Blackburn

VERSO

London • New York

For Honor Elizabeth

This paperback edition first published by Verso 2013
© Robin Blackburn 2011, 2013

1 3 5 7 9 10 8 6 4 2

Verso
UK: 6 Meard Street, London W1F 0EG
US: 20 Jay Street, Suite 1010, Brooklyn, NY 11201
www.versobooks.com

Verso is the imprint of New Left Books

ISBN-13: 978-1-78168-106-0

British Library Cataloguing in Publication Data
A catalogue record for this book is available from the British Library

Library of Congress Cataloging-in-Publication Data
A catalog record for this book is available from the Library of Congress

Typeset in Minon Pro by Hewer Text UK Ltd, Edinburgh
Printed in the US by Maple Vail

Contents

Acknowledgements

Thanking the many people who have helped me in the writing of this book is extraordinarily difficult as my research of the topic spans nearly three decades. I am particularly grateful to Perry Anderson, who once again read the manuscript in its entirety and made a host of valuable suggestions. Stanley Engerman also read the whole book and saved me from serious mistakes. Both found quite a lot to disagree with and thereby helped me to reformulate my argument – but not necessarily in ways that they will approve. Others read parts of the manuscript and I am grateful for their help, particularly John Ashworth, Matthias Röhrig Assunção, John Clegg, Laurent Dubois, James Ingham, Jeremy Krikler, Bruce Levine, Manisha Sinha and Christopher Schmidt-Nowara. I have taught courses on slavery and anti-slavery at the University of Essex in the UK and the New School for Social Research in New York. I am most grateful for the lively discussions with students that often ensued. As for innumerable conversations with colleagues, I know I have learnt a lot without being able to cite precise names and dates. I owe a special debt to Dale Tomich, Ricardo Salles, Rafael Bivar Marquese and the other members of the 'Second Slavery' Research Network. I have greatly benefited from attending their meetings. I would like to thank Lisabeth During and Ross Poole for hospitality, and stimulating conversations, in Brooklyn. I thank Lorna Scott Fox for her superb copy-editing, saving me from many infelicities. Finally I acknowledge a Leverhulme fellowship that enabled me to complete the book.

Robin Blackburn
London, January 2011

TABLE 1. SLAVE POPULATION OF THE AMERICAS

Year	Leading Regions	Number	Main Occupations
1550	Spanish America	7,000	domestic, artisan
1600	Brazil	130,000	domestic, sugar
1700	Caribbean	300,000	sugar, tobacco
1770	Caribbean and Brazil North America	2,340,000	sugar, coffee tobacco
1815	US, Caribbean, Brazil	3,000,000	sugar, cotton
1860	US, Brazil, Cuba	6,000,000	cotton, sugar
1870	Brazil, Cuba	2,000,000	sugar, coffee
1888		none	

TABLE 2. SLAVE-RELATED ATLANTIC TRADE, INCLUDING RE-EXPORTS

£ millions	1720	1750–60	1796–1800	1820	1860
Slaves	0.8	1.8	2.4	3.5	1.0
Sugar	1.8	6.5	12.3	17.5	26.0
Gold	1.5	2.5	0.6	0.1	
Tobacco	0.4	1.0	1.0	1.3	2.5
Cotton	0.1	0.2	8.2	9.0	38.4
Coffee	0.1	2.8	8.3	9.2	10.1
Other	0.2	0.4	1.0	2.0	1.5
Total	4.9	15.2	33.2	42.5	79.5

SOURCES These are my own rough and ready estimates based on combining a variety of sources, chiefly Michael Mulhall, *Dictionary of Statistics*; Manuel Moreno Fraginals, *El Ingenio*, Havana 1977, vol. 3; Alfred H. Conrad and John R. Meyer, 'The Economics of Slavery in the Antebellum South', in Robert W. Fogel and Stanley L. Engerman, eds., *The Reinterpretation of American Economic History*, New York 1971, pp. 342–61; Roberto Simonsen, *Historia Economica do Brasil*, Sao Paulo 1977.

Introduction: Slavery and the West

The conquest and colonization of the New World by the early modern European states was a decisive step in the global 'rise of the West'. The gold and silver which obsessed the conquistadors were just a beginning. America was vast and fertile, and its peoples had domesticated and developed a tempting array of foodstuffs and intoxicants. European traders and colonial officials were able to throw the rich produce of the American cornucopia into what was now – for the first time – a truly global balance of exchanges. Great toil was required to wrest precious metals from the earth, to construct fortified imperial lines of communication, and to cultivate and process such premium products as sugar and tobacco, cotton and indigo. The European conquerors and settlers soon learned how to reinforce and multiply their own efforts by introducing African captives, and using them to strengthen empire and boost the output of the coveted export staples. These processes had their roots in Europe's own needs and desires, and in the emergence of a new political economy – a new type of state, a new class of merchant and a new type of producer and consumer. The Absolutist state and the early capitalist economy drove a process of imperial and commercial expansion which soon overstretched the labour power available to it. The introduction of millions of Africans, and their subjection to a hugely demanding regime of racialized slavery, was seized upon as the solution to the problem. Between 1500 and 1820 African migrants to the New World outnumbered European migrants by four to one.

The Atlantic slave trade and the slave systems it served met resistance from the captives and troubled a few observers, but aroused no public controversy until the last decades of the eighteenth century. During the first century or so after Cortés's arrival, the conquest and enslavement of native peoples, with its tens of millions of victims, constituted one of the great disasters of human history: the number of victims is exceeded only by the total losses of the Second World War. The 'destruction of the Indies' eventually aroused widespread condemnation and, as we shall see in the first chapter, led the Spanish royal authorities to discourage the outright enslavement of the indigenous population. Unfortunately, around the same time, they also licensed a trade in African captives to the New World. At first the sorts of work to which the slaves were put were various. They were domestics, gardeners, masons, carpenters, peddlers, and hairdressers, and some eventually managed to purchase their manumission. But this 'traditional' Mediterranean pattern of slavery gradually gave way to a new type of enterprise, the plantation, which was based on a great intensification of slave work and slave subjection. This institution was to have a career of nearly three centuries during which it was responsible for an extraordinary boom in output, and eventually for great changes in the power and prosperity of the West in relation to the rest of the world.

The present work considers the entire history of the enslavement of Africans and their descendants in the Americas, from the sixteenth to the nineteenth century, explaining why Europeans resorted to slavery and gave it a strongly racialized character. The book also explores the role of resistance and rebellion, abolitionism and class struggle, in the acts of emancipation which finally destroyed the New World slave systems from the 1780s to the 1880s. Slavery and abolition possess their own bibliographies, and are treated as almost separate fields of study. In previous books I have tried to close the gap. But the titles of those books – *The Making of New World Slavery* and *The Overthrow of Colonial Slavery* – show them to have a different focus. The temporal span of the present book is also much wider, since it includes the rise and fall of the new slave regimes of the nineteenth-century United States, Brazil and Cuba. The antebellum US South is sometimes taken to typify the slave order of the Americas but, despite some real parallels, it was very distinctive. The slave regimes were by-products, I will argue, of the rise of colonialism and capitalism, making it all the stranger that the ending of colonialism gave a further boost to slavery. The two leading slave powers of the nineteenth century, the United States and Brazil, had thrown off colonial rule and, together with the anomalous colony of Cuba, gave the slave systems a new lease of life.

Those interested in New World slavery and abolition are fortunate in having two recent overall studies by outstanding scholars upon these topics: *Inhuman Bondage*, by David Brion Davis, and *Abolition* by Seymour Drescher.[1] Like others working in this field, I have a great debt to these two writers. So why the need for another book? The topic is certainly large and complex enough to warrant a variety of approaches.

I focus more attention than Drescher on the plantations, on the consumer capitalism that summoned them into existence and how their extraordinary growth precipitated crisis and provoked slave resistance and nurtured planter rebellion. Whereas I argue that a series of sharp clashes linked to war, revolution and class struggle set the scene for anti-slavery and emancipation in the Americas, Drescher believes that revolutionary excesses led anti-slavery astray, and emphasizes the reformist and parliamentary path to emancipation; however, I believe that he is right to depict a fateful link between abolitionism and the emergence of a new 'public opinion'.

David Brion Davis has written a brilliant study of *The Problem of Slavery in the Age of Revolution* (1975) which, rightly in my view, situates British

---

1 David Brion Davis, *Inhuman Bondage: The Rise and Fall of Slavery in the New World*, Oxford 2007, and Seymour Drescher, *Abolition: A History of Slavery and Antislavery*, Cambridge 2009. Another valuable work is worth signalling: Robert William Fogel, *Without Consent or Contract: The Rise and Fall of American Slavery*, New York 1989, though the focus here is very much on North America, an informative chapter on British abolition being the main exception.

abolitionism in the context of the Revolutionary age. In his recent book he has more on how slavery worked on the ground – in the plantations – than Drescher. However, Davis devotes less space than I do to slavery and anti-slavery in the Iberian world. Another difference in emphasis relates to the economic significance of slavery. I believe that the slave-based commerce of the Atlantic zone made a large contribution to industrialization, furnishing capital, markets and raw materials, tempting consumers with new drugs and stimulants, and adapting to the 'steam age' with remarkable facility. Davis offers a mixed verdict, as when he writes: 'the expansion of the slave plantation system . . . contributed significantly to Europe's, and also America's economic growth. But economic historians have wholly disproved the narrower proposition that the slave trade or even the plantation system as a whole created a major share of the capital that financed the Industrial Revolution.'[2] In Chapter 4 I offer evidence for reaching a stronger conclusion than this.

While Drescher has rightly resisted interpretations of abolition that reduce it to economic interest, I argue that abolitionist movements were intimately linked to the stresses and strains of the industrial revolution.

I shamelessly borrow from these authors where I believe that they have got it right, but my concern is with what was newly forged in the crucible of the Americas, whether it was a more intensely racialized slavery or a reformulated 'rights of man'. My emphasis throughout is on how slavery and abolition in the Americas as a whole were linked to the overall evolution of society, culture and economy in and beyond the Atlantic world – to the functioning of the European monarchies, to the differences between Protestant and Catholic, Iberian and Anglo-Dutch colonialism, to the rise of capitalism, to the succession of revolutions on both sides of the Atlantic, to the colonial racial order and what followed, to industrialization and the logic of Great Power rivalry, and to the emergence of new social values and social rights in the African diaspora and in momentous national and class struggles. (I would have liked to offer a fuller account of the tremendous impact on Africa of the Atlantic slave trade, but that will have to remain a task for another time.)

For nearly 400 years, struggles over slavery were of the greatest importance in the Atlantic region and yet they take place, as it were, offstage. The award to Britain of the *asiento* – the right to supply slaves to South America – by the Treaty of Utrecht in 1714 was one of the rare occasions when it might seem that the Great Powers took some notice; but even this was misleading, since the main story at that time was the hugely larger – and minimally regulated – trade in slaves to the English and French colonies, and to Portuguese Brazil. In my view the emergence and growth of capitalism was very much part of the problem, and not, as some recent accounts would have it, part of the solution. The

---

2 Davis, *Inhuman Bondage*, p. 241.

destruction of slavery, like its initial spread and growth, was a by-product of such central events in the Atlantic world as the American and French Revolutions, British industrialization, the Napoleonic Wars, the Spanish American revolutions, the US Civil War, the rise and fall of the Brazilian Empire, and Cuba's protracted struggle for independence.

The possibility of assessing the contribution of Atlantic history to world history has been greatly boosted by the advance of research and by debates over which models best explain the pattern of events, especially since it is only recently that research had established such basic information as the size of the Atlantic slave trade. There is still unevenness in the literature available on slavery and abolition in the different regions of the New World – but a wave of recent publications, many in Spanish, French and Portuguese, is beginning to change this and assisted me in broadening my account.

The advance of abolition has been central to national historiography in the Atlantic world, and it has typically been couched in celebratory mode. Important protagonists of this history were often neglected, and the sometimes bitter fruits of emancipation were ignored. Descendants of slaves – among them W. E. B. Du Bois, C. L. R. James and Eric Williams – have made a major contribution to supplying a more balanced assessment. In *The American Crucible* I seek to evaluate the controversies their work has aroused. Because of the size and value of the slave systems, and because of conflicts over the future of slavery, the New World became a crucible of new nations, values, institutions and identities. The clashes generated by racial slavery, and the new complexities of commercial and industrial capitalism, gave birth to an age of revolutions and rival conceptions of modernity. While general histories have rightly studied the novel aspirations fostered by the American and French Revolutions, they have too often failed properly to register the contribution of Haiti and Spanish America in extending and re-working the doctrine of the 'rights of man and of the citizen'. African agency and the counterculture of the freed people helped to shape emancipation in major ways, in a pattern that crisscrossed the Atlantic. At the limit, as I hope to show, the new class struggles of the industrial-plantation order put in question the prevailing forms of racial domination and capital accumulation. Unfortunately the achievements of emancipation were limited, checked or even reversed by the weaknesses and divisions of the anti-slavery movements when they were put to the test of success. Racial oppression and inequality took new forms. However, such outcomes were contested, as we will see, and thus contributed to reshaping political programmes and the appeal to basic rights.

The role of both slave revolt and natural rights doctrines in the destruction of slavery has given rise to new controversies. João Pedro Marques argues that abolitionism, especially British abolitionism, should be once again given the entire credit for ending New World slavery, and that the contribution of slave resistance and revolt was minimal and has been greatly exaggerated.[3] In contrast to the account I offer in this book, Marques insists that the world of abolitionism and that of the Haitian Revolution 'do not make part of the same series' since the deliberate action of a parliamentary body is quite distinct from an elemental upsurge of revolt. (However, Marques does make an exception for the revival of British abolitionism in 1804, the year of Haiti's founding). While Drescher and Marques do not agree on all points they share the view that Haiti made a largely negative contribution – it was a horror story – while British abolition was the real saviour of the enslaved.

The Haitian Revolution suppressed slavery three or four decades before the British managed to do so. Some recent authors have seen this as an early triumph for the idea of the 'rights of man' or even 'human rights'.[4] So long as anachronism is avoided I find merit in this idea. However, Samuel Moyn sounds a warning when he writes: 'Of all the glaring confusions in the search for "precursors" of human rights, one must have pride of place. Far from being sources of appeal that transcended state and nation, the rights asserted in early modern revolutions and championed thereafter were central to the construction of state and nation, and led nowhere beyond until very recently.'[5] Exception made of the seven words of the concluding subordinate clause, I very much agree with this and supply many examples of state formation and nationalism frustrating or distorting abolition. I also insist that both slaves and abolitionists could be inspired by values not couched in terms of rights. But the historical record simply does not bear out the claim that struggles against slavery inspired by appeals to natural rights 'led nowhere'. I will pursue this disagreement later in the book and will here simply register, firstly, that the controversy over the contribution of rights is a useful one (as is that over the role of slave revolt), and that Moyn himself may make an exception for anti-slavery, since in a review of Lynn Hunt's *Inventing Human Rights* he does concede that it might be 'worth pondering in what ways the campaign to abolish slavery . . . anticipated contemporary human rights movements.'[6]

While this is not a short book, it is shorter than either of its two predecessors yet covers twice the ground. I do not have space here for the detailed narrative of the *Making* or the *Overthrow*, but I do reconsider their conclusions in the light of fresh evidence and argument.

---

3 João Pedro Marques, 'Slave Revolts and the Abolition of Slavery', in Seymour Drescher and Pieter Emmer, eds, *Who Abolished Slavery?* New York and Oxford 2010, pp. 3–92. I have a response in the same volume (pp. 169–78).

4 Laurent Dubois, *Avengers of the New World: The Story of the Haitian Revolution*, Cambridge, MA, 2004, and Lynn Hunt, *Inventing Human Rights, A History*, New York 2007.

5 Samuel Moyn, *The Last Utopia: Human Rights in History*, Cambridge, MA, 2010, p. 12.

6 Samuel Moyn, 'The Genealogy of Morals', *The Nation*, 29 March 2007. He goes on to say that such 'practices' as 'international mobilization, information gathering, public shaming and so forth' might form elements of a common repertoire.

The larger the slave systems grew, the greater the scope and significance of their eventual overthrow. The first abolitionist victories closed particular territories to the slave traffic, or even banned slavery itself, but the surge of slave output continued and, down to 1860, the numbers of slaves and value of the crops produced by them continued to rise decade by decade, as can be seen in Table 1. When Karl Marx described the momentum of accumulation as having the character of a juggernaut – the war-chariot of the Indian god of destruction ploughing over the bodies of his victims – the image captured the implacable advance of the slave-based Atlantic economy. Yet the Atlantic boom also itself provoked a 'hydra-headed' popular response. Organized anti-slavery drew strength from a diversity of sources – class struggle, slave resistance, a belief in the superiority of 'free labour', the Patriot ideal of civic liberty and a new humanitarian doctrine. Nonetheless it is still necessary to ask why the revulsion from such extreme, large-scale, and officially sanctioned cruelty and exploitation was so belated and selective. The strongly racial character of New World slavery led anti-slavery movements to assert an ideal of human unity, yet the nations responsible for the great acts of emancipation soon abandoned the search for racial equality and allowed new forms of racial domination and colonialism. So the history of New World slavery throws up puzzles to explain – and, notwithstanding mixed results and incomplete achievements, the epic struggle against slavery still offers instruction and grounds for hope.

The rise of slavery in the New World was, to begin with, quite slow, with major growth taking place after 1700 on the basis of a model elaborated in the mid-seventeenth century. The slave population of the Americas reached its height as late as 1860.

The slave systems of the Americas exhibited several sorts of novelty. Europeans built slave systems overseas at a time when outright bondage was disappearing from Europe. Societies and polities claiming to embody a new spirit of virtue and liberty became the most successful practitioners of plantation slavery. Slaves became concentrated in plantations, in contrast to the varied pattern of traditional slavery. American slavery acquired a far stronger *racial* definition than Ancient or medieval slavery. How did consumer demand for exotic produce acquire such scale and force as to require the construction of thousands of slave plantations? Why were planters so passionate about their 'natural rights', and what was their role in the growth of free trade? Why did it take so long for opposition to slavery to surface in public debate, and how was it linked to colonial rebellion? Is the recent emphasis on slave resistance and slave revolt in the advance of anti-slavery exaggerated? What were the limitations of emancipation from above? To what extent did the witness, representations and struggles of slaves and former slaves correct such problems? Why did anti-slavery so often require a revolutionary crisis – or the threat of revolution – to make real headway? If plantation slavery helped to sustain industrialization, why was it so vulnerable in an industrial order? Why did racism thrive in the epoch of emancipation? What did abolitionism contribute to the development of a doctrine of 'human rights', and what does it teach us about how effective such standards can be?

Answers to some of these questions were offered in my previous books, but they are re-examined here with the benefit of further research and with respect to the whole trajectory of slavery in the Americas. As noted above, my main aim will be to bring together the history of slavery and that of abolition, and to do so over the whole span of slavery in the Americas – 1492 to 1888. My conclusions will still be somewhat preliminary and provisional, but at least they will try to address the contradictory impulses and outcomes at work throughout the hemisphere and during both the colonial and the post-colonial periods. I hope to show that the answers require a willingness to scrutinize the history of capitalism and of the social forces which it unleashed. They also require attention to a wider Atlantic and world history. National histories have furnished too narrow a setting for resolving the most important questions with regard to slavery's rise and fall, even though both shaped national identity itself. Twelve million captives were taken from Africa, and many millions of that continent's inhabitants were dispossessed and slaughtered.

From the standpoint of Atlantic and world history, the principles underlying the construction of individual, national, imperial and racial identities should be probed rather than taken for granted. Likewise, the forces making for a 'Great Confinement' of blacks in the Americas emanated from the rivalry of the Atlantic states and from an insatiable demand for exotic spices, drugs, dyes and foodstuffs that was the external consequence of a profound social transformation within Europe itself – the rise of capitalism. While what follows is the history of a peculiar social status, that history was not determined by events taking place wholly within the realm of status, but reflected economic and political imperatives and contradictions.

The slave regimes catered to consumerism and adapted steam-age technology. But American slavery was a modern adaptation of an ancient social institution which it will be convenient briefly to examine.

SLAVERY IN HUMAN HISTORY

If slavery has been ubiquitous in human history, fully fledged slave societies have been quite rare. Indeed Keith Hopkins, an Ancient historian, claims that there have only been five major slave societies known to history, each of which played their part in the history of the West: classical Greece, Ancient Rome, and the slave regimes of the colonial Caribbean, Brazil and the US South. In each of these cases, individually owned slaves were the labour force responsible for producing the bulk of the marketed surplus – of wheat, wine and olive oil in the Ancient world or of sugar, tobacco, cotton and coffee in the New World.[7] If we consider agricultural output as a whole, then small producers were important, but the owners of medium- and large-scale slave estates, and their backers, controlled the major revenue flows and were hence able to act as the leaders of society.[8] The singularity of the New World slave regimes is even greater, since they assigned slaves almost exclusively to menial occupations as field workers, miners or domestics, while in the Ancient world slaves discharged many roles – most of the officials who administered the empire, the *familia Caesaris*, were slaves, as were many tutors. While the slaves in Ancient Greece and Rome were seen as captive strangers they came from many ethnic backgrounds, and were not deemed to be of a special 'race' or colour.[9]

The earliest historical records give evidence that captives have been widely used as slaves. While many certainly carried out menial tasks, they did not constitute the main labour force, and they were used in a great variety of ways, for example as soldiers if they were men, and as concubines if women. The slave status could be transitional, a way of gradually accommodating and assimilating captive strangers as subordinates. Such slavery was often associated with a slave trade, since the trafficking of the slave to some relatively distant place helped to produce the slave condition. Captive neighbours could run away, so they were ransomed, killed or trafficked. In his outstanding survey of slavery in human history, Orlando Patterson has identified a large number of societies where slavery was of structural importance because central to military organization or the bolstering of a powerful lineage. Taking account of the few dozen cases he cites we can add to Hopkins's list of major slave societies.[10] Nevertheless by far the greater part of the slave societies listed by Patterson were either tributary to Graeco-Roman slavery, or were fostered by European empire and commerce, in the Americas, Africa and Asia. The exceptions include various Islamic states dominated by military slavery, and slave systems in Korea, the Celebes and among the Lolo people in China. Islamic rulers acquired European or African slaves, supposedly confining themselves to those who were infidels.

---

7   Keith Hopkins, *Conquerors and Slaves*, Cambridge 1978, pp. 9, 99.

8   In most periods the latifundists and large slave-owners exercised hegemony over the farmers and other small producers, but the latter were often important because of their numbers and actual or potential military significance. Ellen Meiksins Wood, *Peasant-Citizen and Slave: The Foundations of Athenian Democracy*, London 1989. Thus the slave population of Athens may not have been much more than a tenth of the total population, but slaves were nevertheless the critical labour force in the silver mines and on the larger estates. See Geoffrey de Ste Croix, *The Class Struggle in the Ancient Greek World: from the Archaic Age to the Arab Conquests*, London 1981, pp. 31–68.

9   Frank Snowden, *Blacks in Antiquity: Ethiopians and the Graeco-Roman Experience*, Boston, MA, 1972.

10   Orlando Patterson, *Slavery and Social Death*, Cambridge, MA, 1982, Appendix C, pp. 353–64.

There appear to have been the beginnings of slave plantations in Mesopotamia in the ninth century of the Christian calendar, but the great uprising of the Zanj seems to have put an end to this development.[11] While military slaves often played a key role in Islamic states – and individual slaves could rise to become Grand Viziers – there was no large-scale agricultural slavery. Islamic slave traders were meant not to enslave or traffic in fellow believers, a doctrine which the Christian world also adopted at the height of the early Islamic challenge to Christian Europe.[12]

Early hieroglyphs confirm the presence of slaves in the Ancient agrarian empires, sometimes attached to temples or palaces, but not as a principal labour force. The adoption of settled agriculture in fertile and well-watered areas made possible an alternative to outright enslavement in the shape of tribute, and tribute labour, extracted by an elite that could, as Michael Mann has explained, exploit a 'caging' effect.[13] Agriculture led to a massive increase in population density, so these settled communities did not have the option of abandoning their houses, pots, and fields, and returning to a hunter-gatherer existence. They were vulnerable to domination and exploitation by military and priestly elites, but not to thoroughgoing slavery. Elites could control the grain stores, and exact tribute, without incurring the difficult security demands of maintaining large numbers in absolute bondage.

Thus comparative anthropology reveals slaveholding to have been quite common in human societies, and more rarely to have been of structural importance to the ruling group. The Murdoch world sample of 800 societies showed slavery to be present in only 3 per cent of hunter-gatherer communities, 17 per cent of those with incipient agriculture, 34 per cent of those mainly devoted to fishing, 43 per cent of those practising systematic agriculture and 73 per cent of those engaged in pastoralism.[14] While there is a certain correlation between the presence of slaves and economic development, this is often because slaves were a type of 'consumption good', albeit as domestics, and not because they were vital to systems of production outside the home. The gang slavery of the Roman estate or American plantation was distinctive and unusual, though echoed in some prisons in the Americas, or on some colonial plantations in Africa and

11   Alexandre Popovic, *The Revolt of the African Slaves in Iraq*, Princeton, NJ, 1998, with an introduction by Henry Louis Gates.

12   Robin Blackburn, *The Making of New World Slavery: From the Baroque to the Modern*, London 1997, pp. 42–4.

13   Michael Mann, *The Sources of Social Power*, vol. 1, Cambridge 1986. Steven Mithen echoes the 'caging' argument in a review of *On Deep History and the Brain*, by Daniel L. Smail, in the *London Review of Books*, 24 January 2008.

14   See Jack Goody, 'Slavery in Time and Space', in James Watson, ed., *Asian and African Systems of Slavery*, Oxford 1980, pp. 16–44. I have a fuller discussion of comparative slavery in 'Slave Exploitation and the Elementary Structures of Enslavement', in M. L. Bush, ed., *Serfdom and Slavery: Studies in Legal Bondage*, London 1996, pp. 158–80.

Asia, after formal slavery had been declared illegal. Since slaves are potentially a means of production and actually economic property, it is not surprising that their numbers swell in highly commercialized societies – furnishing one clue as to why large-scale slavery marks the 'rise of the West'.

HUMAN UNITY AND SOCIAL DIVISION

But the slave trade, as we have seen, did not only have a purely economic logic. Wherever there was great political fragmentation and warfare there would be a problem of what to do with captives, enslavement being one possibility. However, supervising and controlling the captive was always difficult. Slave trades not only made escape difficult or impossible, they also removed actual and potential enemies and could be seen as more merciful than slaughter. The ransoming of captives seems to have been quite common but the society of origin would have to offer something of value in exchange for the prisoner, and to compensate for the fact that the prisoners' return would very likely strengthen a hostile neighbour. Of course, such calculations did not apply so strongly where there were cultural ties to the defeated. Aristotle urged that a civilized Greek would treat a defeated enemy with generosity. But he was thinking of fellow Greeks here, not barbarians. Likewise Leviticus urges that harsh bondage should not be imposed on fellow children of Israel, but should be reserved for outsiders.

Gabriel Herman sees a progressive softening of manners in the Greek evolution from the Homeric 'age of the heroes' to the later 'age of the citizen'. Aggression was tamed as the citizen was invited to resolve differences by resort to the law, and sources of antagonism were cathartically 'acted out' in sporting contests or in dramatic performance. Yet the pacification achieved by the emergence of a state of laws and 'civilization' was accompanied by a more sharply defined slavery: 'In the case of Ancient Greece this transition also involved certain unique social and technological advances such as the introduction of coinage and writing and the institution of chattel slavery and the phalanx . . .'[15] In Rome as well as Greece, enslavement is portrayed as a humane alternative to the slaughtering of captives, though since the demand for slaves created its own supply – slave-raiding wars and expeditions – this argument was self-serving. We should also be careful not to attribute the more attractive features of the Greek polis simply to the supposed ability of slaves to free the citizen from toil. There were many non-slaveholding citizens in the Greek city states and they helped to sustain the 'democratic' features of those states.[16]

---

15   Gabriel Herman, *Morality and Behaviour in Democratic Athens: A Social History*, Cambridge 2006, pp. 165–6. The author explains that he is following Moses Finley, and drawing, as I will do below, on Norbert Elias, *The Civilising Process*, Oxford 1998.

16   As is argued by Ellen Wood, *Peasant-Citizen and Slave*.

Moses Finley described the slave in Ancient society as 'an outsider', while Patterson defines the slave as 'natally alienated' and dishonoured.[17] In societies where kinship determined identity and honour, the slave was without kin or family – except as a permanently subordinate 'boy' or 'girl' within their master's household. They themselves might cherish family ties, but slave status meant that this had no meaning for the master, who would break up slave families if he found it necessary, or even just convenient. Refusing to recognize the slaves' family ties also allowed for their more intense exploitation, or for their sale. The slave was a 'speaking tool' and a piece of property, an economic asset and beast of burden masquerading as a human being.[18]

Slaves and enemy captives would be feared as 'others' liable to strike out at their captors if the opportunity arose. Fear of the slaves' unruly violence helped to unite all the free population against them, including those who did not own slaves. However, while the other could be thought of as dangerous and barbaric, this arose from awareness of a basic likeness. The slave was a threat not because they were intrinsically alien and different, but for the opposite reason. The enslaved person occupied the same ecological niche, was in competition for the same resources, and could be a sexual mate or rival. Ideologies and cosmologies of enslavement did their best to obfuscate these realities.

Anthony Pagden observes: 'The Hellenistic Greeks who bequeathed to modern Europe the concept of a single human species and the term with which to describe it – *anthropos*, Man – also bequeathed to us the first term capable of making a distinction within that species. The term was *barbaros*, "barbarian". And a barbarian was, before anything else, one who was a "babbler", one who spoke not Greek but only "barbar".'[19] The Greeks thought that all Persians or Egyptians were enslaved to their ruler. Aristotle developed the argument that some were 'natural slaves', a category that embraced those incapable of reasoning, who consequently led a life of pure sensation. Peter Garnsey explains: 'Aristotle "discovered" a body of people who would do nicely as "natural slaves". Slaves in Greece were mainly barbarians . . . Aristotle decided to designate them "natural slaves". This was . . . a popular choice if Aristotle is to be believed.

---

17   Moses Finley, 'Slavery', *International Encyclopedia of the Social Sciences*, 1968, and Patterson, *Slavery and Social Death*.

18   Slaves continually sought to assert family ties and to see themselves as more than just chattels, however difficult this was in a strong slave system. The relatively buoyant slave population of North America, as we will see, is partly to be explained by circumstances which encouraged slave women to have children. But the great surge of nineteenth-century plantation output in the US South was only made possible by a domestic slave trade that massively disrupted the slaves' attempt to build families. See Ira Berlin, *Generations of Captivity: A History of African American Captivity*, Cambridge, MA, 2003; Walter Johnson, *Soul by Soul: Life Inside the Antebellum Slave Market*, Cambridge, MA, 2000, and Walter Johnson, ed., *The Chattel Principle: Internal Slave Trades in the Americas*, Cambridge, MA, 2005.

19   Anthony Pagden, *European Encounters with the New World*, New Haven 1993, p. 120.

The Greeks, he says point-blank, prefer to use the term "slaves" only of barbarians.'[20]

In advancing his 'natural slaves' argument, Aristotle allows that others might question his conclusion. Beyond just a rhetorical device, this allusion to a critic might refer to Alcidamas who asserted around 370 BC that: 'God made all men free; Nature made none a slave.'[21] But there may have been implicit limits to this claim (e.g. it only referred to Greeks), and in any case Alcidamas was a follower of the sophist philosopher Georgias, who delighted in paradox ('Nothing exists and if it did we could not know it').

Hannah Arendt observed that the traditional Roman view was similar to the Greek: 'A human being or *homo* in the original meaning of the word indicates someone outside the range of the law and the body politic of the citizens, as for instance a slave.'[22] Later justifications of slavery by the Stoics broke at least with Aristotle's approach, if not with a pessimistic view of mankind. For them, being a slave was a matter of fate and even the most worthy might find themselves exposed to it. The condition of the slave might be wretched, but each should adjust to the role in life that fortune assigned them. Virtue lay in discharging one's role well, whether it be high or low. The early Christian approach was similar, but with the added considerations that all men were sinners, slavery was the punishment for sin, so slaves were lucky – they were expiating their sin in this world and would have better to look forward to hereafter.[23] In the later Roman Empire the numbers of field slaves declined, but there were still many slave domestics and assistants. The master could motivate the slave by holding out the prospect of eventual manumission. The act of emancipation could be likened to a minor's coming of age, and would still leave the freedman or woman with continuing obligations to the master, who would remain as some mixture of patron, landlord and employer. The social relations of enslavement remained so pervasive in late Antiquity that they were used to

---

20   Peter Garnsey, *Ideas of Slavery from Aristotle to Augustine*, Cambridge 1996, p. 126.

21   Benjamin Isaac, *The Invention of Racism in Classical Antiquity*, Princeton 2004, p. 173. This work documents the plethora of ethnic and proto-racial stereotypes entertained by the Greeks and Romans, but does not quite deliver on its title. The author concedes that in the later empire Roman citizenship was 'liberally bestowed'(p. 148). The multi-ethnic character of the Roman armies eventually produced a very mixed population, with many non-Latins able to claim citizenship. In 212 AD Roman citizenship was conceded to all free men by the Emperor Caracalla (himself a man of mixed Gallic, African and Syrian descent), but it now brought few gains to its possessors. In earlier times it did bestow real protections – against inquisitorial flogging, for example. By the late empire the position of the *humiliores* led them into dependency, but this was essentially a class position, not a racial status. See Ste. Croix, *The Class Struggles in the Ancient Greek World*, pp. 456–62. With fewer hauls of captives for sale in the later empire there was perhaps greater pressure to oppress those who were not enslaved. See Keith Bradley, *Slavery and Society at Rome*, Cambridge 1994, pp. 81–106.

22   Hannah Arendt, *On Revolution*, New York 1975, p. 107.

23   Garnsey, *Ideas of Slavery*, pp. 118–55, 206–142.

express essential spiritual truths. For St Augustine there was an apposition between bad slavery – which had its origin in sin – and good slavery, which was the faith that bound the believer to the Lord. While Christians saw themselves as slaves to Christ, the quite mundane reality of slavery as subordination to a fellow human remained. The Emperor Justinian's sixth-century Code summarized the legal principles of chattel slavery, furnishing a helpful reference point for slaveholders in the New World. But Justinian did not endorse the concept of 'natural slavery' nor associate the slave status with any ethnic group. Rather the fallen state of all mankind lessened the stigma of slavery.[24]

NOTES ON THE HISTORY OF CRUELTY

The belated modern rejection of colonial slavery began by questioning its utility, and repudiating its cruelty, in the second half of the eighteenth century. Slave-traders were despised, slave owners sometimes feared, and slave labour itself seen as limited and rigid. Such criticisms were combined with a new perception that slavery was cruel and inhumane.

In the Graeco-Roman world cruelty was, for the most part, projected externally. The Scythians, for example, were thought a particularly barbarous people and were held to practise cannibalism. The Roman games, later adopted in Greece, offered a spectacle of contained savagery and allowed the crowd, if it wished, to re-enact enslavement by pardoning the defeated. Ancient writers conveyed cruelty using such terms as *crudeliter* – those who are crude or raw – or *saevo*, echoed in the term savage. Any hint of slave insubordination was suppressed with great ferocity (though the term *ferocitas* would be applied to the victims, not the perpetrators). There were repeated slave revolts, but even the most famous – that of Spartacus – did not aim at a complete end to slavery. Perhaps the nearest the Ancient world came to a programme of general emancipation was the revolt of Aristonicus in the Greek kingdom of Pergamon in 132–129 BC. The kernel of this revolt was resistance to Roman rule, but it articulated a utopian vision which attracted support from both slave and free.

Seneca, the Stoic philosopher and servant of the Emperor Nero, was the author of one of the very few Ancient texts that recognized that the civilized could also be violent – for example when they made a spectacle of killing in the Roman games. Seneca also frowned on the abuse of slaves, but his attitude remained paternalist. He cited disapprovingly the Roman saying 'so many slaves, so many enemies', urging that masters would do better to treat them kindly. Seneca's criticism of the abuse of captives and slaves was to be

---

24 For slavery's decline in the Ancient world see Chris Wickham, *Framing the Early Middle Ages: Europe and the Mediterranean*, Oxford 2005, pp. 259–65, 277, 544. For Christianity see Michael Mann, *Sources of Social Power*, vol. 1, Cambridge 1987, pp. 301–40. And for the rediscovery of Justinian's laws, see Perry Anderson, *Lineages of the Absolutist State*, London 1975, p. 24.

rediscovered in the fifteenth and sixteenth centuries when it encouraged a new response to cruelty, seen as not exclusively a property of barbarians and heretics but also as an excess of civilized power itself.[25] Events in the New World were to feed this concern.

The later Stoics and early Christian fathers also deplored delight in violence, though Christian accounts of persecution came to stress their providential character. Echoing a tenet of Jewish faith, they held that the Lord sent tribulations to chastise or test his followers. The persecutions suffered by the early Christians were seen as a punishment just as their fortitude was seen as a proof of their righteousness. The individual slave was urged not to bemoan his misery but rather to see it as the price of sin.

The 'religions of the book' – Judaism, Christianity, Islam – all had a conception of human unity but were also riven by dualism between the 'chosen', the 'elect' and the 'faithful', on the one hand, and the unbelievers, the ungodly and the damned, on the other. While the latter were exposed to enslavement, they could be encouraged to believe that being a slave would actually promote their ultimate salvation. The idea of human unity was accompanied by the idea of the fallen condition of man, and of the original sin which condemned man to toil and woman to be the help-meet of man and to suffer the pain of childbirth.

Two Biblical stories were thought to furnish specific justification for enslavement. Because of his foolishness and immoderation Esau, son of Isaac, was set under the authority of Jacob, his wise younger brother. Likewise Noah condemns his grandson Canaan to be a slave to his brethren because Ham, Canaan's father, has insulted Noah. Christians liked the story of Esau being placed under the rule of Jacob because it showed that the older sometimes needed to be subordinated to the younger. The Jews might be the first-born, but they no longer had the virtue needed to inherit, which had passed to the Christians. Noah's curse was often applied to all the 'sons of Ham'.[26] These stories had a 'just so' logic that seemed to condone the idea of the derogation or enslavement of an entire descent group. This was not the same as modern racism, but in the early modern period such narratives could be mapped onto attitudes toward Jews and Africans, both of whom were seen as a species of natural slave.

In the Ancient Christian Church there was a redeeming aspect to the slave status, since Christians themselves chose to be 'slaves of Christ'. The early Christian Church had a special appeal to freedmen and women, that is, former slaves. In the conditions of the later empire such a condition was no bar to citizenship or dignity.[27] Thus the ideological legacy of the Ancient world was a

25   Daniel Baraz, *Medieval Cruelty: Changing Perspectives, Late Antiquity to the Early Modern Period*, Ithaca 2003, especially pp. 23–6, 29–46, 153–4.

26   Garnsey, *Ideas of Slavery from Aristotle to Augustine*, pp. 44–7, 163–76; Colin Kidd, *The Forging of Races*, Oxford 2006; Blackburn, *Making of New World Slavery*, pp. 64–75.

27   Dmittri Kyrtatis, *The Social Structure of the Early Christian Communities*, London

mixed and contradictory one: it recognized a common human identity, but compromised it by essential dualisms; it justified slavery as a necessary expiation in a sinful world, but also cherished emancipation.

During the European high Middle Ages, say from the eleventh to the fifteenth centuries, slavery steadily dwindled in north-western Europe while even in the Mediterranean Christian lands it survived on a mostly small, domestic scale. *Servus* – the Roman word for slave – persisted in the milder concept of 'servant', while the word 'slave' echoed the 'slav' ethnicity of most medieval slaves. If this development might appear benign, it was unfortunately accompanied by strident assertions of religious and cultural uniformity and a persecution of heretics, witches, Jews and lepers which was to cost the lives of tens of thousands.[28] The advent of the Reformation, and the subsequent cycle of religious wars, saw a ratcheting up of religious intolerance. These developments were ominous for those deemed heathens and savages who stood in the path of European expansion – or could be enlisted to strengthen it.

The conquest of the New World was so destructive – with tens of millions perishing through disease, overwork and dislocation – that it alarmed the Spanish king. A few brave friars warned that the greed of the Spanish colonists was depopulating his newly discovered lands, and giving rise to the heretical doctrine that the New World natives were not really men at all. Charles V eventually promulgated 'New Laws' in 1542 which sought to restrain the rapacity of the colonists, and to ban the enslavement of indigenous peoples. The first chapter considers these arguments and analyses the 'baroque' reorganization of Spanish colonialism in the sixteenth century. While royal protection was extended to the natives, slavery remained legitimate for persistent rebels and for Africans who had been legitimately purchased from the Portuguese. So, despite the worries of some clerics, there was no general rejection of slavery or the slave trade. The royal revenues were swelled by the sale of the *asiento*, that is, the right to introduce a specified number of African captives for sale as slaves in the Americas. So long as these slaves were introduced to the true faith, either on the African coast or upon arrival in the Americas, this was deemed legitimate bondage. While the ceremony of conversion could be a mockery, some clerics – notably Alonso Sandoval and Pedro Claver in early seventeenth-century Cartagena – took it very seriously, baptizing tens of thousands, employing native interpreters and repeatedly running the personal risk of entering the pestilential holds of the slave ships.[29]

1987; see also this author's review of *Freedom*, Vol. I, by Orlando Patterson: 'The Western Path to Freedom', *New Left Review* 197 (January–February 1993), pp. 85–95.

28   R. I. Moore, *The Formation of a Persecuting Society: Authority and Deviance in Western Europe, 950–1250*, Oxford 1987.

29   David Brading, *The First America: The Spanish Monarchy and the Liberal State, 1492–1867*, Cambridge 1991.

The violence of the Spanish conquest was great, so great that it shocked the Dominican priest Bartolomé de las Casas into a new way of looking at cruelty, as we will see. However, New World slavery was to remain unchallenged by philosophers and theologians down to the 1760s, as David Brion Davis argued in *The Problem of Slavery in Western Culture* (1965). One of the central aims of the present work is to explore and explain why and how the legitimacy of slavery was belatedly questioned and rejected.

SLAVERY'S NEW WORLD CLIMAX

By the mid-nineteenth century there were some 6 million slaves in the Americas, a number that probably equals, if not exceeds, the slave population of Roman Italy at the height of empire, around 100 BC to 100 AD. While Ancient slavery was present in the imperial metropolis, the slavery of the Americas developed on the colonial periphery, though eventually most of those colonies were to throw off metropolitan control. The slavery of the New World underpinned an oceanic commerce, and the resulting Atlantic boom for a while dominated European commercial exchanges. Struggles to control the profits of slavery loomed large in eighteenth-century colonial warfare and colonial rebellion, eventually giving openings to slave resistance and fostering the emergence of the anti-slavery idea.

Slaves were present in the New World from the early decades of European colonization up to the late 1880s. The slave plantations, worked by gang labour, powered the rise of the slave systems of the Americas and became hubs of Atlantic commerce. Altogether, some 12 million captives were purchased by European traders on the African coast. Nearly 2 million perished during or immediately after the 'Middle Passage' on the tightly-packed slave ships. Ten million Africans survived to be sold into slavery in the New World between 1500 and 1865. Because of heavy mortality on the plantations, slave numbers in the Caribbean and Brazil were only maintained and increased by a continual stream of new arrivals. In North America a lower death rate and higher birth rate led to a slave population that, by the 1750s or 1760s, was growing even without the new arrivals (reasons for this will be suggested in Chapter 3).

Between roughly 1500 and 1860 the plantation and mining slaves of the Americas toiled extraordinarily long hours to meet European consumers' craving for exotic luxuries. And in order to be able to purchase tobacco, sugar, cotton and coffee, salaried and waged workers subjected themselves to an 'industrious revolution' that, as we will see in Chapter 4, greatly boosted European productivity.

The New World slave regimes came to share some common features, and reflected some conscious borrowing and emulation. Yet at the same time the motive for resort to enslavement, and the pattern of race and slavery, varied.

The different Atlantic powers were locked in mortal combat, leading them to search out productive advantages and seek effective ways of mobilizing their populations. While the Spanish were the first to introduce large numbers of enslaved Africans, they did not employ them, as others were to do, as the producers of an export staple.

Western Europe had a common Latin Christian heritage but was split by the Reformation. It was divided into a plurality of more or less independent kingdoms, principalities, duchies and city states. Towns had considerable privileges and autonomy, even when they acknowledged the ultimate sovereignty of a monarch or emperor. This fragmentation was more conducive to trade than the structures of the great land empires. But this trade grew slowly. The rise of Islam and the fall of Byzantium limited the scope of the Mediterranean trades. The late medieval long-distance trade catered to the luxury tastes of a small elite of great lords and rich merchants. There were still sumptuary laws that prescribed the appropriate clothing of the different ranks of noble, cleric and commoner. But in parts of north-west Europe there were also the germs of a new social pattern based on cash, commodification and rising agricultural productivity. Long-distance trade was no longer solely dedicated to transporting tiny quantities of highly priced luxuries. The English exported woollen cloth and the Dutch built capacious trading vessels which transported such necessities as wheat and textiles from one part of Europe to another. A commercial society based on rent, wages and fees also widened demand for the 'new draperies' (brightly dyed cloth), for tobacco, and for a multitude of confections using sugar and spice. While the social elite could set a certain standard, the late sixteenth or early seventeenth centuries witnessed a burgeoning demand for popular luxuries and a new middle-class culture of consumption. The conquest and colonization of the New World, and new patterns of long-distance trade, are central to this story.

Each of the states that participated in Atlantic development from the sixteenth to the nineteenth centuries helped to shape the practice of colonization and enslavement, and adapt it to contemporary conditions. Likewise each state sought to channel Atlantic commerce. The Portuguese brought spices from the East, and the Spanish fleet the gold and silver of the New World. The seventeenth century saw a rising quantity of plantation goods produced by African slaves in the New World. The European domination of oceanic commerce was based on galleons and caravels whose edge over rivals stemmed from superior naval gunnery and navigation. Whereas only two or three galleons a year returned from the East with spices, the transatlantic plantation commerce soon required many hundreds of ships, and the European states who wished to police the trade had to build fleets of warships ('ships of the line').

Part I contrasts the role of slaves in the construction of the Spanish Empire with the escalating incarceration of slaves in plantations in, first, Brazil and, then, the colonies of the British and the French. An institution that had been marginal but ubiquitous in Mediterranean Europe became central to plantation agriculture in the Americas.

The supposedly sharp distinction between slavery and freedom in the modern world should not be projected back on late medieval Europe or the early modern period, where forms of personal dependence were still widespread and where there were only small pockets of slavery. The Spanish employed indigenous tribute labourers in the American silver mines while the English and French colonies were at first worked by European indentured servants or *engagés*, who were bound to work for those who purchased their contracts for a term of years. However, as the New World slave systems developed, these other forms of labour were often marginalized and the forced labour of enslaved Africans came into sharper focus. Two crucial institutions – the ocean-going sailing ship and the integrated, commodity-producing tropical or sub-tropical estate – made possible a seemingly limitless expansion. At first merchants and planters improvised, but soon rival colonial states entered the picture to channel and tax the resulting trades.

While Part I outlines the logic behind the growth of plantation colonies, Part II explores the consequences of the eighteenth-century Atlantic boom in slave produce. This boom prompted a challenge to European colonial mercantilism and the associated privileges and monarchies of the Old World. The slave-holding planters aspired to a proud independence. The eighteenth-century boom in plantation trades also proved conducive to the spread of industrial production. New textile and metal manufacturers drew on plantation supplies and found outlets in Africa and the New World. After 1776 an 'age of revolution' and industrialization once again reshaped the slave order and set up new strains and conflicts. The colonial elites were divided, and wider layers of the population brought into political life. European control of the Americas began to be dismantled, and – for the first time in an organized and public fashion – slavery was put in question. While the colonial rebels suspended the slave trade, the local representatives of the metropolis urged the slaves of rebel masters to run away.

The first mass abolitionist movement emerged in Britain in the 1780s in a context defined by colonial defeat, acts of slave witness, criticism of 'Old Corruption' (that of the Hanoverian oligarchy with its stake in colonial slavery), and the first combinations and conflicts of a new industrial order. While the emergence of popular and campaigning abolitionism was very significant, it failed to reach its goal during the first big surge, from 1788 to 1792. It was then thoroughly eclipsed by the panic unleashed in Britain by the radicalization of the French Revolution. Indeed, for a crucial period (1792–1804) the baton of anti-slavery passed to the 'black Jacobins' of Saint-Domingue and Haiti.

Part III looks at the pivotal role of the 'rights of man' and the Haitian

Revolution in these momentous events. The mid-eighteenth-century plantation boom had provoked colonial unrest and the beginnings of a widespread questioning of slavery. But it was not until the outbreak of a great slave rebellion in August 1791 in French Saint-Domingue that the system of the New World experienced a challenge it could not contain or suppress. In Chapter 8 I trace the emergence of the goal of 'general liberty' from the tangled struggles involving black rebels, treacherous planters, propertied men of colour, uncertain revolutionaries and outside interlopers. Between 1794 and 1804 the Spanish, the British and the French were each defeated by black insurgency. The defeat of Napoleon led to the proclamation of the Republic of Haiti in 1804, the first major breach in the systems of New World slavery.

While slavery proved difficult to sustain in the Caribbean, the slave order in the United States, Brazil and Cuba demonstrated great vitality in the decades after the advent of peace in 1815. Part IV examines the re-charged plantation slavery in these territories. Slave numbers and slave output rose steadily, despite peripheral victories for abolition in the smaller Caribbean islands and the wide spaces of Spanish South America. Slave-holding planters were initially able to dominate and lead the governments of the United States, Brazil and the Spanish Caribbean, but eventually slavery was to prove vulnerable even in its main mid-century bastion, the United States. Radical abolitionists were never more than a small minority. Given the great national importance of the plantation export trades, it is something of a puzzle how the 'slave power' came to be isolated and distrusted. The sources of anti-slavery are surveyed in Chapter 12, and the last emancipations recounted in Chapter 13. Growing sectional strife was rooted in slavery, but rival concepts of the nation played a major part in exacerbating the clash. Abolitionist agitation, planter paranoia and Yankee intransigence set the scene for a bloody civil war. Helped by pressure from fugitive slaves ('contrabands'), radical republicans and abolitionists, both black and white, Abraham Lincoln used his presidential war powers to issue the Emancipation Proclamation and press for a Thirteenth Amendment outlawing slavery. Despite the disappointing results of postwar Reconstruction, the remarkable events in the United States paved the way for 'free-womb' laws in Puerto Rico, Cuba and Brazil (these laws decreed that the children henceforth born to slave mothers would be free once they reached their mid-twenties). The planters of Cuba and Brazil contrived to squeeze more profit out of their remaining slaves for another two decades, but the authorities, confronting threats of insurgence and mass desertions, opted to wind up the oldest slave systems of the Americas in 1886 (Cuba)and 1888 (Brazil). The fourteenth chapter considers the chief results of emancipation throughout the hemisphere and beyond.

The slave order gave form everywhere to regimes of racial domination. In North America, not only were all slaves supposedly of the same race – one that to begin with the captives were barely aware of – but the great bulk of the slave-holders supposedly also belonged to one race. Though greatly disrupted by the Civil War and Reconstruction, the racial order of the United States was reorganized in the 1860s and 1870s in ways that made a mockery of the equal rights supposedly enshrined in the constitutional amendments that struck down slavery. Throughout the Americas, the persistence of reorganized regimes of racial oppression or exclusion was to compromise many of the gains of the anti-slavery movement. Yet the culture and traditions of the African diaspora in the New World were, in the long run, to prove even more tenacious and to combine in potent new ways with the life forms of indigenous peoples and a 'picaresque proletariat'.

THE THREE EPOCHS AND STYLES OF NEW WORLD SLAVERY

Given that my story extends over more than four centuries, and frequently reflects complex interactions, it will be helpful to offer a preliminary periodization. This will also allow me to challenge a chronology that projects back on the sixteenth century patterns that were not consolidated until much later, or which exaggerate the contribution of state monopoly and colonial mercantilism.

The first century of Spanish conquest gave rise to slaveries that contrast strongly with later developments. The terrible destructiveness of the Spanish colonists was eventually brought under more effective royal control. This led to the elaboration of novel ways of organizing native labour (to be explored in Chapter 1) which have a bearing on slave use – and also show that slavery was far from being the only, still less the best, answer to labour shortages. Outright slavery remained nevertheless, fed by the purchase of African slaves from Portuguese traders. The African slaves worked in the urban centres, and the number arriving each year after about 1570 exceeded new arrivals from Spain itself. But the scale of slave imports to the Americas was still modest compared with later volumes. As can be seen from Table 1, the spread of plantations in the mid- and late seventeenth century led to a scale jump. While some 3,000 new African slaves a year were sold to Spanish Americans in the period 1550 to 1650, by the early eighteenth century the English and French plantation colonies were buying 30–40,000 slaves each year, a figure that often reached 100,000 a year towards the century's end.

The Spanish and Portuguese use of African slaves was heavily influenced by medieval, Mediterranean and Roman legacies. The captives themselves had their own views on how they should be treated, and were sometimes able to strike a bargain that was not completely unilateral. There were thousands of African slaves in Seville and the Canary Islands, just as there were in Lisbon and Madeira, by the time of the conquest of the Americas. In the Peninsula they mainly worked as domestics or artisans' assistants. On the Atlantic islands some worked on sugar estates, a pattern that was tried in the Caribbean with little success at first. However, in the late sixteenth and early seventeenth century, the *senhores de engenho* (sugar mill lords) of Brazil came into contact with wider markets and began to purchase slaves on a greatly increased scale. The development was noted by the Dutch, English and French who set up their own sugar plantations in the Caribbean. The new sugar plantations turned out to be more valuable than silver mines.

While emulating one another, the slave-holders of the main Atlantic states – Portugal, Spain, the Netherlands, England, France, and the United States – each enjoyed a moment of leadership, only to see it snatched from them. At the level of events their fortunes were determined by the outcome of conquest, colonization, war, revolution and economic competition. But such conflicts themselves helped to test and forge new structures and mentalities characteristic of modernity. In the early decades of colonization – the 1510s to 1530s in Spanish America, the 1620s to 1640s in the English and French Caribbean – the weakness of the colonial state in the Americas left huge scope to the colonists. Miners and *encomenderos*, planters and ship's captains, enjoyed great freedom of action, and it was to be in that moment that slave-based enterprises first appeared. The earlier settler communities also nourished a proto-racial identity. But the colonists' neglect of the interests of metropolis and native alike called forth an immediately following epoch of market regulation, taking the form of tighter colonial legislation – Spain's 'New Laws' of the 1540s, Britain's Navigation Acts of 1651 and 1660 and France's *Code Noir* of 1685. A similar 'double movement' of market expansion and regulation was noted by Karl Polanyi in *The Great Transformation* (1944) and *Dahomey and the Slave Trade* (1964), the former dealing with the nineteenth and twentieth centuries, the latter with Dahomey in the seventeenth and eighteenth centuries.[30]

The three epochs of New World slavery were: 1) the household and ancillary slavery of the early Iberian phase of colonization, 2) the colonial mercantilist plantation slavery of seventeenth-century Brazil, Barbados, Saint-Domingue and Virginia, and 3) the era of independent American slavery led by the United States and Brazil, but also involving the strange colony of Cuba – a colonial tail that often wagged the metropolitan dog. These epochs embraced three styles of slavery – the baroque, linked to silver and gold (1500–1650); the mercantile, linked to sugar and tobacco (1650–1800); and the industrial, linked to cotton and coffee (1800–88). Epochs overlap somewhat, and styles mingle, but the differences remain significant within a broader evolution. The first two epochs were systems of colonial slavery, while the third coincided with the retreat of empire and the rise of independent polities within which the planters were well represented.

During the *baroque period* the thirst for silver and gold stemmed from

30   Karl Polanyi, *The Great Transformation: The Political and Economic Origins of Our Times*, London 1944, and *Dahomey and the Slave Trade: An Archaic Economy*, London 1965.

the need to finance dynastic wars, on the one hand, and to finance European purchases of oriental spices, on the other. The subsequent *mercantile era* was marked by the rising importance of the plantation trades and the attempts of rival Atlantic powers to monopolize them. Catering to the consumer tastes of those with money in their pockets or purses had become far more gainful that trying to capture or divert the bullion trade. Finally, the *industrial epoch* saw a slavery freed from colonial dependence and yoked to mass demand and global markets, a slavery that was no longer confined to islands and coastal enclaves but which marched inland and took over great tracts of territory. Yet, however proud the slave-holders might be, at no point did the slave order stand by itself. In every phase it supplied a deficiency in a wider circuit of accumulation.

Thus African slavery was very much an ancillary, secondary source of labour during the baroque era and style which dominated the first century and a half of Spanish colonization. While over 330,000 African captives were sold to Spanish colonists from 1520 to 1650, they played a minimal role in the silver economy, which was seen by European rulers and strategists as the chief prize of colonial acquisition. So who dug the veins of silver and processed the ore? And what social relations made this possible? These questions are addressed in the first chapter.

As silver output boomed in the years 1560 to 1630 the silver fleet became increasingly vulnerable to privateers, and the cost of defending it rose. For most of the sixteenth century Europe's still modest demand for sugar was mainly met by the Atlantic islands – Madeira, the Canaries, the Cape Verde Islands, and São Tomé – where cane was grown and processed with the help of African slave labour. It was not until 1590–1610 that Brazil became a major producer, and it was not until the mid-seventeenth century that sugar and tobacco plantations began to flourish in parts of the Caribbean and, so far as tobacco was concerned, Virginia. By this time capitalism in north-west Europe was pushing wider groups of the population into a cash economy, and stimulating the demand for tobacco and sugar.

The planters and their mercantile sponsors at first sought to work their plantations with European labourers and captive Indians, but by the close of the seventeenth century the implacable and systematic toil of working the new plantations was undertaken almost exclusively by enslaved Africans. The 'plantation revolution' of the mid- to late seventeenth century was based on gang labour, terrifically long hours and a long-term investment in slave skills. This hugely demanding and intense labour regime was linked to a sharper racialization of slavery. The planter needed a labour force that was permanent, highly coordinated, predictable, skilled and regimented. Faced with the scarcity and reluctance of free workers they opted for buying African captives. The decisions of the planters and their backers were at first made without much reference to the guidance of metropolitan authorities. But the latter also found major advantages in the arrangement, as we will see.

Polanyi notes in his study of Dahomey that: 'An epochal event as specific as the invention of the steam engine by James Watt some 130 years later had happened in the Antilles – sugar cane had been introduced to Barbados in 1640. A dramatic transformation of Atlantic trade was set in motion.' Polanyi explains that Dahomey was destined to be greatly affected because it dominated a stretch of coastline favourable to maritime commerce with the interior, there being a gap in the dense tropical forest where the savannah met the sea:

> A shift in international economy had caused a tidal wave to cross the Atlantic and to hurl itself against a twenty-five-mile stretch of the West African coast. This was not the usual kind of exchange of goods which by its nature enriches the people who are engaged in it. The trade that within less than a century was to sweep millions of Africans from villages into slavery overseas was of a peculiar kind. It bore more similarity to the Black Death than to peaceful barter. The ruling strata of the white empires had been mesmerized by the prospect of great riches, if only they were able to provide a labour force for the rapidly spreading sugar plantations. The outcome was the modern slave trade.[31]

During the eighteenth-century 'mercantile' phase the extraordinary surge in plantation output was channelled by the European colonial systems, allowing metropolitan authorities, merchants, manufacturers and consumers to benefit from the forced labour of the slaves. So long as trade could be controlled, duties on tobacco and sugar swelled the receipts of the metropolitan treasuries, and merchants could prosper by selling slaves and marketing slave produce. But the Atlantic boom and the rivalries it engendered could not be contained by mercantilism and imperial rule. The everyday practice of contraband easily developed into principled contestation of metropolitan claims, starting with those colonial elites least dependent on metropolitan support and protection.

Between 1776 and 1825 European rule in the Americas was challenged first by planters and other colonists, and then by slaves and other members of the subaltern classes. While the former slaves of Haiti consolidated their freedom in 1804, slavery survived and flourished as new inland territories were opened up by planters in the United States, Brazil and Cuba. This was a massive wave of market expansion and it was to provoke attempts by society to curb and regulate it. Abolitionism was to be a major expression of this attempt to shield society from unbridled market forces.

---

31   Karl Polanyi, *Dahomey and the Slave Trade*, pp. 17–18.

TABLE 3. AFRICAN CAPTIVE ARRIVALS IN THOUSANDS

Period	Europe	Atlantic Islands	Spanish America	Brazil	British Islands	French Islands	North America	Dutch / Danish	Total
1451–1500	25	9							34
1501–50	20	54	13						87
1551–1600	4	28	63	50					145
1601–50	1	19	128	200	21	3			372
1651–1700		5	165	360	243	153	15	44	985
1701–60			280	950	620	650	170	289	2,959
1761–1810			329	1,020	735	1,060	360	142	3,646
1811–65			660	1,480					2,140
Total	50	115	1,662	4,060	1,619	1,866	545	475	10,368

SOURCES: Adapted from Herbert Klein, *The Atlantic Slave Trade*, Cambridge 1999, pp. 210–11. São Tomé is included under Atlantic Islands. The small Danish trade (47,000) is added to the Dutch trade (it was often Dutch-sponsored).

Table 2 clearly shows the acceleration of the slave traffic after 1650 and its apogee in the period 1750–1810. But the large volume of the trade in the period after 1810 is very striking, with more than 2 million slaves introduced to the New World notwithstanding British and US abolition in 1808 and treaties outlawing the trade between Britain and Spain, Portugal, Brazil and France.

The ending of colonial rule and rising demand boosted the power and wealth of the planters. In the United States and Brazil they were part of the ruling order. In Cuba (and Puerto Rico) Spanish rule survived, but the Cuban *sacarocracia* – a nexus of sugar planters and merchants – exercised great influence and commanded great wealth. This fuelled the last age of slave development in the Americas.

As I have suggested above, I hope to show that the slavery of the cotton plantations of the antebellum US South differed in crucial ways from the social and racial pattern seen in the earlier colonial and mercantile epoch. The advent of industrialism extended the scale and intensified the pace of plantation labour, a feature the US South shared with the new sugar plantations of Cuba and coffee plantations of Brazil. Yet there were also significant differences. Cuban and Brazilian slavery failed to match the growth of North American slave populations, which obviated the need for imports. While the planters of Cuba and Brazil still made large clandestine purchases of slaves from Atlantic traders, US plantation growth was fed by a sizeable domestic slave trade. Despite their prominence in the political structures of the Republic, the US planters faced a very demanding political challenge; they shared a territory and polity with an expansive industrial and agricultural order based on wage and family labour.

Around 1860 the planters of the United States, Cuba and Brazil were among the richest and most influential people in the world. But they had built on a deceptive and dangerous foundation. As will be seen in Part IV, the institution was brought down not because it had ceased to be productive and profitable, but by great political convulsions, class struggles and acts of resistance. I am here only able to offer very tentative interpretations of these momentous events. The present work remains a scouting expedition across this terrain. I hope to return to it with a rounded and substantial treatment before too long. Nevertheless certain conclusions are already possible.

In my previous books I give considerable space to Britain's innovative and leading role as a slave power prior to the American Revolution, and to the importance of British anti-slavery from the 1780s. In this work, British slavery and abolitionism still loom large but are treated rather more succinctly. The rise of capitalism and a distinctive bourgeois and industrial civilization in Britain play a key part in the argument, weaving in and out of several chapters, but without the detailed narrative supplied in earlier works. By contrast I retain a quite extended coverage of the Haitian Revolution. This decision reflects my belief that the British role has received much attention, and is well known, whereas the significance of the overturn in Haiti still needs to be stressed and explored.

Looking at the larger picture, the independence of the United States, the elimination of Saint-Domingue as a major producer, the virtual collapse of mercantilist restrictions and the British-based industrial revolution gave a huge boost to slavery wherever it remained legal in the New World in 1825–60. The triumph of the Haitian Revolution, the only successful large-scale slave revolt in history, and the sponsorship of abolitionism by Britain, the world's premier maritime and commercial power, represented a warning to some and an inspiration to others. But it was not until the ending of slavery in North America by the Thirteenth Amendment in 1865 that the prospect opened up of eradicating slavery throughout the hemisphere. Despite a powerful egalitarian challenge, racial oppression was often reconstructed on a new basis, but the foundering of racial slavery nevertheless represented a historic gain whose complex results are explored in the last chapter.

The story of slavery and emancipation in the New World has lent itself to falsely redemptive interpretations, most of which rely on what one might call the argument from latent virtue. Such accounts ruefully admit enslavement was largely condoned, rather than challenged, by Protestant Christianity, capitalism, 'English liberties' and American patriotism, with the escape clause that each of the above enclosed a latent anti-slavery message that in a few decades – or was that centuries? – would emerge into the light. The plea was that, properly understood, Protestantism, capitalism and patriotism were all in essence abolitionist. Once the initial paradox, irony and contradiction had been resolved, the comforting truth would be clear. Eric Williams – the Trinidadian leader and author of the classic *Capitalism and Slavery* (1944) – referred to a variant of this exculpatory view when he remarked that British historians often wrote as if their country had built up a flourishing system of slavery in order to have the satisfaction of suppressing it.[32]

The latent virtue argument is not merely complacent; it fails to identify what led some Christians, capitalists and patriots – not the majority, but a brave few – to start behaving and thinking in a quite different way. It also fails to identify what it was about the original Christianity, capitalism or patriotism that fitted so snugly with racial slavery. While I hope to be on guard against complacency, there is a genuine difficulty here. Christianity, the market and nationalism did play a part in both the rise and the fall of slavery in the New World. What I hope eventually to illuminate is what were the extra ingredients, and new conjunctures, that allowed slavery to be challenged and dismantled.

At its moments of success abolitionism brought together a strange alliance of religious radicals and radical patriots, black rebels and troubled members of the white elite, businessmen who aspired to be moral and working-class agitators. They were animated by appeals to righteous conduct and to the 'rights of man', the virtues of 'free labour' and responsible government. I explore how this discourse could be appropriated by the oppressed themselves or inspire the 'civilizing mission' of a new colonialism. The modern notion of 'human rights' is a twentieth-century invention, but it resonates with the anti-slavery tradition in important ways. Indeed the historic travails of anti-slavery have great relevance for a world where the conditions needed for human flourishing are too often sadly inadequate or entirely absent. It would be good to know that the right to such flourishing does not have to endure all the disappointments visited upon the former slaves and their descendants. The remarkable culture of the African diaspora offers a glimpse of the way that past suffering can inform, temper and invigorate.

---

32   Eric Williams, *Slavery and the British Historians*, London 1964.

Timeline of Slavery in the Americas

1833   British Slave Emancipation Law
1834   American Antislavery Society founded
1838   Britain ends 'apprenticeship'
1848   Second French Emancipation
1848   Danish slavery ended
1863   Lincoln's Emancipation Proclamation
1863   Slavery ended in Dutch Surinam
1865   US 13th Amendment ends slavery
1865   Morant Bay Rebellion, Jamaica
1868   Equal rights for freedmen in 14th Amendment
1868   Spanish queen ousted; Cubans rebel
1870   Moret Free Womb law in Spain
1871   Free Womb law in Brazil
1873   Slave emancipation in Puerto Rico
1877   Reconstruction in US South ends
1880   Emancipation law for Cuba
1886   *Patronato* in Cuba ended
1888   Emancipation in Brazil
1889   Overthrow of Brazilian monarchy

Part I

EMPIRES AND PLANTATIONS

CHAPTER ONE

The Spanish Conquest:
Destruction, Enslavement and the Baroque

Those who conquered the New World reworked and transformed European and African traditions of bondage. They also improvised in a situation in which they seemed to have virtually unlimited power over the conquered. The indigenous population was forced to supply extremely onerous labour services, but not formally reduced to the status of chattels. The royal authorities at first allowed the colonists to conscript indigenous labour with few controls. But this initial regime proved so destructive that it was eventually reorganized and the outright enslavement of the Indians banned. The status of slave was henceforth largely reserved for captive Africans, sold to the Spanish colonists by Portuguese traders. Tens of thousands of Africans were sold in Cartagena and other New World slave marts and it is sometimes assumed that, as a result, plantation slavery flourished in the Spanish Caribbean or that large numbers of Africans worked in the silver mines. There were, indeed, a few dozen sugar estates, but they did not thrive. And there were a few Africans in the Mexican mines but practically none in Upper Peru, since in both areas the main labour force was indigenous. For nearly a century most African slaves lived in cities, and the institutions which shaped their condition reflected slave-holding in late medieval Spain. The Spanish authorities were obsessed by gold and silver, and for them African slaves were a part of the effort to secure the New World as a providential economic lifeline.

In Spain as in Ancient Rome, the slave was property – a chattel – and the status of slavery was inherited from the mother. The Roman Christian practice of slave-holding, and the Biblical justifications for the enslavement of descent groups, made such ownership seem perfectly acceptable. Slavery helped the captive to become useful and saved them from their own waywardness and laziness. The Spanish practice of slavery drew on the teachings of St Isidore, the seventh-century Bishop of Seville. Isidore wrote compendious but fanciful studies of world history and the nations of mankind. He held that savage, brutish and strange-looking peoples had to be held in bondage for everyone's good. Isidore was the ornament of a highly repressive Visigoth regime that itself kept many in slavery and was soon toppled by an Islamic invasion. Nevertheless his memory was revered by Iberian Christians, especially those who prided themselves on being from Old Christian families, as compared to recent converts from Islam or Judaism. Isidore's severe precepts were softened somewhat by the *Siete Partidas*, the famous thirteenth-century legal code of a Castilian monarch,

Alfonso X 'the Wise'. This codification offered some paths out of slavery to the dutiful slave. He or she might be able to accumulate a *peculium*, or private stash, sufficient to buy their own manumission. Many African slaves in sixteenth-century Spanish America were hired out as skilled workers or allowed to ply a trade as peddlers, bakers or barbers, or in some other semi-autonomous occupation. Masters were further exhorted not to abuse their slaves. In theory a slave who had suffered abuse could ask the courts to be sold to another master, but, while contracts for manumission were common, forced sale was very rare.

The protracted Reconquest of the Peninsula, and Iberian forays down the African coast, involved both the frequent holding of captives for ransom and the acquisition of African slaves. Hence the presence of several thousand African slaves, already engaged as domestics and artisans, in Seville and Lisbon, or on the Atlantic islands, on the eve of the voyage of Columbus.[1] The Iberians had learnt how to extract sugar from cane from the sugar producers of the Levant – Cyprus, Candia, or Outre-Mer (Palestine) – who in turn had acquired this knowledge from the Arab world. Contrary to what is sometimes supposed, sugar was not produced on 'slave plantations' in the late medieval Mediterranean world. Though a few slaves may sometimes have been employed in grinding the cane, it was grown by peasants, and the sugar struck from the boiling cane juice by expert *maestros de azúcar*.[2]

The merchants of medieval Italy and Spain might own a few slaves, but these were usually urban domestics or craftsmen's assistants, and were as likely to be white as black. The very word 'slave' in most Western European languages came from Slav, since many slaves in late medieval Latin Christendom came from Eastern Europe. Latin Christians, like Ottoman Muslims, were not meant to enslave fellow believers, but both saw Orthodox Slavs or Bogomil heretics as fair game. Political fragmentation and in-fighting furnished the background to a slave trade in the British Isles prior to the Norman Conquest, in the Balkans prior to the spread and stabilization of Ottoman rule, and in West Africa in the early modern and modern epoch. As may be expected, the ethnic or religious identity – pagan, heathen, heretic, Angle, Slav, African – foisted upon the captive was not necessarily one that the victim would recognize.

The *Siete Partidas* allowed for the recognition of distinct Moorish and Jewish communities, so long as they paid their taxes and observed the regulations. Religious difference was enforced as well as tolerated. Christians, Jews and Muslims were forbidden from sharing meals together. The captive black

---

1   William D. Phillips, *Slavery From Roman Times to the Early Transatlantic Trade*, Manchester 1985, pp. 88–113.

2   William D. Phillips, 'Sugar in Iberia', in Stuart Schwartz, ed., *Tropical Babylons: Sugar and the Making of the Atlantic World, 1450–1650*, Chapel Hill and London 2004, pp. 27–41; Blackburn, *Making of New World Slavery*, pp. 31–94, 76–9.

Africans who were brought to the Peninsula in the fifteenth century were often willing to embrace Christianity, though this did not mean that they had necessarily abandoned all their former notions. The religious authorities were more concerned to root out Judaism and Islam than pagan beliefs. In 1492 the several thousand black African slaves in Seville and Lisbon were permitted to form their own Christian brotherhoods. African slavery was seen as a useful, if initially minor, element in the institutional repertoire of Christian reconquest and empire.

ABSOLUTISM AND PRECIOUS METALS

The quest to control land and people in the New World was at first driven by the thirst of European states for specie, and the drive of rival dynasties to aggrandize themselves, spread the faith and assert their destiny to be rulers of a new 'universal empire', embracing both Old World and New. Europe's dynastic wars, and the construction of Absolutist regimes with permanent armed forces, were hugely expensive undertakings. American silver supplied a fifth of Spanish royal revenues by the 1570s and in certain years much more, as it supplied the collateral for loans.[3]

Charles Tilly estimates that there were thirty-four wars in Europe involving leading states in the sixteenth century, and twenty-nine in the seventeenth century; these wars only lasted a year or two but accounted for 95 per cent of all years. A sense of the military pressures on the leading states is crudely indicated by the figures in Table 1.1 on the growing size of European armies – crude because size alone fails to convey the growth in the sophistication and expense of weaponry.

TABLE 1.1. MEN UNDER ARMS, WESTERN EUROPE 1500–1700 IN THOUSANDS			
	1500	1600	1700
Spain	20	200	50
France	18	80	400
England/Wales	25	30	292
Netherlands		0	100
SOURCE: Charles Tilly, *Coercion, Capital and European States*, Oxford 1992, p. 79.			

States needed specie to pay for the military, and European merchants also needed gold and silver to buy spices, silks and porcelain from the East. Demand for such exotic luxuries was growing in Europe, and European ships could acquire them in the East. However, there were no European products similarly

---

3   Perry Anderson, *Lineages of the Absolutist State*, London 1974, pp. 70–2.

in demand in Asian markets. Portuguese merchants needed gold and silver if they were to buy pepper, nutmeg and cloves. The Spanish galleon sent from Mexico to the Philippines each year also made its purchases there in silver. When other European merchants began to compete with the Portuguese in the Indian Ocean they, too, needed silver or gold, though sometimes they could earn a little by trading between different eastern ports. Much of the specie mined in the New World eventually served to balance Europe's trade with the East. Italian, Iberian and Flemish merchants also discovered that the sugar craved by European consumers could be grown on the Atlantic islands or in Brazil. Not only were the journey times shorter but, by directly sponsoring sugar estates in the Canary or Cape Verde Islands, the merchants acquired a direct access to producers which often eluded them in the Indian Ocean. The Caribbean also had extensive salt pans and was the source of such new treats as cocoa beans and tobacco. But sugar estates required heavy investments in cane planting, draft animals and equipment – the mill and coppers. Warfare and piracy made the Caribbean a very insecure environment.

The Newfoundland fisheries and the North American fur trade further boosted the maritime exploitation of the New World. But for at least a century the main focus of the European efforts was precious metals – tobacco did not appear as a cash crop until the early seventeenth century, and the quantities of sugar produced in the New World remained very modest. Gold and silver could be directly used to further imperial aims, albeit requiring the construction of an elaborate mining and transportation complex.

The expansion of Christendom into the Baltic or Andalusia had seen monarchs grant considerable autonomy to commanders and military–religious orders because that was effective, and because they were confident that such agents could be reined in once the territory had been taken. The 'discoverers' and conquistadors of the Americas enjoyed even greater latitude once they were the other side of the Atlantic, and proved even more difficult to control. The royal authorities' principal concern was the loyalty of their captains and the size of the flow of returning gold and silver. They conferred *encomiendas* – rights to exploit natural resources and native labour – on the captains they trusted and who seemed most effective. The colonizers needed metropolitan supplies and the legitimacy that came with royal patronage and concessions. At first the authorities were successful in channelling communications and commerce with the New World through Seville. The colonists looked to royal power to arbitrate their quarrels. Such decisive facilities as swords and ships still came from Spain. They had Spanish tastes and relied on the home country for olive oil, wine, clothing and so forth. Controlling the Caribbean settlers remained a challenge, and Queen Isabella expressed alarm at the decimation of the native population of the large islands. The colonists concealed the full extent of the death toll by sending out slave raiding expeditions to the *tierra firme* (mainland) and reducing further hundreds of thousands of natives to slavery. The unremitting toil of panning for gold in rivers, exposure to new diseases, and spiritual demoralization carried off huge numbers. This cycle was repeated on the mainland following the invasion of Mexico, Central America and Peru, with vast silver deposits overshadowing the placer gold mines. The royal authorities' alarm at the widening arc of devastation, and their suspicion of the free-booting gangs of conquistadors, led them to heed critical voices.

'ARE THESE NOT MEN?'

Bartolomé de Las Casas, an eye-witness and former encomendero, told of the heedless rapacity of the colonists, who captured great hauls of Indians and then proceeded to work them to death. The conquerors' lust for precious metals was limitless, relaying European demand. They brought with them not only diseases but an entire way of life which was hugely disruptive to indigenous patterns. European rats, pigs and weeds multiplied, and invaded native lands. The herding of the natives into mining areas also increased their exposure to the deadly ravages of smallpox and other unfamiliar diseases. Europe's population had dropped by a third in the wake of the Black Death in the latter half of the fourteenth century. The natives of the New World were far more vulnerable. The population of the Americas was at least 50–60 million in 1500 but dropped to 8–10 million by 1600, making this one of the greatest disasters in human history.[4]

The arguments and texts used by Las Casas in his defence of the Indians helped to radicalize the Spanish humanist tradition. He disputed the apologetics of such notable colonists as Gonzalo Fernández de Oviedo, governor of the castle at Santo Domingo and chronicler, who insisted that the natives were savages and cannibals, devoid of reason and morality. He claimed that they did not have men's heads: 'They were not heads at all but rather hard and thick helmets, so that the most important piece of advice the Christians gave when fighting them was not to strike them on the head, because that broke the swords. And just as their heads were hard, so their understanding was bestial and evilly inclined.'[5]

Las Casas explained that he had first been moved to reject the colonizers' rapacity when he heard a sermon in 1511 delivered by a Dominican friar, Antonio Montesinos, who expressed his shock at the colonists' devastation of Santo Domingo: '(W)ith what justice do you keep these poor Indians in such cruel and horrible servitude? By what authority have you made such detestable wars

---

4   William McNeil, *Plagues and Peoples*, Harmondsworth 1976, pp. 185–200.
5   Quoted in Anthony Pagden, *European Encounters with the New World*, New Haven 1993, p. 57.

against these people who lived peacefully and gently in their own lands? Are these not men? Do they not have rational souls? Are you not obliged to love them as yourselves?' Montesinos was appealing both to the doctrine of love and to natural rights doctrine. Being human and possessing use of reason would mean that they had rights and an immortal soul. The Friar's words were denounced by the colonists but disturbed Las Casas. However, the conversion of Las Casas into a defender of the Indians took a further three years. He explained that he had been moved to speak publicly by a passage in Ecclesiastes: 'The bread of the needy is their life. He that defraudeth him thereof is a man of blood. He that taketh away his neighbour's living slayeth him and he that defraudeth the labourer of his hire is a blood-letter.'[6] Oviedo scorned the chaotic diversity of languages spoken by the Indians, while Las Casas saw their capacity for speech as further proof of their humanity. Las Casas was inspired by Holy Scripture to refute Oviedo and denounce the colonists, not only because they were themselves ungodly but because they so manifestly neglected their duty peacefully to convey the message of salvation, in contrast – he claimed – to the noble effort of evangelism undertaken by Don Cristóbal Colón. In his view Cortés and Pizarro were guilty of unjustified invasions – the Spanish Christians should instead have been satisfied with peaceful trade and patient witness to Scripture.

Las Casas restated this momentous indictment in his *Brevísima relación de la destrucción de las Indias* (1542), a work that was to be much translated and reprinted. Among the responses it provoked was the defence of the conquest advanced by Juan Gines de Sepúlveda in *Democrates Secundus* (1544): 'these barbarians of the New World . . . who in prudence, intelligence, sobriety and humanity are as inferior to the Spaniards as are children to adults, and women to men. The difference between them is as great as between a wild, cruel people and the most merciful.' He and other defenders of the Spanish conquest and colonization laid great stress on their own version of a 'humanist' argument, namely that the Aztecs practised human sacrifice and that the peoples of the Caribbean would eat their enemies. Las Casas had no truck with the view that massacring the innocent was all right so long as you did not eat them. Indeed he argued that the bloody rituals of the Indians, while barbarous, were at least a form of the sacred. Human sacrifice itself, he urged, placed value on human life, while the pillage and slaughter of the vicious and greedy colonists – or the Roman circus – did not.[7]

Between the polarized views of Las Casas and Sepúlveda there emerged an approach which justified the Spanish monarchy while condemning the excesses of the colonists. Francisco de Vitoria declared that the natives of the New World

---

6 David A. Brading, *The First America: The Spanish Monarchy, Creole Patriots, and the Liberal State, 1492–1867*, Cambridge 1991, pp. 40–2, 58–62; Pagden, *European Encounters with the New World*, pp. 70–2.

7 Brading, *The First America*, pp. 65–7, 79–101.

were humans who needed to be protected and policed by the royal power, just as European peasants did. This allowed for the perception that there was a difference between the more primitive Indians and the relatively more settled and civilized peoples of Mexico and Peru.[8] Just as Christians had seen some merit in the Roman Empire, because it facilitated the work of conversion, so some currents of Spanish humanism saw merit in the Inca and Aztec imperial structures. In this view barbarian empires were an advance over savage nomadism.

Charles V eventually heeded the warnings of Bartolomé de las Casas and a few other courageous friars, at least to the extent of issuing his 'New Laws' banning the enslavement of Indians in the 1540s and organizing a debate at Valladolid on the rightfulness of Spanish dominion in 1550–1. The monarch feared that the sacred imperial mission had gone badly wrong. The conquistadors were despoiling and destroying his new possessions. The allegations of Las Casas not only bore the authority of an eye-witness, they also explained why the flow of specie, large as it was, repeatedly fell short of expectations. As noted above, it tended to average about a fifth of Spanish revenues, large enough to be very important but small enough to disappoint. The colonists were defrauding their monarch as well as the Indians. When Pizarro, the conqueror of Peru, proclaimed himself an independent ruler in 1543 these fears became even more tangible. Pizarro was protesting the New Laws, but his action provoked more rigorous measures to enforce the royal will. The royal bureaucracy became an even more formidable apparatus, with regular rotations of office and inspections. Native caciques were given recognition and 'protectors of the Indians' appointed. The Indians, as *miserables*, were not to be abused or enslaved. But royal warrants of *encomienda* still allowed the colonists to demand tribute labour or goods from the indigenous villages.[9] Royal rule radiated out from a series of towns and fortified strong points along the key sea lanes. The indigenous population continued to decline. Spanish towns were shunned by Indians, who saw them as alien death-traps, creating a severe labour shortage. Indian villages were willing to supply some tribute, as they had done in pre-Columbian times, but not to become the personal property of the conquerors.

From the 1520s the royal authorities authorized the introduction of African slaves to supply the deficiency, so long as they were received into the Christian faith. Even Bartolomé de las Casas urged this approach in a memorial to the King (he later greatly regretted having tendered this advice). So the check to Indian slavery in the New World was accompanied by a growth of African slavery. Both processes were presented as part of a new colonial compact, by which monarchy claimed to be the true guarantor of the religious and secular needs of the ruled.

---

8 Ibid., p. 85.
9 J. H. Elliott, *Empires of the Atlantic World: Britain and Spain in America, 1492–1830*, New Haven, pp. 127–33.

STRUCTURES OF BAROQUE POWER

Some Latin American writers, drawing on the work of José Antonio Maravall, have developed an analysis of what they call a distinctive 'colonial baroque'.[10] The baroque itself can be seen as a celebration of royal power and of its universal destiny. The baroque was the aesthetic of the new Absolutist state, in which over-arching royal power supposedly offered protection to all, and guaranteed an elaborate and differentiated hierarchy. Popular feasting and carnival were absorbed by royal spectacle. The baroque features of empire stressed a harmonious, elaborately articulated constellation of social and ethnic corporations orbiting around the monarch. The baroque responded to the turmoil generated by the Reformation and the Discoveries by re-affirming order and hierarchy, and by recognizing all subjects so long as they reciprocated with the deference owed to clerical and royal authority. Mainly associated with the Counter-Reformation, it also appealed to some Protestant monarchs and mercantile elites. The inclusion of exotic flora and fauna in decorative and sensuous classical tableaux was characteristic, and helped stimulate and impress the populace with the resources of the royal power. Fountains, stretches of water and fireworks were mobilized to the same end. In baroque art the trope of the faithful black servant was to multiply, as if a retinue of supposedly attentive Africans could help to overawe the restive Native American or the wayward European servant.

The black slave in baroque art and spectacle also represented exoticism and luxury. African slaves were associated with sugar and chocolate, whose consumption became a courtly ritual. The imperial state undertook a formidable task of economic coordination, issuing licences to mine and trade, organizing the fleet system, selling tribute goods to wage-earning silver miners and elaborately classifying the relations between the *castas* of *indios*, *negros* and *mulatos*. The colour black was linked to power in baroque paintings in the metropolis. In the colonies the colonial baroque was lavishly encrusted with gold and silver leaf. The cult of the Virgin of Guadalupe in Mexico offered a special channel for the prayers of Indians and creoles.

In the Americas the baroque was sometimes adopted and reshaped, as it were, 'from below'. Though regulated by the Church and royal officials, the festivals of the colonial baroque foregrounded suffering and torment. Subaltern groups and individuals helped to elaborate the colonial baroque when they sought to assert the spiritual power of suffering. Sor Juana Inés de la Cruz in Mexico asserted a feminine dimension of the baroque, which evoked native

---

10   José Antonio Maravall, *The Culture of the Baroque*, Minessota 1987, and Bolívar Echeverría, *Ethos Barroco*, Mexico DF 1997.

resistance to the colonizer.[11] Sor Mariana de Jesús Torres, of Quito, became an intermediary whose help was sought by female believers. (In New France, members of the Jesuit order promoted the beatification of a Huron woman who spoke several indigenous languages but no French.) The conversion – sometimes forced – of the indigenous peoples was a concomitant of the universal ambitions of the baroque. The syncretism of the colonial version allowed for a powerful visual appeal and some adaptation of local customs. In the new colonial centres impressive cathedrals, monasteries and colleges, and fine buildings for the viceroys and captains general, embodied the colonial baroque.

The encounter with the civilizations, peoples and products of the New World represented a challenge to European cosmology that it would require centuries to work through. The culture of the baroque was part of this response claiming a universal mission for the Spanish king. The Hapsburgs with their far-flung possessions – from Spain to the Andes, from Austria to Peru, from Lombardy to the Philippines, from the Low Countries to Mexico (New Spain) – saw themselves destined to unite Christendom.

The overriding preoccupation of the Spanish monarchs of the sixteenth century was with financing their dynastic ambitions and strengthening the bonds that united their distant dominions. The apparatus of imperial administration was geared to these ends. The royal authorities sought to ensure that only Catholic subjects from Castile and Aragon settled in new possessions providentially rich in precious metals. The king had to sign an authorization for each individual or family who wished to emigrate. While the monarch was a Hapsburg and a Catholic, the New World possessions were increasingly thought of as Spanish, a national identity which itself helped to define the compact between ruler and subject. The expulsions of Jews and Moors was deemed to enhance Spanish claims to religious purity and pre-eminence, and hence to territorial dominion. 'Old Christians' who aspired to hold office or land had resented the administrative advancement of 'New Christians' of Jewish extraction, and coveted the land still held by Moriscos, or New Christians of Muslim extraction. The Inquisition served as an instrument of royal power so that when appointing inquisitors, Ferdinand warned them that they could do 'very little' without him. The persecution of heretics, Judaizers, embezzlers and so forth was designed to assist the royal power by rendering the kingdom more homogenous. While witch-hunts in the German lands claimed tens of thousands of victims, the Spanish Inquisition chose its victims in the hundreds and dozens, with the Spanish king himself playing his part in the terrible spectacle of the auto da fé of 1680.[12]

---

11   See, for example, her play 'The Divine Narcissus', in Sor Juana Inés de la Cruz, *Poems, Protest and a Dream: Selected Writings*, edited by Margaret Sayers Peden, London 1997, pp. 194–239.

12   Henry Kamen, *The Spanish Inquisition: An Historical Revision*, London 1997, pp. 137–46; Michael Alpert, *Secret Judaism and the Spanish Inquisition*, Nottingham 2008, pp. 130–1.

The ambitions and resentments of Old Christians had already produced, prior to 1492, the official category of *limpieza de sangre*, or purity of blood, a notion that chimed in with St Isidore's categories but was at odds with Spanish clerical humanism. Nevertheless the monarch had been persuaded to limit office-holding to those who could prove Old Christian descent, whether noble or commoner. The Castilian monarchs were determined to curb municipal autonomy and this concession helped them to achieve that end; in 1520 the revolt of the *comuneros*, or municipal councils, was vigorously and successfully put down. The royal administration in the Americas was staffed by Old Christians. The authorities were obsessed with ensuring that the flow of treasure from the New World was in safe hands, and free from the financial manipulations of heretical European merchants and bankers. While these arrangements reflected the germ of a racial pact between the monarch and the Old Christian families, other principles were also important. Senior posts could only be held by members of the high nobility, others were reserved for the wider category of *hidalgos* or those of gentle birth. Finally, native Indian princes and aristocrats were allowed to occupy certain honourable but symbolic official posts, and some leading Spaniards were able to marry native princesses without losing their credentials as Old Christians. The rules restricting office-holding required elaborate documentation, and individuals could apply to have a stain on their background removed by judicial fiat.

The concept of *limpieza* tainted *conversos* of Jewish or Muslim origin who were thought to be covertly still practicing Judaism or Islam. The decision as to whether an individual had tainted or infected blood was not left to individuals, but had to be sanctioned by the authorities and was laid out in a mass of edicts and regulations. If the charge was made by a given institution and upheld by the Holy Office, the effect was to exclude that person from holding public office, in favour of those who could prove their 'Old Christian' family lines. Henry Kamen points out that while many institutions adopted *limpieza* rules, many did not, and there were also prominent critics who attacked the workings of the *limpieza* rules.[13] The Holy Office itself did not exclude *conversos*, and Torquemada, the famous Grand Inquisitor, was himself of 'remote' *converso* ancestry. The Inquisition only had the power to investigate those who claimed to be Christians, not Jews or Muslims (who were 'protected', controlled and eventually expelled by the secular power). The exaltation of blood-lines nevertheless contributed to a racialization of religious categories.

The huge size of the Spanish possessions meant that the Inquisition faced great problems in the New World. While the Inquisition had a dozen tribunals in Spain it had only three in the Americas. In the period up to 1700 it investigated some 3,000 cases, 80 per cent of which concerned Spaniards or

---

13   Kamen, *The Spanish Inquisition*, pp. 230–54.

their descendants. It is as if the Holy Office was daunted by the prospect of searching for heresy and superstition among Indians or blacks – daunted not because it would be difficult, but because it would be far too easy. The fact that Indians and blacks could not enter the priesthood certainly limited the threat from this quarter. On the other hand the records of the Inquisition suggest that the faith of many Old Christians was becoming dangerously heterodox in colonial conditions. About a quarter of the cases concerned sexual licence, while many others revealed a widespread colonial heresy that the distinctions between Catholic, Protestant, Jew and Muslim mattered little since each could achieve salvation according to their own law. In this and kindred phenomena Stuart Schwartz finds 'evidence of a vibrant culture at odds with the dominant ideologies of Church and state.'[14] The huge gap between the beliefs and customs of the conquered and the conquerors also posed a major challenge, though this was one which imperial strategists could sometimes find effective ways to exploit.

NATIVE TRIBUTE AND THE SILVER REGIME

Many indigenous peoples had formerly been subjects of the Aztecs of Mexico or the Inca rulers of the Andean highlands. They were more inclined to accept a tribute system with which they were familiar than to submit to outright enslavement. On the other hand, those American or African peoples who were hunter-gatherers, or who practised shifting cultivation, proved to be poor workers. If prevented from practising their migratory way of life, they were difficult to keep alive as captives. The Spanish authorities had frowned on enslavement of the native peoples while permitting some great captains to hold slaves, and allowing the enslavement of Indians who were deemed to be in rebellion. But the New Laws tightened up loopholes and were more effectively enforced, even when in some frontier zones raiders still preyed on Indians who had refused to capitulate, such as the Araucans of Chile or the Chichimeca of north-west Mexico. In the lengthy South American frontier zone bordering on Brazil, from the Pantanal to Amazonian Peru, the Jesuits undertook the conversion of Indians who were settled in missionary villages, the *reducciones*. In principle the Spanish Empire sought to give recognition to the monarch's lawful subjects – only excluding heretics and unbelievers.[15]

The system of *encomienda* and *depósito* gave the Spanish colonial elite access to tribute labour, and the Crown itself also exacted a levy from indigenous villages, sometimes as tribute labour but often in the form of food or textiles. The colonial order had a corporate character, comprising not just the *república de españoles*

---

14   Stuart Schwartz, *All Can Be Saved: Religious Tolerance and Salvation in the Iberian Atlantic World*, New Haven 2008, pp. 121–49, 125.

15   Elliott, *Empires of the Atlantic World*, p. 267.

and the *república de indios* but a hierarchy of corporations with their own dignitaries and order of precedence. In the Andean region the native *aylu* were respected. Thierry Saignes cites Juan Polo de Ondegardo, a Spanish official, explaining, in 1571, the necessity of preserving and utilizing indigenous hierarchies: 'The day we decide to count and tax all Indians individually, so that if they have paid they are no longer under the domination of the caciques and under their orders, being free to go where ever they want, we will have taken away the restraint that holds them together in an orderly manner, for this is the way in which they survive and have survived after the Christians obtained these Indians: if one could put this fact to the test for only one year, one would clearly see their destruction.'[16] The colonial state worked through the *aylu* and their caciques, and appointed a 'protector of the Indians', down to the close of the colonial period. In Mexico it was also found that the *indios* were easier to control if left to reside in their own communities, and easier to exploit by means of tribute than by enslavement. While it is true that the royal authorities learned how to adapt and enhance their exactions, the indigenous communities were not at all passive, and significantly helped to shape colonial institutions.[17]

But there was to be a steadily growing intermediary population between the thin layer of Spaniards at the summit and the Indian villages, with their collective obligations, at the base. This included *yanaconas*, reputedly slaves of the Incas, who had collaborated with the conquerors and some of whom became wage workers in the mines and elsewhere. There were also the *castas*, or offspring of unions between Spanish colonists and native women or slaves, or between natives and Africans. However, the baroque order liked to represent even the heterogeneous and hybrid as members of an orderly society of ranks, with their own religious brotherhoods and civic obligations. On royal occasions representatives of the king's faithful native subjects, their caciques dressed as Spanish gentlemen, would be assembled on the central plaza of the provincial capital. A famous painting – *Los primeros mulatos de Esmeraldas* (1599) by Adrián Sánchez Galque – portrays in this way the delegation of a mixed village of Africans and Indians on the Pacific coast: the Africans were survivors of a shipwreck who had themselves merged with an indigenous community. The men carry spears and wear rich cloaks, they have ruffs around their necks and their faces are festooned with gold ornaments.[18] Their respectful presence at a ceremony excused a mixture

---

16   Thierry Saignes, 'The Colonial Condition in the Quechua-Aymara Heartland, 1570–1780', in *The Cambridge History of the Native Peoples of the Americas*, vol. 3, *South America*, Part 2, Cambridge 1999, pp. 59–128, 165.

17   Enrique Semo, *Historia del capitalismo en México: los orígenes 1521/1763*, Mexico DF 1973.

18   The picture is in the Museo de América in Madrid. It is reproduced on the cover to Jack D. Forbes, *Africans and Native Americans: The Language of Race and the Evolution of Red-Black Peoples*, Urbana 1993.

of Indian and African, something that the authorities preferred to avoid by offering recognition to each subaltern group taken separately.

Enslavement had a role in this emerging imperial formula, but not that of native peoples. As we have seen, Bartolomé de las Casas had himself suggested in 1517 that Africans be purchased to relieve the pressure on the natives. The royal authorities saw several advantages. The introduction and sale of African captives would meet a labour shortage and open up a new source of revenue. The Crown sold the *asiento* – the right to ship several hundred captive Africans – to Portuguese merchants who would then sail to Havana or Cartagena where they would sell them to the colonists. Under the terms of the Treaty of Tordesillas of 1494, the pope had ratified a division of spheres of responsibility between the monarchs of Portugal and Castile, with the former allotted the coast of Africa and the latter most of the New World, apart from Brazil. The Portuguese could engage in the slave trade so long as they promoted the conversion of the enslaved.

The slaves sold to the Spanish colonists were chiefly engaged as servants, craftsmen or *mayordomos*. With the indigenous peoples shunning the colonial cities, Africans filled the gap. By 1600 about half the populations of Lima, Havana and Mexico City were African slaves or free persons partly or wholly of African descent. It was not uncommon for urban slaves to buy their freedom over a period of about twenty or thirty years. The owners of slaves reaped good returns by hiring them out or allowing them to ply a trade. They could then multiply these revenues by letting slaves buy their manumission with their own savings over a period of twenty or thirty years. And free people of colour with an income from a trade or craft (masons, carpenters, hairdressers, barbers, cooks and so forth) would also pay good money to buy relatives out of slavery. While this practice of *coartación* was good for extracting service in urban conditions, it was rarer in the countryside. The royal authorities appreciated the fact that captive Africans lacked ties to the indigenous peoples and owed no allegiance to any rival European monarch.[19]

There were a few slaves in the mines and workshops of Spanish America, but they were usually a tiny minority – most of the mining workforce were either indigenous tribute labourers or free wage workers. The *mitayos*, offering tribute labour, comprised a third or less of the Andean mining labour force. The free workers – known as *mingados* – earned a day wage comparable to that of a German silver miner of the time.[20] But their expenditures did not build an autonomous dynamic of consumption, because the royal authorities made sure that as much of the mine workers' expenditure as possible ended up in their

---

19   For general accounts see Rolando Mellafe, *Negro Slavery in Latin America*, Berkeley, CA, 1975, and Herbert Klein, *African Slavery in Latin America and the Caribbean*, Oxford 1986.

20   Pierre Vilar, *A History of Gold and Money*, London 1984.

hands. The tribute food and clothing produced by the indigenous communities was sold by the royal authorities to merchants who supplied the mine workers of the barren *altiplano* with necessary essentials. In this way the authorities managed to convert Inca-style imperial tribute into a mechanism for increasing the flow of silver into the royal coffers.[21] Anxious to boost silver output, the authorities also advanced credit to the owners of mining concessions. The mine owners needed mercury to process the ore and produce silver. The Crown supplied the needed mercury on credit so that the mine owners experienced a gentlemanly version of the debt peonage of the *naborías* or wage workers.[22]

The royal authorities thus had multiple means of ensuring that the royal treasury captured the lion's share of what was produced. There was the *diezmo* of all mined silver, the fees paid by the owners of mining concessions, the silver coins spent by the *mingado* workers in shops stocked by tribute goods, the income received from the freight charges of the *flota* and the money paid by the *asientistas* for the right to sell slaves. But this royal fixation on specie marginalized plantation production and diminished the size of the colonial market.

The imperial fleet system played its part in maximizing the flow of silver and gold, but at the cost of discouraging other types of commerce. Because the *flota* was geared to transporting small quantities of precious metals once or twice a year, its charges were too costly, and its procedures too cumbersome, for items of mass consumption – the Spanish internal market was anyway very shallow. The Spanish authorities did not allow free trade in slaves or anything else. There were a few dozen Spanish sugar plantations in Cuba, Santo Domingo and Mexico in the sixteenth century, and cacao was cultivated in Central and South America, but mainly for local markets. The *Carrera de las Indias*, or fleet system, was not only cumbersome and expensive but attracted a swarm of English, French and Dutch pirates and privateers who devastated the Caribbean in their own search for precious metals.[23]

---

21   Carlos Sempat Assadourian, 'La producción de la mercancía dinero', in Enrique Florescano, ed., *Ensayos sobre el desarrollo económico de México y América Latina*, Mexico City 1979. The Spanish imperial authorities in this period actively and directly coordinated economic activity, in ways similar to those evoked by Michael Mann, *The Sources of Social Power: A History of Power from the Beginning to 1760*, Cambridge 1987 (see especially pp. 437–99). However, the example given here does not figure in his account.

22   P. J. Blakewell, *Silver Mining and Society in Colonial Mexico: Zacatecas 1546–1700*, Cambridge 1971, pp. 121–9. African slaves were sold to mine owners in the early years, but by 1597 black slaves comprised 1,020 of the mining work force compared with 6,229 Indians, with many of the latter being wage workers. See Colin Palmer, *Slaves of the White God: Blacks in Mexico 1570–1650*, Cambridge 1976, pp. 43–5. For the modern presence of African slaves see also Alan Knight, *Mexico: The Colonial Era*, Cambridge 2002, p. 82. Nevertheless Africans and their descendants were prominent in Vera Cruz, Mexico City and some small plantation enclaves.

23   J. H. Parry, *The Spanish Seaborne Empire*, London 1971; Kenneth Andrews, *Trade, Plunder and Settlement*, Cambridge 1984; Eufemio Lorenzo Sanz, *Comercio de España con América Latina en la época de Felipe II*, vol. 1, Valladolid 1979, pp. 614–7. I document the 'false start' of plantation development in the Spanish Caribbean in *Making of New World Slavery*, pp. 129–60.

The urban slavery of Spanish America, with its opportunities for petty accumulation and negotiation, contrasted with the more intense, rural and permanent character of New World slavery in the aftermath of the plantation revolution. But indisputably there are continuities too. The Dutch, English and French were fully aware that the Spanish and Portuguese had used large numbers of slaves to strengthen the authority and resources of the imperial power and to boost the position of the leaders of colonial society. The Iberian states seemed to show that African slavery was a workable and convenient solution to labour scarcity – especially given the difficulty, in New World conditions, of finding enough European labourers willing to work for wages. And while sugar plantation output in Spanish America was very restricted, a few leading men, such as Cortés himself, owned sugar estates worked by a few dozen slaves in areas well-protected from marauders. Sugar estates were vulnerable because they required expensive equipment (the *ingenio* or sugar mill) and a sizeable slave crew. With much less expense some encomenderos cultivated cotton, ginger, and cacao. These items circulated on the internal market and even made it to Spain – indeed spiced chocolate became a prized elite beverage, taken by courtiers and senior churchmen. The Indian custom of smoking tobacco was also gradually taken up by Europeans and became the centre of new rituals, both collective and individual.[24]

Indigenous agriculture had, of course, contributed a variety of highly productive new crops, notably maize, potatoes, yucca, squash, beans and cassava, which were to be vital subsistence crops, helping to feed the settlers and their slaves. While the cultivation of potatoes and maize spread back to the Old World, the impressive yields of these crops and their comparatively modest labour requirements were to fit in well with the construction of plantations devoted to a staple commodity. Maize required between thirty and fifty days of cultivation during the year, yet could supply the main subsistence staple. As Braudel stressed, the Native American success in domesticating high-yield crops broadened the scope for extracting labour from Indian villages or any other fixed and subordinated group of toilers.[25] Relatively high population density in the areas of settled agriculture meant that villagers could not simply abandon cultivation of these crops. So Spanish settlers had assembled many of the essential ingredients of a slave plantation economy, but without succeeding in bringing them together in a permanent and viable form.

---

24   Mercy Norton, 'Tasting Empire: Chocolate and the European Internalization of Meso-American Aesthetics', *American Historical Review* 111/3 (2006), pp. 661–91.

25   Fernand Braudel, *Capitalism and Material Life*, Harmondsworth 1973, and *Civilization and Capitalism in the 15th–18th Centuries: The Structures of Everyday Life*, London 1985, pp. 158–9; and Felipe Fernández-Armesto, *The Americas: The History of a Hemisphere*, London 2004, p. 23.

Besides their use of African slaves, the Spanish also conveyed to other Europeans a warning about the hugely destructive impact of the Conquest and colonization. The brutality of the Spanish towards the native American peoples was widely decried by other Europeans. The *Brief Account of the Destruction of the Indies* by Las Casas was translated into twelve European languages, often in strikingly illustrated editions. By the seventeenth century it was a much-cited text. Horror at the enormity and cruelty of Spanish colonization – the perishing of great multitudes – marks the beginnings of modern humanitarian sensibility. But the new outlook took a considerable time to become differentiated from the tendency of each religious camp to perceive only the excesses of its rivals and opponents.

Cruelty did not rank among the 'seven deadly sins' and, as in the case of judicial torture, could be seen as acceptable if harnessed to a higher purpose. The late medieval period had been marked by ferocious persecution of those viewed as different or threatening. The doctrine that the soul shone through the body suggested that lepers or the disabled were paying the price for some moral defect. Cruel and sacrilegious practices were imputed to Jews, witches and heretics, with many thousands being burned at the stake.[26] Even the apparently kindly teachings of St Francis of Assisi did not squarely oppose such persecutions; the Franciscans stressed Christ's sufferings at the hands of the Jews. In St Francis's legendary dispute with Muslim theologians on his 'peaceful crusade', he challenged them to the test of fire – a stance which existed within the same universe of belief as judicial torture.

Protestants seized on the *Brief Account* without noticing that it, and its reception by the king, was a tribute to at least one important strand of Spanish Catholic 'humanism'.[27] While happy to denounce Spanish misdeeds, the other European powers saw no problem with imitating the Spanish and Portuguese when it came to African slavery and the Atlantic slave trade. For some, Spanish violence towards the Indians was unacceptable because the Spanish colonists were Catholics, whereas for others the problem was that they were not good Catholics (the French Catholic orders sought to protect the natives from English heresy and Spanish malpractice alike).

The recoil from the consequences of Spanish conquest was compounded by the reaction to the horrendous bloodshed and cruelty of the religious wars of roughly 1550–1648, to produce greater recognition of the problem of cruelty – which had been little evidenced in the medieval period. Daniel Baraz writes:

---

26   Robert I. Moore, *Foundations of a Persecuting Society*, Oxford 1987.

27   Fifteenth- and sixteenth-century Catholic 'humanism' was inspired by the Renaissance and the study of classical Hellenistic and Roman philosophy. In addition to inspiring Las Casas, Thomas More and Erasmus, it also influenced some of Las Casas's most determined opponents, notably Juan Ginés de Sepúlveda. See Pagden, *European Encounters with the New World*, pp. 57, 75; and David Brading, *The First Americans*, pp. 58–101.

'Two sets of events, both characterized by cataclysmic violence, mark the transition into the modern period and into essentially different attitudes toward the issue of cruelty: the conquest of the New World and the wars of religion. Historically the violence in America preceded that of the wars in Europe, and it is likely that there is a direct link.'[28]

As with the Mongol Invasions, or the Crusades, the colonizers' violence in America was simply seen as the necessary means to suppress the natives' cruelty. Baraz does not single out Las Casas, as he could have done. The Dominican's willingness to criticize his own fellow countrymen and co-religionists was an important step. It also helped to inform Montaigne's great essays on cruelty and cannibalism, as Baraz does stress. But even these advanced expressions of a new humanitarian sensibility did not focus directly on slavery or the Atlantic slave trade.

By the start of the seventeenth century, slavery underpinned the crucial role of the great colonial cities, and the numbers of slaves entering the empire rose to a total of a third of a million by the middle of that century. Tomás de Mercado, a Dominican who had spent years in Mexico, published a work on the morality of law and commerce in 1569 in which he challenged the legitimacy of the Atlantic slave trade. In Cervantes's *Don Quixote* the wandering knight is deeply troubled by the sight of a coffle of slaves.

The Spanish American slavery of the sixteenth and early seventeenth century was smaller and more varied than the immense, and relentlessly menial, confinement that was to come; but it was still of great significance as a support to the colonization effort. Around 1630 people who were African or of African descent comprised half the populations of Lima, Cartagena, Vera Cruz, Mexico City and Havana, and a half of them were free. The free coloured population was the equal of the slave population not because of the generosity of their former owners, but because they had bought their own freedom (or that of a relative). Freedom was acquired only thanks to many years of saving and hard work. Nevertheless the growth of the free coloured populations, and such institutions as the African brotherhoods, lent a flexibility to enslavement that was soon to disappear from New World slavery.

While Africans and their descendants could build a life beyond slavery in Spanish America, they still belonged to the lower rungs of a very hierarchical society. As marriage partners, blacks and mulattoes ranked below those of indigenous extraction: whereas some Indian lineages were deemed honourable, this was not the case with blacks or mulattoes. Africans showed a tendency to marry other Africans, often those coming from the same cultural area, an outcome that may have been acceptable for many Africans. The lack of *limpieza de sangre*

---

28   Daniel Baraz, *Medieval Cruelty: Changing Perceptions, Late Antiquity to the Early Modern Period*, Ithaca, NY, 2003, pp. 156–7.

barred them from official employments to which they did not aspire anyway. But blacks and mulattoes had to be careful not to arouse the fear of the authorities. The concentration of blacks in the cities, and the fact that half of them were free, was a source of anxiety. Blacks might achieve manumission but they did not enjoy *limpieza de sangre*, and if deemed to be miscreant they became the target of exemplary punishments. In 1612 in Mexico City thirty-three blacks and mulattoes (twenty-six men and seven women) were convicted of gross insubordination, defying their master's orders and plotting to overthrow the government of the Vice-Royalty. Not only were they publicly hanged, but their heads were removed and placed atop the gallows. Six were quartered and displayed in the streets and squares of the city.[29]

29   María Elena Martínez, 'The Black Blood of New Spain: *Limpieza de Sangre*, Racial Violence, and Gendered Power in Early Colonial Mexico', *William and Mary Quarterly*, 61/3 (July 2004), pp. 479–520.

CHAPTER TWO

Mercantile Empire and the Slave Plantation: Brazil Leads, the Dutch, English and French Refine the Formula

Italian and Flemish merchants had sponsored the first sugar estates in the Portuguese Atlantic islands in the period 1480 to 1580. The labour force of the sugar mills (*engenhos*) and cane farms was mixed, with Portuguese wage or contract labourers and native or African slaves. An island which produced 700 tons of sugar a year was doing very well. By the middle of the sixteenth century sugar planting spread to Brazil and began to acquire a new scale. Brazil's northeast had abundant space, and the right soil and climate, for growing cane. Prevailing winds allowed for short sailing times to Europe. The quantities of sugar produced after about 1580 in Brazil escalated to new orders of magnitude, and the colony's total output reached over 10,000 tons a year by the beginning of the seventeenth century, with merchants from Genoa and Antwerp buying much of what was produced. The *senhores de ingenho* employed a mixed Portuguese, Indian and African labour force to process the cane. They allowed *lavradores de cana* (cane farmers) to grow much of the cane they milled. The Brazilian planters were often former office-holders or men who had good ties to officialdom, and all the mills were owned by Portuguese subjects. They were able to draw on the expertise of the planters and skilled workers of the Atlantic islands, some of whom migrated to Brazil, as well as on Italian and Flemish commercial facilities. Merchants helped to bring together American producers and European consumers as the Spanish convoy system, or *flota*, had not done. By the 1620s sugar output had risen to as much as 20,000 tons in a good year.[1]

Portugal's union with the crown of Spain in 1580, and the concessions wrung out of the Spanish King by Portuguese merchants at the subsequent Cortes of Tomar, may have helped to maintain and develop links between European or Portuguese merchants and Brazilian *senhores de engenho*. Flemish agents, some married to Portuguese women, lived in Brazil, and many of the ships taking on sugar cargoes at Bahia were *urcas*, a ship favoured by merchants from Northern Europe. 'New Christians', men of Jewish origin forced to convert by the Portuguese monarch and Inquisition, were active in the sugar trade and

---

1 Stuart Schwartz, *Sugar Plantations in the Formation of Brazilian Society: Bahia, 1550–1835*, Cambridge 1985; Frédéric Mauro, *Le Portugal et l'Atlantique au XVIIe, 1570–1670*, Paris 1960.

had a stake in the *engenhos*.[2] Some retained connections with the Sephardic community in Amsterdam. Such connections linked Brazilian sugar planters to wider European markets and helped them to avoid the suffocation that befell the Spanish Caribbean sugar industry. However, as the value of the Brazilian crop rose it became the target of Dutch, English or French privateers keen to capture a rich sugar cargo.

The Portuguese South Atlantic trading system proved to be resilient. Brazilian planters sent several expeditions to Angola and West Africa, to safeguard the Portuguese coastal trading factories. The Portugese had sunk roots in both West Africa and Brazil, creating Luso-African and Luso-Brazilian communities cemented by marriage and trading links. This helped them to survive military challenges, especially from the Dutch West Indian Company (on which more below). The strong nexus between Portuguese African enclaves, the Portuguese Atlantic Islands and Brazil, with its comparatively short sailing times and transatlantic family business connections, enabled Brazilian plantations to outproduce the Caribbean. It furnished a source of capital as well as labour, as Luso-African traders allowed Brazilians to buy slaves on credit.[3]

The Brazilian producers introduced important innovations in sugar production. A new technique using three millstones turning together ground the cane and boosted the output of each *engenho*; interestingly enough, this new type of mill was brought to Brazil from Peru, where it had been developed by indigenous labourers to grind ore.[4] The average annual output of a sugar estate in the late sixteenth century was 15–24 tons in São Tomé, 23 tons in Madeira, and 10.2 tons in Cuba. Around the same time the output of a sugar estate would

---

2   Stuart B. Schwartz, 'A Commonwealth Within Itself: The Early Brazilian Sugar Industry', in Stuart B. Schwartz, ed., *Tropical Babylons: Sugar and the Making of the Atlantic World, 1450–1680*, Chapel Hill 2004, pp. 158–200, especially pp. 172–6. For the wider commercial context and the growing demand for sugar see also the essay by Eddy Stols, 'The Expansion of the Sugar Market in Western Europe', in Schwartz, *Tropical Babylons*, pp. 237–88. The author supplies fascinating information on the developing culture of sugar consumption and on the ties between the merchants of Italy and Flanders, and the Portuguese Atlantic sugar producers. He talks up the early importance of sugar – e.g. in the early sixteenth century – but the evidence he cites suggests that sugar consumption was an elite affair prior to about 1590, when Brazilian output began to rise. For example, recipes for jam and confectionery appear in the mid-seventeenth century (pp. 146–7) and refineries multiply in the Netherlands after 1600 (p. 273). The author concedes: 'One could even contend that the great sugar boom took place from 1590 to 1630' (p. 266).

3   Luiz Felipe de Alencastro, *O trato dos viventes: Formação do Brasil no Atlântico Sul*, São Paulo 2000. The later evolution of this trading nexus is recounted in Joseph Miller, *Way of Death: Merchant Capitalism and the Angolan Slave Trade*, Madison 1988.

4   António Barros de Castro, 'Brasil 1610: mudanças técnicas e conflitos sociais', *Pesquia e planejamento económico*, vol. 10, no. 3, 1980, pp. 679–712. A fundamental work for understanding the development of Brazilian sugar is Schwartz's *Sugar Plantations in the Formation of Brazilian Society*. But see also Stuart Schwartz, 'Plantations and Peripheries', in Leslie Bethell, ed., *Colonial Brazil*, Cambridge 1987, pp. 67–144, 76.

be several times larger in Brazil – in the range 69–87 tons.[5] There were said to be 192 mills in Brazil in 1612, on the eve of further expansion, compared with twenty to thirty in Cuba and the islands. Dramatic though it was, the Brazilian breakthrough was to be held back by a series of destructive conflicts, stimulated by the new sugar wealth. Inside the colony the labour demands of the new system were met both by purchasing more captives from Africa and by extended slave raiding against the Native American peoples. The labour conscriptions of the new system met resistance from both Indians and Africans in the shape of millenarian *santidade* (holiness) movements, giving religious form to their refusal to submit to the *bandeirantes* and *senhores*. Engaging Indian and African workers side-by-side, and exposing them to a smattering of Christian teaching, risked allying the vision and local knowledge of the Indians with the martial qualities and cultural flexibility of the Africans. The Tupinamba quest for sacred space – a 'Land Without Evil' – inspired one such movement for 'holiness'. For a while it was tolerated by the owner of the sugar mill of Jaguaripe, Fernão Cabral, and his wife, who were said to offer a haven to escaping slaves. The royal authorities and the Jesuits were often at loggerheads, but they readily agreed that this dangerously heretical sect had to be dealt with. The idolatrous centre at Jaguaripe was suppressed, but the heresy lingered and spread.[6]

The Portuguese authorities created militias which offered advancement to both Indian chiefs and capable Africans, but took care to organize them in separate columns. Likewise *mulatos* were organized in special squadrons under a coloured captain to hunt down escaped slaves and to suppress the *quilombos* (maroon communities) that sprang up in the *selva*. Sugar wealth also provoked conflict between the colonists and Jesuit missionaries, with colonial authorities trying to mediate between the two. However, the Church in Brazil had an even weaker ability to regulate everyday life than was the case in Spanish America. The Inquisition made occasional voyages to Brazil but it did not have a permanent establishment there, and the sugar-growing region was regarded as particularly lax.[7] The relative weakness of the Church and Brazil's commercial ethos were also associated with an openness to innovation, at least in the late sixteenth and early seventeenth centuries.

Portuguese pre-eminence was short-lived. The Dutch, English and French merchants and captains saw the African and sugar trades as profitable branches of commerce that should not be left to an unjustified Portuguese (and Catholic) monopoly (many French captains were Huguenots). The colonial entrepreneurs of these nations came to see the advantages of buying slaves who, uprooted

---

5   Schwartz, *Tropical Babylons*, p. 18.
6   Ronaldo Vainfas, 'From Indian Millenarianism to a Tropical Witches' Sabbath: Brazilian Sanctities in Jesuit Writings and Inquisitorial Sources', *Bulletin of Latin American Research*, 24/2 (2005): pp. 215–31.
7   Schwartz, *All Can Be Saved*, pp. 177–208.

from their place of birth, were productive, resourceful and resistant to the disease environment. The long-established Portuguese trade meant that there was already a supply of captives for sale on the African coast.

Brazil's sugar wealth became the target of the Dutch West India Company (WIC). Its first attack on Bahia, in 1624, was beaten off, but a second expedition in 1630 seized Pernambuco in the north-east, a major sugar-producing area. The Dutch also captured Elmina and other forts on the African coast. Some mill-owners cooperated with the Dutch and allowed them to learn the techniques of sugar cultivation and processing. The Netherlanders were good at marketing and competent at sugar-making, but not many were willing to leave their prosperous and tolerant homeland to settle in the tropics. Under Prince Johann Mauritz Dutch Brazil flourished for a while, but Company rule was occasionally heavy-handed. A Portuguese revolt in 1644 led to the loss of much of the sugar-producing hinterland while the Dutch clung to the ports. The Dutch colonists found it difficult to prevail against the tenacious and culturally more rooted and flexible Portuguese, whether in Brazil or Africa. The Portuguese mobilized columns of African and Indian fighters in Brazil in a guerrilla campaign that wore down the Dutch. An expedition led by a Brazilian, Salvador de Sa, recaptured Luanda and Benguela on the Angolan coast. Eventually the WIC withdrew from Brazil in 1654, but retained a large stake in the Africa trade (produce as well as slaves).

Already in the 1640s some Dutch traders and planters, including both New Christians and Brazilians who had cooperated with the Dutch, decided to leave for Curaçao, St Eustatius and Barbados, in a move that helped to disseminate sugar-making skills to the Caribbean. The English and French planters proved to be excellent pupils and soon came up with improvements of their own. While the acquisition of know-how was a great help, the war between the Dutch and the Portuguese reduced Brazilian output and raised European sugar prices, furnishing an incentive for other producers.[8]

---

8   Roger C. Batie, 'Why Sugar? Economic Cycles and the Changing of Staples in the English and French Antilles, 1624–1654', in Hilary Beckles and Verene Shepherd, eds, *Caribbean Slave Society and Economy*, London 1991, pp. 37–55. John McCusker and Russell R. Menard claim that too much has been made of the Dutch role in Barbados and cite the key role of British planters, notably Maurice Thompson, William Penoyer, Thomas Andrews, Richard Bateson and Martin Noel. These are the very same men identified as 'new merchants' by Robert Brenner in *Merchants and Revolution*, Princeton 1993. Brenner stresses their close ties to the Dutch, so it is likely that they tapped Dutch expertise and capital, a possibility that further research may clarify. A notable feature of Barbados was the hundreds of windmills used to power the grinding of the sugar cane. I will itemize some of the original features of the English plantations below, and agree that the Dutch role should not be exaggerated. McCusker and Menard themselves concede: 'We have no interest in denying the contribution of Dutch merchants to the Barbadian sugar boom.' See John J. McCusker and Russell R. Menard, 'The Sugar Industry in the Seventeenth Century: A New Perspective on the Barbadian "Sugar Revolution"', in Schwartz, *Tropical Babylons*, pp. 289–330, 295.

From the mid-seventeenth century the slave plantation drove Atlantic economic growth. The Dutch sponsored this development but were not strong enough to dominate it for long. The Netherlands were comparatively small and vulnerable. Despite a formidable navy and merchant marine, the colonial role demanded large resources and settlers. The Dutch supplied know-how and commercial services to the English and French, but, as we have seen, few emigrants. France and England produced larger numbers of free colonists, who appreciated the opportunities and relative freedom of the colonies. Adventurous individuals did leave the Netherlands for New Amsterdam or the Cape, and many seamen hazarded their lives in the ships of the Dutch East and West India Companies. But, unlike England and France, the Netherlands did not produce a stream of tied labourers – indentured servants or *engagés* – willing to sell three or five years of their life in return for passage to the New World and the hope of eventually becoming smallholders themselves. They persuaded other Europeans to help crew their ships, but they did not themselves migrate in large enough numbers to make Dutch Brazil viable. (Historians debate why the Netherlands failed to produce an anti-slavery movement despite sharing many of the supposed preconditions of abolitionism. I will return to this issue in Part IV, but it is worth considering that Dutch unwillingness to migrate to Brazil may have reflected unease at life in a slave society.[9])

The British and French slave plantations thrived. The planters of Barbados, Jamaica and Virginia, or of Martinique, Guadeloupe and Saint-Domingue, began to produce tens of thousands of tons of sugar, and millions of pounds of tobacco, responding to the new mass markets for exotic produce in north-west Europe. By 1670 the small island of Barbados was producing as much sugar as Brazil. The demand for disciplined labour grew rigorously as Dutch and English merchants had access to the largest markets – those of northern Europe. Spain, as we have seen, had lacked the internal market or commercial resources to sustain large-scale plantation development. The whole system of the *carrera*, whereby the trade of the Indies was reserved to the *Casa de Contratación* in Seville, was designed to keep foreign merchants out. Portugal had an even smaller home market but had been able to shift Brazilian produce via the merchants of Genoa, Antwerp and Amsterdam. Even when Portugal was at war with the Netherlands there was a lively trade between Dutch and Portuguese merchants.[10]

The Iberian merchants had nothing to compare with the extensive networks branching out from Amsterdam, Middelberg, London and Bristol. After 1660 the Portuguese authorities were forced to organize their own cumbersome fleet system, to protect Portuguese ships from capture and to assure metropolitan

---

9   Seymour Drescher, 'The Long Goodbye', in *From Slavery to Freedom: Comparative Studies in the Rise and Fall of Atlantic Slavery*, London 1999, pp. 196–234.

10   C. R. Boxer, *The Dutch War for Brazil, 1624–54*, London 1957.

control. While Portuguese merchants were able to remain as secondary suppliers of sugar to European markets, they could not stem the rise of the English and French plantation colonies. The Brazilian sugar estates – the word 'plantation' was not yet used in Brazil – still had a more mixed labour force, and lower output and productivity than the new plantations which appeared in the Eastern Caribbean. While Brazilian *engenhos* at their best produced about 75 tons of sugar a year, a Barbadian plantation would produce 150 tons, and there were upwards of 600 such plantations by the 1670s. The Barbadian plantation used plenty of metal implements and employed wind or water power for the mills, rather than the animal power used by the Cuban *trapiche* or Brazilian *engenho*. The new English and French plantations were more integrated into North Atlantic circuits than were the Brazilian sugar estates. In the English Caribbean, plantations combined the cultivation of cane with the processing of sugar at the mill, activities that were often separate in Brazil.

While the Caribbean estates dominated eighteenth-century sugar expansion Brazil remained the third-largest producer, lagging some way behind the British and French. It also remained a major purchaser of slaves from Africa. The discovery of gold in Brazil in the 1690s and early 1700s created a new demand for slave labour, as well as allowing Portugal, and its huge colony, their own late-flowering baroque period. Brazil's *fazendas* (sugar estates) were not the most modern, but they had low costs. Slaves could be bought in Brazil for about half the price paid by Caribbean planters, because of shorter transatlantic sailing times, the 'efficiency' of Luso-African trading networks, and their success in cultivating a West African taste for tobacco steeped in molasses. The Brazilian planters were happy to supply this item and receive payment in slaves. The Luso-Africans of Angola – families which united Portuguese and African mercantile branches – coordinated much of the transatlantic traffic from Africa.[11] They would retain ownership of the slaves, transport them to Brazil, and only then put them up for sale. While the Luso-Africans played a key role in the South Atlantic part of the Brazilian slave trade, Portuguese merchants advanced trade goods to the Afro-Brazilians and used this to retain overall control.

The Brazilian pattern of slave-holding spread through the whole colony and embraced a variety of milieus. Brazilian cities had many slave domestics and artisans. In the eighteenth century slaves were widely used to pan for gold – requiring many hours immersed in icy water, this was killing work. Mortality rates on the plantations were also very high, but planters chose to replenish their slave crews by new purchases rather than by easing the workload. In Minas Gerais slaves were also engaged on large estates producing basic supplies for the plantations, while in the interior and south slaves were also bought by cattle ranchers.

---

11   Miller, *Way of Death*, pp. 245–83.

CASH DEMAND, EXOTIC PRODUCE, TIED LABOUR

The struggle for the control of Brazil and the first attempts to cultivate tobacco, cotton and indigo for European markets elsewhere in the Americas, were the sign of a sudden expansion of European demand. Europeans were not only developing a taste for their exotic items but had the cash to pay for them. The distinctively capitalist combination of commodity production and free wage-labour in parts of north-western Europe had set the scene for something very different on the other side of the Atlantic. It was those in receipt of money incomes, whether rents, salaries or wages, who furnished a growing market for plantation products.

Robert Brenner has identified the fateful novelty of English agriculture in the sixteenth century: the rise of the capitalist tenant farmer. Tenant farmers who owed rent to their landlords needed to produce a marketable surplus of wheat or wool. Once they had a revenue from sales they could expand their output by hiring labour and purchasing inputs such as better seed varieties and better tools. The improving landlord also had reason to invest in infrastructure that would allow him to charge higher rents. Rural employers had an incentive to raise labour productivity through innovation, because labour costs were a distinct item borne by the farmer (in contrast, the European serf-lord expanded output by acquiring more villagers owing him labour, or by squeezing more labour from his existing serfs). Rural demand helped to greatly broaden the scope of the market. The towns of Europe west of the Elbe often enjoyed char-ters which gave them a real measure of autonomy. This was propitious for the emergence of capitalism, but the urban market was limited and the prevalence of guilds and of commercial monopolies acted as constraints. The merchants who engaged in long-distance trade favoured a type of commerce based on restricted quantities and high prices. The Asian spice trade had this character. While urban markets continued to expand, the growth of capitalist agriculture and cottage industry was less fettered. The English wool trade, like the Dutch commerce in grain and textiles, reflected a new scale of exchanges and soon involved a growing demand for the produce of the subtropical regions.[12]

---

12   This summarizes a complex argument. See the contributions by Robert Brenner to T. S. Aston, ed., *The Brenner Debate*, Oxford 1986. See also Robert Brenner, 'The Origins of Capitalism', *New Left Review* 106 (July–August 1977). Brenner's argument is endorsed and developed by Ellen Meiksins Wood in *The Origins of Capitalism*, London 1999. England's early agrarian capitalism was critical in terms of the size of the market, the incentive to innovate and the consequent capacity for sustained growth. But there were certainly aspects of feudal Europe and medieval business that helped to prepare for this breakthrough. The spread of the windmill and deep plough helped to raise agricultural productivity, while the comparative weakness and fragmentation of the feudal state allowed for the development of greater urban autonomy. The financial practices and commercial networks of the Italian city states, the Hanseatic League,

The increasing commercialization of the rural economy created opportunities for the state. The Tudor regime, like other European monarchies, had an urgent need of revenue, which it eventually met with help from the dissolution of the monasteries and by allowing the enclosure of common land and royal forests. The waves of privatization in sixteenth-century England were only possible because wage labour was already quite common in the countryside and the rural milieu was already subject to a far-reaching commercialization of wool, dairy products and wheat. The enclosures and sale of Church land expanded the numbers of those who had to sell their labour if they were to provide for themselves and their families; they also helped to stimulate out-migration from the English countryside. While many imposing continental monarchies fell into the clutches of financiers and tax farmers, the Tudors found it gainful to licence the landlords and their tenant farmers. The rise of capitalist farming and manufacture outgrew the residue of natural economy and created a new culture of consumption. The Low Countries and parts of northern France also contributed to commercialized consumption and the spread of wage labour, but these developments were more exposed and vulnerable to military and fiscal pressure than in England, with its strong natural defences.[13]

The lusty figures of Rabelais's Gargantua and Shakespeare's Falstaff can perhaps be seen as caricatures of the new appetites released by the money economy, to be tamed in different ways by the Puritan and the baroque. At first the products of the New World – not only silver, but dried cod, fur and tobacco – were not the fruit of slave labour, though the culture of consumption anyway conveyed little about their precise provenance. But as demand grew for indigo, tobacco and sugar, a new type of merchant saw the advantage of obtaining convenient supplies from the New World.

It is fitting that Robert Brenner, author of a commanding comparative synthesis of the origins of capitalism, also supplies us with an impressive account of the 'New Merchants' who catered to the first stirrings of mass demand. Whereas great merchants had previously preferred to deal in small quantities of highly priced goods, and to enjoy state monopolies, the Dutch and

---

Antwerp and Amsterdam all made a contribution to capitalistic development; but in terms of scale and sustainability the development of a form of rural capitalism in England marks a qualitative advance. For enduring barriers to capitalism elsewhere see, for example, Eric Hobsbawm, 'The Crisis of the Seventeenth Century', *Past and Present* 5 and 6 (1954). See also Luciano Pellicani, *The Genesis of Capitalism and the Origins of Modernity*, New York 1993, for the contribution of the towns, and Eric H. Mielants, *The Origins of Capitalism and the 'Rise of the West'*, Philadelphia PA 2007, for the world market. Though these authors differ over its exact nature, they do focus on capitalism as a highly distinctive economic system. Without such an explanatory category Gregory Clark (*A Farewell to Alms*, Princeton NJ, 2007) is drawn to fanciful speculations about genetic inheritance to explain the sustained growth of English agriculture in the period 1600 to 1800.

13 The peculiar features of British Absolutism are brought out by Perry Anderson in *Lineages of the Absolutist State*.

English New Merchants were evolving a more competitive system which catered to larger volumes and lower prices (on which I will say more below). The spread of capitalism was associated with the rise of experimental rationality at the expense of traditionalism, and of greater care in time-management. Max Weber's famous argument that the Puritan work ethic, the doctrine of the 'elect' and anxiety about salvation helped to promote rationalizing mentalities still has force, even if it remains difficult precisely to identify cause and effect. The planters of the New World also exhibited innovation and the rationalizing approach.[14]

E. A. Wrigley has subsequently explained plantation growth partly by reference to increased productivity and monetization in Europe. He writes:

> The large-scale import of goods such as sugar or cotton was conditional on a matching demand for such products, whether to meet the new wish to smoke tobacco, drink sweetened coffee, or to provide the raw material for a flourishing new textile industry. Such a demand was bigger and more rapidly growing in a country like England, where steadily growing productivity per head in agriculture had permitted a shift of the structure of demand for necessities and comforts and even luxuries, than in a country like Spain, which had been less fortunate.[15]

While fully accepting that the plantation trades reflected metropolitan demand, the plantations were themselves sites of an agricultural revolution and of new approaches to tropical cultivation – unfortunately in ways strongly associated with slave labour. This had much to do with the geographic advantages of the New World, the efficiency of the shipping routes linking the New World to Europe, and the shortage of suitable labour supplies.

Products that could not be grown in Europe had a special appeal and attracted the best prices. Sugar ranked as a premium product because of its many uses as well as its drug-like attractions. It sweetened beverages, cakes, confectionery and puddings. It had preservative properties and came to be widely used in brewing beer. The icing on the wedding or Christmas cake reminds us of its still lingering ceremonial significance. Its purely calorific

---

14   Max Weber, *The Protestant Ethic and the Spirit of Capitalism*, London 1957.

15   E. A. Wrigley, 'The Transition to an Advanced Organic Economy: Half a Millennium of English Agriculture', *Economic History Review*, 59/2 (2006), pp. 435–80, 242. The buoyancy of English agriculture meant more room for the non-subsistence sector. There is evidence that England in the period 1600–1800 was marked by dynamic technological advance in both agriculture and manufacturing, see Gregory Clark, 'The Long March of History: Farm Wages, Population, and Economic Growth, England 1209–1869', *Economic History Review*, 60/1 (2007), pp. 97–135. The English and French plantations also represented a breakthrough regarding the scale of output and productivity of labour, even if the latter had its limits, as we will see below. The planters also purchased supplies and equipment in ways that pumped some demand back into the metropolitan economy.

contribution to diet lags far behind all these considerations. Tobacco was not so versatile – though it could be chewed or snuffed as well as smoked. It was a powerful drug but, unlike alcohol, marijuana or cocaine, did not befuddle the senses or render the user more vulnerable. Still, those who offered a free pipe had to be treated with care. The merchants who spirited away young apprentices to the plantation colonies would invite them first to a smoking party, as a taste of the delights that would supposedly be theirs if they signed an indenture. Sweetened stimulants brightened up the parlour, made possible the coffee house and became the centrepiece of domestic rituals.[16] A new current in English philosophy claimed that there was a natural right to the satisfaction of natural appetites. As Jeremy Taylor put it: 'The right of nature is perfect and universal liberty to do whatsoever can secure me or please me. For the appetites that are prime, original and natural, do design us towards their satisfaction and were a continual torment, and in vain, if they were not in order to their rest, contentedness and perfection. Whatsoever we naturally desire, naturally we are permitted . . . Therefore to save my own life I can kill another or twenty, or a hundred, or take from his hands to please myself if it happens in my circumstances and power; and so for eating, drinking and pleasures.'[17] This author later insists that such 'natural rights' should only be enjoyed if compatible with Christian morality and the law of contract, but he still holds that, subject to this qualification, there is still much that should be permitted and enjoyed. This new emphasis was at variance with Puritan teaching but chimed in nicely with the taste for plantation produce.

Because of the trade winds, plantation products dispatched from the Brazilian North-East, the Eastern Caribbean and Virginia could reach Europe in a little over a month – half the sailing time from the West African or Central African coast. The parts of the Caribbean and Americas chosen by the planters were fertile and, being remote from the centres of Spanish power, secure. The stand-off between the colonists and the Native American peoples could be awkward, but during the first half-century or more of contact the clash was intermittent and containable. Planters were choosy, needing flat, fertile, well-watered land, near the coast. Native peoples who practised shifting cultivation and hunting soon learned to be wary of the aggressive newcomers, seeking to pursue their way of life in the extensive areas that Europeans had yet to settle.

The New World plantation colonies had some dangers, but were much safer than plantations in Africa. European companies and merchants who sought to set up plantations in Africa faced not only lengthy sailing times, but also extremely high mortality from the unfamiliar disease environment. The

---

16   Jordan Goodman, *Tobacco in History: The Cultures of Dependence*, London 1993; Sidney W. Mintz, *Sweetness and Power: The Place of Sugar in Modern History*, New York 1985.

17   Jeremy Taylor, *Ductor Dubitandum*, London 1676, pp. 167–8, 184, quoted in Tuck, *Natural Rights Theories*, pp. 111–12.

European slave-trading companies set up forts and 'factories' on the African coast which survived only thanks to agreements with the local rulers. They commanded a tiny strip of territory and offered protection only against one another. Portuguese inland trading networks and treaties were more extensive, but this was because they formed alliances with such monarchs as the kings of the Kongo.[18]

If New World locations were convenient for setting up plantations, the indigenous peoples were treated as a notable inconvenience. Barbados was uninhabited, but there were constant tensions with the Caribs of the rest of the Eastern Caribbean. Though the French were able to settle Martinique and Guadeloupe, and the English to develop plantations in the Leeward Islands, the Caribs remained a hostile and unconquered presence in the more mountainous islands until the 1770s. The English settlers in North America found it almost impossible to integrate Native Americans into their own culture, but had no such difficulty with their land. Tens of thousands of contracts were drawn up whereby North American colonists and colonial authorities claimed that native chiefs sold them tribal land, notwithstanding the fact that such chiefs, even if genuine, had no authority to alienate ancestral territory. Indeed the Native Americans' relationship to the land, and to flora and fauna, did not conform to English conceptions of permanent individual ownership.[19]

In contrast to Spanish America, the Native Americans were to be dispossessed and displaced rather than subordinated. Some leaders of colonial society sought to instruct willing Indians in the principles of Protestant Christianity, but with only meagre and temporary results. While Spain pursued an inclusive policy towards the Indians, the English colonists preferred to press back and exclude the native peoples. In Spanish and Portuguese America the attempt to construct a caste-like hierarchy of ethnic and class identities had not prevented de facto ethnic mixing on a scale that was not to be repeated in English North America. Men heavily outnumbered women among Iberian migrants to the Americas. In many parts of Spanish America the creole elite itself came to include descendants of the daughters of Indian caciques, and even those with a black great-grand-mother. On the other hand, it was said that any white of Old Christian background (i.e. with no Jewish or Morisco forebears) would be regarded as an *hidalgo*, or gentleman, in the Americas.

The Spanish concept of *limpieza de sangre* had a direct equivalent – *limpeza do sangue* – in Portugal. As we saw in the previous chapter, this notion was initially deployed against *conversos* to assert an 'Old Christian' monopoly of public offices. In the context of colonialism and slavery, it targeted Indians and

---

18 Alencastro, *O trato dos viventes*, pp. 70–7; Hugh Thomas, *The Slave Trade: The History of the Atlantic Slave Trade, 1440–1870*, London 1997, pp. 129–49.

19 The devastating impact is traced by William Cronon, *Changes in the Land: Indians, Colonists, and the Ecology of New England*, New York 1983.

Africans and their descendants. Endowing blood-lines with moral significance chimed in with the practice of enslaving Africans and Indians, but it corresponded more to an official hierarchy of castes than to a generalized, almost spontaneous, construction of race (such as occurred in the English colonies).

The Spanish and Portuguese kingdoms were a jumble of jurisdictions, not a homogenous legislative space. While the rules relating to *limpieza* were oppressive and racializing, they were also an incoherent patchwork.[20] They established ostensibly religious – but also racializing – criteria for holding public office. Sancho Panza prides himself on his identity as an Old Christian, for the effect of *limpieza* was to elevate commoners in an intensely status-conscious society. Like the slave, the tainted individual would be deemed to lack honour, but in the Spanish and Portuguese Americas those with some *converso* or slave ancestry might hope gradually to cleanse themselves of the taint, especially if they were in a position to give money to the Church. The Old Christians retained control of senior posts and of the Church hierarchy, but some well-to-do mulattoes or those with a *converso* grandparent might hold a commission in the militia. While a descendant of Moctezuma could be viceroy of New Spain, the mass of those of commoner indigenous descent were denied *limpieza*. Over time the distinction between *peninsulares* (Spanish-born) and *criollos* (American-born) became more important so far as senior posts were concerned.

The rising importance of Brazilian plantations in the late sixteenth and early seventeenth centuries itself unsettled the official racial order since, as noted above, several of the wealthy *senhores de engenho* came from a tainted or *converso* background. The Brazilian racial regime was to be less clear-cut than that which emerged in the English and French colonies. For a variety of reasons – the greater antiquity of Portuguese settlement, the decision of Brazilian *fazendeiros* to live on their estates and the relative scarcity of white women – Brazil was to be a land where many men of property (*homens boms*) were of mixed race. The Brazilian historian Luiz Felipe de Alencastro writes of Brazil's 'invention of the mulatto' – a strange achievement for a society dedicated to *limpeza do sangue* – and cites the seventeenth-century dictum that Brazil was 'hell for blacks and Indians, purgatory for whites and a paradise for mulattoes'.[21] In Brazil the rapacious *bandeirantes*, themselves of mixed race, undertook slave hunts among the native peoples. The cane fields were often cultivated by tied Indian labourers as well as African slaves. But the labour force of the *engenho* was Portuguese and African.

From the outset the English plantation was a novel enterprise that had little truck with its indigenous context and was narrowly focused on producing the

---

20   For an informative account which overstates the coherence of the Portuguese racial order and its implications for slavery, see Maria Luiza Tucci Carneiro, *Preconceito racial: Portugal e Brasil-colônia*, São Paulo 1988 (2ⁿᵈ ed.), pp. 43–174, 195–256.

21   Alencastro, *O trato dos viventes*, pp. 345–53.

staple. In the early decades English planters relied on imported indentured servants, because there was an acute labour shortage in the colonies and the planters feared the leverage of free labourers during the critical harvest period. It took time for planters to discover the advantage of African slaves. For about fifty years the North American tobacco planters purchased white indentured servants from Britain. During this period, there were as many free blacks as slaves in North America, and the former briefly enjoyed similar rights to white colonists.[22] The Native Americans were systematically displaced from their lands so there was good land available to the recently discharged indentured servant.

Planters in the English colonies discovered that, though good pay would procure an overseer for a large estate, hired labour was simply not available for the basic work of cultivating tobacco, sugar or indigo. So indentured servants for a while filled the gap, in the Caribbean as well as Virginia and Maryland. In the troubled years 1620 to 1660, tens of thousands signed up for plantation work. Somewhere between 170,000 and 225,000 emigrants of all types left the British Isles for America between 1610 and 1660 – more than a half of them indentured servants. Between 110,000 and 135,000 went to the Caribbean, 50,000 to Virginia and 20–25,000 to New England. Many of those sailing for the Caribbean perished before they had worked out their indenture, and of those who did survive most left for North America or returned to Britain. The fact that many hundreds of ships were now needed each year to transport tobacco and sugar from the plantations to England meant that there were cheap berths on the outward journey. English merchants or captains could consequently charge low prices for the servant contracts. Virginia and Maryland encouraged this tied labour by the 'headright' system which allotted a plot of land to those who served out their indenture. The numbers of servants dropped off after 1660, with very few signing on for the Caribbean but a further 30,000 going to Virginia between 1660 and 1690, by which time that stream dwindled to a trickle.

The supply of *engagés* to the French islands was smaller, and amounted to around 40,000 in the years 1630–80. Though France's population was much larger than England's, its agriculture was more labour intensive. The French planters' recourse to captive Africans was emphatic by the time of the promulgation of the *Code Noir* in 1685, and its subsequent implementation was modified by the *conseils* in each colony. The royal authorities distrusted the Huguenot inclinations of French seamen and colonists hailing from the Atlantic ports. The *Code Noir* reserved to good Catholics the right to own colonial property. From the beginning, African captives had been purchased from Dutch, English or Portuguese merchants as a supplementary tied labour force.

---

22   Ira Berlin, *Many Thousands Gone*, Cambridge MA 1998, pp. 29–46; Betty Wood, *The Origins of American Slavery*, New York 1999.

As the English settlements spread, clashes with the Indians meant that there were sometimes hauls of Native American captives. Over several decades in the mid-seventeenth century tens of thousands of such prisoners were taken, and – to be rid of them – dispatched for sale in the Caribbean. But Indian captives did not command good prices, and were deemed unsuitable as field labourers or artisans. Quite apart from the fact that there was no regular supply, the men were not trained for agriculture and would run away. However, in the aftermath of King Philip's War (1675–6) and other such conflicts, many Indian captives were sent to the Caribbean. South Carolina traders fostered rivalries between different Indian peoples by supplying some with firearms and ammunition and inviting them to prey on their neighbours. The captives – men, women and children – acquired in this way could be sold in the Caribbean, or exchanged for African slaves at a rate of two Indians for a single African. The colony's proprietors worried that the traders were exploiting the native 'Covetousness of your guns, Powder, and Shott and other European commodities' to attack their neighbours, 'to ravish the wife from the Husband, Kill the father to get the child and to burne and destroy the habitations of these poore people into whose country wee were Ch[e]arfully received . . . when wee were weak.'[23] One way or another, tens of thousands of Native Americans were sold as slaves to planters, mainly in the West Indies. They could be found niche occupations but were no solution to the quest to expand the plantation labour force. Apart from anything else there were, by this time, only about half a million Native Americans in North America, and only a small number of them were within reach of slave raiders and traders.

African slaves outnumbered white indentured servants on the plantations in Barbados as early as 1650, in Jamaica by the 1670s and in Virginia not until the beginning of the next century. The rise of the plantation was not the result of state initiative. It reflected the competitive and innovatory efforts of hundreds of merchants and thousands of planters as they catered to the developing appetites of civil society. Tobacco became an article of mass consumption with little or no state encouragement and helped to make viable English or French settlements that might otherwise have disappeared. The plantations first appeared as a result of commercial sponsorship in areas beyond the reach of Spanish power. The latter had been driven back onto a well-fortified line of Caribbean staging posts by a plundering swarm of English, French and Dutch privateers and pirates. Between the Treaty of Cateau-Cambresis in 1559 and the Treaty of Ryswick in 1697 a geographical zone referred to as 'beyond the line', that is, West of the Meridian and South of the Tropic of Cancer, was excluded from the scope of European treaties. It was within this no-man's-land that the new plantation developed after about 1630. Many of those inclined to challenge Spanish power,

---

23   Alan Taylor, *American Colonies: The Settling of North America*, New York 2002, p. 231.

whether predators or settlers, were Protestants and Huguenots. Because of domestic strife the rulers of England and France could not spare much attention to the mid-century developments in the Caribbean, allowing the plantations to develop, at least for a while, without interference. Colbert established a colonial company in 1664 which wrested commercial control of the French islands from the Dutch, but the company was soon wound up and replaced by the *Exclusif* system whereby all trade with the colonies was monopolized by Bordeaux and Nantes.

Bristol vied with London as a hub of the new colonial development. The New Merchants did not owe their wealth to royal warrants and monopolies. They catered to mass demand, often beginning as ship's captains sponsored by retailers. They did not belong to the merchant guilds but were in touch with the retailing shopkeepers or even had that background themselves.[24] Several New Merchants also entered the African trade, selling slaves to the planters they sponsored. Such planters might be their junior relatives, or fortune-hunting younger sons of the gentry. Those hoping to make a fortune from planting had a different mind-set from those set on simple plunder. Whereas the planters settled in areas far from Spanish control, the privateers and pirates focused on the silver routes. The colonial systems of England and France only came into the picture after the plantations, with Dutch help, were doing a roaring trade. Seen in this way, the planters and merchants were the prime movers, while colonial mercantilism was a secondary superstructure of exploitation. The new Caribbean slave plantations appeared and made great strides in the years 1630 to 1655, a time when the English and French states were distracted and slow to register the implications of the plantation revolution. However this spontaneous surge of market forces soon called forth an impulse to regulate and control it. The planters themselves needed a new regime of law and order. They also needed protection from enemy privateers and freelance pirates. The English colonies were almost from the beginning endowed with assemblies that could enact their own internal laws.

Plantations were already flourishing on Barbados when the English Commonwealth government first established the Navigation Acts limiting the trade to English ships. The Commonwealth also embarked on the 'Western design' that ultimately led to the acquisition of Jamaica in 1655. The Barbados assembly adopted a law for 'the better governance of negroes' in 1661. The principles of the Navigation Acts were confirmed in the 1660s, restricting the colonial trade to English vessels and English ports. The restored monarchy

---

24   Robert Brenner, 'The Social Basis of England's Overseas Expansion', *Journal of Economic History* 32 (1972), pp. 361–84; Robert Brenner, *Merchants and Revolution: Commercial Change, Political Conflict and London's Overseas Traders, 1550–1653*, Princeton 1993, pp. 30–9, 92–197; and David Harris Sachs, *The Widening Gate: Bristol and the Atlantic Economy, 1450–1700*, Berkeley, CA and London 1991, pp. 251–77.

embodied a colonial order that encouraged independent planters and new merchants, while recognizing some of the privileges of the original colonial proprietors. The Glorious Revolution of 1688 saw the latter further reduced and confirmed a generous margin of colonial autonomy. The London Board of Trade, under the guidance of none other than John Locke, endorsed ferocious Virginia legislation to police the slaves, discourage manumission and control or repress any free blacks.[25]

By the 1660s the planters of the English and French Caribbean had opted for a menial labour force almost entirely comprising African captives, a switch that occurred later in North America, between 1680 and 1710. The planters found it did not make economic sense to offer better prices for the dwindling supply of European contract labourers. They discovered advantages in staffing their plantations with a relatively permanent and increasingly skilled workforce rather than with servants who only stayed for a few years, or with Indian captives who were unused to field labour and likely to run away. The African captives were already inured to agricultural routines, and had much less opportunity to resist or escape than Native Americans or Europeans. They brought with them, or soon acquired, the skills necessary both for the production of the commercial staple and for meeting most of their own subsistence needs. The slave-owners discovered the advantages of what economists today call 'human capital'. While indentured servants left soon after they learned how to be useful, the growing skill and knowledge of the slaves redounded to the benefit of their owners.

The English took the word 'negro' from the Spanish and, with it, a way of thinking which linked the negro to slave-holding. In the process the idea of the 'negro' was taken out of an elaborate hierarchy and eventually placed in simple opposition to 'Christian', 'English' and 'white'. John Hawkins, the first English slave-trader, frequented the Portuguese and Spanish Atlantic islands, and learned how to acquire African captives from the Portuguese. The compilations of travellers' reports assembled by Richard Hakluyt and Samuel Purchas helped to inform English readers of the experience of Iberian colonization. But while the English and Dutch learned something from the Iberians, they were able to supply a stronger impetus to slave-based plantation development in the Americas. They also brought with them a sharper notion of private property, and, since they were urged by Puritan pastors to shun unions with 'strange women', a more narrowly defined sense of religious and ethnic identity. If colonists nevertheless had children by native women, they were punished for the offence but not encouraged to marry the mother of their child, as the Catholic

---

25   See John Locke, *Political Writings*, edited by David Wooton, London 1993, pp. 446–51; David Armitage, *The Ideological Origins of the British Empire*, Oxford 2000; and Blackburn, *Making of New World Slavery*, pp. 263–6.

Church taught should happen in seventeenth-century French Canada or Martinique. The English, whether planters or farmers, formed rather homogenous settler-communities. While some German or Dutch Protestants might be admitted, the native peoples were kept at arm's length. Unsuccessful attempts to convert Indians, or to persuade them to conform to English norms of cultivation, were punctuated by armed conflict. The later adoption of racial slavery in Virginia was both to reflect and to intensify this ethnocentric, racial consciousness; but it is worth noting that, in New England, antipathy to heathens and savages could prompt hostility to the introduction of slaves. Many had ventured to the New World in search of land and were quite prepared to work it with their own hands.

The turn to slavery took place at different times in the different regions. In the English Caribbean it was already quite pronounced by 1670, while it came a little later in the French Antilles. In Virginia and Maryland the tobacco boom was at first based on indentured labour, and the rise of the slave plantation took place between 1680 and 1710.

Indentures and slaves had in common that they were bound to work and could not threaten to leave, or demand more payment, when the time arrived to bring in the harvest. But planters discovered significant advantages in buying slaves, even though they were more costly than indentures. As noted above, the techniques of cultivation and processing were complex and required time to master. While indentures were lost after a few years, the slaves became more productive and valuable. Further, on larger plantations the new slaves could be worked under drivers in gangs which would build up a fierce momentum. It was not thought right for indentures to be driven under the whip in this way. The slave gangs boosted output per labourer and gave slave plantations an edge over cultivators who had no slaves.[26]

These 'productive' advantages rested on the more intense working of the slave. They did not exhaust the advantages of slaves over indentured servants, as the planters saw it. Europeans were more vulnerable than Africans to the diseases of the plantation zone, and might die before their time was up. The hardiness of the slaves had another dimension. Planters or their agents did not always buy in sufficient provisions for their servants; the slaves, if given a plot, were more likely to raise most of the food they needed. Times of drought or pestilence were especially difficult for European labourers. Africans were more likely to have put something aside, partly because they were better acquainted with sub-tropical crops and partly because they did not count on the benevolence of the planter. Consequently in times of drought and dearth – a particular

---

26   For the greater productivity of slaves versus indentures see Lorena Walsh, 'Slave Life, Slave Society and Tobacco in the Chesapeake, 1620–1820', in Ira Berlin and Philip D. Morgan, eds, *Cultivation and Culture: Labor and the Shaping of Slave Life in the Americas*, Charlottesville, VA, and London 1993, pp. 170–201, 176.

problem on the Caribbean islands – the condition of the slaves might appear comparatively better because they had the will and ability to take care of themselves. Observers sometimes said that the indentured servants were treated as badly, or even worse, than slaves. European apprentices and sailors could be physically punished by their masters, and indentures might occasionally be flogged, though certainly not as systematically or harshly as Africans. However, planters were restrained in their treatment of indentures by the opinion of other free colonists, and by custom and contract.

In Virginia indentures were able to sue their masters for ill-treatment, and there were many thousands of such cases in the seventeenth century. The slaves in the English colonies had no such recourse, and no contract to which they could appeal. Small and medium-sized plantations survived and even flourished in the North American colonies and the turn to slavery was slower. The planters of Virginia and Maryland had smaller estates than the planters of the Caribbean. They would work eight to fifteen slaves as a single work group, under their own supervision, and only a few owned over a hundred slaves, as was typical of the West Indian sugar plantations.

With the switch to slaves there was a more intense work pattern, with fewer holidays and work in the evenings. Sundays remained a free day and there was time off at Christmas and Easter. Planters and overseers themselves welcomed such breaks, but slaves quickly seized on any concession, converting it into a custom. Long-serving overseers, who had built up such understandings, obtained more work from the slaves. If there was a valuable crop to be harvested on a Sunday, extra rewards would be demanded. Planters also sought to extract more labour from their slaves by finding secondary and subsistence crops that did not interfere with cultivation of the main staple. The allotting of carefully measured 'tasks' was another device for mobilizing slave labour. This method allowed the slave a little room for manoeuvre and negotiation but, wielded by a competent overseer, it delivered the results the planter wanted. The 'sugar islands' also produced some cotton and indigo, with cattle pens supplying animal power, meat and manure. In Virginia and Maryland slaves were put to cultivating wheat and learned to use the plough effectively.[27]

The precise mix of these various reasons for acquiring slaves varied from place to place, and period to period. They were obviously considerable in the plantation zone in the seventeenth century, and this began to raise slave prices. But potential employers in other parts of the Americas did not buy slaves, perhaps because they could not afford them or because family, free, tribute or indentured labour could meet their needs. Plantation slavery bred new versions

---

27   Walsh, 'Slave Life, Slave Society, and Tobacco Production in the Tidewater Chesapeake, 1620–1820'.

of racial stereotyping and antipathy – but this could also, where free labour was established, discourage a resort to slave labour.

While the Spanish, Portuguese and French royal authorities had a powerful apparatus of administration in the New World and a desire to regulate racial relations in their colonies, the racial regime of the English colonies emerged in a relatively unplanned way. It is true that the Royal African Company for a time had a monopoly on the importation of slaves to the English colonies, but it was supplying an already existing demand. When planters and their fellow white colonists adopted the rule that the children of slave mothers would themselves be slaves, they were following Iberian practice and Roman Law (rather than the descent through the male line of English Common Law). The English colonial practice of the 'one drop rule' – anyone with any African ancestry was 'black' – was distinctive. The various colonial assemblies quickly adopted repressive and racialized slave legislation, which was then ratified by the metropolis. Charles Mills has written of a 'racial contract' shaping the colonial social order.[28] This was, of course, a contract within the white population. While the leading men had the main say in such regulations, the poorer whites were given a stake in a racial order which reserved the hardest toil for 'blacks'.

THE NEW PLANTATION

Elements of the 'industrial revolution' were anticipated by the New World plantation. The implacable, easily invigilated, dangerous, and deeply unhealthy regime of the sugar mill was a dark foreshadowing of the early cotton mill. Both mercilessly consumed the lives of men, women and children. The sugar plantation and the early cotton mill towns had the same high mortality rates; without fresh arrivals they would have rapidly dwindled in size. Both were effectively unregulated and yoked to the seemingly limitless expansion of demand.[29]

The elements of modernity on the plantation came to include tight coordination, a rhythm set by machines, precisely calibrated and invigilated labour, and the application of wind and water power. The physical and human apparatus was financially underpinned by letters of credit, extended networks of trust, insurance, and a voracious but oblivious consumerism. Some of these features were rooted in the fact that the slave plantation was constructed by and for the market, with the aim of maximizing commodity outputs so long as this yielded a surplus of revenues over costs. The slave estate was, of course, based on a 'natural economy' and self-sufficiency which reduced the need for commercial inputs. Slaves grew some of their own food, made their own simple clothing,

---

28   Charles Mills, *The Racial Contract*, Chicago 1998.

29   For a comparison of mortality rates between Leeds and a Jamaican parish in the early nineteenth century, see Michael Craton, *Searching for the Invisible Man: Slave and Plantation Life in Jamaica*, Cambridge, MA, 1978, pp. 94, 116.

constructed the plantation buildings, tended their master and his family, and raised children of their own, all without the planter spending a farthing. But while 'natural economy' limited the planter's purchases, the plantation did still require many productive inputs which often had to be bought in – equipment, hoes, nails, packing materials, extra provisions for the slaves (dried meat or fish), cloth, and, the most expensive single item, slaves themselves. Some salaries and taxes had to be paid and, in the long run, the slave plantation had to justify its cash outlays by turning a profit. Unlike the feudal estate or Spanish American hacienda, its internal organization was deeply penetrated by a commercial logic, and the direct process of production was supervised by the owner or his agent. Unlike a modern business, the plantation could retreat for a few years inside the shell of 'natural economy', with the denizens of the plantation, and its satellite farms and pens, living on their own produce.[30] It could survive disruption to the sea lanes in war, but in the medium or longer run it was vulnerable to foreclosure or bankruptcy. In short it was a hybrid type of enterprise, with modern features (looking forward to the industrial 'plant') but a basis in extra-economic compulsion.

The first planters in Barbados in the 1630s and 1640s had learned slave-trading from the Portuguese and the Dutch, as well as how to make sugar. The English-owned plantations were more productive and 'modern' than those of Brazil, using metal rollers, switching gangs of slaves between field and mill, and employing few or no Native American labourers. The cane fields were manured to sustain their fertility, since land was scarce on the islands. But the secret of the huge surge in plantation output was that the labour of slave gangs could be tightly coordinated, and directed in a timely fashion at the most urgent tasks. Plantation management handbooks stressed that slaves working in gangs could be more easily invigilated by the drivers and overseers, the latter equipped with whips, cutlasses and guns. The slave crew was usually divided, according to age and strength, into three or four gangs. Each gang could then establish a formidable rhythm, with the strongest setting the pace. During the harvest season the slaves on a sugar plantation worked at night in the mill as well as during the day, with extraordinarily gruelling eighteen-hour working days being routine. To avoid the loss entailed by any interruption, the overseer aimed to keep the sugar coppers boiling twenty-four hours a day. The work requirements on a tobacco plantation were spread more evenly through the year and, while there was evening work prizing tobacco or shucking corn, there was no need for the round-the-clock mobilization of the sugar plantation.[31]

---

30   Jacob Gorender, *O escravismo colonia*, Sao Paulo 1988, pp. 81–3, 142.

31   The first handbook to recommend and explain the division of the labour force into gangs was Henry Drax, 'Instructions for the Management of Drax Hall', quoted in Gary Puckrein, *Little England: Plantation Society and Anglo-Barbadian Politics, 1627–1700*, New York 1984, pp. 82–3; for slave gangs in the French islands see Gabriel Debien, 'Les esclaves', in Pierre Pluchon, ed., *Histoire*

The working day on the plantation was divided into spells or watches, signalled by the ringing of bells or the blowing of a horn, as on a ship. Indeed the methodical direction of plantation labour owed something to both maritime routine and the parade-ground drill of Europe's seventeenth-century 'military revolution'.[32] The new notions of military discipline were to include soldiers marching in step, and counter-marching, and learning to reload their muskets with a series of standardized movements. Prince Mauritz of the House of Orange, uncle of the governor of Dutch Brazil, was a pioneer of this military revolution, while Cromwell's New Model Army and Navy also learned from it. Of course, plantation coordination probably reflected African as well as European practices.

The crucial European cultivation tool was the plough, drawn by a horse or an ox. African agriculture often incorporated shifting cultivation and was based on work teams employing hoes. In most of sub-Saharan Africa there were no suitable draft animals and the soil was exhausted too quickly by the deep plough. However, work-teams equipped with hoes, and comprising age cohorts and cousinages, were rhythmic and productive. The slaves of the New World readily wielded the hoe but were very resistant to the plough. And as they worked, they often sang, as did work teams in Africa, with the songs sometimes lampooning the overseer or manager.[33]

Notwithstanding the long hours in the field and mill, the slaves were expected to grow much of the food they ate. They were given small plots away from the plantation to cultivate on Sundays, and in the evenings if they were not working in the mill. Sometimes there were chickens and small gardens tended by the old and infirm close to the slave quarters. The slave's hunger and concern for loved ones was thus enlisted to cut outlays on provisions – although it was usually not possible for slaves to survive on what they produced themselves, and they were still reliant on the planter for extra rations of dried meat or fish. The planter or overseer would often hand rations of food, clothing and rum to

---

des Antilles et de la Guyane, Paris 1982, pp. 141–62. A Brazilian historian emphasizes the crucial importance of the labour coordination and control to be found on English plantations from the 1660s: see Rafael de Bivar Marquese, Feitores do corpo, missionários da mente: Senhores, letrados e o controle dos escravos nas Américas, 1660–1860, São Paulo 2004, pp. 19–86. North American planters were slower to adopt the slave gang, obtaining good results with the task system in both rice and tobacco cultivation. For the evolution of the gang and task system in English North America, see Philip D. Morgan, Slave Counterpoint: Black Culture in the Eighteenth-Century Chesapeake and Lowcountry, Chapel Hill 1998, p. 179. The slave gang was to become crucial to the cotton plantations of the antebellum US South, and its economic significance was at the centre of the argument developed by Robert Fogel and Stanley Engerman, Time on the Cross, New York 1974.

32 William McNeil, The Pursuit of Power, Chicago 1982, pp. 126–33.

33 For the contrast between the plough in Europe and the hoe in Africa see Jack Goody, Technology, Tradition and the State in Africa, Cambridge 1971. For work teams in Africa see John Van D. Lewis, 'Domestic Labor Intensity and the Incorporation of Malian Peasant Farmers into Localized Descent Groups', American Ethnologist 8/1 (February 1981), pp. 53–73.

the head people to distribute, thus reinforcing the internal hierarchy of the plantation. On sugar estates slaves could drink cane juice, a ready source of calories. The rate of labour extraction achieved by the slave plantation with its gang labour and self-provision was extraordinarily high. While the East European serf might work for three or four days for their serf-lord, and much less in winter, the plantation slave worked six days a week during a much longer harvesting-planting cycle. The slaves worked for some 2,500 or 3,000 hours a year directly for their master.[34]

The multiplication of sugar plantations in the Caribbean raised output steeply, and new methods raised output per estate. In the early decades of the eighteenth century a Barbadian or Jamaican sugar estate would produce 150 tons of sugar annually, compared with 75 tons for the seventeenth-century Brazilian estate. By the 1780s the owner of Worthy Park, a large estate with a slave crew of 400, looked to produce 400 tons a year, and in years of high prices (notably 1792–1814) considerably to exceed this goal.[35] In the early seventeenth century the slave on a Cuban sugar estate was producing about a third of a ton of sugar each year. J. R. Ward offers calculations for British West Indian plantations from the late seventeenth to the early nineteenth century, averaging annually a little less than half a ton of sugar per slave. It is not easy to compare like with like, since recently planted cane on new land would give a better yield; the ratoon canes would be cut for another twenty or thirty years, with declining yields. To compensate, planters would improve their production methods, bring new land into cultivation or raise the output of secondary products. By the late eighteenth or early nineteenth century output had risen to one ton per slave; in its best years Worthy Park recorded two tons of sugar per slave.[36] David Watts points to productivity problems in the English Caribbean, and Stuart Schwartz urges that in its early stages the English 'sugar revolution' had only raised output per slave by about 20 per cent.[37] The English West Indian estates produced and sold molasses and rum as well muscovado and refined sugar. Indeed, the sale of molasses and rum to North American merchants often paid for the plantation's direct purchases of provisions and equipment, allowing the planter to live grandly on the sugar sales.

---

34   One of the best studies of the seventeenth-century English Caribbean is Richard Dunn, *Sugar and Slaves*, London 1975. For the new agricultural methods see also David Watts, *The West Indies: Patterns of Development, Culture and Environmental Change since 1492*, Cambridge 1985, pp. 212–32, 319–447. See also *Making of New World Slavery*, Chapters 6 and 8, and Hilary Beckles and Verene Shepherd, eds, *Caribbean Slave Society and Economy: A Student Reader*, Kingston and London 1991.

35   Craton, *Searching for the Invisible Man*, pp. 138–40. Note that Craton's figures are given in hogsheads of 16 cwt, with 20 cwt to the ton.

36   J. R. Ward, 'The Profitability of Sugar Planting in the British West Indies, 1650–1834', in Beckles and Shepherd, eds, *Caribbean Slave Society and Economy*, pp. 81–94.

37   Schwartz, *Tropical Babylons*, Introduction, pp. 19–20.

Planters were chasing revenue, not productivity. They expanded the size of their estates even though hauling the cane longer distances reduced its sugar content. They also needed a slave crew large enough to bring in, and process, the harvest, even if this left them somewhat over-staffed outside the six-month harvest season. Although the plantation resembles the factory in that work on the main crop was supervised by the planter, it had a rigidity about it that made raising productivity difficult. Planters complained that the slaves remained attached to the hoe and worked poorly if asked to use the plough.[38] At any one time at least a half of the English West Indian planters were absent from their estates, and their attempts to introduce new crop varieties or improved methods were fitful and ineffective. They had initiated the plantation revolution, but found that others more fully exploited its possibilities. In the last decades of the eighteenth century there was much concern with 'amelioration', a term that encompassed both measures to encourage female slaves to have more children and improvements in husbandry.[39]

English planting hence owed little to chartered colonial companies. The Royal African Company, with its slave-trading monopoly, established forts on the African coast and supplied some influential planters with credit. Perhaps it helped to consolidate the English presence in the trade, but before long it was the target of planters who were looking for lower prices and larger supplies, and of 'interloping' traders who believed the Company's monopoly to be unjustified. Between 1690 and 1713 parliament received one hundred petitions from traders in the outports requesting the end of the Company's remaining privileges and monopoly. This agitation was eventually successful, and it was proved that 'free trade' permitted a much larger traffic in slaves.[40]

Plantation growth in the British Caribbean surged following the eclipse of the company. The vitality of the English plantation system stemmed from free enterprise and the rise of the new type of consumer society. It embodied the spirit of early capitalism, with its calculation of costs and anticipation of market demand. The thousands of ocean-going ships needed by the Atlantic trades became increasingly specialized and cost-effective. The imperial authorities grasped that they would raise more revenue by levying duties on imports but otherwise interfering as little as possible. A 'draw back' system allowed goods brought to Britain but destined for re-export – such as Virginian tobacco – to be held in bonded warehouses and to pay duty at a lower rate. The French *Exclusif* worked in a similar way.

---

38 Watts, *The West Indies*, pp. 403–4, 429. I discuss limits to productivity gains in *Making of New World Slavery*, pp. 332–44.

39 J. R.Ward, *British West Indian Slavery, 1750–1834: The Process of Amelioration*, Oxford 1988.

40 K. G. Davies, *The Royal African Company*, New York 1970, pp. 122–52.

If the plantation was a key institution in the rise of New World slavery, so was the slave ship which hauled captives across the Atlantic. The kings and merchants of the African coast were well aware that it was the Europeans' ships which allowed them to reap the profit produced by the differential value of captives on the African coast and those same captives in the slave markets of the Americas. Attempts by African monarchs to buy or lease Atlantic sailing vessels were always denied. The slave-trading vessels eventually became highly adept at transporting large numbers of captives, packing them far more densely than was ever considered appropriate for whites, even if the latter were indentured servants. Indeed the typical passenger-per-ton ratio on a loaded slave ship was three times that on a passenger vessel carrying European migrants. The atrocious conditions which resulted raised mortality among the captives, but not by enough to cancel out the profit to be made from overloading, and hence spreading and reducing the unit freight cost. The slavers knew that disease was anyway likely to carry off a tenth or more of those they carried. Racial disregard and economic calculation fitted neatly together. The Atlantic sharks also spotted an opportunity, and followed the wake of the slave ships.[41]

European mariners consoled themselves with the notion of a fickle fate or fortune, which might cast a man down but also raise him up. Portuguese, Dutch and English seamen had reasonable pay and chances to trade on their own account (usually in African or Caribbean produce, not slaves). On a slave-trading vessel, they were as likely to die on the voyage as were the captives. A seaman might himself be captured by North African pirates, to be held as a slave or, if he was lucky, to be redeemed by the charitable societies which existed for the purpose.[42] In Daniel Defoe's *Robinson Crusoe* the hero is himself enslaved prior to escaping and building a plantation in Brazil. Evocation of the capricious 'wheel of fortune' made it easier to take risks and stoically to bear the misfortunes of others.

THE FRENCH OUTPERFORM THE ENGLISH

Louis XIV, the Sun King, was disturbed by the wealth and wilfulness of the French planters, and determined to subject them to a West India Company. This company, devised by Colbert, the arch-mercantilist finance minister, lasted barely a decade, from 1665 to 1674, but during that time it severed the planters' ties to Dutch traders and ensured that the plantation produce was transported in French bottoms to Bordeaux or Nantes, even if it was subsequently

---

41   Marcus Rediker, *The Slave Ship*, London 2007, pp. 37–9.

42   Linda Colley, *Captives: Britain, Empire and the World*, London 2002. That fate might expose the adventurer to enslavement was a recurrent theme of a much-read Portuguese compilation of mariners' accounts. Bernardo Gomes de Brito, *História trágico-marítima*, presentation by Ana Miranda, Rio de Janeiro 1998 (original edition, Lisbon 1735).

re-exported. However, Colbert grasped that the colonial trade would benefit if freed from Company control, while still strictly limited to French ports. The French colonists of Saint-Domingue thought of themselves as an autonomous privateer community which voluntarily submitted to the Crown. But they still needed French protection and legislation to codify slave property and plantation labour. Aware of the success of Barbados, Louis XIV and his ministers were willing not only to allow a measure of planter autonomy but also to award special privileges and assistance to plantation development. Indeed, the new model of slave plantation was to be pushed to a further pitch of development in the French Caribbean colonies.

Saint-Domingue became the richest European colony in the New World by the mid-eighteenth century. French Absolutism achieved a synthesis of colonial mercantilism, plantation slavery and baroque spectacle. To further his New World ambitions, Louis XIV strengthened Saint-Domingue and built a Navy of one hundred ships of the line. Recruitment to the *marine de guerre* was efficiently promoted by means of the so-called *inscription maritime*, which laid a duty of naval service on sailors and caused less friction than Britain's infamous system of impressment.

The court at Versailles played its own part in the promotion of colonial products, serving as an elegant display cabinet for the luxury goods which France and its colonies were so skilled at producing. The merchants of Bordeaux had privileged access to the sugar, coffee, cotton and indigo of the Antilles and were able to sell these to central and eastern Europe side-by-side with the silk and wines of the metropolis. The colonial state subsidized the slave trade. Under the so-called *acquits de Guinée* system, French merchants could use proof of slave purchases to gain exemption from taxes on the importation of plantation produce. The French planters also benefited from the engineering prowess of the French military, since they constructed roads, harbours, bridges, aqueducts and other irrigation works which helped greatly to raise plantation productivity. The plantations of Saint-Domingue overtook those of Jamaica, whose owners struggled to build the irrigation and infrastructure they needed without much help from the authorities.[43]

The king attempted to regulate the slave regime, with the promulgation of an edict of 1685 often referred to as the *Code Noir*. The novelty of New World slavery and the surge of the seventeenth-century Atlantic slave trade had aroused concern among some Catholic clerics, such as Alfonso de Sandoval in

---

43   Jean Meyer, *Histoire du sucre*, Paris 1989, pp. 106–90; Jean Meyer, Jean Tarrade, Annie Rey-Goldzeiguer, Jacques Thobie, *Histoire de la France coloniale des origines à 1914*, Paris 1991, pp. 75–99, 117–47, 235–78; Blackburn, *Making of New World Slavery*, pp. 277–305, 431–56. While the French plantations did outproduce the English islands by the 1780s, the absentee Jamaican planters devised a remarkably effective institution to monitor the performance of their estate managers, the so-called Accounts Produce Department.

Spanish America, Antonio Vieira in Brazil and Father Du Tertre in Saint-Domingue. The rising Protestant contribution to slavery no doubt made it easier for such criticisms to gain a hearing in Catholic Europe. Those in authority came to the view that slavery and the slave trade should be brought more firmly within the scope of rules laid down by the monarch and Church. Following receipt of a petition from Brazil in the early 1680s, the Holy See even briefly entertained the idea that the Atlantic slave trade should be banned. Bishop Bossuet, the eminent French theologian, was quite prepared to defend New World slavery so long as it was duly regulated. Louis XIV was perhaps responding to the concerns of such critics with his elaborate codification of the slave status in the French colonies, emphasizing the duty of planters to provide for the slaves' spiritual and temporal well-being. Jews and Protestants were to be banned from the French colonies. African slaves should be instructed and baptized, and planters were required to supply them with regular rations of bread and meat or fish.[44] There were harsh penalties for disobedience – those who ran away for more than a month were to have an ear cut off. A draft of the *Code* had already been drawn up by Colbert and his officials, with input from the resident planters. The *Code* also reflected the religious concerns of Madame de Maintenon: the king's mistress had once lived in the Antilles.

In practice the French colonists had great latitude in interpreting – and later amending – the *Code*, but it did recognize the existence of a small number of free people of colour. If an unmarried free man had a child with a slave woman, he was encouraged to marry her. Article 59 awarded freedmen and women (slaves who had obtained manumission through good service or payment) the same civic rights as the free-born. Once again, it was not always possible for the free people of colour to make a reality of these provisions, but they did begin to constitute a formally recognized element in colonial society, in marked contrast to the situation in many English colonies – for example Virginia – where manumission was made very difficult and freed blacks were pressured to leave the colony. While French planters successfully elaborated upon the productive organization of their English counterparts, the baroque French state was eager to make clear that it took full responsibility for the workings of such a key institution as the new colonial slavery.

French colonial mercantilism was less state-dominated, however, than that of the Iberian empires. Like them it adopted some features of modernity, namely a courtly spectacle, which displayed the exotic and sought to dazzle the mass of subjects. But while the French colonial system nourished the splendid fortunes of the mercantile elite of Bordeaux and Nantes, it did not succeed in finding a suitable crop for Louisiana, which remained largely undeveloped; the English

---

44   The full text of the *Code* is given in Louis Sala-Molins, *Le Code Noir ou le calvaire de Canaan*, Paris 1987.

colonists, less constrained by regulation, might have done better. French colonial regulations and privileges, with their mixed results of success and frustration, prompted the French colonial entrepreneur Thomas Le Gendre to coin the term 'laissez faire' when he petitioned for a more liberal colonial regime. The French colonial merchants took the lead in the re-export trade and built magnificent houses in Bordeaux and Nantes, but they lacked the deep internal market available to English merchants. The consolidation of French Absolutism rested on a ferocious fiscal system, and this inhibited the growth and integration of the domestic market in the metropolis. Despite its much larger population, France consumed only half as much sugar as England in the mid-eighteenth century. Many colonial merchants and planters keenly resented the *Exclusif*, the monopoly exercised by Nantes and Bordeaux, and engaged in contraband with the English colonies whenever they could. The antagonism between different types of commercial and proprietary interest occasionally led to open revolt, as in Martinique's Gaoulé of 1719, when white *colons* rejected the project of a new colonial company.

CHAPTER THREE

Plantation Hierarchy, Social Order and the Atlantic System

It is clear enough why the slave plantation suited the planters and merchants. But how did the latter secure even a modicum of compliance from free citizens who were not directly involved? How did they contain slave resistance? And how did religious and political authorities justify the new arrangements? The construction of new racial identities supplies a crucial part of the answer to these questions. But this was a multi-layered process, not the simple transfer to a new context of an already-existing formula.

By the close of the seventeenth century nearly all slaves in the Americas were Africans, or of partly African descent, through the mother. The enslavement of rebellious indigenous peoples continued in parts of Brazil, the Spanish possessions, and English North America, but was no longer of much importance as a source of labour for the plantations. In the Spanish, French and Portuguese colonies there were now quite sizeable free coloured or black populations in the towns and cities, but in rural areas where plantations developed, black slaves comprised the great majority of the labouring population. In the English colonies the link between skin colour and social status became tighter, so that any person walking down a country path who seemed to be of African descent was assumed to be a slave unless they could prove otherwise. Slaves travelling outside their plantation were generally required to carry a pass. The existence of larger groups of free people of colour in the colonies of other European powers led to less sharply drawn boundaries, but always involving a demarcation of the African-born and the 'negro' or 'mulatto'. Those who arrived from Africa often preserved a sense of community with all African ethnic groups, as well as with shipmates who had arrived on the same vessel and, eventually, with those on the same plantation.

Although there were repeated episodes of slave resistance, ranging from flight or revolt to a multitude of forms of small-scale evasion or sabotage, they were savagely repressed. The Africans had already passed through the terrible ordeal of capture, march to the coast and Middle Passage; they were then plunged in a forbidding new environment where there were dreadful sanctions for failure to conform, with flogging and torture and deprivation. For those who at least outwardly complied there were modest incentives and those plots of land. Survival itself could seem a form of resistance. The stories told in the slave quarters of Anancy the Spider Man, or of Brer Rabbit, stress the latent strength or cunning of the weak; they are the New World equivalent of the fables of Aesop, another slave.

The planters sought to structure the slave community by creating a hierar-chy. The so-called head people comprised an elite of slave drivers, craftsmen and house slaves, who were given some authority over other slaves and were put in charge of distributing rations of clothing, food and drink. Even the injury of racial stigmatization might be less clear in such circumstances, since slaves on a large plantation might encounter few or no white people, living out their lives within the oppressed but intense slave community. The brutalities of the slave system and endemic waves of reorganization of the slave economy, with the break-up of old estates and the forming of new ones, as planters were squeezed by competition or overtaken by death, acted as a check on the growth of a sense of slave community and, for individual slaves, could reproduce some of the isolation and disorientation of the Middle Passage. We have few slave narratives for the colonial period, and none for the early colonial period. Olaudah Equiano's *Interesting Narrative* offers an account of the shock of enslavement and Middle Passage.[1] Likewise the evocation of uprootedness, vulnerability, and confusion in the autobiographical jottings of Juan Francisco Manzano, the nineteenth-century Cuban slave poet, may, as Susan Willis has suggested, bring us close to formative episodes in the experience of enslavement, at both earlier and later periods.[2]

Coming from a polyglot continent where many different peoples lived side by side, and with frequently shifting frontiers, the culture of Africa inspired pluralism and flexibility, a willingness to try out or adapt new customs and make the best of things. Converting to a new religious practice or belief did not mean abandoning the old ones. Alfred Metraux and Roger Bastide wrote of the conservatism of the slave runaways who preserved African forms in the back-lands of the New World, and there is certainly truth in the observation. But when necessary they innovated. In comparison with the European indentured servant, the African captives showed greater ability to adapt to new surround-ings, partly, no doubt, out of necessity, but perhaps also partly because of a certain cultural suppleness, seen in the development of new languages, religions and skills. Old and new identities coexisted, helping to build a layered, multiple and even contradictory self.[3]

---

1   *The Interesting Narrative of the Life of Olaudah Equiano, or Gustavus Vassa, the African, Written by Himself*, edited by Vincent Carretta, London 1992 (originally 1788). Carretta has subsequently raised the possibility that Equiano was not born in Africa. Nevertheless the account of the Middle Passage given here would still have some authority, since he would certainly have spoken with many who had that experience.

2   Susan Willis, 'Crushed Geraniums: Juan Francisco Manzano and the Language of Slavery', in Charles T. Davis and Henry Louis Gates, eds, *The Slave's Narrative*, Oxford 1985, pp. 199–225.

3   W. E. B. Du Bois famously referred to the 'twoness' of African American consciousness in *The Souls of Black Folk*, New York 1994 (originally 1903), by which he meant their identity as Americans and as people of African descent. It would be wrong to project back this precise double identity, but not perhaps another sort of 'twoness' stemming from Africa and its

There was to be a contrast between those colonies where the majority of slaves soon spoke a European tongue – most of Spanish America and English North America – and Brazil and the Caribbean, where most slaves spoke a creole or patois. In the Spanish colonies and in English North America the slaves did not constitute a majority, and worked in relatively small-scale households. In the Caribbean slaves comprised four-fifths or more of the population and toiled together with hundreds of others on large plantations. In North America only the South Carolina rice country approximated to Caribbean conditions, and here the slaves spoke their own dialect, Gullah. Brazil's connections with Africa were continually replenished and the African presence was quite dense, albeit not at Caribbean levels. James Sweet urges that African culture and religion furnished a matrix for the outlook and belief of many slaves, including the runaways in the *quilombos*, or maroon communities. He cites the priests' complaints that Africans would regard Catholic rites and sacraments as the whites' witchcraft, which would be used simply as a supplement to a still-African system of belief. While priests found this a major problem in Africa, it lingered in the Brazilian plantation and mining districts.[4] There are good reasons to believe that most Brazilian slaves spoke a creole language, something that would limit their exposure to Catholic doctrine.[5] Prior to the nineteenth century, few planters made a serious effort to introduce their slaves to Christianity, and doing so was anyway extremely difficult in the case of slaves who did not speak a European language. English North America, with its white majority and small plantations, was a partial exception. Slaves in North America, even if African-born, soon learned to speak English, but African religious practices and beliefs persisted among them for many decades. The more devout members of the clergy sought to instil Christian faith as they understood it but often worried that the slaves were only superficially touched by their efforts. The Moravians of the island of St Thomas and South Carolina had a little more success in recruiting black helpers but it was only at the very end of the colonial period that there were signs of the beginnings of an autonomous African American Christianity (on which more in Chapter 5 below).[6]

---

heritage, and the new communities of the Americas. For the philosophical implications of this theme, as it appears in the work of Du Bois, see Malcolm Bull, *Seeing Things Hidden*, London 2000.

4   James Sweet, *Recreating Africa: Culture, Kinship and Religion in the African-Portuguese World, 1441–1770*, Chapel Hill 2003.

5   Gregory R. Guy, '*Muitas Linguas*: the Linguistic Impact of Africans in Colonial Brazil', in José C. Curto and Paul E. Lovejoy, eds, *Enslaving Connections*, Amherst, NY, 2004, pp. 125–38.

6   Sylvia Frey and Betty Wood, *Come Shouting to Zion: African American Protestantism in the American South and British Caribbean to 1830*, Chapell Hill 1998, pp. 35–62, and Michael Gomez, *Exchanging Their Country Marks: Transformation of African Identities in the Colonial and Ante-bellum South*, New York 1996.

Slave survival strategies may have implied a tacit acceptance of slavery, but slave-owners knew that they could never rely on the subordination of the mass of slaves. Hence the militia, and patrols, and exemplary punishments. Over time the planters and overseers used concessions – especially to a slave elite – as well as threats and violence to secure compliance. The punishment meted out to recalcitrant slaves was spectacular and bloody. Miscreants were flogged hundreds of times, with gunpowder, pepper or vinegar rubbed in their wounds. Other punishment included burning, and cropping of toes or fingers. The reprisals were meant to cow the entire slave community. To emphasize the implacable will of the planter, they would include injuries that reduced the slave's value.

Planters and supervisors knew the importance of concessions, but the latter could be withdrawn, and favoured slaves could be demoted or sold, to remind everyone who was in charge. The terrain of the slave plantation was a quicksand which offered no secure foothold to the slave. Despite the likelihood of capture, many still ran away, hit back or rose in rebellion if the overseer was deemed to have broken a customary understanding. The element of bargaining should not obscure the crushing advantage that still lay with the planter and overseer.

In the English colonies, even members of the slave elite had little or no prospect of ever achieving emancipation. While Spanish and Portuguese law and custom allowed possibilities of manumission, the latter remained protracted and exploitative. In order to buy manumission, those of African descent had to show extraordinary patience and persistence, and be ready to support one another in the face of owners who would try to wriggle out of agreements they had made. The eventual purchase price paid to the owner would represent the savings of several decades. During this time the slave's unpaid services would have been enjoyed by the master, or the slave would have made money for the owner by being hired out.[7]

If slaves accommodated under duress, what of the non-slave-holding whites? The small numbers who accepted posts as overseers or book-keepers were well paid. In English-speaking America the generality of poorer whites enjoyed skin privileges, since the planters needed them – as hired helpers, as members of the militia, as patrollers and as voters. In North America the white farmers and labourers were usually allowed the 'freedom of the range', which is to say that, in strong contrast to Europe, they could hunt and graze animals on uncultivated land. They could, as the saying went, live 'high on the hog'. Fear as well as privilege prompted cooperation with the slave order, since slave rebels would tend to suppose all whites to be their enemies; colour-coded slavery set up an emotional economy of fear and a calculus of favour which operated irrespective of the private options of the individual. In English-speaking America,

---

7   Manuel Barcia Paz, *La resistencia esclava*, Havana 1998.

each carried around on their face an indelible identity document which even the illiterate could read.

Nevertheless, poorer whites did not love their slave-holding compatriots. As plantation development took hold, large numbers of them emigrated from the Caribbean to North America and from southern colonies to more northerly or westerly ones, where planters were not to be found. Those who remained in the slave colonies complained of the planters' domineering ways. On a few occasions white labourers did make common cause with slave rebels. Irish indentured servants were regarded as particularly treacherous after many defected to the French in St Christopher in 1666, and were closely watched in consequence. In 1676 the Virginian revolt known as Bacon's rebellion occasioned a brief alliance between rebellious whites of varying conditions (planters, small-holders, debtors, indentured servants) and eventually came to include rebellious blacks, though not Native Americans. Indeed the revolt was ignited by Bacon's claim that the royal governor was too indulgent to the Indians, and that an expedition should be mounted against them.

While planters, merchants and the colonial state were ultimately united by religion, nationality and the stream of plantation wealth, the different contingents of oppressed immigrants and displaced natives were divided by language and tradition, and found it difficult to forge a shared vision. Of course this did not rule out individual acts of kindness or solidarity or, indeed, resistance – such as servants and slaves running away together, or Native American communities offering a haven to rebels. But such acts were isolated and did not come together in a challenge to planter power. The notion that there was always some latent 'rainbow coalition' of the oppressed and exploited is, sadly, wide of the mark. It underestimates the complex sources of social identification or the scope possessed by exploiters to gain an advantage by switching to new settings, outflanking direct producers in one place by moving to another. The rise of the plantations was an exercise in what today would be called restructuring, repositioning and social dumping. As African captives were introduced to man the plantations, small white tobacco growers or cane cultivators were forced to leave the market or to become clients of a planter patron.

The slave populations of Brazilian and Caribbean colonies had high mortality and low birth rates. Consequently, without an inflow of new captives the slave population would shrink year on year. So long as the planters made profits and could buy fresh slaves, they could still maintain and expand production. By the mid-eighteenth century the plantation colonies of North America exhibited a new pattern of natural growth among the slave population. Conditions were healthier in North America, with its more temperate climate and abundant land for growing food crops. The work required by tobacco cultivation was intense, but far less so than the night-and-day toil on the sugar plantations. Such factors lowered the mortality rate.

But the slave birth rate was also considerably higher in North America. Slave women had some control over their fertility and faced better conditions in Virginia and Maryland for child-rearing than in most other areas of the New World. The fact that Caribbean and Brazilian slaves were obliged to feed themselves from their plots put intense pressure on the women, who would have difficulty feeding extra mouths. The plots were often some distance from the plantation and cultivating them was arduous. Historians of slavery in the Caribbean stress the solitude of the female slave, only a minority of whom were able to count on the help of a partner.[8] The critical factor here was that the North American planters themselves organized the planting of corn and the raising of hogs, a practice that may have originated in the lengthy period (roughly 1630–1700) when indentured servants were the main labour force. Whatever its origins, it meant that slave mothers could count on a reliable supply of food, and this made child-rearing less daunting. The positive natural growth rate of the slave population of North America contrasted with the Caribbean, where slave numbers shrank each year by 2 per cent or more unless new captives were bought. Infant mortality rates in the Caribbean and Brazil were high in normal times, but in times of drought and dearth they sometimes reached close to 100 per cent. At such times the slave mothers would find that their bodies had, as it were, shut down, and they could no longer produce milk for their infants.[9]

THE COMMERCIAL TRANSFORMATION OF AFRICAN SLAVERY

For the apologists of slavery, the fact that the captives bought on the African coast were already enslaved according to African customs purported to add further justification. Yet there was a difficulty here. If African laws were worth respecting, perhaps Africans were not just savages after all. The Portuguese captains who initiated the coastal African trade in the 1440s and 1450s treated the African kingdoms with respect. Portuguese officials encouraged the kings of the Kongo to convert to Catholicism, and even arranged a marital alliance between the royal families of Portugal and the Kongo. When they entered the traffic in the early decades of the seventeenth century, the Dutch and the English traders were not so attentive, but they still sought to develop relations of trust with their favoured suppliers. On the African coast the colour line never really worked, and whites had to learn to deal reasonably with blacks. For their part, the African coastal merchants and princes thought of themselves as members of a particular people, and not as 'Africans', 'blacks' or 'negroes'.

---

8   Arlette Gautier, *Les sœurs de Solitude. La condition féminine pendant l'esclavage aux Antilles du XVIIe au XIXe siècle*, Paris 1985.

9   The 'natural' growth of North American slave populations had large implications for the future. I discuss the variety of factors making for this in *Making of New World Slavery*, pp. 459–71.

Traditional African slavery was a solution to a number of problems. What should be done with criminals and traitors? Or with captives who, if returned or ransomed, would simply strengthen the enemy? Or with the victims of drought and famine who would sell themselves or family members as a desperate survival expedient? According to custom young men or women might be held as 'pawns' pending discharge of some obligation; in case of default the pawn would be sold as a slave. More broadly, slavery was a mechanism by which an outsider was introduced to a new social context. Slaves would typically be transported some distance and might end up as soldiers or concubines, as well as field labourers. John Thornton identifies many hundreds of African principalities, kingdoms and confederations in West Africa alone.[10] In such a situation generalizations are hazardous, though, as already noted above, political fragmentation itself has often generated the conditions for a slave trade (in England at the time of the Norman conquest, slaves comprised a tenth of the population).

If the slave status was familiar to Africans, the almost uniformly menial and fully inheritable status of the New World slave clashed with African practices. Nevertheless the captives will have recognized aspects of their condition, and will always have hoped that if they managed to survive they would be able to better their lot. Some might hope to escape, others to rise in the plantation hierarchy. The relative fertility of the New World meant that the opportunity to cultivate a plot was worth taking up. But the rigidity of the slave condition and the relentless pace of work could easily make any chance of exit even more attractive.

The widespread presence of slavery in Africa reflected conditions in a vast continent where land was plentiful and labour scarce. This juxtaposition put a premium on labour control. The transport and sale of slaves helped to fix their status, but within Africa slaves gradually acquired a new subordinate identity beyond that of simply being property. The institution of slavery was transitional. While many captives became menials of one type or another, females could become concubines, and male captives could become soldiers or administrators. Enslavement was a stain, but one that could sometimes be gradually washed away by lengthy service, or, so far as women were concerned, the bearing of the master's children. Being held as a slave was the first step of incorporation as a servile member of the slave-holding society; the later steps were uncertain and difficult, but there was nothing equivalent to the exclusionary barrier of 'race' as it became ever more sharply and enduringly defined in the New World.

The slave in Africa was a kinless person whose purchase enabled the master to build his household or clan. The traffic in slaves carried captives to places far

---

10   John Thornton, *Africa and Africans in the Making of the Atlantic World: 1400–1800*, 2nd edn, Cambridge 1998, pp. 103–5.

distant from their origins, making escape and return hugely impractical. A steady trickle of West African slaves were marched in coffles across the Sahara or carried up the East Coast to the lands of the Ottoman Empire. Islam forbade the enslavement of fellow believers, but this was not always an effective protection for sub-Saharan blacks. The Ottoman rulers acquired both white and black slaves to staff their administration and military machine. By the early modern period the piratical statelets of North Africa, owing nominal allegiance to the Turkish caliph, preyed on Atlantic and Mediterranean shipping, seizing cargoes and holding sailors to ransom. Those not ransomed or awaiting ransom would be put to harsh toil. The Mediterranean states sought to defend their merchants' commerce with fleets of galleys, which themselves were manned by chained oarsmen, condemned to this wretched existence because they were criminals, enemy captives or heretics.

In the Atlantic trade the captive men and boys outnumbered the women and girls by two to one. While about a tenth of the captives were children, the great majority were youths and young adults. The traders found that supplies of captives varied greatly in different parts of the coast. Upper Guinea – Senegambia – was the easiest for European traders to reach, but here slaves were scarce and expensive. David Eltis suggests that the diffusion of Islam, with its ban on enslaving co-religionists, was an inhibiting factor in this case, and besides, European manufactures were not in great demand in the region. Senegambia accounted for only 3 per cent of all slave sales but 22 per cent of recorded slave shipboard revolts.[11] However, elsewhere on the coast resistance was widespread, and the volume of the trade subject to sharp fluctuation. Eltis estimates that resistance raised the slave ship's labour costs by two-thirds. In its turn this extra cost raised slave prices and reduced slave sales – by 500,000 in the eighteenth century.[12] But sometimes the African action was even more direct. Whydah was for long an open port thronged with European traders of all nations. But it eventually came to be controlled by the king of Dahomey, who in the 1740s tried to withdraw from the traffic entirely.[13]

The slave ships were the instruments of a terrible baptism for those who had been captured and sold. On major routes losses would average between a tenth and a fifth, but on individual voyages – of which there were some 43,000 between 1550 and 1870 – losses could vary wildly. Girls and women were highly vulnerable to sexual abuse. The tight-packing of the slave vessels, close invigilation by the crew and the often diverse origins of the slaves made resistance difficult, but not impossible. The slaves were usually brought up on deck every day. The holds were often more chaotic than is implied by the tidy diagram of

---

11   David Eltis, *The Rise of African Slavery in the Americas*, Cambridge 2000, p. 159.
12   Ibid.
13   Roland Oliver and Anthony Atmore, *Africa Since 1800*, Cambridge 1994, pp. 53–65.

the *Brookes*. Some of the younger slaves were allowed out of irons to serve food and carry out the slop buckets. In a few cases plots could be hatched, but even where this was not possible friendships would be formed and bonds of solidarity forged with fellow 'shipmates'. The Middle Passage and the slave depots were also places where new pidgins and patois were first encountered and songs learned.[14]

Africa is a large continent, and in the beginning the sale of slaves was limited to comparatively small regions of West and Central Africa. But as the traffic grew it furnished rewards to the most predatory of the African kingdoms and brought about a degradation of traditional African slavery. The lot of the slave was rarely a happy one, though men could become soldiers and women concubines. As the traders were willing to buy tens of thousands of captives each year, an incentive was given to those who practised war principally to acquire slaves.[15]

From the beginning abolitionists were aware that the great majority of slaves had been purchased from 'local' merchants on the coast of Africa. Recently some authoritative accounts have gone further, to stress not just the full extent of African complicity and 'agency' but also to imply co-responsibility and even a near-equality in bargaining power. Thus John Thornton writes: 'We must accept that African participation in the slave trade was voluntary and under the control of African decision-makers. This was not just at the surface level of daily exchange. Europeans possessed no means, either economic or military, to compel African leaders to sell slaves.'[16] This passage is quoted by Jean-François Bayart, the French Africanist, in an important essay, and its sentiments are echoed by the English historian Hugh Thomas, in his impressive magnum opus on the slave trade where he writes of the African slaves: 'This large labour force would not have been available to Europeans in the Americas without the cooperation of African kings, merchants and noblemen. These African leaders were neither bullied nor threatened into making these sales . . .'[17]

---

14   Rediker, *The Slave Ship*, pp. 263–307.

15   For the transformative effect in Africa of the rapid growth of the early slave trade see Paul Lovejoy, *Transformations in African Slavery: A History of Slavery in Africa*, 2nd edn, Cambridge 2000, especially pp. 49–90, 112–39, and Patrick Manning, *Slavery and African Life*, Cambridge 1990, pp. 126–48. For studies which illuminate the pattern of slavery in Africa, see Suzanne Miers and Igor Kopytoff, eds, *Slavery in Africa*, Madison 1977, and Claude Meillasoux, *L'Esclavage en Afrique précoloniale*, Paris 1975.

16   Thornton, *Africa and Africans in the Making of the Atlantic World*, p. 125. Thornton is here referring to the sixteenth and seventeenth centuries, but his own excellent study of the Kongo, and the documents assembled by António Brásio, show the very unequal relationship between the Portuguese and the African monarchs from the outset. See John Thornton, *The Kingdom of the Kongo*, Madison 1983, pp. xiv–xv, 133, and António Brásio, *Monumenta Missionaria Africana, Africa Oriental, 1471–1531*, Lisbon 1952, pp. 291–358.

17   Jean-François Bayart, 'Africa in the World', *African Affairs*, 1999, pp. 217–67, 220; Hugh Thomas, *The Slave Trade: The History of the Atlantic Slave Trade 1440–1870*, London 1997, p. 793.

There is obviously much truth in these observations, but they do not capture the whole picture. As European demand for slaves rose, the Atlantic traffic could exercise a threat over at least some African leaders. The European possession of ocean-going ships, and of increasingly effective firearms and other weapons, gave them a powerful edge. Europeans could not colonize Africa in the seventeenth or eighteenth centuries, but they could dominate its sea-going commerce: there was no level playing field.[18] Those Africans who trafficked in slaves thereby acquired not only valuable goods but cutlasses, gunpowder and guns. The latter were generally of inferior quality but came to number over a hundred thousand a year. At different times, as Thornton and Thomas describe, different African kingdoms sought to withdraw from the slave trade – but they risked being outgunned if they did so for too long. African monarchs sometimes sought to buy a caravel or warship, but the Europeans consistently declined such requests. (Eventually Haiti did acquire warships and was able to detain Spanish traffickers, as we will see in Chapter 10.)

Robert Harms quotes a Dutch memorandum of 1730 which shows awareness of European responsibility for an intensification of slave raiding: 'The great quantity of guns and powder that the Europeans have brought here [West Africa] from time to time has caused terrible wars among the kings, princes and caboceers of those lands, who made slaves of their prisoners of war . . . there is very little trade among the coast negroes except in slaves.'[19] The special character of the slave traffic greatly increased the pressures of commercialization and militarization, strengthening some and weakening others. Harms cites the case of Bullfinch Lambe, an agent of the Royal African Company who was taken prisoner by King Agaja of Dahomey and who persuaded this monarch that, if released, he would arrange with George I for a new 'scheme of trade' whereby the Company would help Dahomey to set up sugar plantations and would agree to buy the resulting crop.[20] This was, of course, a ruse on Lambe's part to escape captivity – the Company had itself discovered that lengthy sailing times made West Africa a poor location for plantations.[21] And perhaps it was reluctant to be any more dependent on African suppliers than was necessary.

European traders were able to monopolize the arbitrage possibilities created by the triangular trade between Africa, Europe and the Americas. The prices obtained by European traders reflected the anticipated productivity gains of forced labour on the New World plantations, and shorter sailing times to

---

18   See J. E. Inikori, 'The Import of Firearms into West Africa, 1750–1807', in J. E. Inikori, ed., *Forced Migration: The Impact of the Export Slave Trade on African Societies,* London 1982, pp. 126–53.

19   Quoting Van Danzig, *Collection of Documents,* Robert Harms, *The Diligent: Worlds of the Slave Trade,* New York 2001, p. 193.

20   Harms, *The Diligent,* p. 242.

21   K. G. Davies, *The Royal African Company,* London 1974.

Europe. All of this meant that another conclusion suggested by Thomas is open to question: 'The memory of Dr Eric Williams [the Trinidadian historian] may haunt the modern study of the Atlantic slave trade, but his shocking argument that the capital which the trade made possible financed the industrial revolution now appears no more than a brilliant *jeu d'esprit*.'[22] In fact the 'Williams thesis' has made a come-back, as we will see in the next chapter.

It is likely that the value of the African produce other than slaves – gold, malagueta pepper, ivory, palm oil and so forth – exceeded the value of the slaves sold until some time towards the end of the seventeenth century. Prior to 1630 the Atlantic traffic in slaves was, in effect, a Portuguese monopoly. The Dutch broke this monopoly in the 1640s and 1650s, but warfare still checked real growth. It was not until 1670 and after that English and French traders entered in a big way, greatly boosting the overall Atlantic slave traffic. By this time if not before, the trade was reshaping African communities and polities on a vast scale. This was not a question of 'African leaders' making this or that decision. It was a transformation of large areas, first on the coast and then further inland, under the pressure of both commercialization and militarization, as European traders offered trade goods on credit in order to secure competitive advantage. Joseph Miller describes a process whereby 'chiefs . . . who had exercised relatively little personal authority . . . but who represented the collectivity to outsiders, obtained imports from the strangers from the Land of the Dead'. He adds that 'the people most receptive to the lure of European commercial credit were most marginal to the African communal ethos'. Europeans gave 'as little as possible . . . seldom investing in enduring relationships of reciprocity'.[23] It is interesting that Catherine Coquery-Vidrovitch, whose work has focused on West as well as Central Africa, also stresses a vicious nexus of credit, slaving and violence – driven by Atlantic capitalist accumulation – and the emergence of new elites and polities shaped by this context.[24]

THE NEW MERCHANTS AND PLANTERS OUTFLANK THE FREE AIR DOCTRINE

The captive Africans who were taken to the Americas were outsiders and did not, to begin with, themselves accept the common identity that was thrust upon them. They knew what it was to be a slave, but might consider that they were themselves not rightly enslaved (because they were soldiers, or of noble lineage,

---

22   Thomas, *The Slave Trade*, p. 795.

23   Joseph Miller, 'The Dynamics of History in Africa', in David Armitage and Sanjay Subrahmanyam, eds, *The Age of Revolution in Global Context*, London 2010, pp 101–24, 16–17.

24   Catherine Coquery-Vidrovitch, 'L'Esclavage en Afrique et l'Atlantique au XIXe siècle', paper presented to the *Nova Fronteira* conference held at the Universidade de Rio de Janeiro, August 2009.

or because they had been born free). They came, as noted above, from a great variety of peoples and cultures; indeed, the idea that they were 'black' or 'African' only took hold slowly, and partly as a result of captivity itself. The identity of the Akan people, or of Islam, could inspire revolt but not unite all slaves.

Europeans saw themselves as united by Christianity and certain practices they dubbed 'civilization'. They lived in political communities where there was a pact according to which the rulers undertook to protect the ruled. However lowly their status, the common people were owed some respect and had been known to rise in rebellion when denied it. All this did not stop Europeans from slaughtering, incarcerating, or torturing one another. It did not stop the rich and powerful from exploiting or abusing those in their charge. But it did prevent European subjects and citizens being enslaved by their enemies or social superiors. The famous treaty of Westphalia (1648) created a European state system, extended to the Americas by the treaty of Ryswick (1697). And even before these treaties there had been a growing tendency for European sovereigns to respect the law-abiding subjects or citizens of other European states.

Most Christians believed that heathens could be legitimately enslaved if there was a commitment to save their souls. In the early English and Dutch colonies some baptized slaves did receive manumission from their owners, but both secular and religious authorities came to deny that baptism would confer freedom. Catholics upheld the codes of Justinian and Alfonso the Wise, to the effect that the children of a slave mother were the property and responsibility of the mother's owner. Calvin and Luther had no problem with slavery, but some early seventeenth-century Protestant clerics were discomforted by the continued bondage of children born in Christian households. The King James Bible often uses 'servant' where 'slave' would have been more accurate, lest Protestant idealization of the Ancient Israelites grate with an English folk-antipathy to enslavement. Notwithstanding such squeamishness, English and Dutch Protestants soon took a leading role in an Atlantic slave trade, and slavery that was less regulated than it had ever been before.

The circulation of Las Casas's *Brief Account of the Destruction of the Indies* in the leading European languages brought awareness of the great tragedy that had befallen the peoples of the New World. Montaigne's fine essays on European colonial arrogance were influenced by it, and expressed a new rejection of cruelty. But neither man focused on African slavery or the Atlantic slave trade – as we have seen Las Casas had even recommended them.

Not until the mid-eighteenth century did there emerge any real philosophical and theoretical rejection of slavery. But the perplexity of Antonio Vieira, a Brazilian priest who had been the king's chaplain and an imperial strategist, is worth noting: 'What theology can there be that would justify the inhumanity and cruelty of the extreme punishments with which these slaves are mistreated? Mistreated, indeed but that is a very short word to cover the meaning that it conceals and hides. Tyrannized we should say, or martyrized. For this is more like martyrdom than punishment for the miserable injured ones, seared with hot wax, slashed, ground up and victims of even worse excesses about which I will be silent.'[25] Vieira abominated the planters' cruelty, but did not reject slavery as such. Instead he believed that, like Christ himself, slaves had been chosen to suffer, and through their suffering to expose the wicked and redeem the virtuous. Sor Juana Inés de la Cruz took issue with Vieira's sermon on Christ's washing of the feet of his disciples (including Judas), an act which the Jesuit saw as a divine example of *fineza* or unprompted benevolence. Sor Juana saw the act not as an example of good done for its own sake, but rather as a kindness accomplished for the sake of humanity in general.[26]

Medieval and early modern Europe witnessed the appearance of a 'free air' doctrine that did reject slavery, albeit in a piecemeal way. This sought to ban slavery in specific municipal and princely jurisdictions within Europe itself. The first wave of assertions of a free air rule was made by municipal authorities in the thirteenth century and after, with the *affranchisement toulousaine* of 1226 being a renowned example. These were an expression of municipal pride and a way of attracting those fleeing lordly oppression – to claim free status the refugee would usually have to remain for a year and a day. The growth of urban centres helped to promote this trend. London, Paris and Mechlin eventually adopted the formula. Jacques Le Goff observes: 'Freedom was an attribute that coincided with the status of a townsman. As a medieval German proverb declared, "the air of the town makes one free" (*stadluft macht frei*)'.[27] In the sixteenth century the 'free air' doctrine was given another twist as it was invoked by those involved in setting up large-scale, incipiently national states. Legal authorities in France and England declared that slavery was banned and that – as the legal phrase had it – the air of their country was too pure to be breathed by slaves. Monarchs and municipalities both saw slave-owning as potentially derogatory to their own authority, so that they were inclined to endorse popular anti-slavery sentiment and embody it in particular decrees and judgements. Attempts to give the doctrine a broader application originated in particular jurisdictions such as the Guyène in south-west France, or Catalonia, but with the aspiration to make them valid throughout the kingdom.[28]

---

25   Antonio Vieira, 'Sermon to the Slaves', in Robert Conrad, ed., *Children of God's Fire*, pp. 163–74.

26   See the discussion in Ilan Stavans, 'Introduction', in Sor Juana Inés de la Cruz, *Poems, Protest, and a Dream*, London 1997, pp. xi–xliii, xiii.

27   Jacques Le Goff, *The Birth of Europe*, Oxford 2005, p. 100. See also Charles Verlinden, *L'Esclavage dans l'Europe médiévale*, vol. 1, Brussels 1955, pp. 814–19, and Barrie Dobson, 'Urban Europe', in Christopher Allmand, ed., *The New Cambridge Medieval History*, vol. 7, *c. 1415–1500*, Cambridge 1998, pp. 121–44.

28   Sue Peabody, *'There Are No Slaves in France': The Political Culture of Race and Slavery in the Ancien Régime*, New York 1996. I am thankful to Sue Peabody for letting me see her article

Another custom which was to have widening implications for free persons was that of access to commons and forests. The English Magna Carta of 1215, revised and incorporated by parliament in 1225, and the Charter of the Forest of 1299, bestowed some highly significant – but nevertheless ambiguous and vulnerable – rights in common land and royal forests.[29] Some of these rights were reserved to free men, a minority of the population, but as serfs and villeins were freed more could claim them. One clause of the Statute of the Forest allowed all men to graze livestock on the 'common herbage'. Edward Coke devoted considerable attention to Magna Carta in his compendium of English Law in 1624, helping to keep its claims alive. Perhaps the real significance of the Magna Carta tradition is that it furnished a first brief summary and revision of how a unified body of law should be interpreted and administered. While access to grazing rights certainly helped to give substance to the liberties of the free man, the widespread enclosure of common land by act of parliament in sixteenth-century England meant that the larger number of free persons actually had less land available to them, and were consequently forced to work for wages or to emigrate, as noted above. (One of the great attractions of the New World colonies was to be the availability of land.)

It is significant that the first philosopher to be critical of the exorbitant powers of the slave-holders was Jean Bodin, the theorist of French Absolutism. However, it would be wrong to conclude that the anti-slavery idea was nothing other than the obverse of the intensifying claims of the modern state. Jean Bodin had himself observed a civic mobilization provoked by such a case coming before the court at Guyène. In *Les Six Livres de la République* (1576) he noted that, whereas philosophers endorsed slavery, 'common sense' did not: 'Lawyers, who measure the law not by the discourses or decrees of philosophers, but according to the common sense and capacity of the people, hold servitude to be directly contrary to nature.'[30] He believed that the wise sovereign would understand this and become the guardian of his subjects' liberties.

The willingness of rulers to adopt the 'free air' doctrine was encouraged by the fact that slavery was not essential to either high feudalism or early capitalism. This latter fact was also registered by a contemporary in another remarkable observation. The British writer Thomas Smith wrote of slaves and serfs as follows in *De Republica Anglorum* (1565): 'Neither of the one sort nor of the

---

forthcoming in *Slavery and Abolition*, which discusses the two waves – municipal and proto-national – of the free air doctrine. See also Paul Freedman, *The Origins of Peasant Servitude in Medieval Catalonia*, New York 1991, pp. 191–2.

29   See J. C. Holt, *Magna Carta*, Cambridge 1992 and Peter Linebaugh, *The Magna Carta Manifesto*, Berkeley and London 2008, especially pp. 283–300. The context is illuminated by Thomas Bissen, *The Crisis of the Twelfth Century: Power, Lordship and the Origins of European Government*, Princeton 2009, pp. 515–28.

30   Jean Bodin, *Les Six Livres de la République*, 4th edn, Paris 1579, pp. 45–66.

other do we have any members in England. And of the first I never knewe any in my time; of the second so fewe there be, that it is almost not worth speaking of. But our law doth acknowledge them in both these sorts.' He attributed this virtual disappearance of servitude to a more humane type of religion and a new political economy: 'I think in France and England the change of religion to a more gentle humane and equal sort . . . caused this old kinde of servitude and slaverie to be brought into that moderation . . . and little by little extinguished it, finding more civil and gentle means and more equal to have done that which in time of gentility (heathenesse) [i.e. pagan antiquity] servitude or bondage did.'[31] These more civil means were the economic pressure on landless labourers to seek work or starve, and on tenant farmers to find rent or face eviction.

The banning of slavery in parts of Italy, France, the Low Countries and England had a fragmentary and contingent character. This is partly because political power itself was still based on fragmented or 'parcellized' sovereignties, and partly because the dominant religious and legal ideologies of the epoch did not endorse any outlawing of slavery. Traditional Catholic teaching had always accepted the legitimacy of slavery, a conclusion that was initially endorsed by most Protestants. The Puritans had a deep sense of mankind's sinfulness, and of the sinner's need for correction. Against this background the suffering of the slave could seem providential. The Renaissance shed no critical light on slavery. Instead it encouraged esteem for the slave-holding Ancients. The natural rights doctrine held that all men were naturally free, but they lived in society not nature. Commerce, property and law were essential to civilized life, and all of these had recognized the slave condition. Luis de Molina, a Spanish natural rights philosopher, insisted that the natives of America and Africa were fully human. Nevertheless, African captives could be bought and sold, so long as provision was made for their salvation, because they had been enslaved according to their own African laws and customs.[32] Molina reached this conclusion at a time when his monarch was also king of Portugal and still responsible for the Atlantic traffic.

Secular considerations prompted both sovereigns and free subjects to celebrate civic freedom in Europe and to uphold personal guarantees for European colonists in the Americas. Prudential motives reinforced popular sentiment, with both limiting the scope of slavery. Rulers did not wish to settle valuable colonies with their enemies, so that, for example, Irish soldiers who surrendered to the English were allowed to leave for continental Europe rather than settled in the Caribbean colonies. Likewise Huguenots were sent to the galleys or allowed to leave, but not deported to the Antilles, while Spain, distrusting the

---

31   Thomas Smith, *De Republica Anglorum*, edited by Mary Dewar, Cambridge 1982, pp. 135–6.

32   See Richard Tuck, *Natural Rights Philosophies: Their Origins and Development*, Cambridge 1979, pp. 53–4.

Jews and the Moors, executed or expelled them rather than consigning them to the Americas.

While all European legislators resorted to racializing doctrines, the construction of racial difference in each colony also reflected the pattern of slave employment and the differing emphasis of Reformation and Counter-Reformation culture. In the Catholic colonies the monarch and the church still claimed the formal right to regulate the condition of the slave, while in Protestant doctrine the condition of the slave was almost exclusively determined within the household by the master and his co-religionists. In the English colonies the condition of the slave was first defined in practice by the planters and local justices of the peace, then codified by local assemblies, and only ratified by metropolitan authorities at a much later date. The colonial courts and assemblies cited scraps of Roman law but took on themselves the responsibility of devising a new institutional structure. The French *Code Noir* in the 1680s at least formally recognized the legal and religious identity of the slave, albeit that in practice the planters were able to flout its provisions when they were deemed inconvenient.

The different Atlantic states were each acquiring a more defined identity in the early modern period, with New World rivalries helping to stimulate this process. The various empires, even when technically dynastic, were dominated by a national identity. The rights of the subject or citizen were held to enjoy the sovereign's respect and protection. But the world of burgeoning national sentiment also allowed for the view that slavery was not right for civilized peoples. When African slave traders offered good prices for Dutch captives, the Portuguese slave-traders explained that they would not purchase fellow Europeans. Even sharp religious differences did not legitimate enslavement of enemy nationals. Curiously enough, slaves were assigned in common parlance the nationality of their owner, so that a 'French slave' or 'French negro' would be a slave owned by a French subject.

By the eighteenth century persons of African descent, held as hereditary chattel slaves, were the critical plantation labour force in the Americas. In peripheral areas of Spanish and Portuguese America there were still indigenous forced labourers, but they were not the basis of the plantation economy. In much of Latin America a free population of colour of African or partly African descent appeared, due to *coartación* and manumission. These *gente de color* began to acquire the elements of a secure social identity, and indeed in a number of cases themselves began to hold slaves. Spanish imperial policy conferred some recognition and petty privileges on a layer of free blacks and people of colour, encouraging them to enrol in special militia regiments and to organize religious brotherhoods. In this way they acted as a counterweight to the aspirations of the white creoles. In times of war the Spanish monarchs were even disposed to issue appeals to the slaves in the English colonies, offering them their liberty if they escaped to Florida and converted to the true Catholic faith.

Barbara Fields has argued that European and African migrants to the New World brought different expectations and traditions, giving advantages to the former that were denied to the latter.[33] As captives and strangers, the Africans were more vulnerable and inherently less able to impose limits to their servitude than European indentured servants. The latter had accepted a short term of service, but had not given up their rights as Englishmen. However, where European colonists and merchants accepted slavery as a fate for Africans, they compromised the 'free air' doctrine that was part of their own tradition of English, French or Dutch liberty. Essentially this compromise held that New England, New France or New Amsterdam were flawed replicas of the original, since their air was quite capable of being breathed by slaves – something not true of the home country. And in so far as slave colonies were part of a single empire and jurisdiction, the liberty of the metropolis had itself been adulterated.

For a considerable time the momentum of plantation slavery outpaced popular understandings. The idea of a world free of slavery was to be a very novel one which took shape only gradually, in and through the groping attempts of slave rebels, unhappy free people of colour, European radicals and revolutionaries, and religious dissidents to establish some common ground. African captives would detest slavery, but the institution was familiar and widespread in Africa, just as it was legal in most of Europe. In the New World the African captive sought to alleviate slavery in tangible ways, by selling rum to peddlers, by producing more from their plots, by rising in the plantation hierarchy, by bargaining or, at the limit, by running away. Both African captives and European servants found that traditional notions of servitude were degraded by the relentless pressure of plantation production, itself reflecting a limitless market rather than the necessarily circumscribed needs of a particular slave-holder. In the slave colonies there was no one who could restrain the planter. Colonial governors or clergymen simply had no capacity to regulate what went on in the plantations. The task of the colonial authorities was to fend off rival powers and to enforce mercantilist restrictions. The planters put up with this, so long as they needed the protection and felt too weak to challenge the metropolis.

We should remember that the decisions embodied in the slave plantations were taken by merchants and planters, not by some democratic vote of the people of England, France, Portugal or Spain. Those who made the decisions certainly took account of popular identifications and prejudices, but typically gave them a sharper and more coherent character. These decisions were then

---

33   Barbara Fields, 'Slavery, Race and Ideology', *New Left Review* 183 (May–June 1990).

ratified by political and religious authorities who were certainly aware of the profitability of the new plantations – indeed they were concerned to make the planters share their spoils.

So slavery and the slave traffic thrived. Rising eighteenth-century demand for plantation slaves drove up prices on the African coast and increased the incentive for slave-raiding in the interior. The European slave-traffickers set out with very valuable cargoes of trade goods. The muskets, swords, cloth and metal implements they carried were to end up in the hands of the most predatory slave raiders. With the volume of slave 'exports' rising from two or three thousand a year to twenty or thirty thousand a year, the traditional sources of slaves were no longer sufficient, and coastal demand prompted ever larger slave hunts in the interior.[34]

TYING THE KNOT OF SLAVERY

In the account I have sketched here, ethno-religious and national-imperial identities and notions definitely play a part – but not racism in its modern sense. Both the common people and the notables harboured feelings of superiority towards many categories of stranger, but this was not the motive force for plantation slavery. The planters and merchants acquired slaves because they found they could make a profit from them. The poorer whites allowed this to happen, partly because they had little leverage in the matter, and partly because they wished themselves to escape the killing toil of the plantations. The metropolitan consumers were interested in smoking the tobacco or sweetening their tea; many had to work very hard themselves to afford such little luxuries, and did not feel responsible for the misdeeds of the planters. We have here a structure of serial alienation similar to that still prevailing in the modern world, and with the same capacity to obscure oppressive processes of production.

La Rochefoucauld was warning against such a trap when he wrote: 'Self-love . . . renders men idolatrous of themselves, and would render them tyrants of others if fortune gave them the means'. Less severely *Dogville*, the film by Danish director Lars von Trier, shows that a community only needs to become accustomed to the services of an obliging stranger to reinvent slavery should the stranger cease to be so obliging. While slavery was routinely condoned by many who found it convenient to have others do the harsh toil, this acceptance could merge with both age-old patriarchy and an age-old devaluation of those who worked in the open. The male slave was unmanned and, like the *femme couverte*, lived entirely in the master's household. And the slave, like the poor labourer, was seen as crude, dark, threatening and uncouth. Racial feeling enters into the mix, but so do gender and class assumptions. What eventually

---

34 Lovejoy, *Transformations in African Slavery*, especially pp. 68–90, 112–39.

emerges under New World conditions is a doctrine of racial supremacy that challenged human unity.

Viewed statically, the knot of New World slavery was tied by three considerations. Firstly, slaves were legitimately acquired property, and property was sacred. Secondly, Africans, or those of African descent, were like dangerous animals who required permanent restraint if they were to be useful to their owners, themselves or the wider community. Thirdly, the new slave plantations were a sinew of national strength, helping to boost trade, revenue and maritime power; in the competitive system of European state relations, each nation or kingdom needed to maximize such resources.

Viewed in dynamic terms, however, the slavery of the New World permanently created, defined and embodied a violent subjugation of blacks by whites, Africans by Europeans, 'heathens' by Christians, one race by another. Inchoate antipathy or unconcern was transmuted into fear and domination. The result was the coalescence of a characteristic racial ideology. Defenders of New World slavery sometimes portrayed it as a state of war. John Locke believed that it could be defended because it embodied 'a just war continued', while Thomas Jefferson declared: 'We have the wolf by the ears and we can neither hold him nor safely let him go'.[35] So one way of describing New World slavery would be to say that it embodied a frozen war of the races. The merit of such an understanding would be acknowledgment of the pent-up violence inherent in the institution.

Feared as wild beasts, and used as beasts of burden, slaves were less than human. Masters often called them by the sort of name – Pompey, Caesar – they might give a horse or dog. Alternatively they had a single Christian name, and the men were 'boys', the women 'wenches'. The slave could not testify in court in the English colonies, and everywhere belonged in the owner's household. Little effort was made to introduce the slaves to Christianity, and the clergy whom the planters tolerated had to teach the virtue of complete subordination. The slaves were taught that they had to subdue their own savage nature and were reminded that, as 'sons of Ham', they had inherited the curse that Noah laid on Canaan and needed special restraint.[36] The more 'enlightened' slave-holders would not credit such tales, but were instead all too likely to entertain pseudo-scientific notions that were still worse – for instance, that the coloured slave was some lower species in the Great Chain of Being.

---

35   Locke's commitment to slavery stemmed from the great importance he attached to the civilized practice of agriculture in validating the English claim to colonial land, rather than from racial animus as such. However, to combine this with disregard for the agricultural toil of the black slave certainly argues the presence of racial blinkers. See David Armitage, 'John Locke, Carolina, and the *Two Treatises of Government*', *Political Theory* 32/5 (October 2004), pp. 602–27; Blackburn, *Making of New World Slavery*, pp. 263–5, 329. For Jefferson see John C. Miller, *The Wolf by the Ears: Thomas Jefferson and Slavery*, Charlottesville, VA, 1991.

36   Blackburn, *Making of New World Slavery*, pp. 64–76; Colin Kidd, *The Forging of Race: Race and Scripture in the Protestant Atlantic World, 1660–2000*, Oxford 2006.

THE DISTINCTIVE CHARACTER OF NEW WORLD SLAVERY

I have urged that the early modern European practice of slavery in some ways echoed Ancient and medieval precedents. But it soon acquired a more intense commercial logic, as well as a sharper racial character, than had ever been seen before. Once they arrived in the New World the Europeans bought their slaves from other Europeans who had in turn bought their slaves from African traders (though the Luso-Africans of Brazil supplied a variant here). The Roman slave trade had some commercial sources of supply, but relied to a great extent on the hauls of captives made by the legions.[37] The Atlantic traffic had acquired the scale and rhythms of a regular business by the mid-seventeenth century, as the Dutch, English and French put up stiff competition to the Portuguese traders. There were other contrasts. Slaves had previously discharged a great variety of roles: some were senior imperial administrators, or respected teachers. Roman slaves were captured from many different outlying parts of the empire and were not thought to be of the same race – very few came from sub-Saharan Africa. New World slavery flourished thanks to market forces, but was defined in racial as well as property terms, and, partly in consequence, established a status that was more permanent than slavery in Ancient Rome. This new slavery was geared to producing commodities in one continent for consumers in another. Slavery in Spanish America was confined to those of African descent but, as we have seen, there were some escape hatches. And whereas slavery in Spanish America was urban rather than rural, the slaves introduced to the English colonies were to be overwhelmingly concentrated in the plantations, and they and their descendants had little hope of ever escaping their servile condition. Slavery was found at the centre of the Roman and Athenian worlds, while it remained vestigial or completely absent in the case of the European metropolis of the Atlantic empires. But given the wealth and dynamism of the colonies, the time came when they saw themselves as the centre.

---

37   The military component is stressed by Keith Hopkins, *Slaves and Conquerors: Sociological Studies in Roman History*, Cambridge 1978; see also Keith Bradley, *Slavery and Society at Rome*, Cambridge 1994, pp. 31–56.

Part II

THE SUBVERSIVE BOOM

CHAPTER FOUR

Slavery and Industrialization

By the 1770s colonial exports and re-exports, most of them the fruits of slave labour, had risen to account for between a third and a half of the trade of the leading Atlantic states. The British and French islands produced over 150,000 tons of sugar annually. The slave produce of Virginia, Maryland, Georgia and the Carolinas comprised three quarters of the exports of the English colonies of North America. The New England and mid-Atlantic colonies were able to buy British manufactures partly thanks to their sales to the Caribbean plantation colonies. And the farmers of these regions were themselves encouraged to produce provisions and equipment for sale to the plantations by the possibility of buying sugar, rum, cottons and tobacco. The impetus of Atlantic trade reflected gains for commodity consumption at the expense of subsistence culti-vation, local exchange and household production by North American farmers. In Britain a wave of parliamentary acts of enclosure of common land was spon-sored by 'improving landlords', encouraging the further expansion of capitalist agriculture and leading to a steady exodus from the countryside. While all the European powers sought to channel their colonial trades, British Atlantic exchanges, both licit and contraband, were the more diversified, fostering a more extensive regime of accumulation. However, the dynamism of the French colonial and export trade furnished strong competition.

The tobacco plantations of Virginia and Maryland had produced 20 million lbs in 1700, which rose to 220 million lbs around 1770, with much of this sold to British merchants for onward shipment to Europe. The numbers of slaves in the Americas had grown from a third of a million in 1700 to some 2.3 million by 1770. The dreadful toll of slave mortality may be gauged from the fact that 1.2 million slaves had arrived in the two decades 1741–60, and a further 1.3 million in 1761–80. European traders laid out prodigious quantities of metal goods, textiles, firearms, shells and cornelian beads to acquire over 150,000 slaves each year on the African coast. The annual value of colonial exports in the early 1770s was £5.6 million for the British colonies, £5.2 million for the French colonies (French Caribbean exports already exceeded those of the British Caribbean by this time, and were to increase their lead in the 1780s). Brazil's exports were worth £1.8 million and the exports of the whole of Spanish America £4.9 million, the latter dominated by silver but also including some slave-mined gold and slave-produced cacao, indigo and sugar.

This surge of slave-related trade meant that Atlantic exchanges were both larger and more balanced than Europe's trade with the East. The New World colonies were vast, fertile and easy to reach, with slaves supplying a mobile labour force. The colonial trade was a major stake in the wars between the Atlantic powers. Yet, notwithstanding the disruption of war, the output of the plantations grew steadily, decade after decade. Britain's trade with North America recovered quickly from the Independence War, and the merchant marine of the new Republic connected planters throughout the hemisphere with wider markets and new sources of supply. Several American territories were greatly to expand plantation output in subsequent decades. Such a sustained and ongoing expansion was to provoke far-reaching transformations in the economic, political, social and intellectual landscape. The plantation trades were reshaping consumption patterns, acting as a spur to enterprise, encouraging more intense work rhythms, breaching the shell of subsistence farming and giving rise to new mentalities. An Atlantic world of rising prosperity, greater interdependence and intense exploitation gave rise to a variety of subversive forces, ranging from colonial liberation to industrial revolution, and from affirmation of the 'rights of man' to a questioning of slavery and the slave trade. We start here by considering the New World contribution to industrialization.

It is tempting to contrast a Dutch and English 'bourgeois' model of development, fuelled by a widening home market and the spread of capitalism, with a French, Portuguese and Spanish Absolutist model, driven by dynastic rather than commercial objectives. There is something to such a contrast, but the various European states were continually competing with and borrowing from one another, jostling for advantage. State regulation and initiative, maritime power, chartered corporations and other features of 'mercantilism' played a role in both formulas. And one way or another an impetus to freer trade was evident in all the colonial systems. But in the Anglo-Dutch model the state was harnessed to commercial objectives, while in the Absolutist model commerce was harnessed to dynastic purposes.[1]

The Anglo-Dutch 'bourgeois state' model inspired more financial confidence, allowing for the more efficient mobilization of public credit.[2] I have stressed that capitalism and consumer appetites drove enslavement and the invention of a new type of plantation. These processes also gave momentum in Britain to a dual process of 'primitive accumulation', on the one hand separating labourers from the land (by enclosure and 'improvement') and on the other using the super-profits of slavery to finance the expansion of industry and credit. In the vital decades from 1760 to 1820 capitalist manufacture itself was

---

1   Perry Anderson, *Lineages of the Absolutist State*, London 1974, pp. 36–7, 41.

2   John Brewer, *The Sinews of Power: War, Money and the English State, 1688–1783*, Cambridge 1990. The Bank of England and the London Stock Exchange were influenced by Dutch prototypes. For the basis of Dutch state finance see Jonathan Israel, *The Dutch Republic: Its Rise, Greatness and Fall, 1477–1806*, Oxford 1995, pp. 285–90.

thoroughly reorganized by an 'industrial revolution', with wage workers toiling in factories, harnessing water and steam power to mechanized processes of production. It seems clear to me – though this has been much disputed – that the expansion of the slave plantations fed into this transformation, and for many decades helped to extend and reinforce it. Less pondered and debated has been the concomitant – and almost undeniable – fact that capitalist industrialization explains the further growth of slavery.

The English and the Dutch enjoyed considerable prosperity in the early eighteenth century, but faced the danger that the 'commercial society' they constituted would be hemmed in by the mercantilist restrictions erected by other states. Britain's hugely important exports of woollen cloth stagnated, and the proportion of total exports going to Europe fell steeply over the course of the eighteenth century. French merchants dominated Europe's luxury trades, and French exports of cotton goods exceeded England's around 1770. Under the Bourbons the Spanish Empire staged something of an eighteenth-century recovery. The Dutch had been thrown out of Brazil and battered by war in Europe. Despite its wealth – some of which found its way into British projects – the Netherlands declined to the status of a second-rate power in the eighteenth century. There was a danger that Britain would suffer the same fate. Britain was an island, and more than double the size of the Netherlands, but still only about a quarter the size of France. The British oligarchy fought war after war to thwart continental combinations and to extend its commercial reach, with a 'blue water' strategy that gave a large importance to Atlantic sea-lanes and American colonial territory. Britain was also able to use its economic strength to find allies, often paying them to keep soldiers in the field. Without the plantations and without industrial advance Britain might very well have been relegated to the second rank.

Britain's internal market was quite large, but still lacked the scale that would really reward innovation and industrial production. In a famous book – *Capitalism and Slavery* (1944) – Eric Williams, the Trinidadian historian (and later national leader), argued that the profits of the slave systems fertilized many branches of the metropolitan economy and set the scene for Britain's industrial revolution. The 'Williams thesis' has fuelled decades of debate and controversy.[3] While it needs to be refined and reformulated, it did quite correctly identify the very great intimacy between the surge of slave produce and slave-trading, on the one hand, and British capitalist development and industrialization on the other.

I argued in Chapter 2 that the early capitalism of the Dutch and English was itself a cause of plantation development, because it put money in the hands

---

3   See Barbara Solow and Stanley Engerman, eds, *British Capitalism and Caribbean Slavery: The Legacy of Eric Williams*, Cambridge 1987.

of new consumers. However, slave plantation growth itself fed back into capitalist and industrial advance in Britain by furnishing novel incentives, wider markets, premium commodities, sources of capital and raw materials. The plantation colonies supplied the metropolis with a growing stream of popular luxuries and cotton, a crucial industrial input. The availability of tobacco, brightly coloured cotton goods, sweetened beverages, cakes and preserves, helped to tempt Britons into greater participation in market exchanges and greater reliance on wages, salaries and fees. Baiting the hook of wage dependence, new consumption goods helped to motivate the 'industrious revolution', that is, the greater regularity, longer hours and reduced holidays that accompanied, and sometimes preceded, the new manufacturing methods.[4] The slave colonies not only supplied premium commodities but were also a captive market for metal tools, textiles and provisions. Indeed the British Empire of the early and mid-eighteenth century became a zone of multilateral exchanges in which the ability of producers in Ireland, New England and Newfoundland to sell provisions to the West Indies, and to participate in the Africa trade, also boosted their ability to buy English manufactures. The boom in Atlantic produce also underpinned a huge programme of commercial ship-building and maintenance, with about a third of the English mercantile fleet being built in the North American colonies.

Before reviewing the British case it will be relevant briefly to consider whether the colonial trade of other powers boosted their manufacturing economy. The answer is, not much. Portugal pioneered plantation development and the Atlantic slave trade, but its metropolitan economy showed no sign of receiving an impetus to capitalism. Portuguese colonialism reflected an entrepreneurial mercantilism as the royal authorities sponsored and regulated long-distance commerce and plantation development. But the domestic market was very small, and wider European markets were only reached thanks to a series of alliances with Italian, Flemish, Dutch, German – and eventually English – merchants and bankers. The sixteenth-century Asian spice trade only required one or two galleons to sail each year, in contrast to hundreds of smaller ships in the late-seventeenth-century Atlantic coastal and island trade. The Portuguese authorities and colonists successfully defended their control of Brazil and of trading posts in Africa and Asia, but they still needed the services of Dutch traders and could not prevent the latter passing along know-how and facilities to the English and French. In 1640 Portugal successfully broke free of the Spanish monarchy (to which it had been yoked since 1580). But in subsequent conflicts Portugal depended on alliance with England to sustain its independence. The price of this was commercial agreements, above all the

---

4   Jan de Vries, 'Between Purchasing Power and the World of Goods', in John Brewer and Roy Porter, eds, *Consumption and the World of Goods*, London 1993.

Methuen Treaty of 1703, which allowed British merchants privileged access to the Portuguese, and, by extension, Brazilian market. Dependence on Britain, and the consequent 'loss' of Brazilian gold to London, could generate antagonism, as it did with the Marquis of Pombal, the strong-willed first minister of the Portuguese king; but it also gave Portuguese wine advantages in the English market.

By the 1770s and 1780s the French Antilles out-produced the English islands, notwithstanding the fact that France's own demand for plantation produce was weaker than that of the more commercialized English market. French plantation development reflected the willingness of the colonial state to furnish subsidies to the slave trade and to use its military engineers to build good roads and an impressive irrigation system. While the French planters were obliged to sell their produce to the merchants of Bordeaux, the latter, with their historic roots in the wine trade, were well connected to the demand for colonial luxuries in Germany, Italy and Eastern Europe. More ambiguous was the growth of a largely illegal trade between the French Caribbean and the New England and middle Atlantic colonies, in which the latter purchased molasses and sold provisions. While there was considerable synergy in this trade, it reflected an impetus towards free trade which could menace the privileges of the merchants of Bordeaux and Nantes.

French colonial development furnished the metropolitan economy with only a modest stimulus. Despite its successes and dynamism, French mercantile advance was not based on an all-round development of the metropolitan economy, which was still hobbled by a patchwork of special exemptions and privileges. Much colonial produce was re-exported, and the slaves, provisions and equipment needed by the planters were often purchased from interlopers, especially North American merchants. By contrast, British merchants and manufacturers had a growing home market, growing colonial outlets and an ability to penetrate – legally or otherwise – the colonial and home markets of their rivals.

The British economy was thus more directly and variously responsive to Atlantic exchanges than was the case for the other European powers. At crucial moments during the early stages of British industrialization, colonial markets, slave-produced supplies and slave-related profits made a strong contribution. Early capitalist manufacturers needed wider markets to reach the levels of output that would allow for the widespread adoption of the new industrial methods. The growth of transatlantic trade more than compensated for the declining ability of British merchants to sell in European markets. The famous triangular trade – whereby merchants from Bristol and Liverpool bartered trade goods for slaves on the African coast, then sailed to the West Indies or North America to sell the slaves and finally took a cargo of plantation produce back to England – was just part of a wider, complex, multilateral pattern. The

French merchants practised a similar triangular trade, but their declining stake in North America gave it a much more restricted character, leaving the French planters reliant on supplies from English North America. During the French Revolutionary and Napoleonic wars (1793–1801, 1803–15) British traders still had good access to South American and Caribbean markets. Napoleon's Continental System sought to deny European markets to British traders. France's own Atlantic ports were badly hit but smuggled sugar, tobacco, coffee and chocolate still found their way to European purchasers. And for several decades after the abolition of the British Atlantic slave trade in 1807, the country's merchants still sold large quantities of textiles and metal goods to the Cuban and Brazilian slave-traders.

The early industrial manufacturers had quite modest capital requirements for the purchase of machinery but they needed extended credit to reach overseas markets. It often took a year or more for the manufacturer to receive payment from overseas. In the meantime they needed credit to pay their workers and suppliers. The buoyancy of the Atlantic trade, including profits on the trade in slaves and slave produce, put merchants and bankers in a position where they were willing and able to supply that credit. Liverpool, England's largest slave-trading port, was adjacent to the Lancashire manufacturing districts, but the merchants of London, Glasgow and Bristol also invested their gains in every type of enterprise, asset and improvement. Canals, roads and wharves were built, manufactories established, land drained or irrigated, and new equipment and plant species purchased. The consequent boost to agricultural production and productivity itself helped to create the space needed for an industrial pattern in which the proportion of the population living on the land was sharply to decline.

Eric Williams anticipated many of these arguments, supplying telling quotations and anecdotes to illustrate the multiple links between planters, merchants, bankers, manufacturers and agricultural improvers. But he did not attempt to quantify the overall contribution of Atlantic exchanges to British industrial growth in the period 1750–1820, nor to present an analytic breakdown of the types of help received by manufacturers from the slave plantations. Some of Williams's formulations were understood to focus only on the contribution of slave trade profits and not on planting profits, but this failed to address Williams's full case. A weak spot in Williams's argument was his belief that the British West Indies had already entered a period of decline by the 1770s. The years of the American War were difficult for British planters, but they made a strong comeback in the years 1783–1803. Some of his formulations seemed to focus only on the contribution of slave trade profits, when there is no reason not to take account of the importance of all aspects of the slave-related trades.

In *The Making of New World Slavery* (1997) I broke down the potential slave-related contribution into the following dimensions: (1) the stimulus afforded to British manufactures by exports to Africa and the Americas; (2) planting and mercantile profits; (3) the provision of finance, credit and financial instruments; (4) the ability of plantations to supply raw materials in great quantity and at a low price; (5) the contribution of plantation products to a new world of consumption, itself linked to more intense work patterns; and (6) the ability of the plantations to ride out periods of disruption and war.

In *The Making of New World Slavery* I could draw on half a century of further research into British industrialization and the dimensions of overseas trade to arrive at a view of the slave-related contribution to overseas demand, and to new comparisons between mercantile and planting profits and the investment needs of the iron and textile industries, and the wider British economy. Thus Elizabeth Schumpeter found that the colonial and African trades around 1770 accounted for 96.3 per cent of British exports of nails, and 70.5 per cent of the export of wrought iron.[5] Around the same time British exports of iron manufactures were equivalent to 15–19 per cent of the country's iron consumption.[6] Textile exports accounted for between a third and a half of total production, with colonial and African markets again looming large. In the period 1784–6 to 1805–7 the growth of exports accounts for no less than 87 per cent of the growth of output.[7] During the French Wars British exporters, obliged to smuggle their goods to Europe, were able to expand their sales to the rapidly growing Atlantic markets. The size and the novelty of the colonial stimulus was such as to suggest that, in its absence, British producers would have been hard pressed to find an alternative.

In the 1970s and 1980s it was common for economic historians to claim that colonial trade and triangular trade profits were simply not large enough to have made much difference to the metropolitan economy.[8] However, even at that time the evidence was ambivalent. In an article published in 1972, Stanley Engerman calculated that annual British slave trade profits running at around £115,000 a year in 1770 could have amounted to 7.8 per cent of total British domestic investment and to 38.9 per cent of total commercial and industrial development.[9] Once plantation production and trade are taken into account, the possible contribution grows very considerably. But were the plantations financially strong?

---

5   Elizabeth Schumpeter, *English Overseas Trade, 1697–1808*, Oxford 1960, pp. 64–6.

6   This calculation is made by Paul Bairoch in an article sceptical of the contribution made by foreign trade to British industrialization: Paul Bairoch, 'Commerce international et genèse de la révolution industrielle anglaise', *Annales* XXVIII (1978), pp. 541–71, 561.

7   These figures are based on the recalculation of the values of British commerce by Ralph Davis, *The Industrial Revolution and British Overseas Trade*, Leicester 1979, p. 88.

8   See for example Joel Mokyr, Introduction to J. Mokyr, ed., *The Economics of the Industrial Revolution*, Totowa 1985, pp. 1–55, and Bairoch, 'Commerce international et genèse de la révolution industrielle anglaise'.

9   Stanley Engerman, 'The Slave Trade and British Capital Formation in the Eighteenth Century', *Business History Review* 46 (1972), pp. 430–43.

Concerned to defend the tariff protection they enjoyed, and to discourage attempts to tax them, planters liked to dwell on the great difficulty they had making ends meet. Times of war and drought could cause real problems, but these do not justify the conclusion that British sugar planting was in some sort of terminal crisis from about 1780 onward. Eric Williams and Lowell Ragatz found evidence of such a crisis in a wave of bankruptcies, but Seymour Drescher, looking at the overall picture from 1780 to 1807 or 1815, argued that the evidence simply did not support the 'decline thesis'.[10] Drescher's scepticism was mainly based on data on output and trade. Working from a sample of West Indian plantation accounts, J. R. Ward came up with direct evidence that British West Indian planters were making robust profits in the late eighteenth and early nineteenth centuries. He computed that aggregate British West Indian planting profits must have been around £2.5 million annually around 1770. According to Roger Anstey, annual British slave-trading profits were around £115,000 at this time.[11] The merchants and planters would have reinvested a portion of these profits back into their enterprises, but this also would have furnished some stimulus to Atlantic circuits. Around this time gross capital formation in Britain each year was estimated at £4 million by C. H. Feinstein, in a contribution to the *Cambridge Economic History of Europe* (1978).[12] Subsequent modelling of the British economy by N. F. R. Crafts and other 'revisionist' historians has urged that overall growth was slower and later than had been thought hitherto, and that capital formation was lower.[13]

The gains of the planters and merchants were so large that, despite themselves, they made a contribution to accumulation. The Atlantic trades and plantations were generating a surplus equivalent to 50 per cent or more of British investment in every branch of the economy – agriculture and infrastructure as well as manufacturing – on the eve of the industrial revolution. Of course absentee West Indian planters often splurged their money on riotous living, finery and grand houses, rather than on the mass-produced goods which were to transform the economy. But they kept their account balances with merchants and bankers who extended credit to manufacturers, or chose to diversify their holdings by investing in canals or improvements to their newly acquired landed estates.[14] Peter Mathias also notes that 'sugar bills and tobacco bills' were 'as freely negotiable at equivalently fine margins as

10   Williams, *Capitalism and Slavery*; Lowell J. Ragatz, *The Fall of the Planter Class in the British West Indies*, New York 1928; Seymour Drescher, *Econocide: British Slavery in the Era of Abolition*, London 1977.

11   Blackburn, *Making of New World Slavery*, p. 536.

12   See C. H. Feinstein, 'Capital Expenditure in Great Britain', *Cambridge Economic History of Europe*, vol. 7, London 1978, p. 74.

13   N. F. R. Crafts and C. K. Harley, 'Output Growth and the British Industrial Revolution', *Economic History Review*, vol., 44, 1992, pp. 703–30.

14   David Hancock, *Citizens of the World, London Merchants and the Integration of the British Atlantic Community, 1735–1785*, Cambridge 1995, supplies many examples.

government securities', with the result that 'short-term credit became the most efficient and mobile factor of production in the eighteenth century'.[15] The merchant and finance houses that facilitated the import of sugar and cotton also helped to extend badly needed credit to textile and metal manufacturers, while their own profits often helped to underwrite expenditure on canals, ports and agricultural improvements. Detailed studies of the mercantile partnerships bring up a host of interconnections.[16]

The orders of magnitude I have cited do not prove that slave-related profits 'caused' the industrial revolution – the prior capitalist context was more important as a cause because it favoured technological advance – but they do show that slave-related profits were large enough to have been a great stimulus, just as colonial and American markets took up the slack when domestic demand faltered, and thus helped prevent interruptions to manufacturing growth.[17] The fact that slaves produced much of their own subsistence meant that the plantations did not collapse during the frequent interruptions to trade.

A distinction can be made between the direct profits of the plantations and slave trade, on the one hand, and the profits made by their suppliers, on the other. The profits made from British metal goods and textiles stemmed from the toil of British wage workers, many of them women and children. But if, in the absence of plantation demand, markets had been lacking for these goods, then one could say that the slave plantation complex enabled British manufacturers and merchants to 'realize' profits that would otherwise have been unavailable to them.[18] As the industrial pioneers, British manufacturers

---

15   Peter Mathias, *The Transformation of England*, London 1979, pp. 97–8.

16   See Hancock, *Citizens of the World*.

17   My argument has been criticized by two distinguished historians of slavery in the Americas, viz David Eltis and Stanley Engerman in 'The Importance of Slavery and the Slave Trade to Industrializing Britain', *Journal of Economic History* 60/1 (March 2000), pp. 123–44. These authors concede that slave-trade profits were equivalent to 8 per cent of total British investment in the later eighteenth century (p. 135), and do not question the data on plantation profits. Nor do they question that Atlantic merchants and finance houses extended credit to Lancashire and Midlands manufacturers. But they remain unconvinced that the British economy needed a boost from colonial slavery. They conclude: 'African slavery . . . did not by itself cause the British Industrial Revolution. It certainly "helped" that Revolution along, but its role was no greater than that of many other economic activities, and in the absence of any one of these it is hard to believe that the Industrial Revolution would not have occurred anyway' (p. 141). The helping-not-causing formulation is very similar to the argument I made in *The Making of New World Slavery*, but the rider downplays the fact that the Atlantic sector was a serious support for the British economy at a difficult time. If Britain had been denied access to all its colonies and Atlantic trades as a consequence of crushing naval defeats in 1782, or 1795, or even 1805, its ability to maintain industrial growth and gain the upper hand against Napoleon would surely have been put in question. I point out in *The Making* that the loss of Saint-Domingue proved disastrous to the French Atlantic economy, and weakened overall French economic performance (pp. 568–78).

18   I further explain the notion of 'realization' of profits in *The Making of New World Slavery*, Chapter 12, n. 47, pp. 575–6. It is really another way of drawing attention to the stimulus of colonial

needed wide markets and could not rely only on industrial consumers. Hence another way of looking at the slave contribution to British capital accumulation is to register that slave toil helped Britain to escape the stagnation of a closed economy.

The exchanges with the plantation zone furnished a resource increment and the actual context of industrialization. Without them the transition might indeed have occurred, but with greater difficulty and over a longer time. It is even possible that France and/or the United States would have seized the lead. Napoleon's attempts to assert control over Saint-Domingue, restore slavery, acquire Louisiana and annex Spain and Portugal, together with their colonies, were a tribute to the perceived advantages bestowed by the plantation trades on the 'nation of shopkeepers'. Napoleon's 'Continental System' could not prevent the suffocation of French Atlantic trade. Britain's naval victory at Trafalgar in 1805 kept open the Atlantic sea-lanes and allowed global markets to compensate for the difficulty of reaching European ones. The US trade boycott of 1806 and the 'War of 1812' brought some difficult moments, but the interruptions proved to be quite short-lived, and in the meantime other American markets helped to sustain Britain's trade. Britain's Atlantic trade reached its peak in the years 1784 to 1825, a period coinciding with industrial take-off. But from the 1820s the domestic market, and exports to India, were to become steadily more important outlets for metal goods and cotton textiles, albeit that down to 1865 American slaves still produced the cotton.

The onset of industrialization was closely linked to new consumption norms and the 'industrious' revolution. Expanding employment in manufacturing was favoured by a growing population, by the privatization of common land by enclosures, and by rising agricultural productivity. But a new consumption package also played a role in fostering the move towards industrial living. The stream of plantation produce helped to transform life and labour in the metropolis. The early industrial workers had to work very hard to feed themselves and their

---

demand. Unfortunately I make a mistake in indicating the size of the 'profits on trade' which relate to the claimed 'realization' effect on p. 535, Table XII.9 of *The Making*. The sentence preceding this table should read 'the Sheridan and Thomas figures on the profits of trade' and the figure £420,000 should be entered as the figure for Jamaican 'profits on trade' in the right-hand column of the table, and the revised total would be £1,220,000. The 'indirect profits' given on pp. 536 and 541 should be correspondingly reduced. While the error is regrettable (and will be corrected in future editions), it does not concern the massive direct contribution of plantation profits. In retrospect I believe that I understated the proportion of direct plantation profits that were remitted to the metropolis by suggesting that for the West Indies as a whole only £1.1 million of the total £2.5 million was remitted back to Britain. It is difficult to believe that the West Indian proprietors ploughed as much as £1.4 million back into their estates, and much more likely that at least £1.4 million was remitted, or £300,000 more than my estimate in *The Making*. Overall the key figure for my argument is West Indian planter profits of £2.5 million, since this was either remitted to Britain or invested in plantation equipment and additional slaves, with both options favouring British Atlantic accumulation.

families. Traditional holidays were suppressed and the habits of seasonal employment penalized. Men, women and children had to toil fourteen hours a day to stay alive and keep a roof over their heads. But while the material conditions of industrial workers and plantation slaves were in some ways comparable – with similar mortality rates – the social relations of slavery and wage labour were still very different. The wage labourer was increasingly tempted by a commodity-based notion of freedom, earning cash to buy necessities and petty luxuries. Such petty luxuries included tobacco, rum, sweetened tea or coffee and indigo-dyed denim cloth, and played a part in the motivation and mobilization of every type of waged and salaried employee (Starbucks and Levi's are modern versions of such consuming habits). The slave's ideal of freedom focused on free movement and an independent life, with stepping stones to the latter including the raising of chickens, fishing, hunting small game, stealing corn, holding a frolic or sing-song in the evening, or even running away. Of course the contrast should not be drawn too sharply, and both types of producer balanced commodified with natural, material with cultural, items of consumption. Wage workers bought newspapers and tended gardens, just as slaves sometimes received small incentive payments and bought little luxuries from itinerant peddlers. But awareness of such qualifications should not lead us to downplay the larger consumption expenditures of wage workers and the role of wage goods in expanding the domestic economy. The fact that the wage worker enjoyed a small but vital margin of mobility and choice contrasted with the figurative – or sometimes real and heavy – chains of the slave. Ultimately slave labour could be a convenient crutch for the accumulation process, but it was wage labour that lent limitless dynamism and autonomy to the capitalist market.[19]

In *The Making of New World Slavery* I calculate that, around 1800, the production of tobacco, sugar and cotton cost slaves around 2,500 million hours of toil annually. In order to purchase these premium goods British households were encouraged to play their part in the 'industrious revolution' which preceded and accompanied the industrial revolution.[20] Plantation products compensated labourers, cottagers, artisans, clerks and factory workers for their drudgery and pinched existence. Cotton goods were pleasant. Sweetened tea, or coffee, or cakes and preserves supplied a little variety and, for some, badly

---

19   C. A. Bayly in *The Birth of the Modern World, 1780–1914*, Oxford 2002, rightly stresses the economic contribution of the slave plantations. But describing this as an aspect of the 'industrious revolution' is a mistake, and muddies the distinction I have drawn here between the toil of the slave and that of the industrial worker. Thus he describes the 'Caribbean slave system' as 'the ultimate, forced industrious revolution' (p. 6), when the value of the concept is precisely that it highlights pressures that did not entail physical force.

20   Blackburn, *Making of New World Slavery*, p. 581; Jan de Vries, 'Between Purchasing Power and the World of Goods', in Brewer and Porter, eds, *Consumption and the World of Goods*, pp. 85–132.

needed calories. Just as merchants used this trade to expand credit, so the government was able to derive a stream of revenue from taxing plantation imports.

The broad case for a plantation trade stimulus to British industrial advance was always strong.[21] It has been further buttressed by the appearance of works which stress the foreign trade advantage enjoyed by Britain in the period 1750–1850, notably Kenneth Pomeranz, *The Great Divergence* (2002), Joseph Inikori, *Africans and the Industrial Revolution in England* (2002), and Ronald Findlay and Kevin O'Rourke, *Power and Plenty* (2008). Pomeranz brings out the contribution of American land and products in easing and hastening industrialization in Britain and Western Europe. He urges that American output gave a vital extra edge to Britain at a time – the later eighteenth century and early nineteenth century – when China was perhaps as rich and productive as Europe. Borrowing the concept of 'ghost acreage' from Eric Jones, he invites us to consider the implications of the fact that Britain, as the industrializing pioneer, had available to it the cotton output of acres of highly fertile (and conveniently located) soil in the New World, helping it over the supply difficulties of early industrialization. European colonization and settlement in the New World had created a huge extension of, and supply base for, the European economy. He estimates that the acreage required to grow the cotton, sugar and timber imported by Britain from the New World in 1830 would have been somewhere between 25 and 30 million acres – or more than Britain's combined arable and pasture land.[22] By this time some European countries were refining sugar from beets, but this too would have required vast acreage. Wood could, perhaps, have been imported from elsewhere, and was anyway not mainly logged by slave labourers. But Pomeranz observes that 'raising enough sheep to replace the yarn made with Britain's New World cotton imports would have required staggering quantities of land, almost 9 million acres in 1815 . . . and over 23 million acres by 1830.'[23] One might add that cotton yarn was much more suitable for early industrial processes than wool, that the price paid for each pound of raw cotton dropped by one half between 1790 and 1820, and that consumers found that cotton textiles were more washable, and more comfortable next to the skin.

The geographical factors highlighted by Pomeranz supply a powerful argument, but they do not sufficiently register the enormous all-round contribution

---

21   See also Patrick O'Brien and Stanley L. Engerman, 'Exports and the Growth of the British Economy from the Glorious Revolution to the Peace of Amiens', in Barbara E. Solow, ed., *Slavery and the Rise of the Atlantic System*, Cambridge, 1991.

22   Kenneth Pomeranz, *The Great Divergence: China, Europe and the Making of the Modern World Economy*, Princeton 2000, p. 276. The concept of ghost acreage was introduced by Eric Jones in *The European Miracle*, Cambridge 1963.

23   Pomeranz, *The Great Divergence*, p. 276.

of slave labour.[24] While European conquest, colonization and settlement – including dispossession of the native peoples – are an important part of the story, so, as we have seen, was the coercive mobilization of millions of slaves, and their organization as a plantation labour force. The profits – indeed super-profits – generated by slave labour for planters, merchants and financiers stemmed from the demand for plantation produce, the effectiveness of coerced gang-labour, the rapidity with which new land in the Americas could be opened up by slave-owners, and the scope for obliging the slaves to cover much of the cost of their own direct subsistence. Slave prices and the profits reaped by slave traders reflected the anticipated gains of exploiting slave labour in New World conditions. E. A. Wrigley has argued that Pomeranz's claims for 'ghost acreage' are true only in a trivial way.[25] Yes, he concedes, Britain's economy was able to annex this extra land. But this was simply a measure of the productivity of the new industrial order (and of British agriculture which had opened space for it). But the British economy was annexing not only land but the produce of the forced labour of a few million slaves.[26] And if industrial output measured British productivity, then buoyant plantation output and rising slave prices reflected the productivity of the slave gangs.[27]

Joseph Inikori's work supplies a massively documented account of the intimacy between slave-owners and slave-traders and the key agents of British economic growth in the seventeenth, eighteenth and nineteenth centuries. He brings out the importance of a very demanding African market for textiles and metal goods.[28] While Inikori is surely right to stress the contribution of trade – and the labour of Africans and their descendants – he somewhat underplays the growth of a British domestic market rooted in increased commodification, and

---

24   While stressing 'ghost acreage' Pomeranz denies that profits from slavery or the stimulus of colonial demand played a significant role, arguing that there were many domestic sources of profit and that Europe could have supplied a wide enough market (ibid. pp. 3, 23). Yes, there were many sources of domestic credit, but was the banking system good at channelling them to where they were needed? And were not the capital needs of infrastructure investments truly immense? Many of the profits of the Atlantic trade went to Lancashire and the Midlands, from the manufacturers' point of view just where they were required, and, beyond that, into the hands of the very merchants and banks from whom they needed credit. While it is true that Europe 'could' have supplied a major export market for Britain, the fact remains that European markets were increasingly closed to British exporters by quite effective mercantilist policies (and wartime restrictions) during the vital early decades of the industrial revolution.

25   E. A. Wrigley, 'The Transition to an Advanced Organic Economy', *Economic History Review* LIX/2 (2006), pp. 435–80, especially pp. 471–4.

26   Pomeranz's chapter is entitled 'Abolishing the Land Constraint', but he shows that it was slaves who supplied the key labour force (p. 264), a point that Wrigley does not seem to have noticed. If Britain's annexing of 'ghost acres' was unproblematic, as Wrigley claims, would annexing millions of slaves have been equally unobjectionable?

27   Robert Fogel, *Without Consent or Contract: The Rise and Fall of American Slavery*, New York 1989, pp. 21–34, 60–113.

28   Joseph Inikori, *Africans and the Industrial Revolution in England: A Study in International Trade and Economic Development*, Cambridge 2002.

the dynamics of an early capitalism based on wage labour in agriculture as well as manufacturing.

Findlay and O'Rourke's *Power and Plenty* (2008) consolidates much of the foregoing argument and shows that the profits of slavery, and the scale of the plantation trades, were indeed large enough to facilitate Britain's industrial take-off. They do not deny that innovation was critical to the advance of labour productivity, but they insist that 'the remarkable innovations of the industrial revolution would not have had the deep and sustained consequences that they did if British industry had not operated within the global framework of sources of raw materials and markets for finished products that had been developed during the heyday of mercantilism . . . Slavery and the plantation economy of the New World, supplying first sugar and then cotton, the two major British imports over two hundred years, was an integral part of this Atlantic system'.[29]

Arguing that it is most unlikely that a 'closed' British economy would have witnessed the surge of technical improvements that ensured sustained industrial growth,[30] Findlay and O'Rourke develop a triangular model of the Atlantic economy embracing Europe, Africa, and the plantation Americas which captures the dynamic interaction of these zones. It shows that, in the absence of market outlets in Africa and the plantation zone, British manufactures would have faced steeply declining prices, inhibiting further investment. They also write that 'the model allows us to see that African labour was important as well as New World land.'[31]

Findlay and O'Rourke's model would have captured even more reciprocal and self-reinforcing effects if it had been quadrilateral rather than triangular, and if it had allowed for technical development in the Americas. The farmers and merchants of North America sold provisions and packing materials to the planters, buying the latter's molasses to use in rum-making. North American farmers, drawing on their earnings in the provisions trade, also purchased manufactures and textiles from Britain. Dried fish from Newfoundland and dried meat from the mid-Atlantic colonies (and South America) further swelled and diversified Atlantic exchanges. Importing metal implements from Britain, the farmers and planters were also able to boost their own productivity.

In contrast to the classic Marxist accounts associated with the work of Maurice Dobb, Eric Hobsbawm and Robert Brenner, these authors fail to situate British industrialization and colonial development firmly in the context of the prior growth of capitalism in English agriculture in the sixteenth and

---

29   Ronald Findlay and Kevin O'Rourke, *Power and Plenty: Trade, War and the World Economy in the Second Millenium*, Princeton 2008, p. 339.
30   Ibid., pp. 311–64.
31   Ibid., p. 342.

seventeenth centuries.[32] In a strange relationship that might be called 'asymmetrical complementarity', a primitive, hybrid capitalism in both metropolis and colonies created the conditions for the later breakthrough to industrialization. While social relations played a critical role, so did the transformation of the state in the course of the English Civil War and Glorious Revolution. The new state forged by these events enjoyed the confidence of the possessing classes and was able, when necessary, to raise huge sums – and consequently to win its hugely costly wars with France.[33]

The slower rate of growth of the British economy detected by 'revisionist' accounts of the industrial revolution, by Nicholas Crafts and others, has the effect of highlighting the significance of export markets in the whole period 1750–1840. Stanley Engerman has urged that so multiple were the connections between metropolis and plantations that the latter were really part of the British economy. When William Pitt introduced the first British income tax in 1799, income from the plantations was treated just as if it was a domestic income source and was taxed in Britain. Looked at as part of the British economy, the plantation colonies made a strong contribution, because of high sugar prices, down to 1815, and thereafter maintained output levels quite successfully, though increasingly overtaken by Cuban and Brazilian planters. The British merchants found that the planters and slave-traders of Brazil and Cuba were also keen to buy their textiles and metal goods. The slave plantation was perhaps not the perfect complement to capitalism: the fact that slaves received no payment limited the size of the market in the plantation zone. But if our interest is in the global rise of a new order – whether capitalism or industrialism – it makes no sense to assume away the old. Slave plantations were hybrid and transitional

---

32   Maurice Dobb, *Studies in the Development of Capitalism*, London 1946, and Rodney Hilton, ed., *The Transition Debate*, London 1982; Eric Hobsbawm, 'The Crisis of the Seventeenth Century', *Past and Present* (1954), and T. H. Aston, ed., *The Crisis of the Seventeenth Century*, Oxford 1964; Robert Brenner, 'Agrarian Class Structure and Economic Development', *Past and Present* (1977), and T. H. Aston and C. H. E. Phillips, eds, *The Brenner Debate*, Cambridge 1976. Findlay and O'Rourke criticize 'Marxist' accounts of the origins of capitalism or progress towards industrialization for focusing on 'profits' instead of innovation. While there is no monolithic Marxist account, the Marxist approaches I cite follow Karl Marx in distinguishing between 'absolute' and 'relative' surplus value, with the latter referring to the specifically capitalist incentive to make technical investments which raised both productivity and profits. By contrast the serf-lord did not directly control the whole labour process, and instead sought to extract surplus by squeezing the direct producer or by seizing new villages. Slave-owning planters were intermediate social agents, who episodically pursued technical progress but who were generally addicted to the pursuit of absolute surplus value.

33   Findlay and O'Rourke follow Gregory Clark (*Farewell to Alms*, Princeton 2006, pp. 241–2) in denying that the Glorious Revolution was a watershed event, greatly enhancing the credit-worthiness of the British state and hence its ability to advance Britain's commercial and colonial interests. But the evidence Clark supplies actually confirms that tax rose from 2.2 per cent of GDP prior to 1688 to around 10 per cent in subsequent decades. For the real importance of 1688 see Brewer, *Sinews of Power*.

enterprises, partly rooted in 'natural economy' but also anticipating features of
the new industrial 'plant' (short for plantation) of the future. The non-commodified
element of natural economy – which included slave labour on subsistence
and the investment of slave labour on building works – somewhat limited the
scope of the market in the plantation zone. But many producers in the early-
nineteenth-century world were far less responsive to market pressures and
industrial demand than the slave plantations of the Americas, just as a few,
based exclusively on wage labour, were even more attuned to such pressures. In
the circumstances the cotton manufacturers paid a sincere compliment to the
planters – they bought growing quantities of slave-grown cotton and at a stroke
solved their most pressing supply problem. The mechanization of work
processes has never proceeded evenly. When it advances rapidly at one point,
the market will exert a pressure upon another, upstream, for labour intensification. Even planters who were embarrassed to own slaves believed that slave
gangs were their best solution. Some cotton was cultivated by small farmers and
delivered to the planter, at a cost, for ginning, but it was the multiplying slave
gangs that explained the surge in output.

Steam power turned out to be a technology that could be adapted to a wide
variety of uses. In the plantation sector steam power was harnessed to processing and transport. Contrary to the belief of some economists at the time, slave
labour could be highly skilled and could be combined with some of the new
industrial methods.[34] Plantation production and trade absorbed some mechanical advances, such as the new cotton gin, or the 'vacuum pan' used to extract
sugar from boiling cane juice. Steam transport opened the inland regions.
While the acres of fertile land were an 'ecological windfall', only Indian removal,
and the forced labour of several million slaves, brought them swiftly into
cultivation.

Planters were not fully capitalist agents, since they only employed a small
number of paid workers. Nevertheless they contributed to an expanded regime
of capitalist accumulation. This was a process whereby capitalism grew by integrating more primitive sources of exploitation. The world's first industrializing
capitalists could not find already-existing partners like themselves. They and
their merchant suppliers and backers were consequently happy to seek outlets
and supplies from the plantations. And even when capitalist development took
hold elsewhere in Europe and North America, the manufacturers and merchants
responsible also found exchanges with the plantation and farming zone of the
Americas to be a convenient, sometimes even essential, market outlet and
source of stimulants and raw material.

---

34   Robert Starobin, *Industrial Slavery in the Old South*, New York 1970. The liberal case
against slave labour was summarized effectively by J. E. Cairnes, *The Slave Power*, London 1860.
Although these specific criticisms were mistaken, his overall argument that enterprises relying on
slave labour faced strict productivity limits still has merit, as will be argued below.

In the eighteenth century, and even well into the nineteenth, Britain's commerce with the planters and farmers of the New World was more extensive and dynamic than its exchanges with either the serf-lords of Eastern Europe or the zamindars of Bengal. This is because the planters traded with the farmers, and both were good customers for English manufactures, something that could not be said of Prussian Junkers and Indian landowners. The Junkers bought some wines and silks but not nails, hoes, clothing or provisions. The zamindars were ferocious exploiters but desultory customers. The flood of New World plantation produce in the eighteenth century was much larger than the trade in spices or tea. However, by the mid-nineteenth century, with the spread and consolidation of British rule, Indian markets, raw materials and revenues were to become hugely important – a further illustration of the fact that capitalism generally advances most unevenly, and through sometimes bizarre mixtures of the modern and the pre-modern.

I have suggested that if slavery had been effectively banned – with, perhaps, Catholics and Protestants shaming one another into observing it – then one or other of the leading Atlantic states might have been spurred to organize a labour supply which did not depend on, and itself reproduce, racial bondage. In *The Making of New World Slavery* I urged, as a 'counterfactual' speculation, that if free, wage-earning labourers could have been found then the pattern of growth, while slower to start with, might have been more sustainable in the long run. I pointed out that the French navy was recruited by the *inscription maritime*, an efficient administration, with special inducements for the skilled. The organization of indentured labour also showed how outright slavery could have been avoided; when the supply of English indentures dried up, similar terms – with freedom, land and tools after a three-year period – could have been offered to emigrants from Africa, India or Eastern Europe. The vital point to register here is that such arrangements would not have simply appeared as a consequence of market forces, but would have required careful planning, as did the *inscription maritime*. While slave-traders would have been deprived of their profits, a plantation regime that eventually fostered a free labour supply could have fostered better markets, and equivalent or better chances for long-run productivity gains. If the authorities had scrupulously respected the treaties negotiated with the Native Americans, this would have greatly limited the availability of land and made wage labour more attractive. Unfortunately the simple pursuit of profit by individual merchants and planters was not going to come up with the institutional package needed. As it was, the colonial authorities created conditions favourable to a supply of slaves, rather than to one with free labourers. This counterfactual was doomed by the lack of imagination and class blinkers of seventeenth-century elites, not, as some seem to suppose, by the eternal impossibility of organizing sugar cultivation without slave labour.[35]

The story of Britain and its colonies was to be reprised, within the borders of one country, by the United States. New England's early-nineteenth-century 'lords of the loom' depended on the South's 'lords of the lash' and their slave-produced cotton. New York's merchant houses catered to planters throughout the plantation zone and, like their English and Scottish counterparts, invested at least some of the proceeds in canals, garment factories and railways.[36] While not always the perfect fit, the economies of the South, North and West displayed many synergies and complementarities in the first half of the nineteenth century. The South sold cotton and purchased machinery, the farmers of the North West bought sugar and sold wheat, and slave labour contributed to these domestic circuits.[37]

The brokers of New Orleans – with their links to the City of London, the Paris Bourse and Amsterdam – were another hub of plantation development. For many decades slave-produced goods, especially cotton, furnished the country's chief export. The United States produced 55 million lbs of cotton in 1802, 331 million lbs by 1830 and 2,241 million lbs, worth $249

---

35   There is, of course, something artificial about my 'free-labour' counterfactual. It was framed as an alternative to a counterfactual developed by David Eltis which postulated that European elites could have made even greater profits, and developed their plantations even more quickly, if only they had been willing to enslave their own people. I urged that such a proceeding would have been so costly as to be impossible. Seymour Drescher also questions the feasibility of Eltis's counterfactual, but is no more persuaded by mine: 'Blackburn's scenario requires the reversal of what most scholars have taken to be the primary motive in the choices made by the planters and princes . . . Theirs were choices for maximal productivity, higher output, cheaper commodities and greater economic opportunities for Europe.' Seymour Drescher, ' "White Atlantic"? The Choice for African Slave Labour in the Plantation Americas', in David Eltis, Frank Lewis, Kenneth Sokoloff, eds, Slavery in the Development of the Americas, Cambridge 2001, p. 33. This objection does not register my argument that a well-organized (not 'spontaneous') free labour system would have led to higher productivity and output, and hence to lower prices and greater opportunities than did the slave plantation. The slave gang only permitted a 'once and for all' boost, while a wage labour system, supposing one to have been organized, would have led to continuous gradual improvements. We will see later that the abolition of slavery did not everywhere lead to higher prices, lower output and so forth, though of course there was no automatic free labour replacement – and some of the substitutes resorted to, even if nominally 'free', were just as inhuman. It is true that the ending of slavery in Haiti led to a sharp drop in sugar output, but the black state also suffered from war devastation, the loss of skilled personnel and a trade boycott. Notwithstanding this, Haiti remained a major supplier of coffee cultivated by free labour, sometimes with the help of the cooperative labour practice known as the coumbite. The latter was a benign version of the African work team, just as the slave gang was a cruel version. I have more on Haiti in Part III, but see Alex Dupuy, Haiti in the World Economy: Class, Race and Underdevelopment since 1700, Boulder 1989, pp. 88, 108.

36   For a broad-brush indication see Anne Farrow, Joel Lang and Jenifer Frank, Complicity: How the North Promoted, Prolonged and Profited from Slavery, New York 2005.

37   Connections evident in Douglass North, The Economic Growth of the United States, 1790–1860, New York 1980.

million, by 1860.[38] Very little of the $249 million was spent on the slaves who produced it, and the little that was, was spent in ways determined by their owners. This impressive sum went to enrich planters, brokers, merchants and suppliers, both in the US and Europe. And just as British employees had to work long hours to earn the wages and salaries which they spent on plantation produce, so the farmers, labourers, artisans and professionals of the US West and North had to work hard to afford their daily cup of coffee or pipe of tobacco, and the purchase of blue denim overalls or cotton blouses.

The planters of the Americas were a hybrid social type, more implicated in market exchanges than feudal landlords but still resting to a great extent on 'natural economy'. They purchased equipment and provisions, and paid wages or fees to supervisors and agents, so long as this would generate more net revenue from the staple. They sustained a maritime complex based on free workers. On the other hand they extracted huge quantities of unremunerated labour from hundreds of thousands – eventually millions – of slaves. They earned surplus-profits on the sale of slave produce, but had to share them with merchants and shippers. They were very wealthy men but often owed large sums to suppliers. Most of their wealth was tied up in slaves who they did not want to sell. Any disruption to trade could force difficult choices on them. Their dependence on merchants and factors was a source of considerable bitterness and frustration to the planters, who grumbled at the high price of provisions, the uncertain price of the staple, and the high rates of interest charged if they got into debt. The merchants had access to sophisticated insurance, giving them a greater ability to manage risk. The planter felt himself lord of everything he surveyed, yet could be entangled in debt and paying exorbitant rates of interest. The tension between planters and merchants, especially metropolitan merchants and colonial planters, was a strand in the revolutionary events of 1775–1825.

The link between slave plantations and economic growth was a complex and many-sided affair. I have stressed that those using the new industrial methods needed credit, and the sponsors of improvements needed capital. From one point of view it is the intrinsic advantages of a project that determines its creditworthiness, and not the source of credit or capital. But good projects still need the backing of people or institutions with financial resources. Creditworthiness cannot be sustained without cash flow. The plantation trades were a major source of cash flow. Merchants and financiers had greater ability to back promising enterprises and projects because their investment in the plantation-related trade earned good returns. Those earnings, in their turn, reflected the profitability of the plantations, which rested on the unpaid and unremitting exertions

38 Alfred H. Conrad and John R. Meyer, 'The Economics of Slavery in the Ante-bellum South', in Robert W. Fogel and Stanley L. Engerman, eds, *The Reinterpretation of American Economic History*, New York 1971, pp. 342–61, 358.

of the slave gangs. Rising sales and profits drove up the price of slaves. With other sectors advancing even more strongly, the diverse recipients of the revenues generated by slavery had some incentive to diversify and to invest in the North and West. Merchants, brokers and financial backers siphoned off some of the strong cash flow generated by plantation exchanges and devoted it to sectors more in need of fresh capital than the plantations. Investors also knew the advantages of diversification. British sugar planting in the years 1780–1820, and US cotton plantations for much of the period 1840–60, seem to have acted as a 'milch-cow' sector, part of whose large profits could be devoted to investments in communications, infrastructure and industry. During these decades plantation maintenance and expansion still needed, and received, some reinvestment. But in many years profits on the sale of the premium staple were so ample that there was a surplus available for investment elsewhere. Merchants and bankers were also aware that, while very profitable, the slave economy had strict limits. Gang labour was good for producing plantation staples but had no special edge in general farming or manufacturing. The slave states of the Upper South became large producers of wheat. They achieved some development of general farming and manufacturing using slave labour. But the prices of wheat or pork belly futures on the Chicago exchange were set by the efforts of prairie farmers using family and wage labour, not slave-owning planters.

The steam engine was to become in many ways the symbol of the dawning industrial era. It harnessed a gigantic new source of power, speeded up communications and allowed land transportation to compete with waterborne commerce. In the long run the steam age was to nurture a many-sided development which slave plantation societies were unable to match. But the planters could be content simply to form a subordinate part of the new industrial system. They were among the first to adapt steam power to grind sugar cane, to bale cotton and to carry their products to market on trains and steamships. Scientifically-minded planters sought to develop steam-driven machines to cut the cane, or to plant and harvest the cotton, but these tasks proved resistant to thorough mechanization. The human eye and hand proved superior at coping with the untidiness of the cotton or cane field. However, the French authorities in Saint-Domingue had shown that it was possible to use collective resources – the Engineering Corps – to irrigate the land and improve communications.

Short of a collectively devised new context, nothing could compete with the productivity of the coerced armies of the slave gangs, notwithstanding the argument of some political economists that slave labour could never be as productive as free labour.

The use of slave labour did not prevent semi-mechanization of the processing and transportation of the premium staples, but the very profitability of the slave plantations and the appropriation of some of those profits by brokers, bankers and merchants tended to generate unevenness and uncertainty in the growth process. Slave plantations might be compared to oil fields in more recent times, with the high profits made from 'black gold' inhibiting diversification and industrialization in the producing zone and the profits of financial intermediation fuelling speculation and cycles of boom and slump. At all events, during some periods, slave plantations absorbed capital in the plantation zone, draining it away from industrial investment.[39]

A significant portion of the massive slave-produced surplus was siphoned off to the metropolis instead of widening the local market, as happened with capitalist farming and manufacture in Britain and the United States. I have stressed that mercantile profits generated by slavery could allow merchants, banks and brokers to extend more credit to manufacturers or farmers who needed it. But a credit system can magnify, instead of correcting, underlying imbalances, as the history of the trade cycle and the financial panic repeatedly shows. The growth of slave plantations added a source of 'over-accumulation', with its consequential imbalance and instability, because it increased the mass of mercantile profit without correspondingly widening monetary demand in the plantation zone.[40]

The sustained importance of plantation output and profits prompted some observers to wonder whether permanent forms of bondage might not be needed if national prosperity was to be sustained. The history of economic thought gives little attention to this line of speculation, and has preferred to dwell on remarks by Adam Smith and Benjamin Franklin insisting that slave labour, because of its expense, yielded poor returns – a conclusion not based on a study of plantation finances. That many shied away from celebrating the achievements of slave-based enterprise probably reflected a widespread unease. However, Sir William Petty in his *Treatise of Ireland* (1687), John Locke in his work for the Board of Trade (1690s), Sir James Steuart in his *Inquiry into the Principles of Political Economy* (1766) and Jeremy Bentham in his *Pauper Management Improved* (1797) believed that compulsion would prove indispensable to sustained national prosperity. Petty's notions were the target of Swift's withering satire in his *Modest Proposal* (1729). The enslavement accepted by Locke was challenged by many of the writers of the Scottish enlightenment. Sir James Steuart preferred the Spartan model, in which an educated, disciplined and gentlemanly elite would direct a subject population of helots. This was not

---

39   See Ralph Anderson and Robert Gallman, 'Slaves as Fixed Capital and Southern Economic Development', *Journal of American History* 64/1 (1977), pp. 24–46, and Gavin Wright, *Slavery and American Economic Growth*, Baton Rouge 2007.

40   The importance of finance as a precipitant of crisis is argued by Giovanni Arrighi in *The Long Twentieth Century*, London 1994. For 'over-accumulation' as an expression of geographical unevenness, imperialism and unfree labour, see David Harvey, *Limits to Capital*, 2nd edn, London 2006, pp. 326–45. I return to these points in Chapter 12, below.

outright chattel slavery, but it would entail compulsory, onerous, and lengthy engagements. Steuart was aware that the labour market could restrain wage pressure, especially where there were many workers in competition with one another. But the existence of a class of helots would also help to reduce the wage workers' expectations and leverage. For his part Bentham proposed that the 'whole body of the burdensome poor', amounting to some half-million persons, be placed at the service of a joint stock enterprise, the National Charity Company, which would put them to work in hundreds of industry houses. The interest which sections of the elite took in the Spartan model and schemes of workhouse 'reform' was to put wage workers on their guard.[41]

---

41   Michael Perelman, *The Invention of Capitalism: Classical Political Economy and the Secret History of Primitive Accumulation*, Durham 2000, pp. 20–2, 124–9, 139–70.

CHAPTER FIVE

Black Aspirations
and the 'Picaresque Proletariat'

The new Atlantic system had been consolidated thanks to multiple fragmenting divisions – between black and white, captives of one nation and those of another, Africans and creoles, the slave elite and the field labourers, blacks and mulattoes, slaves and free people of colour. On the other hand planters, merchants and colonial officials had overcome their initial differences and worked together. In practice even the ever-warring colonial powers generally respected property in slaves. English or French privateers or commanders seized slaves as part of the spoils of war, but then resold them. Some commanders declined such plunder, instead using the capture of an enemy colony as a trading opportunity. When the British captured Havana in 1762–3 they seized prize goods but did not burn the plantations. Instead they brought in British merchants who sold over 4,000 slaves to the Cuban planters. The Spanish king invited slaves in the English colonies to flee their captivity and seek refuge in Spanish lands, where they would be given the opportunity to fight the English. But when Spain acquired title to new territory in North America in 1763 and after, it did not disturb the slave order.

Conflicts within the imperial and slave-holding order multiplied after 1763, eventually allowing insurgent slaves to find some surprising allies. The period 1776–1848 was to witness a gradual growth of community and solidarity among those slaves whose labour was driving the Atlantic boom. There were fewer plantation revolts, but more concerted resistance to the slave condition. As plantations matured the slave complement began to develop greater cohesion, nourished by family ties and claims to provision and burial grounds. Planters and overseers liked to think that they were in command of the allocation of these land rights but, the more mature the plantation, the larger the role of the slave community in such matters. Numbers of slaves were also able to reach outside the plantations, as they traded surplus provisions in local markets and used the proceeds to make small purchases. Furthermore many were brought as domestics or artisans to the great Atlantic ports.

In the early eighteenth century there were struggles in the Caribbean colonies over whether slaves should be permitted to bring the surplus produce of their plots to the Sunday market. Poor white farmers often objected but eventually had to give way, because the planters found the arrangement meant savings for them and a more diversified diet for everyone. By the 1780s the produce of the slave plots in Saint-Domingue and Jamaica furnished the bulk of the food consumed by the whole colony. Attendance at the Sunday market facilitated communication between the favoured slaves allowed to participate, beginning to breach the fragmentation of the slave communities of different plantations. Another, very sensitive area of contested autonomy, was that of burials and burial grounds. Planters and overseers found it impossible to deny burial to dead slaves, but later might wish to use the land for construction or cultivation. As generation succeeded generation, and notwithstanding heavy mortality rates and new arrivals, the slave crews really did become communities, rather than collections of captives.[1]

In the plantation zone the passage of a couple of generations allowed the slave community to begin to discover itself. In the Caribbean, creole languages and patois took hold, and part-African religious cults acquired a following. The locally-born poor whites would sometimes speak the patois and practice the cults. In Saint-Domingue a new language – Kréyole – was widely spoken by slaves and free people of colour who also participated in vodou ceremonies. Such developments were also found in other French colonies and in Brazil, where the free people of colour belonged to brotherhoods sponsored by the Church. In parts of the Caribbean and mainland, free people of colour joined Freemason lodges, or formed their own religious cults. Jamaican slaves spoke their own patois and practised obeah.

The slaves' provision grounds would be bequeathed to descendants, and land used for burial would become the focus for familial and communal rites. The slave community or specific kin groups would seek recognition of customary claims to 'free time', as well as land. Sometimes planters or overseers chose to go along with this, in the expectation that the cost of the concession would be more than compensated by enhanced slave cooperation. These pressures and negotiations often suggest the aspirations of an emergent peasantry.[2] Some planters saw a pattern of concessions and 'amelioration' as a wise and enlightened policy that would raise productivity and the birth rate. Others recognized that the plantation and slave order rested on implicit understandings – or 'hidden transcripts' as they are called by James Scott[3] – which it would be foolish to ignore. Planters, overseers and drivers knew that they would get better work if they held to certain understandings relating to the availability of extra rations, the pace of work, the timing of breaks, the use of slave plots and time to cultivate them. But in the conditions of slavery these were fragile, temporary and conditional. Concessions made at one moment would be withdrawn at another.

---

1   For an excellent study of Antigua which brings out such trends, see David Barry Gaspar, *Bondmen and Rebels*, Baltimore 1985.

2   The 'proto-peasant' aspect of Caribbean slavery has been analysed by Sidney Mintz in, e.g. *Caribbean Transformations*, Chicago 1974.

3   James C. Scott, *Domination and the Arts of Resistance: Hidden Transcripts*, New Haven 1990.

The implacable logic of commercial pressure on the slave enterprise, and the turnover of personnel, set narrow limits on all concessions and customary rights. Market conditions periodically destroyed understandings between planters or overseers and the slave elite, or mass of slaves. Any implicit – unwritten – 'contract' was vulnerable to a succession of likely events. Financial distress, fear of foreclosure, the death or departure of a planter or overseer, or the effect of drought or war, would undo supposed concessions and agreements within the plantation. The internal slave trade was there both to dispose of troublemakers and to encourage a reallocation of slave labour towards new sectors of the planting economy. At the limit the slave community would be broken up and sold. The slave order, with its patrols and slave-catchers, was there to cope with physical resistance. To run away or commit suicide could still impose a cost, but a very unequal one. The owner lost the value of the slave but was rid of a problem.

The social relations of slavery allowed the planter to make concessions to the slaves' desire for comfort and survival which, nonetheless, benefited the slave-holder. If the slave took time on Sunday to cultivate food crops, or bring them to market, then the planter – who needed to keep his slaves alive and well – gained economically.[4] Likewise if the slaves were allowed to sing their own songs as they toiled, the work would go better. But beyond the economic calculus, such concessions could help to strengthen the collective morale of the enslaved. The major slave markets which grew larger and larger in Jamaica and Saint-Domingue over the decades certainly embodied concessions which allowed the slave community to discover itself, and to develop its own identity and means of communication.

The North American tobacco plantations were distinctive both because they were quite small and, as discussed in Chapter 3, because of high slave birth rates. Most tobacco plantations had around one or two dozen slaves, and the high birth rates led to a rapidly growing population of American-born or creole slaves. The gap between the slave elite and the mass of slaves was here much narrower than on the Caribbean plantations. In North America slave drivers were usually white; in the Caribbean they were black. North American conditions fostered a somewhat greater homogeneity among the slave community, but inserted this community into a stronger, more defined and policed system of racial subjection. The slaves were a large minority of the population in the Southern plantation zone, not a majority. White males were armed and organized – under planter leadership – to hold down the slaves. In the last chapter it was noted that by the 1770s North American slaves were likely to speak English, and often adopted Christianity. These were elements of partial

---

4 The logic here is explained by G. A. Cohen, *Karl Marx's Theory of History: A Defence*, Oxford 1978, p. 67.

cultural assimilation which were to allow the plantation slave better chances of escape to Northern towns when turmoil paralyzed the colonies during the Independence War.

When Lord Dunmore, the governor of Virginia, offered freedom to the slaves of any rebel master who made it to the British lines, several hundred responded within a few weeks of the proclamation (14 November 1775). The fact that fifteen to twenty thousand slaves eventually responded to such appeals by British commanders shows that many were following the white men's quarrel quite closely. The freedom they could claim was not only a passport to personal liberty, it also promised to remove the stigma of slavery by making them soldiers of the Crown. Though such hopes might be disappointed, it seemed to many an opportunity worth seizing.[5] Such action, rather than plantation revolt, seemed to offer a way out.

In several of the Caribbean colonies, such as Jamaica and Surinam, there were communities of escaped slaves known as maroons. In Brazil, Cuba and Spanish South America communities of escaped slaves – *quilombolas* or *cimarrones* – had successfully withstood attempts to suppress or capture them. The Jamaican authorities acknowledged their inability to defeat the rebels when they negotiated a treaty with the maroons in the 1730s. However, the maroon chiefs, in return for a recognized status as free negroes, committed themselves to return future runaways. Large-scale *marronage* was uncommon on the French islands, but in Saint-Domingue at least slaves would use *petit marronage* – absconding to the hills but keeping in touch with friends and relations who stayed put – as a way to apply pressure on the planters.[6] In a 1789 revolt on a Brazilian plantations the slaves left as a body, and took vital equipment with them. They were willing to return if given the right to veto the choice of overseer, to have two extra free days a week, to be given canoes and fishing nets, to hold festivities, and to have increased food rations. They also wanted more slaves to be acquired to lighten the collective load. The interest of the incident is not that the slave system could tolerate such demands, but rather that they give us a glimpse of the very tangible goals to which these rebels aspired.[7] I have urged that the slaves who wanted to control their own time and plots of land were a sort of proto-peasantry, but this should be qualified by adding that as workers in plantation gangs – and sugar mill work-teams – they were also very much a contingent of the working class.

---

5   Cassandra Pybus, *Epic Journeys of Freedom*, New York 2006. Gary Nash cites appeals made to the British by African Americans which considerably predate Dunmore's declaration. See Gary Nash, *The Unknown American Revolution: The Unruly Birth of Democracy and the Struggle to Create America*, London 2004, pp. 157–65.

6   Richard Price, ed., *Maroon Societies: Rebel Slave Communities in the Americas*, Baltimore 1979.

7   Robert E. Conrad, ed., *Children of God's Fire*, Princeton 1983, pp. 68–9.

While the growing number of creole (American-born) whites and free people of colour was to expand the milieu favourable to assertions of civic liberty, the main groupings of native Americans, whether tribes or indigenous villages, played little or no part in the growth of Patriot politics. Indeed the metropolitan authorities, who sometimes protected Indians from the predatory encroachment of the creoles, were apt to have better understandings with the Indian peoples than did the patriots, notwithstanding the latter's willingness rhetorically to evoke the former's nobility and fighting spirit – and the simplicity and real freedom of their way of life. The virtues of 'noble savages' were also celebrated by French *philosophes* in contrast with the corruption of European life and institutions, a theme that patriots in the Americas happily echoed – while scheming to displace and dispossess these same savages.

The 1760s and 1770s saw a rash of 'freedom suits' brought in England, North America and France – that is, legal actions against wrongful enslavement, of a type which had been known for some time in Brazil and Spanish America. Such actions usually arose when a black person claimed that they were really free but were being held as a slave due to mistaken identity, or kidnap, or because the owner had cheated them of a promised manumission. In some famous cases, such as that which freed James Somersett in England in 1772, the claim was that slavery itself had no legality outside the plantation zone. These freedom suits always required the support of a free person, as slaves had no access to the courts. Those pleading their freedom usually drew on sympathetic lawyers and the support of friends, relatives and work-fellows, both white and black.

The English judgment in the Somersett case was bound to be a source of concern to American slave-holders, even though it had no bearing on the legality of slavery in the colonies. The author of the judgment was Lord Mansfield, the lord chief justice, who himself owned land in Virginia. The progress of the case had been followed by the newspapers and a crowd of a few hundred, including some of London's free people of colour. Several lawyers donated their services to the plaintiff and much was made of a flourish in William Blackstone's *Commentaries on the Laws of England* (1765) to the effect that breathing England's air freed the slave. Mansfield sought to make his ruling as narrow as possible – focusing only on the owner's right to return Somersett to Virginia – but it nonetheless served as a warning shot to the already restive American slave-holder.[8]

While Mansfield's judgement has often been held up as an example of the distinctive British commitment to liberty, it is less well known that scores of

---

8   Lord Mansfield delivered his judgment reluctantly, aware that it was difficult to square with Britain's imperial interests and practice of the slave trade. See David Brion Davis, *The Problem of Slavery in the Age of Revolution*, Ithaca 1975, pp. 474–8. Mansfield had a coloured niece – daughter of his brother and a Jamaican woman – who lived in his household as one of the family.

slaves in France pursued freedom suits in courts at Paris, and did so with great success. The lawyers engaged by these slaves argued that they were free by virtue of the traditional principle that 'there are no slaves in France'. An Edict of 1716 and a Royal Declaration of 1738 had tried to circumvent this by specifically allowing French colonists to bring slave domestics to France. But the Paris *parlement* refused to register the law, rendering it invalid so far as the Paris courts were concerned – in particular the Admiralty Court, which heard 154 cases between 1730 and 1790 and freed a total of 257 enslaved men and women in that time, finding for the plaintiff in nearly every case. The legal opinion obtained by the *parlement* when it first refused to register the Edict of 1716 referred to the doctrine that all France's inhabitants were free, and that Henri II had issued a decree in 1556 freeing all serfs in the Dauphiné in such sweeping terms that it was impossible to reintroduce slavery. The freedom suits gave an opportunity to the *parlement* and the Paris courts to demonstrate their independence and zeal for French liberties. The language used in the opinions seems to echo the positions of the Jansenists, a current within the French Church that increasingly regarded slave-holding as unchristian.[9]

The plantation boom had given rise to hundreds of thousands of mariners and dock workers, mainly white but also significant numbers of people of colour. Those of different backgrounds learned from one another. Faced with the rigours of shipboard discipline, they also learned to stick together. When the sailors in the Port of London went 'on strike' in 1768 – that is, struck their ships' sails – they added a word to the English language.[10] They could easily see that it was better to negotiate with employers who did not have slaves. Slaves in such major ports as London, Glasgow, Boston, Philadelphia and New York found supporters willing to help them bring freedom suits. And there were enough victories to deter slave-owners from bringing more slaves to these centres. This helped check the spread of slavery in areas where it was marginal, and served as a necessary prelude to abolitionism. The proportion of slaves fell, and the proportion of free coloured workers grew, in most of the major Atlantic ports. By the last decades of the eighteenth century the authorities were worried that these concentrations of 'masterless men' (and women) constituted a danger to the status quo and that the port towns were a haven for runaways.[11]

The Methodists and Baptists were able to attract hearers and worshippers from this milieu and from among those, white or black, whose existence was

9   Sue Peabody, *'There Are No Slaves in France': The Political Culture of Race and Slavery in the Ancien Régime*, Oxford, 1996, p. 55.

10   Marcus Rediker, *Between the Devil and the Deep Blue Sea: Merchant Seamen, Pirates, and the Anglo-American Maritime World*, Cambridge 1993, p. 110.

11   Many examples are given in a marvellous study by Julius Scott, *The Common Wind: Currents of Afro-American Communication in the Era of the Haitian Revolution*, Duke University PhD thesis 1986, pp. 26–42.

being transformed by the Atlantic boom. The 'non-conformist' churches offered self-help and community in a fast-changing and upsetting world. The Methodists held open-air meetings at which all were welcome, while the Baptist ceremonies, with their uninhibited emotionality, attracted a mainly plebeian following. While slave-owners rarely encouraged participation in such gatherings, they found it difficult to forbid Sunday worship. The colony of Georgia had been established with a formal ban on the entry of slaves; after a planter-led campaign this ban was lifted in the 1740s, in return for assurances that the slaves could go to church. This colony and state was to become a centre of African American Christianity.

The Patriot crowds calling for liberty in the 1760s on both sides of the Atlantic also gained a following among the artisans, journeymen and port workers, mostly white but some coloured. Peter Linebaugh and Marcus Rediker have coined the term 'picaresque proletariat' to refer to a maritime workforce that was distrustful of constituted authority and which detested the arbitrary exactions of the Royal Navy's press gangs.[12] The American cause came to embrace a diverse popular constituency. John Adams famously described a Patriot mob which had attacked British soldiers as a 'motley rabble of saucy boys, Negroes and mulattoes, Irish teagues and outlandish jack tars'.[13] Adams was here appealing to the class prejudice of a respectable jury. People of colour were, overall, probably a smallish component of the Patriot mob, because their numbers were anyway modest. But we do know that Crispus Attucks, the first colonist shot by the redcoats, was an African American. Racial sentiment was not absent, but it was inchoate. Both the Methodist followers of John Wesley and the agrarian-radical followers of Thomas Spence opposed slavery and welcomed coloured members. Many picaresque proletarians wanted to settle down as independent artisans, shopkeepers or farmers, an aspiration not so different from the slave's desire for land and freedom.

In the French and Spanish colonies the social gains of a larger free coloured population were resented by the colonial whites. While the latter craved more freedom from metropolitan regulation, the colonial authorities saw free people of colour as a useful resource, whether in defending the colony from the British, or as a check on colonial autonomy. The large French Caribbean colony of Saint-Domingue was shaken by *révoltes blanches* in the 1760s, as colonial whites claimed greater freedom and privileges for themselves but strongly disputed the need for a coloured militia.[14] The French regime of slavery had led to the emergence of a free coloured population that was nearly equal in size to the white

---

12   For the role of the crowd in the agitations leading up to the American Revolution see Peter Linebaugh and Marcus Rediker, *The Many-Headed Hydra: The Hidden History of the Revolutionary Atlantic*, Boston and London 2000, pp. 211–47.

13   David McCullough, *John Adams*, New York 2002, p. 67.

14   Charles Frostin, *Les Révoltes blanches à Saint-Domingue*, Paris 1975.

population. Coloured proprietors owned a fifth of the colony's slaves and there were also many free coloured notaries, administrators, shopkeepers, domestics, barbers, carpenters and stone masons. There were also the so-called *libres de savane*, former slaves who had been freed by their master but who had not acquired the costly freedom papers. The colony's flourishing markets were places where members of the slave elite would sell slave produce and free peddlers would sell other articles of consumption. As noted above, the white population itself was largely dependent on food purchased in these markets.

Since the later seventeenth century, Jamaica had been the scene of repeated and sustained slave revolts. This island also had two tenacious maroon communities. Yet following the suppression in 1760 of Tacky's Rebellion – with its strong 'Coromantee' character – there was to be over two decades without a major upheaval.[15] The bustling French colony of Saint-Domingue also escaped a major slave uprising during these years. These were decades of headlong plantation growth as well as of widespread political controversy. Leaders of the slave community followed these disputes – perhaps waiting to take advantage of them. In the meantime, planter power was heavily concentrated close to sea and rivers. In the backlands, mountainous regions and mangrove swamps there were many indigenous holdouts and hybrid groupings. This is where runaways could hide and maroons establish themselves. In Florida, the Eastern Caribbean and along the northern Pacific coast of South America were autonomous communities of black Seminoles, Caribs and the part-African Indians of Esmeraldas.

The slave trade reached unprecedented heights in the last decades of the eighteenth century. There were shipboard risings, and parts of the upper West African coast where the traders found they were not welcome. David Eltis shows that such factors had a large impact on trading patterns.[16] The jihadi wars and revolts in West Africa in the 1770s – including the overthrow of the king of Fuuta Jalon in 1776 – seem to reflect resistance to the slave trade in parts of West Africa where Islam was strong.[17] The price of captives rose during those years, but so did the flood of captive humanity. Because the Atlantic was so large and the slave traffic so destructive, it was most unusual for even free blacks in the Americas to develop connections back in Africa itself, though it was not unknown in the South Atlantic.

I have mentioned a number of the gradual processes whereby the slaves and freed people of colour in the Americas gradually achieved a greater degree of collective identity, and also noted some points of resistance to the slave

---

15   For Tacky's Revolt see Michael Craton, *Testing the Chains: Resistance to Slavery in the British West Indies*, Ithaca 1982, pp. 125–39.

16   David Eltis, *The Rise of African Slavery in the Americas*, Cambridge 2000, pp 164–92.

17   James Searing, *West African Slavery and Atlantic Commerce*, Cambridge 1993, pp. 91–2, 155–62.

condition. The slaves and free people of colour took an interest in religious revivalism as well as in the growing conflict between metropolis and colonies. Both parties to these conflicts allowed themselves anti-slavery gestures – ranging from the colonial boycott of slave imports to British celebration of the Mansfield judgment in the Somersett case – but both remained committed to a flourishing slave order. Because slave resistance had always existed, its growing potential for coherence was not immediately noted by the planters and colonial authorities. While always prone to paranoia about slave conspiracies, neither colonists nor metropolitan authorities saw them as any reason to moderate their own quarrels. They may have been somewhat reassured by the lull in major slave uprisings, unaware that it was merely a pause before a new and more directly politicized type of resistance appeared.

CHAPTER SIX

The Planters Back Colonial Revolt

The imperial projects of the different European states, with their cycle of wars, helped to stimulate the beginnings of national awareness in the metropolis. While these states comprised many different jurisdictions at home, overseas they claimed sovereignty over their colonies. Spanish, British, French or Dutch identity was clearer in the New World than it was in the Old. While those born in Europe could contemplate their colonial possessions with pride, those of American birth, even if white, were a sort of second-class citizen or subject. They might have their own colonial assembly or municipal council, but these had limited powers and were subject to metropolitan regulation. And it was also the metropolis which distributed the plum jobs in colonial administration. As colonies matured, and the numbers of creoles multiplied, they were drawn to assert their own identity against imperial rule. The wave of colonial 'reform' that followed the Seven Years War (1756–63) accentuated the problem because it was based on unilateral metropolitan fiat, including exercise of far-reaching powers to tax, regulate militia and distribute commercial privilege. Examples included the attempted imposition of the Stamp Tax in English North America, the organization of a coloured militia in the French Caribbean, and the introduction of *comercio libre* in Spanish America, all in the 1760s.

By fostering the wealth, population and self-confidence of the English North American colonies, the Atlantic boom set the stage for the American Revolution. Like any long-term market boom it was disruptive, generating ups and downs, winners and losers. Support for action against the imperial power came from all those who felt that the imperial power was arbitrary, intrusive and constraining. The extent of the revolt among the colonial elite is shown by the fact that the rebels won a majority in the assemblies of each of the thirteen North American colonies (English Canada, with its precarious hold on Quebec, stayed clear). The bold appeals launched by this elite succeeded in rallying a broad swathe of support from white colonists, whether propertied or not, and whether their mother tongue was English, German or Dutch.

Slave-holding planters and plantation merchants were prominent in the leadership of the Revolution. Success in North America was eventually to encourage a great arc of rebellion throughout the Americas in the years 1776–1825 which was to reshape the slave order. The planters of the New World were proud of what they had accomplished, and believed that they could do even better if the royal officials were sent packing. They were angered by restrictions on their trade and resented the impositions of metropolitan officialdom.

Merchants and professionals based in the Americas were prone to sympathize with them. The planters and their allies saw themselves as protagonists of a movement to check arbitrary royal power, and to promote learning and liberty. Planters and American-based merchants favoured free trade and limited government. They had a sense of the great things they could accomplish if only metropolitan despotism could be swept away.

At crucial points in the unfolding of the crisis of empire, the generality of planters came to see the metropolitan authorities as unreliable defenders of slavery. Many of the leading planters had their own ambivalence about the institution, but this was something they wished to see addressed in a suitably responsible and cautious manner.

The planters of the different regions and colonial orders were not equally positioned. Planters in Virginia, Maryland, Georgia and the Carolinas were far better placed to mount a challenge to their colonial status than were those of the Caribbean or South America. In North America the southern planters had forged an alliance with the leaders of the northern colonies, and could count on the support of the white majority in the southern plantation zone itself. In the British and French Caribbean planters were often absentees, and whites in a small minority, circumstances which dictated great caution.

The colonists of English North America no longer needed the protection of the mother country. The French had been driven from the mainland, and the thirteen colonies were more than capable of defending themselves. Virginian planters saw no good reason why their tobacco had to be shipped to Glasgow rather than sent directly to their French customers. Those who directed the mature plantation economy felt no dependence on the metropolis. They had their own satellite pens and farms as well as being able to count on supplies from other regions of the Americas. Virginian planters grew wheat, North Carolina planters rice, and the more northerly colonies could supply every type of provision. Keeping their estates going required the purchase of some extra foodstuffs, wooden packing cases or casks, rope, building materials, nails and so forth, but by the mid-eighteenth century these items could be obtained from American suppliers. The planters on the small Caribbean islands were still dependent on outside supplies and – given the huge racial imbalance of their populations – on the ultimate guarantee represented by the garrisons and warships of the colonial powers.

The colonial elites of Spanish and Portuguese America were slow to challenge imperial rule, largely because they were themselves so embedded in, and beholden to, imperial structures. In Spanish America, as we saw in the first chapter, the colonial state was a directly productive force, organizing tribute labour, distributing tribute goods and granting mining concessions and trading monopolies. This was the silver skeleton over which was draped the finery of the colonial baroque, and the creole elite was not disposed to jeopardize it. In both Mexico and the Andes, creole leaders also had cause to fear that divisions within the elite would trigger popular explosions. The 1780s had been marked by a chain of indigenous uprisings in the Andes, while in Mexico the elite's uncertainty in the wake of Napoleon's invasion of the Peninsula led to popular but localized uprisings led by two priests, Fathers Hidalgo and Morelos. The elite in Mexico and the Andean region was committed to the mining complex and the royal administration, and there was only a tiny sprinkling of planters in these areas. Planters and independent merchants were more common in Venezuela, Colombia, La Plata, and on the Pacific coast of South America, and it was in these regions that the liberation armies would prepare for the final assault on the colonial power.[1]

The North American spirit of independence was encouraged by many circumstances – the buoyant and self-sufficient economy, the spread of newspapers and magazines, the circulation of pamphlets, long-standing traditions of representative government, the cult of 'patriotism' and 'English liberties', popular opposition to metropolitan restrictions, exactions and pretensions, as well as the removal of the French threat in 1763. The restrictive policies of the metropolis were particularly galling to an 'expansionist' group of planters, merchants, and professional men, who believed that the mother country was denying them their rightful opportunity to spread out over the continent and establish their sway over the American hemisphere.[2] Frontiersmen and land speculators resented colonial attempts to prevent westward expansion beyond the 'Proclamation line' or other arbitrary limits. The planters' and merchants' desire to trade freely with the world was likewise a strong impulse, and one that was shared by other colonists. The subordination of the colonies to the merchants of Glasgow and Liverpool was greatly resented. British attempts to levy taxes and duties were seen as an even more intimate threat. Colonists held that taxation without representation would reduce them to the miserable condition of 'slaves', despite their inherited rights and their vital contribution to the empire. Exaggerated as this rhetoric now sounds, it expressed strong convictions stemming from a distinctive and widely held doctrine of 'republican' liberty, seen as the absence of dependence.

In Quentin Skinner's account, seventeenth-century Englishmen saw the arbitrary element in royal power, even if mildly and benignly wielded, as a threat of 'abject slavery'.[3] The ideological spokesmen of the Virginia planters

---

1   John Lynch, *The Spanish American Revolutions*, London 1978.

2   Marc Egnal, *A Mighty Empire: Origins of the American Revolution*, Ithaca 1988.

3   This has been expounded in a number of studies but see Quentin Skinner, *Hobbes and Republican Liberty*, Cambridge 2007. The rebel leaders' concern to rally support among the 'multitude' would bear out some of the points made by Ellen Meiksins Wood in a review of this book; see 'Why It Matters', *London Review of Books*, 25 September 2008. However, in the colonial

found the unilateral acts of the colonial power no less menacing. The language of republican liberty had the further advantage that it reached out to articulate the fears and hopes of small-holding farmers, frontiersmen and the urban multitude – the hydra-headed, motley crew denounced by Adams. When it is borne in mind that American sailors were the favoured targets of the press-gangs of the Royal Navy, it will be seen that for some colonials the threat of 'slavery' was quite tangible.[4]

In the 1760s a few individuals in both colonies and metropolis began openly to criticize slavery. Viewed in the perspective of the great outpouring of debate and polemic in a burgeoning public sphere, with its thousands of pamphlets and hundreds of newspapers and almanachs, the attention devoted to slavery was relatively modest. In the long run, of course, the very existence of this public sphere had unsettling implications for slavery. But so far as North American slave-holders were concerned, Lord Mansfield's 1772 judgment in the case of Somersett was far more worrying. This denied the right of a Virginian planter to exercise the rights of a slave-holder over his servant, James Somersett, and most particularly the power to order him back to America against his will. Mansfield held that the power of a slave-holder was so odious that it would have to be expressly sanctioned by a positive law; he somewhat reluctantly concluded that no such law was to be found in English statutes. Britain's rulers wished to protect the property of loyal colonial subjects, but saw that the rebels' dependence on slavery rendered them vulnerable. In November 1775 Lord Dunmore, the governor of Virginia, went onto the offensive against wavering planters when he incited slaves to desert disloyal owners and enlist in his forces, with several hundred responding. The Continental Congress's first move towards concerted military action was prompted by this threat. Without the British government ever making military emancipation a systematic policy, several commanders followed Dunmore's example.

The leading men of New England, New York and middle Atlantic colonies, and those of the plantation colonies, were, in principle, equal partners in the revolt. Each of the new states preserved their own laws and finances, but were ready for sacrifices and compromise in the common struggle against colonial tyranny. From the outset the rebels challenged 'taxation without representation' by non-importation boycotts as well as a flood of pamphlets. The first rebel Congress was united in extending the trade boycott to slaves, but pointedly refused to give this act abolitionist significance. In the long run

---

case such leaders as Thomas Jefferson did not fear the multitude but did wish to enlist it in the 'republican' cause (on which more below).

4   For the popular pressure on the revolutionary leadership, see Gary Nash, *The Unknown American Revolution: The Unruly Birth of Democracy and the Struggle to Create America*, London 2007, pp. 1–150. See also Merrill Jensen, *The Founding of a Nation*, London 1965.

many Northern merchants had a stake in the plantation trades and some had participated in the slave trade (and were to do so again when it was legalized in the 1780s).

THE DECLARATION OF INDEPENDENCE

The drafters and signers of the Declaration of Independence wished to justify their action in ways that would both confirm their probity and patriotism, and reach out to the broadest alliance against the colonial power. Their detailed litany of the injuries and slights to which they had been subjected conveyed the idea that they and their assemblies had been treated as lesser beings, or as children, certainly not as equals. The 1760s and early 1770s witnessed an extraordinary radicalization of opinion in North America, explained in Thomas Paine's *Common Sense* but most authoritatively expressed in the Declaration itself, and most especially in its opening paragraphs.

The Declaration of Independence has no equal in the prior history of rebellion and revolt. The abjurations and remonstrances of the Estates General of the Netherlands in the 1560s and 1570s, or of the English parliament in the 1640s, or the declarations to be found in the 'Putney debates' of 1649, are important precedents but they cannot compare with the clarity, confidence and universalism of the Declaration of Independence. The Declaration is the key document for anyone interested in the origins of modern freedom and democracy. It helped to inspire the great French Revolution, and it announced the grand theme of universal human rights. In the latter respect it contrasts with the US Constitution of 1787 as well as with all prior attempts to lay down the principles of human political association. US historians and political leaders are sometimes so reverential in their attitude to the Constitution that they miss this striking contrast. Though the Declaration belongs, in the first place, to the American people, it also belongs to Atlantic and world history.

Let us remind ourselves of the famous opening passage:

> When in the course of human events it becomes necessary for one people to dissolve the political bands which have connected them with another, and to assume among the powers of the earth, the separate and equal station to which the Laws of Nature and Nature's God entitle them, a decent respect to the opinions of mankind requires that they should declare the causes which impel them to the separation. We hold these truths to be self-evident, that all men are created equal, that they are endowed by their Creator with certain unalienable Rights, that among these are Life, Liberty and the Pursuit of Happiness. – That to secure these rights, Governments are instituted among Men, deriving their just powers from the consent of the governed. – That whenever any Form of Government becomes destructive of those ends, it is the Right of the People to alter or abolish it, and to

institute new Government, laying its foundation on such principles and organizing its powers in such form, as to them should seem most likely to effect their Safety and Happiness.[5]

There follows an important passage conceding that such action should not be lightly undertaken, but this renders no less remarkable the quoted sentiments. When assessing the meaning of the Declaration it is essential to grasp that its principles apply to 'a people', and not simply to a number of individuals. It was asserting that Americans, as a people, were fully the equal of the English, and not to be subjected to laws they had no hand in framing. To those being asked to renounce the condition of 'free-born Englishmen', the broad principles invoked in the Declaration were a necessary compensation.[6]

Thomas Jefferson, the slave-holder who wrote the first draft, intended the argument of the Declaration to culminate in a vigorous paragraph denouncing the monarch for having endorsed a British slave trade that was tantamount to piracy. This passage attacked the British king for 'having waged cruel war against human nature itself, violating its most sacred rights of life and liberty in the persons of a distant people who never offended him, captivating and carrying them in another hemisphere, or to incur miserable death in their transportation hither . . . the CHRISTIAN king of Great Britain . . . is now inciting those very people to rise in arms amongst us, and thus to purchase the liberty of which he deprived them, by murdering the people upon whom he also has obtruded them . . .'[7] The paragraph thus awarded the status of a 'distant people' to the Africans, a people deserving of natural rights and comparable in this respect to the people of Britain or North America.[8]

Most of the rebellious colonies had at least temporarily banned slave imports, but as part of a general trade embargo. The delegates were uneasy at the proposed paragraph, so it was entirely removed. Jefferson himself later explained: ' The clause . . . reprobating the enslaving of the inhabitants of Africa

---

5   Lynn Hunt, *Inventing Human Rights: A History*, New York 2007, pp. 215–6 (also 113–46).

6   My argument here is similar to Samuel Moyn's insistence, in *The Last Utopia: Human Rights in History*, (Cambridge, MA) 2010, that eighteenth-century ideas of 'the rights of man' defined the state's relationship to its own citizens. These citizenship 'rights' are not to be equated with twentieth-century notions of 'universal human rights' (pp. 17–43). While I agree with this, the Declaration's opening passage did, surely, have great resonance because of its generous promise of equality and liberty? Jefferson understood that something with a universalist ring was needed, both at that moment and for a boundless future.

7   Thomas Jefferson, *The Declaration of Independence*, presented by Michael Hardt, London 2007, p. 13.

8   David Armitage notes this and adds that Jefferson was to reiterate it in his *Notes on Virginia* (1785), where he characterizes African Americans as an essentially alien people – who should consequently be returned to Africa whenever that might prove possible. David Armitage, *The Declaration of Independence: A Global Study*, Cambridge, MA 2007, pp. 59–60.

was struck out in complaisance to South Carolina and Georgia who had never attempted to restrain the importation of slaves and who, on the contrary, still wished to continue it. Our Northern brethren also I believe felt a little tender under those censures, for tho their people have very few slaves themselves yet they had been pretty considerable carriers of them to others.'[9] Jefferson, like other Virginian planters, despised the slave trade (it was eventually ended when he was president). He had imbibed the writings of the Scottish and French Enlightenment, which denounced or deprecated slavery as well as the slave trade. As a lawyer the young Jefferson had undertaken to back a freedom suit. He was also very much aware of the battle for legitimacy that was in prospect. The concerns of the free-born Englishman needed to be expressed in a new language and in universal terms that could appeal to those of German or Dutch origin. This also expressed the planters' own 'republican' sense of liberty.

The framers of the Declaration were quite aware of Lord Dunmore's appeals to the slaves of rebel masters to join the British forces, and the consequent danger that their cause could be compromised by the slavery issue. The lofty principles of the Declaration – and of subsequent statements of this kind – allowed the perspective of a boundless future to overshadow current practices that might be at odds with those principles. The planters, merchants and lawyers assembled in Philadelphia were familiar with the device of the promissory note, and with the resonant implications of the expression 'my word is my bond'. The Declaration had something of the function of a promissory note, issued to enlightened opinion everywhere, that the new Republic would strive to respect self-evident truths and unalienable rights. While of great delicacy, the problem of what to do about slavery was not in fact urgent or immediate in 1776. Public agitation on the question had not yet really commenced. The Quaker pioneers were still mainly concentrated on persuading other Friends to give up slave-holding, using the pressure of a Manumission Society to promote this end.

The Declaration made a strong appeal to what was owed to natural rights and human nature, but without addressing race or slavery. Jefferson may have taken satisfaction in being the boldest of the delegates on the slave trade in 1776, but that did not mean that the formulae of the Declaration applied to African slaves, since they could be regarded as, like Indians, not part of the American people.

Thus, with or without the slave trade clause – but especially without – the Declaration was easier to reconcile with enslavement than might be thought. The rights it asserted were collective and institutional, and could only be claimed by members of 'a people' with their own properly organized government. Slaves of African descent were part of the household of their owner, not members of

---

9 Quote from Thomas Jefferson, *Autobiography*, in Jefferson/Hardt, *The Declaration of Independence*, p. 9.

the political community. The revolt of the thirteen colonies was the collective act of their assemblies, not the refusal of isolated individuals. Jefferson did not see the slaves or their descendants as part of the American people, and probably already believed that most of them should find their own liberty somewhere else, perhaps in Africa. Even Thomas Paine in *Common Sense* praised America as a providential home for persecuted Europeans, without mentioning its other inhabitants.[10] Paine was anti-slavery and had a hand in Pennsylvania's Emancipation Law of 1780, which was to free the children of slave mothers when they reached adulthood; but in this, his most influential text, there is an unthought exclusion of Africans and Native Americans.

On the other hand the disruption of the war, and the disposition of some British commanders to offer freedom to slaves who would fight for them, furnished conditions where tens of thousands could escape their masters.[11] Gary Nash goes so far as to describe this exodus as 'the greatest slave rebellion in North American history.'[12] This is true so long as exception is made of the mass flight of slaves from rebel (and loyal) masters in the years 1861–5 (which, as we will see in Chapter 13, numbered around half a million). During the war both sides enlisted some black soldiers while tending to assign them to them service roles. As many as 4,000 may have fought with the rebel forces, often serving as substitutes. While more than 40,000 may have fled their masters during the war, only about 15,000 left with the British. British commanders salvaged some pride from their own defeat by insisting on the freedom of those to whom they had offered haven. The advent of peace made escape much more difficult, and brought the need for appeals to free blacks.

In my *Overthrow of Colonial Slavery* I placed the Revolution at the start of my story, but did not sufficiently register the intense wartime fraying of master–slave relations and the eventual impact in both Britain and the US North of the presence of many self-emancipated blacks.[13] The flights showed that slaves would take great risks to escape their captivity. They brought an anti-slavery message to a wider public. But in the new nation this was a two-edged sword, making issues connected with slave flight a source of lively concern. Critics of

---

10   See Thomas Paine, 'Common Sense', *The Thomas Paine Reader*, edited by Michael Foot and Isaac Kramnick, Harmondsworth 1987, pp. 65–115, 81–3.

11   Simon Schama, *Rough Crossings: Britain, the Slaves and the American Revolution*, London 2005.

12   Gary Nash, *The Forgotten Fifth: African Americans in the Age of Revolution*, Cambridge, MA, 2006, p. 23; this aspect of the war is a major theme of Sylvia Frey, *Water from the Rock: Black Resistance in a Revolutionary Age*, Princeton 1991.

13   Blackburn, *Overthrow of Colonial Slavery*, pp. 109–30. The significance, extent and consequences of slave flight are covered by Nash, *Forgotten Fifth*, Schama, *Rough Crossings*, and Cassandra Pybus, 'Jefferson's Faulty Math: The Question of Slave Defections in the American Revolution', *William and Mary Quarterly*, April 2005; see also Cassandra Pybus, *Epic Journeys of Freedom*, London 2006, for the later exploits of some of those who escaped – such as George Washington, formerly the property of a leading Virginia planter.

slavery sought to secure more favourable manumission laws on a state-by-state basis.

In the more conservative post-Revolutionary moment when the Constitution was drawn up – 1787 – race lost its semi-conscious character. The presence of slaves and Indians was indirectly – but explicitly – affirmed in the clause dealing with fugitives, and in the clauses which awarded slave-holding states representation in proportion to their white population plus three-fifths of the number of their slaves, with untaxed Indians not counted at all. It is commonly said that the Constitution thus treated slaves as only three-fifths of a person. But it is more accurate to say that the slaves were not represented at all, or, even worse, were represented by their masters. The consequence was that the voting weight of whites in the slave-holder states was inflated by a third in the House of Representatives and the Electoral College, and that the weight of the free states was diminished by a similar proportion. Given the size of the two sections, the boost given to the South often gave it decisive leverage.[14] The fugitive slave clause further implicated all states in the defence of slavery. Above all, the Constitution made no promises to slaves and left it to the states to allot a status to free African Americans and to regulate slavery if they wished.

The North West Ordinance of 1787 took the fateful step of barring slaves – and fugitives – from that large territory. This was a concession made to non-slave-holding whites, not to free blacks, who were denied the right to settle there. So far as possible slavery was to be a domestic issue for the states, not a proper topic of Congressional legislation, though the disposition of federal territory was inescapably a subject of Congressional concern. In this way the Constitutional Convention inaugurated a pact of silence with regard to slavery, albeit that there were certain awkward issues that had to be adjudicated relating to 800,000 slaves – and nearly 100,000 free blacks – spread out unevenly across the new federation. It was widely agreed that the United States did not need further slave imports: the slave population was reproducing itself, and the Virginian slave-holders stood to gain from a ban leading to higher prices. However, as a concession to the minority of slave-holders or traders who disagreed, Congress was forbidden to regulate the Atlantic slave trade for twenty years. The Federal arrangements of the 1780s did not recognize blacks even hypocritically, as happened to the Indian nations whose wishes were supposedly to be consulted before the seizure of their lands.

Neither the Declaration nor the Constitution offered any institutional guarantees to the Indian nations. Indeed the former attacked the British monarch on the grounds that he had 'excited domestic insurrections amongst us, and has endeavoured to bring on the inhabitants of our frontiers, the merciless Indian Savages, whose known rule of warfare is an undistinguished destruction of all

---

14   Garry Wills, 'Negro President': Jefferson and the Slave Power, Boston 2003, pp. 1–13.

ages, sexes and conditions'. When the Bill of Rights was appended to the Constitution, none of its clauses offered protection to slaves or free African Americans or any of the Indian nations. The Ordinances concerning the North West and South West constituted a disposition of these territories which was, in effect, simply to be imposed on their native inhabitants.[15]

In denying Indians any rights the patriots were betraying their own fondness for invoking the Indian peoples' spirit of independence. Throughout the New World the leaders of creole society sought to glorify the original Americans and their resistance to conquest, while in practice robbing them of their lands and withholding from them rights or representation.

The Declaration's references to equality were to be at odds with the practice of the state it founded. Recoiling from imperial arrogance, they uphold equal human worth and the equal worth of different human communities. Of course the phrase 'created equal' implies an equality of opportunity, not condition. Nevertheless such a standard would be incompatible with racial privilege. Natural rights doctrines had traditionally declared that all men were born free, but had immediately qualified this notion by insisting that liberty could only be realized in specific communities organized by the law of peoples (*ius gentium*).[16] The slaves lacked a community that would recognize their freedom. There is here an echo of the notion of Christian freedom, which is open to all but can only be attained by becoming a servant of Christ and a faithful member of his church. When Rousseau observed that man is born free but everywhere he is in chains, he was signalling a secular and generalized version of this logic, as was Edmund Burke, from the other side of the argument, when he wrote that he infinitely preferred the rights of Englishmen to the rights of man.

One strand of republican thinking held that, since slaves lived and toiled under the direction of their owner, they displayed a degree of acquiescence in their condition. François Furstenberg argues that American patriots characteristically believed that their liberties were the product of their own virtuous resistance to tyranny, and that any slave community not heaving with revolt could be deemed to have condoned the slave regime. The living slave could thus be seen, in this view, as having refused the test of the patriot cry of 'liberty or death'. He argues that this line of thought furnished a justification of slavery that was internal to liberal-republican ideology, not, as standard references to 'paradoxes', 'ironies' and 'contradictions' in the standpoint of the Founders suppose, in opposition to it. Furstenberg suggests that even those who deprecated or

---

15   The explicit and implicit exclusions of the Constitution and subsequent amendments are thoroughly analysed by Rogers Smith, *Civic Ideals: Conflicting Visions of Citizenship in United States History*, New Haven 1997. See also the forum on 'Rethinking the American Revolution', with contributions from Edward Countryman, Sylvia Frey and Michael Zuckerman, in *The William and Mary Quarterly* LII/2 (April 1996), pp. 341–86.

16   Richard Tuck, *Natural Rights Theories: Their Origin and Development*, Cambridge 1979.

opposed slavery implicitly subscribed to this reasoning, as in a remark attributed to Samuel Adams by Benjamin Rush: 'Nations were as free as they deserved to be.'[17]

In those parts of the new Republic with large slave populations the institution emerged essentially unscathed and, notwithstanding slave escapes and a temporary rise in manumissions, overall slave numbers climbed as the plantation economy recovered in the 1780s and the cotton boom began in the 1790s. The Constitution of 1787 went far towards entrenching slavery as an institution, by limiting the power of the federal authorities, by recognizing white representation of slaves in the Southern states and by requiring all states to respect each other's slave property. The emergence of a larger free coloured population, especially in the North where some states limited or repudiated slave-holding, gave openings to anti-slavery ideas. There were prominent slave-holders in Maryland and Virginia who publicly deplored slavery and patronized Manumission Societies. The idea gained ground that the citizens of these states, if left to their own devices, would themselves eventually find voluntary ways to redeem their bondsmen. The assemblies of New York and New Jersey rejected 'free-womb' laws in the 1780s, but slavery was sufficiently marginal in these states to make consensual emancipation more likely – one day. The several tens of thousands of black people who made good their escape from bondage and stayed in the United States or Canada helped to establish or enlarge the African American churches, with great implications for the future. In the Independence and post-Independence era, planters became more likely to encourage their slaves to participate in supervised religious instruction and worship.[18]

The anti-slavery measures taken by some states and the Enlightened planters' readiness to attack the vices of slavery – as Thomas Jefferson did in *Notes on Virginia* – led some French writers, like the Abbé Mably, mistakenly to believe that the Americans were embarked on an abolitionist path.[19] While some British observers shared this view, others judged that the colonists' concern for liberty had been very narrow, and used anti-slavery themes to discredit the rebellion. Both reactions strengthened anti-slavery in Britain. Indeed the American Revolution, carried out in the name of defending 'English liberties', dealt a heavy blow to the legitimacy of the Hanoverian order and persuaded many Britons of the need for thoroughgoing national and imperial reform. British abolitionism was born of defeat in America (on which more in the next chapter).

---

17   François Furstenberg, 'Beyond Slavery and Freedom: Autonomy, Virtue and Resistance in Early American Political Discourse', *Journal of American History* 89/4 (March 2003), pp. 1,295–330.

18   Frey, *Water from the Rock*, pp. 243–83.

19   See Bonnot de Mably, *Observations on the Government and Laws of the United States*, London 1790.

From the outset there was tension between the states containing a sizeable slave population and those whose prosperity came from farms and workshops based on family and wage labour. Within a month of the Declaration of Independence, a Southern delegate was threatening an end to the Confederation if any attempt was made to tax slave-holding wealth. The Northern delegates were sharply critical of what they saw as the hypocrisy of the slave-holders, who wanted to see slaves counted to inflate their representation in Congress but not counted as taxable wealth. Yet as Robin Einhorn makes clear, this Northern scorn was not abolitionist in character, which is why it could lead to the notorious 'three-fifths' compromise, with slaves to be counted as three-fifths of a free person towards both representation and taxation.[20] But the Southern slaveholders got the better of the bargain, since their representation in Congress and the presidential electoral college was raised by a third and, in normal times, they were able to block direct federal taxes. Though the tariff supplied a stream of revenue, the slave-owners' antipathy to taxation remained intense – they did not want inspectors on their land, and they did not want to cough up cash because so much of their wealth was sunk in their slaves. In the long term both the federal state and the individual slave states were unable to fund improvements for this reason, and the Southern states were to lag far behind the Northern states in areas such as public education.

Gordon Wood argues that the American Revolution set off a wave of development throughout the new Republic, based on the expansion of interstate commerce. This brought Southern planters and Northern merchants, farmers, manufacturers and sea captains into even closer connection.[21] The tobacco planters had a difficult decade following the defeat of the British. However, by the 1790s the conditions had been created for a prodigious expansion of plantation slavery. The invention of the cotton gin in 1792, and the Louisiana Purchase of 1802, set the scene for the expansion of slave plantations to the inland areas and the construction of a mighty 'cotton kingdom' in the South and South West. Less well known is that the American Revolution – a historic blow to mercantilism – stimulated plantation development throughout the Americas, with US markets and commercial facilities now more easily available to planters elsewhere in the Americas. The young republic's large and growing merchant marine hauled slaves from Africa, and offered to buy all the sugar, cotton, coffee and cacao that the planters of the Caribbean and South America could produce. There was a plantation boom in Saint-Domingue, until it was brought to an end by the great slave revolts of 1791. The devastation of Saint-Domingue in turn gave huge openings to planters in Cuba, Brazil and Louisiana. The possibilities were so great that they persuaded the royal authorities of Spain and Portugal to relax or suspend restrictions on colonial trade, even before war and political

20   Robin Einhorn, *American Taxation, American Slavery*, Chicago 2006, pp. 120–36.
21   Gordon Wood, *The Radicalism of the American Revolution*, New York 1994.

turmoil themselves allowed the planters of Cuba and Brazil to secure good conditions for export agriculture.

The momentous victory achieved by the Americans impressed planters elsewhere in the Americas, but it was not until after Napoleon's invasion of Spain that they raised the standard of armed rebellion. In the British West Indies, one half of the planters were absentees and all of them were aware that the colonial system protected them from French competition. The modest white colonial population of the British islands was anyway fearful of slave unrest and bound to respect the power of the Royal Navy. The French planters of Martinique, Guadeloupe and Saint-Domingue aspired to a relaxation of the *Exclusif* and much greater autonomy, but it was not until the downfall of the monarchy in 1792 that they threw off allegiance to France.

What was the real planter ideal? As patriots they sought to build a new society, free of the vices of the Old World. In the heartlands of the slave systems, slave-owning planters came to see themselves as champions of a new civilization that would spread liberty and prosperity. But even those who deprecated slavery – as many of the Revolutionary era did – regretfully concluded that they would have to retain the slave regime, at least for a period. Where else would they find the hands they needed? And how could they free slaves who would run amok if released? Whereas colonial mercantilism had favoured the metropolis by appropriating a portion of the slaves' surplus product, the planters of the Americas aimed to build on what a Brazilian historian has recently called 'endogenous accumulation'.[22] Rather than being dependent upon, and exploited by, merchants or a metropolis, they hoped to encourage local suppliers and sources of credit, and extend their links to social allies outside the plantation zone. They aimed at an accumulation based on slave plantations and satellite farms, ranches, workshops, mines and fisheries, employing slaves where necessary. In pursuit of this ideal Thomas Jefferson wasted large sums seeking to develop a nail factory on his estate.

The goal of planter self-sufficiency was congruent with at least one strand of early abolitionism – the aspiration to end the Atlantic slave trade. Planters did not want to be dependent on the slave traders. The termination of the trade would raise the value of their holdings, and reward those planters who promoted the security and well-being of slave mothers. The more enlightened or patriotic planters, whether in North or South America, felt that capping the limitless influx of Africans would foster a better racial balance and prove conducive to nation-building. Among the first acts of the rebellious North American assemblies was a ban on slave imports. Though conceived as part of a wider boycott, there was still a special resonance and meaning to this blow against the metropolis and its slave traders. While the planters of South Carolina, who

---

22   João Luís Fragoso, *Homens de grossa aventura*, Rio de Janeiro 1998.

depended on the trade to keep up slave numbers, were only prepared to accept such a ban as a temporary wartime measure, the planters of Virginia and Maryland saw it as a valuable measure promoting virtue and self-sufficiency. Leading planters in Brazil, Cuba and Spanish South America entertained the same ideal, though they were not to retain the upper hand in Cuba and Brazil. In sum, the more 'enlightened' planter ideal was a free trade in plantation produce and necessities, not a free trade in slaves. But this still implied a domestic slave market, and hence a domestic slave trade.

Following the momentous defeats inflicted on European colonialism in the half-century after 1775, Atlantic commerce passed from mercantilism and closed commerce to something very close to a free trade in plantation goods. The leading planters and merchants of the US and Brazil, were, circa 1830, installed at the heart of the state and in a position to bid for slave-holder hegemony in the Americas. The Cuban planters could sell wherever they wanted, but had to pay tariffs on their imports and an export tax on sugar. While US planters accepted a complete ban on slave imports from 1808, the clandestine slave traffic to Cuba and Brazil survived for another half-century.

CHAPTER SEVEN

From the Critique of Slavery to the Abolitionist Movement

In the English-speaking Atlantic world, Patriots and imperialists both liked to appeal to the conceits, ideals and language of the 'free-born Englishman'. The rights of the free-born Englishman were celebrated by Daniel Defoe and upheld by the philosophy of John Locke. The American patriots, no less than their metropolitan counterparts, cherished civic freedom as a central value. That this English freedom coexisted with, or even depended upon, colonial slavery was a paradox rarely addressed. Yet imperial conflicts nourished a new patriotic sentiment summed up in the lines of a popular anthem of the 1740s: 'Rule Britannia, Britannia rules the waves, Britons never, never, never, shall be slaves.'

That Britons might be slave traders and slave-holders remained unquestioned for a while, but the pressures of popular mobilization for war, and the controversies over domestic and colonial rights and duties, created a context where it became increasingly difficult to keep colonial slavery and national destiny in wholly separate compartments. Imperial conflict was destructive and expensive, and its expedients, from new taxes to the press gang, encroached on the rights of the subject. Britain and France had greater natural security than other powers – Britain because it was an island, and France because of its size and geographical position. British and French wars were wars of choice, with colonial wealth a major prize. The war party could more easily be seen as the tool of mercantile and dynastic interests. Both those who backed war and those who opposed it were led to question colonialism and mercantilism. The Seven Years War (1756–63) brought these issues to a head, and witnessed the first real questioning of New World slavery.

If war and nationalism prompted a new concern for the principles of social being, so too did the cosmopolitan – and supposedly peaceful – world of learning and scholarship. The Enlightenment, whether French, German, Italian or Scottish, at least strove to probe human nature and the principles of social institutions and morality. The *philosophes* did not produce a coherent or rigorous critique of European colonialism, slavery and racism. Voltaire, the Enlightenment's most brilliant publicist, wrote that Europe's sweet tooth was fed by the suffering of plantation slaves. But he also scorned blacks and confidently declared that the Hottentots were an 'entirely different' race, with a different 'intellect' as well as 'squat noses'.[1] Emmanuel Chukwudi Eze has compiled an

---

1 [François-Marie Arouet] Voltaire, *The Philosophy of History*, New York 1965, p. 5.

anthology of Enlightenment writings on race which shows the distressing frequency with which some of its most prominent thinkers endorsed ideas of racial difference, and stereotypes of savagery, that could easily justify severe restraint and rigorous exclusion – and were of course devoid of scientific value.[2]

Nevertheless, some Enlightenment thinkers did lay the basis for an indictment of slavery, racism and European colonialism. The cruel treatment of the indigenous peoples of the Americas was widely deplored and seen as undermining Europe's claim to represent a superior civilization. The work of Las Casas and Montaigne still carried great resonance. The defence of the natural equality of all humans by Baron Lahontain (1666–1715) enjoyed authority because of his vivid account of life among the Hurons in Canada – which also described the baleful consequences of colonization. Montesquieu satirized the racial fantasies of French colonists and mocked justifications for slavery in the *Esprit des lois* (1748), but his critique targeted the pretensions of the colonists more than the imperial vision itself. The Scottish Enlightenment widened and deepened the agenda of social analysis in the direction of a reflexive study of commercial society. Capitalism had developed unconsciously and accidentally, as it were, but the Scottish thinkers – Francis Hutcheson, John Millar and Adam Smith – believed that it was now possible to discern the institutional and functional principles of commercial society, and that these rendered obsolete both slavery and colonial mercantilism. A somewhat fiercer critique of the destructive consequences of British, French and Spanish colonialism came from Giambattista Vico and Paulo Mattea Doria, the leading lights of the Neapolitan Enlightenment.[3] Vico's claim that human history differs from natural history because we can make the former, not the latter, pushed thought in the direction of action, guided by his famous watchword: 'pessimism of the intellect, optimism of the will'. Doria argued that women were the equal of men in all respects except brute strength, and that they should consequently enjoy an equal education. Because slavery infantilized and feminized the captive, the questioning of male privilege tended to undermine the patriarchal assumptions which sought to justify slavery.

In 1760 George Wallace, a Scottish jurist, devoted one chapter of his book on the principles of Scottish law to a direct and powerful indictment of slavery, the first substantial treatment from any writer. Wallace denied that 'men and their rights' could ever be proper objects of commerce. He concluded:

---

2   Emmanuel Chukwudi Eze, ed., *Race and the Enlightenment: A Reader*, Cambridge, MA, 1997. See also the contributions on Rousseau and Kant in Julia Ward and Tommy Lott, eds, *Philosophers on Race: Critical Essays*, Oxford 2002.

3   Jonathan Israel, *Enlightenment Contested: Philosophy, Modernity and the Emancipation of Man, 1670–1750*, Oxford 2006, pp. 520–9, 610–11. For slavery and the 'early Enlightenment' see pp. 603–9. I discuss passages on slavery in Montesquieu and the Scottish thinkers in *Overthrow of Colonial Slavery*, pp. 47–54.

For these reasons every one of those unfortunate men, who are pretended to be slaves, has a right to be declared free, for he never lost his liberty, he could not lose it; his prince had no power to dispose of him. Of course the sale was *ipso jure* void. This right he carries about with him and is entitled everywhere to get it declared. As soon, therefore, as he comes into a country in which the judges are not forgetful of their own humanity, it is their duty to remember he is a man and to declare him free.[4]

Wallace added that it was abominable that humanity be abused 'that our pockets may be filled with money and our mouths with delicates'. Instead he urged the superiority of free labour: 'Set the Nigers free, and in a few generations this vast and fertile continent would be filled with inhabitants.' Wallace cites an unresolved freedom suit brought before the Scottish courts by 'a niger boy', Montgomery Shedden, and this incident may have helped to prompt his reflections. Wallace's chapter on this theme was to appear in two influential places. Somewhat reworked, it became the entry under 'Traite des esclaves' in the *Encyclopédie* (1765). It was also integrally reproduced in a much reprinted collection edited by Anthony Benezet, the Quaker and pioneer abolitionist, and well known to the early anti-slavery campaigner Granville Sharp. Wallace's text was marked by a clarity and directness which was often lacking in the voluminous literature of abolitionism.[5]

The single most widely circulated work of the French Enlightenment was the *Histoire des Deux Mondes*, compiled by the Abbé Raynal and first published in 1770. Its ten volumes conveyed the powerful ambivalence of the Enlightenment on issues connected to slavery and colonialism. On the one hand it contained eloquent denunciation of these practices, written by Denis Diderot and Jean de Pechmeja. On the other it recommended the wisdom of establishing new plantations and allowing greater freedom to the slaves to amuse themselves with dances and song on their weekly day of rest. Raynal himself was to be given a stipend by the colonial administration, and some of his reformist ideas were drawn upon in new regulations in 1784 that infuriated the planters.

Sankar Muthu has urged that the notion of a universal human 'cultural agency', possessed by all peoples, is to be found in the work of Denis Diderot, Immanuel Kant and Johann Gottfried Herder, and that it constituted a powerful critique of European colonialism.[6] In Herder's case the criticism of empire focused on the working of the commerce in slave produce. Herder, as much a

---

4 George Wallace, *A System of the Principles of the Laws of Scotland*, Edinburgh 1760, pp. 94–5.

5 The significance of Wallace's text was established by David Brion Davis, 'New Sidelights on Early Anti-Slavery Radicalism', *William and Mary Quarterly* XXVIII/4 (October 1971).

6 Sankar Muthu, *Enlightenment Against Empire*, Princeton 2003.

critic of the Enlightenment as a contributor to it, was inspired to similar bitter irony by the path-breaking study of a Scottish philosopher, John Millar's *The Origin of the Distinction of Ranks* (1771). This work combined a questioning of the productivity of slave labour, and the profitability of slavery, with praise for the growing refinement of commercial society and the impressive growth of the system of commerce. Montesquieu had already used satire to assail the hypocrisy of racial 'thinking'. Herder responds similarly to celebrations of the prosperity and liberality of civilized Europe:

> 'Our system of trade!' Can one think of anything higher than the *refinement* of this all-*encompassing science*? How wretched were the Spartans who needed their Helots for agriculture, how barbaric the Romans who locked their slaves into prisons inside the earth! In Europe slavery has been abolished because it has been calculated how much more these slaves cost, and how much less they yielded than free men. There is only one thing we continue to permit ourselves, to use and *trade three continents as slaves*, to banish them to silver mines and sugar mills. But these are not Europeans, not Christians, and in return we receive silver and gems, spices and sugar – and secret disease. All this for the sake of trade and for *mutual fraternal assistance* and *community* among nations. 'The system of trade!' The greatness and uniqueness of the project is obvious. *Three continents devastated* and *regimented* by us, and we *depopulated* by them, emasculated, sunk in luxury, exploitation and death: what a rich and happy transaction! Who could do other than claim his share in this great *whirling cloud*, that is sucking the life out of Europe, than to press for his place within it and to deliver his own children, if not another man's, to it as the *greatest man of trade*. The old name, shepherd of the peoples, has been changed to monopolist, and when the great cloud will one day burst and unleash a hundred tempests, then help us the great God Mammon, whom we are *all serving now.[7]*

These strenuous images do not always find the right target – the 'whirling cloud' was surely sucking the life out of Africa, not Europe – and reveal an obsession with 'secret disease'; yet Herder faces up to the enormity of the Atlantic traffic, something which cannot be said of the Scottish writer he was criticizing. While Herder writes in stronger language than Millar, neither offers any practical path towards the suppression of these slave systems. Raynal's *Histoire des Deux Mondes* pointed to the existence of communities of runaway slaves, such as the maroons of Jamaica, and predicted that before long a great man would arise from among the slaves, a black Spartacus, who, if he considered only the wrongs perpetrated upon blacks who had been 'tyrannized, mutilated, burnt,

---

7   Johann Gottfried Herder, *Another Philosophy of History*, trans. Ioannis D. Evrigenis and Daniel Pellerin, Cambridge 2005, pp. 62–4.

and put to death', would be entitled to wreak bloody vengeance.[8] This was a rhetorical flourish, not a programme of emancipation.

Condorcet's *Réflexions sur l'esclavage des Nègres* of 1781 distinguished itself from the criticisms of slavery that now began to appear by combining denunciation with a practical programme for phasing out the institution. Condorcet's stance was anti-slavery but not anti-imperial, since it was the imperial power that was to organize the emancipation. In order to preserve the good order and value of the colonies, the ending of slavery was to be, as Olivier Le Cour Grandmaison and Louis Sala-Molins have emphasized, an extraordinarily lengthy and moderate affair. Despite all that he had said about the cruelty of the slave-owners, the latter were given a key role in a most protracted transition. The emancipation was only to free the children born to slave mothers when they reached thirty-five years of age – about the life expectancy of a plantation slave. Taking account of the children born to such unfree parents, it was going to take seventy years before slavery disappeared.[9] While Condorcet did envisage restraints on planter behaviour, previous slave regulations had always proved to be a dead letter. Condorcet hoped that the general crisis of empire and regime would open the way to thoroughgoing, but judicious and gradual, imperial reform. The reform process was not to jeopardize the French 'system of trade', and for this reason was far less radical than the approach taken by Scottish jurist George Wallace.

While Condorcet was to accept the idea of the coloured or black citizen, his lengthy deferral of emancipation stemmed both from an unwillingness to risk French colonial wealth and from a sense that many of the enslaved Africans could not be trusted with their own freedom; besides, they were aliens, with no automatic claim to French citizenship.

If one scans the entirety of the debates and investigations stimulated by the Enlightenment, one can identify radical critiques of European empire, white racism, enslavement and rampant commercialism, with plans gradually to free the slaves. But neither critiques nor plans are urgently combined in an emancipationist programme. Instead there is rhetorical radicalism combined with marginal, protracted or unconvincing ameliorations. And those who do back an abolitionist programme typically envisage its very gradual introduction by means of expanding colonial rule. Even the most liberal – perhaps especially

---

8   Guillaume-Thomas Raynal, *Histoire des Deux Mondes*, vol. 9, pp. 22–4. Jean de Pechmeja and Diderot are believed to have drafted this passage of Raynal's book.

9   Olivier Le Cour Grandmaison, *Les Citoyennetés en Révolution*, *(1789–94)*, Paris 1992, pp. 191–238 and Louis Sala-Molins, *The Dark Side of the Light: Slavery and the French Enlightenment*, Minneapolis and London 2006. Notwithstanding its exaggerations the latter book, published in France in 1992, does convey the great timidity of even the best abolitionist thinking before the uprising in Saint-Domingue. In order to contemplate general revolt and emancipation, Louis-Sébastien Mercier had to place it in *L'An 2440*.

the most liberal – doubted the civic capacity of slaves or native peoples.[10] The more conservative thinkers are no better. Edmund Burke denounced the slave trade, but declared that it would be preferable to regulate it humanely than to decree its total and immediate suppression.

POPULAR ANTI-SLAVERY AND THE BIRTH OF ABOLITIONISM

The rejection of slavery had been first articulated not by philosophers but by scattered protests throughout the Atlantic world, mainly from persons who observed the workings of the institution while having no stake in it. These diffuse anti-slavery reactions are tinged by religious and political radicalism, by the 'free air' doctrine and by disgust at wanton cruelty, or the predatory sexual activity of sailors and plantation whites. If radical religious impulses play a part, it is that of those, like the Quakers, who heed their 'inner light' and have renounced both sin and violence, whether in wars of religion, wars of conquest or even wars of liberation. While cruelty in the service of the true religion was once held to be in the best interests of its victims, a more chastened sensibility was beginning to find it unacceptable. Nevertheless the new sensibility made slow progress within an intimidating colonial order and with rising financial incentives deriving from the plantation complex.

The Quakers would not doff their hats to secular authority, yet they were respectful of colonial power. Following his visit to Barbados in 1671, the Quaker leader George Fox wrote to the governor and Assembly denying the 'slander and lie' 'that we should teach the negroes to rebel', when in truth they taught them to 'be sober and to fear God, and to love their masters and their mistresses'. But Fox did denounce the 'wicked and the debauched, whoremongers and adulterors' and warn that 'negroes and tawny Indians make up a very great part of families here in this island for whom an account will be made . . . when everyone shall be rewarded according to the deeds done in the body'.[11] This was a teaching which spoke to the individual and focused on regulating behaviour and belief. But under some conditions it could be politicized, especially in colonies that had been set up with a religious purpose. This seems to be the case with the Germantown resolution of 1684, and the petition of Highland Scots in Georgia in 1739. The latter attacked the bringing of slaves to Georgia, a colony set aside for free settlement. It denounced the coercion of the slaves since 'freedom to them must be as dear as to us', and declared it 'shocking to human

---

10   Liberal abolitionists who favoured enlightened empire include Zachary Macaulay, James Mill, Thomas Babington Macaulay, and John Stuart Mill for Britain, and, for France, Condorcet, Benjamin Constant and Alexis de Tocqueville. See Uday Singh Mehta, *Liberalism and Empire: British Liberal Thought in the Nineteenth Century*, Chicago 1999. And not all liberals were anti-slavery, see Domenico Lusardo, *Liberalism—a Counter History*, London 2011.

11   John Nickalls, ed., *Journal of George Fox*, London 1975, pp. 604–6.

nature, that any Race of Man, and their Posterity, should be sentenced to perpetual slavery'.[12]

These were generous sentiments. Popular anti-slavery could also be self-
serving, stemming from the fact that slave-holding planters often encroached
on the free man's space and introduced the danger of slave violence or collusion
with the enemy (the leaders of the Stono rebellion of 1739 were responding to a
Spanish appeal). While the prospect of slave resistance nourished anti-slavery
sentiment, slave rebels were themselves quick to appropriate undercurrents of
criticism of the slave regime.

The popular 'common sense' of the metropolis was allergic to slavery, and
slave trading found even fewer defenders. The political cultures of France and
Britain both supposedly upheld the liberties of the subject. Serfdom had dwindled to being a curiosity, and many towns took pride in the centuries-old
promise that any man who lived within their jurisdiction for a year and a day
would be free. These same ideas were to be found in North Italy, the Low
Countries, Scandinavia and Germany, but they had been crushed in Spain at
the time of the revolt of the *comuneros* in 1520 and, because of the strength of
the royal power, had never recovered. Eighteenth-century patriotism saw itself
as rooted in civic freedoms. While there was certainly something particularistic
about the West European cult of liberty, it did offer some vantage points from
which slavery could be rejected.

In the last chapter I cited Charles Mills's concept of the 'racial contract' by
which whites tacitly agreed to restrict harsh colonial labour to blacks.[13] But the
contract could seem unwise as well as barbarous to those who were not planters, merchants or well-paid overseers, with a stake in the slave system. Where
slavery flourished it boosted the power of the rich and fostered an atmosphere
that most non-slave-holders found disagreeable, leading many to leave the
plantation zone. Moreover, anti-slavery could itself appeal to 'aversive' rather
than 'dominative' racial feeling – hostility to the slave trade and slave-holding
because it would introduce 'swarms of Negroes'.[14]

Thus popular antipathy to slavery and slave-holders was already evident
before the philosophers and theologians addressed the issue. But it belonged to
an everyday world that was supposedly policed by private morality and self-
control, and was very rarely politicized. In the colonial order only those with a

---

12   I quote the whole petition and several similar documents in *The Overthrow of Colonial Slavery*, pp. 45–6.

13   Mills, *The Racial Contract*.

14   The distinction between aversive and dominative racism is proposed by Joel Kovel, *White Racism*, New York 1978. Granville Sharp, who befriended and helped black people, nevertheless warned of 'swarms of negroes' coming to England if slave-holding was upheld at the time of the Somersett case. See Christopher Brown, *Moral Capital: The Foundations of British Abolitionism*, Charleston 2006.

direct stake had a right to express a public view, and the slaves themselves were members of the household or family of their owners. The mid-century colonial wars and the eventual outbreak of the struggle for independence intensified both Patriot celebration of the rights of the free-born Englishman, and the pacifism of the Quakers and of some evangelicals. Already in the 1760s some radical Friends denounced slave-trading and slave-holding as practices saturated by violence and sin, and hence just as bad as war-making. Indeed Anthony Benezet and John Woolman claimed that the Atlantic slave trade had become the chief cause of African wars. While their writings reached beyond Quaker ranks, their aim was to change the behaviour of Quakers, and others who aspired to a righteous life. A campaign to change public policy was not yet in their sights, and remained a concern typical of politically minded Patriots.

Both the Reformation and the Counter-Reformation expressed new approaches to the self-understanding of the believer. While Protestants dwelt on individual sin and redemption, the Catholic Church offered itself – and the newly important confessional – as necessary mediations to such salvation. In the seventeenth century Catholics and Protestants had both reconciled themselves to the reappearance of large-scale slavery in the Americas, albeit that a brave handful of clerics denounced the horrendous consequences. It was not until the mid-eighteenth century that such concerns became more widespread and, as David Brion Davis noted, not until 1760 that philosophers and jurists began to denounce slavery.[15] But once slavery became exposed to public debate, the inclination to attack or disavow it spread quickly.

Lynn Hunt points out that at almost the same time that the slavery critique surfaced, there was a rejection of the judicial use of torture in continental Europe, and that many of those who attacked the one also criticized the other (as did Louis de Jaucourt and Brissot de Warville in France). The anti-slavery impulse shared something with the rejection of the judicial practice of torture, which was subjected to a thoroughgoing philosophical critique by the twenty-five-year-old Italian aristocrat, Cesare Beccaria, in his *Essay on Crimes and Punishment* (1765). The revulsion against this practice was such as to lead to its abandonment in France prior to the overthrow of the monarchy.[16] But in the case of plantation slavery the interests at stake were more formidable, and daunted even high-minded theologians and philosophers.

What was it that triggered a new politics of sensibility and the rejection of cruelty? The explosion of print culture helped to thrust such practices into the light of day, and undermined the localism of convention and habit. Print culture

---

15   David Brion Davis, *The Problem of Slavery in Western Culture*, Ithaca 1965.

16   Lynn Hunt, *Inventing Human Rights*, pp. 70–112. John Locke urged the Board of Trade, of which he was a member, to decree that 'sturdy beggars' should have their ears cropped for the second offence and be transported for forced labour in the colonies for the third, but his colleagues overruled him.

– images as well as the printed word – had already played a mighty part in the Reformation and Counter-Reformation. As we have seen, Protestants found in Las Casas's *Brief Account of the Destruction of the Indies*, with its vivid illustrations, an indictment of (Catholic) cruelty. Michel de Montaigne's essays offered a secular rebuke to European conceit and brutality. Judicial torture was formally suppressed in England in 1640, and in 1689 the Bill of Rights rejected 'cruel and unusual punishment'. Nevertheless public flogging, of women as well as men, remained legal in Britain, and far worse tortures were visited upon slaves in the British colonies.[17] The French and Scottish Enlightenments deplored the bloody excesses of the sixteenth- and seventeenth-century wars of religion. Reservations about slave-holding and slave-trading became a distinctive feature of evangelical Protestantism. In France, followers of Jansenism supported the freedom suits mentioned in Chapter 5 and Jaucourt, one of the early critics of slavery, had a Protestant background.

That the institution of slavery might be barbarous rather than civilized was also a conclusion that could be drawn from the accounts of those who had been held as slaves by Algerian pirates. In Chapter 2 it was suggested that such accounts, by emphasizing the capriciousness of Fate, served to excuse European slave-holding. But the appeals made by associations for the freeing of white slaves in North Africa developed views of the institution that might eventually trigger critical reflections. However, the latter were scarcely in evidence in 1694 when a royal proclamation complained: 'A great number of our good subjects peaceably following their employment at sea [are now] slaves in inhuman and cruel bondage . . . driven about by blackamoors'.[18]

Print culture and the spoken word – sermons and public reading, novels and poetry – were eventually to express a generalized humanitarian sentiment that tried to break with the prevailing language of commerce, civilization and racial difference. Catholic theologians and philosophers such as Tomás de Mercado and Andrés Suárez had debated the morality of Atlantic trade, but had not directly investigated its humanity. Grotius, the Dutch Protestant philosopher, had urged the rightfulness of the *mare liberum*, or freedom of the seas, against Spanish monopoly. Willem Usselinx, founder of the Dutch West India Company, had unsuccessfully opposed its involvement in the slave trade. In the late seventeenth and early eighteenth century the merits and demerits of rival trade policies were debated in mercantilist terms – would they or not enhance national prosperity and power? In the early 1700s the various English port towns had successfully petitioned parliament for the right to breach the slave-trading monopoly of the Royal African Company.[19] By the 1760s and 1770s, trade

---

17   George Riley Scott, *A History of Torture*, London 1940, pp. 134–5.
18   Quoted in Linda Colley, *Captives: Britain, Empire and the World*, London 2002, p. 64.
19   K. G. Davies, *The Royal African Company*, London 1974.

boycotts were instruments in the quarrel between metropolis and colonies, and there was a flood of pamphlets, travel literature and autobiography bearing on the workings of the Atlantic world and helping to inform the consuming public.

Thomas Haskell has argued that the greater intensity and scope of market exchanges also prompted a widening horizon, and an interest in institutional 'recipes' that might apply at a distance.[20] This helps us to grasp the popular reaction only if it is recognized that the new awareness was often hostile to market processes, and looked to the state to restrain and temper them. The workings of a complex network of international exchanges could baffle the consumer, but little by little popular awareness grew, with political and commercial rivalries and print culture playing their part. A popular 'moral economy' was prone to resist the swings of the market, particularly at times of shortage and high prices. Edward Thompson writes: 'There is a deeply-felt conviction that prices ought, in times of dearth, to be regulated, and that the profiteer put himself outside society.'[21] Willingness to drive home the critique of slavery and the slave trade required a challenge to a section of the wealthy. It is interesting to note that in the months prior to the first Emancipation Law – Pennsylvania, 1780 – Philadelphia had witnessed an outpouring of popular hostility to profiteering and 'forestalling merchants'. Price committees were set up to establish fair values and prevent price gouging.[22] (The link between anti-slavery and anger at market forces also appears in Rhode Island in 1784, and Paris in 1793–4).

In this context, poetry and the novel played their part in promoting and sustaining anti-slavery feeling – and in checking the self-centred and heedless response that the market alone was likely to encourage. The novel, Lynn Hunt argues, endowed the reader with a new sensitivity. She traces the emergence of a concern with 'human rights' as much to the psychology of the novel-reader as to the arguments of the philosophers – with Rousseau, the philosopher-novelist, scoring on both counts.[23] While political pamphlets appeal to the faculty of reason, novels or poems encourage the reader to imagine her- or himself in the situation of another. Literature directly arouses empathy and sympathy. The 'golden rule' – do as you would be done by – acquired new dimensions in the realm of print culture (autobiography as well as fiction). Readers could be invited to identify with those unlike themselves. The very modesty of Laurence Sterne's 'poor negro girl' in *Tristram Shandy*, who brushes aside flies with a feather rather than kill them, catches the reader off-guard. The Corporal asks '(doubtingly)' if 'the negro has a soul?' to which Uncle Toby

20   Thomas Haskell, 'Capitalism and the Origins of the Humanitarian Sensibility', Parts I and II, *American Historical Review* 90/2 (April 1985), 90/3 (1985).

21   Edward Thompson, 'The Moral Economy of the English Crowd in the Eighteenth Century', *Customs in Common*, New York 1991, pp. 185–258, 229.

22   Eric Foner, *Tom Paine and Revolutionary America*, New York 1970, p. 134.

23   Lynn Hunt, *Inventing Human Rights: A History*, New York 2007, pp. 35–69.

replies: 'I am not much versed in things of that kind; but I suppose God would not leave him without one, any more than thee or mee. – It would be putting one sadly ahead of another, quoth the Corporal'. The Corporal then asks whether a black wench is to be used worse than a white one? When Uncle Toby says he can see no reason why, the Corporal replies that she had 'no one to stand up for her'. Uncle Toby responds: ''Tis that very thing . . . that recommends her to protection – and her brethren with her: 'tis the fortune of war which has put the whip into our hands now – where it may be hereafter, who knows.'[24]

However, *Tristram Shandy* opens with a gently satirical passage which suggests that the notion of 'human rights' may not quite fit. The very first page furnishes the reader with a graphic account of the sexual act which gave birth to its protagonist. This account has his mother suddenly enquiring of her husband whether he has allowed the fire to go out – and it says of Tristram that even as a 'homunculus' in the womb he already enjoyed 'all the claims and rights of humanity'.[25] In fact there were to be currents of abolitionism which, for whatever reason, did not use the language of rights, but preferred the golden rule and basic human sympathy. Radical patriots like Thomas Paine certainly saw slavery as a violation of the 'rights of man', but this idiom did not appeal to John Wesley or William Wilberforce. Jeremy Bentham, critical of slavery on the ground of its inefficiency, thought that talk of 'natural rights' was 'nonsense on stilts'. These men were doubtful about the novel and little influenced by poetry. However, Hunt's emphasis on literature still helps to explain aspects of the new mentalities that were helpful to anti-slavery, one being interest in life outside the metropolis.

The early history of the English novel gives us clues to new subjectivities and other worlds, though their bearing on slavery was not immediately critical. John Bunyan's *Pilgrim's Progress* (1678), Daniel Defoe's *Robinson Crusoe* (1719) and Aphra Behn's *Orinooko* (1688) appealed to the reader's imagination in new ways. These works reached huge audiences (Behn's indirectly through a stage adaptation). *Orinooko* has a denunciation of West Indian slavery put in the mouth of a princely rebel, albeit that the suppression of the revolt suggests that the mass of slaves was not capable, as was Orinooko, of rising to the level of the heroic. *Robinson Crusoe* positively endorses enslavement, but the vividness of its first-person narrative furnished an effective model that was to be appropriated by the exponents of the slave narrative, a literary form that was to make a major contribution to abolitionism, enabling readers to imagine slavery from the standpoint of the slave. The evangelical churches

---

24   Laurence Sterne, *The Life and Opinions of Tristram Shandy, Gentleman*, London 2003 (originally 1760–7), p. 552. Its significance is discussed in Srinivas Aravamudan, ed., *Slavery, Abolition and Emancipation: Writings in the British Romantic Period*, vol. 6, *Fiction*, London 1999, pp. vii–xx, 111, 1–7.

25   Laurence Sterne, *Tristram Shandy*, p. 7.

also encouraged members of the congregation to explain their individual journey of redemption. The first such slave narratives appeared in the 1780s, with the most widely read being *The Interesting Narrative of the Life of Olaudah Equiano, the African* (1788).

Equiano was certainly aware of Bunyan and Defoe, but managed to adapt both the religious and the secular impulses in these works to his own purposes and the campaign against the slave trade. From the 1780s there were to be a host of attempts to portray slave suffering. Paintings, drawings, poems, short stories and novels all contributed. While the result sometimes betrayed a false sentimentalism, there were also eloquent contributions from Blake, Cowper and Wordsworth. The anti-slavery logo adopted by British abolitionists depicted a freed slave on his knees, thanking an unseen liberator and with the inscription 'Am I Not a Man and a Brother?' An outpouring of pamphlets and newspapers also carried the anti-slavery message, reflecting the growth of literacy and interacting with the improving debates of philosophical and literary societies. Many of London's several thousand free Africans in the 1770s and 1780s found work as musicians – Equiano played the horn and the violin, and James Somersett knew Granville Sharp because he played in the Sharp family ensemble. The musical milieu often supported early abolitionism.

Alexander Pope did not directly attack slavery, but in his *Essay on Man* (1739–44) he insisted that Virtue could not be elated 'as long as one man is oppress'd', and was optimistic that an enlightened happiness and self-love would refuse to lose itself in pleasure, but identify with the fate of all humanity. To wit:

> Self-love but serves the virtuous mind to wake,
> As the small pebble stirs the peaceful lake;
> The centre moved a circle strait succeeds,
> Another still and still another spreads,
> Friend, parent, neighbour, first it will embrace,
> His country next, and next the human race,
> Wide and more wide, th'o'erflowings of the mind
> Take ev'ry creature in of ev'ry kind.[26]

Norbert Elias argues that the value placed on a pacified social life, with brutality suppressed or pushed out of sight, reflected the rise of a state that could monopolize legitimate violence across its territory.[27] For him it is the state, and the law, rather than the market or the novel, that conduces to the 'civilizing process'. Such a state was supposedly dedicated to upholding the liberties and security of the subject – and capable of enacting impartial legislation in the public interest. Even Absolutist monarchs liked to see themselves as the

---

26   Alexander Pope, 'Essay on Man', in *The Poems of Alexander Pope*, edited by John Butt, New Haven 1963, pp. 500–47, 546.

27   Norbert Elias, *The Civilizing Process*, Oxford 1998, pp. 161–71, 365–447.

guardians of their subjects' liberties, and sought to establish a framework of public security. Elias saw the Absolutist monarchs as agents of a 'civilizing process' that sought to suppress judicial torture and to restrain and educate the brutal manners of the warrior.[28] While these monarchs might succeed in taming the aristocracy, they had difficulty enforcing their will in a uniform way throughout their dominions – and especially in the colonies. Elias did not properly register the 'de-civilizing' concomitants of a very uneven 'civilizing process'. The ideal of the gentleman might soften the manners of comfortably situated Europeans, but it could also widen their sense of distance from those less favourably placed, whether the poor at home or savages overseas. Elias was well aware that civility might dictate the use of the fork, or ways of blowing the nose, and a restraint on personal aggressiveness, but it did so in ways that justified dreadful punishments on those who were deemed to lack civility. In *The Making of New World Slavery* I cite Père Labat, a French Catholic priest, Hans Sloane, an English savant, and a self-described 'Lady of Quality', each of whom witnessed the mortification of slaves by pitiless flogging and burning, yet felt that this was necessary because Africans were not sensitive to pain – and what is more, according to the 'Lady of Quality' slave women were not even attached to their children.[29]

Africans were often portrayed as lacking emotion when punished or separated from one another. Rather than seeing stoicism in this behaviour, or a desire to cheat the punisher of satisfaction, it was interpreted as a sign that they were less than human. John Woolman insisted on the necessity and difficulty of seeing the African's point of view: 'To come at a right Feeling of their Condition, requires humble serious Thinking; for in their present Situation they have little to engage our natural Affection in their favour. Had we a Son or Daughter involved in the same case as many of them are, it would alarm us and make us feel their Condition without seeking it.'[30]

The wretched situation of the enslaved inhibited identification. So did 'self-love' in the view of Woolman and Benezet. In *The Rape of the Lock*, Pope had furnished a piquant portrait of how the taste of English ladies and gentlemen for the little indulgences of the tea-table sent maritime fleets scouring the planet. The Quaker moralists construed Pope's *Essay on Man* as a most unfortunate and misconceived celebration of 'self-love', with the poet elaborating the idea (similar to that of Jeremy Taylor discussed in Chapter 3) that God would not have endowed us with appetites if He had not meant us to satisfy them, and that God's hidden hand ensured that in pursuing our own pleasure and happiness we fulfil His great design. Pope's twinning of reason and passion

28   Ibid.
29   Blackburn, *Making of New World Slavery*, pp. 345, 424–5
30   John Woolman, *Considerations on Keeping Negroes*, quoted in Nicole Eustace, *Passion is the Gale: Emotion, Power and the Coming of the American Revolution*, Chapel Hill 2008, p. 39.

nevertheless struck a chord found in both patriotism and abolitionism. Woolman knew that untutored passion might only confirm prejudice and fear; it needed to be tempered by 'serious Thinking'. The Patriot message also combined an appeal to passion and the intellect. Nicole Eustace observes: 'Yet, the man who gave us the catchphrase 'the Age of Reason' did so only in 1794, nearly two decades after inciting revolution with a call to "every man whom Nature has given the power of Feeling".[31]

Below is an example of anti-slavery sentiment written by a young woman who manages to infuse her almost Augustan rhyming couplets with true feeling. It evokes a new public aware that their own ease of life was uncomfortably related to the misery and violence of the slave traffic, and the remorseless driving of the slave gangs. These lines – by the seventeen-year-old Mary Birkett – are from a 1792 poem 'addressed to her own sex'.

> Sisters! Here – I must, I dare, I will be warm –
> Shall we who dwell in pleasure, peace and ease,
> Shall we who but in meekness, mildness please,
> Shall we surrounded by each dear delight,
> To soothe the heart, or gratify the sight,
> Say, shall for us the sable sufferers sigh?
> Say, shall for us so many victims die?
>
> Say not that small's the sphere in which we move,
> And our attempts would vain and fruitless prove;
> Not so – we hold *a most important share*,
> In all the evils – all the wrong they bear;
> And tho' their woes *entire* we can't remove,
>
> We may th'*increasing* mis'ries which they prove,
> Push far away the plant for which they die,
> And in this one small thing our taste deny.[32]

The argument that all were implicated in the workings of slavery was stronger than the claim that boycotts would be effective. Anti-slavery themes inspired some good poetry – from Wordsworth, Cowper and Blake, as I have said – but not novels, at least in English. Eventually abolitionism did produce a classic of

---

31   Eustace, *Passion is the Gale*, p. 3.

32   Mary Birkett, 'A Poem on the African Slave Trade', in Alan Richardson, ed, *Slavery, Abolition and Emancipation: Writings in the British Romantic Period*, vol. 4, *Verse*, London 1999, pp. 196–217. The editor points out that William Cowper's anti–slave trade ballads (reprinted pp. 74–82) were very popular. Cowper complained that it was difficult to make poetry from such material, because depressing and predictable, but the editor writes that they have 'enduring appeal'. In his *Critique of Taste* (London 1983), Galvano della Volpe insists on the capacity of poetry to convey argument as well as feeling; the relative success of abolitionist verse bears this out. Anti-slavery also appealed to the Romantics, see Helen Thomas, *Romanticism and the Slave Narrative*, Oxford 2001.

the didactic kind, Harriet Beecher Stowe's *Uncle Tom's Cabin*; but a taboo on representing interracial passion inhibited novelists writing in English in the eighteenth and nineteenth centuries, something not true of Cuba (Cirilo Villaverde) or Brazil (Machado de Assis).

SOVEREIGNTY, SENTIMENT AND ORDER

Elias saw the spread of ball games as a sign of the pacification of social life accompanying his 'civilizing process'. The gentlemanly British slave-trading cartel, which maintained a base at Bance Island on the Sierra Leone river, entertained themselves and visiting slave-trading captains by playing golf on their one-hole course, attended by African caddies. The slave colonies were replete with savage punishments. Though protected by British warships, those who ran the plantations seemed a law to themselves so far as their management of slaves was concerned. However, the consortium of slave-traffickers on Bance island became ornaments of English and Scottish polite society (with their historian thanking an extraordinary bevy of dukes, earls, marquesses, barons and baronets for their permission to consult the family records).[33] The huge gulf – yet intimate connection – between stately home and plantation, the metropolitan drawing room and the African coastal slave factory, was to be integral to the Great Divergence.

Elias's argument is that it was the emergence of a new type of metropolitan state that proved conducive to a softening of manners. But the new, more autonomous and distinct realms of civil society and polity produced by Britain's seventeenth-century revolutions allowed for the emergence of domains of 'policy' and 'public opinion' which were to be the privileged sites of the challenge to slavery and the slave trade. The legislation of most eighteenth-century European monarchs did not have the consistency and evenness of modern lawmaking, but had to be separately negotiated in each jurisdiction. Britain's Hanoverian regime was different. In the aftermath of the Glorious Revolution (1688–9) its landed and mercantile oligarchy recognized a central authority – the 'Crown in Parliament' – which was a first approximation to a modern unitary state based on policy and rule of law.[34] Laws were publicly debated, enacted in parliament and applied throughout the kingdom. To the relative strength of law corresponded the relative weakness of royal authority. (The only

---

33   David Hancock, *Citizens of the World*, Cambridge 1995, pp. 1–2.

34   I attempt to sketch the specificity of the Hanoverian regime in *The Overthrow of Colonial Slavery*, pp. 69–74, using the term 'illegitimate monarchy' since the monarch's weak personal legitimacy was linked to the strength and autonomy of the legal system. In its turn this also allowed for the relative autonomy and independence of property and commerce. For such features of the Hanoverian regime see also Perry Anderson, *English Questions*, London 1994; Edward Thompson, *Whigs and Hunters*, London 1975; and John Brewer, *Sinews of Power*, London 1982.

European state that sometimes resembled the British in these respects was the Dutch, but with extended interruptions and no equivalent to colonial revolt and war, which brought matters to a head in the British case.[35])

PATRIOTISM AND ANTI-SLAVERY

Mid-eighteenth-century Britain witnessed great public controversy over the scope of liberty and empire, and demands for constitutional reform based on manhood suffrage and an end to the exclusion of the Nonconformists (Protestants outside the Anglican communion). The war for public opinion was waged through pamphlets, newspapers and petitions. Policy towards the colonies was a major focus, with domestic issues lurking behind it as metropolitan reformers like John Wilkes and his supporters backed the Americans.[36] The campaigns against slavery and the slave trade were born in this milieu, but sometimes cut across the division between ministry and opposition, as the former noticed that slave-holding weakened rebel claims. Meanwhile Quaker pacifism and Methodist reluctance to back either side in the conflict led them to highlight their anti-slavery critiques.

British abolitionism should be seen, in part, as allied to the attempt to reform the state by purging it of corruption and arbitrary violence and establishing it on a more responsible, representative basis. But the abolitionist leaders and committees were all insistent on the need to promote their goal by peaceful and constitutional methods, including legitimate methods of mobilizing civil society and pressuring parliament. The West India interest nevertheless branded abolitionist agitations as dangerous attacks on property, order and national prosperity, and rallied much elite support for this view.

On both sides of the Atlantic radical Patriots had opposed ministerial high-handedness and despotism, and had often received planter support when they did so. But a strand of radical Patriotism in both the metropolis and the colonies had an antipathy to slave-traders and slave-holders, since slavery seemed to menace the rights of the free-born Englishman, whether in the metropolis or colonies. Thomas Paine published an attack on the slave trade just before the outbreak of the Independence war. However, the conflict between colonial rebels and metropolis was of such overwhelming and absorbing importance that, for a time, it marginalized concerns over slavery, which were anyway quite limited. The years after 1763 saw the publication of tens of thousands of pamphlets and articles by Patriots, which is why it is significant that so few

---

35 Political controversy only rarely touched on slavery in the Netherlands, for reasons to be explored below. But see Jonathan Israel, *Enlightenment Contested*, pp. 590–609.

36 Kathleen Wilson, *The Sense of the People: Politics, Patriotism and Imperialism in England, 1715–1785*, Cambridge 1995, especially pp. 206–36. See also G. D. H. Cole and Raymond Postgate, *The Common People 1746–1946*, 2nd edn, London 1961, pp. 156–270.

mention the slavery issue – aside, that is, from the 'abject slavery' of the colonists. In England itself the Mansfield judgement of 1772 was the result of the courage and tenacity of James Somersett, the slave fighting return to the US, and Granville Sharp, the eccentric member of a distinguished ecclesiastical family, who abominated slave-keeping and believed in frankpledge, the equality and freedom that Englishmen had supposedly enjoyed before the imposition of the Norman yoke. The case received wide publicity, and drew a large and diverse public who made clear their hostility to slave-holding. Sharp was a devout Anglican but favoured constitutional reform, including the lifting of the exclusion of Nonconformists. In 1780 he supported the Society for Constitutional Information, and represents a mingling of secular and religious radicalism (the later abolitionist organizer Thomas Clarkson was to reflect similar impulses).

Notwithstanding the priority of defeating the British, some relatively obscure American Patriots were responsible for translating anti-slavery into specific acts of public policy – the Vermont Constitution of 1777, the Pennsylvanian Emancipation Act of 1780, and similar legislation in Rhode Island in 1784. These gains were significant as expressions of a radical species of Patriotism at times of great social and political tension within the Patriotic camp itself. Vermont was seceding from New York, while Pennsylvania and Rhode Island were trying to contain intense hostility to mercantile profiteering. Vermont's Constitution barred both slavery and indentured servitude. Under Pennsylvania's cautious Emancipation Law of 1780, children of slave mothers had to wait until they were twenty-eight before they could claim their freedom. The Pennsylvania Emancipation was the work of Painites and took the Quakers pleasantly by surprise, but there were few slaves in that state and perhaps none in Vermont. In New York and New Jersey, two Northern states where slaves comprised about 5 per cent of the total population, similarly moderate measures of emancipation foundered. In the main slave-holding states no such attempt was ever made. The North West Ordinance of 1787 excluded slaves from the territory, a rule that was later used to bar all blacks, free or otherwise, even though the 'free air' doctrine had been invoked at the time of its enactment.

The modest anti-slavery measures achieved in the new Republic helped to start the abolitionist ball rolling. They encouraged abolitionism as an organization and a campaign, the first of its type. Yet this impact was to be in Europe, not the United States, where there was no national abolitionist movement or campaign until much later. In the 1780s and 1790s there were scattered, small-scale, uncoordinated representations, gatherings and societies, in some states but not in others. The Manumission Societies set up in New York, Massachusetts and Virginia are sometimes referred to as abolitionist organizations, but this is misleading since they were mainly devoted to persuading slave-holders voluntarily to free their slaves, and to promulgating easier manumission laws within their own state. While a few petitions were submitted, there was no concerted or sustained abolitionist campaign to influence the proceedings of the Constitutional Convention or Congress. Yet the 1780s and 1790s were to see abolitionism emerge centre-stage in British and French politics, in the British case attracting hundreds of thousands of supporters. Just at the time when the new Republic embraced the slave-holder, it helped to convey an anti-slavery message to Europe.

The shock of defeat in North America had an extraordinary impact on British politics, and jolted British Quakers into a more radical and activist stance on the slave trade helping to explain why they played the key role in founding the Society for the Abolition of the Slave Trade in 1787. Prior to the 1782 Yearly Meeting, the London Quakers had been reluctant to press the issue – even though Quakers in other parts of the country, notably Yorkshire, had been influenced by John Woolman and Anthony Benezet over the previous two decades. Swayed by the Quaker example, John Wesley, the Methodist leader, had published his highly critical *Thoughts on Slavery* in 1774. But for the next decade both Quakers and Methodists were mainly preoccupied by the war. The Quakers gave no support to either side; the Methodists were not rigorous pacifists but still favoured negotiation, compromise and peace. The leaders worried that their neutralism or pacifism would expose them to repression. A stance against slavery and the slave trade helped to explain and justify such positions, but, while war raged, neither Quakers nor Methodists were in any position to lead public campaigns – hostilities ruled out all other questions.

ABOLITIONISM AND REFORM

The defeat of the British government changed everything. Whereas victory in the Seven Years War had boosted Patriotism, the outcome in North America suggested that something was seriously amiss with the British monarchy and empire. This legitimacy crisis gave openings to radical dissent and reform. The Quakers – highly successful business people pledged to pacifism and formally excluded from the political system – took the lead. There was a generational revolt within the ranks of the London Quakers, and in 1782, for the first time, the Yearly Meeting committed itself to lead a public campaign against the slave trade. The new policy was adopted in direct response to representations from the Philadelphia Meeting. Such prominent London Quakers, as David Barclay had declined to raise the awkward issue of the slave trade in their dealings with political notables like Lord North, on the grounds that it would do no good and would simply reduce Quaker influence on issues where they could be effective. But at the London Yearly Meeting in 1782, a younger generation responded to the appeal from Philadelphia and cast aside such caution. Whereas the Philadelphia Quakers were still thinking mainly in terms of their obligation to lead more rigorous lives of witness, the English Quakers helped to lay the basis for the first modern social movement. The Quaker leaders, including Barclay, found that their first public representations against the Atlantic traffic were very well received, leading them to find allies to assist in the work of society for the abolition of the slave trade.[37]

Quaker representations chimed in well with the preoccupations of thoughtful members of the British elite who saw abolitionist proposals as a way of reproving the arrogance of rebellious slave-holders. Lord North, Charles James Fox and William Pitt agreed on little, but each took a stand against returning to slavery blacks who had rallied to the loyalist cause. Pitt formed his first administration in 1784 and almost immediately encountered the slave issue. When John Adams, the American envoy, explained that the British had agreed to return American property, including absconding slaves, Pitt refused, saying that to hand over blacks freed by British commanders was contrary 'to the dictates of the higher law of humanity'.[38]

Among those who had already identified colonial slavery and the Atlantic slave trade as evidence that Britain and its empire were in urgent need of reform were Sir Christopher Middleton, Comptroller of the Admiralty, James Ramsay, his aide, Thomas Robinson (Baron Grantham), president of the Board of Trade, Peter Packard, vice chancellor of the University of Cambridge, several bishops and the philanthropist Hannah More, already a respected authority on questions of public morality. Also highly significant was the cautious interest taken by William Pitt and his friend William Wilberforce.

British abolitionism was soon to become a genuinely popular movement – indeed the first social movement with really broad support and involvement – so it is important to register the prominence of its early supporters. These leading individuals were members of the Church of England who had great respect for the Evangelicals, but were preoccupied with the urgent need for imperial reform. As Christopher Brown explains: 'anti-slavery measures promised not only to redress moral wrongs; they promised as well to assist in the rehabilitation of metropolitan authority. No writer defined this agenda with greater clarity than the Reverend James Ramsay. Ramsay understood that slavery reform could occur only by centralizing sovereign power within the British empire'.[39] However, the considerable weight of slave-holding and mercantile interests within the Hanoverian oligarchy meant that those who could see the merit of anti-slavery measures were very much in the minority.

---

37   The role of the American Quakers and the background to the Yearly Meeting of 1782 is explained by Christopher Brown, with the help of valuable new research, in *Moral Capital: Foundations of British Abolitionism*, Charleston 2006, pp. 351–490. Brown brings out well the link between British abolitionism and defeat in North America. See also Colley, *Britons*, and Blackburn, *Overthrow of Colonial Slavery*, pp.131–60.

38   Quoted in Brown, *Moral Capital*, p. 312.

39   Brown, *Moral Capital*, p. 244.

Quakers had the resources to furnish the initial funds and staff of the Abolition Society, and to finance a flood of abolitionist publications. But they were happy to work with and publish Anglicans who shared their concerns. Thus Granville Sharp chaired the Abolition Society Committee and helped to link it to abolitionist currents within the established church. The Committee also recruited Thomas Clarkson, a Cambridge student who had won the university prize for an essay answering a question set by the vice chancellor: 'Is it lawful to makes slaves of others against their will?' Clarkson was later to be described by Coleridge as a 'steam engine of the moral sphere', a description that captures his ability to combine moral suasion with empirical research and popular mobilization. Clarkson embarked on travels round the country, holding meetings and helping to establish local branches. He also visited as many ports involved in the slave trade as he could, with the aim of documenting its real human cost.

The Abolition Committee found that the imperial crisis gave them an extraordinary opportunity. William Pitt, now prime minister, became more open in expressing support and urged Wilberforce to take up the cause and introduce forward legislation to accomplish a ban. Pitt, Wilberforce, Clarkson and the new Quaker leaders were all still in their twenties. When the issue was first debated in the Commons in 1788 it also attracted support from such noted orators as Charles James Fox, the radical Whig, and Edmund Burke.

Sir Charles Middleton, his wife and their friends, especially James Ramsay and Hannah More, contributed special expertise and influence to the cause. Ramsay had spent two decades in the West Indies and could supply detailed and authoritative information about the workings of the slave regime, while Hannah More enjoyed great success as a publicist for moral reform. The 'Barham Court' connection inclined towards evangelical Anglicanism but Middleton, with his Admiralty post, combined this with secular preoccupations. Indeed Brown writes of both Middleton and Ramsay – who was taken on as a confidential secretary at the Navy Board – that 'there is less evidence, in their papers, of a pronounced concern with their own sinfulness, or of a transformative conversion or awakening'.[40] The reverses suffered by the Navy during the American war pointed to the need for reform. Middleton wanted to remodel naval regulations and improve the quality, conduct and conditions of naval ratings. Ramsay also gave evidence to a Board of Trade investigation into the slave trade.

Defenders of the slave trade urged that it was a 'nursery for seamen'. Thomas Clarkson's exhaustive researches into ships' manifests and log books in the slave-trading ports established that there was heavy loss of life among the crew as

---

40   Brown, *Moral Capital*, pp. 344–5.

well as the captives on the Atlantic voyages. From the records of over 300 slave-trading vessels he established that the African trade was a graveyard rather than nursery of seamen, with proportionally more sailors than captives dying on the lengthy voyages. The Abolition Committee also sponsored the circulation of a diagram showing the tight-packing of the captives aboard a typical slave-trading vessel, the *Brookes*. Clarkson explained that this shocking image helped the viewer to go beyond a vague distaste for the slave trade and become aware of the 'enormity of the Commerce'.[41]

Defeat in North America was a blow to British self-regard, and provoked doubts concerning both the domestic regime and the nature of empire.[42] The idea that those who paid taxes deserved representation is one which struck a chord in Britain itself, encouraging the re-emergence of demands for a more representative political system. Several of the champions of reform had been sympathetic to the American rebels, a stance that still jarred with many. But abolitionism was a new cause which allowed its supporters to respond to the need for renewal without challenging head-on the entrenched institutions of oligarchic power. The impeachment of Warren Hastings, the East India Company's former governor of Bengal, was a kindred expression of the impulse for imperial reform. Of course the slave trade had its defenders who argued that it was wrong to tamper with such a mainstay of national prosperity. In the first parliamentary debate a back-bench MP declared: 'The leaders, it is true, are for Abolition. But the minor orators, the pygmies, will, I trust, succeed this day in carrying the case against them. The property of the West Indians is at stake; and though men may be generous with their own property, they should not be so with the property of others.'[43] Even though it was a trade, not property as such, that was directly in question, this speaker's argument seems to have registered with his fellow MPs, who defeated the bill.

As it gathered strength the abolitionist campaign gave an opening to secular radicals to attack the shameful origins of the fortunes of the most

---

41   Marcus Rediker, *The Slave Ship*, London 2008, p. 309.

42   Seymour Drescher denies a connection between the advent of abolitionism in 1787–8 and any legitimacy crisis triggered by the North American defeat, as I suggested in *The Overthrow of Colonial Slavery*. See Seymour Drescher, *Abolition: A History of Slavery and Antislavery*, Cambridge 2009, p. 212. However, I am encouraged to persist in my view, since Christopher Brown and Linda Colley also make such a connection. Brown writes: 'The American Revolution did not cause abolitionism in Britain . . . The crisis in imperial authority did, however, make the institution of slavery matter politically in ways that it had never mattered before. It turned the slave system into a symbol, not just an institution, the source of self-examination as well as the fount of wealth.' (*Moral Capital*, p. 27.) A parallel reflection is found in Linda Colley, *Britons: Forging the Nation 1707–1837*, London 1992, pp. 132–46, 350–61. Recent writing on the extent of military manumission by the redcoats in the American War adds a further dimension to the argument. See Schama, *Rough Crossings*, London 2006.

43   Reginald Coupland, *Wilberforce: A Narrative*, London 1923, pp. 144–5.

corrupt, cruel and conservative components of the ruling oligarchy. The fact that parliament was debating the slave trade ban itself encouraged those outside parliament to take up the cause, and subscribe to petitions that were to be laid before the legislators. This right of petition had long been allowed to citizens who might be affected by a piece of legislation. In the early 1700s there had been a hundred petitions from English ports for an end to the Royal African Company's slave-trading privileges, so that all could engage in the traffic if they wished. Now, eight decades later, the right of petition was being used in a new way, to assert a principle – and the moral existence of the petitioners – rather than an interest. Tens of thousands of artisans and labourers signed abolitionist petitions in the new manufacturing centres of the North and Midlands. Hundreds of meetings were held in towns and cities across Britain in 1788. Sometimes an African and former slave would speak from the platform – Olaudah Equiano being the favourite – and sometimes a motion to abolish slavery as well as the slave trade would pass by acclamation. By early 1792, petitions carrying 400,000 signatures were presented to parliament.

While it had a popular following, the Abolition movement was led by reform-minded members of the middle and upper class. The new daily newspapers in Manchester, Leeds, Leicester, Birmingham and Exeter gave their support to the cause. Plates and cups stamped with the anti-slavery logo enjoyed a brisk sale. It was sometimes claimed that the ending of the slave trade would necessitate a reform of slavery itself, and some abolitionist writers developed the argument that wages, be they ever so modest, were vastly preferable to the cruelty of the whip. The anti–slave trade cause had great appeal for women, though in this first phase they did not organize and agitate independently, as they were to do later.

A gender reading of abolitionism is not difficult to make, but needs to be nuanced and qualified. Patriotic anti-slavery – such as the freeing of male slaves to fight as soldiers – had a 'manly' character, rescuing them from the feminized status of the slave. The enlargement of the sphere of civil society in eighteenth-century Britain saw women claim public roles, as authors and as participants in public events. Aphra Behn, Catherine Macaulay, Mary Wollstonecraft, Hannah More and Harriet Martineau challenged female stereotypes as much by their lives as by what they wrote. While female participation in abolitionism might seem simply an outgrowth of the prescribed female role, it was soon to escape beyond such limits and assert a new public role for women.[44]

---

44   Moira Ferguson, *Subject to Others: British Women Writers and Colonial Slavery, 1670–1834*, New York 1992. While saluting the appearance of a 'feminist vanguard', Ferguson insists that colonial stereotypes often survive in this writing.

The abolitionist petitioners of the late 1780s and early 1790s claimed a voice as subjects or citizens. Several of the leading Quakers had made their fortunes in the Atlantic trade, but they were now rejecting this and dedicating themselves and their Society to a radical reform of the Atlantic and industrial order. Religious Nonconformists, entrepreneurs from the new industrial districts, and political radicals – all were staking a claim to be legitimate participants in the political system. This is not to say that their horror at the slave traffic was insincere; it is simply to understand that they were asserting not their interests but their values. For some the claim was not to a political voice as such but to the view that the political sphere should itself acknowledge the moral feelings of the country, something which the presence of a bench of Anglican bishops in the House of Lords did not achieve.

The American example and the English agitation over the slave trade encouraged the formation of a French abolitionist society, the *Amis des Noirs*, in 1788. For a while the crisis of the French monarchy favoured the abolitionist cause, since it could be argued that France would join Britain in banning the trade. Popular and parliamentary support for a ban both reached a high point in the early months of 1792, but the House of Lords blocked the measure, with members of the royal family making clear their opposition. However, in deference to the concern expressed in the Commons a motion was passed that sought to regulate the loading ratios of the slave ships. Outside parliament campaigning continued for a while and became caught up in a polarization of opinion stimulated by events in Paris. Thomas Paine's *The Rights of Man*, capturing the new radical spirit, sold 200,000 copies in the two years following its publication in 1791.

But in 1792–3 large sections of British opinion recoiled from the Jacobin phase of the French Revolution, with Terror in Paris and reports of bloody strife in Saint-Domingue. Before long Britain was at war with France, at the urging of French planters hostile to the Republic. The British parliament had appeared on the brink of endorsing slave-trade abolition in early 1792, yet, within little more than a year, the British government had dispatched a huge fleet to the Caribbean to seize the French islands, with orders to defend the slave-holding French planter royalists. While Wilberforce was convinced that the aims of the expedition were aggressive – to acquire more slave colonies – the governor of Jamaica saw it as essential to defend the island and 'its all-important commercial credit'.[45] However, there was a little-noticed abolitionist gain in Upper Canada in 1793, when the governor successfully obtained approval of a 'free-womb' law. (The governor had left

---

45   David P. Geggus, *Slavery, War, and Revolution: The British Occupation of Saint Domingue, 1793–1798*, Oxford 1984, p. 284.

London at the height of the abolitionist campaign.) While gratifying to the black refugees, this ruling did not prepare them for the arrival in 1796 of 600 deported maroons from Jamaica.[46]

At home, curbs on freedom of expression and association were introduced, and anti-Jacobin 'Crown and Anchor' mobs set on radicals who tried to defy the repression. The abolitionist campaign withered away, a casualty of the anti-Jacobin panic.

Abolitionism in the English-speaking world had made only very modest gains. Its main achievement had simply been to publicize and politicize the slave trade and slavery. It had failed to overcome the three central ideological supports for slavery identified in the previous chapter – respect for property, racial fear and concern for the national interest. The British parliament chose to regulate but not abolish.

In explaining the government's position, Henry Dundas told the Commons that he still believed the slave trade to be 'incompatible with the justice and humanity of the British constitution', but that were the motion to abolish it 'agreed by the House it would endanger the peace of the country'.[47] A sign of the new prudence surrounding this topic was Hannah More's story, published in the first volume of her *Cheap Repository Tracts* in 1796, 'A True Account of a Pious Negro'. Moira Ferguson summarizes the story:

> [T]he Pious Negro is a slave who is never freed. An 'English Gentleman' who meets the slave in North America discusses slavery with him, only to discover that the Negro's Quaker master is so kind that this unnamed slave does not need freedom. Reading the Bible avidly has taught him what a 'very great sinner' he is. After questioning the bondsman closely, the 'gentleman' finds him 'perfectly charming', a man with a 'heavenly' disposed mind. In the course of this intimate dialogue they grow mutually attached, the slave weeping because of God's mercy . . . They part on the understanding that they will meet and 'live together, and love one another throughout . . . eternity'.[48]

Ferguson points out that by this time Quakers were forbidden to own slaves, so that the story was a libel. More was not an abolitionist leader – women did not play a public role in British abolitionism at this time – but she had once supported the movement, so the invisibility of the abolitionist content in this trite little tale was sign of a great falling-off.

The US Constitution (1787) had entrenched the rights of slave-holders, as we have seen, and allowed at least another twenty years of slave imports. The

---

46   R. T. Naylor, *Canada in the European Age, 1453–1919*, Vancouver 1987, p. 156.
47   Quoted in Ferguson, *Subject to Others*, p. 211.
48   Ferguson, *Subject to Others*, pp. 215–16.

numbers of free people of colour did grow considerably in North America in the Revolutionary decade as a result of freedom suits, escape, emancipation legislation and private manumission. But the social and political rights of free people of colour, never extensive, were to be increasingly circumscribed by racially discriminatory legislation. The crisis of empire had aired and disseminated the critique of slavery, but only tiny numbers of slaves were freed in consequence. The events in Saint-Domingue in 1791–1804 were to change everything.

Part III

THE HAITIAN PIVOT

CHAPTER EIGHT

Haitians Claim the Rights of Man

In the sequence of revolutions that remade the Atlantic world between 1776 and 1825, the Haitian Revolution is rarely given its due; yet without it there is much that cannot be accounted for, especially if we are concerned with slavery and colonialism. The revolutions – American, French, Haitian and Spanish American – should be seen as interconnected, with each helping to radicalize the next. The American Revolution launched an idea of popular sovereignty which, together with the cost of the war, helped to provoke the downfall of the French monarchy. The French Revolution, dramatic as was its impact on the Old World, also became a fundamental event in the New, since it was eventually to challenge slavery as well as royal power. This was not because of the French Assembly's resounding 'Declaration of the Rights of Man and the Citizen' in 1789, since neither the Assembly nor its successor, the Convention, moved on their own initiative to confront slavery in the French plantation colonies. Indeed the issue was not to be addressed for another five years, by which time the French Caribbean colonies were engulfed in slave revolts and threatened by British occupation.

In mid-1791 Saint-Domingue, the richest slave colony of the Americas, was torn apart by struggles between supporters and opponents of extending citizenship to free coloured proprietors. This set the scene for a massive slave uprising in August 1791 in the colony's Northern plain, involving about 30,000 slaves and leading to the formation of large bands of rebels. Several of the main black commanders were subsequently persuaded to join the Spanish army – Saint-Domingue shared the island of Hispaniola with the Spanish colony of Santo Domingo, and relations between republican France and royalist Spain were deteriorating. With other black chiefs retreating to the hills and mountains, the colonial authorities lost control of important areas. Influential planters invited the British to intervene. On 29 August 1793 rival decrees of emancipation or 'general liberty' were issued by the Revolutionary Commissioner in northern Saint-Domingue and one of the black generals, Toussaint Louverture. The National Convention in Paris was eventually brought to issue the decree of 16 Pluviôse An II (4 February 1794) which abolished slavery throughout the French colonies. The Convention was spurred to action by delegates from Saint-Domingue who argued that, faced with a British invasion of the colonies and the defection of many royalist planters, only such a radical step could save the Republic by rallying more black insurgents to its side.

The National Convention struck down slave property at a time when the pressure of the sans-culottes on the Convention was at its height. Perhaps only the Revolution at its most radical could have embraced the policy, but, following Robespierre's overthrow in Thermidor, it was to be sustained by the Directory down to the end of the 1790s. An expedition of 1,500 men led by Victor Hugues ejected the British from Guadeloupe with the help of several thousand local coloured troops, including former slaves. Among those sent packing was Benedict Arnold, who had joined the British expedition as a war contractor. Victor Hugues, the 'Robespierre of the Islands', encouraged slave revolts in neighbouring islands and converted Guadeloupe and its dependencies into a privateering base.

In Saint-Domingue the black army led by Toussaint Louverture, a former slave, deserted its royal Spanish patron in April 1794 and joined the republican ranks. The French commander General Laveaux supported the emancipation policy and welcomed Louverture. In 1796 Louverture was appointed lieutenant governor, and in the following year commander in chief. With materiel sent from France, Louverture created a well-armed and disciplined force which drove first the Spanish and then the British from the colony. Overall the British, who had to fight hard to regain Saint Lucia, Saint Vincent and Grenada, lost 80,000 soldiers between 1793 and 1799, half of them in Saint-Domingue, half in the Eastern Caribbean, and more in this theatre than in Europe.

Toussaint Louverture insisted that Saint-Domingue remained French, but he dealt with Britain and the United States like a sovereign power. His army included white and coloured, as well as black, commanders. He invited émigré planters to return. In 1801 he drew up a Constitution for the colony whose first article declared that it was part of the French Empire, but subject to 'special laws'. The third article declared: 'There can be no slaves in the territory; servitude is forever abolished. Here all men are born, live and die free and French.' Another clause insisted that all residents, 'whatever their colour', could pursue any employment and that the only distinctions would be those based on 'virtues and talents'.

In 1802, with British and US encouragement, Bonaparte sought to reassert metropolitan power and re-establish slavery and white supremacy in Saint-Domingue. He sent a large expeditionary force under the command of General Leclerc, his brother-in-law, to accomplish this mission. Louverture resisted but was eventually captured, and died in France. However, the expeditionary force encountered escalating resistance, with a loss of some 50,000 men, including Leclerc himself.

In January 1804 the victorious black generals established the new state of Haiti. A Constitution adopted in the following year outlawed slavery and declared that all citizens were legally black – probably an attempt to forestall conflicts between black and mulatto groupings.[1] The French Republic's anti-slavery stance had delayed the onset of national consciousness in Saint-Domingue by tapping into the titanic forces of revolt in the most extreme and concentrated slave system that had ever existed. But with the overthrow of the Directory and Bonaparte's dispatch of a large and threatening expedition, the only way to defend the liberty of the former slaves was to proclaim a new state. The name Haiti was a homage to the island's pre-colonial inhabitants, signalling the break with empire; the Republic's flag was the tricolour with the white band removed. Colour distinctions, especially between black and mulatto, continued to be important but had no legal force, and citizenship extended to all, including Poles and Germans who had defected from the French army. The term *blanc* (white), as employed in Haiti, does not describe a person by reference to the colour of their skin. Instead it became – as it remains to the present day – the vernacular term for any foreigner, even if they are Jamaicans or Brazilians of dark complexion.

In 1816 Haiti's President Alexandre Pétion helped Simón Bolívar to mount the invasion that was ultimately to defeat the Spanish Empire in the Americas, giving him arms and ammunition and allowing hundreds of Haitian fighters, known as *los franceses*, to sail with him. In return Bolívar promised to adopt measures to extinguish slavery in the lands he was to liberate. Bolívar had already freed his own slaves. He was only able to persuade the Congress of Angostura in 1819 of limited measures – an end to the slave trade, and the release of male slaves who were enrolled in the liberation forces. Against continuing opposition from many of his fellow planters, he persuaded the Congress of Cúcuta in 1821 to go further and decree that all children born to slave mothers would be free when they reached eighteen years old. Former slaves and free men of colour were to make up a high proportion of the main liberation armies, usually between a third and a half; they were also strategically vital because they were more willing to serve outside their native region.[2] The years 1776 to 1848 in the Atlantic world witnessed the creation of a string of new states and administered a revolutionary shock or challenge to the old order, and to the colonialism and slavery which were so important to it. Slave produce was driving commercial expansion, yet slavery sat uncomfortably with the popular ideal of the nation or *patrie*.

---

1 For the text of Haiti's 1805 Constitution with a commentary see Sibylle Fischer, *Modernity Disavowed: Haiti and the Cultures of Slavery in the Age of Revolution*, Durham, NC 2004, pp. 227–44, 275–82.

2 I supply a far more detailed account of the sequence in *The Overthrow of Colonial Slavery*. For the high proportion of black soldiers in the Spanish American armies see Nuria Sales de Bohigas, *Sobre Esclavos, Reclutas, y Mercaderes de Quintas*, Barcelona 1974. The record of the Spanish American republics will also be discussed in Chapter 10.

RECOGNIZING THE HAITIAN REVOLUTION

The fact that the first major breach in the hugely important systems of slavery in the Americas was opened, not by English or American abolitionists, but by Jacobin revolutionaries and the black peasantry of Saint-Domingue/Haiti, has taken a long time really to register in English-language historiography. Outside the world of academe, C. L. R. James, the Trinidadian political activist and journalist, had already made the case in his superbly vigorous and well-researched book, *The Black Jacobins*, first published in 1938.[3] Decolonization in Africa and elsewhere helped attract attention to the Haitian Revolution from the 1960s, and in recent years historians have begun to study the revolution as an event in the history of ideas, and of the moral imagination, as well as a dramatic political episode with a wide impact.

In 1959 Robert R. Palmer published a brilliant and influential study of the 'age of the democratic revolution', giving detailed attention to the American and French Revolutions – and indeed to lesser upheavals in the Low Countries, Switzerland and elsewhere – but entirely neglecting the struggles which led to the proclamation of the Haitian Republic.[4] The notion of an 'age of revolution' is well worth retaining, but we should be careful not to impose upon it a ready-made, seemingly predestined character. The democratic and anti-slavery impulses of the French Revolution found their way with difficulty to a brief but momentous common focus, only to be threatened by bloody counter-revolution. Ignoring or minimizing the Haitian Revolution robs these contradictory events of their historic denouement. Without Haiti, the sequence of revolutions is falsified and diminished, as we will see.

The Haitian historian Michel-Rolph Trouillot has argued that the events leading to the foundation of Haiti have suffered from either 'erasure' or

---

3   C. L. R. James, *The Black Jacobins: Toussaint L'Ouverture and the Santo Domingo Revolution*, London 1938.

4   Robert R. Palmer, *The Age of the Democratic Revolution: A Political History of Europe and America, 1760–1800*, 2 vols, Princeton 1959 and 1964. Such classical historians of the French Revolution as Jean Jaurès and Georges Lefebvre included some discussion of the momentous events in the Caribbean, but François Furet had very little to say on this topic. Simon Schama's best-selling *Citizens*, London 1988, has one reference to events in Saint-Domingue. But the appearance of a US paperback edition of James's *Black Jacobins* in 1963, and the retreat of European colonialism, rekindled interest in Haiti in the English-speaking world. Eugene Genovese's *From Rebellion to Revolution: Afro-American Slave Revolts in the Making of the Modern World*, Baton Rouge 1979, and Eric Foner's *Nothing But Freedom: Emancipation and Its Legacy*, Baton Rouge 1983, were significant attempts to integrate Haiti into the wider history of slavery and emancipation in the Americas. Recently Garry Wills, *'Negro President': Jefferson and the Slave Power*, Boston 2003, pp. 33–46 foregrounded Haiti's impact on US politics, while David Brion Davis devotes a chapter to the French and Haitian Revolutions in *Inhuman Bondage: the Rise and Fall of Slavery in the New World*, Oxford 2006, pp. 157–74.

'banalization' in general histories of the Americas and the West, because they were seen as lacking sufficient coherence and meaning. They were merely a confused disorder that did not rise to the level of a national or social revolution.[5] Just as Haiti was diplomatically shunned by the Great Powers – the US did not recognize it until 1862 – so scholars paid it little or no attention for at least another century. Spanish American historiography acknowledged Haiti's assistance to Bolívar, but general histories of the 'age of revolution' often dealt briefly with these liberation struggles themselves.[6] Yet the fate of Saint-Domingue was a strategic stake in the statecraft of Pitt, Adams, Pickering, Jefferson, Talleyrand, Bonaparte and Bolívar. The survival of Haiti had implications for the future of slavery in the Americas, and tested and tempered the outlook of the abolitionist movement. While faint-hearted abolitionists recoiled in horror at the bloody consequences of slave revolt, others saw the latter as no reason to tolerate a slave regime which was intrinsically violent. Indeed certain intellectual and moral conclusions seemed to flow from these momentous and tragic events, capturing the imagination of writers and artists from Romantics like Wordsworth and Lamartine to Moderns like Alejo Carpentier and the artists of the Harlem Renaissance. Finally, and whatever view is taken of Haiti's achievement, the revolution which established it is a vital piece of the jigsaw without which no good picture of Atlantic politics in this period can be produced, a fact known to Henry Adams but neglected by many of his successors.[7]

We have seen that, by the mid-eighteenth century, slavery was integral to an Atlantic social order based on a booming commerce in plantation produce. Slaves were a form of property, a component of patriarchy and, as Africans or descendants of Africans, members not of the polity but simply of the households of their owners. The racial definition of who could be enslaved stemmed from entrenched religious and secular ideas about the different nations of man and the Great Chain of Being.

But we have also seen that slavery had become – for the first time – the object of public controversy and criticism in the middle decades of the century among sections of 'enlightened' and 'awakened' opinion. On both sides of

---

5   Michel-Rolph Trouillot, *Silencing the Past: Power and the Production of History*, Boston 1995, pp. 88–107.

6   Eric Hobsbawm, in his masterful but avowedly Europe-focused work *The Age of Revolution*, London 1964, excludes the American Revolution as well as the Haitian from detailed attention; however, his brief passages on Haiti and South America make several essential points (pp. 69 and 110). A late entrant to the 'age of revolution' literature, Lester Langley's *The Americas in the Age of Revolution*, New Haven 1997, takes the contrary approach – focusing on the New World and giving little attention to Europe.

7   Henry Adams, *The History of the United States during the First Administration of Thomas Jefferson*, vol. 1, New York 1890, pp. 377–98. However, the language used by Adams when writing about Louverture is both patronizing and inaccurate ('the sensitivities of a wild animal', 'the unhappy negro found himself face to face with destruction', the rat versus the ferret and so forth).

the Atlantic the new Patriotism celebrated liberty and denounced despotism. The Patriots were uncomfortable with both slavery and the African presence. The American War of Independence and its immediate aftermath had helped to put the issue of the slave trade, and even slavery itself, on the agenda, but both sides had shied away from decisive action. By the end of the 1780s plantation slavery was recovering and, by the 1790s, positively thriving: at the beginning of this decade the Atlantic trade in slave produce and slaves had never been larger.

SLAVERY AND THE FRENCH REVOLUTION

French colonial slavery had been initially sponsored by royal Absolutism but became a major component of French capitalist and bourgeois development. When the Estates General assembled in 1789 many members of the Third Estate, and quite a few of the nobles, were colonial merchants or planters. About a tenth of the members of the National Assembly were colonial proprietors, and the two Atlantic ports which virtually monopolized the colonial trade (Bordeaux and Nantes) were the hubs of the Jacobin and Girondin network of revolutionary clubs. When the Abbé Sieyès declared that the productive forces in society should sweep aside the parasites and establish their own leadership, it was an appeal which had resonance for colonists and colonial merchants who saw themselves as the victims of ministerial despotism.[8] The Massiac Club, a lobby mounted by colonial proprietors, espoused a moderate but constitutional royalism, but above all focused tenaciously on the defence of white slave-holders. On the other hand, the colonial merchants backed the Girondin Club and were prime exponents of the discourse of 'bourgeois revolution'.[9] Given these facts, it is not surprising that classic accounts of the revolution paid so much attention to conflicts related to slavery and the colonies, and bizarre that Furet and Schama should neglect them. Of course, classic notions of bourgeois revolution found in the work of Guizot and Marx failed to register that France's bourgeoisie – a term that applied to lawyers and officials as well as businessmen – included a large contingent with a stake in the colonies and colonial trade. This was a source of weakness and vulnerability, as well as a challenge to bourgeois revolutionaries who were anxious to lead society as a whole and to frame their aims and values in universalistic terms.

The French Revolution at first presented barriers to slave emancipation as strong as those found in North America. The discourse of 1789–92 made liberty

---

8   The classic study of the powerful colonial lobby is Gabriel Debien, *Les colons de Saint-Domingue et la Révolution*, Paris 1953. But see also M. B. Garrett, *The French Colonial Question, 1789–1791*, New York 1970.

9   William H. Sewell, *A Rhetoric of Bourgeois Revolution: The Abbé Sieyès and 'What is the Third Estate?'*, Durham, NC, 1994.

conditional on public utility, property and membership in the community. Only propertied French men could be 'active citizens'; French women and children were 'passive' citizens. The enslaved were treated as both minors and aliens. The first clause of the Declaration of the Rights of Man stated: 'Men are born, and always continue, free and equal in respect of their rights. Civil distinctions, therefore, can be founded only on public utility.' The last clause of the Declaration reinforced 'public utility' as a potential qualification of freedom by insisting: 'The right to property being inviolable and sacred, no one ought to be deprived of it, except in cases of evident public necessity, legally ascertained, and on condition of a previous just indemnity.'[10] Since slaves were indubitably a sort of property, as well as arguably a prop of public utility, the qualification of natural liberty seemed robust enough to reassure the many colonial proprietors in the Assembly. The duc de La Rochefoucauld proposed freedom for slaves during the famous session that made a bonfire of feudal privileges, but the proposal was brushed aside.

By this time slave-holders were on the alert. In 1788 a French abolitionist society, the *Amis des Noirs* had been formed. Patronized by prominent philosophers, financiers and political leaders, it enjoyed cordial relations with the British Abolition Society. The *Amis des Noirs* opposed the slave trade but came to focus mainly on defending the civic rights of the free men of colour. When the slaves of Saint-Domingue launched their historic uprising in August 1791, the *Amis des Noirs* had yet to propose the ending of slavery.

The founding in Paris of a *Société des Citoyens de Couleur* in 1789 added another ingredient as free men of colour demanded equal rights, pointing out that the Declaration said nothing about skin colour and that as sons of French soil, many of them well-educated and propertied, they deserved active citizenship. The Abbé Grégoire, a member of the *Amis des Noirs*, composed a 'Letter to Philanthropists', urging that this case was undeniable and that it would be disgraceful to refuse to honour the principles so recently and solemnly proclaimed. From this moment equality for free people of colour became a defining issue for the *côté gauche*, or left wing of the Constituent Assembly.[11]

The eventual French decree of emancipation in 1794 certainly reflected the pressures of slave revolt and war, but also a change in the metropolis, with a

---

10 'Declaration of the Rights of Man and of the Citizen', in Merryn Williams, ed., *Revolutions, 1775–1830*, Harmondsworth 1971, pp. 97–9. The limits of the French Revolutionary concept of citizenship are explored in Olivier Le Cour Grandmaison, *Les Citoyennetés en révolution 1789–94*, Paris 1992, especially pp. 191–238 so far as slavery is concerned. The idea that men are not only born free and equal but remain so potentially headed off the idea that, though naturally free and equal, men lost these attributes once they entered society. But in the 1789 Declaration this improved formulation is already mortgaged to property and public utility.

11 Florence Gauthier, *L'aristocratie de l'épiderme: Le combat de la Société des Citoyens de Couleur, 1789–1791*, Paris 2007, pp. 211–43.

surge of republican and national sentiment imposing a new egalitarian order and denouncing privilege, including that of the rich and of the 'aristocracy of the skin'. The radical social patriotism of 1793–4 helped to weaken the claims of property and race, and of intermediary bodies like the colonial assemblies.[12] The emancipation policy was put on the agenda by Léger-Félicité Sonthonax, the French republican comissioner to Saint-Domingue, and by the delegation he sent to Paris. It was then taken up by the Hébertists, the most radical grouping in the National Convention and, at this time, the main force in the Paris Commune. The cause was endorsed somewhat hesitantly by Danton and eventually backed by Robespierre and the Committee of Public Safety, even though they had not originated the policy and initially had reservations about it. The argument that the Republic must free the slave and make itself the standard-bearer of general emancipation proved to have a broad appeal to nearly all in the republican camp. The revolutionary emancipationism of 1793–4 survived Robespierre's downfall and endured until nearly the end of the decade. It echoed Raynal's *Histoire des Deux Mondes*, which had declared that the first European sovereign to declare war on slavery would enlist the mighty cause of humanity on their side.[13] (This can be seen as a species of national striving for 'moral capital'.) The emancipationist policy was both inspiring and effective, but also likely to antagonize all the other powers, and hence add to France's enemies. The policy was to be abandoned by Bonaparte as First Consul when he sought a peace settlement with Britain in 1802 and better relations with the United States. But emancipation was not a policy that could be simply dropped when convenient. In the French Caribbean it was now embodied in a new social order which rejected the first consul's attempt to destroy black power and restore slavery, and proclaimed instead the independence of Haiti.

HAITI AND THE RACE BAR

Laurent Dubois argues that the events in the former French colony mark a watershed. 'They were', he writes in *Avengers of the New World* (2004), 'the most concrete expression of the idea that the rights proclaimed in France's 1789

---

12   The radicalism of the Jacobins was greater than that of the American Revolution because, while still affirming a patriarchal family model, they were to question racial hierarchy and affirm the equality of all citizens. See William H. Sewell, 'The French Revolution and the Emergence of the Nation Form', in Michael A. Morrison and Melinda Zook, eds, *Revolutionary Currents: Nation Building in the Transatlantic World*, Lanham 2004, pp. 91–126. See also Sewell, *A Rhetoric of Bourgeois Revolution*.

13   Abbé Raynal, *A Philosophical and Political History of the Settlements and Trade of the Europeans in the East and West Indies*, 2nd edn, London 1776, vol. 3, pp. 466–7. This passage appeared in the first edition. The passages attacking slavery, mainly written by Diderot, grew longer and sharper in each successive edition. See Yves Benot, 'Diderot, Pechmeja, Raynal et l'anti-colonialisme', in *Les Lumières, l'esclavage, la colonisation*, Paris 2005, pp. 107–23.

Declaration of the Rights of Man and of the Citizen were indeed universal. They could not be quarantined in Europe or prevented from landing in the ports of the colonies, as many had argued that they should be. The slave insurrection in Saint-Domingue led to the expansion of citizenship beyond racial barriers despite the massive political and economic investment in the slave system at the time.'[14] He sees the revolution in Haiti as an intellectual and cultural as well as a political event, holding out the ideal of a society in which, in principle, 'all people, of all colours' were granted social freedom and citizenship. While this ideal was difficult to live up to, the Haitian Revolution also had a very tangible success. It struck a mighty blow against slavery where it was strongest, in the plantation zone. 'If we live in a world where democracy is meant to exclude no-one, it is in no small part because of the actions of those slaves in Saint-Domingue who insisted that human rights were theirs too.'[15]

Dubois's judgements arise from his detailed narrative of revolutionary events in the French Caribbean and France itself, and chime in with conclusions drawn in work by Lynn Hunt and Florence Gauthier.[16] These judgments challenge traditional Western histories of liberty, including accounts of Anglo-American abolitionism which had little or no space for black anti-slavery, and for the impact of black resistance and witness on the maturing of the abolitionist movement.[17] More problematic might be the proposed link between slave liberation in Haiti and modern 'human rights' doctrines – is it not anachronistic to attribute to the black leaders or freed people a concept of 'human rights' which only flowered in the mid- or late twentieth century? Was not the Haitian Revolution defined by the founding of a new state, even at great cost to observance of individual rights? What was the link between the 'rights of man' and Caribbean innovation in the course of the Haitian Revolution? These are issues to which I return later in this chapter.

The first decade of the century, helped by Haiti's bicentennial, was marked by publication of important new works by Haitian and overseas historians.[18]

---

14 Laurent Dubois, *Avengers of the New World: The Story of the Haitian Revolution*, Cambridge, MA 2004, p. 3.

15 Ibid., pp. 6–7. See also pp. 165–70.

16 Florence Gauthier, *Triomphe et mort du droit naturel en Révolution, 1789–1795–1802*, Paris 1992, pp. 155–238; and Lynn Hunt, 'The Paradoxical Origins of Human Rights', in Jeffrey Wasserstrom, Lynn Hunt and Marilyn Young, eds, *Human Rights and Revolutions*, Lanham 2000, pp. 3–18.

17 The British and US abolitionist movements accorded great importance to black witness, but many historic accounts paid little attention to this. Decolonization and the US civil rights movement began to change this in the 1960s and 1970s. However, as late as 1992 Thomas Bender's important and interesting collection, *The Anti-Slavery Debate*, New York 1992, saw black abolitionism largely neglected. I return to this in Chapter 12.

18 Notably Vertus Saint-Louis, *Mer et liberté: Haiti 1492–1794*, Port-au-Prince 2009, and *Aux origines du drame d'Haiti: droit et commerce maritime (1794–1806)*, Port-au-Prince 2008. Another essential work is Michel Hector and Laennec Hurbon, eds, *Genèse de l'Etat Haitien (1804–1859)*,

They yield a richer knowledge of the French Caribbean during the Revolutionary epoch, enabling some clearer answers to be given. However, there remains a danger that, as we will see, the 'silencing of the past' is giving way to a 'scolding of the past'. Nevertheless new research and controversy should help to reconstruct the narrative of emancipation, to establish the decisive turning points, and grasp the nature of the contending notions of freedom at stake in the age of revolution, and the ways in which they were eventually redeemed and pushed to a further limit by the former slaves of Saint-Domingue. Once the focus is on the Haitian Revolution, the case for black agency is undeniable but, as will be seen, its meaning and influence remain very much subject to dispute.

At what point did the revolutionary challenge to racial slavery emerge? Was it the first large-scale slave uprisings in 1791? Or the proclamations against slavery made by Sonthonax, the Jacobin commissioner, and Toussaint Louverture, the black general, on 29 August 1793? Or the eventual decree of 4 February 1794 (16 Pluviôse An II), declaring the ending of slavery in the French colonies? Or the French defeat in Saint-Domingue, and the proclamation of the black Etat de Haïti on 1 January 1804? Or even the subsequent drawing up of a constitution or adoption of a republican form? These were certainly each important stepping stones, and it will be useful briefly to sketch the narrative that connects them. Such an account has to explain both why the leaders of the French Revolution took so long to abandon slavery and rally to revolutionary emancipationism, and why they eventually did so. It also has to weigh the contribution and diversity of social revolution in the colonies, above all that of the enslaved majority.

SLAVERY OVERTURNED, 1791–94

I have already noted that Saint-Domingue was in turmoil on the eve of the great slave uprising of August 1791 that swept through the Northern plain. The colony was gripped by intense battles between supporters and opponents of the metropolitan Revolutionary authorities. The latter had announced modest concessions to the free people of colour, sparking intense opposition from many of the resident *petits blancs* and *grands blancs*. The slave uprisings were seen by many Jacobins as the result of a royalist provocation and plot, and the rebels as dupes

---

Port-au-Prince 2009. Important studies by foreign historians included, besides those already cited: Laurent Dubois, *A Colony of Citizens: Revolution and Slave Emancipation in the French Caribbean, 1787–1804*, Williamsburg 2004; David Geggus, *Haitian Revolutionary Studies*, Bloomington 2001; Frédéric Régent, *Esclavage, métissage et liberté: la révolution francaise en Guadeloupe, 1789–1802*, Paris 2004: Benot, *Les Lumières, l'esclavage, la colonisation*. See also David Geggus and Norman Fiering, eds, *The World of the Haitian Revolution*, Bloomington 2009; Jeremy Popkin, ed., *Facing Racial Revolution: Eyewitness Accounts of the Haitian Revolution*, Chicago 2007, and Jeremey Popkin, *You Are All Free: The Haitian Revolution and the Abolition of Slavery*, Cambridge 2010.

of the counterrevolution. While the mass of rebels were certainly motivated by their own yearning to throw off enslavement, some of the leaders may have received encouragement from royalists or Spanish agents. Within a week or two of the slave uprising some 30,000 rebels had fanned out across the Northern plain, burning plantations and urging slaves to join them. The French Revolutionary garrison and militia were just strong enough to venture outside the provincial capital, Le Cap, and to restore a very fragile control over some of the devastated estates. The poorly armed rebel columns headed for the hills or made their way to the eastern frontier with Spanish Santo Domingo. The Spanish authorities had long been prepared to offer the life of a soldier to male slaves willing to abandon Spain's enemies and serve their king. (As noted in the last chapter, St Augustine in Florida had been garrisoned by such a force.) By the summer of 1791 it was clear that Europe's most powerful and glittering monarchy – that of France – faced a mortal threat, and that any weak point in the posture of the revolutionaries was to be exploited as much as possible. However, while it was only natural for the Spanish authorities to seek to use slave insurrection in this way – they were to repeat the stratagem in Venezuela in 1814 – they were playing a dangerous game.

Yves Benot, in a survey of contemporary accounts of the great uprising, highlights a significant phrase used by the rebel leaders, one that echoes revolts in other parts of the colony. The leaders proclaim their intention is to 'seize the country'.[19] Carolyn Fick describes a somewhat similar idea conveyed by a French soldier in his description, in a letter home, of the outlook of slave rebels in the South: 'They come and treat us as if we were the brigands and tell us "*nous après tandé zaute*", which is to say, we had expected you, and we will cut off your heads to the last man; and that this land is not for you it is for us.'[20] Documents relating to the slave uprisings occasionally describe their goal as 'liberté', a word and concept much in play but not the same as universal emancipation or 'liberté générale'. The leaders of the Northern revolt negotiated for the liberty of their immediate followers, and for three free days a week (so they could cultivate their plots) and a ban on the whip, rather than for general emancipation.[21]

Pierre Pluchon cites a report that the black leaders were demanding 'liberty' as early as September 1791.[22] Of course, the term itself traditionally referred to the special liberties or privileges of the favoured subject, and only gradually gave way to the modern notion of general liberty. The fact that many rebel

---

19   Benot, 'Les insurgés de 1791', *Les Lumières, l'esclavage, la colonisation*, pp. 230–41. See also Benot's contribution to Geggus and Fiering, *The World of the Haitian Revolution*, pp. 99–110.

20   Carolyn Fick, *The Making of Haiti: The Saint Domingue Revolution from Below*, Knoxville 1990, p. 156. This remains an important work for grasping the meaning of the Haitian Revolution.

21   Ibid., pp. 114–15.

22   Pierre Pluchon, *Toussaint Louverture*, Paris 1984, p. 26.

leaders were ready to settle for a highly selective emancipation may only mean that they had yet to understand what was happening. Carolyn Fick shows evidence for hostility to the French and their *colons* related to a widespread revolt around Les Platons in the South, which preceded the rising on the Northern plain by nearly eight months. However, as we have seen, it was not to be until two years later, in August 1793, that the rival leaders issued unambiguous and quite general proclamations calling for a complete end to slavery.

With his customary scruple, Benot did not construct a stereotype of the slave revolutionary. These leaders have not yet committed themselves to ending slavery. Indeed many enlisted with a Spanish monarch who upheld it. In the situation created by the revolt, very tangible objectives – such as three free days a week, the freedom of this person or that, a ban on the harshest punishments, the fate of this garden or plot – had more purchase and meaning than French legal categories. The black leaders had a notion of kingship, and a willingness to exploit it for a variety of ends. This is something common to African and French political culture. The willingness of the rebels to invoke the distant king against local masters, unworthy officials, and racist colonists persisted for a while, but it weakened as French royalists and Spanish royal authorities upheld slavery.

Despite the occasional presence of the *fleur de lys*, the diffuse royalism of the black leaders was never pledged to a particular king. However, rumours that royalists were behind the slave revolt were widely credited by metropolitan Patriots. Some connected to the colonial lobby sought to portray the slave rebellion as a traitorous *vendée*, and such were the blinkers of the Patriot imagination that the charge was widely entertained. Racist Jacobins were dupes of their own conceit if they failed to notice that the British – the Republic's most dangerous enemy – responded in a very different way to these two revolts, encouraging the *vendée* while attempting to put down the slave uprising at the cost of the lives of tens of thousands of British soldiers. The moderate republican chronicler Garran-Coulon had no doubt that the slave rebels had an agenda of their own: 'One would have to have little understanding of human nature, if one were to believe that . . . the blacks needed any other inspiration than that irresistible impulsion of all living beings which . . . speaks perhaps even more to the hearts of those who are closest to nature.'[23] (In acknowledging the main point here we do not, of course, have to endorse the author's trope of Africans being 'closest to nature'.)

The slave community included both literate creoles and newly arrived Africans. Kréyole was far more widely spoken than French, and varieties of

---

23   Quoted in Jeremy Popkin, 'The French Revolution's Other Island: The Impact of Saint Domingue on Revolutionary Politics in France', in Geggus and Fiering, *The World of the Haitian Revolution*. pp. 199–222, 313.

African culture still had great importance. A famous Kréyole saying insists that *tou moun se moun*, which may be rendered as 'everyone is a person'. If this was already current in the Kréyole of the early 1790s, then we have the philosophical premises of a doctrine favourable to general liberty. Another approach would be a direct reworking of the French discourse of liberty, and this is found in a letter reputed to have been sent by three rebel leaders in July 1792 to the colonial assembly. In it they ask: 'Have you forgotten that you have formally vowed the Rights of Man?' and present as their first demand 'general liberty for all men detained in slavery'.[24] The appeal was ignored by the assembly. It is believed to have been drafted by Toussaint. Its conclusions were not subsequently sustained by its signatories. Biassou and Jean-François continued to serve the Spanish King, never subsequently attacked slavery and were even implicated in slave trading. So for a little while longer the genie of general liberty floated above the conflict, waiting to be claimed by its rightful possessors.

The *Amis des Noirs* had battled for the civic equality of free people of colour rather than the freedom of the slaves. In so doing they at least weakened the racial constraints on rights and citizenship, even if their attachment to the colonial system led them to great caution on slavery. The decision of the *Amis des Noirs* to focus on coloured rights was influenced by the *Société des Citoyens de Couleur*, for whom this was the key issue. It was the spokesmen of this club who – by coining the term *l'aristocratie de l'épiderme*, or 'aristocracy of the skin', to describe colonial racism – found a juncture between revolutionary discourse and their racially egalitarian concerns. They also persuaded the Girondins that the people of colour were the true friends of the Republic in the colonies. Finally they educated some of the Montagnards to adopt more enlightened positions on racial and colonial issues.[25]

Distracted and divided by the controversies over the free people of colour, the colonial authorities had failed to spot the preparations for slave revolt. When Camille Desmoulins declared 'Let the colonies perish rather than a principle', he was supporting a decree which extended full civic rights only to free coloured proprietors both of whose parents had been born on French soil (it was believed that only 400 qualified).[26] Eventually full recognition of the civic

---

24   Letter to the General Assembly from Biassou, Jean François and Belair (nephew of Toussaint Louverture). For an English translation see Toussaint Louverture, *The Haitian Revolution*, London 2008, pp. 5–8, 7. David Geggus warns that royalists sometimes fabricated documents linking slave insurrection to republican doctrine. See David Geggus, 'The Caribbean in the Age of Revolution', in David Armitage and Sanjay Subrahmanyam, eds, *The Age of Revolutions in Global Context, c. 1760–1840*, Basingstoke 2010, pp. 83–100, 96.

25   Florence Gauthier, *L'Aristocratie de l'épiderme*.

26   Yves Benot, *La révolution française et la fin des colonies*, Paris 1988, p. 76. This remark is sometimes wrongly attributed to Robespierre, who was not consistent on the subject. On 11 May 1791 he pertinently observed: 'the rights you offer the coloured proprietors can only strengthen the rights of the masters over their slaves' (p. 79). Conversely, as late as 18 November

rights of free men of colour was promoted by many Girondins. It may seem puzzling that a political network based in Bordeaux, France's premier colonial port, wished to enhance the status of the free people of colour. Generous sentiments played their part, and local pride in the 'free air' tradition of Guyène, but there was an important further consideration: recognition of mulatto rights would encourage the latter to support the colonial administration, and resist colonial whites who hankered for free trade and autonomy. The free coloured community in Saint-Domingue, now 30,000 strong, had long been seen by colonial officials as a check on the white *colons* and their wish for autonomy or even separation. The colonial whites' habit of flouting metropolitan authority and controls, and lording it over the free people of colour, meant that the ministry and the free coloured were natural allies. The colonial whites had created a great rumpus when the authorities created a coloured militia in the 1760s. By the later 1780s there were scores of coloured militia officers, several of whom had fought in North America against the British during the War of Independence. The coloured elite also comprised educated men and women, and planters who owned a fifth of the colony's slaves. Naturally the coloured population wished to enjoy the same rights and status as their white counterparts.

The Girondins backed the principle of coloured citizenship because they saw this as a righteous cause, as well as one which would cement the loyalty of the free coloured population. Jacobin counsels were more divided but eventually they, too, rallied to the cause of free coloured rights. On 4 April 1792 a decree was approved which extended active citizenship to all free coloured men, together with provisions to enlist them in militia battalions. White and coloured resident planters had been tentatively negotiating a common front against the metropolitan authorities, but the great bulk of the free coloured rallied to the incipiently republican camp, with only a handful of large coloured proprietors being prepared to throw in their lot with the royalists and the British. A new order began to form that would advance coloured rights while defending slavery. But with many of the whites, whether *grands* or *petits blancs,* opposing mulatto rights and republicanism, the factional division that favoured slave rebellion spread. Though all sides remained committed, in principle, to upholding slavery, some proprietors freed and armed some of their own slaves. In the course of 1793–4 the British occupied about a third of the colony with the assistance of the planters; they found a fragile slave order still in existence. While some slaves had run away, others remained attached to the plantations, and staple crops were still being produced.[27]

1793 he attacked the defeated Girondins for having tried to reduce the French poor to the status of helots, while wishing 'in an instant to liberate and arm the Negroes in order to destroy the colonies' (p. 81).

27   David Geggus, *Slavery, War and Revolution*, especially, pp. 100–14. This account makes good use of British military records, sometimes deflating claims concerning the impact

Sonthonax had published articles denouncing slavery and the white *colons* in *Révolutions de Paris*, one of the few journals to focus strongly on colonial issues.[28] Those who chose him to be commissioner of the Northern Province after the new law of 4 April 1792 will have counted on him vigorously to promote the Convention's strategy of allying with the free people of colour against the treachery of white colonists conspiring with the royalists and the British. The commissioner for the West was the like-minded Etienne Polverel. French Revolutionary political culture, however prone to paranoia, was not wrong to suspect that the *grands blancs* were in cahoots with the enemy. Sonthonax formed new coloured battalions and cracked down on counter-revolutionary conspiracies, causing much anger among the white colonists. This opposition was encouraged in mid-1793 by the arrival of a new military governor, General Galbaud, whom the white colonists hailed as a saviour. Though a republican, he had both property and family in Saint-Domingue, and was soon persuaded that Sonthonax and Polverel were ruining the colony with what he described as their 'negrophile system'.[29] The commissioners had simply pursued the construction of multi-racial order in conformity with metropolitan instructions. They appointed coloured officers both to a new legion of coloured troops and to the white garrison regiments. They freed slaves willing to fight for the Republic and arranged 'republican marriages', whereby a slave woman who married such a republican soldier was also freed. With Eugénie, his mulatto partner, on his arm, Sonthonax presided over official receptions at which – to the scandal of many white colonists – men and women of all colours would mingle.[30]

In June 1793 the commissioners ordered Galbaud to return to France, but this only spurred the governor to attempt to seize Le Cap, the capital of the Northern plain. His forces comprised sailors from the fleet in the harbour, some members of the garrison and companies of the white militia. On 20 June, the governor mounted an attack on Government House, the commissioners' headquarters, but the commissioners' forces – some whites but many more coloured and black – put up a strong resistance. Retreating to the Bréda plantation on the outskirts of Le Cap, Sonthonax took a string of fateful steps. He promoted black officers like Jean-Baptiste Belley, Henri Christophe and

---

of Revolutionary rhetoric, so that it is interesting when he registers the startling impact of Toussaint Louverture's 'volte face' in 1794 (p. 116) or the breakdown of the slave order by 1796 (p. 203).

28   Benot, *La révolution française et la fin des colonies*, pp. 142–3 and Robert Stein, *Léger Félicité Sonthonax: The Lost Sentinel of the Republic*, London 1985.

29   Jeremy Popkin, *You Are All Free: The Haitian Revolution and the Abolition of Slavery*, Cambridge 2010, p. 177.

30   Elizabeth Colwill, '*Fêtes d'hymen, fêtes de la liberté*': Matrimony, Emancipation and the Creation of the New Man', in David Geggus and Norman Fiering, eds, *The World of the Haitian Revolution*, pp. 125–55.

Pierre Michel to key commands in Le Cap.[31] Some important commanders remained loyal to the commissioners, notably General Etienne Laveaux and the mulatto veteran Jean Villate. Sonthonax also forged an alliance with Louis Pierrot, an African commander and insurgent chief who maintained an independent column in the hills flanking the Northern plain. Pierrot descended to the environs of Le Cap and helped to secure it for the commissioner. Galbaud and a few thousand of his supporters clambered aboard the ships in the harbour and sailed for the United States. The struggle in Le Cap was marked by looting and the burning of most of the city's buildings. The sailors began the pillage but many took part. Even more significantly, slavery itself was put to the torch. Sonthonax offered freedom and citizenship to black insurgents held in Le Cap's prisons and to the remaining residents of the Northern capital, numbering several thousands, so long as they joined the fight. The cry went up: 'You are all free!'[32] As the commissioners were well aware, further steps were necessary to confer full republican legitimacy on what had been an emergency measure.

The trouncing of Galbaud was celebrated in late July at a republican military parade outside Le Cap comprising 100 whites, 300 mulattoes and 6,000 black soldiers. Pierrot swore an oath of loyalty to the Republic. Sonthonax was adamant that the Republic was the indispensable vessel for equality: 'It is the kings who want slaves. It is the kings of Guinea who sell them to the white kings.'[33]

The Commune of Le Cap held a mass assembly of 15,000 'souls' on 26 August which passed by acclamation a call for the freeing of all slaves. The idea of 'general liberty' which had first surfaced a year earlier, in the appeal of three rebel leaders to the colonial assembly, was now adopted by a representative institution. On 29 August, Sonthonax issued a decree of general emancipation throughout the North.[34] Toussaint Louverture, then the commander of a large black force who still served the Spanish King, issued his own laconic declaration – on the same day – asserting that he was fighting to end slavery.

At a desperate moment for the Republic, Sonthonax had gone far beyond his instructions and powers. The Girondins who had sent him were moderate abolitionists who wanted to save the colonies from slave revolt, as well as prevent them declaring independence. Indeed the decree of April 1792 had

---

31   Belley, later to be elected to the Convention, has become the iconic 'black Jacobin'. Attired in his French deputy's uniform he proudly gazes out of Anne-Louis Girodet's 1797 painting, a bust of Raynal by his side. These events are recounted in Dubois, *Avengers of the New World*, pp. 155–65.

32   Popkin, '*You Are All Free!*', pp. 1–22.

33   Quoted in Dubois, *Avengers of the New World*, p. 159.

34   Ibid., pp. 156–63. Florence Gauthier, *Périssent les colonies plutôt qu'un principe!*, *Contribution à l'histoire de l'abolition de l'esclavage, 1789–1804*, Société des études robespierristes, Paris 2002, p. 108.

been in part a response to the great revolt of August 1791, as well as to the treachery of the white colonists; it was hoped that the free people of colour, who included quite a few slave-owners, would be a source of stability as well as loyalty.[35] But when the clash with Galbaud obliged Sonthonax to choose, he had decided that the best way of saving Saint-Domingue for France was to appeal to the black rebels and commit the Republic to emancipation. His decision chimed in with – perhaps inspired, perhaps reflected – the appeal for general liberty which the Commune of Le Cap had adopted six days before.

Beneath the legal and political terminology of competing decrees of general liberty was the reality of a massively exploitative slave system, a system detested by all blacks and many mulattoes because it exposed them to abuse. The slave-order was only held in place by force – that of the militia, *maréchaussée* (slave-catcher brigade), overseers, and elite slaves, including slave-drivers. In Saint-Domingue in 1792–4 all political actors had eventually to explain whether they wished to maintain, reform or abolish this regime. Once a degree of disorder reigned, the reliability of the slave elite vanished, and sometimes the whole crew would decamp at once. On the other hand, whether they thought of themselves as slaves or not, there was an attachment to land and family that led many to stay put.

The boldness of Sonthonax and Toussaint is that they were willing, as no abolitionist had been before, to end slavery immediately, without delay, compromise or compensation. In the rush of events, both men had exceeded their powers. But once the great assembly of the Commune at Le Cap on 26 August had called for such action, the die was cast. Sonthonax had perhaps set up this event, though we cannot be sure that he directly inspired the sweeping motion it passed.[36] He coupled his anti-slavery radicalism with a concern to ensure that the former slaves would continue working. New labour regulations required them to do so for at least another year. The whip was to be banned, and the cultivators were promised compensation equivalent to a third of the value of the crop. Cultivators also retained possession of their provision grounds, so long as they remained on the plantation. Polverel, who was based in Port Républicain (formerly Port-au-Prince) issued regulations which confiscated the property of enemies of the Republic. These estates were supposedly to be held in common by the cultivators and warriors, with a codicil that the land

---

35   A point made by Frédéric Régent, *Esclavage, métissage, liberté*, p. 437.

36   While Sonthonax may have persuaded the Commune to adopt general liberty – wishing to be seen to be responding to their call – it remains to explain the commissioner's preoccupation at this time with promoting marriage as a route to emancipation. If he intended to issue and implement a decree of general liberty, why concern himself with partial emancipations via marriage to enlisted men? For the latter see Colwill, '*Fêtes d'hymen, fêtes de la liberté*', pp. 125–55.

might be distributed after order had been restored.[37] While the French commissioners were preoccupied with ensuring continuing plantation labour, Toussaint, at this point, had no such concerns. His appeal simply offered an end to slavery.

While such decrees and pronouncements have their own powerful significance, they do so partly because they point us elsewhere – to what is happening in the countryside, hills and towns throughout the colony. The oath taken by Louis Pierrot in Le Cap, the rescue of Sonthonax by Jean-Baptiste Belley and his men, the parades and concerts in Le Cap, the calls for universal emancipation, all signal the emergence of a new racial order in response to counter-revolution – the British threat – and the surging tide of slave revolt. It was far from inevitable that the French Republic would catch this tide rather than being crushed by it. The sweeping proclamations and the insistent ceremonies were devices for transforming both the Republic and the slave insurgency. They were tributes to the pressure of the slave rebellion but, as such, they were still very incomplete – the Convention had not spoken – and the commissioners were in competition with Toussaint's simultaneous appeal.

The delegates dispatched by the commisioners to the National Convention – Louis Dufay, a white proprietor, Garnot, a mulatto, and Belley, the black commander – arrived at their destination thanks to the good offices of Edmond Genet, the French minster to the US, who welcomed them in Philadelphia, despite the intense hostility of the many French émigrés in the city. The delegates arrived shortly after news that the British had been cordially welcomed to Jéremie and other ports by royalist planters. Genet urged the French minister of foreign affairs not to worry about this since – so long as Paris responded boldly – the volcano of the slave insurgency would soon overwhelm these miserable traitors and lay the basis for a 'new France in the midst of the Mexican archipelago'.[38] The Convention's decision to seat black and brown representatives from Saint-Domingue in February 1794 was dramatic.[39] At this time the election of a black member to the British parliament or US Congress was unthinkable. When they first arrived, the delegates from Saint-Domingue had been arrested at the prompting of slanderous Patriots who claimed they were royalist agents. But they had been speedily freed. Their seating as deputies was a blow to the friends of slavery and the 'aristocracy of the skin'.

The positive reception of the delegates may have reflected awareness of the need for a quite new strategy. A memorandum submitted to the Committee of

---

37   Dubois, *Avengers of the New World*, pp. 165–70. See also one of the earliest histories of Haiti and its revolution, Gaspard Théodore Mollien, *Haiti ou Saint-Domingue*, 2 vols, vol. 1, Paris 2006, pp. 81–6.

38   Quoted in Popkin, *You Are All Free*, p. 322.

39   Popkin, 'The French Revolution's Other Island', in Geggus and Fiering, *The World of the Haitian Revolution*, pp. 199–222.

Public Safety on 28 December had urged: 'send the [blacks] arms and munitions. Confirm the rights extended to the mulattoes and the Negroes. Then the
genius of liberty will spur these new republicans to prodigious feats . . . Proud
Albion and old Spain will then pay for their sins.' Louis Dufay delivered a
lengthy address in the course of which he described his own journey from slave-
holder revolutionary to republican abolitionist: 'a friend of liberty and equality
had to also be a friend of humanity'. But, taking the justice of the emancipation
policy as given, he urged the huge advantages that would accrue if it was
adopted. The emancipated would become good customers for French goods:
'You will see your colony of Saint Domingue, cultivated by free hands will
become more flourishing . . . that soon it [Saint Domingue] will dominate the
entire archipelago of the Gulf of Mexico.'[40]

The debate led to the passage of a motion on 16 Pluviôse which pronounced
the end of slavery in the French colonies. This was itself a transformative
moment, but one which was over-determined by the insurgency in Saint-
Domingue, the outbreak of war and the radicalization of the sans culottes. Here
is perhaps one of those rare occasions when a text can redefine context and
subtext, because it is establishing a new horizon.

The motion passed read as follows: 'The National Convention declares slavery abolished in all the colonies. In consequence it declares that all men, without
distinction of colour, domiciled in the colonies, are French citizens and will
enjoy all the rights assured under the Constitution.' The ending of slavery and
the extension of citizenship offer a more clear-cut verdict on the institution
than any earlier declaration of rights. If we look at the words with a lawyer's eye,
the motion could be construed as being less radical than it might seem. Since
the Constitution was suspended, the precise import of the last promise was not
clear, while the phrase 'domiciled in the colonies' could be linked, via regulations that had already been reported, to continuing labour obligations laid on
the former slaves. But while some colonial proprietors may have comforted
themselves with such interpretations, the plain meaning of the motion is what
counts, and what counted at the time.[41] Levasseur of Sarthe, the man who
framed the motion, seems to have had no ulterior motive and, as 'an obscure
Montagnard', found it a 'sweet and consoling' memory.[42]

---

40   This is from *Le Moniteur*, quoted in Popkin *You Are All Free*, pp. 351, 357, 361.

41   The attempt of pro-slavery forces to somehow amend or stymie the motion is explained
by Yves Benot, 'Comment la Convention a-t-elle voté l'Abolition de l'esclavage en l'An II', in *Les
Lumières, l'esclavage, la colonisation*, pp. 252–63. See also Jean-Daniel Piquet, 'L'Emancipation des
Noirs dans les débats de la Société des Jacobins de Paris (1791–94)', in Marcel Dorigny, *Esclavage,
Résistances, et Abolitions*, Paris 2002, pp. 187–98. In *Mer et Liberté* Vertus Saint-Louis points to the
key role of the policeman André Amar in seeking to frustrate anti-slavery initiatives. The legal
dimensions are stressed by Miranda Frances Spieler, 'The Legal Structure of Colonial Rule During
the French Revolution', *William and Mary Quarterly*, April 2009, pp. 365–408.

42   Popkin, *You Are All Free*, p. 364.

Here is an account of a ceremony celebrating the decree, cited by Popkin:

> Despite his connections to the pro-slavery colonists, the elderly diarist Guittard found the ceremony impressive. He described the march of 'all the sections, the revolutionary committees of the sections, the clubs sent deputations with their banners, along with women and drummers, the members of the city assembly, a deputation from the National Assembly accompanied by veterans and grenadiers of the Convention, the musicians from the opera and a procession of Negroes and Negresses who live in Paris, along with three deputies who came from Saint Domingue to obtain this decree . . . Speeches were given, odes and appropriate songs sung. There was a big crowd. I was there and I had a good view.' Similar festivals were held in almost twenty other French cities and towns, sometimes at the behest of local Montagnard leaders, but sometimes as the result of an apparently spontaneous initiative.[43]

Ceremonies such as this ensured that a decree, once agreed, would actually be implemented. Foreign policy considerations seem to have occasioned a slight delay, but only of a few weeks.

The decree of Pluviôse was the Republic's offer of alliance to the black insurgents, and to the sizeable slave populations of the colonial territories still controlled by the royalist planters and their allies, the British. The decree was no doubt understood in this way by Toussaint when he declared for the Republic, a few months later. Laveaux's promotion of the black general, the dispatch of 30,000 muskets and much ammunition from France, and the offensive of Victor Hugues's forces in the Eastern Caribbean, all helped to spell out the meaning of 16 Pluviôse. Since the Constitution was suspended, the motion, together with instructions for its implementation, had the force of a decree.

It has always been clear that the French commitment to revolutionary emancipation gained support because it constituted a response to the large-scale British expedition to seize the French islands. But it cannot be dismissed as mere realpolitik. While emancipation fitted well with resistance to Britain, it also posed a great strategic risk – that of antagonizing the 'sister republic', the United States, the Republic's sole remaining friend. When the Convention had been debating the resolution on slavery, Robespierre was closeted with Page and Bruley, Jacobins from Saint-Domingue who energetically opposed Sonthonax and his emancipation policy. The hesitations of Robespierre and the Committee of Public Safety are likely to have stemmed as much from concern for the international situation as from the blind spots of republican discourse, and its obsession with plots. The friendship of the US would inescapably be threatened by an emancipation policy.

---

43   Popkin, *You Are All Free*, p. 371.

Robespierre delivered one of his most striking and eloquent addresses to the Convention, 'On the Principles of Political Morality', on 18 Pluviôse An II, two days after the emancipation decree. In it he celebrated the fact that the French people had at last displayed their true character, but warned that ultra-revolutionaries were jeopardizing the security of the Republic. France was by this time already at war with Austria, Prussia, Britain, Spain, Holland and a phalanx of princely states. Robespierre attacked hotheads who had no concern for France's allies and who wanted to go to war with the governments of the whole world.[44] He was, perhaps, thinking especially of the vital bond of friendship between the two 'sister republics', France and the United States. Vertus Saint-Louis, the Haitian historian, observes that concern for US reactions restrained the Jacobins: 'Up to 4 February 1794 they neglected the slaves as the Republic's best friends in the New World, and counted on the United States . . .'[45]

However, news was shortly to reach Paris that dashed hopes of continuing US friendship. Thomas Jefferson had stepped down as secretary of state in December 1793, and Washington had chosen to entrust to John Jay the task of negotiating a rapprochement with the British. Exactly when and how Robespierre and the Committee of Public Safety became aware of the new course of US policy is unclear. But reservations concerning the emancipation policy were swept aside, and in March–April 1794 the decree of Pluviôse was carried to the New World by the Hugues expedition to Guadeloupe and by another to republican Saint-Domingue, along with a large quantity of munitions.

The British expedition had seized the French islands of the Eastern Caribbean as well as significant territory in Saint-Domingue. The Hugues expedition recaptured Guadeloupe and its neighbouring islands, freeing slaves and enrolling them in the republican forces. But Martinique remained in British hands. The French republican forces also fostered slave unrest through the Caribbean and supported major insurgencies in Antigua and St Lucia. The Republic's emancipation policy showed boldness, not narrow calculation. It encouraged Toussaint Louverture to turn on the Spanish forces and rally to the Republic. The Revolution's prospects in the Caribbean were transformed. The policy of revolutionary emancipation was maintained after Robespierre's downfall, and inflicted heavy losses on the British. It also helped to trigger the 'Quasi-War', the undeclared naval conflict between France and the United States of 1796–9, and, as late as 1800, Denmark Vesey's conspiracy may have received some French encouragement.

---

44   The text of the speech is given in *Virtue and Terror: Slavoj Žižek Presents Robespierre*, edited by Jean Ducange, London 2007, pp. 108–26.

45   Vertus Saint-Louis, *Mer et Liberté*, p. 353.

In both metropolis and colonies, new mentalities emerged from the collapse of the *ancien régime*. Robespierre himself had already explained that revolution dissolved the 'dominion of habit', habits of subordination that were nourished by the culture of despotism and needed to be uprooted.[46] By the late eighteenth century racial slavery had instilled habits and assumptions that, it seemed, only a revolution on both sides of the Atlantic could challenge and change. In one of the earliest histories of the Haitian Revolution, Thomas Madiou explained that by 1792 the new revolutionary order had already brought about a profound change in everyday 'habits, customs and language'.[47] The crisis of the traditional order and the Revolution's own discourse of 'droits de l'homme' had combined with undercurrents of slave resistance to destroy the habits of subordination.[48]

The Jacobins were in the ascendant at the time the emancipation decree was passed, but the Girondins must be given credit for having sent Sonthonax to Saint-Domingue in 1792 and for educating the Convention on the need for anti-slavery measures.[49] The maintenance of the policy for several years after Robespierre's overthrow in Thermidor reflected both a Girondin echo and the emergence of a 'neo-Jacobin' current.

The French republican anti-slavery offensive lasted for a relatively brief period, from mid-1794 to late 1799, with a few wobbles. But given its audacity, the surprise should be that it lasted so long. The Directory which took charge after Robespierre's overthrow has a reputation for great moderation, abandoning Jacobin orientations. But so far as the Americas are concerned this is misleading. The Directory maintained the emancipationist strategy in the Caribbean, and reappointed Sonthonax. The Constitution it adopted held that the colonies were an integral part of the republic, governed by the same laws.

---

46   *Virtue and Terror*, p. 19. Žižek stresses the significance of these words.
47   Thomas Madiou, *Histoire de Haiti*, vol. 1, Port-au-Prince 1988 (originally 1847), p. 263.
48   Lynn Hunt, *Inventing Human Rights*, especially pp. 160–70.
49   Florence Gauthier points out that, following arguments put by Julien Raimond and Brissot, the *côté gauche* or left wing of the National Assembly had defined itself by opposing the racially exclusive approach of the Barnave ministry. See Florence Gauthier, *L'aristocratie de l'épiderme*, pp. 211–26. She also pays tribute to the educative role of some Girondins and of the Société des Citoyens de Couleur. Sibylle Fischer criticizes my account in *Overthrow of Colonial Slavery* for explaining Girondin colonial policy too much in economic terms. Sibylle Fischer, *Modernity Disavowed*, pp. 223–4. She sees this as contrary to my refusal of economic reductionism (pp. 15–16); but the impressive prosperity of Bordeaux and the Gironde did stem from its huge stake in the colonial complex. The most immediately effective elements of Girondin policy were those calling for the return of the colonies to metropolitan control, but there were different ways of pursuing this goal, and we may say that the strategic alliance the Girondins forged with the free people of colour was one of the more progressive. Moreover there was an emancipationist 'surplus' here which communicated itself to their Jacobin opponents, which informed the choice of Sonthonax and which was to animate the policy of the Directory. My account in *Overthrow of Colonial Slavery* may be a little too dismissive of Brissot but I did try to rescue the Directory's positive record, something which is often overlooked.

The radical anti-slavery policy gave a vital breathing space to Toussaint's republican black power in Saint-Domingue and helped him to defeat the Spanish, the British and the royalists. The Republic's offensive in the Eastern Caribbean tied down 45,000 British troops who could otherwise have been deployed in Saint-Domingue – and the British forces committed to the Caribbean exceeded those sent to fight in continental Europe. The British were able to occupy a large swathe of territory around Port-au-Prince, Môle St Nicolas and other enclaves, which they could sustain and connect by using their naval power. The plantations within the British-occupied zone in Saint-Domingue were still worked by slave crews and producing sugar. Slavery also survived in Spanish-occupied territory bordering Santo Domingo, the Spanish half of the island. Military pressure obliged Madrid to come to terms with the French Republic, and Toussaint managed to drive many Spanish forces back across the border. The British took longer to repulse. Nevertheless tens of thousands of British soldiers perished from illness and the difficulty of making headway against Toussaint, eventually leading the British commander to nego-tiate a withdrawal with the black leader. Albeit with further heavy losses, the British did succeed in regaining control of St Lucia and Antigua. In the British-controlled areas of Saint-Domingue some slaves had been freed and enrolled as military auxiliaries. Following the withdrawal from Saint-Domingue, thou-sands of slaves were specially purchased by the British to create a military force more resistant to the disease environment and to strengthen the defences of Jamaica and the islands of the Eastern Caribbean.

Toussaint, by himself, would have found it very difficult to build a black power capable of defeating the Spanish and the British and of uprooting slavery throughout the colony. While some black soldiers still fought for the Spanish, others confined themselves to defending a locality. Systems of slavery have usu-ally survived, though not unscathed, even huge revolts, such as those associated with Spartacus in Ancient Rome or the Zanj in eighth-century Mesopotamia. The French envoy Gaspard Théodore Mollien, writing in the 1820s after several years studying the history of the revolution, argued that if an expedition like Leclerc's in 1802 had been sent in 1795 to save slavery rather than re-establish it, the effort might well have succeeded.[50] Emancipation in the French colonies was a messy affair, with planters and commanders sometimes being able to seize freedmen or women and carry them beyond the reach of republican law. Given the dangers and uncertainties, some slaves were content to be evacuated to a place of safety.

The French Republic of 1794–9 should be given credit for sealing an alli-ance with black emancipation and giving it a few years to consolidate itself in Saint-Domingue. Nevertheless, the cause of black emancipation remained

---

50   Mollien, *Haiti ou Saint-Domingue*, vol. 1, p. 143.

fragile so long as it depended on the fluctuating fortunes of the Directory and its 'neo-Jacobins'. The rise of Napoleon Bonaparte, with his personal ties (via Josephine) to colonial planters, merchants and bankers, boded ill for the emancipationist policy. So did the prospect of peace, since it would give the French authorities an opportunity to restore control over their colonies. Bonaparte's decision to destroy black power in Saint-Domingue and attempt to restore slavery followed an ending of the 'Quasi-War' and the conclusion of the Peace of Amiens. The freed people of the French Caribbean needed a state to defend their new civic condition, with its vital element of personal autonomy. If the French state abandoned them they would need to found one of their own.

The black revolt contained a germ of independence from the outset, as Yves Benot noted. Toussaint's conclusion of a treaty with General Maitland, securing British withdrawal in 1798, was an act of sovereignty. Shortly thereafter Toussaint accepted help from US warships when moving forces to crush the mulatto general Rigaud – a rival who was closer to France. Finally he devised, and unilaterally proclaimed, a Constitution for Saint-Domingue in 1801. These acts, too, were those of a sovereign power. But it remains significant that Toussaint did not declare a formal breach with the French Republic – not even in his last battle with Leclerc. Perhaps he still harboured hopes of an agreement with Bonaparte, or a change in Paris; or he may have believed that, with the leading powers anxious for peace and fearful of slave revolt, no government would recognize an independent, black-led Saint-Domingue.

Toussaint himself had no difficulty in seeing that the Leclerc expedition was Bonaparte's bid to crush black power in the Caribbean, though many black and mulatto commanders were at first misled by the French general's assurances. Without the defeat of Leclerc, the anti-slavery idea would have been contained and relegated once again. Toussaint's attempt to resist the expedition was soon overwhelmed. So the core resistance to the French came not from the famous black and mulatto generals – most of whom accepted commissions from Leclerc – but from grass-roots leaders, many of them African-born. Toussaint himself, it is true, had held out for a while, but even he had capitulated and was captured, leaving the struggle to be continued by local commanders. The African-born were, after all, in a majority among the slave population. They supplied many, perhaps most, of the local leaders and soldiers at every stage, but especially in the resistance to Bonaparte in 1802–3. After a few months Henri Christophe, Alexandre Pétion and Jean-Jacques Dessalines abandoned the floundering French forces and, taking with them most of their troops, assumed the leadership of the fight against France. The new state of Haiti was to adopt European trappings, but Haiti's African roots were to be affirmed in the rites of the vodou, which give a central role to a re-enactment of the midnight ceremony at the Bois Caïman that had prepared the attendees for the great uprising in August 1791.

CURRENTS OF CARIBBEAN ANTI-SLAVERY

I have pinpointed the period July 1793 to May 1794 as being critical for the emergence of revolutionary emancipationism. Toussaint Louverture and Sonthonax made crucial decisions, but Pierrot, Polverel, Laveaux, Michel and Belley also played key roles. Only several years of sustained slave revolt and increasing metropolitan radicalization had produced the option for revolutionary emancipationism, followed by nearly a decade of battles against the Spanish, British and French which tempered and shaped the new black power, and set the scene for the proclamation of Haiti. The whole sequence was a triumph for the revolutionary concept of 'the rights of man'. But this should not be seen simply as a tropical vindication of the new values. The Caribbean setting radicalized the rights of man and anti-slavery ideas, in part by giving them a very tangible and specific content. The war-torn former colony, with a capsized economy, no foreign friends and lingering communal antagonisms, offered a difficult space for realizing its own lofty ambitions. But at least it gave tangible examples of what was needed, and broke once and for all with the endless procrastination of the European legislators and philanthropists for whom slavery had to be dismantled at an excruciatingly slow pace – in order not to jeopardize an economy of plantation colonies which produced the ingredients for a civilized existence.

The Haitian Revolution channelled mass longing for freedom into a ban on slavery. The existence of these longings can be inferred from the whole organization of colonial society. Planters acted as if their slaves might flee or hit back at any moment. That is why they and their retainers were armed to the teeth, and why they hired slave-catchers and cultivated the slave elite. While nearly every slave will have known resignation and defeat, they also knew that the overseer and planter depended on them and needed their compliant effort, and that individual resistance was limited and very risky, such that the freedom they sought could not be won without collective support. In Saint-Domingue in the 1780s there were very few maroon communities. The *maréchaussée* (slave-catchers) and their dogs were so effective that rebels preferred either to flee across the border to the Spanish half of the island or to practise *petit maronnage*, that is, taking refuge in nearby woods and hills, remaining in touch with the slave community and even negotiating with the overseer. The outbreak of factional war and the spread of slave revolt changed the context of slave resistance radically, allowing it to become more ambitious.

TOU MOUN SE MOUN

Charting the changes in slave mentalities at a time of revolution is very difficult. To take the measure of the Haitian achievement we have to dig beneath ready-made notions – whether of purely heroic rebels or of implacable caste hatreds – to bring to light the forging of new identities and new ideals in a colony where they already spoke a new language (Kréyole) and practised a new religion (vodou).[51] Sonthonax's decision to issue official decrees in Kréyole, the language spoken by the great mass of the slaves, as well as French was highly significant and a mark of his seriousness.

The waves of revolt which swept Saint-Domingue after August 1791 wrought great damage on slave-owners, but their emancipationist outcome was not preordained. The Haitian Revolution appealed powerfully to the Romantic imagination, but understanding it is not helped by the seductive and romantic notion that slaves were bound to rebel, bound to champion a general emancipation and bound to triumph (or to fail). Resistance has been ubiquitous in slave systems, but it has usually been particularistic – demanding freedom for a given person or group – and usually defeated.

The slavery encountered in Saint-Domingue and throughout the New World had been invented by planters and colonial officials, using European legal notions. Rather than dispute a legal concept, slaves often sought to extend concessions they had already won. Much slave resistance in Saint-Domingue in the early 1790s, as noted above, took the form of a demand for land and for three days off a week (instead of one). While the slaves on some plantations freed themselves simply by running away, others remained, unwilling to leave provision grounds which they saw as rightfully theirs. The decision to abandon a plantation or to stay put reflected local circumstances, but eventually it was the old or the young who were left.[52]

The slave community had a reality, notwithstanding the hierarchy and heterogeneity within it between creoles and African-born, or between different African nations. The racialized structure of exploitation fostered a countervailing solidarity, since only those of African descent were enslaved. The previously cited Kréyole saying *tou moun se moun* (everyone is a person) perhaps echoed African notions of *ubuntu* – a person is a person through other people.[53]

---

51   Laurent Dubois, *Colony of Citizens*. While Dubois focuses on the oceanic sweep of revolution in France and the French Caribbean, with considerable attention to the role of Guadeloupe, Frédéric Régent's welcome recent study *Esclavage, métissage et liberté* focuses more exclusively on events in Guadeloupe itself.

52   David Geggus, *Slavery, War and Revolution*, pp. 302–15.

53   For ubuntu (*ubuntu ngumuntu ngabantu*) see Jean-Bertrand Aristide, 'Introduction', Toussaint L'Ouverture, *The Haitian Revolution*, p. xxxiii. Aristide's own potent blend of Catholicism,

Mulattoes and poor whites born in the colony also spoke Kréyole and would consult vodou seers.

The African background of so many of Saint-Domingue's slaves meant that African values and concepts animated the liberation wars. The African influence was not, of course, itself homogenous. It would have been reworked in the New World context by young men and women who came from different parts of Africa. A widespread feature of African cultures was their multilingual, syncretistic, flexible and 'open' character compared with European societies, with their generally monoglot populations and comparatively uniform and rigid religious orders. The *ubuntu* tradition is only one strand of African thought, linked to Bantu culture, and should not itself be essentialized.[54]

While most of the well-known leaders of the revolution in Saint-Domingue were American-born, some commanders were African-born (Macaya, Sans Souci, Belley), and the same was true for many of the rank-and-file soldiers and middle-level leaders. They brought with them African ideas and methods of struggle. The insurgents often employed guerrilla tactics that they might well have practised as soldiers in Africa, prior to capture. The hierarchy of the plantation would typically favour creoles over Africans, but it stamped them both as *nègres* and menials, subject to the whims and cruelty of whites. Creoles were interested in Africa. New arrivals felt a special bond to those they had been shipped with, and an affinity to those who came from the same African nation. But creoles and Africans soon spoke the same language, participated in the same festivals and cults, and helped one another to survive the oppression they shared. While some would run away and others not, the planters believed that the maroons were in constant touch with those they left behind. Divisions and conflicts among the slave-holders gave opportunities to the slave community and brought into focus common aspirations. The failure of well-armed British, French and Spanish forces in Saint-Domingue testified to the former slaves' deep aversion to slavery, whatever the disappointments of freedom. At decisive points the *anciens libres* shared this aversion, since they knew that slavery was racially constructed and construed. Thus Henri Christophe, when still a French general in 1802, explained to his colleague General Pamphile de Lacroix that the danger faced by the authorities was not the scattered armed bands but 'the general opinion of the blacks'.[55]

Kréyole and 'African philosophy' was itself a synthesis of the religious and the secular, the European and the African. While very much belonging to its own epoch, it may also furnish some broad interpretive themes that may put us in touch with aspects of that lost world. There are fanciful aspects to the cited text by the former Haitian president, but it does pose sharply the problem of how tiny minorities of whites could have tyrannized colonies of blacks, and of the role of ideology ('mental slavery') in explaining this (pp. xviii–xxi).

54 See V. Y. Mudimbe, *The Invention of Africa: Gnosis, Philosophy and the Order of Knowledge*, London 1988.

55 Quoted in Fick, *The Making of Haiti,* p. 216.

The logic of racial polarization in Saint-Domingue was complicated, but not removed, by the fact that free coloured masters had owned about a fifth of the slaves in the colony. The coloured proprietors, unlike the whites, lived in the colony. While some threw in their lot with the white proprietors, most of the *anciens libres* came to oppose slavery. Louverture himself had been a freedman and his wife a slave-owner. Nineteenth-century Haiti proclaimed republican equality and decried caste distinctions, but the tension between black and mulatto endured and had to be negotiated anew within each generation.

The title of C. L. R. James's classic study, *Black Jacobins*, unsettled both the idea that emancipation had been a gift bestowed by the Republic and the idea that slave revolt was its own programme. The 'black Jacobins' found something in the discourse of the French Revolution which helped them to elevate and generalize their struggle. But at the same time they brought experiences of slave society and memories of Africa which radicalized the ideas they appropriated from, and eventually defended against, France itself. The travail of Africa's sons and daughters in the New World gave a new scope and meaning to the freedom they claimed. In citing the diversity of black revolutionary inspiration, Dubois cites the example of one captured and killed insurgent who was found in possession of a pamphlet on the Declaration of the Rights of Man, a packet of tinder, phosphate and lime, and a sack of herbs, bone and hair – a fetish in the Haitian vodou religion. Dubois comments: 'The law of liberty, ingredients for firing a gun, and a powerful amulet to call on the help of the gods: clearly, a potent combination.'[56]

VIVE LA RÉPUBLIQUE?

In *A Colony of Citizens* Dubois tells the little-known story of a revolt in April 1793 in the Trois Rivières district of Basse Terre, Guadeloupe. The royalists on three or four plantations had armed their slaves and told them that the time had come to move against the godless Republic. The slaves had instead risen against their masters, slaughtering more than twenty whites. A militia commander sent to find out what was happening reported: 'We saw a column of about two hundred men armed with rifles, pistols, sabres and axes. This column advanced in silence and in fairly good order; their movements did not seem hostile; they were allowed to approach within rifle range. When the advance sentinel called out, "Who goes there?", the negroes responded, "Citizens and friends!"'[57] Acting as Patriots, the rebels had decided that they must be citizens. The republican authorities, impressed by the 'surprising and almost unbelievable' patriotism

56   Ibid., p. 103.
57   Dubois, *Colony of Citizens*, p. 128.

and discipline of the citizen-slaves (since they were still formally enslaved) condoned their revolt, but their exact status was to remain uncertain until the following year, with the arrival of Hugues's expedition.

Under the Directory (1794–9) republican France was engaged in constant hostilities, including the so-called Quasi-War, or naval conflict, with the United States. From his base in Guadeloupe, Hugues sent out over thirty privateering vessels to prey on enemy shipping. The effectiveness of this policy, and the stream of prize goods he sent back to France, may help to explain why the Thermidorian regime pursued such a bold policy in the Caribbean. The *Amis des Noirs* was reconstituted, and offered support to slave emancipation throughout the Caribbean. This was a sign of the influence of a 'neo-Jacobin' current, to which Sonthonax (the former commissioner) and Laveaux (the general who had welcomed and supported Toussaint) both belonged.[58] Admiral Laurent Truguet, the minister for the navy and colonies, was a key member of this grouping. He nurtured an alliance with the coloured peoples of the Caribbean against the various slave powers, organizing supplies to the insurgents in the Eastern Caribbean and fostering a string of anti-slavery conspiracies and uprisings. (In Europe he gave backing to the United Irishmen.) But notwithstanding their Caribbean successes, Bonaparte had no time for the neo-Jacobins and their revolutionary strategies. He preferred to listen to the insistent advice of colonial proprietors who dreamt of a come-back – his wife, the daughter of a wealthy planter from Martinique, was well acquainted with this social circle. Truguet sent a letter to Bonaparte in 1799, defending the emancipation policy and denouncing those who 'dared to call themselves French' while supporting slavery.[59]

In a study of the *Guerre des Bois*, or 'Brigand's War', which inflicted such heavy casualties on the British in the Eastern Caribbean, David Barry Gaspar quotes the celebrated British commander General John Moore, directing operations in St Lucia, as declaring: 'The Negroes in the island are to a man attached to the French cause; neither hanging, threats or money would obtain for me any intelligence from them. Those on the estates are in league with those in the woods.' He later added: 'Their attachment and fidelity to the cause is great; they go to death with indifference. One man the other day denied, and persevered in doing so, that he had ever been with them or knew anything of them. The instant before he was shot he called out "*Vive la République!*" '.[60] This anti-slavery 'République' may have lasted barely half a dozen years, and the

---

58   Bernard Gainot, 'La Société des amis des noirs et des colonies, 1796–1799', in Marcel Dorigny and Bernard Gainot, *La Société des amis des noirs, 1788–99*, Paris 1998, pp. 299–396.

59   Dubois, *Colony of Citizens*, p. 352.

60   David Barry Gaspar, 'La Guerre des Bois', in David Barry Gaspar and David Geggus, eds, *A Turbulent Time: The French Revolution and the Greater Caribbean*, Bloomington 1997, pp. 102–30, 115–17.

considerations which animated it may often have been instrumental or even sordid; but without it, and the breathing space it allowed to the emancipation regime in Saint-Domingue, Haiti might never have come into existence.

In critical remarks aimed at those who see the Haitian Revolution as a contributor to modern concepts of human rights – notably Lynn Hunt and Laurent Dubois – Samuel Moyn contrasts this claim with what he takes to be the more hard-headed approach of C. L. R. James: 'He [James] did not think of presenting Toussaint Louverture and his confederates as human rights activists before their time. A Trotskyist, James' view of *droits de l'homme*, instead, seems to have been as the "wordy" promises of eloquent "phrase makers" who, driven by the true economic motor of history to "perorate", were in the end only willing to give up the aristocracy of the skin at the point of the gun.'[61] James was certainly scathing about those who prated about the 'rights of man' while upholding a vicious slave system. But James was neither a cynic nor one to reduce everything to 'the true economic motor of history'. He acknowledged the power of revolutionary ideals. He notes approvingly that Toussaint invokes 'liberty and equality' in his declaration of 29 August 1793.[62] Likewise James stressed the huge importance of the moral factor, insisting: 'It was the colonial question which demoralized the Constituent Assembly . . . If they had limited the franchise they had done so openly. But to avoid giving the Mulattoes the Rights of Man they had to descend to low dodges and crooked negotiations that destroyed their revolutionary integrity.'[63] In successive chapters James – who was indeed a Trotskyist – saw the conflict in Saint-Domingue as one involving *class struggle* as well as – eventually – national liberation. Hence he has successive chapters entitled 'The San Domingo Masses Begin' and 'The Paris Masses Complete'. Moyn elsewhere gives an account of the ending of slavery in Saint-Domingue/Haiti that simply skips the revolutionary emancipation period (1794–9) as if it was of no significance: 'Tousaint Louverture and others were spurred by the French Revolution to seize citizenship when Frenchmen did not live up to their rhetoric. But when the "cascade" did not happen by itself it had to be forced by violence, and what these radicals insisted on was mainly their right to be masters of their fate. Hunt pays homage to the "soft power of humanity".

---

61   Samuel Moyn, *The Last Utopia*, Cambridge, MA, 2010, p. 92.

62   James, *Black Jacobins*, rev. edn, London 1980, pp. 125–6. On another occasion James writes about the supporters of the decree of Pluviôse with a warmth that belies Moyn's interpretation of this author: 'Noble and generous working people of France and those millions of honest English Non-conformists who listened to their clergymen and gave strength to the English movement for the abolition of slavery! These are the people whom the sons of Africa and the lovers of humanity will remember with gratitude and affection'. *Black Jacobins*, p. 139. Notwithstanding this tribute, James cautions against the tendency to sanctify Toussaint or to portray him as 'an admirable example of a Protestant clergyman turned revolutionary' (p. 389).

63   Inid., p. 81.

Toussaint, for his part, found it necessary to resort to weapons.'[64] Yet for a vital period, as I have shown, Republican France did help – and arm – Toussaint Louverture, and did so, at least in part, because of the ideology – 'soft power' – of the 'rights of man' and 'liberty, equality and fraternity'. Toussaint's greatest achievements, after all, were made when he was a French general. Nevertheless, the French republican authorities were in many ways unworthy, and the time came when the blacks of Saint-Domingue had to defend themselves from a French army and to go beyond Toussaint by declaring independence.

The discourse of the 'rights of man' clearly did have an impact in Saint-Domingue, but there were other strands too, some of which I have noted already. I readily grant that it would be anachronistic to attribute modern human rights doctrines to revolutionaries in Saint-Domingue or Haiti in the 1790s, but putting it the other way round, considering anti-slavery's impact on modern political culture, and the diverse attempts to appropriate the abolitionist legacy, is another matter. (These are themes I return to in later chapters).

The discussions between French and US diplomats which ended the Quasi-War, and those with the British that led to the Peace of Amiens (December 1801–October 1803), enabled Bonaparte to move against the revolutionary order in Guadeloupe and Saint-Domingue. The Americans claimed that these colonies were piratical states akin to Algiers, one of the notorious rogue statelets of the Mediterranean.[65] The British and French both encouraged Bonaparte to restore slavery. Indeed, in returning Martinique to France with its slave order intact, the British made the restoration of slavery a consequence of the treaty.

After his negotiations with the North Americans, Toussaint Louverture discouraged privateering and undertook not to promote slave insurrections. This was sufficient for Adams, but not for Jefferson. When Toussaint's troops annexed Spanish Santo Domingo in 1801 he did not, Dubois tells us, immediately free the slaves. He even urged white proprietors to return, aware that they possessed needed skills and capital. Toussaint Louverture favoured the doctrine of the Catholic Church, especially since most of the priests left in the colony were prepared to accept his patronage – and to allow him to speak to their congregations from the pulpit. Toussaint Louverture's chief of staff, General Pierre Agé, was white, and overall his forces included around 800 whites in 1801.[66] None of the foregoing alters the fact that Toussaint ruled because he commanded a mainly black army. Whites who accepted the new order were welcome.

---

64   Samuel Moyn, 'The Genealogy of Morals', *The Nation*, 29 March 2007. The reference to 'cascade' is directed at Hunt's idea of a cascade of rights-claims.

65   A US naval expedition to Tripoli in 1801–4 to release American sailors held for ransom by the Bey explains why its 'shores' figure in the first lines of the Marine anthem.

66   Frédéric Régent, *La France et ses esclaves: De la colonisation aux abolitions*, Paris 2007, p. 265.

DECLINE OF THE PLANTATION

The colony's immensely profitable past and the rising prices of sugar, cotton and coffee led its new rulers to seek to restore the plantation economy. Both Toussaint and the French commissioners tried to devise incentives and penalties that would ensure that the cane was cut and ground. Cultivators were told that they would receive a share of the proceeds once the harvest was in, but few responded. Military commanders were converted into plantation managers and an attempt was made to confine the *cultivateurs* to obligatory labour and a narrow 'plantation citizenship'.[67] While black soldiers were honoured, black labourers were forced to stay on the plantation and work for the doubtful prospect of a small share of future revenue. Some commanders resorted to violence to keep the *cultivateurs* at work. That plantation output reached as much as a quarter of pre-revolutionary levels around 1800 shows that militarized labour was not entirely unproductive. But a coercive labour regime proved enormously difficult to enforce and sustain. Soldiers and *cultivateurs* did not see themselves as separate species, and both had witnessed the breakdown of authority. 'Slavery without the whip' proved an empty formula, while forced labour provoked rebellion.

Toussaint, desperate for the cash that would allow him to buy supplies, attempted to enact a coercive labour regime in 1801 but encountered stiff resistance led by his nephew Moyse. Toussaint's difficulty in rallying resistance to Leclerc stemmed in part from this failed experiment in unfree labour. Later rulers of Haiti made the same mistake. Henri Christophe, ruler of the short-lived Northern kingdom, had some limited success with a military mobilization of workers for plantation labour and construction projects, including his famous Citadel or palace at Sans Souci. His overthrow in 1820 reflected the difficulty of sustaining a forced labour regime among a people who had rejected slavery. In 1827 President Boyer issued a severe labour code, with provisions against vagrancy similar to those found in most European countries, but he lacked an administrative apparatus capable of implementing it. The peasants of Haiti simply refused to be dragooned, and armed irregulars (*piquets*) sometimes came to their aid. The revolution persisted thanks to their tenacity in the struggle for the control of time, land and movement, in and through several changes of formal jurisdiction, and whatever the stance of their leaders. While the Republic of Haiti presented a façade worthy of recognition by the Atlantic diplomatic world, the peasants of the interior were creating their own distinctive culture, with its own language, religious cults

---

67   The concept of plantation citizenship – *citoyenneté d'habitation* – is elaborated by Vertus Saint-Louis, *Mer et Liberté*, p. 315.

and music.[68] However, the exact relationship between *pays réel* and *pays légal* remains difficult to establish. The peasants had some need of a world of exchange, and the state was able to tax trade.

The more radical abolitionists, both white and black, were not abashed by evidence that slavery could be profitable since their indictment focused on the inhumanity and oppression of slave-holding. Whether white or coloured, they still found confirmation of their beliefs in the history of Saint-Domingue/Haiti, which showed both that slavery would breed violence and that former slaves would never tolerate a return to their earlier condition. Under slavery, slave births were always outnumbered by slave deaths, and the population of African descent only increased because of slave imports. In the half-century after emancipation the population roughly doubled. An autonomous peasantry established itself.

The new political economy of the late eighteenth century had encouraged anti-slavery thinking by insisting that free workers were more productive than slaves. But Bonaparte was not the only one to doubt this. The former slaves of Saint-Domingue and Guadeloupe abandoned plantation toil wherever they could, instead devoting themselves to subsistence cultivation.

Dubois cites several attempts to grapple with the problem of devising a post-slavery plantation regime. Etienne Polverel offered cultivators a share of the proceeds of the plantation, but had no way of ensuring that this would be carried out in a fair way. Julien Raimond, a leading man of colour who served as a revolutionary commissioner, appealed to the newly liberated in the following terms: 'It is necessary that you continue to work after acquiring your liberty, not only to procure all the things necessary for your new state but further to acquire property that will protect you in later years from want and insecurity.' He added that they would soon discover other obligations: 'in order to be equal to the free you will have to work . . . to procure all the objects of luxury and convenience that distinguish the free from the slave.'[69]

As noted above, most former slaves were deaf to such appeals. It was because they appreciated the luxury of free time, the convenience of meeting their own needs through their own efforts and, in many cases, the security of a parcel of land they were prepared to defend. Only force, not unreliable offers of pay, kept some at work. Guadeloupe's small size, and the special role of Hugues's expedition in bringing emancipation, made it easier for authorities there to keep the former slaves working, and later to return some of them to slavery.

---

68   A point often made for the revolutionary period by C. L. R. James in *The Black Jacobins* and Carolyn Fick in *The Making of the Haitian Revolution*. The continuing importance of peasant autonomy in the Republic of Haiti is stressed in influential work by Gérard Barthélémy, notably *Le Pays en dehors*, Port-au-Prince 1989. The latter's ideas are extensively discussed in the special issue of *Revue de la Société haïtienne d'histoire et de géographie* (January–June 2009).

69   Dubois, *Colony of Citizens*, pp. 183–4.

However, the reimposition of slavery in Guadeloupe in 1802 was only achieved after a bitter struggle. Just as British losses in the Eastern Caribbean had helped persuade them to negotiate with Louverture, so the heroic stand of Guadeloupe's coloured commanders and soldiers at Matouba helped to raise the alarm in Saint-Domingue. Dubois notes that in Guadeloupe several whites took part in what became a protracted war of resistance.[70] It is significant that the planters never succeeded in restoring night-work in the sugar mills on this island.

Raimond's idea of freedmen and women building their own consumer society was a fantasy, but his reasoning did appeal to many in the mulatto or black elite. When more settled conditions returned, a new middle-class stratum of merchants and officials, medium and small landowners and notaries began to emerge – though this process was stronger in the South and West, with their coloured proprietors, than in the North. However, any incipient Haitian bourgeoisie had to contend with formidable obstacles. The surplus generated by the trade with France was siphoned off first by French *rentiers* and then by Haiti's own political and military class. The small-holding peasantry was vulnerable to official exactions and many preferred to devote themselves to a local subsistence and barter economy. Haiti's internal market simply did not achieve the dimensions that would have been needed to fulfil Raimond's vision.

FRENCH RECOGNITION, CIVIL SOCIETY AND A TRIPLE REVOLUTION

Michel Hector and Laennec Hurbon argue that the Haitian revolution was a triple revolution – against 'slavery, colonialism and racial oppression' – and that its social base in the former slaves gave it 'a strong orientation towards rejection of the plantation system', and that this opened the way to a challenge to both feudal and capitalist property forms.[71] These formulations helpfully underscore the different but complementary role of race and exploitation. There were racial components to slavery and colonialism, and all these structures would not have existed unless they boosted national and planter wealth and swelled the output of plantation produce. So the triple revolution had a double consequence. It suppressed plantation slavery and affirmed racial equality.

Over successive decades, and in the course of rivalries within the Haitian elite, the former slaves and their descendants defeated various attempts to conscript them for plantation labour. Factions which insisted on disciplining the peasantry lost out. Medium and small farmers could not produce sugar, but they could cultivate coffee and some other secondary crops. The rehabilitation of sugar production would have required expensive mill machinery – and by

---

70   Ibid., pp. 415–16.
71   Michel Hector and Laennec Hurbon, eds, 'Introduction', *Genèse de l'état haïtien (1804–1859*, Port-au-Prince 2008, pp. 11–24, 16–7.

the 1820s, steam engines – and large-scale public investments in irrigation and communications. Saint-Domingue had been the richest colony only because of the elaborate irrigation and road works built by French engineers with slave labour. These had fallen into disrepair, and finding the labour, skills and materials to maintain them was a huge challenge.[72]

During the period 1804 to 1820, Haiti faced commercial blockade and diplomatic isolation at the hands of France and the United States, and even, in 1814, moves to restore French rule. For much of this time Haiti was politically fragmented but by 1820 the country was reunited and subsequently enjoyed a degree of recovery. While the slave population of Caribbean plantation colonies, if new arrivals are excluded, declined each year by one or two percentage points, Haiti's population grew. The country's French-educated notaries and lawyers applied the principle of partible inheritance, leading to the fragmentation of holdings, albeit that political and military chiefs sometimes carved out larger holdings for themselves.

In 1825 President Boyer obtained recognition, at a price, from the French monarchy. The Haitian government broke its diplomatic isolation and secured entry to the French market by agreeing to lower the tariffs on French imports, and to pay 150 million francs in compensation to the French proprietors of Saint-Domingue, their estates valued at prices current in 1789. In return France was to recognize Haitian independence and to admit Haitian produce, especially coffee. The estate valuations supposedly did not directly include the slaves but, of course, plantation land values certainly reflected the availability of slave labour to work them. The labour code enacted in 1827 was partly designed to reassure foreign bond-holders that Haiti had a disciplined work force, and did not tolerate idlers and vagrants. The first tranche of the indemnity was financed by floating a bond on the Paris bourse. In 1838 the debt would be restructured to make the payments more manageable. Nevertheless servicing the debt was an onerous drain on Haiti's public finances for many decades, and was not wound up until the 1880s.

The Franco-Haitian Treaty allowed Haitian coffee exports to rise to £1 million a year in the 1830s, making Haiti one of the leading producers. Unfortunately, the mere existence of the compensation debt prevented Haiti from floating any other bond on the Paris bourse to pay for badly needed investment in roads, bridges or waterways.[73] This constraint was the more

---

72   See Blackburn, *Making of New World Slavery*, pp. 402, 434–7. In my view too many studies neglect the role of economic factors in constraining the outcome of the Haitian Revolution.

73   Alex Dupuy, *Haiti in the World Economy: Class, Race and Underdevelopment since 1700*, London 1989, pp. 93–4. Dupuy is careful to put the debt problem in a wider context of neocolonial dependence on France. When President Aristide requested return of this compensation in 2003, Chirac, the French president, established a commission headed by Régis Debray, whose report found that even though Haiti had been 'impeccable' in its servicing of the debt, the repayment

significant since Haiti's constitution barred foreigners from making direct investments in land.

As Atlantic demand for coffee grew by leaps and bounds, it was to be the planters of Brazil who proved capable of doubling the size of their crop each decade, thanks to slavery and a spreading rail network. In an increasingly free market, slave labour in Cuba, Brazil and the US South proved more effective than Haiti's peasant smallholders at producing the coveted items of an expanding consumer culture, whether it was coffee, cotton or sugar.

Nevertheless Haitian producers had a niche market in better-quality coffee. The country's export earnings helped to sustain a modest but educated middle class. The Liberal Revolution which swept the ageing Boyer from power in 1843 was almost bloodless, following a campaign against him in the press, in the national assembly and eventually in the streets. While the former president sought exile in Jamaica, a 'Society for the Rights of Man and the Citizen' decried his dictatorial tendencies. The Haitian military sought to arbitrate disputes within the political elite but had to take care not to provoke the *piquets*, or autonomous peasant militias. The various elite factions invariably claimed that they opposed any racial caste regime, accusing their opponents of favouring either blacks or mulattoes. Whichever faction prevailed all subscribed, at least formally, to a new and very unusual doctrine: that of racial equality.[74]

The recovery of the population of Haiti in the period 1804 to 1840 reflected a sharp drop in deaths due to overwork and the burdens placed on slave mothers. The ending of captive arrivals from Africa reduced death from disease – though the demanding disease environment had still made a huge contribution to the losses of British and French invaders. In the years 1791 to 1804 the ravages of war had involved heavy loss of life, but thereafter conflicts between Haitian factions were often settled by shows of force and some periods – such as 1822–43 – were largely peaceful.

Military conflicts, revolutionary ideology and nationalism all contributed to giving a strongly masculine character to Haiti's political system. There were some female soldiers and the exploits of a few of these, notably Marie Jeanne's heroism in the defence of Crête-à-Pierrot, were celebrated. Suzanne Simone, Toussaint's wife, and Claire Heureuse, Dessalines's wife, were public figures.[75]

---

proposed by Aristide was wholly inappropriate. See Peter Hallward, *Damming the Flood: Haiti and the Politics of Containment*, London 2010, pp. 228–9.

74   The apparently diverse accounts supplied by Beaubrun Ardouin, Thomas Madiou, David Nicholls and Mimi Sheller suggest such a common discursive matrix even though they do not themselves draw this conclusion. See Beaubrun Ardouin, *Etudes sur l'histoire d'Haïti*, Paris 1860; Thomas Madiou, *Histoire d'Haïti*, Port-au-Prince 1845–7; David Nicholls, *From Dessalines to Duvalier: Race, Colour and National Independence in Haiti*, London 1987; Mimi Sheller, *Democracy After Slavery: Black Publics and Peasant Radicalism in Haiti and Jamaica*, London 2000, pp. 49–61.

75   Sabine Manigat, 'Le Rôle des femmes', in Hector and Hurbon, *Genèse de l'état haïtien*, pp. 331–7.

But the real changes for women were not at the elite level. The overthrow of slavery had brought fundamental changes in women's position. Fewer women than men obtained privileges under slavery. With the suppression of slavery they still had to work hard, but were better able to enjoy the rewards. Men comprised two-thirds of the slaves arriving from Africa, and the attempts that were made to keep these Africans working focused on the men as well as the women. However, the crumbling of the plantation system freed both sexes from the toil of the slave gang. The position of women improved a little once a degree of pacification was achieved. Women, while certainly excluded from all political roles, were not absent as social and economic agents. While the elite aspired to an observance of the family norms preached by the Catholic Church, the family structure practised by the mass of the population was more flexible. The 1805 Constitution devoted twenty-five pages to the question of divorce and the status of children born out of wedlock. These laws envisaged women having custody of their children, and required former husbands to contribute to their upkeep. Women were not allowed to divorce men absent on military service, but they could unilaterally divorce husbands who had emigrated. These laws, if applied, were more liberal than those prevailing in Europe at this time, while remaining broadly patriarchal nonetheless.[76]

Population growth testified to a revival of family life, with considerable responsibility in the hands of women. It was widely observed that women held the purse strings and – West African style – dominated local markets. The *revendeuse* bought and sold a vast range of produce, while the coffee *spéculatrices* were women who bought the crop from the peasant and sold it to the export houses. In 1843 some women came out openly against Boyer: allowing this looked weak, but it would have been worse to fire on them. In 1867 a march of market women brandishing their butcher's knives supported President Salnave; he appointed two as army generals.[77] Furthermore women were often respected because of their knowledge of sorcery and the secrets of vodou. The *manbo* or vodou priestess could cast out a zombie or restore a *petit bon ange*.[78] Some would be recognized as the *Reine de la rara*, or Queen of the shrine. Women's spiritual power could also be misused or subordinated in various ways, but it did command some respect. Altogether Haiti's civil society was by no means mono-lithically patriarchal.[79] A common sight in Port-au-Prince, persisting into the

---

76 *Lois et Actes sous le règne de Jean-Jacques Dessalines*, Port-au-Prince 2006, pp. 77–105.

77 David Nicholls, 'Holding the Purse Strings: Women in Haiti', *Haiti in Caribbean Context: Ethnicity, Economy and Revolt*, London 1985, pp. 121–9.

78 Laennec Hurbon, *Le Barbare imaginaire*, Paris 2007, p. 181.

79 I believe that the foregoing qualifies the conclusions of a text which, though posing some very necessary questions, underestimates the changes in women's position in Haiti. See the 'Introduction' to Pamela Scully and Diane Paton, eds, *Gender and Slave Emancipation in the Atlantic World*, Durham, NC 2005, pp. 1–33.

twenty-first century, was that of women carrying baskets of produce, or piles of washing, on their heads. This image perhaps sums up the ambivalent position of Haitian women carrying a special burden, but also thereby commanding respect and acquiring influence.

A 'NEARLY GENOCIDAL' REVOLUTION?

Haiti's belated admission to the Pantheon of revolutionary history has been followed, at no lengthy interval, by a wave of revisionism which questions the claims that have been made on its behalf. The leaders of the Haitian Revolution have been accused of 'quasi-genocidal' actions, and of labour coercion tantamount to outright slavery. Such claims, if justified, would contradict the idea that the Revolution signalled a victory for the rights of man. Before looking at the detail of the events of 1803–4, the background should be considered.

The revolution in Saint-Domingue was marked by great loss of life, much destruction and many violations of the rules of war. Slave uprisings, war to the death against the British, Spanish and French, the struggle for power between black and mulatto leaders, led to atrocities and bloodshed. The predatory European states had evolved rules of war when fighting one another, but such rules did not apply to colonial situations or to the repression of slave uprisings. New World slavery was a violent, arbitrary and racialized institution, imposed on a diverse population of captives. Attempts to escape it, overthrow it, or restore it thawed the state of frozen race war which it represented. Slave-owners and their henchmen fought to keep their slaves in subjection, and their actions were to be backed by the strongest Atlantic states. Some historians even reach the pessimistic conclusion that the Haitian Revolution, despite freeing half a million slaves, was a setback rather than a victory, because its bloodshed and racial violence undermined the claims of abolitionists.[80]

Toussaint's rise had reflected not simply his prowess as a commander but also his awareness that political and moral factors were at stake in the conflicts engulfing Saint-Domingue. As a black general he was known sometimes to urge a policy of clemency towards prisoners, and his staff numbered several key white and mulatto aides. He conducted his former owner and his family to safety in August 1791, before joining the rebels. On one occasion he addressed a magisterial rebuke to a British officer, General John White, whose troops had executed prisoners: 'I feel that though I am a Negro, though I have not received as fine an education as you and the officers of His Britannic Majesty, I feel, I say, that such infamy on my part would reflect on my country and tarnish its glory.'[81]

---

80   It is to the credit of the key abolitionist leaders – Wilberforce, Clarkson, Garrison, Schoelcher – that atrocities committed by insurgent slaves in Saint-Domingue or elsewhere did not mitigate their hostility to slavery or respect for the leaders of the Haitian Revolution.

81   Quoted in James, *Black Jacobins*, p. 201.

Louverture's willingness to join forces with the French Republic was also consistent with this approach. He explained his conduct to the Directory in terms of a stern new moral order: 'Whatever their colour only one distinction must exist between men, that of good and evil. When blacks, men of colour and whites are under the same laws, they must be equally protected and equally repressed when they deviate from them.'[82] With some exceptions (mainly the war against Rigaud), Toussaint generally sought to frame broad alliances, to abstain from race war, to concentrate overwhelming force, and avoid disproportionate violence. Other leaders were less deliberate and strategic. The wives of Christophe and Dessalines appealed for clemency, but their husbands practised exemplary violence, often racially targeted.

Colonial wars and civil wars have been notoriously pitiless, and the fighting in Saint-Domingue partook of both types of conflict. Seymour Drescher not only rejects the idea of a Haitian contribution to the 'rights of man', he also argues that 'in the end it was the Haitian victors who were to carry the conflict to its nearly genocidal climax, massacring most of the French who had not reached the blockading British warships and surrendered.'[83] This episode is often cited as proof of the bloodthirsty character of the Haitian Revolution, and it does seem likely that many hundreds of French were slaughtered and that the victims included women and children, and whites who were not French. But what was the context and scale of this deplorable event? In the preceding weeks Rochambeau's forces had been besieged in Le Cap. In November there were talks between the defenders, the besiegers and the envoy of the commander of the British warships off the coast (Britain was once again at war with France). A truce was arranged on 19 November, allowing for the evacuation of Rochambeau's forces and those civilians who wished to leave. A total of 18,000 refugees, including 8,000 soldiers, were taken off by

---

82   Toussaint Louverture to the Directory, 28 October 1797, George F. Tyson, *Toussaint L'Ouverture*, Englewood Heights 1973, p. 43.

83   Seymour Drescher, *Abolition: A History of Slavery and Antislavery*, Cambridge 2009, p. 166. I should make it clear that Drescher has been quite consistent over several decades in his scepticism concerning a positive Haitian contribution to abolition. In 1997 Drescher argued: 'In . . . late twentieth-century perspective, the age of the democratic revolution was also recognized as an age of racial and genocidal conflict. In that respect . . . the Haitian Revolution anticipated more of the world's future than . . . could have [been] imagined a century ago.' Drescher, 'The Limits of Example', in David Geggus, ed., *The Impact of the Haitian Revolution on the Atlantic World*, Charleston 2001, pp. 10–14, 13. I would instead urge that it is wrong to single out the independence movements. The events in Saint-Domingue/Haiti in 1802–4 prefigure the colonial repression and anti-colonial resistance seen in Cuba in the 1890s, China in the 1930s, Algeria in the 1950s and Vietnam in the 1960s, much more closely than they do the genocidal extermination of Armenians in 1916, of Jews in Nazi Germany or Tutsi in Rwanda in the 1990s. There are no cases I am aware of where the colonized have perpetrated genocide against the colonizers. Colonizing powers have usually been restrained by the wish not to destroy the value of their colony, but in Saint-Domingue they were thinking of importing tens of thousands of new slaves. On modern genocide see Michael Mann, *The Dark Side of Democracy: Explaining Ethnic Cleansing*, Cambridge 2005.

thirty vessels. Dessalines had just defeated Rochambeau's forces in a pitched battle, so allowing this evacuation was an act of signal moderation. However, with this operation nearly complete the insurgents occupied the Northern capital, pillaging the town and killing any who stood in their way. Given the evacuation – and the prior siege – the number of whites still remaining cannot have been very great. When the insurgent forces captured Port-au-Prince, they found ninety-two whites left in the town and killed most of them.[84] Since whites who remained were probably willing to accept the new authorities, their slaughter was the more reprehensible. As the insurgents moved towards independence, whites did confront a new and difficult choice: as French citizens, did they want to abandon their nationality and actively support secession? Even those opposed to the First Consul could find these questions difficult to answer. The suspicious Dessalines no doubt drew his own grim conclusions.

Echoing Drescher, David Geggus writes that the actions and decrees of the Haitian leaders in 1803–4 were 'quasi-genocidal'.[85] The Declaration of Independence branded the French as 'monsters' whose crimes justified vengeance. Geggus does not mention a half-apology for excesses which this document also contained. An anonymous account quotes a decree of January calling for the death of the remaining French – 'exterminate the tygers' – but notes that the populace failed to respond. The decree itself was composed in a blustering French style which could have meant little to the black soldiery.[86] Was there ever a Kréyole version of this decree? It is as if it was chiefly intended to scare the remaining French, who would have been able to read it. Thomas Madiou, the mid-nineteenth-century historian, accepts that, under orders, black troops did slaughter some thousands of whites during this period.[87] While the influential book *The Present State of Haiti* (1828), by James Franklin, harped on racial violence with the stated goal of rebutting prior accounts 'too much coloured by the zealous advocates of negro independence', many Haitian writers belonged to that strong current in the country's civil society which wished to disavow the partisans of racial violence and unending vengeance.

Mulatto and *ancien-libre* writers agreed that Dessalines had been the most ferocious commander, whether fighting for Toussaint against Rigaud in 1799, in 1802 for Leclerc or against the French in 1803. While there were violent clashes after Dessalines's removal, they were much less bloody. The convenience of blaming Dessalines, especially after his death, is evident enough. But the earlier bloodshed reflected not factional squabbling over the fruits of office, but the

---

84   Thomas Ott, *The Haitian Revolution, 1789–1804*, pp. 176–9.

85   Geggus, 'The Caribbean in the Age of Revolution', in Armitage and Brahmanyam, *The Age of Revolutions in Global Context*, p. 99.

86   *History of the Island of Santo Domingo*, London 1818, reprinted New York 1824 by Mahlon Day, pp. 177–81.

87   Madiou, *Histoire d'Haïti*, vol. 3, pp. 159–79.

refusals of the white Atlantic powers to accept black freedom and independence. David Geggus is too good a historian not to be aware of this. In 2004 he explained: 'Dessalines had been responsible for the death of many blacks and *anciens libres*. However he was the ideal person to lead the struggle to expel the French, and not only because he was the senior general. A menial slave under the old regime he had none of the liking for white society which Toussaint and the former domestic Christophe, shared with the *anciens libres*. He spoke only *Kréyole*, language of the cultivators. And he was possessed of demonic energy: his battle cry was "Burn houses, cut off heads!".'[88]

The portrayal of Dessalines rings true. But was he the sort of bloodthirsty warrior that national and civil wars throw up, or was he something worse? It is important not to devalue the term genocide, which refers not simply to racial violence but to racial violence on such a sustained and broad scale as to threaten the very existence of the target people or ethnic group, or a significant part of such a people or group. Nearly all the whites slaughtered by Dessalines' forces were born in France, and many of the adult males among them will have been party to French repression. The Haitian government had reason to fear the French because neighbouring Santo Domingo remained under French military occupation, and was thus a continuing threat. Slaughtering prisoners and civilians is ethically wrong, but not necessarily genocidal or 'quasi-genocidal'. British actions in the Caribbean theatre were brutal, involving exemplary violence and almost certainly the use of torture, but they were not genocidal. Leclerc's desperate arguments and actions, by contrast, aimed to kill huge numbers and often targeted his own coloured troops. He aimed to destroy the black community, and to replace it with a new one transported from Africa once that had been done. The discourse of early Haitian nationalism was intolerant of the French, but this intolerance was fed by continuing French threats, especially the ominous clause in the Treaty of Paris which proclaimed French sovereignty over 'Saint-Domingue'.

As Geggus is well aware, the insurgent massacres were a direct response to French massacres on a considerably larger scale.[89] The insurgent claim that the French forces killed 60,000 in 1802–3 has not been challenged. In September 1802 the increasingly isolated Leclerc wrote to Paris: 'We must destroy all the blacks of the mountain, men and women, and spare only children under twelve years old. We must destroy half of those in the plains, and must not leave a single coloured person in the colony who has worn epaulettes.'[90] He was promised reinforcements. Shortly thereafter Leclerc began to arrest and imprison the

---

88   Geggus, 'The Haitian Revolution', *Haitian Revolutionary Studies*, pp. 5–32, 26.

89   See Geggus, 'The Caribbean in the Age of Revolution', note 68, p. 245, where he writes of the 'genocidal tactics' used by the French in the war of independence.

90   Leclerc to Bonaparte, 7 October 1802. Cited in Dubois, *Avengers of the New World*, pp. 291–2.

coloured soldiers still in French ranks. One of Leclerc's officers lamented that 4,000 coloured troops had been loaded on hulks and drowned off Le Cap: 'This is how we are fighting this war.'[91] Leclerc nominated Rochambeau as his successor, explaining that he 'hated the blacks'. Indeed Rochambeau had already won a reputation as the expedition's worst butcher.[92]

The years 1791 to 1804 were certainly very bloody. But the British and French leaders bear the main responsibility for the violence, which stemmed from their own attempts to defend or restore Saint-Domingue's slave order. In 1790 there were 30,000 whites in Saint-Domingue. While some were killed, often no doubt because they were white, most fled to the United States, Cuba, France and other destinations. The British and French troops certainly suffered heavy losses, nine-tenths of which were from disease, some from fighting and a few from massacres. While it is virtually impossible to give exact figures, it is likely that at least 150,000 black and coloured people died in Saint-Domingue as a result of the invasions. The prime responsibility for all these losses must reside with the British and French leaders who ordered or conducted them. The racial strife and communal bloodletting which attended the collapse of the old order in Saint-Domingue stemmed from the attempt to defend and uphold racial slavery and colonialism. This having been said, the combatants on all sides committed atrocities and slaughtered innocents. Jean-Jacques Dessalines, Haiti's first ruler, had contributed to this wanton bloodshed, as we have seen. While guilty of ordering racial massacres, he did not elaborate a consistent racial ideology, and a number of his fellow leaders sought to disown, not endorse, racial violence.

Despite the bloodthirsty sentiments attributed – not without reason – to the authors of Haitian independence, the official documents of the new state sound a different note: the Declaration of Independence issued in 1804 both acknowledged and apologized for 'the cruelty of a few soldiers and cultivators too much blinded by memories of their past sufferings'.[93] Allowing that it was not just a few, any such admission and apology is nevertheless highly unusual in documents of this type.

The Haitian Constitution of 1805 was prefaced by the declaration of its signatories that they stood 'In the presence of the Supreme Being before whom all mortals are equal and who has scattered so many beings over the surface of the earth, with the sole goal of manifesting his glory and his might through the

---

91   Cited in ibid., pp. 289–90.

92   Fick, *The Making of Haiti*, pp. 219–29. See also Carolyn Fick, 'La résistance populaire au Corps Expéditionnaire', in Yves Benot and Marcel Dorigny, eds, *Rétablissement de l'esclavage dans les colonies françaises*, Paris 2003, pp. 127–48.

93   'Declaration of the Independence of the Blacks of St. Domingo', 29 November 1803, reprinted in *The Haitian Revolution, 1784–1804*, catalogue of an exhibition at the John Carter Brown Library, May–September 2004, edited by Malick W. Ghachem, Providence 2004, p. 26.

diversity of his works. Before the whole creation, whose disowned children we have so unjustly and for so long been considered: We declare that the terms of the present Constitution are the free, spontaneous and determined expression of our hearts and of the general will of our fellow citizens.'[94]

Dessalines endorsed the Constitution, though his actions in the previous year had utterly belied its lofty sentiments. In October 1804 he crowned himself Emperor; within less than two years he was ambushed and killed by fellow generals who claimed that he was too violent and erratic. Thereafter political change often involved shows of force or brief military clashes, sufficient to establish who was strongest.

Thus the final stages of the Haitian Revolution were marked by racial slaughter, but the Republic to which it had given rise aspired to repudiate such violence. Dessalines's brutality stimulated a counter-doctrine of racial and civic harmony. The Republic echoed the Revolution by defining itself against the slavery and caste spirit of the colonial order – a caste spirit which Bonaparte had tried so recently to revive. The Haitian elite and the mass of Haitians were reaching for a new life and a new nation. The number of remaining Europeans was small, with succeeding governments actively seeking to attract overseas school-teachers, doctors, missionaries and specialists. Haitian political life and civil society included tenacious currents which decried racial violence, because they saw it as destructive and inimical to the best ideals of the nation's founding.

Thomas Madiou's very critical account of the bloodshed in 1803–4, in the third volume of his *Histoire d'Haïti* (1847), was itself a contribution to a republican culture which deplored and rejected race war.[95] The republican doctrine of racial reconciliation and harmony was to be constantly frayed in the first century of independence by bickering between blacks and mulattoes – and also constantly reaffirmed through compromise within the elite, and between the elite and the peasantry. The military and landed elite had a significant black component, though mulattoes were the majority of the educated. The somewhat black National Party and the somewhat *mulâtre* Liberal Party were both elite outfits, and both adopted European models. The *politique de doublure* meant that if a grizzled black veteran held the presidency then he was bound to be a front for a mulatto faction, just as a *noiriste* administration would be sure

---

94   'Imperial Constitution of Haiti' in Fischer, *Modernity Disavowed*, pp. 275–81, 274. Article 13 declared that whites would not be able to own land, article 14 that this did not apply to already naturalized white women or to naturalized Germans and Poles, and article 15 that '[a]ll distinctions of colour will by necessity disappear . . . Haitians shall be known from now on by the generic denomination of blacks.' (p. 275). The latter clause was dropped from future constitutions. Although Haiti would be an empire, succession was to be 'elective not hereditary' and any ruler who departed from the Constitution was 'to be considered in a state of war with society' and the Council of State was to remove him (p. 276). For the French text, see *Lois et Actes sous le règne de Jean-Jacques Dessalines*.

95   Thomas Madiou, *Histoire d'Haiti*, vol II1, Port-au-Prince 1988 (originally 1847).

to find a prominent post for a mulatto poet or historian. (Baron Vastey, the chief ideologist for Henri Christophe's black monarchy, was a light-skinned *jaune*).[96]

In the years after 1806, Dessalines's sanguinary rule was widely portrayed as the aberrant prehistory of the Haitian state; after all, the Republic was not founded until after his death. In the early decades the bloodthirsty emperor had few defenders. But by the 1850s Madiou began to have qualms about the country's attitude to its past: 'Let us show that we have a memory; it is time we did.' He had a duty, he said, to speak about 'the man of the past, the serf who became an emperor. Giant of Antiquity he raises his monument by blood and sweat alone. His work is the result of this profound conviction that only independence could make the people of our island happy . . . Shuddering with horror and admiration we do not know whether to condemn or absolve him. Moral standards condemn him, but does not the logic of national salvation cleanse him? The enemies of independence saw in him a merciless being. The very incarnation of the principle of freedom, he was barbaric in the face of colonial barbarism.'[97]

The meaning of such a reassessment in mid-nineteenth-century Haiti was not an incipient apologetics for 'quasi-genocidal' actions or watchwords, but rather a greater willingness on the part of the largely mulatto, educated elite to acknowledge the black majority. The Haitian national pantheon had to find room for Dessalines, just as British history has to find room for Oliver Cromwell and his Irish campaign, or Robert Peel and British responsibility for the Irish famine. Likewise, US history has to face up to the Indian-removal policies of Thomas Jefferson and Andrew Jackson. If there was a 'quasi-genocidal' element in the Haitian Revolution, and the charge is far from proven, then at least Haitian nationalism sought to confront its own demons – already in the nineteenth century – rather than deny or obfuscate them.

The overthrow of Dessalines in 1806 had a further significance. It was a turning point in a complex struggle within the Haitian elite. This struggle pitted creoles against the African-born, blacks against mulattoes, and – last but not least – supporters against opponents of the conscription of labour for plantation agriculture. Fundamentally these disputes saw *anciens libres* (former free blacks or mulattos) struggle to contain and control black generals who were *nouveaux libres* (former slaves). Many of the *anciens libres* recoiled from the violent excesses of the liberation struggle. The war between black and mulatto military leaders in 1799 bequeathed a tangible fear of race war. The official documents of 1804–6 give evidence of contradictory impulses. Beyond signing his name, Dessalines was illiterate and had to rely on secretaries and advisers in drawing

---

96   David Nicholls, 'Class, Caste and Colour in Haiti', *Haiti in Caribbean Context: Ethnicity, Economy and Revolt*, London 1985, pp. 21–35.

97   Quoted by Carlo Célius, 'Neo-classicism and the Haitian Revolution', in Geggus and Fiering, *The World of the Haitian Revolution*, pp. 339–51, 381.

up official communications and documents. The Declaration of Independence had been signed overwhelmingly by *anciens libres*, some military men, others lawyers or journalists. The Declaration's generous sentiments and tentative apology seem to reflect an aspiration for a fresh start, with Haitians putting behind them the bloody expedients of the liberation wars. The adoption of the name Haiti also helped to suggest this.

Dessalines endorsed these fine sentiments because the consolidation of his authority required a constitution and laws. In October 2004 he declared himself emperor in a move that rather worried many of the other leaders. Dessalines still had the allegiance of many *nouveau-libre* commanders. He stood not only for war to the death, but also for the reconstruction of plantation agriculture. In Toussaint's regime he had been inspector of agriculture, conscripting labourers for the plantations. As a French general he had executed labourers who refused to work. He and a number of his fellow commanders had acquired estates of their own. They saw that only export sales and taxes would pay for military equipment and salaries. It was even alleged that he had approached British slave-traders to supply captives to serve in the army or rural police. Following Dessalines's overthrow, Christophe's Northern regime did buy Africans to serve as members of a rural police – the Dahomets – with those involved acquiring formal freedom after three years' service (the British had already formed several black West Indian regiments in this way).

Opposition to Dessalines was strongest in the South and West, where *ancien-libre* proprietors and *nouveau-libre* peasants had less scope or need for militarized labour. Pétion, a Southern mulatto and *ancien libre*, took the lead in the plot against the emperor and later adopted a land distribution policy, awarding small farms to his soldiers. Christophe colluded in the overthrow of Dessalines but continued to promote plantations and labour coercion in his Northern kingdom. Christophe may have believed that Haiti needed British support and that he, not Dessalines, was the man to bring this about. But if Dessalines had made the mistake of too enthusiastically embracing the plantation model in a country determined to repudiate it, Christophe was himself later to repeat the error.[98]

Haiti's role in the radicalization of the 'rights of man' does not require us to endorse all the actions of the Revolution's leaders, or to excuse their offences. The accounts by James, Benot, Dubois, Fick, Trouillot, Manigat and Hector allow the grandeur of the Revolution to emerge without any need to conceal the excesses committed on all sides. Even admitting that the process as a whole unleashed a deplorable racial violence, the fact remains that a powerful current of Haitian opinion reacted against this by elaborating an anti-racist ideology.

98   Vertus Saint-Louis, 'L'assassinat de Dessalines et les limites de la société haïtienne face au marché international', in Benot and Dorigny, *Rétablissment de l'esclavage*, pp. 161–78.

Abbé Grégoire, the French abolitionist and constitutional priest, gave preliminary and tentative expression to the rejection of racism, but it was to be a Haitian, Anténor Firmin, who published the first really substantial critique of racism in 1886. In doing so he reflected Haitian civil society, an entity which in its various forms, both urban and rural, often acted as a corrective to vices of the political and military elite.

While forswearing wars against their neighbours, the leaders of Haiti were to offer their territory as a haven to the oppressed. In 1816 Pétion issued a Constitution which included this article: 'All Africans and Indians, and those of their blood, born in the colonies or in foreign countries, who come to reside in the Republic, will be recognized as Haitians, but will not enjoy the right of citizenship until after one year of residence.'[99]

In the essay already quoted Geggus refers to Christophe's purchase of slaves to serve as rural police, a practice discontinued after his overthrow. However, the specially commissioned 'Afterword' to the volume in which he writes goes much further. In it Christopher Bayly observes that 'The revolutionary shine has . . . been taken off the "black republic" of Haiti where . . . the survival of an African and mixed-race slave-holding ruling class has attracted recent scholarly attention.'[100] That there was a landholding mixed-race ruling class in Haiti is very clear, but the notion that it was 'slave-holding' is quite wrong. If slave-holding really had been restored it would not just have taken the shine off the Haitian Republic, but would have contradicted its essential achievement. That such an idea can now gain credence suggests that Haiti, after its brief moment of glory in the literature on the 'age of revolution', is threatened with relegation back to the shadows. The last Atlantic revolution to be recognized now becomes an early victim of what Bayly calls the 'conservative turn' in that historiography.

David Geggus, who has contributed so much to the study of Haiti and its Revolution, still draws up a schedule of achievements which many will find deeply impressive, and is worth quoting:

> Of all the Atlantic revolutions, Saint-Domingue's most fully embodied the contemporary struggle for freedom, equality and independence, and it produced the greatest degree of economic and social change. Beginning as a home-rule movement among wealthy white colonists it quickly spread to militant free people of colour seeking political rights and then gave rise to the largest slave uprising in the history of the Americas. Its narrative is a succession of major precedents: colonial

---

99   Quoted in Fischer, *Modernity Disavowed*, p. 238. This Constitution limited white access to citizenship to those already covered in the 1805 clauses, but since this comprised all the whites in the country it should not be equated with the restrictions on black citizenship in the United States.

100   C. A. Bayly, 'Afterword', in Armitage and Subrahamyan, *The Age of Revolutions in Global Context*, pp. 209–17, 212.

representation in a metropolitan assembly, the ending of racial discrimination, the first abolition of slavery in a major slave society, and the creation of a Latin American state. By 1804 colonialism and slavery, the defining institutions of the Caribbean, were annihilated precisely where, for three hundred years of unchecked growth, they had most prospered.[101]

The next two chapters survey the impact of the Haitian Revolution on the Great Powers, and on Spanish and Portuguese America. Once again, there are now those who see this as very limited and, so far as anti-slavery is concerned, even counter-productive.

---

101   Geggus, 'The Caribbean in the Age of Revolution', p. 87.

CHAPTER NINE

Results and Prospects I: Slave-Trade Abolition

If the British abolitionist movement was, in part, a response to defeat at the hands of the North American rebels, its eclipse in 1793 had been caused by the onset of war with Revolutionary France. In the 1780s a group of young Quakers had persuaded first their own Society and then broader layers of the British public that the traffic in captive Africans was cruel and destructive, carrying off tens of thousands of Africans, and many hundreds of British sailors, each year. Within the ruling elite itself a number of key individuals – notably Pitt, the prime minister, and Middleton, the comptroller of the navy – became convinced that a ban on the slave trade would signal a serious intent to reform the regime and empire. The vested interests of 'Old Corruption' were too strong to be overcome by an open assault but they could be weakened, and thrown on the defensive, by defeat on the highly symbolic issue of a ban on the Atlantic slave traffic. The cause had attracted support from both evangelicals and advocates of constitutional reform. The West Indian planters and merchants were well represented in parliament, and managed to foil the first abolitionist challenge, but they furnished an egregious instance of dubious wealth buying privilege. The West Indians controlled many 'rotten boroughs' and had secured preferential tariffs for their produce. The Abolition Society had made impressive headway in 1789–92 with hopes that the new French authorities would also join a move to end the slave traffic. But the *Amis des Noirs*, as we have seen, concentrated on the rights of free men of colour. Then the radicalization of the Revolution led to a convulsive anti-Jacobin reaction in Britain and to the collapse of the abolitionist campaign. Edmund Burke accused the Jacobins of direct complicity in cannibalism in his 'Letter on a Regicide Peace' of 1796. With the outbreak of war the government closed down every sort of democratic agitation and reignited colonial rivalry. Wilberforce persuaded Pitt to allow a right of petition but the abolitionists were in no position to make use of it. The effort to ban the slave trade was dropped, and parliament instead sought to regulate loading ratios. The Committee of the Abolition Society met fitfully from 1794 and then not at all after 1796. Clarkson, afflicted by demoralization and illness, ceased campaigning. For a while Wilberforce continued to present annual Abolition Bills to parliament, but between 1799 and 1803 he let the issue rest.

The overthrow of the French monarchy and the upheavals in Saint-Domingue led many French colonial proprietors to appeal for British help.

Henry Dundas, a master of patronage and imperial connections, persuaded Pitt that the immensely valuable French colonies could be easily acquired. It took a few years for this expectation to be dashed. The loss of 80,000 men in the West Indies in the years 1794–9 showed the expedition to be a great error. In its negotiations in 1801–2 the London government encouraged Napoleon to restore order (and slavery) in the French colonies. But the attempted Anglo-French rapprochement at the Peace of Amiens (1802–3) proved short-lived. Napoleon's bid to restore French control – and slavery – in Saint-Domingue put black resistance there in a new and sympathetic light. General Maitland, the commander of the British forces in Saint-Domingue, had already anticipated such a shift in 1798 when he negotiated a handover to Toussaint Louverture and the withdrawal of his own troops. Maitland's action was a de facto recognition that black victory had far-reaching implications for the imperial powers. Vertus Saint Louis, a Haitian historian, argues that Maitland's accord with Toussaint turned a French victory into a French defeat.[1]

Events in Saint-Domingue created a new strategic context for Britain which allowed a revived campaign to present abolition as an act of sound policy, as well as high morality. The character of war was changing. Between the Treaty of Westphalia in 1648 and the outbreak of the North American rebellion in 1776, European and Atlantic wars had pitted one power against another in a struggle for revenue, trade and other colonial assets. The Anglo-Dutch Wars of the 1650s and 1660s, pitting the two premier Protestant states against one another, proved that the age of wars of religion was over. The Glorious Revolution (1688) and the accompanying Anglo-Dutch alliance sealed a Protestant succession, but did not signal any new Puritan crusade. Britain assumed the leading role and Dutch capitalists were happy to invest in British bonds. It was left to the American rebels and their Declaration of Independence to imbue war with principle by asserting that peoples had a right to defy their monarch and fight for representative government, albeit that the expedient American alliance with the French king qualified this a little. The European wars of the 1790s found Britain's unreformed Hanoverian order allied with the European monarchies and counter-revolutionary princes in an attempt to restore the French Bourbons. The warfare that produced French victories in Europe and British defeat in the Caribbean had a new and revolutionary character, embracing the *levée en masse*, the declaration of the rights of man, the Marseillaise, the decree of Pluviôse and the emergence of that new phenomenon dubbed *idéologie* by the philosopher Destut de Tracy. For its part the British government had been able to rally popular sentiment at home against the French threat, but the debacle in Saint-Domingue, the Spithead naval mutiny in 1797 and the Irish rising in 1799

---

1   Vertus Saint-Louis, *Aux origines du drame d'Haïti: Droit et commerce maritime, 1794–1806*, Port-au-Prince 2005, pp. 94–121.

all showed the need for a new imperial narrative. To add a further disturbing note, unrest in the industrial districts was soon to take the form of General Ludd's machine-breaking.

While Napoleon Bonaparte had a thoroughly instrumental attitude towards ideology, sections of the British elite were drawn in the opposite direction to a new stress on the need for war goals going beyond national interest. Vocal sections of the middle class – the 'Friends of Peace' – began questioning the need for and purpose of any new hostilities. The naval victory at Trafalgar (1805) encouraged Patriots, who remained numerous – but also removed the threat of French invasion, thus handing an argument to those who opposed war.[2]

The new conjuncture led both to a revival of abolitionist agitation and to recognition that the war against the French dictator needed to be framed and fought in a new way. Some began to see the cause of abolition as the perfect banner for a new Pax Britannica, based on free trade but respectful of the cause of humanity.

With Britain once again at war with Napoleon – and Napoleon in difficulties in the Caribbean – the anti–slave trade cause began a strong recovery. William Wordsworth published a fine tribute to Toussaint Louverture in the *Morning Post* following the news of the black leader's death. Around this time the gains of the insurgents moved *The Times* to change its line and come out against the slave trade. The Committee of the Abolition Society met again and began to press for new initiatives inside and outside parliament. In a significant move the Committee was determined to show that abolition was sound policy, that it would bring a great gain of principle at little cost, that it would rally public opinion and elevate Britain's struggle with the French dictator in the eyes of the world.

In devising the new approach, the Committee drew on the thinking of two men who had expertise in colonial matters: James Stephen, who had worked as a lawyer in the West Indies, and Henry Brougham, a prolific contributor to the *Edinburgh Review* and author of a two-volume study of the British Empire. Stephen, married to Wilberforce's sister and shortly himself to become a member of parliament, devised a strategy which successfully persuaded parliament, with the consent of most West Indian proprietors, to accept a ban targeted only against the foreign slave trade – especially the trade to Cuba. This foreign slave trade was, he urged, simply aiding Cuban competitors, and the Spanish or American merchants involved were fraudulently claiming to be neutral when in reality they were happy to break the British blockade, and carry plantation produce to France. Acceptance of this argument paved the way for a

2   See J. E. Cookson, *The Friends of Peace*, Cambridge 1982, and for the broader setting the masterly study by David Brion Davis, *The Problem of Slavery in the Age of Revolution, 1770–1823*, Ithaca 1975.

universal ban. British planters in the older islands (Barbados and Jamaica) could be brought to see advantage in a general ban, since it would firm up slave prices and constrain the growth of more efficient producers in Demerara. While these arguments played a key role in widening parliamentary support, Stephen also published popular pamphlets stressing that the African heroes in Saint-Domingue were heaven-sent allies in the fight against Bonaparte.[3] The fact that Santo Domingo – the Spanish half of the island – remained under French control until 1809, and that Haiti had not been recognized by France, lent some substance to this alliance. Indeed the British authorities were happy to encourage Dessalines and Christophe.

Henry Brougham rounded out the case for abolition in a pamphlet that was sent to every MP. He urged that suppression of the traffic would not reduce the value of a single West Indian estate, rather the reverse. West Indian proprietors could insure themselves against future labour shortages by promoting family life and child-bearing. Abolition would disappoint few merchants, since the execrable slave traffic comprised less than 5 per cent of Britain's commerce. Brougham also declared that it was folly to import large numbers of captive Africans, 'prone to explosion', to the British islands at a time when slave insurrection was 'flaming to windward'. Security should be paramount. His overall argument was that the cost of abolition would be slight but the social gain would be very great.[4]

In 1804, after a debate in which several members referred to Brougham's pamphlet, the House of Commons passed a bill suppressing the trade – but it thereafter foundered in the Lords. In 1805 the disgrace of Dundas and the death of Pitt created a new situation in which the Whigs would be able to form a government. Brougham's role became pivotal, as he enjoyed good relations with both the Saints and the Whigs. Wilberforce's previous disappointments made him appreciate that a cross-bench approach was more likely to succeed. Thanks to Brougham, Wilberforce was invited to write an article on the slave trade for the *Edinburgh Review*, a journal of pronounced Whig inclination which was setting new standards for serious and documented argument. A resolution against the slave trade which passed in 1806, during the short-lived Whig administration of Lord Grenville and Charles James Fox, was turned into a Bill which passed both Houses by large margins and obtained the royal assent in

---

3   James Stephen's contribution was highlighted by Roger Anstey, *The Atlantic Slave Trade and British Abolition*, London 1969, pp. 344–6. See also Davis, *The Problem of Slavery in the Age of Revolution*, especially pp. 346–86.

4   Henry Brougham, *A Concise Statement of the Case Regarding the Slave Trade*, London 1804; Robert Stewart, *Henry Brougham: His Public Career, 1778–1868*, London 1985, pp. 28–37; Chester New, *The Life of Henry Brougham to 1830*, Oxford 1961, pp. 21–31, and Blackburn, *Overthrow of Colonial Slavery*, pp. 300–16. While Brougham's later role as a leader of Abolition and Reform is widely acknowledged, this early contribution to abolition, emphasized by his biographers, is seldom given its due by historians of anti-slavery.

March 1807.[5] Fox was dead by this time but Grenville, as a Whig peer, played a critical role in the Lords.

Why had abolition won at last? The overall positive reason was parliament's need to rally opinion at a critical juncture, but it certainly helped that several obstacles had been removed. The elimination of Saint-Domingue as a major sugar producer made it much easier for British parliamentarians to vote down the slave trade, secure in the knowledge that British planters now faced easier market conditions and that they would not be undercut by French producers.[6] Seymour Drescher, who is generally sceptical concerning Haiti's influence on abolition, nevertheless concedes that the movement's revival in 1804 was greatly helped by the French defeat in Saint-Domingue. However, he believes that this impact had faded by March 1807. João Marques, who otherwise questions the importance of slave resistance, sees the Haitian Revolution as the great exception. He finds it incredible that 'the spectre of Haiti played a major role in the revival of abolitionism in 1804, but played no role at all in the approval of the Abolition Act in March 1807'[7] While Marques makes an important point here, Haiti was no longer seen as a 'spectre' but rather as an ally, with Stephen entitling one of his pamphlets, *The Opportunity, or Reasons for an Immediate Alliance with Santo Domingo* (1804).

The Abolition Society had gathered petitions, and urged its supporters to demand of candidates in the November 1806 election where they stood on the slave traffic. Parliamentary advocates were this time careful to argue that suppressing the traffic was not just a noble gesture, but a measure favourable to the stability and prosperity of the British plantation colonies. Several MPs with military experience of the West Indies spoke in favour of the measure.[8]

But, as already suggested, Britain's rulers needed a lofty cause and the abolitionists offered one. Reasons needed to be given to a war-weary people for continuing a draining conflict. British sea-power contrasted with the collapse of

---

5   Chester New describes Brougham's role as that of a 'go-between' concerting the efforts of the Saints (Abolition Committee) and the Whig leaders of the government. See also Stewart, *Henry Brougham*, p. 37.

6   David Geggus, 'The Caribbean in the Age of Revolution', in David Armitage and Sanjay Subrahmanyam, eds, *The Age of Revolutions in Global Context*, pp. 82–100, 89–90. Geggus asks for further 'direct connections' between Haiti and British abolition. I would urge that the previously cited contributions of James Stephen and Henry Brougham furnish precisely such connections. I came across Brougham's pamphlet in the British Library and was surprised that it had not figured more prominently in the debate on British slave-trade abolition. New observes that the first Commons debate where abolition regained strong support saw many MPs carrying the pamphlet and echoing its arguments. New, *Life of Henry Brougham*, pp. 29–30.

7   João Pedro Marques, 'Afterthoughts' in Seymour Drescher and Pieter Emmer, eds, *Who Abolished Slavery? Slave Revolts and Abolitionism: A Debate with João Pedro Marques*, Oxford 2010, pp. 185–200, 193.

8   Adam Hochschild, *Bury the Chains: Prophets and Rebels in the Fight to Free an Empire's Slaves*, London 2006, pp. 280–308.

its position in continental Europe. Napoleon defeated Britain's allies in a string of brilliant victories in 1805–6, and moved to reach an agreement with the Russian Tsar. Britain was completely isolated. The British government believed that it must mobilize its people for a further difficult war with the French. The long-mooted abolition of the Atlantic slave trade furnished a potent symbol of a better world, a world thriving thanks to free labour and free trade. The 1807 bill was first introduced in the Lords in December 1806, the idea being to secure victory in the House that had twice before turned down abolition bills that had passed the Commons. Grenville had always insisted that abolition must be supported on grounds of policy. He promised that abolition would not be allowed to benefit foreign competitors. He was, he assured their lordships, animated not by doctrinaire philanthropy but by concern for the safety and prosperity of British proprietors. The planters were, he urged, wrong to think that they needed to purchase more slaves – they had enough already, and should look to methods of ensuring natural growth of the existing slave population.[9] He did not spell out that great credit would accrue to the Lords if it at last relented, nor did he explain that the British people detested and despised the slave traffic or that the government desperately needed popular backing: some things are best left unsaid.

At the close of the Commons debate on suppression of the slave traffic in 1807, as victory was at last secured, Romilly, the solicitor general, pointed to the contrast between the dictator Bonaparte, the 'common enemy of mankind', and the true nobility and benevolence of William Wilberforce. The House had been assured that abolition was not only 'sound policy' but would bring great credit to it as well. As enrolment in the British armed forces swelled to number 700,000 – by far the largest in its history – the country's leaders could assure the 'Friends of Peace' that their country was fighting for a noble cause.[10]

Unlike some Whigs Henry Brougham had no soft spot for Napoleon, but he did have strong views on the type of war that should be fought, believing that the emergency dictated radical measures. In an *Edinburgh Review* article which caused great controversy, he saluted the popular character of the Spanish resistance to Napoleon's invasion in 1808. Who, he asked, had led resistance to Napoleon?

> The people, then, and of the people, the middle and above all the lower orders, have alone the merit of raising this glorious opposition to the common enemy of national independence. Those who have so little of what is commonly termed

---

9   A recent study gives a useful summary of Grenville's arguments and their role in finally winning the argument for the bill; see David Beck Ryden, *West Indian Slavery and British Abolition, 1783–1807*, Cambridge 2009, pp. 182–4, 255–7. Ryden does not say so, but Grenville's arguments echoed Brougham's; the two men worked closely together in the next few years.

10   Davis, *The Problem of Slavery in the Age of Revolution*, pp. 448–9.

interest in the country, those who have *no stake* in the community (to speak the technical language of the aristocracy), the persons of *no consideration* in the state – they who could not *pledge their fortunes*, having only lives and liberties to lose, the bulk, the mass of the people, nay, the very odious, many-headed beast, the multitude – the mob itself – alone, uncalled for, unaided by the higher classes – in spite of those higher classes, and in direct opposition to them, as well as to the enemy they so vilely joined – raised up the standard of insurrection.[11]

Brougham was not, in fact, as radical as he sounded (in Chapter 12 I will cite his moderate reflections on property). An *Edinburgh Review* colleague argued that the role of the magazine in British politics should be to 'side with the most respectable and sane of the democrats [and that] by so doing [we] will restrain and enlighten them'.[12] Brougham's article expressed his frustration that the war against Bonaparte was not being prosecuted in a different way – a way favourable to popular involvement and political reform. At least the Abolition Act lent the conflict a worthier purpose. Brougham saw reform as a portfolio of issues – including anti-slavery – which came to define the oppositional agenda and went far beyond constitutional change. In 1808 and 1811 he became the spokesman of opposition to any widening of the war. He attacked the government for adopting rules of naval engagement ('Orders-in-Council') that would lead to war with the United States. Brougham's book on colonial policy had pointed to Britain's buoyant trade with the US as proof that the country's manufacturers and merchants did not need mercantilist privileges. Brougham had learned free-trade principles in Edinburgh from Dougald Stewart, a disciple of Adam Smith. However, he was no doctrinaire free-trader, seeing slave-trade abolition as a necessary qualification and corrective.

Following Brougham's entry to parliament in 1810, Wilberforce invited him to take the initiative in drafting legislation that would close damaging loopholes in the 1807 Act. He introduced a bill that changed the crime committed by slave-traders from mere felony – attracting a £20 fine – to piracy, which could mean death. Brougham succeeded in gaining the support needed for this tougher sanction. Around the same time Brougham successfully defended Leigh Hunt from a libel charge incurred when he published an article, 'One Thousand Lashes!!!!', attacking the brutal orgies of whipping which played such a part in the discipline of the British armed forces. While Brougham won the libel case, an attempt to end punishment by the lash failed, with only twelve MPs voting in favour; however, the parliament did agree that no punishment should exceed 300 lashes. (Britain's military code thus remained far more severe than

---

11   Quoted in New, *Life of Henry Brougham*, p. 46.
12   Ibid., p. 52.

that of the French or Prussian armies.[13]) In another noted case, he secured the acquittal of thirty men accused of being Luddite agitators. The Whigs had been turned out shortly after passage of the Abolition bill, and Brougham worried that the Whig role was simply to come up with ideas, every once in a while, that got the Tories out of a tight spot.

The British government remained anxious to ensure security in the Caribbean. The heavy losses incurred in Saint-Domingue had persuaded them to form black regiments under white officers. African men in their prime were specially purchased for this force, on the understanding that, though still technically slaves, they would eventually be freed. In 1802 the soldiers of one of these West Indian regiments mutinied believing that, with peace in prospect, they were about to be relegated to agricultural toil. The regiment involved was broken up, the leaders executed and those who had not joined the mutiny distributed to other regiments. In 1806 the government decided that the soldiers in these regiments should be declared free, albeit that they still owed service to the army.[14] The black regiments contributed to security in the short run, but eventually they swelled the size of a free coloured population that was hostile to slavery.

It is in the nature of war that it concentrates attention, reorders priorities and imposes sacrifices. In the conditions of 1806–7 it boosted the strategic case for abolition. Most particularly it helps to explain how abolition could suddenly attract support from the great mass of MPs and peers who had earlier voted it down many times. Another dimension of the strategic case stemmed from deteriorating relations with the United States.

US SLAVE-TRADE ABOLITION

British slave-trade abolition was certainly favoured by the knowledge that US action against slave imports was imminent. The Jefferson administration was moving to boycott trade with Britain because the Royal Navy was harassing US merchantmen suspected of trading with the French. Jefferson had also announced that he would urge Congress to end slave imports as soon as the twenty-year moratorium adopted in 1787 had ended.

The idea of banning the Atlantic traffic had itself arisen from the initial conflict between Britain and its North American colonists, and neither power would be comfortable continuing the traffic if the other banned it. The Virginian planters had long wanted this and would lose nothing by it – indeed, slave prices would probably rise. Stopping slave imports would also, it was held, reduce the

---

13   Stewart, *Henry Brougham*, pp. 65–75.
14   Roger Norman Buckley, *Slaves in Red Coats: The British West India Regiments, 1795–1815*, New Haven 1979.

'Haitian' danger and avert the controversies among whites which had made it possible. South Carolina's reopening of the traffic in 1803 was widely decried in the South, as well as the North. As noted in Chapter 6, the allocation of representation according to the 'three-fifths' rule would mean that the Southern states could acquire more clout *simply by importing Africans*, upsetting the balance between North and South. In 1803 Congress passed a bill forbidding ships' captains from bringing free Negroes to those states which had barred slave imports. British abolitionists saw signs that the US Congress was planning to end the traffic as soon as possible. By ending further legal slave imports in 1808, Britain and the United States were each ensuring that they retained the moral high ground in their difficult relationship. While the action taken was fairly effective so far as slave imports were concerned (some exceptions are noted below), slavery and an internal slave trade remained. Moreover English and US merchants still sold trade goods to Cuban and Brazilian traffickers, and helped them in other ways.

The ending of US slave imports had been preceded by measures that reduced the importance of slavery in the North. In the 1780s moderate emancipation measures had been defeated in New York and New Jersey. Slaves comprised only about 5 per cent of the population in these states, but their owners were influential. In the immediate aftermath of the 1791 rising, such measures had not even been proposed; but with the stabilization of a new black power in Saint-Domingue/Haiti, there was a new reality. American and British merchants were happy to do business with the black authorities. Federal politicians rarely avowed support for abolitionism, but at state level matters were different. Political leaders in New York and New Jersey once again came forward with proposals for a gradual phasing out of slavery in their own states. A 'free-womb' law passed in New York in 1799 which freed the children of slave mothers once they reached the age of twenty-eight. It was sponsored by a Federalist, but attracted some Democratic–Republican support as well. In 1804 New Jersey also adopted a gradual emancipation law. The sons of slave mothers were to be freed when they reached twenty-five years of age, with daughters freed at twenty-one. To those with no stake in the slave system, such a moderate approach was in tune with the 'spirit of the times'. Without requiring expropriation they removed an institution that was awkward as well as marginal.

In Britain, slave-trade abolition was a dramatic event and was subsequently much celebrated. The US suppression of the slave trade was not preceded by a public abolitionist campaign, and was treated as a non-event (curiously, historians often agreed). If there was any abolitionist significance to the US action – and at some level there was – it was convenient to ignore it. The Virginians were strong supporters of an end to the slave trade, but not as part of any abolitionist agenda. Indeed the problem faced by the Virginian political elite was a quite different one: their concern was to insulate the institutions of their region from all dangers. So far as the US was concerned, the implicit ideal of a white man's republic (on which more below) was quite compatible with setting limits on slavery, and ending the slave trade – just as it was with establishing a *cordon sanitaire* around Haiti.

THE BRITISH ABOLITIONIST CAMPAIGN OF 1814

The importance of Haiti for British abolitionism was not over. The abolitionist petitions sent to parliament in 1806–7 carried less than a third the number of signatures as those submitted [at the height of the agitation] in 1792. But the latter figure was to be exceeded in 1814 when wide sections of the British public were outraged to learn that the draft Treaty of Paris was about to recognize 'Saint-Domingue' (i.e. Haiti) as rightfully the possession of the newly restored French monarch. The victorious allies were contemplating this action in order to strengthen Bourbon legitimacy and encourage France to forsake military adventures, devoting itself instead to peaceful commerce. The draft treaty even envisaged a five-year period during which French merchants would be able to undertake a slave trade to restock its plantations. But if Britain's rulers still believed in the pacific virtues of trade, the public was more discriminating. Almost every sector of British opinion was horrified – even West Indian propri-etors did not favour restoring Saint-Domingue to France, still less allowing it to rebuild the plantations.[15] Parliament received 800 petitions containing 750,000 signatures protesting at the proposed treaty terms.[16] Henry Brougham, as a director of the African Institution, helped to organize the massive campaign. The government of Lords Liverpool and Castlereagh hastened to distance itself from the plan. During his 'hundred days' in 1815 Napoleon himself, recognizing the symbolic charge of the issue, issued a decree banning the French slave trade. 'Saint-Domingue' was not restored to France by the Vienna Congress and Settlement of 1815. At British insistence the treaty instead incorporated the first international declaration repudiating the Atlantic slave trade. The extent of the popular protest in 1814, and Napoleon's attempt to emulate the British ban in the following year, both tend to confirm the claim that abolitionist initiatives accrued

---

15   Betty Fladeland, 'Abolitionist Pressures on the Concert of Europe', *Journal of Modern History* 37 (1966), pp. 117–24. Jane Austen's *Mansfield Park*, in which Fanny Price asks her plantation-owning uncle his views on the slave trade, was written just at this time. Fanny's query is followed by a dead silence. Edward Said rightly argues for the significance of this episode in *Culture and Imperialism*, London 1996. The idea at work in this novel is that Britain's traditional rulers need to regain their moral compass, which has been disturbed by parental negligence or absence, juvenile pleasure-seeking and waywardness and the irreligion of too many of Britian's rulers. The exchange on the slave trade is very brief, but this redemptive notion pervades the novel. Sir Thomas Bertram's attempt to impose an unwise marriage on Fanny also offers a gentle questioning of patriarchal power.

16   Seymour Drescher, *Capitalism and Antislavery*, Oxford 1986, pp. 93–4.

'moral capital' to those taking them and set up a sort of 'hegemonic compact', by which rulers bound themselves to respect certain vital undertakings.

The allies' plan to return 'Saint-Domingue' to France only acquired a momentary plausibility because Haiti itself was at this time divided into three, with Henri Christophe ruling a kingdom in the North, and Pétion and Goman republics in the South and West. However, all Haitians rallied against the French threat and Christophe entered thereafter into a cordial correspondence with Thomas Clarkson and William Wilberforce.

At the time of the passage of abolition in Britain and the United States, tensions between the two countries – exacerbated by the 'Orders in Council' which authorized the Royal Navy to search neutral vessels, and to impress American sailors, claiming that they were British deserters – led first to a US commercial boycott and then to war, the 'War of 1812'. In the course of this conflict British commanders once again offered freedom to Virginian slaves willing to fight with them. Admiral Lord Cockburn seized Washington in 1814, and torched the White House with the help of 300 black soldiers who had responded to this appeal. Both this exploit and British appeals to the Seminole dramatized situations in which slavery was a source of vulnerability.[17]

That Britain, the major power of the age, favoured an end to the oceanic slave trade became a factor in the political calculations of all Atlantic states. London followed up the Vienna declaration against the Atlantic slave trade with a string of bilateral negotiations with the European Atlantic powers. Spain, Portugal and France signed treaties agreeing to end the traffic within a short time, but a continuing illegal traffic brought tens of thousands of new slaves to the Americas each year in the 1820s. Britain stationed a squadron on the West African coast whose instructions were to seize these slave-traders, but its effectiveness was reduced by the lack of cooperation from other powers, especially the United States, Spain, Portugal and Brazil. While the US had stopped importing slaves – or at least reduced their entrance to a clandestine trickle – it had refused to allow the Royal Navy a 'right of search' of US vessels (the British were willing to allow British merchant vessels to be searched by its treaty partners). The Spanish–Cuban and Luso-Brazilian authorities were prepared to grant a right of search, but nevertheless turned a blind eye to a continuing and flourishing traffic, partly because they were bribed to do so and partly because the slave-traders could afford to buy the fastest ships and became skilled at evading the squadron. Between 1808 and 1860 some 2 *million new slaves* were brought to the Americas, with Cuba and Brazil being by far the most important destinations. The US and British bans did not extend to those who supplied the slave-traders with 'trade goods'. While only a few British merchants risked indictment by taking a direct part in buying and selling slaves, many respectable trading

---

17   Reginald Horsman, *The War of 1812*, London 1969, p. 78.

houses in London and Liverpool supplied trade goods to the slave-traders (that is, textiles, manufactures, guns and other products which were strongly in demand on the African coast).[18]

The British nevertheless made a large commitment to the West African squadron, which usually numbered between a dozen and two dozen vessels. In the whole period 1815–1865 the squadron apprehended nearly 486 ships, carrying 145,000 slaves. Its vessels stopped a further thousand ships with no slaves aboard. Impressive as this effort may seem, the ocean was vast, the coast-lines extensive and Britain's treaty partners duplicitous, so the already-noted 2 million were trafficked despite the squadron's patrols.[19]

British attempts to impose an anti–slave trade policy generated a degree of nationalistic resistance, and were resented even by governments – like that of Louis Philippe in the 1830s and 1840s – who were quite sincere and effective in suppressing the traffic. The failure of the US to concede the 'right of search' led to clandestine Cuban, Spanish, Portuguese and Brazilian slave-traders adopting the stars and stripes as their flag of choice. In the years 1808–1819 Spanish Florida furnished the basis for a semi-legal importation of captives from Africa – their arrival in Florida being legal, but not their sale to US buyers. Richard Drake, a notorious slave-trader, boasted that he had continued to use Florida as a base for contraband trade for several decades after it became US territory.[20] It would be good to know more about the dimensions of such slave smuggling, but it was probably greatly exceeded by covert and illegal slaving voyages in US-built ships that were skippered by Spanish captains but financed by US merchants. Such ships would use real or fraudulent US papers, and fly the stars and stripes, in order to evade inspection by the Royal Navy. In the 1840s the US minister to Rio de Janeiro reported that about half the slaves arriving in Brazil – numbering over half a million in that decade – did so aboard ships flying the US flag. This was an illegal use, but the US naval patrols – comprising just four second-rate warships – were neither large enough nor vigorous enough to suppress the practice; and there must have been US agents willing and able to acquire the needed documentation.[21]

In 1819, British abolitionists were gratified when the Haitian warship *William Wilberforce* apprehended a Spanish slave-trading vessel in Caribbean waters. Haiti's achievement was also saluted by British abolitionists in 1823,

---

18   David Eltis, 'The British Contribution to the Nineteenth-Century Transatlantic Slave Trade', *Economic History Review* 52/2 (1979); Marika Sherwood, *After Abolition: Britain and the Slave Trade Since 1807*, London 2007.

19   David Eltis, *Economic Growth and the Ending of the Transatlantic Slave Trade*, Oxford 1981, p. 98.

20   Richard Drake, *Revelations of a Slave Smuggler*, New York 1860. See also Jane Landers, 'Slavery in the Spanish Caribbean and the Failure of Abolition', *Review* XXXI/3 (2009), pp. 343–72.

21   Leslie Bethell, *Britain and the Abolition of the Brazilian Slave Trade*, Oxford 1970, p. 128.

when Fowell Buxton and others announced the opening of their campaign for slave emancipation.[22] The brazen continuance of a supposedly illegal slave traffic confirmed the view of many abolitionists that without emancipating the slaves there could be no lasting and comprehensive suppression of the slave traffic.

PLANTERS LOOK FOR ALLIES

The awesome scale of the events in Saint-Domingue and their unexpected outcome had far-reaching consequences, even though it was to be a long time before they were fully registered. The fear of slave insurrection – especially if backed by a hostile state – instilled a sort of deliberate panic in the minds of New World slave-owners, leading them to redouble their security and to fortify their links with potential allies.

So far as planters in the Americas were concerned, there was no question of abandoning plantation slavery. The sharp decline of plantation output in Saint-Domingue after 1791 raised prices and opened large opportunities to rival producers. Emigrés from Saint-Domingue brought their expertise to these rivals. The planters of the United States, Brazil and Cuba were the main beneficiaries, partly because they had huge areas that could be brought into cultivation, but also because they proved capable of maintaining slave subjection. The slaves were only a third of the population in the US South, 45 per cent in Cuba, and at most, and briefly, 50.5 per cent in Brazil – not 89 per cent, as in Saint-Domingue in 1789. The large slave-owners needed the support both of other free citizens, organized in militia and patrols, and of the state. Their hegemony was enhanced by some dispersal of slave-ownership among the free population and by the fact that a diverse institution of slavery had long been embedded in their social structure. Despite – or perhaps because of – their closeness to Saint-Domingue, the planters, merchants and officials of Cuba were most aware of the opportunities that were opened to them by the destruction in Saint-Domingue. Cuba received many thousands of refugees, both white and coloured, from Saint-Domingue, helping greatly to improve the technical level of Cuban plantations.

In Brazil and Cuba the big planters and merchants reduced the danger of conflict by cleaving loyally to the reigning monarchy, thus obtaining new security measures while persuading the authorities to encourage the export economy (on which more below). In the United States the slave-holders of the South needed the support of local white, non-slave-holding fellow citizens, who outnumbered the slave-holders by four to one. But this still left the task of ensuring slave-holder security at both Federal and local level.

---

22 Seymour Drescher, *The Mighty Experiment: Free Labor versus Slavery in British Emancipation*, Oxford 2002, pp. 100–5.

JEFFERSON AND SOUTHERN LEADERSHIP

Thomas Jefferson's campaign against what he saw as the conservative, even crypto-monarchist, politics of Adams and the Federalists in the 1790s expressed his deep republican convictions and, on the face of it, had nothing to do with defending slavery. Yet the National Republicanism which emerged triumphant from this campaign was to secure Virginian control of the White House for a generation (1800–24). Jefferson considered that the Jay treaty with Britain had been far too accommodating. Genuine as they were, Jefferson's republicanism and continuing defence of the French Revolution also consistuted a response to the plumes of smoke rising from the plantations in Saint-Domingue. Jefferson believed that an alliance with the republicans of the North could anchor the political order far more effectively than a policy of repression. Jefferson, Madison and Monroe saw themselves as defenders of a good republican order, not champions of slavery, but in practice the two stances were aligned. By forging a Democratic-Republican cross-sectional alliance, these enlightened planter-statesmen were reaching out to the most radicalized sectors of the population and securing support for the prevailing order. Democratic Republicanism offered enhanced rights and status to white citizens and, in so doing, helped to adapt the colonial patronage complex binding 'American slavery' to 'American freedom', to the new circumstances of an independent republic, more specifically of a 'White Man's Republic'.[23] A small but telling sign that the free people of colour were not to be full citizens was conveyed by the wording of the Militia Act of 1792, which called for the enrolment of all 'free, able-bodied, white citizens'.[24] (The framers of the motion were perhaps aware of the agitation raging at this time over the rights of the men of colour in Saint-Domingue.) In Brazil and Cuba, slave-holders were concerned to retain the support of the free people of colour, but in the United States, with its white majorities, it was the disposition of the free whites that was of critical importance.

In the colonial period, the leading men of Virginia and Carolina had accorded racial privileges to non-slave-holding whites as a way of enlisting their social support. Yeoman farmers had the vote, and their younger sons and

---

23   I am here referring to two crucial interpretations of the articulation of class, race and power, one focused on colonial Virginia, the other on the nineteenth-century republic. See Edmund Morgan, *American Slavery, American Freedom*, New York 1975, and Alexander Saxton, *The Rise and Fall of the White Man's Republic*, London and New York 1992. Jefferson's radicalism is well conveyed in the introduction to Thomas Jefferson, *The Declaration of Independence*, edited and with an introduction by Michael Hardt, London 2007.

24   Rogers Smith, *Civic Ideals: Conflicting Visions of Citizenship in United States History*, New Haven 1997, pp. 142–4.

daughters might work for a planter. In sharp contrast to the English farmer or labourer, any white could graze an animal on extensive areas of uncultivated land, allowing them to live 'high on the hog'. They served in the militia and patrols in units commanded by planters or professional men. During the Revolution the slave-holders of the South were allied to the leading men of the North in joint defiance of the imperial power. In the 1790s, Jefferson broke with the tacit assumption that the gentlemen of the South should allow their cross-sectional alliances to be mediated by the gentlemen of the North. He instead pioneered an alliance with subaltern members of Northern society, such as the artisans, mechanics and smallholders of Philadelphia and New York, against key members of the Northern elite. He was also happy to win the endorsement of the United Irishmen, some of them Catholic.[25]

Jefferson was a slave-holder but shied away from endorsing slavery as a positive good. Indeed his best-known text, *Notes on the State of Virginia*, presents slavery as a highly regrettable institution. Originally written for a French friend in 1783, it celebrates American virtues. Buffon had claimed that the New World had such an extreme climate that it was inhospitable to either natural abundance or the progress of civilization. In such a dank and inclement environment, only small creatures like insects and snakes could thrive, and there were none of the larger, noble beasts, such as elephants and lions. Drawing on Spanish American writers like Francisco Clavijero and Antonio de Ulloa, Jefferson set out to show that this was utterly mistaken, that the natural landscape of the New World was awesome and spectacular, that it teemed with species and that the size of its larger animals was in no way inferior to those of the Old World. In this context Jefferson also insisted on the admirable qualities of Native Americans, and expressed confidence in their capacity to improve. But the black descendants of Africans were another matter. Physically, morally and politically, they were a threat, an unstable and alien presence. They were intellectually limited and aesthetically unpleasing. Did not black males themselves prefer white women, just as 'uniformly as is the preference of the Oranootan for the black women'?[26] If this was the verdict of 'science', it followed that America would be better off without those of African descent.

Jefferson claimed himself to share the deprecation of slavery which was gripping political and religious radicals alike. He understood that the practice of slave-holding compromised the Republic's international reputation, and that it was a source of internal weakness and external vulnerability. It will be

25   David Hackett Fischer, 'Patterns of Partisan Allegiance', in Lance Benning, ed., *After the Constitution: Party Conflict in the New Republic*, Belmont 1989, pp. 143–70; Sean Wilentz, *Chants Democratic: New York City and the Rise of the American Working Class, 1788–1850*, New York 1984.

26   Thomas Jefferson, *Notes on the State of Virginia*, edited by Frank Shuffleton, London and New York 1999, p. 145.

recalled that he had tried to insert a denunciation of slave-trading into the Declaration of Independence. In 1784 he had supported the North West Ordinance which barred slaves from the North West territory. (The fact that the North West bordered British Canada, and that the British had tried to use emancipated slaves against the rebels, could well have been a factor.) Jefferson also believed that slave-holding corrupted the manners of the young whites and taught them contempt for work. His ideal was the yeoman farmer, working his own land. But he warned that if the slaves were simply freed and left in the country, it would produce 'convulsions that will probably never end but in the extinction of one or the other race'.[27] The slave was so injured by, and resentful of, his condition that he could never become a Patriot. In the long term, the only solution was to ship all the blacks back to Africa or some other haven. Until that should prove possible the priority was to keep the slaves in a proper subordination – to keep holding 'the wolf by the ears', as he put it in one of his last writings.[28] There was a brutality and candour about *Notes* – a supposedly private communication that became very public – that shattered the decorum and euphemism of public discourse. Unlike most apologists for slavery, Jefferson, writing at a time when many thousands of blacks had deserted their masters, did not offer the consoling fiction of the grateful slave. Political discourse requires multiple layers of 'make-believe', as Edmund Morgan has pointed out; but Jefferson's unsparing conclusions could find no room for blacks even in the world of make-believe.[29]

In the early years of the French Revolution, Jefferson, as secretary of state, gave cautious encouragement to the reformist hopes of the planters of the French Caribbean who wished to enjoy greater autonomy and self-government. The event that would, as a later historian was to put it, 'upset all calculations' and necessitate 'an entirely new policy' was neither the uprising of August 1791 nor the emancipation decree of 1794.[30] It was instead the rallying of insurgent blacks in June 1793 to defend Sonthonax, the commissioner in Saint-Domingue, from a white colonists' revolt. This marked a new, 'revolutionary' type of threat to the slave order.

Jefferson had little sympathy for the first refugees from Saint-Domingue. He believed them to be royalists and aristocrats, and privately opined that if

27   Ibid.

28   John C. Miller, 'The Wolf By the Ears': Jefferson and Slavery, New York 1972, pp. x, 38–45; see also Robert McColley, Slavery and Jeffersonian Virginia, New York 1978.

29   Edmund Morgan, Inventing the People: The Rise of Popular Sovereignty in England and America, New York 1989, p. 13.

30   Dudwell Lee Montague, Haiti and the United States, Durham, NC, 1940, pp. 34–5, quoted by Michael Zuckerman, 'The Color of Counter-Revolution: Thomas Jefferson and the Rebellion in Saint Domingue', in Loretta Waltz Mannucci, ed., The Languages of Revolution, Milan 1989, pp. 83–108, 91. Winthrop Jordan in White Over Black, Chapel Hill 1968, p. 375, also draws attention to the impact of Saint-Domingue on Jefferson but does not pinpoint this particular event.

SLAVE-TRADE ABOLITION   237

they were sent to live among the Indians they might learn something about liberty and equality. In 1792 and the first months of 1793 it also seemed that the rebellious blacks had become instruments of the royalist cause. But everything changed in June 1793, with the defeat of Galbaud. About 6,000 colonists, together with several thousand of their coloured servants or slaves, set sail from Saint-Domingue and sought haven in North American ports. They brought stories of atrocities and of narrow escapes from rampaging blacks. Like other white North Americans, Jefferson was affected by the plight of these refugees, many of whom, being destitute, threw themselves on the charity of the American authorities. Jefferson did not see how the Federal government could help, but he urged the governor of Virginia to do what he could to offer succour.[31]

The events of the summer of 1793 in Saint-Domingue prompted Jefferson to take the measure of new threats and new opportunities. The juncture between black revolt, coloured rights and the policy of a major power greatly alarmed the Virginian, but without leading him to abandon his public stance in favour of the French Republic. He had justified slavery by insisting that the slaves were too wild and unruly ever to be good citizens. The uprising of August 1791, and the subsequent decision of many black chiefs to enlist under the banner of the Spanish Bourbon king, did not challenge this view. But the events of July 1793, in which black Jacobins had foiled a military plot, was the beginning of a powerful challenge to Jefferson's line of argument. With the rise of Toussaint Louverture – who became lieutenant governor of the French colony in 1795 – it became clear that, so long as the republican power based itself on the former slaves' aversion to bondage, it could count on the support and discipline of most blacks. Indeed, the good order of Toussaint's *demi-brigades* was widely noted by observers. Jefferson evidently found the discipline and republicanism of free blacks more disturbing than the unruliness of slaves. Whatever his high-minded protestations about republican liberty, and some future emancipation, Jefferson's determinate allegiance was to the slave order.[32]

On 14 July 1793 Jefferson wrote to James Monroe: 'I become daily more convinced that all the West Indian islands will remain in the hands of the people of colour, and a total expulsion of the whites sooner or later take place. It is high time we should foresee the bloody scenes which our children, certainly, and possibly ourselves (south of the Patomac [sic]) have to wade through, and try to avert them.'[33] Jefferson has not completely abandoned his previous model, but

---

31   The impact of the refugees is brought out vividly in Ashli White, 'A Flood of Impure Lava': *Saint Dominguan Refugees in the United States, 1791–1820*, Columbia University PhD thesis 2003.

32   Garry Wills, *'Negro President': Jefferson and the Slave Power*, Boston 2003, gives many examples. As we will see, Haiti and Louisiana furnished critical tests of the sincerity of his claim that he would act against slavery if the right opportunity presented itself.

33   'To James Monroe', 14 July 1793, in John Catanzariti, ed., *Papers of Thomas Jefferson*, vol. 26, Princeton 1995, p. 503.

he is now writing about the 'people of colour' as a protagonist of history – and identifying a need for a counter-strategy. Ending the importation of slaves as soon as was constitutionally possible was certainly one aspect, but this would not be until 1807.

Unlike President Adams and the Federalists, Jefferson rejected a rapprochement with Britain. France must certainly be persuaded to abandon its unworthy representatives – Toussaint as well as the inept and provocative envoy Citizen Genet – and to give up its emancipationist policy. But joining the former colonial power in fighting the French Republic, as President Adams did during the Quasi-War of 1797–1800, Jefferson thought to be a great betrayal and a great error, whatever the provocations offered.

Jefferson's decision to stick with the French Republic, while having no truck with its emancipation policy, demonstrated remarkable sangfroid. Jefferson's antagonism to Hanoverian Britain and the royalists was in no way feigned, and was strong enough to explain why he took up this stance to begin with. But as the situation unfolded, a pro-French tilt also served a number of other ends. It could dissuade the French Republic from targeting the US slave order, and it could help the Southern planters to reach out to new allies in the Northern states. And later, with rising French influence over Spain, it might have a bearing on the fate of Spain's New World possessions.

The excesses of the Jacobins in 1792–4 thoroughly alienated George Washington and John Adams, but did not dampen enthusiasm for the French Revolution among the shopkeepers, artisans and labourers of Philadelphia, New York and other Northern districts. Washington and Adams were alarmed at the sight of tens of thousands parading in the streets to commemorate French Revolutionary anniversaries. But Jefferson persisted in seeing these partisans of the French Republic as allies. While his friend Madison had explained that an expansive republic could escape the dangers to property represented by popular organization ('faction') in the *Federalist Papers,* Jefferson was now to endorse popular politics. Eventually many of the patrician Republicans of the South, including Madison, reached out to the plebeian 'democrats' of the North and West. In Britain and France, artisans and sans-culottes had been drawn into the anti-slavery campaigns, sometimes with momentous results; but their North American counterparts were more circumspect. The Democratic-Republican agitation had a powerful national-populist strain. Virginian planters were part of the nation, and slaves were not. Even radicals uncomfortable about slavery, as Jefferson himself claimed to be, could grasp that this issue threatened the integrity and existence of the new Republic. A few known anti-slavery radicals, such as Abraham Bishop, participated in the Democratic-Republic agitation of the 1790s, but they were unable to promote the issue in this milieu. Philip Foner tells us that Jefferson's *Notes on the State of Virginia* was popular with members of the Democratic-Republican Societies, and that 'although there were scores of resolutions adopted by the popular societies in hailing and supporting the French Revolution, not one was passed supporting another revolution occurring at the same time – the black revolts of slaves in the French West Indies.'[34]

The exacerbation of partisan conflict brought little benefit to the free blacks in the North. 'Free-womb' measures wound down slavery, and free blacks could gingerly seek to exercise the rights of citizens, but they received few friendly invitations. Instead each party portrayed the opponent as the favoured vehicle of Negroes or 'colored citizens'. Thus a famous Federalist cartoon, entitled 'A Peep into the Antifederal Club', showed a desperate crew of ruffians including a pirate, a devil, a Jacobin and a black man, who is asked: 'What do you think of this?' and replies 'tink! Fine ting Broder bockra [brother whitey] our turn nex.'[35] The Federalist jest here is as much at the expense of the Republicans as it is of the black. Waldstreicher writes that Republicans 'portrayed blacks as degraded, dependent and unworthy of citizenship.'[36] He cites a Republican editor who, on the eve of a parade, warned that the Federalists would 'hire Negroes and vagabonds who are in their service to join the procession, to throw ridicule on it'.[37]

Around this time (1793–4) the sans-culottes were cheering slave emancipation in Paris, and, at a Sheffield meeting called to support a wider franchise and 'the total and unqualified abolition of Negro slavery', thousands of metal workers endorsed freedom for the slaves in order to 'avenge peacefully ages of wrongs done to our Negro Brethren'.[38] In rallying to the abolitionist cause British workers were perhaps seeking to confer respectability on their gathering. Soon, unlike their US counterparts, they were to be banned from holding such public assemblies because of the anti-Jacobin panic of the mid- and late 1790s. Meanwhile the demagogy of the US Democratic-Republicans also abated. By the late 1790s or early 1800s the Democratic-Republicans even began to soft-pedal their earlier revolutionary rhetoric. By 1800, as Simon Newman puts it, 'toasts to Thomas Paine, liberty, equality and fraternity, and to the rights of man were all but forgotten'.[39] The language of Democratic-Republicanism had very rarely challenged the slave-holder, but now this was less likely than ever.

---

34 'Preface' to Philip Foner, ed., *The Democratic-Republican Societies, 1790–1800*, Westport 1976, pp. 3–32, 13. See also Simon P. Newman, *Parades and the Politics of the Streets: Festive Culture in the Early American Republic*, Philadelphia 1997, pp. 120–51. Using the pseudonym J. P. Martin, Abraham Bishop published a radical defence of 'The Rights of Black Men' in the Boston *Argus*, November/December 1791.

35 David Waldstreicher, *In the Midst of Perpetual Fetes: The Making of American Nationalism, 1776–1820*, Chapel Hill 1997, p. 231.

36 Ibid., p. 232.

37 Ibid.

38 Hochschild, *Bury the Chains*, p. 245.

39 Simon Newman, 'American Political Culture and the French and Haitian Revolutions', in Geggus, *Impact of the Haitian Revolution*, pp. 72–89.

The 'revolution of 1800' was not socially radical, and some Northern gentlemen certainly supported it, but this was perhaps the first time in history that a partisan clash led to a change of government with a large number of white males having the right to vote. However, not all those votes carried equal weight. Jefferson owed his victory to the 'three-fifths' clause which boosted his support in the Electoral College. Jefferson never uttered the word slavery, but in the election of 1800 he was to win the electoral college votes of all the Southern states. When the election was deadlocked in that college, Southern Federalist leaders like Charles Pinckney of South Carolina knew that the slave-holder was their man.[40] Both the radical Northern farmers and working men, and the Southern slave-holders, were obliged by the pressure to find allies to form cross-sectional ties. In so doing Northern Democrats might hope to escape from the tutelage of Northern patricians, while Southern slave-holders acquired an extra line of defence for their 'peculiar institution'. The gentlemen of Virginia and Carolina were inclined to a fierce independence and liked to think of themselves as stout defenders of liberty and the common man. If this patriotic stance helped to win friends in the North and West, this was an added bonus. The slave-holders were comforted by the knowledge that each state decided the boundaries of citizenship. And since physical security was such a tangible issue to them, they would also have been reassured by the Second Amendment, with its confirmation of the people's right to bear arms and to form a 'well-ordered militia'.[41] But states' rights were not enough: slave-holders also needed to have confidence in the national power. Democratic-Republicans claimed to embody the national idea and the true spirit of Patriotism, imbuing these with implicit, and sometimes explicit, racial exclusion.[42] The anti-slavery impulse of Patriot radicalism was more effectively smothered by the Virginian embrace than it could have been by outright suppression.

The two US parties said very little about slavery, but if there was a difference then it was the Federalists who seemed most uncomfortable with the institution. The Northern Federalist leaders patronized Manumission Societies and were more likely to support 'free-womb' laws, such as those in New York and New Jersey. Sometimes moderate anti-slavery initiatives served to unmask or divide the Republicans, but foreign policy differences were more dramatic.

The Adams administration favoured doing business with the new leader of Saint-Domingue so long as he welcomed US traders and abandoned French attempts to export slave insurrection. Toussaint, alarmed by signs that the *colons* were regaining influence in Paris, was happy to accept US help. The

---

40   Peter S. Onuf and Leonard J. Sadowsky, *Jeffersonian America*, Oxford 2002, p. 56.

41   The right to bear arms was collective as well as individual; it extended to militias organized at state level as well as to county patrols.

42   For the prevalence of racial imagery in the early republic, see Waldstreicher, *In the Midst of Perpetual Fetes*, especially pp. 294–322.

secretary of state, Timothy Pickering, sent a secret envoy to the black general in 1798 offering support. Subsequently US warships helped Toussaint to overpower an opponent – the mulatto general André Rigaud – who was more faithful to France. Toussaint, as noted in the last chapter, agreed to end attempts to export slave insurrection.

Both Britain and the United States were intensely concerned at the French Directory's aggressive pursuit of a revolutionary anti-slavery policy. British losses in the Eastern Caribbean had shown just how devastating this could be. The French Republic hoped to use André Rigaud, the mulatto commander of Southern Saint-Domingue, to mount an expedition to seize Jamaica. The Republic's commissioner in the South, Hédouville, was in charge of this plan, a Caribbean counterpart to the French attempt to link up with the revolt of the United Irishmen. The British feared that a battle-hardened force of a few thousand coloured troops could inflict great damage on Jamaica, and even lead to its loss. The US authorities were greatly disturbed by this policy. Pickering favoured backing Toussaint against Rigaud, partly because Toussaint's victory would open Saint-Domingue's ports to US merchants, but also for reasons of fundamental security. Pickering was, in his own way, an abolitionist, making it easier for him to offer help to Toussaint. But he also believed that 'the Blacks of St. Domingo will be incomparably less dangerous [under Toussaint] than if they remain subjects of France'. He feared that the French revolutionary authorities would use black soldiers to attack 'all the British [Caribbean] isles and put in jeopardy our Southern states.'[43] Animated by such fears, the US navy offered vital supplies and transport to Toussaint, in return for trade concessions and a promise to abort all attempts to spread French Revolutionary influence. Whether or not this particular compromise was justified – although it probably was – Toussaint's skill in playing off the powers against one another was necessary to the survival of the emancipation regime. The significant help extended to Toussaint by the Adams administration might have become a source of US national pride but, as David Brion Davis observes, it has instead usually gone unnoticed.[44]

If the Federalists secretly tilted to Toussaint, the Republicans openly inclined to France. By 1796 those interested in such matters would be aware that France's ascendancy over Spain might allow it to repossess Louisiana. But it is not yet clear when this first began to dawn on US leaders. In 1798 Mississippi's territorial governor, Winthrop Sergeant, warned Secretary of State Pickering

---

43   Quoted in Carolyn Fick, 'Revolutionary Saint-Domingue and the Emerging Atlantic Paradigms of Sovereignty', *Review* 31/2 (2008), pp. 121–44. This essay is fundamental for understanding these events, but I respectfully disagree with the author's suggestion that there was something 'paranoid' in Pickering's fears, since the French did have such plans (more evidence on this below). Anyway, the actions of statesmen are often prompted by paranoia.

44   Davis, *Inhuman Bondage*, p. 7.

that if France regained Louisiana, 'a few French Troops with a Cordial cooperation of the Spanish creoles, and arms put into the hands of Negroes, would be
formidable indeed'.[45] In allowing the United States to be drawn into the 'Quasi-
War', President Adams was inciting France to consider such a highly alarming
move. French encouragement of subversion continued. Gabriel Prosser, the
ringleader of a slave conspiracy discovered in Richmond in 1800, believed that
the French would support the anti-slavery cause in North America. But
President Adams became aware of many signs that moderation was in the
ascendant in France. During his last year in office he came to doubt the wisdom
of the Quasi-War, dismissed Pickering and moved to make peace with France.

When Jefferson became president in 1801, he went further than Adams and
promised Napoleon every assistance in isolating Saint-Domingue and, as the
French envoy reported, 'reducing Toussaint to starvation'.[46] This was quite
consistent with Jefferson's willingness to describe Toussaint and his supporters
as 'cannibals of the terrible republic'. But in a letter to Monroe dated November
1801, he made a significant admission in the course of a discussion as to where
it would be best to deport unruly blacks: 'The most promising . . . is the island
of St. Domingo, where the blacks are established into a sovereignty de facto. &
have organized themselves under regular laws & government.'[47] Notwithstanding
this judgement, Jefferson opted to deny Toussaint any recognition and to
support a return to slavery and French rule.

NAPOLEON, LOUISIANA AND THE ATLANTIC CHESS BOARD

Napoleon was lured into his attempt to restore slavery by Britain and the United
States. Dubois cites a note from Henry Addington, the British prime minister,
on peace negotiations with France, in which he explains: 'The interest of the two
governments is absolutely the same, the destruction of Jacobinism and above all
that of the Blacks.'[48] It is easy to see why Britain, the United States and Spain,

---

45   Quoted in Adam Rothman, *American Expansion and the Origins of the Deep South*, New
York 2004, p. 16.

46   Dumas Malone, *Jefferson the President, First Term 1801–1805*, Boston 1970, pp. 252–3; and
Charles Tansill, *The United States and Santo Domingo*, Baltimore 1938, p. 87. For Jefferson's evolving
policy towards Toussaint and Napoleon see Tim Matthewson, 'Jefferson and Haiti', *Journal of
Southern History* 61/2 (May 1995) and the same author's *A Pro-Slavery Foreign Policy: Haitian–
American Relations during the Early Republic*, Westport 2003. These events show Jefferson readily
conceding to the pressure of slave-holder opinion and expose the hollowness of his occasional
wistful expressions of a commitment to emancipation.

47   Letter to James Monroe, 24 November 1801, appendix to *Notes on the State of Virginia*,
pp. 276–9, 278.

48   Du Bois, *A Colony of Citizens*, pp. 366–7. For the metropolitan context following
Napoleon's seizure of power see also the contributions by Yves Benot, Marcel Dorigny, Bernard
Gainot, Thomas Pronier and Sabine Manigat, in Benot and Dorigny, eds, *Rétablissement de
l'esclavage dans les colonies françaises*, Paris 2003.

with their valuable slave plantations, would welcome the destruction of the new black power, more difficult to see why Napoleon allowed himself to be lured into this disastrous enterprise. The Revolutionary policy in the Caribbean had inflicted huge losses on his main enemy, the British. Some, such as Mississippi's previously quoted governor, Winthrop Sergeant, feared that Napoleon would ally himself with Toussaint Louverture and use Saint-Domingue as a base from which to launch a new anti-slavery offensive in the Caribbean with the help of coloured troops. Talleyrand, the French foreign minister, reported to the French ambassador in London in November 1801 that Napoleon was in two minds. If the British did not allow a large French expedition to sail for the Caribbean unmolested, then it might be necessary to 'recognize Toussaint' and the new 'black Frenchmen', since this would create 'a formidable base for the Republic in the New World'.[49] He will have counted on the French envoy using this threat to bring the Anglo-Saxons to accede to French demands.

In fact, Napoleon was anyway loath to recognize black leaders he thought of as 'gilded Africans'. Instead of simultaneously alienating the rulers of Britain, Spain and the United States, he counted on pleasing them all. As he noted, since 'the Spanish, the English and the Americans also are dismayed by the existence of the black republic', they would see the 'common advantage' to the 'Europeans' of 'destroying the rebellion of the blacks'.[50] The attempt to restore slavery was bound to make it far more difficult to regain control in Saint-Domingue. The British had protected and maintained slavery following their occupation of the French island of Martinique in 1794, so their offer to return the island to France in 1801 was as compromising as it was tempting. Jefferson was, to begin with, disposed to encourage Napoleon in a course of action that would yield advantage whatever the outcome – weakening or destroying either Toussaint or Napoleon, or both, and perhaps facilitating a deal over Louisiana.

Given the French undertaking to destroy the black government in Saint-Domingue, neither the British nor the Americans objected to the dispatch of the Leclerc expedition. Napoleon later complained that émigré colonists and merchants, and their suborning of his ministers, led him into the trap. But to him the plantations of the New World were a glittering prize and he saw the vulnerability of Spain and Portugal, together with their valuable colonies. The secret treaty with Spain for the retrocession of Louisiana was part of this grand vision, and in 1802 he gave orders for another large French force to sail to the Caribbean: supposedly reinforcements for Leclerc, but in reality ready to sail onwards to New Orleans. At this point he clearly meant Louisiana to again become a French colony, but events conspired to frustrate him. Freak weather

49   Dubois, *Avengers of the New World*, p. 260.
50   Ibid., p. 256.

prevented the expedition sailing.[51] Even more ominously, the Leclerc expedition went badly and black resistance in Saint-Domingue (and Guadeloupe) demanded all the troops that could be spared. In these difficult circumstances the alternative option of selling Louisiana came under consideration. From his recent sojourn in Philadelphia, Talleyrand was well aware that members of the American elite – his own friends – took an acute interest in Western lands.[52]

Jefferson, who distrusted Napoleon, had been concerned at the size of the Leclerc expedition and worried that Louisiana might be its real aim. Even if slavery was restored, this was an alarming prospect. The US authorities did not attempt to stop their merchants trading with Toussaint. Later, as Leclerc became bogged down in an increasingly difficult struggle, Jefferson was made aware that he might acquire Louisiana if he offered a large sum to the cash-strapped consul and raised the hope of US support in the likely event of renewed conflict with Britain. Napoleon accepted the deal, and it is possible that someone on the French side (Talleyrand?) first mooted it. Although apparently a huge sacrifice of territory, the French knew that Louisiana would be difficult to defend from British attack, and that such a handsome bargain would earn much goodwill from the US government while offering French forces a last hope of retrieving the situation in Saint-Domingue.

The United States thus acquired vast new territories suitable for planta-tions. Congress and president not only ratified the Treaty, but Louisiana territory was to be permitted to import slaves from other states, thus boosting demand for, and the prices of, slave imports from Virginia. Given a buoyant slave popu-lation, planters did not need Atlantic slave imports, and their ending helped to increase the value of slave-holdings.[53]

Jefferson had nearly doubled the land-area of the United States thanks, in part, to the tenacious resistance of the freedom fighters of Haiti.[54] But the black state remained the target of unremitting hostility. It was denied recognition and became the object of a formal mercantile blockade in 1807. At one point Jefferson proposed to the British ambassador that 'all governments who have colonies in the West Indies' should negotiate 'an agreement not to suffer the former slaves to have any Kind of Navigation whatsoever or to furnish them, with any Species

51   See Robert L. Paquette, 'Revolutionary Saint-Domingue in the Making of Territorial Louisiana', in Gaspar and Geggus, eds, *A Turbulent Time*, pp. 204–25.

52   François Furstenberg supplies a fascinating account of this milieu in a forthcoming article.

53   I discuss the reasons for the rapid increase in Virginia's slave population in *Making of New World Slavery*, pp. 465–71, and the motives that prompted most planters to support the ending of the Atlantic slave trade in *Overthrow of Colonial Slavery*, pp. 286–7.

54   As famously argued by Henry Adam, *History of the United States of America During the First Administration of Thomas Jefferson*, New York 1962, pp. 391–2. Essentially the same point was made by Alexander Hamilton at the time (see Paquette, 'Revolutionary Saint-Domingue', p. 211).

of Arms and Ammunition'.[55] Jefferson's attempt to quarantine Haiti elicited a remarkable letter of protest from Timothy Pickering, the former secretary of state, now a Massachusetts senator: 'the wretched Haitians ('guilty' indeed of skin not colored like our own), emancipated by a great national act and declared free – are they, after enjoying freedom many years, having maintained it in arms, resolved to *live free or die*; are these men not merely to be abandoned to their own efforts but to be deprived of those necessary supplies which for a series of years, they have been accustomed to receive from the United States, and without which they cannot subsist?'[56]

A domestic colour line matched that in foreign policy. The wave of national feeling that accompanied US successes in the War of 1812 did not lead to a more catholic definition of the nation so far as blacks were concerned. Other than in Louisiana, black attempts to rally to the war effort were rebuffed. That there might be a slavery problem was suggested by the formation in 1816 of the American Colonization Society, a body dedicated to promoting the manumission of slaves, with an undertaking that, once free, they would agree to be shipped to Liberia or some other African destination. The sponsors included many leading figures, starting with Andrew Jackson, the commander at the battle of New Orleans, Henry Clay, and Richard Rush.[57] This solution had a certain appeal for slave-owners in the Upper South, where there was a 'surplus' slave population, and its aim may be compared to the projects to 'whiten' the population entertained by leading planters like Arango y Parreño in Cuba and Andrada e Silva in Brazil. In practice the Colonization Society never succeeded in freeing and deporting more than a few hundred slaves. Planters in declining regions, with too many slaves, sold them at good prices to expanding inland areas. The internal slave trade was to dispatch a million slaves to the plantation frontier.[58]

The norms of a 'White Man's Republic' were becoming more explicit. Immigrant and native whites had considerable success in excluding free blacks from desirable employments and in denying blacks any space in the public sphere. When free blacks in the US North sought to participate in political life, for example by demonstrating on the anniversary of the slave-trade ban or other such occasions, they often met with derision and hostility. On one occasion a spoof advertisement, supposedly imitating African American dialect, appeared in the press announcing the 'Bobalition of Slavery And "Great Annibersary

55   Matthewson, 'Jefferson and Haiti', *Journal of Southern History* 61/2 (May 1995), pp. 209–48.

56   Quoted in Wills, *'Negro President'*, p. 44.

57   Waldstreicher, *In the Midst of Perpetual Fetes*, p. 302. The Louisiana coloured militia fought under Jackson's command but he regarded their existence as a concession to local attitudes, not as an example to be followed elsewhere. Coloured American prisoners of war in Britain who wished to join in celebration of the US victory were not welcome to join the whites, but had to organize their own column. See W. Jeffery Bolster, *Black Jacks: African Americans in the Age of Sail*, Cambridge, MA, 1997.

58   Ira Berlin, *Generations*, Cambridge 2003, pp. 246–70.

Fussible," by de Africum Shocietes of Boston'.[59] Free blacks were barred by law from acquiring Federal land, and by state law from settling in Ohio, Indiana, and Iowa, while exclusion, harassment and segregation were their lot in Northern cities. They lost the right to vote in New York in 1827. By the late 1820s only a fifth of the free black men living in the 'free states' had the right to vote (a figure that was to shrink to 5 per cent by 1860). Since they were counted in the census for representation purposes, Northern white men enjoyed a 'five-fifths' bonus at the expense of black men.[60]

HAITI AND THE IDEA OF REVOLUTION

The revolt in Saint-Domingue and the setting up of a coloured, but European-style, republic had a large impact on the nineteenth-century imagination, especially on abolitionists and the Romantics. In France it inspired Victor Schoelcher, the abolitionist organizer and colonial minister, who paid tribute to Toussaint, and Alphonse de Lamartine, poet and president, who wrote a verse drama devoted to the black leader. In the United States the example of Toussaint was invoked by the veteran white abolitionists William Lloyd Garrison and Wendell Phillips, as well as by black leaders. The Haiti of Pétion and Boyer offered a haven to people of colour, something appreciated by African American sailors and a source of vexation to US officials.[61] The very existence of Haiti emboldened African Americans to reach for freedom, as Denmark Vesey, William Wells Brown and Frederick Douglass testified.[62] When free Northern blacks organized picnics, parades or funerals it was a common precaution for young men to form into an honour guard, sometimes with martial details evoking the black state. In the months before and after blacks were enrolled in the Union Army, the Republic's would-be soldiers frequently sported Haitian insignia and mementoes of Toussaint Louverture.[63]

Haiti contributed to an idea of revolution which haunted the political imagination throughout the Americas. The idea of revolution as a cyclic return to a

---

59   Waldsteicher, *In the Midst of Perpetual Fetes*, pp. 339–42.

60   David Gellman and David Quigley, eds, *Jim Crow New York: A Documentary History of Race and Citizenship, 1779–1877*, New York 2003, pp. 1–199. See more generally the survey by Donald R. Wright, *African Americans in the Early Republic, 1789–1831*, Arlington Heights 1993, pp. 127–48. For the even more miserable situation of free blacks in the South see the classic study by Ira Berlin, *Slaves Without Masters*, New York 1974, especially pp. 51–107. Berlin cites the panic reaction to Haiti as a significant factor in the drastic curtailment of the rights of free blacks in the South (p. 81).

61   Bolster, *Black Jacks*,

62   Alfred N. Hunt, *Haiti's Influence on the Antebellum United States*, Baton Rouge 1988.

63   Jeffrey R. Kerr-Ritchie, 'Rehearsal for War: Black Militias in the Atlantic World', *Slavery and Abolition* 26/1 (April 2005) 1–34; Matthew J. Clavin, 'American Toussaints: Symbol, Subversion, and the Black Atlantic Tradition in the American Civil War', *Slavery and Abolition* 28/1 (April 2007), pp. 87–113.

nobler order of things had almost disappeared, its only residue being the name Haiti itself. The American Revolution had destroyed British power in North America. The French Revolution had indelibly associated the idea of revolution with that of a fundamental overturn, contested and bloody. The English had had a 'Glorious Revolution' in 1688, and in the late-nineteenth-century US there would develop very respectable societies of Daughters of the American Revolution. But the events of 1789 and after set up different associations, from fear of upheaval to longings for a world made anew. Theda Skocpol points out that 'ideological models of "revolution" and "counter-revolution", based on understandings of earlier revolutionary upheavals, have been available to proponents and opponents of revolution, especially since the French Revolution.'[64] In the slave-holding Americas one should add: 'and the Haitian Revolution'.

In Europe the crowned heads feared a French-style republican revolution. The American planters had no fear of republicanism – they worried about an undermining of the slave order by 'philanthropic' meddling and slave insubordination. In the United States the idea of a revolution against slave-holding could be in the air even though there were no organizations, and scarcely any individuals, committed to it. The fear that the Republic could break up was often stronger, but a spectre of revolution was never entirely absent. The American Anti-Slavery Society called on slave-holders voluntarily to give up their slaves and, if they refused, for a peaceful 'dis-union' and Northern secession. But Southern slave-holders feared that the vehemence of the anti-slavery critique would eventually become known to the slaves, and encourage uprisings.

The success of the Democratic-Republican party in putting together a cross-sectional alliance that implicitly protected the slave order impelled several of those influenced by the Federalists to become more critical of slavery. But the Federalist party never recovered from its failure to back the War of 1812. However, its tradition did supply one strand which entered into the later constitution of organized anti-slavery, with both William Lloyd Garrison and Lewis Tappan having a Federalist background in their youth. Such men sometimes equated the violence of slavery and the violence of Jacobinism.[65] Following Jefferson's death there were to be very few planters who had any esteem for the Jacobins. And in the fullness of time the anti-slavery impulses evident in the work of Abraham Bishop, the US Jacobin of the 1790s, found an echo in the political anti-slavery of the 1840s.

---

64   Theda Skocpol, *Social Revolutions in the Modern World*, Cambridge 1994, p. 8.

65   Rachel Hope Cleves, *The Reign of Terror in America: Visions of Violence from Anti-Jacobinism to Anti-Slavery*, Cambridge 2009. While offering a subtle and well-documented account of Federalist elements in the anti-slavery critique, this author ignores the significant non-Federalist input to the emergence of political anti-slavery in the 1840s.

In Virginia and the rest of the Upper South, many slave-owners thought that the dangers of a too numerous slave population could be reduced by a policy of 'diffusion', or sale of slaves to other states. However, the economic gains they made from this must be added as motive to their satisfaction at what was a fairly modest 'whitening' of the population of their states. In the deep South some planters urged that the 'domestication' of slaves by means of paternalistic practices was the best way to forestall revolutionary impulses, while others warned that the slaves would take advantage of any loosening of the bonds to hatch conspiracies like those associated with Gabriel Prosser (1800) and Denmark Vesey (1820). The violent uprising of Nat Turner in 1831 fuelled the slaveholders' 'rational paranoia'. The real reassurance for planters was the size of the white population, its organization and commitment to slavery. John Calhoun insisted that American planters had nothing to fear from 'the disorganizing effects of French principles' because the mass of slaves were 'ignorant': 'I dare say that not more than half of them ever heard of the French Revolution.'[66] Calhoun had a point but, again, it was not as reassuring as he intended.

Several black abolitionists were themselves committed to the 'metaphor of revolution', as Manisha Sinha puts it, while others, together with many white abolitionists, warned that slave-holding would provoke a revolution and could only be averted, if at all, by an unlikely conversion of the Southern slave-holders to emancipation.[67] Eventually such an idea animated Gerrit Smith's political abolitionism and led to John Brown's assault on Harper's Ferry. But Southern radicals saw the danger – or perhaps one should say imagined the danger – too. The relationship of social forces in the antebellum United States did not favour a slave uprising, but – partly thanks to Haiti – the idea of a revolutionary overturning of the slave order was nevertheless abroad and itself became an element of the political drama that led to the Civil War. Just before the election of 1860 Chief Justice Roger Taney confided to a friend: 'I am old enough to remember the horrors of St. Domingo and a few days will determine whether anything like it is to be visited upon any portion of our own southern countrymen. I can only pray that it may be averted.'[68]

The slave-holders of the South had become so alarmed that in 1861 they opted for the huge gamble of secession. The fear of slave violence had always been a fundamental ingredient of the slave order, helping to cement solidarity

---

66   This statement is quoted in a survey that shows that nagging worries about security prompted a variety of responses from slave-holders. See Lacy Ford, 'Reconfiguring the Old South: "Solving" the Problem of Slavery, 1787–1838', *Journal of American History* (June 2008), pp. 95–122, 104.

67   Manisha Sinha, 'An Alternative Tradition of Radicalism: Black Abolitionist Ideology, 1775–1865', forthcoming in a volume of which the author is editor.

68   Quoted in Timothy Heubner, 'Roger B. Taney and the Slavery Issue', *Journal of American History* in 97/1 (June 2010), pp. 17–38.

among those not enslaved. But with French emancipation and the Haitian Revolution there was a new fear – a fear of emancipation as a state policy – and it was one slave-holders found much more difficult to live with.

With the onset of Civil War the topic became of keen interest to Northeners as well. On 18 March 1862 Wendell Phillips delivered one of the most commented upon lectures of his career when he addressed the Smithsonian on the lessons to be drawn from the life of Toussaint Louverture. His theme was that, while slavery was always liable to provoke bloodshed, a deliberate policy of emancipation would be conducive to military recruitment, speedy victory and good order. Around the same time William Whiting, a lawyer, drew attention to the history of Saint-Domingue and the decisive conduct of Sonthonax in his influential study of *The War Powers of the President, and the Legislative Powers of Congress in Relation to Rebellion, Treason and Slavery* (1861).[69] Whiting's work attracted Lincoln's interest, as will be seen in Chapter 13.

---

69   These examples are studied at length in Mathew Clavin, *Toussaint Louverture and the American Civil War: The Promise and Peril of a Second Haitian Revolution,* Philadelphia 2010.

CHAPTER TEN

Results and Prospects II: Latin America

The turmoil of the American, French and Haitian revolutions had some echoes in Spanish and Portuguese America, but the watershed event was Napoleon's decision to invade the Peninsula and to place his brother on the Spanish throne. The creole elites initially proclaimed their fidelity to the captive king, but their unavoidable autonomy impelled them to a de facto independence. The British fleet enabled the Portuguese ruler and court to sail for Brazil and to make Rio de Janeiro the administrative hub of the empire. The decapitation of the colonial systems gave many opportunities to US, British and freelance merchants, but the British authorities expected them all to comply with the terms of its Continental blockade. While the British could not hope to stop all European trade with the Americas, the blockade was quite effective enough to ruin Bordeaux and create acute shortages of plantation produce throughout Europe. The British government used its sea power, and commercial and financial leverage, to press slave trade bans on both new and old authorities. Once Britain had abolished its own slave trade it was, of course, very much in the interests of its West Indian planters that other nations should subscribe to a ban. If this was one powerful consideration, another was supplied by Haiti, both as an example and as a source of material support. The epoch of the Peninsular War contributes two new words to the political vocabulary – guerrilla warfare, and Liberalism.[1] These terms took up aspects of what had transpired in Haiti, and both were to have echoes in Spanish America.

Neither in Brazil nor in any of the Spanish colonies was the social order as polarized and lopsided as in Saint-Domingue. But the actual and potential plantation development of Brazil and Cuba was large enough to supply both with hopes of filling the hugely profitable gaps left by the removal of Saint-Domingue without suffering the fate of the French proprietors. In the last chapter we already noted that, despite continuing slave imports, the slave proportion of the total population in Cuba and Brazil did not reach 51 per cent. The local elites believed that, so long as they avoided adventures and internecine conflict, they would be assured of a brilliant future. Elsewhere in Spanish America matters stood very differently. While there were enclaves of plantation development in Venezuela and Peru, residues of urban slavery in the major

---

1 See Ronald Fraser, *Napoleon's Cursed War: Popular Resistance in the Spanish Peninsular War*, London 2008, pp. 335–47, 383–4. Fraser urges that the gap between the 'liberals' and the 'guerrillas' explains much of the tragedy of the war (pp. 480–1). For 'Liberal' see also Raymond Williams, *Keywords*, London 1983.

cities, some slave ranching in the La Plata region and slave mining in New Granada (Colombia), the total number of slaves on the mainland was no more than about 200,000, the same as in Cuba, and only around 2 or 3 per cent of the total population. But the Spanish American struggles over slavery and the slave trade in the years 1808–1824 were nonetheless hugely significant, for a variety of material and symbolic reasons. Former slaves were to play a very disproportionate part in the independence wars, and Haiti itself would supply valuable assistance. More generally the advent of free trade – which the British and Americans both warmly supported – was bound to mean the proliferation of slave plantations throughout Spanish America, especially in Gran Colombia and central America, if the Atlantic slave traffic continued. The social content of the struggle for liberation was thus of great importance for the fate of New World slavery.

Benedict Anderson has written of the relative 'social thinness' of the Spanish American revolutions, as the creole elites sought to avoid capsizing the social order. But they were, nevertheless, radical enough to put slavery on the road to extinction.[2] The Spanish American republics evolved into oligarchies characterized by wide inequalities and a racial hierarchy. But, in principle, they offered citizenship to all. Many black and *pardo* (mixed race) soldiers received commissions in the republican armies. However, if any such officer appeared to show special favour to people of colour he would be accused of aiming at *pardocracia* – coloured rule or 'black power' – and this could lead to summary execution. (In Brazil there were similar anxieties about what was termed *haitianismo*.) The potential for social conflagration varied, but it sprang from the imbalance between a small creole elite, comprising only a few per cent of the population, and a sizeable and growing *mestizo* or *pardo* population, speaking Spanish and keen for social advancement and recognition. *Pardos* were of partly African descent, *mestizos* partly Indian, and together the *castas* could comprise over half the population. The indigenous workers in their villages or on large estates remained the most oppressed and exploited social layer; in the Andean highlands and parts of Central America, they were also still the most numerous.

While events in Haiti and British abolition certainly put pressure on the creole elites to explain where they stood on slavery, they were both constrained and encouraged by internal considerations. For some, abolitionist declarations served to symbolize republican nation-building. Claudio Lomnitz has argued that Benedict Anderson's account of creole nationalism fails to register the inscription of race, gender and class within the republican order.[3] He maintains

2   Benedict Anderson, *Imagined Communities*, 2nd edn, London 1995, Chapter 5.
3   Claudio Lomnitz, *Deep Mexico, Silent Mexico: An Anthropology of Nationalism*, Minneapolis 2001, p. 33.

that 'nationalism does not ideologically form a single, fraternal community, because it systematically distinguishes full citizens from part citizens or strong citizens from weak ones (e.g. children, women, Indians, the ignorant). Because these distinctions are by nature heterogeneous, we cannot conclude that nationalism's power stems primarily from the fraternal bond that it promises to all citizens. The fraternal bond is critical, but so are what one calls *bonds of dependence* that are part of any nationalism.'[4] Lomnitz is right to draw attention to the heterogeneity of such 'internal' bonds of dependence. The patriarchal family and estate, spreading out through a network of patron–client relations, helped to constitute many of these bonds. But nonetheless a type of modern nationalism still permeated the whole and asserted a mythic national community. Spanish American nationalism tended towards an inclusive definition of citizenship, embracing all those who were making their life on the soil of the nation. This arose from the logic of challenging the colonial order.

Benedict Anderson notes that the boundaries of the new nations were to correspond to the administrations and jurisdictions of colonial times. As we have seen in previous chapters, the colonial state played a much larger role in organizing the colonial order in Spanish America than had ever been the case in English North America. Periodically sections of *indios* and *castas* would revolt, but this only served to reinforce the loyalty of the creole elite, notwithstanding their resentment at the privileges enjoyed by Spaniards (*peninsulares*). The independence movements were slow to develop, and only emerged decades after the North Americans had shown the way.

Jeremy Adelman stresses this slow development of national movements, since the link to the metropolis was already cut after the breakdown of the Peace of Amiens in 1802, and a new order did not really emerge until the early 1820s.[5] The elites sought to maintain the forms of the monarchy for quite a while, especially in Mexico and Upper Peru where, as we saw in Chapter 1, they were quite dependent on tribute systems orchestrated by the colonial authorities. The cacao planters of Venezuela and the merchants of Cartagena and Buenos Aires were somewhat bolder. When the 'Cortes de Cádiz' were convoked in 1810, the colonial elites were invited to come forward with their own proposals.

As the Spanish American elites moved tentatively beyond loyalism, they still retained an attachment to hierarchy. However, more radical leaders, notably Simón Bolívar, drew on a creole patriotism which had developed over decades, nourished by outcast Jesuits and the spread of Enlightenment ideas within the educated classes. This creole patriotism placed a symbolic value on all things American, including the heritage of indigenous peoples. The resulting republican

---

4   Ibid., pp. 12–13.
5   Jeremy Adelman, 'An Age of Imperial Revolutions', *American Historical Review* 113/2 (April 2008), pp. 319–40, "especially" 337.

ideology retained the royal aspiration to furnish a template for the whole social order, but without its formal hierarchy of privilege and exemption.[6]

In Mexico the first wave of revolt in 1810–11 was led by a pair of radical priests, Miguel Hidalgo and José María Morelos. They claimed to be faithful subjects at a time of usurpation. The emergency required local initiative and far-reaching measures to end the tribute system and slavery, and to end caste distinctions by establishing a true equality. These men mixed revolutionary watchwords with invocation of the sacred compact between monarch and subject.[7] The royal authorities and the creole elite joined in repressing these movements. Although the popular revolt was extinguished by 1815, it marked the entry into political life of hundreds of thousands of *indios*, *mestizos*, *mulatos* and *negros*. While there may have been no more than 10,000 slaves in Mexico by 1810, this was the residue of what had been a sizeable slave population – there were at least ten times as many free *mulatos* of partly African descent. The latter participated enthusiastically in subsequent political battles, including elections, and furnished a key constituency for General Vicente Guerrero, a man who was himself a *casta*, with both indigenous and African forbears. During his brief presidency between April and December 1829, Guerrero issued a decree which freed all slaves without indemnification. (The decree took effect on 16 September, the anniversary of the Congress of Chilpancingo in 1813, at which Morelos had declared Mexican independence.) Proprietors in Texas and Yucatán were outraged. Guerrero offered to negotiate, but was overthrown before this could come to anything. The emancipation decree was upheld by subsequent Mexican governments at a time when the Bolívarian states of South America were only committed to 'free-womb' laws.[8]

---

6   An illuminating study here is David Brading, *The First America: The Spanish Monarchy, Creole Patriots and the Liberal State, 1492–1867*, Cambridge and New York 1991, pp. 293–313, 447–63, 514–620. I discuss the 'baroque' structures of the Spanish imperial order in Chapter 1, above.

7   For the interlacing of tradition and modernity in Spanish American revolutionary thought, see François-Xavier Guerra, 'The Spanish-American Tradition of Representation', *Journal of Latin American Studies* 26/1 (February 1994), pp. 1–36.

8   Patrick J. Carroll, *Blacks in Colonial Vera Cruz*, Austin 1991, especially pp. 130–42, and Theodore Vincent, *The Legacy of Vicente Guerrero*, Gainesville 2001, pp. 195–9. For the extensive mulatto population see Gonzalo Aguirre Beltrán, *La población negra de México, 1519–1810*, Mexico City 1946, pp. 223–45. The neglected, if undeniably subaltern, African undercurrent in Mexican popular culture, which can be detected in its music and wrestling, also found, in this epoch, an echo in the political sphere. The Bishop of Valladolid denounced Morelos and Hidalgo for following the Haitian example. In 1829 Vicente Guerrero may also have believed that an abolitionist gesture would go down well in advanced liberal circles in the Atlantic world. With this in mind I am sceptical of the claim by Eric Van Young that 'the further down colonial Mexico's socio-ethnic hierarchy we travel, the more remote the relationship of an Atlantic revolutionary tradition to the well-springs of the popular insurgency appears to have become.' Eric Van Young, ' "Throw Off Tyrannical Government": Atlantic Revolutionary Traditions and Popular Insurgency in Mexico, 1800–1821', in Morrison and Zook, *Revolutionary Currents*, pp. 127–72, 135. (This valuable volume has studies of the United States, France and Mexico, but not Haiti.) For the impact of French

The formal suppression of slavery by Mexico became a powerfully complicating factor when slave-holders proclaimed the independence of Texas, a Mexican province, in 1836, and when the United States subsequently seized huge chunks of Mexican territory in 1846–8.

In colonial Spanish America there had been a coloured militia, and there were religious and self-help associations formed by people of colour. It was even possible, using a royal warrant known as *gracias al sacar*, for the free man of colour to purchase the status of a white person. Francisco de Miranda, the first Venezuelan Liberator, adopted North American models and failed to attract the support of the *castas*; indeed, the Spanish royal authorities themselves successfully practised what was called *revolución de otra especie*, stirring up *castas* and *negros* against their Patriot masters. Miranda capitulated to the Spanish in 1813 at a time when his main forces were still intact – his baffling decision seemed to reflect hesitation before a struggle that threatened not only to free the slaves but also to up-end the racial order by promoting the coloured majority. Bolívar was contemptuous of Miranda's decision, and insistent that civic equality was the path to victory.[9]

Bolívar's approach to Pétion stemmed from his conviction that a more radical strategy was needed, one that would hold out the promise of racial equality to the *mestizos* and *pardos*. Bolívar wrote in 1815 that racial diversity was no obstacle, since all 'the children of Spanish America, of whatever colour or condition, preserve a reciprocal and fraternal affection for one another.'[10] This myth of racial harmony was far too glib. Nevertheless, if treated as an aspiration, it was a decent one. Bolívar held that just as Spanish rule had promoted caste distinctions and a weak civil society, so strong public measures were needed to promote civic equality and an active citizenry. The aims he proclaimed at Angostura and Cúcuta were to prove very difficult to achieve, but they did signal the beginning of a transformation of Patriotism, with its conscious and unconscious exclusions, in the direction of a variant of modern nationalism, with an inclusive definition of the people, notwithstanding 'bonds of dependence' within it. Interestingly, women were present as mothers and wives in public mobilizations against the royal

revolutionary doctrines on Mexico see Maryse Gachie-Pineda, 'Résonances de la Révolution française au Mexique: 1789–1857', in Michel L. Martin and Alain Yacou, eds, *De la Révolution française aux révolutions créoles et nègres*, Paris 1992, pp. 195–206.

9 John Lynch, *Simón Bolívar: A Life*, New Haven 2006, pp. 57–64; Clément Thibaud, *República en Armas: Los Ejércitos Bolivianas en la Guerra de Independencia en Colombia y Venezuela*, Bogotá 2003, pp. 107–115, 134–5.

10 Simón Bolívar, *Obras*, Havana 1950, vol. 1, p. 181, quoted in Anthony Pagden, 'The End of Empire', *Spanish Imperialism and the Political Imagination*, New Haven and London 1990, pp. 133–53, 170, n. 73. This critical but not unsympathetic account of Bolívar's ideas does not directly address the implications of his anti-slavery positions. The anti-slavery appeals made by Bolívar and other leaders are noted by John Lynch, *The Spanish American Revolutions*, London 1967. See also the classic biography, Gerhard Masur, *Simón Bolívar*, Albuquerque 1949, pp. 271–3 and Jorge Velázquez Delgado, 'La enjundia del Libertador en el ojo de Maquiavelo', *Cuadernos Americanos*, year 15, 3/87 (May–June 2000), pp. 53–65.

authorities in New Granada (Colombia): an entire room is devoted to celebrating their deeds in Bogotá's museum of liberation.

The Spanish American liberation struggle prominently featured coloured soldiers and sailors. Since the Spanish royalists were using coloured troops, the case for doing likewise was not difficult to make. Once it was clear that they were welcome – and would be rewarded with freedom – those of African descent inclined to join the rebels. Former slaves and free people of colour comprised as much as a half of the troops which marched with Bolívar to establish Gran Colombia and to overturn the last redoubts of the colonial power in Peru. The southern army marshalled to carry the torch of liberty from La Plata to the Andes and Pacific also contained many former slaves and free blacks. It joined forces with Bolívar's columns for the final assault.[11] White soldiers were often less willing to fight outside their own native province. In Cartagena, and elsewhere along the coast of Gran Colombia, the *pardos* and *negros* were very much part of the Patriot milieu and helped to shape the course of the liberation struggle.[12] As sailors and port-dwellers, the *costeños* received ideas from all over the Caribbean. Bolívar's liberation army also had a large contingent of British veterans; though often fighting for pay and prizes, many also liked to think that they were soldiering in the cause of freedom.

In the light of the large black contribution to independence in Spanish America, the anti-slavery consequences, while not negligible, were certainly disappointing. The Atlantic slave trade was ended, and 'free-womb' laws were agreed everywhere but in Paraguay. Chile ended slavery itself, but elsewhere many planters did their best to sabotage the free-womb laws. Tens of thousands of slaves remained in various parts of Spanish South America and the institution was not wound up until the 1850s.[13] But with the defeat of Spain, at least it was now impossible for slave systems to develop in huge areas of the Americas.

---

11   Nuria Sales Bohigas, *Sobre esclavos, reclutas y mercaderes de quintos*, Barcelona 1974. See also Peter Blanchard, *Under the Flags of Freedom: Slave Soldiers and the Wars of Independence in Spanish South America*, Pittsburgh 2008. I supply a more detailed account of slavery and the South American Revolutions in *Overthrow of Colonial Slavery*, pp. 331–80.

12   Marixa Lasso, 'Revisiting Independence Day: Afro-Colombian Politics and Creole Patriot Narratives, Cartagena, 1809–1814', in Mark Thurmer and Andrés Guerrero, eds, *After Spanish Rule*, Durham NC, 2003, pp. 223–47 and Marixa Lasso, 'Haiti as an Image of Popular Republicanism in Caribbean Columbia', in Geggus ed., *Impact of the Haitian Revolution in the Atlantic World*, pp. 176-89. See also Alfonso Múnera, *El fracaso de la nación: región, clase y raza en el Caribe colombiano*, 1717–1821, Bogotá 1998, and Marixa Lasso, *Myths of Racial Harmony: Race and Republicanism During the Age of Revolution, Colombia 1795–1831*, Pittsburgh 2007.

13   Harold Bierke, 'The Struggle for Abolition in Gran Colombia', *Hispanic American Historical Review* 33/3 (August 1953), pp. 365–86; John Lombardi, 'Manumission, *Manumisos* and *Aprendizaje* in Republican Venezuela', *Hispanic American Historical Review* 69/4 (November 1969), pp. 656–78. I have more on the slaves and the independence of South America in *Overthrow of Colonial Slavery*, pp. 331–80.

SLAVERY, RACE AND CITIZENSHIP

Racial feeling remained quite pervasive in the new states and, as noted above, there was great fear of *pardocracia*. Still, persons of colour could obtain public office, and *pardo* merchants or farmers could achieve a degree of social recognition which was out of the question in the US South, except during Reconstruction, and extremely rare even in the North. The collective expressions of a coloured identity that had existed in the colonial era either disappeared – as did the *pardo* militia – or withered – as did the religious orders. Meanwhile, in the antebellum United States, racialized caste distinctions were as strong as ever.

Bolívar's turn to Haiti and anti-slavery discourses greatly alarmed some influential North American observers. In or around 1818 General Andrew Jackson composed a memorandum on the dangers occasioned by revolution in South America. He wrote:

The condition and prospects of an important Spanish American district, Venezuela, suggest the most sober consideration in relation to the subject. The state of that district or country may neither be a return to the condition of a Spanish province; nor its establishment as a free white civilized state. It is possible, that there may not be enough of white materials for either of these forms of civil society at the end of the present war, and that fine country, near to the Floridas and capable of very prompt water communications, may become like the black and coloured communities of the late French St. Domingo. The United States have a right to be prudent & energetic on such subjects. The isles and coasts of the Atlantic Archipelago give solemn warnings. We cannot witness with folded arms even the jeopardy much less the subversion of the moral order of our country by the convulsions of well-intentioned communities in contiguous & adjacent neighbourhoods.[14]

With Spain facing defeat in America in 1823, and the restored Bourbon in France sending forces to shore up the position of his Spanish cousin, the president of the United States, James Monroe, opposed any naval intervention by France in the Caribbean, especially if linked to Cuba. Some US leaders hoped eventually to acquire Cuba by purchase. Until that deal could be reached, its possession by Spain, a third-rate European power, was deemed acceptable – but not its sale to France, or any attempted liberation by Gran Colombia or

14 From a memorandum in Jackson's hand found among his papers entitled 'Spain, Floridas, Louisiana, The Missouri Territory', with Washington indicated as the place of composition. It is unsigned and undated, but appears to have been drafted in or around 1818–19. I would like to thank Jane Landers of Vanderbilt University for drawing my attention to this document and supplying me with a copy.

Mexico. It is not often noticed that the Monroe doctrine, while warding off French intervention, actually sanctioned the continuance of Spanish rule in Cuba.[15] In 1829 Secretary of State Martin Van Buren explained: 'Other considerations connected with a certain class of population, make it the interest of the Southern section of the Union that no attempt should be made in the island to throw off the yoke of Spanish dependence, the first effect of which would be the sudden emancipation of a numerous slave population, the result of which could not but be very sensibly felt upon the shores of the United States.'[16]

For his part Bolívar thought that Gran Colombia was large enough already, and counselled Santander that the federation should not seek to include the extremes of North and South (the United States and La Plata), nor should it create 'another Republic of Haiti', as he rather ungratefully put it, by revolutionizing Cuba.[17] (Bolívar's misgivings may have been strengthened by the fact that President Boyer had just invaded Santo Domingo, the Spanish half of the island, and incorporated it into the Republic of Haiti.)

Gran Colombia was still rhetorically committed to ending slavery, but this was only slowly, incompletely and reluctantly translated into fact in the early decades of independence, while the promised extension of citizenship to all racial groups proved even more difficult to realize. But at least the Spanish American independence struggles established a more generous and inclusive horizon of expectation than did their North precursor. Contradictory approaches to slavery were to be a major source of conflict along the border between Anglo- and Hispanic America between 1829 and 1845. Clashes over slavery between Mexico and the Anglo-Texans contributed to the secession of Texas as an independent state, and eventually to the war between the United States and its neighbour.[18]

The whole issue of slavery and revolution presented a very different aspect to the landowner and mercantile classes of Cuba and Brazil. The destruction of the plantations of Saint-Domingue raised sugar and coffee prices and created a huge opening which they sought to fill. In 1802, during the Peace of Amiens, a thousand ships crammed the port of Havana. The planters of Brazil and Cuba

---

15   An illuminating study concludes: 'US officials opposed the liberation of Cuba because they feared that it might become a second Haiti.' Piero Gleijeses, 'The Limits of Sympathy: the United States and the Independence of Latin America', *Journal of Latin American Studies* 24/3 (October 1992), pp. 481–505, 493. See also Herminio Portell Vilá, *Historia de Cuba en sus relaciones con los Estados Unidos y España*, Havana 1938, 5 vols, vol. 1, pp. 276–88.

16   Quoted in Louis Pérez, *Cuba and the United States*, Athens, GA 1997, p. 109.

17   Letter to Santander, 25 May 1823, in Vicente Lecuña, compiler, *Selected Writings of Bolívar*, edited by H. E. Buerke, New York 1951, p. 499. See also Blackburn, *Overthrow of Colonial Slavery*, pp. 395–7.

18   Sean Kelly, '"Mexico in his head": Slavery and the Texas–Mexico Border, 1810–1860', *Social Science History* 37/3 (Spring 2004).

had seen new opportunities in the 1780s and 1790s flowing from the opening of the US market and the collapse of output in Saint-Domingue. In both colonies the royal authorities were persuaded to relax trade restrictions and to allow continuing slave imports (in Cuba's case this included, for the first time, a direct trade to and from the African coast). The size, long settlement and social composition of these colonies emboldened the elite to put aside fears of slave insurgency. As previously noted, slaves had made up as much as 89 per cent of the population of Saint-Domingue, in contrast to a half or less of the populations of Cuba and Brazil. Reassuring as this might be, it was still only prudent to avoid the internecine strife that had given slave rebels their opening in Saint-Domingue.

While the planters and merchants of Cuba and Brazil had prudential reasons peacefully to settle their differences with one another and with the metropolis, there were positive incentives too. From the period of the Seven Years War onward there had been efforts to stimulate plantation growth in both colonies. The reforms undertaken during the ministry of the Marquis of Pombal in Portugal (1750–77), and by José de Gálvez (various posts 1763–87) in Spain and Spanish America, aimed to help the colonial elites to develop plantation agriculture by loosening trade restrictions and encouraging technical modernization.[19] Whereas reform sparked conflict in the English colonies, it was seen as helpful by the *hacendados* of Cuba and *fazendeiros* of Brazil. Colonial companies helped to diversify agricultural output (from sugar to cotton and coffee in Brazil, from tobacco to sugar in Cuba, from cattle to cacao in Venezuela). Pombal encouraged technical education at the University of Coimbra, nursery of the elite in Brazil as well as Portugal. By 1773 matriculations at Coimbra included 162 in mathematics, 62 in medicine, 78 in philosophy and none in theology (there had been 14 in this discipline in the previous year). The advent of these disciplines was a major development, but the most favoured degree was law, with 531 matriculations.[20] In 1773 Pombal repealed the laws relating to *limpeza de sangue* which had restricted all senior offices to Old Christians and men of noble blood. Young nobles were encouraged to acquire professional training in the Naval Academy or Military School. And while Pombal sponsored plantation development in Brazil, he made Portugal the first Atlantic state to ban slavery (in 1759). Before he became first minister Pombal served as ambassador in London, where he was both impressed and disturbed by Britain's aggressive pursuit of its commercial interests and its sense of superiority over foreigners.

---

19 For José de Gálvez see J. H. Elliott, *Empires of the Atlantic World: Britain and Spain in America, 1492–1830*, New Haven 2006, pp. 304–5; for Pombal see C. R. Boxer, *The Portuguese Sea-borne Empire*, London 1969, and Blackburn, *Making of New World Slavery*, pp. 390–1.

20 José Murilo de Carvalho, I, *A Construção da ordem*, and II, *Teatro de sombras*, 2nd edn, in one volume, Rio de Janeiro 1996, p. 57.

The Pombaline period prepared the Luso-Brazilian elite to take advantage of the great upheavals which overtook the Atlantic world after 1776. These eventually culminated in 1808, when Napoleon's invasion of the Peninsula led Dom João, the Portuguese prince regent, together with his incapacitated mother, Queen Maria, and several thousand administrators and courtiers to sail from Lisbon and to settle in Rio de Janeiro. In developments of far-reaching significance, Brazilian ports were thrown open to trade with all nations, and Rio became the capital of the empire. While the British welcomed the free-trade policy, the prince regent had little choice. The measure chimed in with the wishes of Brazilian planters, notably the Bahian planter José da Silva Lisboa, who had advocated this in his landmark laissez-faire treatise, *Princípios de Economia Política* (1804). In this way the full panoply of a European Absolutist monarchy was established on the basis of an open, free-trading economy. Hundreds of ships brought some £2 million of British goods, and their captains were willing to buy Brazilian sugar and cotton at good prices. Soon the British were demanding – and receiving – the protection of preferential tariffs. Rio's city life was enhanced by the foundation of public libraries and scientific institutes, the opening of theatres and the presence of thousands of refugees from Spanish America, the French Caribbean and Germany. A new, more scientific and businesslike spirit began to infuse Brazilian plantation agriculture. Dom João, who became João IV, stayed in Brazil until 1821, when he returned to Portugal, responding to urgent requests from assemblies in Lisbon and Oporto. João left behind his son Pedro as regent, who moved to declare Brazil's independence under himself as emperor in the following year. While Pedro was quite strong-willed enough to act for himself, it was important that he was assisted by Portuguese-educated Brazilian leaders, notably José Bonifácio de Andrada e Silva. However, Brazil's leaders were unhappy at Dom Pedro's capitulation to crucial demands made by the British when negotiating London's recognition of Brazilian independence. He agreed to pay Portugal compensation of £2 million, of which £1.4 million was to be earmarked to allow Lisbon to discharge a Portuguese debt to Britain. He also agreed to end the Brazilian slave trade within three years.[21] In 1831 the Brazilian elite forced Pedro to abdicate in favour of his infant son Pedro II. The subsequent consolidation of the empire as the hemisphere's second sovereign slave power will be considered in the next chapter. In some ways Cuba, though still a colony, was a decade or two ahead of Brazil.

In Cuba and Puerto Rico, as in Brazil, the invasion of the peninsula led to de facto autonomy, encouraging cooperation and compromise between royal

21   Leslie Bethell, 'The Independence of Brazil', in Leslie Bethell, ed., *Brazil: Empire and Republic, 1822–1930*, Cambridge 1989, pp. 3–44; Kirsten Schultz, *Tropical Versailles: Empire, Monarchy and the Portuguese Royal Court, 1808–21*, London 2001; and Emilia Viotti da Costa, *The Brazilian Empire: Myths and Histories*, Chicago 1985, pp. 1–24.

officials and the mercantile and land-holding elites. In the 1790s the leaders of Cuban society had harnessed the typical institutions of the Enlightenment to the task of building an extensive slave-based agriculture capable of filling the yawning gap left by the collapse of plantation output in Saint-Domingue. There was the *Sociedad de Amigos del País*, dedicated to scientific and technical knowledge, and the journal *Papel Periódico*, carrying reports of such discussions. The direct slave trade from the African coast to the Caribbean was encouraged by acquisition of Fernando Po, an island off the African coast, as a slave depot. Refugees from Saint-Domingue helped the *Sociedad de Amigos del País* to raise the technical level of the sugar industry and to spread knowledge of coffee cultivation. The Real Consulado was reorganized as a professional administration under the stewardship of Francisco Arango y Parreño and José Pablo Valiente. The Cuban elite paid close attention to events in Saint-Domingue. While some endorsed the bold strategy of offering army commissions to the black generals, others were not convinced. Arango y Parreño warned that the loyalty of the free coloured militia was suspect.[22]

When Spain was invaded the Cuban elite was to prove wily rather than courageous, extracting valuable concessions from the metropolis while steering clear of formal independence. A succession of able Spanish officials fostered the development of Cuban plantation agriculture. The Marques de Someruelos (Captain-General 1799–1812) and Alejandro Ramírez (Intendente 1816–1821) allowed Cuban planters the freedom to sell where they wished, and to buy large numbers of African slaves. The expenses of the Cuban Captaincy had often been met from Mexican silver in the eighteenth century, but from at least 1803 the island's administrators were able to pay for the upkeep of a sizeable garrison and naval squadron in Cuba and Puerto Rico; indeed the time came when Cuban revenues began to contribute significantly to Spanish finances. The Real Consulado established a prize of 2,000 pesos for the best essay on sugar-mill construction, and established a botanical gardens to improve cane varieties. In 1805–6 the authorities carried out a successful campaign of smallpox vaccination, starting with 20,000 vaccinations and subsequently covering the whole population, including slaves. The *hacendados* obtained direct title to their land, and their sugar works were protected against seizure for debt (the *privilegio del ingenio*). Though the planters could sell their sugar where they wished – most of it went to New York – they had to pay an export tax. Spanish merchants retained protected access to the

---

22   Manuel Moreno Fraginals, *El ingenio, complejo económico social Cubano del azúcar*, 3 vols, Havana 1977, vol 1, pp. 105–11. (This author's *The Sugar Mill*, New York 1978, is the English version of the first volume of this work.) The memoranda of Arango y Parreño and several other key documents are available in Hortensia Pichardo, ed., *Documentos para la Historia de Cuba*, vol. 1, Havana 1964. For the background see Márcia Berbel, Rafael Marquese and Tamis Parron, *Escravidão e política: Brasil e Cuba, 1790–1850*, São Paulo 2010, pp. 95–182.

island's market for imports. The royal tobacco monopoly, the *estanco*, was suspended in 1810 and abolished in 1817.[23]

Spain's Liberal interludes in 1810–14 and 1820–23 saw radical delegates to the Cortes raise the issue of abolition. Hispanic abolitionism is usually given short shrift by historians, but there was to be a significant undercurrent of abolitionism in Hispanic and Hispanic-American social and political thought. The 'Liberals' who emerged at Cádiz were to become, in a variety of national guises, a fascinating feature of Atlantic history in the nineteenth century, promiscuously intermingled with colonialism, free trade, regulated slavery and moderate varieties of abolitionism. While the Cádiz delegates debated, representatives of the Cuban oligarchy worked behind the scenes to make sure that the key Peninsula officials, politicians and military men were in no doubt of the necessity to protect the slave-trade and the slave order of the Spanish Caribbean. Anti-slavery themes were ventilated by Joseph Blanco White's London-based journal *El Español*, and a slave-trade ban was proposed in the Cortes by Agustín Argüelles – the Cuban sugar lobby helped to ensure its defeat and Argüelles was jailed when Fernando VII suppressed the Cortes in 1814. Only intense British pressure persuaded the royal authorities to agree to end slave imports in 1817, and to set up joint courts to supervise this. But this was a sham. The large merchants and *hacendados* easily reached a covert understanding with the royal authorities for the latter to allow massive slave imports.

However, there was another Cuba, as became clear in the second Liberal interlude, 1820–3. On this occasion the Liberal leaders in Madrid compromised with slave-holder interests, but the *menu peuple* of Havana and Pinar del Río elected Félix Varela, an opponent of slavery, as their deputy. The king squashed the Cortes with the help of French troops and Varela was forced into exile. The somewhat more moderate deputy Tomás Gener, of Matanzas, also opposed the slave trade and suffered exile for a while. The Cuban scholar José Antonio Saco, who wrote a massive tome on the history of slavery, saw himself in the humanist tradition of Bartolomé de las Casas. He expounded a moderate blend of abolitionism and nationalism, and his researches were patronized by the more liberal planters. Another critique of slavery was expressed by the political economist Ramón de la Sagra, who, after a spell as secretary to the captain-general, found inspiration in the French Revolution and utopian socialism.

British recognition of the Spanish American republics – and their abolitionist gestures – aroused the anger and contempt of governments in Madrid,

---

23   Christopher Schmidt-Nowara, *Empire and Anti-Slavery: Spain, Cuba, and Puerto Rico, 1833–1874*, Pittsburgh 1999, pp. 1–13; Josep M. Fradera, *Colonias para después de un imperio*, Barcelona 2005, pp. 17–60; Sigfrido Vásquez Cienfuegos, *Tan Difíciles Tiempos para Cuba: El Gobierno del Marqués de Someruelos, 1799–1812*, Seville 2008, pp. 169–95; Imilcy Balboa Navarro, 'Las Luces en la Agricultura', in José Piquera, ed., *Las Antillas en la Era de Luces y la Revolución*, Madrid 2005, pp. 215–46.

who saw London's display of disdain for the slave trade as no more than a smokescreen for its commercial objectives. Britain's ostentatious support for slave-trade abolition and its claim to a right to inspect any suspect ship on the high seas fuelled nationalist resentment not only in Spain but in France, the United States, Portugal and Brazil.

The Spanish and Brazilian authorities were quite willing to accommodate the interests of planters, so long as they remained loyal. Appointments for creole leaders such as Francisco de Arango y Parreño in Cuba and Bonifácio de Andrada e Silva in Brazil helped to promote loyalty to their respective monarchs and planter-friendly decision-making (on which more in the next chapter). Meanwhile staple exports surged and the slave population swelled. Refugees from Saint-Domingue helped to disseminate expertise. Cuba exported 40,000 tons of sugar in 1802, and between 1790 and 1821 registered imports of no less than 240,000 slaves, with at least a further 60,000 unregistered imports. A count in 1816 reported that the island's slave population had risen to 310,000 and that the coloured population, free as well as enslaved, now just outnumbered the white population. These proportions might counsel caution, but scarcely alarm. The white population of Cuba still outnumbered the slave population and was relatively homogenous, with substantial numbers of smallholders and about 20,000 soldiers in the Spanish garrison.[24] Brazil also now returned to the front rank of plantation production, with large exports of sugar, coffee and cotton. The slave population of Brazil grew from 1,582,000 in 1798 to 1,930,000 – or just over half the total population – in 1817–18, a peak from which it was gradually but steadily to decline.[25]

The Brazilian elite was not drawn to seek security in racialization. The elite and the 'white' population were probably somewhat less homogenous than the white population of Cuba. But anyway they comprised only about a quarter of the population and, for security, needed the support of the free people of colour. The authorities in Brazil had been lax in enforcing *limpeza de sangue*, and besides the Portuguese technique of colonization placed great value on cultural assimilation and social cooptation. Both Portuguese and Brazilian leaders embarked on fundamental constitutional debates in the years leading up to 1822. While these culminated in Brazilian independence, neither side favoured a racial definition of citizenship. There was considerable agreement that those born on Portuguese or Brazilian soil, so long as they were not enslaved, should be accounted at least 'passive' citizens, possession of property or income being the decisive criteria for 'active' citizenship. However, the African-born were another matter and, even if manumitted,

---

24 Fernando Ortiz, *Los negros esclavos*, Havana 1916, pp. 18–19; Moreno Fraginals, *El ingenio*, vol. 1, pp. 95–102.
25 Robert Conrad, *The Destruction of Brazilian Slavery 1850–88*, Berkeley 1972, p. 210.

would not be granted citizenship. By downplaying or ignoring descent, the Brazilian slave-holders were in a better position to align the whole free popu-lation – a half of the total – against a slave population divided by multiple occupational, ethnic and religious identities. Brazilian leaders learned to take pride in this, as may be gleaned from the remarks of a member of the Brazilian Legislative Assembly in 1823, in which he referred to reports of support in US ruling circles for the 'colonization' of manumitted blacks to Africa: 'Gentlemen, may we not wish to be more philanthropic towards our slaves than the North Americans: as we know they are trying to abolish slavery, but they don't want them to play any role in American society, rather they want to get rid of them . . . In fact their repugnance is so great that they won't even grant free men of colour political rights or access to public posts. On this point they are . . . unreasonable and we are superior to them'.[26]

Symbolic of the civic potential of the literate and professional mulatto was the knighting of André Pereira Reboucas, son of a freedwoman, as a *Cavaleiro* of the Order of the Cross in 1822, and his appointments as secretary of Sergipe province in 1824 (briefly), as a member of the chamber of deputies (from 1830) and eventually as *Conselheiro do Imperador* – imperial counsellor – in 1861.[27] The old rules of *mancha de sangue* were not very strictly enforced, but they would certainly have prevented a coloured man from holding such posts. The ascent of Reboucas was, of course, highly unusual, but men of colour who were Brazilian-born and otherwise qualified could advance them-selves, while foreign-born whites, especially Portuguese, found doors closing against them.

The planter elites of Cuba and Brazil were manifestly not paralysed by fear of their slaves but, mindful that a further twist of war and revolution could compromise or destroy their wealth, they acted with due caution. The Cuban planters were better prepared but in some ways faced a more difficult situation. In 1812 a conspiracy was uncovered in Cuba, involving both free men of colour and slaves; it was supposedly inspired by the arrival of Jean François, the former insurgent from Saint-Domingue.[28] In this context a strengthening of the Spanish garrison in Cuba aroused no opposition. By the early 1820s both Arango y Parreño and Andrada e Silva were urging that the time had come to halt slave imports and to encourage European immigration. The Havana

---

26   Marcia Regina Berbel and Rafael de Bivar Marquese, 'The Absence of Race: Slavery, Citizenship, and Pro-Slavery Ideology in the Cortes of Lisbon and the Rio de Janeiro Constituent Assembly (1821–4)', *Social History* 32/4 (November 2007), pp. 415–33, 415. This is a key article for understanding the slave order in Brazil in the early nineteenth century.

27   Hebe Maria Mattos, *Escravidão e cidadania no Brasil monárquico*, Rio de Janeiro 2000, pp. 35–54, 62–3; and Keila Grinberg, *O fiador dos brasileiros*, Rio de Janeiro 2002.

28   Matt Childs, *The 1812 Aponte Rebellion in Cuba and the Struggle against Atlantic Slavery*, Chapel Hill 2006.

cabildo showed no inclination to risk a struggle for independence in the troubled years after 1810; and even less in the 1820s, by which time the build-up of a large Spanish garrison and the presence of many loyalist refugees would have made it a very demanding undertaking indeed.[29] Similar considerations explain why the much smaller island fortress of Puerto Rico failed to join the independence movements. Puerto Rico was a strong-point in the Spanish New World defences, and had in the past successfully withstood Dutch and British attempts to seize it.

In Brazil there had been republican and nationalist stirrings in the North East in 1817 and 1822, but these were swiftly suppressed and an essential continuity preserved when Pedro I declared the independence of the Empire of Brazil in 1822. Pedro was governor of Brazil as well as heir to the throne, facilitating the move. Portugal was in the throes of a liberal revolution and the assembly had rejected Brazilian demands for fair representation. After some localized skirmishes, the remaining Portuguese forces in Brazil swiftly adjusted to the new situation.[30] The title 'emperor' was no doubt designed to evoke a type of modernity, but it was to take a further two or three decades to consolidate the imperial order (on which more in the next chapter).

The remaining colonial authorities in the Caribbean – British, French, Dutch and Danish – also recognized the potentially crucial role of the free people of colour in the 1820s. David Geggus draws attention to a striking and shared improvement of the position of free people of colour in the Caribbean and South America in the 1820s and early 1830s:

> [O]ne epoch-making change affected almost all colonies in the Caribbean. That was the abolition of legal racial discrimination that the British, French, Dutch and Danish extended to their Caribbean colonies between 1828 and 1832 ... Like abolition [British slave emancipation] in 1834, it was a product of reform rather than revolution, even if it is hard to exclude the French Revolutionary experiment with racial equality in the years 1792–1802 as a possible causative influence. Those who have studied this transition depict it primarily as a reaction to the rapid growth of the free non-white population, to metropolitan abolitionist pressure, to colonial whites' reluctant search for allies against the enslaved and, above all, to the persistent petitioning for reform by the free coloured themselves. Since their campaigns for

---

29 The Cuban elite paid close attention to events in Saint-Domingue from 1791 onwards, with a Cuban *hacendado* serving as governor of Santo Domingo. The policy of integrating black rebels as officers will have been one they supported. In the next chapter the concessions obtained by the Cuban elite will be explored. But see also Moreno Fraginals, *El ingenio*, vol. 1; Larry R. Jensen, *Children of Colonial Despotism: Press, Politics, and Culture in Cuba, 1790–1840*, Tampa 1988; Ada Ferrer, 'La société esclavagiste cubaine et la révolution haïtienne', *Annales* 58/2 (March–April 2003), pp. 333–56; and Blackburn, *Overthrow of Colonial Slavery*.

30 Emilia Viotti da Costa, *The Brazilian Empire: Myths and Realities*, José Murillo de Carvalho, *Cidadania do Brasil, o larga caminho*, Rio de Janeiro 2001.

reform generally date from the period 1810–13, one wonders if the simultaneous . . . emergence of 'racial democracy' in the new Spanish American republics also helped to inspire this free coloured activism.[31]

Clearly these various impulses should each be given weight, but it is difficult, as Geggus concedes, to separate out the influence of revolutionary and reformist pressures on such unbalanced social structures. Colonial authorities – and some local whites – were eager to 'find allies' and accept reform, because they were fearful of black revolt. This fear was present whether or not they were nerving themselves for emancipation. While Haiti certainly concentrated minds, the very existence of oppressed slave/black majorities in an age of great hopes was the basic source of anxiety on the part of slave-holders and governments. (In the next chapter I will suggest that a perceived near-revolutionary threat in both colonies and metropolis was very much present in the minds of British legislators in 1831–3.)

Matters stood differently in both Cuba and the United States during these years. There were increasing numbers of free people of colour, and many pressed for social equality but were denied it. As plantation wealth and slave numbers grew in Cuba the authorities became more cautious. While not wishing to alienate free people of colour, they trusted them less. The coloured militia and brotherhoods were subject to greater invigilation – and in the case of the militia, eventually disbanded. The situation in the United States was different, because coloured rights had never been very considerable. In the immediate post-revolutionary period a few gains had been made, but subsequently past gains were often lost or compromised. In New York in 1821 and 1827, new provisions deprived all but a tiny number of free blacks of the vote. In North American conditions the majority of slave-holders felt no need for black or mulatto allies, because there was a white majority. An influx of European immigrants in the North meant that there was no shortage of labourers. Some migrants brought with them anti-slavery ideas, but many were seduced by the appeal of white citizenship and privilege.

Britain confronted an embarrassing paradox. It had banned the slave traffic and, together with Haiti, had helped to persuade the new Spanish American states to do likewise. But the Spanish American authorities who followed British advice, signing free-trade agreements and conventions against the slave trade, did not prosper commercially. With the collapse of colonial coordination, and exposed to international competition, their economies made a declining contribution to Atlantic exchanges. British merchants recorded some gains in these lands and there were hopeful investments in public

31   David Geggus, 'The Caribbean in the Age of Revolution', in David Armitage and Sanjay Subrahmanyam, eds, *The Age of Revolution in Global Context*, pp. 83–100, 87–8.

infrastructure, but nothing to compare with the buoyancy of the Cuban and Brazilian economies.

By the 1850s British and US trade with Brazil and Cuba, each running at £5 million annually each way, was several times the size of the sales to, or imports from, the rest of Spanish America put together.[32] It was, of course, no secret that the dynamism of the Cuban and Brazilian trades derived from slavery. In the aftermath of 1815 British statesmen had also urged that constitutional monarchy was the ideal political form for oligarchic rule, especially where the monarch lacked the dynastic legitimacy to impose a personal rule. The regimes of Louis Philippe in France and Leopold I in Belgium conformed to this model, as did the Spain of Isabella II and Pedro II's Brazil.[33] Britain was the hegemonic Atlantic power – yet it found itself implicated overseas in the very institution many of its people insisted on rejecting. In the post-1815 Atlantic free-trading world, British merchants and manufacturers seem indissolubly wedded to American slave-owning planters.

SLAVERY ON NOTICE

The Haitian Revolution and the British commitment to slave-trade abolition threw slavery onto the defensive. Haiti had saved the honour of the Atlantic revolutions by striking down racial slavery. The white North Americans had declared a new ideal of popular sovereignty but reserved its benefits for themselves, with none for enslaved African Americans or dispossessed Native Americans and precious few for free blacks. The French Revolution first ignored slavery, then accorded civic rights to coloured proprietors. Only in 1793–4, at a time when the wealth and patriotism of the planters was suspect, did it forge an alliance with insurgent blacks and strike down what remained of slavery in the colonies it still controlled. The slaves had taken advantage of the turmoil to reach for freedom by myriad revolts, escapes and demands for the control of their land and time. A small group of black and white military and political leaders committed themselves to an emancipationist policy in mid-1793 and eventually, under the leadership of Toussaint Louverture, they defeated the British. When France under Napoleon changed its mind the new citizens fought tenaciously to defeat him, eventually establishing the first state in the world to be founded on the rejection of slavery and citizenship for all.

The bloody struggle in Saint-Domingue raging for most of the period 1791–1804 prompted slave-holders and public authorities to look to extra guarantees

---

32   James Dunkerly, *Americana*, London 2000, p. 319.
33   I discuss the fit between slave-holding and 'illegitimate monarchy' in *Overthrow of Colonial Slavery*, pp. 69–74, 413, 490–2, 523–4, 545.

and new political alignments. However, the failure of all attempts to crush the new black power also encouraged slave rebels, free people of colour and other opponents of slavery. Napoleon Bonaparte lost France's richest colony. Jefferson had doubled the size of the United States and safeguarded planter power – domination without hegemony over the slaves – by extending planter hegemony within the white man's republic.

By 1807 Haiti added an extra reason for Britain and the United States finally to commit to the long-mooted ending of the Atlantic slave traffic. The help extended to Bolívar by Pétion in 1816 had helped to radicalize the Spanish American independence struggle. Slavery was not suppressed outright, as we have seen, but a vast territory – much of it suited to plantation crops – had been closed to slavery expansion. None of the new Spanish American republics would be based – as were colonial Cuba, imperial Brazil and the antebellum US – on a slave economy.

The Haitian revolt had showed the great vulnerability of slave colonies where slaves comprised more than four-fifths of the population, while encouraging US, Cuban and Brazilian planters to take precautions and establish a broader social basis. The British and French islands were soon again to be shaken by slave resistance and abolitionism.

A pan-American and transatlantic perspective is required to make full sense of these events or of what they might portend, whether one considers the attempts to shore up the slave systems, or reactions against the new slave power, or the outlook of the now more numerous free people of colour. The blinkers of national historiography are always a problem, but never more so than in an epoch where 'nations' were still very unstable, or in formation, and there was a many-sided intercourse between them. This is perhaps obvious enough in South and Central America, or on the island of 'Santo Domingo'. It also applies to the ever-expanding borders and uncertain identity of 'these United States' and such entities as Texas and the 'Bear Republic' (as California was briefly known). In the early nineteenth century some preferred to think of the United States as 'Columbia' (hence Washington 'District of Columbia', and the magazine and university of that name).

In 1811 John Adams almost ruefully observed to Benjamin Rush: 'Did not the American Revolution produce the French Revolution? And did not the French Revolution produce all the calamities and desolations of the human race and the whole globe ever since? I meant well, however . . . I was borne along by an irresistible sense of duty.'[34] Was he regretting that, as president, he had helped Toussaint Louverture? Probably not. He was writing at a time when the United States, under Virginian leadership, was on a collision course with Britain. Many in his own section, New England, were actively considering secession. They

---

34   John Adams to Benjamin Rush, 28 August 1811, quoted in Davis, *Revolutions*, p. 49.

included Pickering, the man who had served as his secretary of state and whose abolitionist disciple, William Lloyd Garrison, was to dub the US Constitution a 'covenant with Hell and pact with the Devil' in the *Liberator*, the abolitionist journal he launched in 1831.

Adams's stoical despair and foreboding contrast with a very different assessment of the events considered here, made eight years later by an editorialist in the *Quarterly Review*. This conservative British magazine abominated Jacobinism, yet declared in 1818:

> The abolition of Negro slavery and the civilization of this long oppressed race of human beings will probably in later ages be considered to date from the era of the French Revolution. In the midst of all the mischief and misery occasioned by the eruption of that volcano of the moral world, the first germ of Negro emancipation was unintentionally planted in the island of Santo Domingo . . . whence it can hardly fail to spread its roots, in the course of no very distant period, through the whole of the . . . Antilles.[35]

If this striking and unusual perception is rearranged and coupled with Pickering's above-cited tribute to the 'Haitians', we could conclude that the latter had themselves authored an advance in 'civilization' and obliged the Atlantic powers to respect it.

Immanuel Kant did not live to see the founding of the Republic of Haiti but, despite the racial speculations of his notebooks, he abominated the colonial slavery of the Caribbean islands and saluted the positive moral impact that the French Revolution triggered in distant lands. In 1798 he wrote:

> In human affairs, there must be some experience or other which, as an event which has actually occurred, might suggest that man has the quality or power of being the *cause* and (since his actions are supposed to be those of a being endowed with freedom) the *author* of his own improvement. But an event can be predicted as the effect of a given cause only when the circumstances which help to shape it actually arise. And while it can well be predicted in general that these circumstances must arise at some time or another (as in calculating probabilities in games of chance) it is impossible to determine whether this will happen within my lifetime and whether I shall myself experience it and thus be able to confirm the original prediction. We must therefore search for an event which would indicate that such a cause exists and that it is causally active within the human race, irrespective of the time at which it might actually operate; and it would have to be a cause which allowed us to conclude, as an inevitable consequence of its operation, that mankind is improving. This inference could

---

35 *Quarterly Review* 42 (1819), cited in Gaspar and Geggus, *A Turbulent Time*, p. vii.

then be extended to cover the history of former times so as to show that mankind has always been progressing, yet in such a way that the event originally chosen as an example would not itself be regarded as the cause of progress in the past but only as a rough indication or *historical sign*. It might then serve to prove the existence of a tendency within the human race as a whole, considered not as a series of individuals (for this would result in interminable enumerations and calculations) but as a body distributed over the earth in states and national groups.[36]

Kant particularly stresses the impact that events at a distance can have on public opinion. He also sees it at work in the psychology of the event's protagonists: 'No pecuniary rewards could inspire the opponents of the revolutionaries with that zeal and greatness of soul which the concept of right could alone produce in them, and even the old military aristocracy's concept of honour (which is analogous to enthusiasm) vanished before the arms of those who had fixed their gaze on the rights of the people to which they belonged, and who regarded themselves as its protector.'[37] While these remarks were prompted by the French Revolution, I would suggest that, had he lived just a little longer, he might have deemed them apposite in the case of the Haitian Revolution as well. Over and above the special configuration of slavery in each New World territory, the structures of slavery, race and colonialism had certain broadly oppressive characteristics which were bound to arouse resistance. And at the level of development reached by Atlantic communications, long-distance effects were also likely.

While new expedients had secured an extra term for slavery in the Americas in the US, Cuba and Brazil, the institution was still haunted by what had happened in Saint-Domingue. The sequence of revolutions meant that there were narrower limits to the New World slave system – and a growing free coloured population that was to agitate for equal rights and against slavery. Anti-slavery laws enacted in Mexico and South America encouraged abolitionist movements in Europe. And US debates about the status of slavery in conquered Mexican lands would have been very different if slavery was already flourishing there. As it was, abolition's victory in Mexico in 1829 handed a powerful argument to North American 'free soilers'.

---

36   Immanuel Kant, 'A Renewed Attempt to Answer the Question "Is the Human Race Improving?"', *Political Writings*, edited by Hans Reiss, 2nd edn, Cambridge 1991, p. 179.
37   Ibid., p. 183.

HAITIAN EPILOGUE

Christophe ruled the North Kingdom of Haiti as King Henri I until overthrown in 1820, and Pétion ruled the Republic of Haiti in the South from 1805–18, to be succeeded by Jean-Pierre Boyer. After the collapse of Christophe's monarchy, the Republic reintegrated the North. Pétion and Boyer were both mulatto generals, but their republican ideology sought to assert the unity and equality of all Haitians. Boyer enjoyed a long presidency (1818–43), during which time, as noted in Chapter 8, there were the stirrings of a modest but not negligible civil society. Half a dozen newspapers (among them *Le Manifeste, Le Patriote, Le Temps*) disputed the country's future direction. Some even questioned what they called the 'new aristocracy of finance', who organized the national debt and the *fisc* or tax office, with its new species of bondage. Intra-elite disputes were conducted in French, and the distribution of political favours often reflected membership in Haiti's twenty-three Masonic lodges.

Following agitation against Boyer's lengthy incumbency, the elections of 1842 saw victory for the opposition. The president sent soldiers who prevented many of the new deputies from entering the National Assembly. This action was denounced by the newly formed Society for the Rights of Man in its *manifeste de Praslin*, which declared that Haitians now had no alternative but to take up arms. The agitation against Boyer snowballed and his officers found it increasingly difficult to maintain control. The general commanding at Port-au-Prince denounced the role of women in spreading rumours and warned that they would be held responsible. Secret meetings were held on country estates, with the workers exhorted not to abandon cultivation. The 'Liberal' opposition made soundings of military opinion and attracted the support of Charles Hérard, a general who owned the Praslin estate. With military units defecting to the Liberals, Hérard marched on Port-au-Prince. Boyer took refuge on a British ship and sailed for Jamaica. A Liberal provisional government, headed by Hérard as president, was established in April 1843, but it soon became clear that the overthrow of Boyer had aroused the expectations of the peasantry and urban poor, who wanted tax reductions, debt forgiveness and further land distribution. An 'army of sufferers' or *armée souffrante* arose, with backing from black proprietors and *piquets*. Hérard had to make way in 1844, but the popular rebellion failed to stabilize and the regular army retained control. However, the elite now chose a succession of black generals (Guerrier and Pierrot) to occupy the Presidential Palace. The *piquets* retreated to the interior. The Liberal Revolution had unintentionally provoked a popular rising, but this had been contained.[38]

---

38 The most succinct account of these events is Sheller, *Democracy After Slavery*, pp. 11–44.

The episodic and limited violence of the country's politics was deeply disappointing, but not so different from the chequered history of nineteenth-century Spain and most of Spanish America. The violent expansion of the French in North Africa, the English in India, or the United States across the North American continent was to involve violence and racism on a far larger scale than anything seen in Haiti after it gained independence. From the standpoint of the Haitian people that did not render the oppressions to which they were subject any more acceptable, and many of them undoubtedly cursed their own rulers' unfortunate attempts to emulate the other powers.

Christophe and Pétion had based their rival concepts of a new order on the suppression of slavery and mayhem. Boyer had trod the same path. African and creole, *anciens* and *nouveaux libres*, black and mulatto, could all unite against projects to reimpose slavery, and could also discover that they needed one another. As a Haitian saying has it, *Chak nwa gen mulat li, chak mulat gen nwa li* ('Each black has his mulatto, each mulatto has his black'). The country's rulers, whether black or mulatto, knew that they could only govern with the implicit consent of the *piquets*, or armed peasant militias. As a result of the Haitian Revolution, men and women had a degree of social freedom which was far greater than that which people of colour enjoyed anywhere else in the Americas. Haitian men were citizens, but it was military rank, landownership and – to a lesser extent – education which conferred real political power. These were male power structures, with women having leverage in both the household and peasant economy. The relative ineffectiveness of the Haitian state was not a matter of great concern to the peasants and town-dwellers, who used their new freedom to elaborate a rich folk culture. The weakness of the state limited civic participation, but it also limited the state's capacity to interfere in the lives of the common people.

The leaders of Haiti in the first decades of its existence, whether monarchical or republican, went to considerable lengths to adopt the prevailing state forms and styles of the European and American world. Their public buildings, dress, and legal arrangements reflected this, and French remained the official language. Henri Christophe invited Protestant missionaries and educators while the Catholic Church continued to function, often with official blessing, in the Republic. Writing in 1830, Hegel remarked that the Negroes of Haiti 'had formed a state built on Christian principles'.[39] While this was certainly meant as a tribute, it also pointed to what might be seen as a defect. Formal state structures typically misrepresent their citizens, but the gulf was quite glaring in the case of Haiti.

---

39   G. W. F. Hegel, *The Philosophy of Subjective Spirit*, Dordrecht 1979, vol. 2, p. 55, quoted in Susan Buck-Morss, 'Hegel and Haiti', *Critical Enquiry* (Summer 2000), p. 854.

Dubois suggests that the soul of Haiti is still found in a religious ceremony, not in a Declaration of Independence, a Constitution or a Pantheon.[40] It could further be urged that this ceremony – the nocturnal gathering in the Bois Caïman which planned the great rising of 1791 – is also enshrined in nationalist historiography, and that there are secular as well as religious bearings for Haitian nationalism. The spirit of the revolution lives on in the people, and their stubborn defence of an autonomous personal realm, but not yet – despite the efforts of such reformist leaders as Anténor Firmin and Jean Price-Mars in an earlier epoch, or Jean Dominique, Aristide and René Préval more recently – in the formal arrangements of the state. It is only the efforts of the country's own citizens, not foreign intervention, that could mend this absence of a properly functioning and legitimate state.

Though Haiti is dirt poor, its people do not define themselves by waged employment and consumption. In Haiti the legacy of the descendants of slaves and rebels comprises echoes of both a pre-capitalist past and a memorable refusal of the first globalization.

---

40   Dubois, *A Colony of Citizens*, pp. 430–7. See also Gérard Barthélémy, *Le Pays en dehors*, Port-au-Prince 1989.

Part IV

THE AGE OF ABOLITION

CHAPTER ELEVEN

Abolitionism Advances –
But Slavery is Resurgent

The ending of New World slavery lends itself all too easily to notions of an irresistible advance. Yet the outcome was often in doubt, and only unevenly and imperfectly attained. Nevertheless abolitionism, slave resistance, patriotic mobilization and class struggle did eventually combine to destroy the slave systems. Slavery went from respectability to widespread odium in Europe in a few short decades. There were times when even many planters heartily regretted their dependence on slaves. Slavery did not simply wither away in the Americas, as it did in many parts of late medieval Europe. The Atlantic slave trade and the slave systems it created in the New World were destroyed through definite acts of legislation and resistance. Emancipation was not a localized or hole-and-corner affair but something to be incorporated in resounding and self-consciously historic decrees. Large social movements against the slave trade and slavery grew up outside the slave zone, and the discourse of abolition became entangled with major political conflicts, shaping and reshaping the polities and cultures of the major Atlantic states. All of this requires systematic explanation – as does the often very disappointing limits of emancipation. Acts of emancipation were seen as proof of moral superiority and as conferring a right to supervise lesser breeds. The discourse of liberty too often became the rhetoric of a new articulation of power, wealth and race. In what follows I can offer only a very tentative outline of an approach to understanding abolition – at some points just a checklist, at others generalizations which strive not to be too general, or simply wrong.

ABOLITION ADVANCES

New World slavery was suppressed in one territory after another, from Vermont in 1777 and Pennsylvania in 1780, to Cuba in 1886 and Brazil in 1888. At the beginning of this period slavery was legal and seemingly unassailable in all European New World colonies. Prior to 1760 it had never been questioned by anyone who seemed to matter, and slave produce was the basis of an Atlantic commerce which was, in turn, the lifeblood of the European empires in the New World, as we saw in Chapter 4. The emergence of the anti-slavery idea from an initially unpromising context was traced in Chapter 7. Despite some small-scale gains, such as tighter regulation of slave ships, the first mass abolitionist campaign in Britain (1787–1792) was brought to an end by the anti-Jacobin panic. The Haitian revolution (1791–1804) secured the freedom of half a million former slaves and encouraged the reawakening of British abolitionism. The British and US bans on the Atlantic slave trade in 1808 were gratifying to abolitionists, as was the denunciation of the traffic by the Congress of Vienna in 1815. This was followed in the 1820s, as we saw in the last chapter, by the emergence of new republics in Spanish America which banned slave imports and enacted 'free-womb' laws. Abolitionist sentiment was stimulated by such gains – but also by the knowledge that an illegal Atlantic traffic continued and that slavery itself still flourished in parts of the Americas. Though it had only minor abolitionist consequences – enforcement of the ban on slave imports to France's remaining colonies – the French Revolution of 1830 signalled the rebirth of an idea of progress, as Condorcet had sketched it.

The rekindling of anti-slavery agitation in Britain in the 1820s and its eventual success in the 1830s seemed to confirm the forward march of abolition. Britain was the Atlantic 'superpower', and emancipation in the British West Indian colonies freed 700,000 slaves. The abolitionist breakthrough itself reflected the new vulnerability of the Caribbean slave order, at a time of profound social and political crisis in both metropolis and colonies.

Slave revolts in Barbados in 1816, British Guiana in 1823 and Jamaica in 1831–2 both reflected and radicalized metropolitan debates on slavery. The rebels were aware that the workings of slavery were controversial. Some believed that local planters or officials were concealing or obstructing metropolitan measures favourable to the slaves. In truth the action of the rebels themselves helped to encourage and reanimate a dormant movement. In Barbados in 1816 some rebels saw an attempt to draw up a slave register as a metropolitan effort to regulate or restrain slave-holders. The slaves who led the disturbances in the British West Indies in the years 1816–32 typically sought negotiation rather than slaughter or pillage. The metropolis and colonial authorities were seen as a potential check on the planters or estate managers. The slave rebels sometimes demanded more free time, or payment for extra work. The colonial authorities had no instructions to negotiate such questions, and the colonial whites called for revolts to be crushed and their leaders summarily executed. The arrival of Methodist and Baptist missions had opened some unofficial channels of communication between metropolis and colony, notwithstanding the missionaries' insistence that slaves should be obedient to their masters. That Baptists, Methodists and other 'nonconforming' Protestants were themselves denied public office or the vote in Britain underlined the appropriateness of their campaigns on behalf of the slaves.

In Demerara in 1823 John Smith, a missionary, was arrested and imprisoned on a charge of having encouraged the slave rebels, but died in prison before he could be brought to trial. British Nonconformists were outraged, and redoubled their anti-slavery agitations. The parliamentarians who had championed abolition had deplored slave rebellion as much as planter repression. But as they learned more about the nature of the disturbances in Demerara, it transpired that the rebellion was not a blind act of vengeance. The abolitionist leader Henry Brougham explained to parliament in 1824 that the slaves were 'inflamed with the desire for liberty', and that it was only natural that they believed that a metropolitan attempt to ameliorate the slave condition would promote their liberty. He drew attention to the restraint of the rebels and to the fact that they had parlayed with the governor, explaining that they wished only for freedom, not bloodshed.[1] In 1816 there had been no organization aiming at slave emancipation; in 1823 a Society for 'Mitigating and Gradually Abolishing the State of Slavery' had been set up. In 1830 the Society was persuaded to adopt immediate emancipation as its goal and to undertake mass campaigns.

The so-called 'Baptist War' in Jamaica (late December 1831) saw some 30,000 slaves, armed only with machetes, desert their plantations to mount a demonstration for freedom. Many of the leaders had an involvement with the Baptist Churches. While the slave rebellion had the character of an armed demonstration with specific demands, the planter reaction was bloody and indiscriminate, with hundreds killed. Four missionaries were deported by the colonial authorities, notwithstanding the absence of proof they had in any way instigated the revolt.

The campaign against the abuses of West Indian slavery, and mounting outrage at the persecution of missionaries, injected a powerful moral and symbolic theme into the campaign against 'Old Corruption' just as the Reform crisis was coming to a head in 1832.[2] This was the most acute crisis of the British political order between 1688 and modern times. Vested interests were against anything but the most minimal change, with the Duke of Wellington at one critical moment constituting himself as a one-man Cabinet in order to defy the popular outcry. Demonstrations, petitions, riots and strikes expressed widespread and disparate civic unrest. With no modern police force, and the bulk of the army in Ireland, there were only some 5,000 troops in London and the Home Counties.[3] In Birmingham the partisans of Reform took to drilling in public. The countryside was swept by 'Captain Swing' riots while the capital witnessed huge – indeed unprecedented – demonstrations by the 'working

---

1   Gelien Matthews, *Caribbean Slave Revolts and the British Abolitionist Movement*, Baton Rouge 2008, pp. 87–8. This work helpfully brings out the dialogue between abolitionists and slave rebels which marked the years 1816–38 and which changed both parties. For the revolts see Michael Craton, *Testing the Chains: Resistance to Slavery in the British West Indies*, Ithaca 1982, and Mary Turner, *Slaves and Missionaries: The Disintegration of Jamaican Slave Society, 1787 to 1834*, London 1982.

2   Hochschild, *Bury the Chains*, pp. 333–54; see also Drescher, *Abolition*, pp. 245–66.

3   For the seriousness of the Reform Bill crisis, see Malcolm Thomis and Peter Holt, *Threats of Revolution in Britain, 1789–1848*, London 1977, pp. 87–8.

classes' demanding 'reform', by which they meant the vote. The country was not heading for a 1789-style revolution; the Hanoverian order was a bloated and corrupt bourgeois regime, not a feudal Absolutist apparatus. A closer and more worrying parallel was the French Revolution of 1830, with the added menace of something more like 1848. Such a denouement was avoided when the king, William IV, had the common sense to give way to Grey, Macaulay and Brougham. The reform they proposed, after all, might sweep away the rotten boroughs, remove religious disabilities and give the vote to £10 freeholders, but it retained the monarchy and House of Lords, and only a little over a tenth of the adult male population would be enfranchised. Edward Thompson writes of this period:

> Viewed from one aspect, England was passing through a crisis in the twelve months (to May 1832) in which revolution was possible . . . The enormous demonstrations, rising to above 100,000 in Birmingham and London in the Autumn of 1831 and May 1832, were overwhelmingly composed of artisans and working men . . . And viewed from another aspect, we can see why throughout these crisis months a revolution was in fact improbable. The reason is to be found in the very strength of the working-class Radical movement; the skill with which the middle-class leaders, Brougham, *The Times*, the *Leeds Mercury*, used this working-class force and negotiated a line of retreat acceptable to all but the most die-hard defenders of the ancien régime . . . The industrial bourgeoisie desired, with heart and soul, that a revolution should not take place, since they knew that on the very day of its commencement there would be a dramatic radicalization . . .[4]

The clamour for slave emancipation chimed in perfectly with responsible reform. It gave credence to the view that the Reform Act was just the beginning of a more far-reaching transformation, achieved by constitutional means.[5]

Both middle-class and working-class representatives welcomed anti-slavery as a terrain on which they could collaborate in ways that might position them better for future trials.[6] The 'moral capital' which the bourgeois

---

4   E. P. Thompson, *The Making of the English Working Class*, revised paperback edn, Harmondsworth 1968, pp. 889–900.

5   On this occasion I find myself in agreement with C. A. Bayly when he writes: 'Arguably, the concession of parliamentary reform, the end to slavery and Catholic emancipation . . . saved Britain and its empire from more dangerous turbulence during the 1840s.' Bayly, *The Birth of the Modern World*, Oxford 2004, p. 140. There is an echo here of Elie Halévy on the Nonconformist contribution to British gradualism in his classic work, *The Liberal Awakening*, London 1949.

6   Betty Fladeland, *Abolitionists and Working-Class Problems in the Age of Industrialization*, London 1984. Edward Thompson's classic work, *The Making of the English Working Class* (1963), vividly documents the reality of class antagonism in these years but says little about anti-slavery, perhaps because it was seen as almost a distraction from the path of class confrontation. The references to Wilberforce are very critical – understandably, because they concern not anti-slavery but Wilberforce's support for an often highly repressive social order.

or middle-class leadership earned in their struggle for slave emancipation could be deployed to contain political radicalization and to demonstrate their bona fides. The Reform Bill awarded parliamentary representation to the new manufacturing centres and established the House of Commons as the leading organ of government. But its moderate features allowed it to be strongly supported by the City of London. Indeed the Reform Act and the Reform parliament were so clearly and narrowly 'middle class' or bourgeois in character that they needed the flourish of some dramatic and generous act to prove that they were not irredeemably selfish and corporatist. A wider appeal had to be made, because popular pressure was required to gain parliamentary and royal assent even for this much reform. Slave Emancipation added something lofty and disinterested to what was otherwise a distinctly moderate and selfish middle-class agenda.[7]

The anti-slavery campaign itself was an intense one, with thousands of meetings, editorials, solemn processions to Downing Street, and massive petitions to parliament. Women's abolitionist societies emerged for the first time in the 1820s, and the Birmingham Ladies Negro's Friend Society led the way in demanding immediate, not gradual, emancipation in 1825. An abolitionist editor published a powerful slave narrative, *The History of Mary Prince*, a vivid account of the vulnerability and unending toil of the female slave. The Methodists and Baptists strongly supported the agitation. Abolitionism had great resonance in British political culture. British governments had made suppression of the Atlantic slave traffic as much a preoccupation of British foreign policy as free trade and the balance of power. In response to abolitionist pressure, governments had introduced a register of the slave population and had proposed regulations – such as a ban on the flogging of female slaves – to render the workings of the slave regime more humane. These measures in their turn had provoked planter resistance and inspired hopes in the slave quarters.

Following the dramatic passage of the Reform Act in 1832, the first major legislation adopted by the Reform parliament was the 1833 Slave Emancipation Act. To the disappointment of many abolitionists, the planters received substantial compensation for their 700,000 slaves, both in cash – just under £20 million – and in the obligation laid on slaves to work for their masters as 'apprentices' for a further six years, on nominal pay. Any who refused were not to be whipped

---

7 I supply a fuller account of the wider meaning and context of British slave emancipation, embracing both slave resistance and metropolitan crisis, in *Overthrow of Colonial Slavery*, pp. 419–72. This larger context and meaning is not offered in an effort to belittle the British abolitionists, still less the vast popular anti-slavery mobilization, nor to diminish the significance of British emancipation. The best recent narratives now pay due attention to slave revolt but there is, perhaps, a lingering feeling that slave emancipation was only briefly and contingently related to the crisis of the oligarchic regime, while it is harder to miss the link between the French Revolution and the birth of Haiti, or US emancipation and the Civil War.

but instead handed to the courts, where they would be sentenced to terms in prison working a gigantic treadmill, which punished the shins of any who failed to keep pace. A 'fact finding' mission sent by the Anti-Slavery Society exposed many abuses. The Emancipation act also provided for the dispatch to the West Indies of English 'stipendiary magistrates' in the hope that this would protect the courts from the planters. The former slaves resisted the terms of 'apprenticeship', and were encouraged by Dissenting missionaries to demand proper wages. The institutions of apprenticeship embodied the latest penal theory, with its concern to administer a 'just measure of pain' to the recalcitrant. But the reluctant West Indian 'apprentices' were not – in their own eyes – malefactors. Their experience of the slave gang and sugar mill had instilled a powerful aversion to the principles of the 'panopticon' prison.[8] A combination of worker resistance, missionary protest, judicial disquiet and abolitionist outrage led to a parliamentary crisis back in Britain as the 'Mighty Experiment' unravelled. In 1838 the government brought the apprenticeship system to a summary end.

The £20 million compensation paid to the West Indian proprietors was, on its own terms, a more successful expedient. Of course, elementary justice should have dictated that this money be paid to the former slaves – it would certainly have helped them to establish themselves as independent farmers. The compensation clause was added partly to appease the West Indian proprietors, but partly too to gain the support of the British merchants and bankers who held large amounts of West Indian debt. (In 2009 the news that Nick Draper, a researcher at University College, London, had found detailed records showing that many City of London banking houses had claimed and received compensation for slaves who they had accepted as collateral on loans extended to planters, made the front page of the *Financial Times*.[9]) As much as a half of the compensation money went to the planters' creditors – with London's merchant banks at the head of the queue – or to planters who had no intention of investing it in the West Indies. However, at least some of the remaining money went to smaller resident proprietors, or to planters who were still committed to their West Indian estates. Sugar output was maintained in British Guiana and Barbados.[10]

Plantation output sagged in Jamaica, where the women largely withdrew from plantation labour, and both men and women sought to cultivate the

---

8   Michael Craton, *Searching for the Invisible Man: Slaves and Plantation Life in Jamaica*, London 1978.

9   Carola Hoyos, 'Paper Trail Loosens Shackles on Hidden Past', *Financial Times*, 26 June 2009, and 'Businesses Regret Links with Slavery', *Financial Times*, 1 July 2009. See also Nick Draper, '"Possessing Slaves": Ownership, Compensation and Metropolitan Society in Britain at the Time of Emancipation 1834–40', *History Workshop Journal* 64/1 (2009), pp. 74–102.

10   Kathleen Mary Butler, *The Economics of Emancipation: Jamaica and Barbados, 1823–1843*, Chapel Hill 1995.

provision grounds they had worked as slaves. While some missionaries saw justice in this demand, it was resisted by both the governor, Lord Glenelg, and by the planter-dominated assembly. The result was a stand-off that left most former slaves without land and the planters without sufficient workers.[11] From the 1840s tens of thousands of contract labourers from India were introduced to the British West Indies to boost the workforce. The labourers bound themselves to work for three years for modest wages and a return fare (though many chose not to return). Plantation output stagnated in Jamaica but grew in British Guiana. While the overall story was of relative decline, the reason for this was that the British islands did not have the space needed for a new 'extensive' pattern of sugar cultivation. Even if slavery had survived in the British Caribbean, its sugar output could not have kept pace with production levels in Cuba or Louisiana. In the circumstances abolitionists were able to argue that the overall results of emancipation were quite positive, with rising plantation output in British Guiana, many estates elsewhere surviving, and former slaves asserting a claim to patches of land that had once been their provision grounds. Slavery had been abolished without massive bloodletting or general social collapse. Pro-slavery writers were less impressed, but moderate partisans of abolition could declare British emancipation a success.[12]

With the triumph of British emancipation, speakers at the World Anti-Slavery Convention in London in 1840 claimed that abolitionism was the cause defining progress in the Atlantic world. Britain was not only the world's leading commercial and maritime power, but its recently reformed institutions were regarded by influential foreign observers as a model. This was an epoch of property franchises, constitutional monarchy, cautious 'reform' and Britain's 'empire of free trade'. New governments in France, Spain, Portugal and Spanish America had agreed to cooperate in stamping out a continuing Atlantic slave traffic. Racial tensions remained in the British West Indies, but emancipation had belied the slave-holders' warnings that emancipation would lead to race war.

The British government maintained the squadron on the West African coast to intercept slave-trading, but many abolitionist leaders did not support the use of military means and instead sought to spread the abolitionist message by attacking slavery itself and fostering anti-slavery literature – not only pamphlets and tracts but also poems, novels and slave narratives.

The British example helped to inspire the birth of a more radical anti-slavery movement in the United States in the 1830s. A large American delegation

---

11   Thomas Holt, 'The Essence of the Contract', in Frederick Cooper, Thomas Holt and Rebecca Scott, *Beyond Slavery: Explorations of Race, Labour and Citizenship in Postemancipation Societies*, Chapel Hill 2000, pp. 33–60.

12   W. G. Sewell, *The Ordeal of Free Labor in the British West Indies*, New York 1862. The suppression of Jamaica's Morant Bay rebellion in 1865 was to qualify this fairly positive view and add to the 'ordeal' noted in the book's title – on which more below, in Chapter 13.

attended the 1840 World Anti-Slavery Convention in London. The British organizers, drawn mainly from the churches, refused to allow the female members
of the US delegation to play an active role as participants, relegating them
instead to the gallery, as observers. William Lloyd Garrison and the more radical wing of US abolitionists protested and joined the women in the gallery.
Despite this note of dissension there was satisfaction that the movement was
spreading. The dispute over the role of women at the Conference really
confirmed that the movement was, despite its apparent conservatism, an
element of the social vanguard. And though the British and Foreign Anti-
Slavery Society was to agitate on behalf of the slave for many years to come, the
torch had now passed to the US abolitionists.

In Britain the Liberal government still campaigned for suppression of the
Atlantic slave trade (later extended to all international waterways) and the
African Institution, an elite organization, sponsored free labour colonies in
West Africa. Many British Liberals saw the anti-slavery cause as inextricably
bound up with the pursuit of free trade and with the sanctity of contracts. So far
as the British colonies were concerned this meant an end to tariff protection for
colonial produce, notably West Indian sugar, in the home market. The free-
trader wing of the Conservative party agreed. Two notable Liberal spokesmen,
Cobden and Bright, urged that tariffs were nesting-grounds for privilege and
waste and that British consumers should be free to buy sugar from the cheapest
supplier – which by this time was Cuba. After a public debate in which leading
members of the BFASS argued to protect 'free sugar', parliament voted in 1846
to phase out the sugar duties. At this period Joseph Sturge, a prominent
Birmingham abolitionist, was a leader of the 'moral force' wing of the Chartist
movement, demanding manhood suffrage and annual parliaments. British
governments, whether Liberal or Conservative, insisted that Her Majesty's
government was still strongly committed to stamping out the international
slave traffic.[13] As we saw in the last chapter, it committed real resources to this
effort. Moreover in the 1840s, 1850s and 1860s the British consuls in Havana and
ambassadors in Rio de Janeiro engaged in most undiplomatic efforts aimed at
encouraging local anti-slavery activity. London's zeal against the slave traffic
hoped to obscure, or even atone for, the massive boost brought to New World
slavery by British capitalism and its 'empire of free trade'. But the loftier liberal
doctrines are anyway difficult to square with British foreign policy or imperial
goals as embodied in the Opium War (1839–42), the relentless fiscal exploitation
of India, or the reserving of its market for British textile manufacturers.[14] The

---

13   Howard Temperley, *British Antislavery 1833–1870*, London 1974.

14   J. Gallagher and R. Robinson, 'The Imperialism of Free Trade', *Economic History Review*
6/1 (1953), pp. 1–15; Eric Hobsbawm, *Industry and Empire*, London 1964; P. J. Cain and A. G.
Hopkins, *British Imperialism: Innovation and Expansion, 1688–1914*, London 1993, pp.
276–315 (Latin America), 316–49 (India).

dogged pursuit of the slave traders supplied a more attractive theme, and justified maintenance of a West African squadron that had a latent strategic value.

A French abolitionist campaign in the 1840s and the French Revolution of 1848 further encouraged the idea that abolition was integral to the progressive 'spirit of the times'. With radical abolitionists in key positions in the early months of the new French Republic – the poet Lamartine as president and the veteran anti-slavery advocate Victor Schoelcher as colonial minister – a law emancipating the slaves was only to be expected, especially after the procrastinations of the Orleanist governments. Before the decree could arrive, the slaves in Martinique simply deserted their plantations, obliging the governor to declare them free even before receiving official instructions to that effect.

However, abolitionist successes in the small island colonies of the Caribbean – or in regions of the United States or Spanish America where there were no plantations – did not stop slavery from advancing with giant strides, in step with Atlantic capitalism, across extensive regions of the US South, Cuba and Brazil. Abolitionist gains were belied by a steady rise in slave numbers and output.

While the French and British island colonies lacked the extensive and fertile land that steam-age plantation development required, it was found in abundance in the inland areas of the US South, or around São Paulo in Brazil, or on Cuba's sizeable central plain. New plantation zones were linked by rail lines or rivers to the coast. These regions were to become – and to remain for many decades after slavery ended – the world's main suppliers of cotton, coffee and cane sugar. The Spanish colony of Puerto Rico, often bracketed with Cuba, developed a much more modest plantation economy – with around 40,000 slaves compared to Cuba's 340,000 – since it was of small size and much of its terrain was either rocky or swampy, or suitable only for smallholder cultivation.

THE NEW AMERICAN SLAVERY: A SKETCH

The planters of the United States, Brazil and Cuba believed themselves perfectly capable of handling their own slaves so long as they were protected by the authorities from mischief-making philanthropists. These American slave-holders lived on or near their estates, not, like so many West Indian proprietors, on the other side of the Atlantic. They were the acknowledged leaders of society, commanding the militia and occupying important political positions. The slaves produced the key export staples but they were outnumbered by the free population, and slave-holding was quite widely distributed among the latter. The median slave-holding in the US South, Cuba and

Brazil was just five slaves.[15] As these were slave societies, with a dearth of free labourers, any professional or middle-class person would own a few slaves as household servants. The majority of holdings were composed of more than a dozen slaves, but in the US South and Brazil holdings were of medium size. While there were typically a few hundred slaves on a British or French West Indian sugar plantation, the US cotton plantation or the Brazilian or Cuban coffee or tobacco plantations were much smaller, with many using just twelve to twenty-four slaves. Cuba did have large sugar estates but then it also had many small tobacco farms, and medium-sized ranches and coffee estates. In these lands the leaders of slave society exploited stories of slave conspiracy and revolt to spread fear, curtail civic rights and impose an even harsher regime on the slaves. The Gabriel Prosser conspiracy in Richmond in 1800, the Aponte conspiracy in Cuba in 1812, the Denmark Vesey conspiracy in 1822, the Nat Turner rebellion in Virginia in 1831, the rebellion of the Malés in Bahia in 1835, and the claimed discovery of the conspiracy known as La Escalera in Cuba in 1844, were the signal for greater repression and much alarmist scaremongering aimed at the planters' fellow citizens or subjects. The latter might not always love the larger planters, but in the plantation zone were bound to them by fear of the slave as well as by planter patronage.[16]

The conquest of independence by the United States inaugurated the new regime of American slavery. New York and other US ports became the commercial hubs of the hemisphere and US merchants enabled Cuban and Brazilian planters swiftly to fill the gap left by the decline of Saint-Domingue. The perfection of the cotton gin and the Louisiana Purchase allowed cultivation of this crop to spread inland. The proclamation of the Empire of Brazil in 1822 created another new American state wedded to slavery and free trade. However, Pedro I ruled in quite an autocratic way and moves against him by the Brazilian political class led to his departure for Portugal in 1831, in an almost equally bloodless completion of the independence process. The imperial politicians, most of them slave-holders, upheld the monarchy as a symbol of a central power that offered continuity and stability. The infant son of the departed emperor was recognized as his successor, with senior political figures as regent. As in the United States, the constitutional structures of the empire gave planters political representation and local command of law and order.

---

15   Laird Bergad, *The Comparative Histories of Slavery in the United States, Cuba and Brazil*, New York 2007, p. 86.

16   Matt Child, *The 1812 Aponte Conspiracy and the Struggle Against Atlantic Slavery*, Chapel Hill 2006; Douglas Egerton, *He Shall Go Out Free! The Lives of Denmark Vesey*, revised edn, New York 2005; Robert Paquette, *Sugar Is Made with Blood: The Conspiracy of La Escalera and the Conflict of Empires over Slavery in Cuba*, 1988; João José Reis, *Slave Rebellion in Brazil: The Muslim Uprising of 1835 in Bahia*, Baltimore 1995.

While the United States and Brazil achieved independence, Cuba remained a colony of Spain, albeit one which enjoyed considerable autonomy and metropolitan influence. Cuban planters knew that the island had the geographic and political conditions for a flourishing slave system so long as it avoided the hazards of a fight against Spain. The early 1820s showed that many free Cubans would welcome separation, but the leading men of the island believed that they could manipulate the Spanish link. Spain itself was strong in Cuba because it maintained a formidable garrison of some 20,000 troops. The dominant Cuban faction of merchants and large sugar planters – the *sacarocracia* as Moreno Fraginals, echoing a contemporary usage, calls them – had demonstrated quite different qualities from the martial patriotism of their North American counterparts.

The Cuban planters could export their sugar wherever they wanted, but had to pay an export tax that raised serious amounts of revenue; import tariffs raised less, since their aim was protectionist. Spain sent a string of prominent generals to govern the island, but the *sacarocracia* was generally able to bind them to its interests, as they acquired a sugar estate or married a Cuban heiress. Moreover the colony's Intendancy, in charge of economic administration, was invariably held by a Cuban. This office was shaped by Arango's protégé Claudio Martínez de Pinillos, later Conde de Villanueva, who occupied it for most of the time between 1825 and 1851. Under his management the Cuban Treasury paid for much of the naval budget as well as all the costs of a large Spanish garrison. It also sent substantial cash subventions to the Madrid Treasury.[17] The island's Havana-Guines railroad was opened before there was a rail line in the metropolis. Villanueva also built a modern prison at Havana, to which special Spanish prisoners were sometimes sent. By the mid-1820s Arango y Parreño came to regret the support he had given to Villanueva, probably because the latter was willing to sacrifice Cuban autonomy. In his own sinister way Villanueva still asserted the interests of Cuban slave-holders by his skill at manipulating metropolitan institutions. He forged a pact between the *sacarocracia* and the metropolis based on defence of a now-illegal slave traffic, the suppression of representative bodies and a flow of remittances to Madrid.[18] By mid-century the pact was strongly supported by the Havana-based newspaper, *Diario de la Marina*.

The Spanish authorities – for a consideration – ignored the treaties banning slave imports. Queen Isabella herself was said to receive a silver peso for every

---

17   I document these impressive contributions in *Overthrow of Colonial Slavery*, p. 398, but for their wider significance see Josep Fradera, *Colonias para despúes de un Imperio*, Barcelona 2005, pp. 327–439, 707–8.

18   Manuel Barcia, 'El Conde de Villanueva de la Cuba Grande. Una aproximación a la labor de Claudio Martínez de Pinillos al frente de la Intendencia de la Isla de Cuba, 1825–1851', Oficina del Historiador de la Ciudad de La Habana, Havana 2002.

slave landed. The wealth of the Cuban planters and merchants, their connections to former captains general and their allies in Catalonia and elsewhere, often allowed them to pull strings in the metropolis and to veto any metropolitan initiative they did not like. Cuba was, in truth, a colony like no other.[19]

The post-independence American slave order was far less vulnerable than the colonial slavery of the French and British Caribbean. The planters were not at the mercy of a distant metropolis, nor did they confront a large slave majority. North American planters had helped to lead the fight for independence and had played a more robust role in the War of 1812 than the 'free states' of New England. Martial heroes like Andrew Jackson and Zachary Taylor embodied the young Republic's will to expand at the expense of both Native Americans and its neighbours. Planters and planters' sons were all too eager to leave their comfortable life on the Eastern seaboard and open up the interior. With the help of a dozen or so slaves, such men could bring new land into cultivation more quickly and effectively than a family homesteader with no slaves.[20] If their land could grow cotton then merchants from Louisiana and New York would be happy to use steamboats and freight trains to bring their product to market. While there were a total of 400,000 slave-holders in the US South in 1860, there were about 40,000 who owned enough slaves to count as planters. Around 1830 there were about 2,000 *hacendados* in Cuba (then producing coffee as well sugar) and perhaps 10,000 *fazendeiros* in Brazil. In all three countries there were a great variety of small and medium estates and enterprises, worked with the help of a few slaves and helping to create a much more diversified and self-sufficient pattern than was possible on the small islands of the Caribbean. This new American slavery furnished a much tougher target for abolitionism, in part because it had already weathered the stormy Age of Revolution.

Rail companies built 600 miles of railways in Cuba between 1837 and 1860. The number of steam-powered sugar mills rose from twenty-five in 1827 to 286 in 1846, and 949 in 1861. Sugar exports grew from 105,000 tons in 1830 to 429,000 tons in 1860.[21] By this latter date only one of the island's 1,442 *ingenios* lacked the Derosne train, a sophisticated piece of equipment – invented by a free man of colour in Louisiana – that mechanized the sugar-boiling process. Sugar cultivation advanced most rapidly in central and western Cuba, with

19   See Fradera, *Colonias para después de un Imperio*, pp. 183–326; Márcia Berbel, Rafael Marquese, Tamis Parron, *Escravidão e política: Brasil e Cuba, 1790–1850*, São Paulo 2010, pp. 200–19, and the concluding essay in Manuel Tuñón de Lara, *Estudios sobre el siglo XIX español*, Madrid 1973.

20   This is well conveyed in James Oakes, *The Ruling Race*, New York 1978, and confirmed by Gavin Wright, *Slavery and American Economic Development*, Baton Rouge 2006.

21   Heinrich Friedlaeder, *História Económica de Cuba*, vol.1, Havana 1979, pp. 234–6; Antonio Santamaría García and Alejandro García Alvarez, *Economía y colonia: la economía cubana y la relación con España, 1765–1902*, Madrid 2004, p. 182.

development being much weaker in the eastern part of the island. By 1880 Cuba had 1,382 miles of public railway, with many large estates having their own internal tracks. Brazil had 745 miles of track in 1870, rising to 3,398 miles in 1880 – the US South had no less than 15,000 miles of railroad in 1860.[22] In each case the lines ran from the plantations to the ports. If the US South led the charge, slave-holding Cuba was not far behind. Brazil took a few further decades but was impressive nonetheless.

The slave-owners of the US South, Cuba and Brazil were more self-sufficient than the colonial planters had been. In North America they grew wheat as well as cotton, tobacco and sugar. There were factories and steel plants which used slave labour. However, the overall balance of the Southern economy remained very agricultural and export-oriented at a time when industry and the home market were developing apace in the North. Some Cuban and Brazilian slave-owners ran ranches or cultivated foodstuffs for the plantations, but plantation exports were still by far the leading sector. Indeed Dale Tomich has described the flourishing of the nineteenth-century slave systems of the US South, Brazil and Cuba as a 'second slavery', contrasting with the former colonial slave regimes.[23] Anthony Kaye has developed this line of research by citing the selective dimensions of modernity deployed by the slave-holders.[24] Thus they were interested in finding the most effective and appropriate plant and seed varieties, as well as the best processing equipment and the cheapest transportation. Competitive pressure spurred even conservative producers to adopt innovations or be forced out of business. While patent laws were difficult to enforce, the planters did have a motive for discovering improvements or purchasing steam engines or Derosne vacuum pans from metropolitan

---

22 B. R. Mitchell, *International Historical Statistics: The Americas 1750–1993*, London 1998, pp. 539–42.

23 Dale Tomich, 'The "Second Slavery": Bonded Labor and the Transformation of the Nineteenth-Century World Economy', in Francisco O. Ramirez, ed., *Rethinking the Nineteenth Century*, New York 1988, pp. 103–37. This essay helpfully links the new American slavery to wider circuits of capitalist accumulation. Christopher Schmidt-Nowara also picks up the terminology of a 'second slavery' – echoing the 'second serfdom' of the seventeenth century in Eastern Europe – and a 'second empire' in *Empire and Anti-Slavery: Spain, Cuba and Puerto Rico, 1833–1874*, Pittsburgh 1999, pp. 3–36. In the context of the present study I prefer to propose three periods of New World slavery, as outlined in the Introduction. The first (baroque) period being the diverse forms of slavery which accompanied Iberian conquest and colonization in the sixteenth and seventeenth centuries, the second (or colonial mercantilist) phase corresponding to English and French plantation development in the period 1650–1783, and the third phase ('the new American slavery') being the slave systems of the US South, Spanish Cuba and Brazil in the nineteenth century. In my schema colonial Brazil would be a hybrid, and I am happy to accept the argument of Tomich and Schmidt-Nowara that the nineteenth-century slave plantations of Cuba, Brazil and the US South represented a more intense mobilization of unfree labour corresponding to the advance of industrial capitalism at this time.

24 Anthony Kaye, 'The Second Slavery: Modernity in the Nineteenth-Century South and the Atlantic World', *Journal of Southern History* 75/3 (August 2000), pp. 627–50.

suppliers. Planters' need for credit and insurance often meant that they were also dependent on metropolitan finance houses. The planters of the US South showed a lively interest in potential improvements, with such publications as *De Bow's Review* (Louisiana), *Southern Agriculture* (South Carolina), *Southern Cultivator* (Georgia), and the *Farmers Register* (Virginia) carrying many articles on agronomy and technology as well as politics and political economy.

While the US planters were able to count on a naturally rising slave population after the cessation of legal slave imports in 1808, the Brazilian and Cuban slaves still suffered very high mortality and low fertility. The authorities in Madrid and Rio were willing to turn a blind eye to a continuing illegal slave traffic down to the 1850s. Indeed the departure of Pedro I in 1831 reflected tension between the major slaving interests and the emperor when the latter signed an anti–slave trade treaty with Britain. The treaty was subsequently widely flouted.

The United States had survived the half-hearted secession mooted at the Hartford Convention because of determined Virginian leadership and the surge of nationalism unleashed by the War of 1812. Independent Spanish America broke into first nine, and later fifteen, different republics, but Brazil remained united, notwithstanding the Regency necessitated by the underage status of Pedro II between 1831 and 1840. A sequence of five significant regional revolts severely tested the empire's integrity, but in the end served to reassert rather than destroy it. These revolts by local notables drew on disparate social layers, reflecting patron–client relations as well as some reshaping of the delicate socio-racial balance. Pedro I had reorganized the militia into a National Guard that amply represented the planters but granted commissions to some of the officers of the coloured militia. The Constitution of 1825 also gave the vote to many *pardos libres*, or free people of colour. Hebe Maria Mattos de Castro argues that such concessions strengthened the slave regime because they gave the *pardos* a stake in it.[25] However, coloured military men who played a part in later regional revolts had to be careful not to presume too much, or they would be accused of fostering race war. The supporters of the Sabinada revolt of 1837–8 were denounced as a *pardo* rabble when they called for an independent republic. The insurgencies were suppressed by the National Guard at the cost of thousands of lives and some compromise with regional elites.[26] Matthias Röhrig Assunção argues that the need to conserve the central guarantee of the slave-holding order supplied a strong motive for retaining the imperial order. The relative strength of the slave economy supplied resources to the imperial authorities in

---

25   Hebe Maria Mattos de Castro, *Escravidão e cidadania no Brasil monárquico*, São Paulo 2000.

26   Matthias Röhrig Assunção, 'El Imperio bajo amenaza: la Regencia y las revueltas regionales: Brasil, 1831–45', in Universidad de Salamanca, *Acuarela de Brasil: 500 años después*, Salamanca 2000, pp. 51–66.

Rio de Janeiro. It also meant that planters in declining regions could sell surplus slaves to new producers, while the latter also purchased dried meat from the south and other provisions from Minas Gerais. (In North America such factors helped to consolidate the ties between Upper and Lower South.)

The Brazilian planters' success in securing independence and safeguarding national unity was also associated with a strong process of indigenous accumulation, with investments in communications and the ancillary inputs required by the plantations, especially foodstuffs. Between 1821 and 1833 the price of sugar fell by 7.4 per cent a year while the volume of exports rose by 13.8 per cent, yielding an overall growth of revenue of 5.0 per cent annually.[27] With the departure of Pedro I in 1831 and the ten-year Regency over his infant son, Pedro II, the power of the emperor was whittled down and the leading *fazendeiros* and merchants rallied to sabotage the anti–slave trade law and to defend their slave order. Brazil became by far the world's largest coffee producer and exporter, with output tripling between 1830 and 1870 to reach 30 million sacks (of 60 kilos) at a time of rising prices.[28] Prior to the 1830s, the process whereby Brazilian planters had learned about agricultural improvements had remained somewhat haphazard – but manuals appeared by Miguel Calmon du Pin e Almeida in 1834, Carlos Augusto Taunay in 1839, Francisco Peixoto de Lacerda Werneck in 1855 and Antonio Caetano da Fonseca in 1863, focused on agricultural technique as well mobilizing labour. A journal, *O Auxiliador da Indústria Nacional*, began publication in 1833.[29]

The wealthy *fazendeiro* or rancher, as a colonel in the militia, commanded many *agregados* or henchmen. In Brazil, as in the US South and Cuba, many 'middle-class' urban and rural dwellers had a double stake in slavery, firstly because they would own a few slaves themselves and secondly because they depended for custom or advancement on the large *fazendeiros*. Most of the latter tired of the strife of the 1830s and early 1840s and hankered for greater security. In 1848 Pedro II called on a Conservative ministry to stabilize the federal power after the regional turmoil of the preceding period. The *saquarema* grouping sought to end internecine conflict and to put a stop to British interference. It offered a pardon to all those who accepted the emperor's authority.

José Murilo de Carvalho probes the new configuration of power in Brazil in a two-part study, the first part entitled 'The Construction of Power' and the second 'Theatre of Shadows'.[30] The construction of order involved what he terms

---

27   João Luis Fragoso, *Homens de Grossa Aventura, Acumulação e hierarchia na Praça Mercantil do Rio de Janeiro, 1790–1830*, Rio de Janeiro 1988, p. 19.

28   Virgílio Noya Pinto, 'Balanço das transformações', DIFEL, São Paulo 1968, pp. 156–7.

29   Rafael de Bivar Marquese, *Feitores do corpo, missionários da mente: Senhores, letrados e o controle dos escravos nas Américas, 1660–1860*, pp. 259–98, 388–9.

30   José Murilo de Carvalho, I, *A Construção da ordem*, II, *Teatro de sombras*, 2nd edn, in one volume, Rio de Janeiro 1996.

a 'primitive accumulation of power' by means of which the large proprietors sought to mobilize their tenants and employees. The upsets of the 1820s and 1830s illustrated the danger of separatism, fragmentation and social unrest, including slave revolt. The measures necessary to organize and finance the militia and National Guard helped to establish the elements of a functioning social order and federated state. The power of the big *fazendeiros* and ranchers in their regions depended on their ability to dominate a following of henchmen (*agregados*) and clients, with some of the latter being smallholders who might own a few slaves of their own. But the raw power of the landlords and rural bosses was also articulated in complex ways by the provincial and national structures of the empire. The imperial authorities derived their principal revenues from customs duties, supplemented from time to time by floating bonds on the international bourses.

Brazil's political elite, as we have seen, had a shared experience of higher education. *Fazendeiros* with no higher education made up at best a tenth of the Senate and the Council of Ministers. About a half of the members of these bodies were magistrates and nearly a fifth were practising lawyers. These men were also members of landholding families, but their education and qualifications helped to secure advancement and furnished a common culture. Colonial Brazil had no universities, in contrast to colonial Spanish America, with its twenty-seven universities and colleges, many of which were over one hundred years old by the time of independence. The Brazilian elite in the empire's first decades were Coimbra law graduates. The empire subsequently established its own universities, but elite education remained a factor of cohesion. The party system, with its Liberals and Conservatives, offered differentiation within a shared basic framework. Those who called themselves Liberals were supposed to support free trade and oppose the slave trade, but ideological labels could never be trusted – they were part of a 'theatre of shadows'. The Emperor Pedro II presided over this shadowy realm by ostentatious acts of sympathy for the cause of the slaves – usually freeing dozens on his birthday – while remaining the linchpin of a slave-holding order.

Richard Graham sees class power in the empire – the power of the propertied – as woven into a hierarchy of dispersed binaries that underpinned slave-holder rule. A person's status would be raised or lowered according to whether they could claim the desirable first position in the following couplets: rich/poor, master/slave, graduate/lacking credentials, educated/illiterate, white/coloured, free/unfree, male/female, adult/child, Brazilian/foreign-born, Christian/heathen, voter/non-voter. If one point is awarded to the first term in each couplet and zero to the second, then a person's total score would give a good approximation to their position on the social scale. (This is my own interpretation of Graham's subtle analysis, and overlooks the different specific weight of the various items). Graham concludes: 'The acceptance of a multi-layered social hierarchy − by focusing attention all along its extent rather than between two groups − further aided the propertied in exerting control.'[31] There is a certain legacy of the baroque order here, but no longer an Absolute ruler at the summit. Indeed, as Graham makes clear, the ability to mobilize votes, by whatever means, was a crucial dimension of the power of the propertied. And while members of the elite had to be very assertive, disorderly conduct by those lower down in the social scale was sternly repressed. The social order of Spanish Cuba has parallels with that of Brazil, with the difference that American birth brought no advantages.

The new American slavery had been born into an Atlantic world where abolitionism was already a force. Several of the leading planter-statesmen were rueful about slavery and regretted their dependence on it. But how else, they asked, could they continue to produce the flow of plantation commodities which helped to define a civilized existence? The more respectable planter-politicians were prepared to accept a ban on new slave imports and to accept some nominal regulation of abuse. But it would be wrong to conclude that the new American slavery was in any essential way an improvement over the old colonial version. The North American slave population reproduced itself and grew, but this had begun in colonial times. Outrageous punishments may have declined, but any sign of slave resistance or revolt was answered with great savagery, the corpse of the malefactor being often dismembered and exhibited. Slave-trade bans had a limited effect. Because slavery continued to flourish, so did an internal slave trade, with its abuses and destructive impact on families. Slavery, based on the 'chattel principle', remained linked to a commerce in human beings long after the suppression of the Atlantic trade. The threat of sale and family break-up gave a powerful weapon to the planter or manager, and the sight of the slave coffles and slave markets was demeaning and menacing to every person of colour.[32]

Furthermore the Atlantic slave traffic to Brazil and Cuba proved remark-ably resilient, mainly because the authorities did not seriously try to stop it but also because the major naval powers did not act concertedly against it and sometimes failed to control their own merchants. While both British and US warships were sent to patrol the West African coast, US administrations rejected

---

31   Richard Graham, *Patronage and Politics in Nineteenth-Century Brazil*, Stanford 1990, p. 30. For the patrimonial articulation of class power in Brazil, see also Ilmar Rohloff de Mattos, *O tempo saquarema*, São Paulo 1987, and Berbel, Marquese, Parron, *Escravidão e política: Brasil e Cuba*, pp. 257–346.

32   See Ed Baptist, ' "Cuffy", "Fancy Maids" and "One-Eyed Men"' in Walter Johnson, ed., *The Chattel Principle: Internal Slave Trades in the Americas*, 2004, pp. 291–324. Many of the essays in this collection are − like this one − both informative and shocking. Robert Slenes and Richard Graham write about the Brazilian internal trade. For the US see also Walter Johnson, *Soul by Soul: Life Inside the Southern Slave Market*, Cambridge MA 1999, and Aidiya Hartman, *Scenes of Subjection*, Oxford 1997.

a mutual right of search. A further source of Anglo-US tension was the presence of slaves aboard US ships plying the internal trade from the east coast to the Gulf. When, in 1841, the slaves on one such vessel – the brig *Creole* – revolted, captured the ship and sailed to the Bahamas, the British declared that they were free. The US secretary of state, John Calhoun, was outraged, declaring the British action a violation of the 'law of nations' which required respect for slaves being transported by a fully legal slave trade. Just a few months earlier Calhoun had set out his view that other countries were bound to uphold US claims in such a case and had obtained the backing of the Senate by thirty-three votes to zero, with eight abstentions. Nationalism was here intertwined with respect for property in slaves. In such an atmosphere Washington turned a blind eye to the role of US merchants and captains in the massive illegal slave trade to Brazil and Cuba. Fast clippers could be built in North America, sailed to Cuba and Brazil – where they took on textiles and metal goods, often of British origin – and then sent to the West African coast where, dodging British and US patrols, they would take on hundreds of slaves. While the London government was acutely embarrassed, the US administrations saw no reason to give in to what they deemed unwarranted British pretensions to command the high seas. Indeed Calhoun declared that the British were simply trying to salvage the disaster which emancipation had brought to their own islands by forcing their competitors to forgo the advantages of slave labour. Several hundred thousand captive Africans seem to have been illegally transported with American participation to non-US destinations in the mid- and late 1840s.[33] In South Carolina there were to be ultras urging a reopening of the Atlantic traffic, but most Southern opinion remained opposed.

The British government's frustration at this gaping hole in the Atlantic slave trade ban helps to explain the escalation of its attempts to punish Hispano-Cuban and Brazilian slave-trafficking. A naval expedition was sent to Brazil to enforce compliance. In 1850 the shelling of Brazilian ports, and the imposition of a blockade, persuaded the imperial government at last to bring in effective measures to stamp out the importation of slaves.[34] Despite some complex sparring between Britain, Spain and the US in the 1850s, the Cuba traffic continued until the mid-1860s, when the advent of the Lincoln administration finally made joint British/US enforcement effective.

---

33   Drescher, *Abolition*, pp. 314–6. Drescher suggests that as many as 500,000 slaves could have been brought to Brazil in the 1840s with some degree of 'American participation' (p. 316). For further light on this murky business see also Gerald Horne, *The Deepest South: the United States, Brazil and the African Slave Trade*, New York 2007, pp. 3–4, 33–51.

34   Leslie Bethell, *Abolition of the Brazilian Slave Trade: Britain, Brazil and the Slave Trade Question*, Cambridge 1970. The imperial politicians who believed that the time had come to make a reality of Brazilian slave-trade abolition did so because they saw this as necessary, in prevailing Atlantic conditions, to the country's independence and integrity. The fact that many prominent slave-traders were Portuguese lent colour to the argument.

The new American slavery is modern if we consider the miles of railway or telegraphic cable which served it. But this also meant a harsher, more demanding pace of work than had sometimes obtained in the epoch of the colonial baroque. Slavery in the steam age was even more implacable than its predecessor, with the productivity of the slave gangs pushed up another notch, and with women and children being ever more systematically incorporated in the labour force. (We will see below that US planters forced slave women to maintain a strenuous cotton-picking rate into the last month of pregnancy.) In Cuba the possibilities of slave manumission dried up as planters faced a labour shortage. The white racism of the Anglo-Saxons began to foster a Cuban and Brazilian equivalent, though the latter still allowed wealth to have a limited 'whitening' effect. Whether in the US South, Cuba or Brazil, there was a degradation in the position of the free black. As slave prices rose the proportion of slaves concentrated in the export sector grew, and obtaining artisanal notes became far more difficult than had been the case in seventeenth- or eighteenth-century Cuba and Brazil.[35]

The slave-holders of Brazil and Cuba navigated political crises with some success in the first half of the century. In their different ways – supporting independence in Brazil, renouncing it in Cuba – they had managed to avoid the risks of war. Reaping the advantages of continuity, they also secured an end to the most onerous features of the old mercantilism. In Cuba in 1825 the civil liberties of the brief Liberal interlude (1820–3) were suppressed when Madrid conferred *facultades omnímodas* – absolute power – on the Spanish captain general in Cuba. In the 1830s a renewed Liberal interlude led to some discussion of representation for Cuba, but this eventually came to nothing, and free Cubans found themselves denied political rights. In 1843–4 the alleged discovery of a widespread slave conspiracy backed by the British consul – known by the name of the instrument of torture, 'La Escalera' or staircase, used to extract confessions – was exploited to alarm the free whites and to deprive the numerous free people of colour of privileges they had previously enjoyed. The sizeable Spanish garrison, and the huge profits made from sugar, slavery, and a supposedly illegal slave trade, furnished a strong guarantee to this distinctive colonial pact.[36]

Pro-slavery arguments were adjusted to the epoch of industrialism. While abolitionists claimed that the labour of free men was always more productive than that of slaves, defenders of the new slave systems pointed to

35   The consolidation of a new order in Cuba and Brazil is conveyed in an outstanding essay by Matthias Röhrig Assunção and Michael Zeuske, '"Race", Ethnicity and Social Structure in Nineteenth-Century Brazil and Cuba', *Ibero-Amerikanisches Archiv* 24 (1998), pp. 375–444.

36   Robert Paquette, *Sugar Is Made with Blood: The Conspiracy of La Escalera and the Conflict between Empires over Slavery in Cuba*, Wesleyan 1988, and Fradera, *Colonias para después de un Imperio*, pp. 220–51.

their productive momentum and urged that the plantation boom required disciplined toil. The early and mid-nineteenth century witnessed a debate on what was called 'the organization of labour' and the 'social question', with some affirming that slavery was required to mobilize and subject the needed armies of toilers, while others instead argued the motivational advantages – and hence productiveness – of free labour. Thus 'free labour ideology' was pitted against a defence of the necessity of slavery. While the advocates of free labour displayed an admirable generosity, hard-headed statesmen in Washington, Madrid, Rio and Paris were often persuaded that, at least for the time being, slavery was essential to plantation development. After all, in the aftermath of emancipation, plantation output had crumbled in Saint-Domingue and stagnated in the British West Indies. The anti-slavery economist J. B. Say, a former Jacobin, reluctantly concluded that, while very inhumane, slavery was still profitable.[37]

The momentum of New World slavery seemed unstoppable. The slaveowners of the Americas were rich and powerful, and their institution remained dynamic and expansive. The number of slaves in the Americas continually grew, roughly doubling between 1815 and 1860, when it reached 6 million (of which just under 4 million were in the United States, about a quarter of a million in Cuba and 1.75 million in Brazil). The value of slave produce grew even more rapidly. US cotton output rose from 43.6 million lbs in 1801 to 387 million lbs in 1831, and reached 1,125.4 million lbs in 1850. Cuban sugar output grew from 63,000 tons in 1821–5 to 501,400 tons in 1861–5. Brazilian coffee exports grew from $13.3 million in 1840 to $60 million in 1880.[38]

The rising value of slave produce exported from the Americas was maintained despite falling prices (the volume and value of slave-produced Cuban sugar and Brazilian coffee was to rise even more strongly in the 1860s and 1870s).

The new American planters found allies among the free population both inside and outside the plantation zone. Their business partners in the financial and manufacturing centres were natural allies. They also felt, not without reason, that the governments of Britain and France, whatever their

---

37   We will return to 'free labour ideology' below, but see Eric Foner's influential study *Free Soil, Free Labor Free Men: The Ideology of the Republican Party Before the Civil War*, Oxford 1970. For Hispanic contributions see Fernando Diez, *El trabajo transfigurado. Los discursos de trabajo en la primera mitad del siglo XIX*, Valencia 2006. See Drescher, *Mighty Experiment*, for economists' growing caution concerning the productivity edge of free over slave labour; yet this remained a theme for many abolitionists, a classic statement being J. E. Cairnes, *The Slave Power*, New York 1860.

38   For the US and Cuba, see David Eltis, *Economic Growth and the Ending of the Transatlantic Slave Trade*, Oxford 1987, pp. 284–8; and for Brazil, see Boris Fausto, *A Concise History of Brazil*, Cambridge 1999, pp. 103–117 and EH.net, 'Statistics on Developing Countries'.

stance on the Atlantic slave traffic, showed every respect for the plantation trades. They were perfectly willing to buy slave produce, to furnish loans and to sell their own best machinery and manufactures. In 1861 the secessionists believed that such considerations would lead to French and British recognition for the Confederacy. In the end a resurgent popular abolitionism headed off such a move, but the idea did enjoy considerable elite support.

TABLE 11.1. NINETEENTH-CENTURY SLAVE-RELATED ATLANTIC TRADE

Value in £ millions	1796–1800	1820	1860
Slaves	2.4	3.5	1.0
Sugar	12.3	17.5	26.0
Tobacco	1.0	1.3	2.5
Cotton	8.2	9.0	38.4
Coffee	8.3	9.2	10.1
Other	1.0	2.0	1.5
Total	33.2	42.5	79.5

SOURCES: These are my own rough and ready estimates based on combining a variety of sources, chiefly Michael Mulhall, *Dictionary of Statistics*, London 1884; Moreno Fraginals, *El ingenio*, vol. 3, pp. 43–6, 82–9; Conrad and Meyer, 'The Economics of Slavery in the Antebellum South', pp. 342–61; Roberto Simonsen, *História Económica do Brasil*, São Paulo 1937. These valuations often include customs, insurance and freight.

From the planters' vantage point, New World slavery did not appear doomed in 1815 or 1830, or even 1850. The US defeat of the British at the battle of New Orleans in 1815 could easily seem a more substantial event than the very superficial abolitionism of the Great Powers at Vienna in the same year. The US victory was not about slavery, but it vindicated a Southern-led patriotism. The ending of slave imports and the feeble efforts of the Colonization Society allowed even enlightened planters to feel more comfortable about slaveholding, in contrast to the doubts that had produced a surge of manumissions in Virginia in the 1780s. For a while after 1815 there was scarcely any organized anti-slavery in the United States, Brazil or Cuba. Respectable opinion in these states held that 'philanthropy' would lead to race war, as in Haiti. The fact that the British invaders had armed Virginian slaves in the War of 1812, and led a few hundred freed slaves in sacking and burning the nation's capital, discredited British abolitionism in the eyes of many Americans. Slave-holders everywhere in the Americas thought that the British government's abolitionism was dreadful humbug, in reality a ruse to advance its own interests and to meddle in the affairs of others.

The master class of the US South, because of its size and historic role, was essential to slavery's future in the hemisphere. Its initial success in marginalizing anti-slavery showed a position of great strength. Not only did it wield enough votes to quash any abolitionist initiative in Washington, it also had the leverage to prevent any such initiative being taken in the first place. Unvarnished abolitionism made no headway at all in official politics. William Lloyd Garrison, editor of the *Liberator*, founded in 1831, maintained that the Constitution was a 'covenant with Hell' and 'pact with the Devil', and exhorted the free states to abandon the Union.[39] He believed that slavery was impregnable in Washington. However, as Alexis de Tocqueville and others foresaw, the division between 'slave' and 'free' states remained a critical fault line. Sectional antagonism was contained rather than dissolved by the Missouri Compromise of 1820 (which allowed slavery expansion to the South-West, but not north of 36° 40'). One sign of latent sectional tension was Southern insistence that the White House should be occupied either by a slave-holder or by a 'dough face', a Northerner who had proved his fidelity to 'Southern principles'. John Quincy Adams, who served one term (1825–9), was to be the only exception. Martin Van Buren (president 1837–41) had been closely attached to Jackson and upheld slave-holders' rights (for example favouring return of the *Amistad* rebels to their Cuban owners), but he was deemed less than fully reliable and, like Adams, denied a second term. The Southern master class as a body was notable for its distrust of the Federal power, despite its strong grip on Washington.[40]

Prior to secession, no anti-slavery measure stood a chance of success. Even more remarkable is that so few such measures were ever proposed. In 1830 the Massachussets senator Daniel Webster became embroiled in a debate on the principles of the Union with Robert Haynes of South Carolina, in the course of which he drew attention to the forbearance of Northerners on the topic of slavery. Since the first meeting of Congress in 1790, Webster observed, the latter had demonstrated great restraint: 'from that day to this . . . no Northern gentleman, to my knowledge, has ever proposed any legislation or resolution inconsistent with that principle [silence over slavery]. It is the original bargain – the compact – let it stand.'[41] (Garrison, an admirer of Webster, was shocked by this statement, and his famous attack on the Devil's pact seems to echo it.)

So long as it lasted, the cross-sectional logic of the national party system offered further guarantees. Andrew Jackson (president 1829–37) took over the torch of 'democratic republicanism' from the Virginian founders, helping to

---

39   Henry Mayer, *All on Fire: William Lloyd Garrison and the Abolition of Slavery*, New York 1998, pp. 303–8.

40   Elizabeth Fox Genovese and Eugene Genovese stress the abiding impact of the Revolutionary epoch on the Southern imagination. See Elizabeth Fox Genovese and Eugene Genovese, *The Mind of the Master Class: History and Faith in the Southern Slaveholders' World View*, Cambridge 2005, pp. 11–69.

41   Quoted in Drescher, *Abolition*, p. 100.

mobilize a populist politics of race and nation that supplied a buttress to the slave power. His campaign against the Second Bank of the United States and in favour of the common man made it difficult to see him as the leader of a wealthy slave-owning elite. His military exploits and championing of Indian removal encouraged a type of nationalism well-adapted to the 'white man's republic'. Even more moderate species of anti-slavery were swiftly marginalized, as it became clear that abolitionism of any kind was anathema to Southern slave-holders and consequently posed a threat to the Union. Indeed public protests against slavery, even if limited to specific targets – such as the presence of slaves in Washington, DC, – provoked a national and racial backlash which pro-slavery forces energetically exploited. Northern political and church leaders were concerned not to alienate or anger their Southern colleagues. There were violent, and partly successful, attempts to silence the abolitionist agitators, some of whom were thrown in jail, others tarred-and-feathered, and one, Elijah Lovejoy, killed. In several cases the riots were the work of self-described 'gentlemen of property and standing'.[42] This was not at all the world of peaceful British abolitionist petitions. The US abolitionists certainly collected petitions, but large Congressional majorities refused to accept them. By modern standards the racial views of abolitionists were often paternalistic and condescending, but the majority of them insisted on human unity and the humanity of the Africans at a time of hardening racism.

THE NEW RACISM

Throughout the Atlantic zone – and notwithstanding the advances of abolitionism – the period 1815–88 saw a growing tendency to use racial categories and to assume a racial hierarchy, with 'whites' at the top, 'blacks' at the bottom, and the 'coloured' in between. Indeed many claimed that there were further hierarchies within these broad categories, so that, for example, in the English-speaking world the 'Anglo-Saxons' were seen as the elite of the white race.[43] The nineteenth century was both the century of abolition and the time when modern racism was born, and a racially-informed nationalism and colonialism elaborated and celebrated. Not all racists supported slavery, and racial arguments could be used to prevent slaves entering territories where there were none. Nevertheless the intensification of both educated and popular racism bolstered the slave order.

---

42 Leonard Richards, *'Gentlemen of Property and Standing': Anti-Abolition Mobs in Jacksonian America*, Ithaca 1971.

43 Reginald Horsman, *Race and Manifest Destiny: The Origins of American Racial Anglo-Saxonism*, Cambridge, MA 1981, pp. 116–39; Alexander Saxton, *The Rise and Fall of the White Man's Republic*, New York 1993; Röhrig Assunção and Zeuske, ' "Race", Ethnicity and Social Structure'.

The early decades of the nineteenth century saw a broadening of white manhood suffrage in the US, but a reduction in the proportion of free black men with the right to vote in Northern states, until it stood at 16 per cent in 1860. Free blacks were also denied rights of assembly in several Northern states.[44] Appeals to racial pride and privilege were accompanied by an insistent harping on sexual fears and the dangers of 'racial amalgamation'.[45] Throughout the Atlantic world racial slavery was now defended in secular as well as religious terms, either with elaborate pseudo-scientific arguments for black inferiority and the necessity of permanently restraining the savage negro, or with the 'sociological' argument that the freedom-enhancing accoutrements of modern civilization could not be produced without a considerable amount of degrading toil, and that racial slavery allowed this to be carried out by blacks, freeing the white man for a comfortable and civilized existence. It was claimed that the Africans and their descendants belonged on a lower rung than Europeans. Such notions were proclaimed almost as blatantly in the US North as in the South. They were echoed in Europe, especially among those who regarded the decline of plantation output in Haiti and Jamaica as proof that emancipation was a ruinous policy and that black people were congenitally lazy and self-centred. These sentiments were held by some abolitionists or former abolitionists, as well as by defenders of slavery.

The new racism found champions in Europe, notably Thomas Carlyle in England and J. A. Gobineau in France. Notions of racial hierarchy and difference were propounded in the United States by Louis Agassiz, a Swiss naturalist, in his well-received Lowell Lectures in Boston in 1846, and were to infect many currents of nineteenth-century thought.[46] The racial teachings of Agassiz were welcomed by Southern opinion – even though he disliked slavery because he thought it brought white and black into too great a proximity. The appearance of books justifying and elaborating racial notions, such as *Crania Americana* (1839) by George Morton and *The Races of Men* (1850) by Robert Knox, and the absence of strong rebuttals, bolstered the respectability of racialist ideology. Morton's work inspired the self-described 'American School of Anthropology'.

---

44   Rogers Smith, *Civic Ideals*, New Haven 1997, pp. 178–81, 203–5, 252–71. Smith carefully explains the intertwining – but also contrasting – exclusions relating to blacks, Native Americans and women in the 'White Man's Republic'.

45   The prominence of sexual anxieties in pro-slavery discourse invites psychoanalytical readings. See Joel Kovel, *White Racism*, New York 1982 and Mark Smith, *Hour Race Is Made*, Charleston 2006.

46   For the general spread of racial doctrines see Léon Poliakov, *The Aryan Myth: A History of Racist and Nationalist Ideas in Europe*, London 1974, pp. 215–53. For Louis Agassiz see Louis Menand, *The Metaphysical Club: A Story of Ideas in America*, New York 2001, pp. 97–116. The pattern of racial ideologies in the US, Brazil and South Africa in the nineteenth century and after is surveyed by George Fredrickson in *Diverse Nations: Explorations in the History of Racial and Ethnic Pluralism*, London 2007, pp. 137–67.

Members of this school persuaded Agassiz to contribute to *Types of Mankind*, a racial compendium, in 1854. Robert Knox, a medical doctor, gave a pseudo-scientific veneer to Anglo-Saxon bigotry, and pronounced racial slurs on the dispositions and capabilities of Jews and Celts as well as blacks, with all of these races being arranged in an elaborate hierarchy.[47] Such ideas rested on a rampant empiricism and essentialism, finding racial destiny inscribed in existing conditions, and predicting that, in accordance with their inherent characters, lesser races were doomed to either exploitation, exclusion or extinction. Skin colour, anatomy and craniology offered the visible signs of racial identity.

The supposedly more 'commonsensical' and casual racial slurs and stereotypes of the British traveller and novelist Anthony Trollope, in his much-reprinted book *The West Indies and Spanish Main* (1859), may have done more to spread and support the new racism than Carlyle's crude polemics or Knox's arcane sophistries. Trollope's work could be cited by open defenders of slavery, but it also had an insidious influence on those abolitionists who were obsessed with ensuring that the emancipated became regular and reliable wage workers.[48] Edward Bean Underhill, secretary of the British Missionary Society, did not accept the 'prejudiced' views of Carlyle and Trollope, and blamed the 'ruin' of Jamaica on its feckless planters and incompetent colonial officials. His report of an extended visit, *The West Indies: Their Social and Religious Condition* (1862), stressed the considerable achievements of black and coloured Jamaicans while still measuring their progress by the paternalist standards of English Nonconformist Christianity. Other British missionaries were less generous. They were not only disappointed by the freed peoples' supposed lack of a work ethic, their sexual mores and home life, but also alarmed by the assertiveness of native pastors in laying claim to leadership roles. In this and other contexts the rise of racist sentiment was a response to the fact that former slaves and their descendants were rejecting white authority and claiming a wider civic role, which disconcerted their erstwhile patrons.[49] (By 1865 the 'Underhill movement' of peasant protest was to be crushed by vicious colonial repression – the Morant Bay rebellion and its consequences to be considered in Chapter 13.)

White racists in the US, whether Northern or Southern, did not require the authorization of a Harvard professor or English novelist. They regarded the racial hierarchy as self-evident and self-sufficient. Racial prejudice emerged in a spontaneous and overdetermined fashion. The onset of the 'market revolution' in North America in the decades after 1820, allied to the pressures of

---

47   Michael Banton, *Racial Theories*, London 1987, p. 59; Patrick Brantlinger, *Dark Vanishings: Discourse on the Extinction of Primitive Races, 1800–1930*, Ithaca 2003, pp. 39–44.

48   Catherine Hall, *Civilising Subjects: Metropole and Colony in the English Imagination, 1830–1867*, Oxford 2004, pp. 210–23.

49   Ibid., pp. 47–9, 209–64.

industrialization, mass immigration and urbanization, fostered both group differentiation and competition for desirable land, resources and employment.[50] Millions of newly arrived European immigrants came to the New World to improve their situation and soon spotted that blacks were marginalized and excluded, or admitted only to menial employment. Imbibing racial sentiments became part of the invention of an American identity. Of course the new immigrant and the free black might carouse together in a tavern, but the new world of the market revolution taught them to find a place of security if they could. People with similar backgrounds and affiliations, whether geographical, ethnic or religious, tended to help one another out. In some cases this led to trade unionism, but it could also lead to communalism and racism, each striving for a type of closure. Whiteness was constructed as a claim to better wages and superior status. Racial ideology, Michael Banton argues, offered a way to respond to market society and, as Joel Kovel points out, could take either aversive or dominative forms, with pro-slavery representing the latter while Northern racism was more likely to favour the former.[51] Some currents of Protestantism were troubled by racial doctrines, since they clashed with Christian teaching concerning the common descent of mankind and the injunction to treat others as one would hope to be treated by them. The abolitionist criticism of slavery had an impact on the larger Protestant churches, but most of the latter included many Southern worshippers and were, at first, reluctant to condemn slavery too harshly. (Quakers and Unitarians were quite different, of course. The evolution of the Churches' positions on slavery will be examined in the next chapter.)

In the early and mid-nineteenth century, criticism of slavery could be muted by patriotism, by respect for the law and private property, or by racial interpretations of the Bible – notably the story of Noah's curse on Canaan and his descendants.[52] Convention, convenience and peer-group pressure can powerfully shape beliefs and behaviour.

---

50   The 'market revolution' was a period when the majority of the free Northern population became dependent on market exchanges for their daily existence. See Charles Sellers, *The Market Revolution: Jacksonian America, 1815–1846*, Oxford 1991, pp. 125–30, 271–8, 396–427, and Melvyn Stokes and Stephen Conway, eds, *The Market Revolution in America: Social, Political and Religious Expressions*, Charlottesville 1996. Michael Banton, *Racial Theories*, 2nd edn, Cambridge 1998, suggests a strong link between markets and race-formation.

51   See Kovel, *White Racism*, and David Roediger, *The Wages of Whiteness*, London and New York 1988.

52   David Brion Davis, *Slavery and Human Progress*, London 1984, p. 337, n. 144. A racial understanding of Noah's curse was common in the US South, but offhand references also appear in the discourse of British missionaries in Jamaica; see Hall, *Civilising Subjects*, pp. 142, 237. Mark Noll observes that in the antebellum US the idea of the curse as applied to African Americans 'still flourished among the people at large', though he claims that intellectual elites were more sceptical. See Mark Noll, 'The Bible and Slavery', in Randall Miller, Harry Stout and Charles Wilson, eds, *Religion and the American Civil War*, Oxford 1998, pp. 43–73, 62.

The racial order in Latin America was less rigid and intolerant, though it still saw most blacks as suited for subordinate roles. The legacy of a traditional racial order and weaker penetration of marketization help to explain this. Spokesmen of the liberal wing of the Brazilian and Cuban elites – men like José Bonifácio Andrada e Silva in Brazil and José Antonio Saco in Cuba – espoused a more moderate racism which aimed to 'whiten' the population through increased European immigration. They deplored slavery, but regarded the practice of slave-holding in their own countries as comparatively humane. They favoured such alternatives as European immigration and Asian contract labour. But these men were marginalized as plantation growth surged. Most planters remained strongly committed to a racialized slave system and were prepared to justify and defend it. Indeed, the mobilization of slaves by the sugar boom actually meant that conditions in Cuba were harsher than in previous centuries. The coffee boom in Brazil transferred slaves from the toil of the sugar mills to coffee groves, where conditions were somewhat easier because there was no need for night work. Nevertheless racial ideology became more insistent in Brazil too, albeit that it focused most strongly on those of African birth and allowed some recognition to free coloured proprietors and professionals.

In the baroque period Spanish slavery had been more flexible and diverse than the slavery of the English colonies, with their rigid racial definitions based on the 'one drop rule'. The doctrine of *limpieza de sangre* had excluded those of African descent from senior posts in Spanish America, but had not prevented them from organizing religious brotherhoods or receiving commissions in the militia. Manumission rates were higher in the Spanish colonies and there were niches for free people of colour. The doctrine of *limpeza de sangue* had not been consistently applied in Brazil and, as noted in the previous chapter, had been suppressed in the Portuguese Empire by Pombal in 1773. But the nineteenth-century sugar and coffee booms tended to strengthen racial definitions and make manumission more difficult. The rise in slave prices itself made self-purchase (*coartación*) and the purchase of relatives much more expensive.[53] The United States was hugely important to Cuba and Brazil, as their most important market and as a beacon of American development. North American practices had considerable prestige. By the middle decades of the century, Cuban and Brazilian planters were resorting more frequently to racial arguments.

The planters of the US South, Cuba and Brazil could not understand the willingness of respectable opinion in Europe or the US North to indulge abolitionist treason and incitement. The situation was the more puzzling in that the main centres of abolitionist agitation – Britain and the US North – were also the

---

53   Laird Bergad, Fe Iglesias García, María del Carmen Barcia, *The Cuban Slave Market, 1790–1880*, Cambridge 1995, pp. 143–54.

prime markets for US cotton, Cuban sugar and Brazilian coffee. In the early days of abolitionism there had been attempts to boycott slave-grown produce, though to little perceptible effect. By the 1830s there were few calls for a consumer boycott. In Britain several former abolitionists led a campaign in the 1840s to remove the duties placed on Cuban and Brazilian sugar. And, as we have seen, while British cruisers patrolled the West African coast, British merchants happily supplied Cuban and Brazilian slave-traders with the trade goods they needed to do business on the African coast.[54]

Fear of slave revolt helped to cement the racial slave order in the plantation zone, and lurid accounts of bloody outrages perpetrated by rebels undercut support for abolitionism even in areas where there were few or no slaves. Slave revolt was seen to threaten civil society with race war – and if they were freed, where would the slaves go? Slave unrest reminded planters that they needed an entirely reliable state to buttress their peculiarly vulnerable institution by suppressing resistance, returning runaways and gagging the abolitionists. Ensuring all this without alienating fellow citizens who did not own slaves was a difficult and delicate undertaking, with the consequent compromises being disrupted by the dynamism of the slave economy and planter fears for the security of the slave regime. The settlement achieved in the United States by the Missouri Compromise of 1820[55] – allowing slavery in the southerly territories acquired by the Louisiana Purchase – was strained by controversies over how to handle abolitionist agitation, and then disrupted by the Mexican War, leading to the even more unstable Compromise of 1850.

CAPITALISM AND SLAVERY: AN IRREPRESSIBLE CONFLICT?

Richard Graham – who as we have seen registers the many patrimonial features of the Brazilian slave order – nevertheless makes it clear that the social order of the empire was no longer feudal or Absolutist. In fact it was rather a hybrid – the illegitimate progeny of the Age of Revolution and extended primitive accumulation, the patrimonial out-works of a capitalist system of which it was a subordinate component. While Brazil was 'closely tied' to capitalism, it was not fully a part of it.[56] Brazil was contributing to capital accumulation without being fully transformed by it. Slavery in Brazil – and Cuba – in the nineteenth

---

54   David Eltis, 'The British Contribution to the Nineteenth-Century Transatlantic Slave Trade', *Economic History Review* 52/2 (1979); Marika Sherwood, *After Abolition: Britain and the Slave Trade Since 1807*, London 2007.

55   Robert Pierce Forbes, *The Missouri Compromise and Its Aftermath: Slavery and the Meaning of America*, Chapel Hill 2007.

56   Graham, *Patronage and Politics in Nineteenth-Century Brazil*, p. 73. However, Graham perhaps exaggerates the logic of freedom at work in Brazilian liberalism. The articulation of class power and capitalist accumulation is traced in Ricardo Salles, *E o Vale era o escravo: Vassouras, século XIX. Senhores e escravos no coração do Império*, Rio de Janeiro 2008, pp. 41–76.

century was increasingly focused on field labour and commodity production. Yet in the end the slave labour force largely fed and clothed itself by its own efforts, and this limited the slave order's capacity for rationalization, growth and development. Max Weber underestimated the scope for rationalization in the slave order, but he was not wrong to see slavery as setting limits to productivity.[57]

Classical social science maintained that slavery was incompatible with a rising industrial capitalism and that this explained why abolitionism appealed not only to the idealistic, and those capable of great empathy, but also to hard-headed – and hard-hearted – governments, supported by the new business elite and their professional helpmeets. Auguste Comte, Karl Marx and Max Weber all believed that industrial progress would sweep slavery to oblivion. The propertied classes were seen as divided into conservative and radical wings, with the conservatives rooted in mercantilist privilege and landowning, while the more progressive and liberal wing included merchants and manufacturers linked to the introduction of industrial methods, based on free wage labour.

Such a schema should not be wholly rejected, but needs to be heavily qualified. Business interests in Bristol and Liverpool, New York and Barcelona, enjoyed profitable connections with the plantation zone. They were opposed to abolitionism and, where they could, used their influence with the press to stir up popular hostility to the cause. On the other hand, aristocratic landowners like Earl Grey and Earl Stanley could take the lead on abolitionism at Westminster, convinced that this cause was both valuable in itself and symbolic of a new epoch of progress and reform. William Wilberforce came from a leading mercantile family in Yorkshire, a county with a strong woollen industry and few links to slavery or the slave trade. The abolitionist cause could be supported on the grounds that it promoted a philanthropic restraint on predatory profit-taking. Richard Oastler, a leading British factory reformer who campaigned for limits on working hours, was also a supporter of British slave emancipation in the 1830s.

Adam Smith judged that wage labourers were more economical, better motivated and more flexible than slave labourers, and hence more productive. Harriet Martineau, a popularizer of the new political economy, was a convinced abolitionist but also saw the critique of slavery as an excellent way to highlight the virtues of wage labour.[58] Likewise, Joseph Conder explained in *Wages or the Whip* that the employer could lay off workers when he did not need them, without having to pay for a costly apparatus of coercion; the propertyless factory hand was obliged to work because the alternative was starvation.[59]

---

57 Max Weber, *General Economic History*, London 1924.
58 Harriet Martineau, *The Tale of Demerara: Illustrations of Political Economy*, London 1833.
59 Joseph Conder, *Wages or the Whip*, London 1834.

By this time the British government had had its own experience with convict labour in Australia. So long as the colony was forced to rely solely on convict labour, it had to be supported by the British Treasury. But a system was devised in the period 1800–20 which allowed convicts to be assigned to land-holding sheep farmers. The convicts – or 'government men' as they were usually called – were encouraged to work by fear of being sent to harsh penal colonies such as Norfolk Island or Van Deimen's Land. While these penal colonies were not themselves profitable, they deterred the mass of government men from disappointing their employers. As convicts served out their time and became 'emancipi', wage labour spread and the colony thrived. Australia's subsequent prosperity was also encouraged by limiting the availability of land so that there were always landless labourers looking for work.[60] Within a few decades Australian wages were among the highest in the world. Edward Gibbon Wakefield, who secured a charter for the New Zealand Company in the 1830s, argued from the beginning for a colonization plan founded on free labour and restrictions on access to landownership. In both Australia and New Zealand this 'free-labour' colonization was, of course, based on ejecting indigenous peoples from possession of their lands. (In the New Zealand case the colonial power conceded significant rights to the natives by the Treaty of Waitangi, though in practice the colonizers often seized land and fishing rights suppos-edly reserved to the Maori peoples.) Had the treaties made with native peoples been respected, less land would have been available to migrants and there would have been a greater incentive to become a wage-earner.

It was anticipated that wage labour would also create a broader market. The expenditures of the wage worker, however modest, enlarged the size of the market in the colony or metropolis, in contrast to slaves, who grew much of their own food and made most of the clothes they wore. The slave plantations often fostered traditional craft skills, the skill of masons, coopers, sugarmakers, tobacco-prizers, cooks, drivers, coffee-pickers and so forth. Slavery was compatible with craft skills, but not with the literate and educated employees and customers of an industrializing region. The planter feared the acquisition of literacy and education by slaves, since this would facilitate resistance and escape.[61] Cuban and Brazilian planters sometimes encouraged their slaves to acquire skills, but not literacy. Their reliance on slave imports meant many slaves had limited command of

---

60   Robert Miles, *Capitalism and Unfree Labour: Anomaly or Necessity?* London 1987, pp. 94–117. See also Robert Hughes, *The Fatal Shore*, New York 1987, pp. 282–302. While conveying the brutality of the 'system' Hughes distinguishes it from slavery, since the convicts still had some rights and a time when, if they were lucky enough to reach it, their sentence would expire. While emancipi suffered caste discrimination many managed to become farmers themselves, so that class eventually could eclipse caste.

61   G. A. Cohen plausibly sees this as an inherent fetter on productivity, and hence the development of the 'forces of production' in a slave regime. See G. A. Cohen, *Karl Marx's Theory of History: A Defence*, Oxford 1978, pp. 65–73.

spoken Portuguese or Spanish. The Southern US states not only made it illegal to teach slaves how to read or write, but made little effort to educate the poor whites. The University of Virginia was there for the elite, but the plantation economy had no need of a flourishing public education system. While literacy rates were grow-ing in Europe and the US North, they remained low in the US South, Cuba and Brazil. The resulting paucity of 'human capital' retarded the technical level of industry in the slave zone. Asian contract labourers were sometimes introduced, but while they were less likely to attempt escape they would usually leave when their contracts ended. And, as noted above, the ethos of the slave societies proved unattractive to immigrants, skilled or otherwise – a consideration that lay behind the rapid growth of the North- and North West in the United States.

Do such considerations mean that anti-slavery was driven by economic forces? British and US abolitionism served as crucial reference points for the 'economic interpretation' of anti-slavery offered in Eric Williams's well-researched and powerfully written book *Capitalism and Slavery* (1944).[62] While Williams drew attention to economic motives, he did allot some weight to slave resistance and to the idealism of the abolitionists. But he saw broader consider-ations of economic structure and imperial reorganization shaping British colonial and commercial policy, with a demotion of the British West Indies as a result of a surge of trade with India and Latin America. British governments could not ignore such commercial realities but the US, Brazilian and Spanish governments had a quite different set of calculations to make. However, beyond the specificities of the British case the new liberal political economy developed a case against slavery which, with appropriate modifications, identified economic limitations on the new slave regimes of the Americas as well. Many Northern observers came to see the plantation slavery of the US South as a barrier to a healthy and all-round growth path and accumulation process. This was certainly the conclusion of Frederick Law Olmsted in his widely read reports of visits to the South (first appearing in the *New York Daily Tribune*, some were collected in the volume *Reports and Journeys in the Cotton Kingdom*, 1861). This line of thought was elaborated by the liberal political economist J. E. Cairnes, in his book *The Slave Power* (1861).

In the early twentieth century the US historians Charles and Mary Beard developed their own economic explanation of the US Civil War.[63] They argued that the conflict was not really about slavery but instead stemmed from the relentless expansionism of Northern capitalism, menacing the South's agrarian and patriarchal way of life. They noted that while British liberals tended to favour free trade, with its promise of cheap food, the US Republicans favoured higher tariffs on manufactured imports, to encourage the growth of US

---

62   Reprinted half a century later: Eric Williams, *Capitalism and Slavery*, Chapel Hill 1994.
63   Charles and Mary Beard, *The Rise of American Civilization*, New York 1927.

industry. While slavery was downgraded as a cause of conflict, the Beards' approach shared the sense of a clash of social systems lying beneath the apparent sources of conflict.

Writers on the American slave systems influenced by Marx have typically seen them as constrained by the inherent limitations of slave labour, albeit that they still leave room for class struggle and the clash of ideologies. Thus Eugene Genovese's early study, *The Political Economy of Slavery* (1967), pointed out that the plantation tended to be overstaffed because the planter had to have enough hands to bring in the harvest, but there was difficulty in keeping them fully occupied during periods of the year when the demand for labour was less intense.[64] Similar rigidities were identified in writings on Cuban slavery by Raúl Cepero Bonilla and Manuel Moreno Fraginals, and on Brazilian slavery by Jacob Gorender. They stressed the greater flexibility of wage labour and the emergence of an elite faction which favoured a transition from slavery, with 'free-womb' laws, assisted immigration and agreements with Asian labour contractors.[65]

Studies of French colonial slavery in Guadeloupe and Martinique in the 1840s suggest that it was holding back progress towards a new, more integrated coordination of plantation output.[66] More recently Howard Winant, in a powerful account of the successive reworkings of the racial order in the West, portrays plantation slavery as an economically outmoded institution by the time of emancipation.[67] Alternatively, slavery can be seen as a micro-method of labour mobilization directly controlled by the planter which is eventually superseded by macro-methods of labour conscription, as embodied in colonial taxes or post-emancipation laws against vagrancy.

The argument that slave labour was becoming a barrier to the growth of productivity and the internal market did not involve a denial that, in its heyday, it had made possible a surge of Atlantic trade, and the incorporation of some modern machinery in the plantation zone. Moreno Fraginals and Gorender shared Williams's view that plantation slavery had made a large, albeit humanly very destructive, contribution to the rise of Atlantic capitalism. However, they each saw the plantation economy as entering into crisis.

Modern research has shown that slave plantations were still highly profitable in the period before emancipation, and hence that there was no purely

---

64   Eugene Genovese, *The Political Economy of Slavery: Studies in the Economy and Society of the Slave South*, London 1967, pp. 43–69.

65   Raúl Cepero Bonilla, *Azúcar y abolición*, Havana 1957; Moreno Fraginals, *El ingenio*, and *La Historia como arma*, Madrid 1999; Jacob Gorender, *O Escravismo Colonial*, São Paulo 1988.

66   Christian Scknackenburg, *Histoire de l'industrie sucrière de Guadeloupe*, vol. 1, *La Crise du système esclavagiste*, Paris 1980; Dale Tomich, *Prelude to Emancipation*, Madison 1978.

67   Howard Winant, *Beyond the Ghetto: Race and Democracy in the Postwar World*, New York 2003.

economic reason to abolish slavery.[68] The buoyancy of nineteenth-century slave prices was a sign of this.[69] The slave gang and task system supplied a crucial industrial input – cotton – in quantities and at a price that could not be matched by farmers using only free labour. Such farmers did sometimes produce a little raw cotton, to provide themselves with pocket money, but they could not be relied upon to bring in the huge harvests the merchants were looking for. Cotton brokers also found it convenient to help finance the planters. In the aftermath of slavery cotton was to be produced mainly by a share-cropping system, not wage labour. It is also striking that cotton-picking, cane-cutting and coffee-harvesting proved recalcitrant to mechanization – it was not until the mid-twentieth century that mechanization made real advances with the harvesting of these crops. However, after emancipation, planters using wage labour did succeed in greatly expanding the output of sugar and coffee. The idea that slavery entailed some productivity blockages retains some force, but it cannot be denied that this labour regime remained profitable, often very profitable, in the mid-nineteenth century.

The slave-based economies produced core items of a new regime of mass consumption, itself linked to waged labour. Slave plantations were still a dynamic pole of Atlantic trade in 1860. Slaves were driven to work very hard, and the incorporation of women and persons of all ages meant a very high labour-force-participation ratio compared with free populations. The collective rhythm of the slave gangs achieved an exceptionally high rate of exploitation, and could always be supplemented by the task method for aspects of the labour process that were ill-adapted to gang labour. Integral to the exploitation of the slaves was that they also supplied many of their own needs, leaving to the planter only the provision of a few incentive goods. In the nineteenth century, as before, the US planters achieved greater predictability and higher reproduction rates by themselves organizing the slaves' subsistence cultivation, rather than leaving the slaves to fend for themselves. And the nineteenth-century slave population of Minas Gerais,

---

68   Bergad, *Comparative Histories of Slavery in Brazil, Cuba and the United States*, pp. 143–54. Alfred H. Conrad and John R. Meyer, 'The Economics of Slavery in the Antebellum South', in Fogel and Engerman, eds, *Reinterpretation of American Economic History*, pp. 342–61. See also Robert W. Fogel and Stanley L. Engerman, *Time on the Cross: The Economics of American Negro Slavery*, Boston 1974; Robert Fogel, *Without Consent or Contract: The Rise and Fall of American Slavery*, New York 1989. Though *Time on the Cross: The Economics of American Negro Slavery,* was by no means the first work to claim that slavery was profitable, it did identify the slave gang as the reason for the productivity and profitability of slave labour. Although the book was very controversial, the argument that slavery was profitable is now widely accepted. See also the adoption, albeit incomplete, of capitalist business procedures by the slaveholders described by James Oakes, *Slavery and Freedom: an Interpretation of the Old South*, New York 1990, pp. 40–79.

69   Information on all parts of the Americas is assembled in Bergad et al., *The Cuban Slave Market*, pp. 143–54. Prices rose strongly in the decade after 1815 and in the 1850s.

an area by then dedicated to cultivating foodstuffs, seems also to have demonstrated positive growth.[70]

The rising productivity of slave labour in the nineteenth century stemmed from a number of causes – agricultural improvements, higher-yielding plant varieties, the mechanization of processing, the more intensive working of slaves and the harnessing of steam power among them. Output per slave on the US cotton plantations grew from 436 lbs per plantation worker in 1801 to 516 lbs in 1831 and 620 lbs in 1850. The increase in productivity was the more impressive in that it accompanied the rapid growth of total output (noted above). Cuban sugar output per slave rose from 1.06 tons a year in 1827 – roughly double the output typical of the seventeenth-century sugar plantation – to 2.36 tons per slave in 1861.[71] The development of a hulling machine, and the use of asphalt drying grounds, facilitated the processing of coffee beans. The tremendous expansion of Brazilian coffee output was based on a more extensive regime of cultivation than was found in the Caribbean, with some sacrifice of quality for quantity. Instead of picking individual berries when ripe, the Brazilian slaves picked whole branches, leaving the sorting process to be part-mechanically accomplished by the hulling machines. Whereas Caribbean slaves had tended 1,500 bushes, the Brazilian slaves were expected to tend 4,000 bushes or more – planted in long lines reaching up the hills, since this best enabled the overseers to monitor the pace of work.[72] This extensive pattern of cultivation was made possible by the abundance of land in the Paraiba Valley and the Paulista West. So far as the slaves were concerned the work was more intense than in the Caribbean coffee groves. Brazilian slaves experienced heavy mortality, but planters could always buy replacements – from Africa up to 1850, and from the internal traffic thereafter.

The positive ring to reports of rising productivity should not obscure that for the slaves this meant that they were being more intensively driven, especially the field slaves whose work was not mechanized but who were forced to match the rhythm of semi-mechanized processing (cotton-ginning, cane-grinding, coffee-hulling and so forth). The new American slavery was increasingly defined by a stress on clock time and close invigilation. Accurate watches were now available. Inventories show that, by 1839–43, 93 per cent of US masters owning

---

70   Laird Bergad, *Slavery and the Demographic and Economic History of Minas Gerais, Brazil*, Cambridge 1999.

71   Eltis, *Economic Growth and the Ending of the Transatlantic Slave Trade*, pp. 284–8.

72   Rafael de Bivar Marquese, 'African Diaspora, Slavery and the Paraiba Valley Coffee Plantation Landscape: Nineteenth-Century Brazil', *Review* 31/2 (2009), pp. 195–216. For coffee plantation methods in Saint-Domingue/Haiti see Pierre Buteau, 'L'Evolution de la notion de liberté sur les plantations de Saint-Domingue', *Revue de la Société d'Histoire et de Géographie* 209 (October–December 2001), pp. 1–16. Haitian farmers retained a quality niche, but in Cuba the owners of *cafetales* sold their slaves to the sugar *haciendas* as they were unable to compete with Brazilian planters. See Francisco Pérez de la Riva, *El café*, Havana 1944, pp. 77–98.

from six to ten slaves owned a timepiece.[73] This enabled a 'scientific' tightening of the task system.

In the traditional task approach used in South Carolina's rice plantations, the slaves had been given a job to do that was thought likely to require a day's work. If they finished earlier, they could enjoy some extra free time. The philosophically inclined planter would tell himself that the slave would use much of this extra time cultivating food or fishing, so the planter gained anyway. The traditional task system also allowed the planter to encourage, and to profit from, the acquisition of craft skills. As we saw in Part I, about a third of the slave crew on a colonial eighteenth-century plantation were skilled or responsible slaves. The nineteenth-century slave regimes were more tightly focused on field work and mechanical processing.

In the cotton fields of the US South-West the planters developed a more exacting species of task system, by first measuring how much time a productive worker needed for a given task and then punishing those who failed to achieve their assigned quota. The punishment could be an extra task, or a beating – or both. In the new plantation, as in the old, the whip was essential equipment and had to be in regular use.[74] The modern watch enabled punishment to be targeted more exactly. The timing of every operation helped the masters to subordinate the slaves' time to their own.

While some plantation productivity growth came from machinery and improved varieties, much of it was the result of squeezing more toil out of a given slave crew, with the threat and infliction of pain driving the pace of work. Many also offered individual slaves petty incentives, extra rations or, at critical points in the harvest, tiny cash prizes. The rewards and concessions could also be collective and 'customary', designed to establish and reinforce hierarchy rather than reward individual effort. Planters and overseers would encourage slaves to sing while they worked, and would give them a dinner at Christmas

---

73   Mark Smith, *Mastered by the Clock: Time, Slavery and Freedom in the American South*, Charlottesville 1997, p. 105.

74   For the extent of the use of the whip and other punishments see Herbert Gutman and Richard Sutch, 'Sambo Makes Good, Or, Were Slaves Imbued with the Protestant Ethic?', in Paul A. David, Herbert Gutman, Richard Sutch, Peter Temin and Gavin Wright, *Reckoning With Slavery*, Oxford 1976, pp. 55–93, especially pp. 57–77. In a critique of Fogel and Engerman's *Time on the Cross*, these authors show that, in one of the rare cases where punishments were systematically recorded by a planter, whipping and humiliation were inflicted as punishment for 'inefficient labor' or other disobedience. The more productive workers, both men and women, were, on average, whipped more often, presumably because their work was most important. These authors do not see evidence of a 'system' of positive incentives, though they do observe that the planter in question would occasionally note that he had given clothes, money or 'a dinner' as a reward. Some of these seem to have been customary presents (e.g. at Christmas) rather than incentive payments. But the examples cited were probably widespread and various enough (pp. 69–77) to act as somewhat haphazard 'incentives'. While slave-holder violence could have its own economic rationality, the power and impunity enjoyed by whites made sadistic excess inevitable.

and 'presents' of clothing. However, planter paternalism was never capable, by itself, of driving plantation work. Well-meaning attempts to dispense with the whip – whether by philanthropic planters or reforming governments – soon led to the collapse of labour discipline.[75]

Planters and overseers ensured that all save infants and toddlers were incorporated in the labour force. Work was found for the young and the old, the halt and the lame. Women played a key part. The following table throws light on how the output of a slave crew was raised: it gives the cotton-picking rates of pregnant or nursing women in the weeks around childbirth on plantations in an antebellum Southern US plantation, expressed as a percentage of the cotton picked by women who were neither pregnant nor nursing. Southern planters were interested in the fertility of their women slaves, but they evidently felt that pregnant and nursing women should be picking cotton almost to the moment of childbirth and should return to their field gang as soon as possible. And many of them kept the sort of records that permit such 'cliometric' analysis.

TABLE 11.2. COTTON-PICKING RATES OF PREGNANT AND NURSING WOMEN AS % OF PICKING RATES OF WOMEN NEITHER PREGNANT NOR NURSING

Weeks Before (-) or after (+) Childbirth	Age			
	20	25	30	35
-12 to -9	82.3	83.3	84.1	84.8
-8 to -5	77.4	78.8	79.8	80.6
-4 to -1	74.8	76.3	77.4	78.3
+2 to +3	3.9	9.8	14.1	17.4
+4 to +7	64.9	67.1	68.6	69.8
+8 to +11	91.3	91.8	92.2	92.5

SOURCE: Robert W. Fogel and Stanley L. Engerman, 'Explaining the Relative Efficiency of Slave Agriculture in the Antebellum South', *American Historical Review*, June 1977, pp. 275–96, 292.

The very high female labour participation rate – of which the information in Table 2 provides just one aspect – greatly contributed to raising the output from a slave crew of a given size, while only slightly reducing per capita slave output. The women working in the cotton fields bore enough children to reproduce the slave population, but their fertility declined. When white women moved to the South-West they had more children than those who stayed behind

---

75   An example is 'Monk' Lewis's attempt to do without the whip on his Jamaican plantation: M. G. Lewis, *Journal of a West India Proprietor*, London 1929. Attempts to ban or limit physical punishment were to contribute to the collapse of labour discipline in the British West Indies during 'apprenticeship', in Martinique in 1848 and in Brazil in 1888.

in the East. With slave women it was the other way around. The slave women of the South-West had fewer children than those in the East, with the intense work regime of the cotton (and sugar) plantations of the South-West contributing to their reduced fertility.

Plantation productivity growth was raised by machinery and improved plant varieties but also required squeezing more toil out of a given slave crew, and more intensive working of the land. Resort to intensive methods of cultivation led to soil exhaustion, land hunger and a moving slave frontier. However, land was quite plentiful in North America, Brazil and Cuba, and planters could also purchase guano and other fertilizers. The real constraint on the slave economy related to its typical labour processes and political economy. The gang and task systems could not be applied to every process, and the climate of intimidation and violence did not foster respect and cooperation, or attract skilled free immigrants.

The slave plantation rested on a sphere of uncommodified 'natural economy' that was beyond the rationalizing pressures of marketed production and consumption. The reproduction of the plantation and of its slave crew rested on a sphere of self-provision that reduced planters' outgoings but was not exposed to competitive pressure. The slaves grew their own food and made their own clothes, often in laborious ways and without mechanical help (such as the sewing machines that now graced the comfortable Northern home). The plantation zone furnished only a very shallow market for other producers. Altogether the new American slavery lagged behind the advancing regions of the Atlantic world.

The growth of slave output was quite impressive in absolute terms, as was seen in Table 1. But in comparative terms the American slave zone was not keeping pace with the rising tide of global exchanges in the period 1820–60, as Table 3 makes clear.

TABLE 11.3. SLAVE-RELATED ATLANTIC TRADE AS % OF WORLD TRADE

£m	1720	1750	1800	1820	1860
'World Trade'	88	140	302	341	1,489
Slave-Related %	4.8	10.8	10.9	12.6	5.3

SOURCE: as for Table 11.1.

The labour of slave gangs and crews was highly effective in plantation agriculture, and in some branches of mining, but it had no special advantages, and some drawbacks, in general farming, manufacture or commercial transport. The growth of productivity in these latter branches kept pace with, and eventually overtook, the productivity advances achieved on the plantations, even where the latter were able to use industrial machinery and steam-power. The slave economies remained overwhelmingly agricultural, and highly specialized – even their commercial dynamism depended on externally supplied financial and transport facilities. From one point of view this was certainly a symptom of economic weakness and rigidity. But there was no systemic contradiction here, but rather every evidence of complementarity. There was no economic reason why plantations could not continue to supply cotton to the new textile mills, or coffee and sugar to the industrial populations. True, the internal market in the plantation zone was modest. But then it was to remain so post-emancipation, as planters offered meagre wages or squeezed share-croppers to supply cheap raw cotton.

It will not be possible fully to explain here all the obstacles to productivity growth under slavery, but I should add to those already noted the limits on mechanization on the plantations. If the cotton and sugar planters had been able to mechanize the cane and cotton harvest they could have raised output for a given slave crew, or reduced its size, and hence its cost. Some have seen the slave plantation as 'over-capitalized' in that acquiring the slave labour force was expensive, soaking up the capital that might have been invested in machinery. But such considerations did not prevent planters buying very expensive sugar-processing machinery. As I have already argued, the high price of field slaves reflected the coerced but productive character of the slave gang. If mechanization had been achieved, it would have allowed planters to make do with fewer of these expensive slaves. In part the difficulty of mechanizing cane-cutting and cotton-harvesting had a technical dimension – effective means of mechanizing these processes were only implemented seventy or more years after the suppression of slavery. Yet the types of labour contracts available to the producers after slavery probably contributed to the failure to mechanize. Warren Whatley has pointed out that the first patent of a cotton-harvesting machine based on the picking principle came in 1850 but that, prior to the availability of the general tractor, it did not pay to install it. The advent of share-cropping after emancipation did nothing to make mechanization more attractive. Whatley quotes the minutes of a development meeting at International Harvester in 1907, rejecting a proposal for a picking machine which the company was eventually to adopt (in 1922) and market (in 1942); the picker could be mounted behind a tractor, and was favoured by wartime labour shortages.[76] Post-slavery sugar plantations in Cuba relied on a core of skilled workers and a large number of poorly paid casuals, so there was little incentive to mechanize (the first systematic efforts to mechanize cane-cutting had to wait until the 1960s).[77]

---

76   Warren Whatley, 'Southern Labor Contracts as Impediments to Cotton Mechanization', *Journal of Economic History* 47/1 (March 1987), pp. 45–70, 65–6.

77   Charles Edquist, *Capitalism, Socialism and Technology: A Comparative Study of Cuba and Jamaica*, London 1985.

The early capitalist organization of farming, manufacture and transport was itself not based on pure wage labour: the labour of family members, apprentices, indentured servants and tied tenants all made a significant contribution to capitalist accumulation in this epoch, though successive approximations to wage labour did supply a crucial edge of flexibility, a capacity for expansion and elements of an internal market. The free wage worker might work simply to keep the wolf from the door, but even this supplied more motivation than was often present with an unfree labour force.

The fairly comfortable fit between the slave systems of the New World and the emerging industrial capitalist order led Karl Marx to observe that the veiled wage slavery of Britain's new capitalist industries was raised on the pedestal of the naked slavery of the Americas, and in particular that of the cotton districts of the US South.[78] Marx believed that capitalism was a flexible and expansive economic system, and that it would be able to find alternative sources of labour and cotton if it was obliged to. Capitalists did not need to rely on slave labour, and yet they did so. Marx also argued that employers did not need to keep their workers – including children – toiling for twelve or more hours a day. He was contemptuous of the employers' claim that they made all their profit in the last hours of the working day. He supported legislation limiting the hours of labour, arguing that this would favour the more efficient capitalists, who aimed for greater 'relative' rather than 'absolute' surplus value. He supported emancipation in the US, and the cause of the North in the US Civil War, because he held that capitalists should be denied resort to extreme forms of exploitation, and because he believed that white workers would never be free so long as black workers were in chains. But while he favoured placing limits on capitalists, he warned that they were likely to search for new ways to outflank their employees and suppliers – through colonial forced labour, for example. In the 1860s Marx was quite happy to endorse an anti-slavery cause which also attracted the support of John Stuart Mill and other liberals. But he also saw this campaign as a way of spotlighting oppressive terms of labour or aspects of the labour contract.[79]

Marx contended that wage workers were exploited because they received only the value of their labour power, not the actual value of the products that they made. In this way the capitalist employer reaped the gains of a cooperative labour process. Slaves were super-exploited because they did not receive even the market value of their labour – indeed, they did not receive any monetary

---

78   Karl Marx, *Capital*, vol. 1, Penguin Marx Library, London 1976, pp. 333ff. See also Jorge Ibarra Cuesta, *Marx y los historiadores ante la hacienda y la plantación esclavistas*, Havana 2008.

79   Marx's analysis of slavery is well discussed in G. A. Cohen, *Karl Marx's Theory of History; A Defence*, Oxford 1978, pp. 65–73, 88–92, 199–202 and Robert Miles, *Capitalism and Unfree Labour: Anomaly or Necessity?*, London 1987.

reward for toil which yielded a huge flow of premium commodities. While the wage workers received much less than the value of their work, they were able to shape their own 'extended reproduction', that is, not only to reproduce themselves and their families but to achieve a level of discretionary spending above that – for example by buying newspapers.[80] The slave was by contrast permitted only 'simple reproduction', a subsistence based on the use values that they received or could themselves produce. The enhanced 'surplus value' produced by the slave crew was siphoned off not only by the planters but by the merchants, brokers and bankers who advanced credit to them. Marx did not further examine the consequences of the vast scale of 'super-exploitation' for the accumulation process. But if 'pure' capitalism was gripped by a trade cycle, the workings of 'super-exploitation' could only aggravate the phenomenon of what David Harvey calls 'over-accumulation'.[81]

The slaves furnished a flood of produce, but were not themselves a market for other producers. Because the planters needed credit to finance production and because they competed with one another, they had to share the surplus value they extracted from the slave crews with the bankers, brokers and merchants whom they dealt with. When Andrew Jackson and his followers railed against the bankers they expressed a resentment at the power of finance felt by many indebted planters and farmers. The super-exploitation of the slaves was a source of instability as well as resentment, because financial intermediation was required to realize it. The plantation economy inflated profits in circulation just as it forced down the cost of reproducing the slave. This fuelled speculation and asset bubbles, unsafe lending and financial panics, rather than balanced growth and the matching of demand and supply. Workers were thrown out of employment, small and large producers faced ruin and banks failed. The ballooning cloud of capital generated by super-exploitation thus exacerbated the strains and swings of the 'market revolution'. The resulting financial panics of 1837 and 1857 led to heavy losses. The failure to reward the direct producers of such premium crops as cotton, sugar and coffee was a major factor in generating these wrenching dislocations, which in their turn provoked class struggles.

If such factors led to instability, differences in regional growth also had large political consequences in the United States, most starkly because population affected the distribution of votes in the House of Representatives and Electoral College. By 1860 the Southern population, at 11 million, was only a little over half the size of the Northern population of 20 million. In 1800 the two sections had been equal, at 2.6 million. The growth of the North Central

---

80   Karl Marx, 'Results of the Immediate Process of Production', published as an appendix to Karl Marx, *Capital*, pp. 949–1,065, 1,033.

81   David Harvey, *The Limits of Capital*, 2nd edn, vol. 1, London 2006, pp. 326–45.

population from a mere 50,000 to 9 million was decisive in allowing the North to outpace the South. Canals and railroads led to multiple links between the North-East and North-West or Central. The growth of the latter was greatly assisted by immigration, which the territorial authorities encouraged by building roads, bridges, schools and other improvements. The North-Western farmer also purchased mounting quantities of reapers, churns and sewing machines. Immigrants promoted the all-round development of the North-West and undoubtedly appreciated the fact that they would neither have to compete with slaves, nor scrimp and save to purchase one. Buoyant land values were, of course, also a part of this story. The South received modest numbers of immigrants and was, of course, barred from importing slaves. The planters and merchants of the Old South sold slaves to the South-West, and native growth rates were quite high, but overall the South was falling behind and even the threadbare device of the 'three-fifths' clause could no longer conceal that the North was nearly twice as large.[82] The success of the North in hegemonizing the most rapidly growing central and western areas was particularly ominous to a slave-holder regime which set such store by its control of Washington, DC.

Gavin Wright, drawing on the work of Roger Ransom and Richard Sutch, makes another point concerning the limitations of Southern wealth: namely that the institution of slavery tended to soak up Southern wealth in ways that did not develop productive capacity. Free white Southerners in 1860 were richer than Northerners if the value of their slave holdings was included, but poorer if slave holdings were excluded. He writes: 'slavery retarded regional economic growth by absorbing the savings of slaveowners, "crowding out" investment in physical capital – including the forms of capital formation represented by improvements in the value of land.'[83] The value of farmland in the North and North-West rose more steadily than that of most Southern plantations and farms, notwithstanding the fact that, if the value of slaves is added, Southern estates were much more valuable. Wright observes: 'the average free southerner was 50 per cent wealthier than the average northerner in 1850 and 80 per cent richer in 1860. But the accumulation of *non-slave* wealth by the southern economy was 40 to 45 per cent below the northern standard. Slaveowners accumulated wealth in a form that had no counterpart in non-slave societies, a form that vanished when slavery was forcibly ended.'[84] Compared to an alternative scenario in which it had been settled by free family farmers, the South was impoverished by slavery.[85]

---

82 Wright, *Slavery and American Economic Development*, pp. 57–9.
83 Ibid., p. 61. See also Roger Ransom and Richard Sutch, 'Capitalists Without Capital: The Burden of Slavery and the Impact of Emancipation', *Agricultural History* 62 (1988), pp. 135–60.
84 Wright, *Slavery and American Economic Development*, p. 61.
85 Ibid.

These observations also help to explain three important aspects of the antebellum US South: (1) the depth of its commitment to slavery, (2) its weak economy compared with the North, and (3) the relatively poor endowment of its economy after emancipation.

FREE LABOUR AND THE BOURGEOIS REVOLUTION

The tension or contradiction between slave labour and the social relations of industrializing capitalism, based on wage labour, was not only, or even primarily, economic – at least in a narrow sense of the term. Instead, I would urge, *slavery turned out to be vulnerable in an environment dominated by the aspirations, anxieties and strife of an advancing capitalism.* The class struggle of the early industrial epoch focused on the ability of the owners of an enterprise to dictate terms to their workers, as well as on the instability of the accumulation process. This standpoint could put in question the widespread idea – always a key prop of the slave system – that private property was sacred. Wage workers knew that they were better off than chattel slaves, but they began to challenge the powers and privileges of capitalist employers, and yearned for the independence of owning a small farm or workshop. And whereas slave-holding planters were averse to state intervention, wage earners often supported regulation, such as proposals to limit the length of the working day.

My argument here chimes in with that of those historians – especially Eric Foner and John Ashworth – who have stressed the spread of 'free-labour' ideology as a factor in the challenge to slavery and the master class. In the wake of economic development there were artisans and craftsmen, wage workers and specialists, professionals and technicians, who were moved to assert their status as independent citizens. They upheld the rights of labour and of humanity, and saw the slave-holder as inimical to them.[86] At times abolitionism furnished a form of 'surplus consciousness' generated by the Atlantic economy. The slave-holder was also seen as a potential bully by smallholders, labourers and domestic workers, especially women.[87] (The

---

86   Rudolf Bahro, the East German dissident, wrote of how the social regime in the DDR produced what he called 'surplus consciousness', by which he meant that the regime needed capable workers but then could not satisfy their aspirations. See Rudolf Bahro, *The Alternative*, London 1982. In terms of the Atlantic economy of this period, abolitionism was a sort of 'surplus consciousness'.

87   For the huge contribution of free labour ideology to political anti-slavery see Eric Foner, *Free Soil, Free Labor, Free Men*, and 'Abolitionism and the Labor Movement in Antebellum America', in *Politics and Ideology in the Age of the Civil War*, New York 1980, pp. 15–33; see also John Ashworth, *Slavery, Capitalism and Politics in the Antebellum Republic*, vol. 1, *Commerce and Compromise, 1820–1850*, Cambridge 1995, pp. 125–91. I discuss below David Brion Davis's suggestion in *The Problem of Slavery in the Age of Revolution* that Gramsci's concept of 'hegemony'

appeal of abolition to free and independent workers is explored in the next chapter.)

The powers exercised by slave-holders were uncomfortable to all free citizens. They also seemed overweening to most varieties of modern political and legal authority, since the slave (and hence his or her owner too) stood outside the law – subject to private physical punishment, and incapable of giving testimony in a court. Fugitive slave laws claimed the compliance of all free citizens in ways that they could easily find intrusive, compromising and threatening.

In *From Rebellion to Revolution* (1979), Eugene Genovese has argued that slavery was attacked in the course of a 'bourgeois democratic revolution', referring us to another systemic context combining struggles over the form of the state with the advance to a new phase of capitalist development.[88] This, too, is an approach which foregrounds the rights of man and the citizen, and of the claims of labour, emerging in the course of a bourgeois or middle-class revolution. The 'democratic' aspect evokes the presence of popular pressure from below for wider political participation and a class alliance centred on the new bourgeoisie, not only merchants and manufacturers but also lawyers, teachers and other professionals, leading to a new political order geared to reproducing capitalist relations and promoting accumulation. The 'bourgeois democratic' phase could be understood as a stage through which all societies would have to pass; or it could be seen as the progressive option, in contrast to an 'undemocratic' bourgeois revolution, carried through on a basis which sought to limit the scope of workers' rights while still encouraging wage labour. (At this point Genovese's thinking is strongly influenced by Antonio Gramsci and other Marxist theorists of the anti-fascist struggle.) Genovese writes that slave revolts 'must be primarily understood as part of the most radical wing of the struggle for a democracy that has not yet lost its bourgeois moorings'.[89] In this view a radical democratic impetus, if maintained, would eventually demand a break with those moorings and a questioning of the capitalist context.

Genovese did not just adopt the classical schema of the bourgeois revolution, but sought to adapt it to the reality of the Atlantic societies. He was well aware that capitalist manufacturers and merchants were deeply implicated in exchanges with the slave plantations while, on the other hand, democratic struggles against colonialism, oligarchy or Absolutism led radical bourgeois to seek coalitions with artisans, farmers and labourers. The Girondins and Jacobins, Miranda and Bolívar, had reflected, and wrestled with, the competing attractions of aligning with the planters or committing themselves to wholehearted anti-slavery. British

---

helps to explain the appeal of abolition to British ruling circles. Davis's argument here fits well with the concept of 'free labour ideology', as he has himself noted.

88   Genovese, *From Rebellion to Revolution*.
89   Ibid., p. 2.

Liberals and Conservatives faced the same choice, as did US Whigs, Democrats and Republicans.

In the nineteenth century republicanism seemed the natural form of democratic revolution, though liberalism and constitutional monarchy could also offer a (more moderate) promise of political progress. While for some the rise of the bourgeoisie was a punctual affair, carried through in decisive revolutionary events, for others it was rather epochal in character, with successive approximations and the slow construction of a bourgeois hegemony. In a related Marxist idiom, the appropriate container for the bourgeois-democratic revolution was the nation-state. This was a state of a new type, based on general legislation and public taxation, and subject to administration. It did not tolerate the 'parcellized sovereignty' of the Absolutist regimes and it was uncomfortable with the special exemptions claimed by slave-holders, many of whom believed themselves to be lords of all they surveyed.[90] The planters could be outstanding Patriots, but consorted ill with nationalism. Having helped to construct the national container, the rising bourgeoisie also wished to infuse it with bourgeois values.

David Brion Davis's subtle and penetrating study, *The Problem of Slavery in the Age of Revolution*, furnishes great insight into how British abolitionism in the late eighteenth and early nineteenth centuries allowed for the burgeoning of a 'bourgeois hegemony' that indicted the oppressions of slavery, celebrated the advantages of wage labour and demonstrated the virtue of the country's leaders at times of great difficulty.[91] British abolitionism, as Davis points out, enjoyed governmental approval almost from the beginning, and embodied the hope for legitimate reform. But abolitionism in the United States, as we have seen, faced a far more powerful foe, and threatened disunion or revolution. The fact that both British and French planters had received compensation made it even more difficult to envision the US Congress ever considering emancipation: such an extraordinarily expensive undertaking would require a huge public debt (around $3 billion), and stiff tax rises to meet the cost of servicing it.

The concept of bourgeois revolution remains indispensable, and helps to explain the formation of the Dutch and British states and then the US and French states.[92] But this bourgeois and national revolution was not, by itself, a

90   For 'parcellized sovereignty' see Perry Anderson, *Lineages of the Absolutist State*, London 1974, and for nationalism and the national revolution as a force of democratic modernity see Tom Nairn, 'The Modern Janus', in *Faces of Nationalism*, London 1999.

91   Davis, *Problem of Slavery in the Age of Revolution*, especially pp. 346–85.

92   The concept has a Marxist ring but Marx did not invent the idea of a 'bourgeois revolution'. He adopted and adapted the idea from the writings of such notable historian-politicians as Guizot and Macaulay. As mentioned above, the 'democratic' and the 'bourgeois' did not always fit well together; nevertheless we do need to focus on the social setting of democratic struggles. Without necessarily accepting the term, historians of a variety of persuasions see revolutionary political

plausible champion of anti-slavery. As we saw in the second chapter, the seven-teenth-century revolutions associated with the spread of capitalist social relations and the setting up of states geared to defend them were, at the outset, part of the story of the rise of plantation slavery. The toil of the slaves furnished merchants with a quick way to meet the surging demand for tobacco and sugar. As Eugene and Elizabeth Fox-Genovese put it in the title of another important book, slave plantations were *The Fruits of Merchant Capital* (1983).[93] Indeed the slave colonies only came into existence as dependent formations sponsored by the type of commercial, manufacturing, and agrarian capital found in the Atlantic world in the seventeenth and eighteenth centuries. This new pattern was facilitated and promoted in the plantation zones of the New World by the Dutch state, the English state of the post-1650 period, and, later, the early United States. The Dutch revolt, the English Civil War of the 1640s, the Glorious Revolution of 1688, and the American Revolution were thus all in at the making of New World slavery. In its early years even the French Revolution attracted much support from colonial planters and merchants. Plantation slavery received its first impetus from the mercantilist phase of colonialism in the seventeenth and eighteenth centuries. It then received a second wind from the break-up of the European empires in the New World in the period 1776–1824. Indeed plant-ers and merchants based in the Americas played the key role in challenging mercantilist restrictions and monopolies. The beginnings of creole nationalism, nourished by a new print culture and local interests, helped to shape the nation-states that sought to plug into Atlantic circuits.

The course of revolution in the French Caribbean, as we saw in Part III, showed that a second, more radical phase of 'bourgeois revolution' might ensue, when a still-bourgeois leadership responded to the pressures of sans-culottes in the metropolis and black insurgents in the Antilles. In the case of the English seventeenth-century revolutions, there was a great geographical and social distance between Diggers or Levellers in the New Model Army, on the one hand, and the black maroon fighters who resisted the English occupation of Jamaica. Likewise after the American Revolution, Shay's Rebellion had no point

---

events as removing obstacles to capitalist growth: see Robert Brenner, *Merchants and Revolution*, Princeton 1993; Gordon Wood, *The Radicalism of the American Revolution*, New York 1991; and John Markoff, *The Abolition of Feudalism*, University Park, PA, 1996. See also Perry Anderson, 'Bourgeois Revolutions', in *English Questions*, London 1992, and 'Civil War, Global Distemper', in *Spectrum: From Right to Left in the World of Ideas*, London 2005. Eric Hobsbawm's classic studies – *Age of Revolution*, *Age of Capital* and *Age of Empire* – portray the complex interweaving of these forces and phases of capitalist growth. See also the same author's 'Crisis of the Seventeenth Century', *Past and Present* 4 & 5 (1954) for the obstacles to capitalist growth which the revolutions removed or outflanked. Manuel Moreno Fraginals writing on Cuba, Florestan Fernandes writing on Brazil and John Ashworth writing on the US Civil War have also made use of this interpretive framework, as we will see below.

93   Elizabeth Fox-Genovese and Eugene Genovese, *Fruits of Merchant Capital: Slavery and Bourgeois Property in the Rise and Expansion of Capitalism*, Oxford 1983.

of contact with slave rebels in Florida. But five years of revolution in France and Saint-Domingue plunged sans-culottes and slave rebels into a common quandary, leading both to endorse, in their own way, the passage and application of the decree of Pluviôse An II.

Bourgeois revolution is best understood in general as a complex, epochal process, requiring repeated attempts to reform and revise the results of the first phase. The epoch of revolution was invariably heralded by the emergence of great public controversies and a burgeoning print capitalism. Sermons and pamphlets, later almanachs and newspapers, ventilated the great issues of public concern. The abolitionists helped to inaugurate a new phase, with open public campaigns on the secular fate of the slave trade or slavery. The successive waves of abolitionism were examples of the new importance of 'public opinion', as expressed in newspapers and journals, sermons and speeches, petitions and insignia.[94] Rousseau's concept of the general or popular will was, perhaps, an attempt to seize this new autonomy of opinion-formation. Likewise De Tocqueville was impressed that American democracy was characterized by the tyranny of majority opinion.[95]

The anti-slavery idea showed an ability to cross borders, but even so it was ultimately tested by its ability to influence the policy of states, and it was wars and revolutions which shaped the contours of these containers of national feeling and aspiration. The connection between anti-slavery and 'imagined community', already suggested in the last chapter, was to be a general theme of the advance of emancipation and the revision of the workings of the state associated with this.

Britain's seventeenth-century revolutions established a state more responsive to independent property and trade, but the 1832–3 Reform crisis was needed to oblige the oligarchy to admit a fairer representation of bourgeois Britain.[96] The US Civil War has been called the 'Second American Revolution', or an 'Unfinished Revolution', with both concepts implying that revolution was not a once-and-for-all affair but needed to be re-visited, renewed and revised.[97] While

94   Seymour Drescher rightly stresses the new importance of 'public opinion' in *Capitalism and Antislavery*.

95   Alexis de Tocqueville, *Democracy in America*, London 1994, pp. 261–2.

96   The scope and character of bourgeois revolution in Britain was powerfully debated by Perry Anderson, Tom Nairn and Edward Thompson in the 1960s and after. See Anderson, 'Origins of the Present', in *English Questions*, and Edward Thompson, 'The Peculiarities of the English', in Ralph Miliband and John Saville, eds, *Socialist Register* (1965). See also Perry Anderson, *Arguments Within English Marxism*, London 1980. Though I find Anderson and Nairn largely persuasive on the question of 'peculiarities', I see merit in Thompson's notion of bourgeois revolution as an epochal process.

97   The democratic moment is stressed in the most systematic account of the US Civil War as 'bourgeois revolution': John Ashworth, *Slavery, Capitalism, and Politics in the Antebellum Republic*, vol. 2, *The Coming of the Civil War, 1850–61*, Cambridge 2007, especially pp. 628–49. The blockage of Reconstruction meant defeat for many of the democratic goals of Radical Reconstruction, but opened the way to 'robber baron' capitalism, as we will see below (Chapter 13).

outright chattel slavery was swept away, the democratic aspirations associated with Reconstruction were to be cruelly disappointed (on which more below, in Chapters 13 and 14). More generally, however useful the concept of 'bourgeois revolution' may be, it needs to be recast to take full account of diverse impulses and refinements 'from below'. These might include a coloured bourgeoisie but they also involved social layers that were not at all urban or middle-class. My schematic view of a first and second wave of bourgeois revolution also needs to be qualified, because there were significant emancipatory stirrings during the first wave, even if they were usually contained. After all, the Quakers emerged as precisely such a current during the Engish Civil War.[98] The revision of the first wave by the second (or third) could be botched or incomplete. Thus each wave contained contradictory impulses and – crudely put – the outcome depended on the relationship of forces, on political skill and on the fortunes of class struggle.

The classic task of the bourgeois revolution was to create the conditions necessary for capitalist advance; yet in Brazil and Cuba the era of war and revolution permitted a largely peaceful rupture with the past, and produced a hybrid in which the demand generated by advancing capitalism elicited an extension of slavery and the frustration or denial of democratic hopes. Florestan Fernandes has portrayed Brazil's secession from the mother country in 1822–31, the popular revolts of the 1830s, the ending of slavery in 1888, and the overthrow of the empire and birth of the Republic in 1889, as episodes in a protracted bourgeois revolution.[99] In the Cuban case there was evidently a qualitative move to a new colonial regime between the years 1790 and 1825, with the most important measures concerning land tenure and freedom of commerce being devised in the wake of the Constitution of Cádiz in 1814.[100] Absolute property rights encouraged *hacendados* to invest in their estates without fear that the Crown could reclaim the improved land. The suppression of the *estanco* (tobacco monopoly) freed this sector for the development of capitalist farming. The *privilegio del ingenio* was more ambiguous, since it protected sugar mill owners from the swings of the trade cycle (the advent of a somewhat less adulterated capitalism in the 1880s saw the suppression of the *privilegio*, allowing freer rein for mergers and acquisitions in the sugar sector). While the colonial regime was modernized it was on terms acceptable to the slave-owning and mercantile elite. It was not until the outbreak of armed rebellion in 1868, and the cycle of revolution and restoration in Spain, that slavery was challenged, and eventually finally abolished by the constitutional monarchy in the 1880s.

---

98   For some fascinating examples see Linebaugh and Rediker, *The Many-Headed Hydra*.
99   Florestan Fernandes, *A Revolução Burguesa no Brasil*, São Paulo 1974.
100   Moreno Fraginals, *El ingenio*, vol. 1, pp. 105–11.

Slavery did not disintegrate and decline as a necessary result of the rise of industrial capitalism but this dynamic new context, and the outbreak of political class struggles against racial exclusion and pre-democratic forms of the state, help to explain both the rise of abolitionism and the willingness of a section of the elite to back or accept it.

Thomas Haskell has argued that abolitionism was stimulated by the new cognitive and ethical implications of the market. The market justified outcomes that were rooted in contract and it encouraged greater awareness of policy 'recipes' and action at a distance.[101] These observations may help to identify one source of abolitionism, but do not identify the market's ambivalence. At every stage, wider markets had helped to encourage the growth of the slave plantations. Partly in consequence, popular fear of market processes also made a contribution to abolitionism, leading many to look to state regulation as the necessary response. The rise of British abolitionism was in part a response to the rising 'dynamic density' of a society in the throes of capitalist industrialization. The same could be said of the Northern states of the US in the years 1830–60, which were strongly affected by the experience of the 'market revolution'.[102] France in the 1840s was also to undergo some of these strains. Haskell's approach does not explain why abolition was sometimes sponsored by royal Absolutists or radical Patriots or outright socialists, all of whom, for various reasons, actively distrusted or even detested the market. A further source of ambivalence relates to the role of market competition in fostering racial identities, as suggested by Michael Banton (and noted above). Finally, the anti-slavery of the slaves themselves was sometimes nourished by their participation in local markets, a point to be elaborated later, even though freedmen and women were to shun plantation labour wherever they could.

The various systemic flaws, strains and contradictions added up to serious problems for the slave-owners of the Americas – and their own impulsive and high-handed response was to complicate their situation. The US imperialists of 'Young America' in the 1840s and 1850s yearned to annex Cuba or grab Nicaragua; after invading the latter in 1858, William Walker actually proclaimed himself its president, and legalized slavery. But this adventure ended with Walker's capture and execution by Nicaraguan forces in 1860. While the US was preoccupied by its Civil War, Spain reacquired Santo Domingo, backed a French debt-collecting expedition to Mexico and fought a brief war with Chile – the Cuban *sacarocracia*

---

101   See Thomas Haskell, 'Capitalism and the Origins of Humanitarian Sensibility', in Bender, 'The Anti-Slavery Debate', *American Historical Review* 90 (April and June 1985); and his reply to David Brion Davis and John Ashworth published together in *American Historical Review* 92 (October 1987). The whole exchange was republished in Thomas Bender, ed., *The Anti-Slavery Debate,* New York 1992.

102   See the contributions by Eric Foner and John Ashworth in Melvyn Stokes and Stephen Conway, eds, *The Market Revolution in America: Social, Political and Religious Expressions,* Charlottesville 1996, pp. 99–148.

had a hand in these ultimately fruitless adventures. In 1865 the Brazilian Empire unwisely attacked the formidable state of Paraguay, led by Francisco Solano López. Despite the country's small size and the fact that it was pitted against the Triple Alliance of Brazil, Argentina and Uruguay, the Paraguayan forces kept up an effective resistance for five years. The Brazilian war-weariness that resulted played a part in the subsequent questioning of the Empire's social and political institutions, and, centrally, of the influence of slavery. The febrile impulsiveness of the various regimes of American slavery made a signal contribution to their destruction, with the Southern US Secession being the most flagrant example.

The ideology of progress cherished the 'modern' and scorned backward-ness and tradition. We have earlier seen that the slave-holders of the Americas were scarcely traditionalists: they had selectively utilized signature devices of nineteenth-century technology, such as the steam engine, stopwatch and tele-graph cable, without giving up either slavery or an agrarian way of life. The plantation staples – cotton, sugar and coffee – themselves supplied vital ingre-dients of a 'modern' existence. Some historians of slavery in the Americas have seen it as menaced by a mid-nineteenth-century wave of 'modernization' and 'nationalization', processes seen as homogenizing social relations and clearing away all the residues of quaint localism and rural idiocy. The slave-owners were far too dependent on the world market – for inputs as well as sales – to be genu-ine feudal lords. But they did regard themselves as gentlemen, and in Cuba and Brazil often sported aristocratic titles. To Raimundo Luraghi they were obsta-cles to further modernization, and the Northern mission in the Civil War was a struggle for the future of the nation. Eric Foner cautions: 'Within the context of modernization, one can agree with Luraghi that it [the Civil War] became part of the process of "building a modern, centralized nation-state based on a national market . . . controlled by an industrial capitalist class". But is there not a danger here of transposing causes into consequences? It might be easier to say that both sides fought to preserve a society they thought was threatened.'[103] While Southerners 'fought to preserve the world the slave-holders had made', the radi-cal Republicans were attempting to preserve a society that was also 'pre-modern – the world of the small shop, the independent farm, the village artisan.'[104]

But once a desperate struggle to prevail had been engaged, then it could only be won by resort to Luraghi's 'modernization' of the 'nation-state'. In the US Civil War, the North eventually proved better at this in a process that some-how combined bourgeois revolution 'from above' with a version of the national unification seen around the same time in Italy and Germany. Unionism was a new species of US nationalism capable of mobilizing the North, integrating the

---

103   Eric Foner, 'The Causes of the American Civil War', in *Politics and Ideology in the Age of the Civil War*, pp. 15–33, 32. Foner is citing Raimundo Luraghi, 'The Civil War and the Modernization of American Society', *Civil War History* (September 1972).

104   Foner, *Politics and Ideology in the Age of the Civil War*, p. 32.

West and subordinating the South. C. A. Bayly has described the advent of the modern as leading to the 'growth of uniformity between societies and the growth of complexity within them'.[105] This is misleading. Rival attempts to modernize might prompt elites to wear trousers and top hats, and broader layers to wear cotton shirts and drink coffee for breakfast – but the struggle for capitalist and military modernization was in deadly earnest. To the winners went the spoils, and the losers found themselves on the wrong side of the Great Divergence and its international division of labour. And the real internal complexity of the new industrial capitalist order gave rise to the relentlessly homogenizing force of consumer capitalism.

The implication of the various analyses I have discussed above is that the overall position of mid-nineteenth-century American slave-owners was not as strong as it looked. They were among the richest people in the world and yet their wealth was far too narrowly based, others could produce their staples if necessary, and they had fewer real friends than they supposed. The willingness of the planters of the United States, Brazil and Cuba to embrace free trade, combined with the weak development of locally rooted finance and manufacture, undercut the autonomy of these slave regimes. However much they flattered themselves by references to 'King Cotton' and 'His Majesty Sugar', their capacity to impose their will on the Atlantic world was undermined by the fact that their great wealth stemmed only from the sale of one or two export crops – and that it required a frightening intensification of toil. The slave states of the US South had nearly 15,000 miles of rail track in 1860, but this was only one third of the US total, and the lines ran mainly from plantation to coast. There was some manufacturing in the South but it accounted for only a tenth of total US manufacturing. In Cuba and Brazil the manufacturing sector at mid-century was even weaker than in the US South. By the 1870s, with slave numbers in decline, Brazil experienced the beginnings of industrial development in the last years of slavery.

The arrogant slave power of the early and mid-nineteenth century did not measure up to the power of the new industrial capitalism in Britain and some parts of Europe and North America. This was the truly expansionist force of the age, even if it did have to contend with the literally unprecedented strains associated with the new type of boom and bust, of urbanization and proletarianization, of unemployment and demographic growth, of crime and the beginnings of mass communications. While the new capitalism involved substantial exchanges with the plantations it also disposed of other markets and sources of supply, in the Near East and in India. This did not mean that capitalist interests in the metropolis were positively hostile to slavery, and indeed few were. It did mean that if the slave-holders became awkward or inconvenient

---

105   Bayly, *The Birth of the Modern World*, pp. 88–9.

partners, then alternatives could be found. The slave-holders of the United States, Brazil and Cuba proved to be less masterful and expansionist than was feared. The political leaders of the US South could have greatly strengthened their position within the Union by annexing Cuba – it would have made up three new slave states – but they failed to follow through their annexationist initiatives, because they knew it would put the US on a collision course with Britain and France. Eventually Southern economic weakness also contributed to the defeat of the Confederacy.

Abolitionism as a mass movement arose principally in societies undergoing capitalist industrialization, and the large-scale banning of slavery itself required the apparatus and legitimacy of a modern state. The amalgamation of capitalism, industrialization and the market revolution was a watershed in human history, comparable to the Neolithic Revolution but far more concentrated and universal in its effects. Marx believed that capitalist advance would lead to alienation, class conflict and insecurity as 'all that is solid melts into air'. Emile Durkheim warned that it would, or had, generated anomie, a pervasive sense of normlessness. Ernest Gellner also drew attention to the tremendous disruption of traditional social patterns provoked by industrialism, and saw this as setting the scene for the rise of nationalism and the nation-state.[106]

Britain in the years 1780–1840, and the United States in the years 1820–70, were in the white heat of industrial revolution and both witnessed struggles over the form and character of the state. Both also witnessed the rise of abolitionist movements and their contribution to the formation of public opinion. France in the 1840s experienced elements of the same conjunction.

There is also the vital question of agency. Even where there are deep systemic contradictions, these can remain latent for lengthy periods until strains in the tectonic plates produce earthquakes and volcanic eruptions (the latter was an image much evoked in the Age of Revolution but will not be pursued further here). Once the slave order was in question then abolitionists, slave rebels and revolutionists and statesmen in a tight corner could see the possibility of bold action. Two books published by black scholars on the eve of the Second World War – *The Black Jacobins* by C. L. R. James and *Black Reconstruction in America* by W. E. B. Du Bois – sharply posed the question of the agency achieved by black people as authors of emancipation politics. This was a much-needed corrective to the traditional whites-only narrative. But these authors were well aware that those who make history do not do so in conditions of their own choosing, and often have to bequeath to later generations the completion of their work. The next two chapters seek to identify the tortuous advance of emancipation and its diverse constituencies.

---

106   Ernest Gellner, *Thought and Change*, London 1972.

CHAPTER TWELVE

Anti-Slavery: Its Scope, Character and Appeal

Abolitionist movements made a crucial contribution to anti-slavery. They educated a wider public opinion which gave openings to key leaders. But they could not, by themselves, achieve emancipation, and sometimes did not even aim at other than a very gradual erosion of the slave status. The strong surge of abolitionism in Britain in the 1780s and 1790s limited itself to ending the slave trade. As we have seen, British colonial slavery itself was not suppressed until 1834–8, half a century after the first agitation. The manumission societies of the revolutionary and early republican period in North America were moderate and gentlemanly, usually focusing on freeing individuals and helping them to adjust to life as freed-people. The state-level emancipation laws and judgments of the time, and the ending of the US slave trade in 1808, owed little to organized abolitionism. The Federalists' reaction against Jeffersonian 'Jacobinism' led some to be critical of slavery, but Federalism itself disintegrated in the years after it had opposed the War of 1812. So it was not until the 1830s and 1840s that US abolitionists engaged in open public agitation against slavery itself, and there were to be precious few practical results until the Civil War.

In the early days moderate abolitionist goals were supported by highly influential personages within the political elite, including William Pitt, the British prime minister, and such outstanding leaders of the American and French revolutions as Benjamin Franklin and Brissot de Warville. But these men achieved few of their extremely modest goals. Indeed early abolitionist literature was replete with arguments denying that immediate freeing of the slaves was either possible or desirable. At the moment of victory in the parliamentary campaign for abolition of the slave trade, William Wilberforce emphasized that this had nothing to do with immediate freeing of the slaves, declaring 'insanity alone would dictate such a project'.[1] Condorcet, unlike Wilberforce, at least had a scheme for emancipation but, as we have seen, he planned for it to take seventy years to complete. On the eve of the Civil War Lincoln supported a plan that would have allowed some still to be held as slaves into the twentieth century.

Brissot de Warville and his Girondin colleagues were founding members of the *Amis des Noirs*, yet when they dominated the National Convention their anti-slavery measures were modest. However, they can be credited with

---

1 William Wilberforce, *A Letter on the Abolition of the Slave Trade*, London 1807, quoted in James Walvin, *A Short History of Slavery*, London 2007, p. 192.

appointing Sonthonax to the post of civil commissioner in Saint-Domingue, and defending racial equality as an ideal. Girondin Liberalism was given a second chance during the reign of Louis Philippe (1830–48). A sort of diluted abolitionism was part of the reigning ideology, and the plantations were subject to regulation, yet slavery survived. The feebleness of French abolitionism contrasted with the vigour of the French colonial mission in North Africa, with Alexis de Tocqueville being an exponent of both causes.[2]

The French Revolutionary emancipation of 1794 was achieved at a time when the *Amis des Noirs* dispersed. While there was a genuinely abolitionist strand to the decree of Pluviôse An II (February 1794), it was by no means the only one. Likewise the Spanish American Emancipation laws of the 1820s were not the product of abolitionist movements. The British government of Lord Liverpool claimed in 1815 to be animated by abolitionist principle, yet largely confined itself to actions against the slave trade. The British Anti-Slavery Society made a strong contribution to the emancipation of 1833–8, but the details of the legislation were at variance with their wishes. French abolitionism played a role in 1847–8, as did the slaves in the Caribbean, but eventually Louis Napoleon shaped the post-emancipation order. Several of the governments of Isabella II of Spain also paid lip-service to abolitionism. The Revolution of 1868 arose in reaction to the corruption and hypocrisy of Isabella and led to the 1870 free-womb law. The Spanish and Puerto Rican abolitionists persuaded the Republic to end slavery in that island in 1873. But Cuban slavery was to survive, albeit not unscathed, and would eventually be suppressed by the restored monarchy. During the reign of Pedro II the Brazilian monarchy itself was surrounded with a decorous aroma of abolitionism. The emperor had endorsed the ending of the slave trade in 1850. But the empire still rested on what Pedro termed 'the servile element' for its continuing coffee boom for more than a generation thereafter. When it is remembered that the United States banned the slave trade in 1807, and that Jefferson was by no means the only slave-holder to deplore slavery, then it could well be argued that a species of mild abolitionism was the official ideology of the nineteenth-century Atlantic world. Those mid-century US slaveholders who proudly upheld their peculiar institution were exceptional and their response defensive, a defiance of what was often called 'the spirit of the age'.

In the history of abolitionism there were radicals and statesmen, reformers and revolutionaries. The English pioneer Granville Sharp and the American pioneer Anthony Benezet were clearly radicals who repudiated slavery, but could only hope to register a protest, make small gains and present an example

---

2   See the texts assembled in Seloua Luste Boulbina, ed., *Alexis de Tocqueville sur l'esclavage*, Paris 2008, and Seloua Luste Boulbina, ed., *Alexis de Tocqueville sur l'Algérie*, Paris 2003.

that others would follow. In different ways Condorcet, Wilberforce, de Tocqueville and Samuel Chase were abolitionist statesmen, whose aims often fell far short of immediately freeing all the slaves and recognizing them as full human beings and citizens. The European abolitionists not only abstained from criticizing colonialism, but were often among the warmest advocates of their country's colonial destiny. Evangelical ideas had a large impact on abolitionism, and the movement often saw itself in missionary terms. While this could at the limit lead to a recognition of independent black churches, it often implied conde-scension and an assertion of the need for spiritual tutelage by whites.

Paying attention to the discrepancy between abolitionism and emancipa-tion can help to spotlight the inhibitions and frustrations of the former and the forces really active in the latter. Why was abolitionism so often blocked, despite having won widespread acceptance? Why did tame species of abolitionism develop which accommodated so easily to the slave power?

The defence of slavery was stiffened by commitment to (1) *the inviolability of private property* – slaves were legitimately acquired property, and legislatures did not have the right to tamper with the property of citizens; (2) *commitment to the racial order* – the blacks were seen as dangerous and alien, unsuited, or unready, for freedom; if freed they would be a menace to others and themselves, and (3) *the primacy of national interest* – slavery or the slave trade constituted an important branch of national wealth and any decision to give it up would simply benefit competitors. Circumstances which undermined, challenged or counter-balanced these considerations gave openings to anti-slavery.

Vested interests weighed heavily with governments and the elites from which they were drawn. The latter were typically zealous in defence of property, keen to uphold lawful subordination, blinkered and prejudiced in their views of those unlike themselves, and solicitous of the national interest, as they conceived it. Such inhibitions defined conservatives but also weakened and undercut the proposals of moderate abolitionist leaders, and were not wholly absent from the outlook of some radicals. More broadly, patriarchal notions and disdain or contempt for those who worked with their hands were also generally supportive of slavery. However, in the United States many leading planters took their cue from Jefferson and Jackson, expressing esteem for the yeoman farmer and those who worked the land. The existence of something like white manhood suffrage in the United States helped to encourage a positive valuation of labour, albeit with racial restrictions.

At times of social crisis abolitionism could exert a strong appeal to the enlightened wing of the propertied classes. It had many of the elements of a bourgeois utopia. It projected an idealized vision of the freedom of the wage worker, of respect for contract and self-ownership, and of civil institutions supportive of the foregoing. Many early abolitionists were also prison reformers and advocates of educational experiments and public improvement. Abolitionism helped to build a hegemonic, or would-be hegemonic, ideology in which the wisdom of employers and public authorities would make class struggle unnecessary.[3] An anti-slavery stance could, under the right circumstances, vindicate the claims of a central power or colonial government.

The limited forms of abolitionism were not always hypocritical or completely ineffective. It was possible genuinely to deplore slavery, yet to respect property more, or to believe that abolitionist principle should not be set above the vital interests of the nation, or to believe, like Edmund Burke, that modest ameliorative measures were to be preferred to any abrupt ending of slavery or the slave trade, since the latter would be bound to encourage disorder. The half-measures promoted by the more responsible and elite-oriented abolitionists played a modest, sometimes even necessary, part in the ending of New World slavery. They were to include the ending of slavery in metropolitan areas where it was economically marginal or insignificant; the ending of the slave trade to the plantation zone; the defence of the rights of free people of colour in the slave zone; attempts to limit and regulate either the slave trade or the powers of the slave-holder. There were many half-measures whose main utility was educational, in that their failure showed the necessity for a radical attack on slavery as such. Other half-measures somewhat destabilized or delimited the slave-holders' power or threw them on the defensive, as was often to prove the case with laws that upheld the rights of free people of colour. The barring of the North-West territory to slave-holdings in 1784 and the ending of US slave imports in 1808 were both laws that somewhat constrained the slave system. However much it might be denied by established opinion, these decisions did imply that there was something wrong with slavery.

The more significant of the half-measures of moderate abolitionism rarely triumphed without considerable external pressure being exerted on the political system by slave revolt and popular unrest. There was thus a continual dialectic between reformist and revolutionary varieties of anti-slavery, and between anti-slavery itself and other challenges to, or tensions within, the social order.

Two measures falling short of abolition should be singled out: prohibition of the Atlantic slave trade, and 'free-womb' laws. Early anti-slavery advocates sometimes hoped or believed that the ending of the Atlantic slave trade would persuade slave-owners to take greater care of their slaves, and even gradually to erode the institution itself. Yet while the slave trade was certainly an easier target, we know from the United States that its suppression could prove compatible with a flourishing slave system. Of course, the slave population of North America was self-reproducing even before the ending of the Atlantic slave

---

3   See the many subtle illustrations of this in Davis, *The Problem of Slavery in the Age of Revolution*.

trade. In the British West Indies the size of the slave population dipped after the ending of the Atlantic trade, but there was a long-run increase in reproduction rates and planter interest in policies of 'amelioration' that might have contributed to the eventual attainment of a 'naturally' self-reproducing slave labour force. The Cuban and Brazilian slave-owners had longer access to the Atlantic trade. Between the effective ending of the trade and the introduction of free-womb laws there was only a brief period – too short to establish whether they would have been able to find ways of reproducing their slave labour force in satisfactory numbers.

Bans on the Atlantic slave trade were often not regarded as a fundamental threat by American slave-owners. So long as slavery existed it was going to produce slave trades. The Cuban and Brazilian planters were able to buy over 2 million slaves between them in the years 1820–65, notwithstanding agreements made by their governments outlawing the trade. Following the Atlantic ban, British and US planters had been able to acquire slaves from a large-scale and quite legal internal trade. Planters in declining sectors were happy to sell, and those in new areas to buy. There was also the possibility that the bans might be reversed by legislation – reinstating the Atlantic slave trade was likely to be far easier than reintroducing slavery. In this regard it was not until the defeat of the Confederacy that the various agreements banning the Atlantic traffic became fully effective and irrevocable for those areas where slavery survived.

The campaigns against the Atlantic slave trade did help to discredit slavery, to limit its growth and to concentrate slave-ownership in ways that made it more vulnerable; but by themselves these consequences were far from fatal. Indeed for a time trade bans reduced pressure for more fundamental measures, and their contribution to rising slave prices acted as a spur to the more efficient organization of slave labour. The free-womb laws, if adhered to, did promise an eventual end to slavery, however gradual. To begin with, such laws were only endorsed in areas where there were few slaves. But in the plantation zone they implied the transition to a new labour regime. Planters in Martinique, Guadeloupe, Cuba and Brazil were eventually brought grudgingly to accept free-womb laws, but they certainly hoped to supplement and replace outright slavery with other forms of tied labour. And many of them intended to evade the rigour of these laws by resort to fraud. The struggles against the slavery which survived the free-womb laws were of great importance because they led to this legislation being enforced – sometimes in ways more favourable to the ex-slaves and remaining slaves than had been originally envisaged.

One of the difficulties in winning elite support for emancipation was explaining what would then become of the freedmen and women. Many abolitionists feared that slavery had degraded the slaves and that it would take a long time to teach them how to handle their liberty. A number of abolitionists urged that they should be helped to return to Africa, with moderates cautioning that they should not be freed until a suitable colonization plan had been devised and financed. Granville Sharp's early support for such a plan chimed in with the yearnings of some African American refugees following the War of Independence. But these colonization ventures usually disappointed all those involved, and the colonies struggled to survive. Even white sponsors with the best of intentions were loath to permit black self-government.[4] American slaves were highly suspicious of offers to settle them in a strange land, even if some friends and family would accompany them. Because it implied that slaves should be released from bondage it counts as a form of abolitionism, but it was very weak and compromised, tending to rely on planter goodwill to secure manumission and pandering to racial prejudice in its insistence on black removal. Nevertheless it did supply a way-station for some whites who disliked slavery but could see no future for free blacks in America. The latter considerations mattered to Abraham Lincoln, who supported colonization plans for a long time but was eventually persuaded, as we will see in Chapter 13, that it was impractical and perhaps unjust to ask African Americans to leave the land of their birth and a country enriched by their toil.[5]

Abolitionism was by no means always limited or self-serving. More radical strands of abolitionism arose precisely as a reaction against the inconsequential piety of the moderates, leading to such developments as the emergence of a more consistent Jacobin anti-slavery in 1793–4, or the struggle for 'immediatism' within British anti-slavery in the mid- and late 1820s, or William Lloyd Garrison's battle against the dubious abolitionism of the advocates of 'colonization' in the early 1830s. Radical abolitionists played an important part in challenging racial stereotypes and in making sure that the voice of slaves and former slaves was heard.[6] The more moderate abolitionists could be patronizing and timid, or easily swayed by the hostile reaction of middle-class public opinion to slave revolt. The radicals practised salutary provocations which disturbed the ideological universe that upheld slavery; this was a hallmark of both Garrison in the US and Antonio Bento in Brazil. The thrust of radical abolitionism challenged the moral credentials of the slave-holders to be seen as reputable proprietors, and refused a conception of national interest which excluded the slaves. Radical anti-slavery played an important role in that it prepared the way for the emergence of an emancipation policy, though the latter was only likely to be placed on the agenda by a wider crisis.

Struggles over slavery were invariably bound up with a sense of crisis and with disputes over the leadership of society and control over the state, or

---

4   As Simon Schama shows with respect to Sierra Leone in *Rough Crossings*, London 2006.

5   See Eric Foner, 'Lincoln and Colonization', in Foner, ed., *Our Lincoln*, New York 2007.

6   Paul Goodman, *Of One Blood: Abolitionism and the Origins of Racial Equality*, Berkeley 1998; Gauthier, *L'Aristocratie de l'épiderme*, Paris 2007.

'hegemony' as Antonio Gramsci called it. The assertion of leadership requires the capacity to focus on the requirements for the flourishing of society as a whole, not the pursuit of narrow class interest. During the 'century of abolition' there was a recurrent fear that the social order faced a mortal threat and that property itself might be in danger. The fear may have been exaggerated but it was keenly felt at the time, posing a challenge which hegemonic strategies sought to contain.[7] In a struggle for leadership, the political forces linked to the more expansionary sector were at an advantage, since they could offer more generous concessions. In the struggles against colonialism and mercantilism, patriot slave-holders sometimes felt able to offer a more ample political representation to the mass of free citizens – the Jefferson moment. In their struggle with Napoleonic France, Britain's rulers were eventually brought to feel that their own Atlantic slave trade was a disposable asset. Slave-trade abolitionism gave them moral capital – it was more suited to Britain's new global responsibilities, and more gratifying to its people. In the nineteenth century the main centres of capitalist advance did not positively or necessarily require either abolition or slavery, but their superior resources gave them an advantage; the antebellum US Republicans represented such a current, celebrating the virtues of free labour and making a more generous appeal to Northern voters. But hegemony can never be reduced to a calculus of material advantage. Indeed leadership entails a willingness and ability to accept sacrifice. Whereas hegemony is about leadership and power, the search for 'moral capital' is more limited – and more disinterested. In the Britain of the Reform parliament and its Emancipation Act, the middle-class abolitionists garnered moral capital but the gentlemanly elite retained hegemony. Indeed, it renewed it for the epoch of industrial capitalism.[8]

The appeal of 'free-labour' doctrine in the construction of a new hegemony was more constant, although in some circumstances – such as those of 1793 – it could suddenly slump if thought to be too radical and demanding. The doctrine offered rights and status to the working man, but also insinuated the superiority of capitalism at a time when the ultimate shape and destiny of the market revolution was still far from clear. The rise of the English working class posed new hegemonic challenges. Henry Brougham, who played an important role in the abolitionist campaigns, was firm on the need to inculcate the virtues of capitalism. He attacked 'the strange delusions propagated by some wild visionaries . . .

---

7   David Brion Davis's use of the concept of hegemony takes note both of the fluctuating imperial and military crisis facing Britain's rulers in the years 1776–1815 and of the social crisis and class antagonisms which surfaced in the 1790s but escalated in subsequent decades. See Davis, *The Problem of Slavery in the Age of Revolution*, pp. 443–96.

8   Perry Anderson, 'Origins of the Present Crisis', *New Left Review* 23 (January–February 1964); see also the same author's *English Questions* and 'The Antinomies of Antonio Gramsci', *New Left Review* 100 (November–December 1976).

that labour alone gives a right to enjoyment, and that the existence of accumulated capital is a grievance and an abuse'.[9] He believed it was imperative to teach working men otherwise, arguing that the wild utopians 'could not have the least success with men who had been taught that . . . no classes have a stronger interest in the protection of capital than the labourers whom it must necessarily be employed in supporting'.[10]

In identifying the intra-elite conflicts which rendered New World slavery vulnerable, it is important not to diminish the role of the social forces which pressed for emancipation or contrived to place their stamp upon it. The terms anti-slavery, abolitionism and emancipation each stress the negative; they tell us the condition to be done away with, leaving it to be understood that the persons emancipated will now enjoy some species of freedom. Yet, as we know, that freedom might be specified or denied in a great number of different ways – enjoyment of the personal autonomy implied by family life, freedom of movement, freedom from forced labour, access to means of subsistence, protection by the law, participation in the political system, and so forth. The diversity of the forms and results of emancipation point to a clash of social forces and rival notions of legitimate civil rights, bearing in mind that slavery had to be replaced as well as destroyed. Hitherto systemic explanations of anti-slavery have tended, like the term itself, to be stronger on the negative side. The slave relation and the power of slave-holders were suppressed and broken because they were obstacles to industrial capital, or offensive to the humanitarian world-view of the new middle classes. This tells us something about what was happening in the metropolis, or in the areas where slavery had long been marginal or absent. It does not explain the variable outcomes in the plantation zone itself, nor even identify this as a problem. Slaves and freed-people were invariably interested in the control of land and time, in reproduction as well as production, and in equal access to public facilities. The ending of slavery was just the beginning of the struggle to define 'the rights of man', as the French put it in the revolutionary epoch, or to establish 'public rights', as the Louisiana State Convention put it in 1868.[11] According to the latter, the racial segregation of public space was a denial of 'public rights' – an argument as novel as the terms of the Haitian constitution.

The concept of emancipation suggests the presence of an emancipator. Originally this referred to the paterfamilias who enacted the emancipation, and who could claim some continuing sense of obligation on the part of the son after his reaching majority. Manumitted slaves were in an analogous

9 Quoted in Robert Stewart, *Henry Brougham: His Public Career, 1778–1868*, London 1985, p. 203.

10 Ibid.

11 Rebecca Scott, 'The Atlantic World and the Road to Plessey v. Ferguson', *Journal of American History* (December 2007), pp. 726–33, 729.

situation of obligation to the master who freed them, especially where this manumission had not been purchased. Where an emperor or king was the sponsor of manumission or emancipation, a residue of civic obligation also remained. Royal officials in the Americas sometimes offered specific emancipations at times of foreign invasion or planter revolt to those slaves who would fight for the monarch; in such cases loyal slave-holders would be compensated or exempted. The emancipations of the century of abolition were carried through as measures of general legislation. But while this was their novelty, there was still an expectation that the act of emancipation would ensure the loyalties of the freed-persons and command the respect of all citizens. The processes of emancipation argued the presence of a new type of state, capable of undertaking it. On the whole the expedient emancipations promised by royal officials came to little; those sponsored by political leaders founding or renewing the state proved more significant. The ending of slavery embodied in the Haitian constitution was highly unusual because it was not the gift of an emancipator.

Even quite sincere variants of European abolitionism twinned anti-slavery with colonial projects, both in Africa and the New World. Abolitionism required state enforcement and the colonial state needed legitimation, with Christian missionary work sometimes bringing the two together.[12]

ABOLITION AND THE COURSE OF HISTORY

It was only at rare moments that the abolitionists really influenced the policy of states. Anti-slavery often presented itself as a single-issue moral campaign with no wider political implications, and yet, I have argued, its success critically depended on the wider political and social context. It should be seen as part of a wider 'democratic revolution', albeit that instalments of anti-slavery could sometimes be offered, as in Britain in 1833, as compensation for the modesty of democratic reform. The 'democratic revolutions' of 1776–1848 and beyond were not a simple forward march but complex affairs with their dark sides, with their detours and zigzags.[13] Patriotic rebellions, social unrest, civil war, revolutions and major slave revolts offered opportunities, but could also provoke social panic and racial backlash. At the same time the emergence of abolitionism was part of a sea-change in sensibility, embracing concern at social evils, novels of sentiment, black witness and peaceful civic protests. For reasons to be explored, initiatives against slavery marked wider turning points in national life in the main Atlantic states. Some of these – the Haitian Revolution and the American

---

12   A theme explored by Catherine Hall, *Civilising Subjects: Metropole and Colony in the English Imagination, 1830–60*, Oxford 2002, and François Vergès, *Abolir L'Esclavage*, Paris 2003.

13   See Michael Mann, *The Dark Side of Democracy: Explaining Ethnic Cleansing*, Cambridge 2003, pp. 70–110.

Civil War – were very bloody affairs. Yet abolitionists typically yearned for a pacification of social existence. The association between abolitionism, pacifism, and the aspiration to racial equality prompts the question of whether the abolitionist goal could have prevailed with less bloodshed – and with more satisfactory overall results for the former slaves and their descendants.

In some accounts of abolition, the British anti-slavery crusade has been normative, setting a moral benchmark which no other nation proved able to emulate – the orderly and peaceful suppression of slavery in the Caribbean territories of the world's strongest empire. The elevating story of Britain's unprompted virtue left no need to consider the role of British defeat in the Caribbean in the 1790s, slave resistance, a new type of class struggle, or the crisis of 'Old Corruption'. Partly thanks to the critical legacy of Eric Williams, smug self-regard was challenged during the bicentennial of British slave-trade abolition[14] – but it had by no means entirely disappeared.[15] Britain's dedication to 'abolition' should not obscure the fact that the emancipation of the slaves in the British West Indies took place three decades after the founding of Haiti, forty years after the emancipation decree of Pluviôse An II, and some six decades after the Vermont Constitution and Mansfield judgment. Notwithstanding this chronology, it is not only British historians who have been seduced by the notion of Britain's singular and pre-eminent role in 'abolition'.[16]

The national historiography of the United States is now usually more

---

14   Williams, *Slavery and the British Historians*.

15   The most striking example being a lavish biopic of William Wilberforce, *Amazing Grace*, whose flaws were dissected by Adam Hochschild in the *New York Review of Books*, July 2007. While infatuated with Wilberforce and misleading about Thornton, the movie does contain rare flashes of a truer narrative in glimpses of Thomas Clarkson and Equiano.

16   This has been the consistent theme of Seymour Drescher's work and it is also evident in the argument of João Pedro Marques, 'Slave Revolts and the Abolition of Slavery', in Seymour Drescher and Pieter Emmer, eds, *Who Abolished Slavery?*, New York and Oxford 2010, pp. 3–92, 195–7. I am happy to endorse compliments to British abolitionism where they are deserved – and where they are real compliments. Marques in the work cited brushes aside the idea that black witness (Equiano) or resistance (Toussaint Louverture) had any impact on British abolitionism. I don't think this is true and do not regard Clarkson's map of the river of abolitionism as clinching Marques's argument. Clarkson had a long life and his direct contact with Haiti post-dated the river chart. But even supposing it to be true that Clarkson was impervious to black testimony and example, would this have been to his credit? In praising British abolitionism Marques is also praising the largely peaceful character of British emancipation (in contrast to the revolutionary path taken in Haiti). He also somehow assimilates US emancipation to the British model, despite its bloody and extra-constitutional character (to be considered in the next chapter). While it is appropriate to consider each national case of emancipation in its own context, it is also necessary to consider the sequence, and cumulative momentum, of New World emancipations. The peaceful path to emancipation was certainly desirable, for its own sake and because of its more hopeful legacy. But the slave-owners were prone to resist emancipation violently. In the British case, as we have seen, the largely absentee planters did not have this option and were generously compensated anyway.

chastened, though one can still find claims such as 'The greatest republican reform of the period [that of the early Republic] was this anti-slavery movement', or 'By attacking slavery more fiercely than ever before, Revolutionary Americans freed tens of thousands of slaves.'[17] These statements fail to register the weakness of anti-slavery in the early Republic, the awkward fact that the British military freed far more slaves than the Revolutionaries, and the absence of fanfare surrounding the suppression of the external slave trade in 1808. Even those who are more candid about the failures of the Revolution with respect to slavery still sometimes like to argue that the inherent virtues of US institutions, above all the Constitution, enabled slavery eventually to be suppressed. Yet the ending of slavery was only secured by the bloody ordeal of a fratricidal Civil War. The Constitution and Supreme Court were part of the problem, not part of the solution.[18]

Both British and US historical traditions have in the past downplayed the role of black resistance and foreign example. Studying the chequered progress of anti-slavery, one is also studying the evolution and vicissitudes of the national idea itself. British and US governments in the post-emancipation era – indeed even in the pre-emancipation era – saw themselves as the global champions of a new type of freedom.

The national mythologies of Spanish South and Central America have also been written in such a way as to flatter the founders, many of whom – in contrast to most of the North Americans – came out against slavery. While President Vicente Guerrero deserves credit for emancipating Mexico's tiny slave population, and Simón Bolívar for his abolitionist efforts, the former slaves rarely thrived, and slavery did not disappear in most of Spanish South America until the 1850s. The Brazilian Empire, established in 1822, did not manage to end slavery until 1888, one year before it was itself overthrown. The patriotic and republican ideology of the Spanish Americans and Brazilians was not based on the harsh dichotomy of 'white' and 'black' that succeeded slavery in the Northern Republic, but the bulk of the former slaves and their descendants languished at the margins of society and were regarded as racial inferiors. Spanish Americans of African descent did not suffer lynch law and segregation. Wealthy mulattoes could acquire social recognition, and some obtained public office. But the mass of blacks were poor and excluded.

The history of abolition is inescapably a history of the struggle of ideas. On rare occasions even hardened slave-traders and slave-owners could see the

---

17 Gordon Wood, *Empire of Liberty: A History of the Early Republic, 1789–1815*, Oxford 2009, p. 508. The Philadelphia Abolition Society presented a petition to Congress in 1790 but was reprimanded by the president for doing so, and no British-style campaign followed.

18 I return briefly to this in the next chapter, but see Dan Lazare, *The Frozen Constitution*, New York 1995, and Bruce Ackerman, *We, the People: Transformations*, Cambridge, MA 1998, pp. 269–70.

light. Less rarely, the partners, fellow-citizens and descendants of slave-holders and slave-traders sought to distance themselves from what came to be seen as a compromising association. But these ideas arose in a context of wider commerce, new sensibilities, mounting slave resistance, critical nation-building and raw class struggle, processes which themselves require attention – and need to be thought through in their interconnections, not simply in isolation. The fate of slavery and abolition reflected wider social antagonisms and new solidarities generated by processes of exploitation and exchange. Racial definitions of the people or nation were pervasive, but the defenders of slavery found that race was not always a trump card.

AMBIGUOUS PROMISES

The suppression of the Atlantic slave trade and acts of emancipation often supply key reference points in a narrative of the spread of liberty and human rights. In the Ancient Greek and Roman worlds the freedom of the citizen was offset by the unfreedom of foreign captives held in servitude. In Christendom there arose the notion of Christian freedom, but this related to the spiritual realm, and was balanced by the duty to become a slave of Christ. The medieval 'free air' doctrine and the 'freedom suits' pursued by those claiming to be wrongfully held in bondage supplied further challenges to the slave order.

In many societies a sense of identity encompasses the notion of a particularistic right or freedom to be 'who one is', and to be a member of the collective. Africans and Native Americans felt this no less intensely than Europeans, and their communal values often revealed the limitations of the individualism characteristic of much abolitionist thinking. The novel conception associated with anti-slavery was that all members of a given society should enjoy personal freedom, and that the sovereign power was obliged to respect and protect that freedom. In practice this idea was qualified from the outset by the patriarchal notion that freedom was the special right of adult males, with women, children, juniors, servants and other dependents allowed only a vicarious or lesser freedom. The north-west European and North American notion of freedom also held that freedom required economic autonomy, such as would be conferred by ownership of a farm or workshop, possession of a skill, or membership of a profession. However, the anti-slavery idea also challenged the harsher forms of patriarchy. The Scottish Enlightenment thinkers – notably John Millar – who were among the first philosophers to question slave-holding, also urged an abatement of the authority of husbands and fathers; later, as abolitionist movements developed, women came to play an important part in them.[19] The

---

19   John Millar, *The Origin of the Distinction of Ranks*, London 1781. I discuss the significant Scottish Enlightenment contribution to anti-slavery thought in *Overthrow of Colonial Slavery*, pp. 48–54.

workings of the New World slave systems were plausibly represented as threatening to family life, robbing the slave father of his manhood and exposing the slave female to abuse. The disposition to set limits on patriarchal power had an appeal to many women, whether wives or, like many British Methodists, domestic servants.

Abolitionism was a product of the 'age of reform' as well as the 'age of revolution'. The abolitionists often hoped that their goal could be reached by peaceful means and that it was part of a package which included wider suffrage, free public education, improved communications, public parks, good sewage systems and prison reform. The British example was attractive but difficult to reproduce. The anti-slavery cause could appeal to the virtues of 'freedom' and 'free labour' but still did not have a simple and straightforward social meaning. Its complex message requires us to decipher the political and social clashes and shocks of a world in the grip of industrialization and democratic revolution, and reaching for new forms of empire and domestic order. Abolitionism was associated with a vision of a moderate and responsible modernity, and with institutions that would equally restrain the market and the mob, and foster a Protestant work ethic. Max Weber's 'spirit of capitalism' and Michel Foucault's theses on 'governmentality' both address key features of the species of abolitionism which emerged as an official doctrine. The masterless freedmen and freedwomen were, it was hoped, to discover sources of discipline within themselves that would render them even more productive plantation workers than before (the ex-slaves' preference for subsistence agriculture over wage labour was to be a source of great disappointment to some abolitionists).

In looking for the wider meaning of abolitionism, we simply acknowledge something well-known to the abolitionists themselves, namely the strong symbolic charge of issues of slavery and freedom. When the British House of Lords at last brought itself to support a bill suppressing the Atlantic slave traffic, Wilberforce, who listened to the debate from the visitors' gallery, remarked how gratifying it was to see young aristocrats impress themselves on the public mind with such generous sentiments. While there was always a core of enthusiasts for whom the cause needed no embroidery, its fate as a political movement drew strength from an appeal to political and social actors who saw it as elevating their own concerns.

ABOLITIONISM AND PACIFICATION

The growth of anti-slavery sentiment tracked a rejection of systematic violence and cruelty, and a growing willingness to acknowledge the dignity of labour. The cruelty the abolitionists exposed was not just the behaviour of a vicious individual but the violence of an institution which fostered cruelty, or gave it great latitude. The rejection of cruelty was prompted by empathy and the golden rule, or by insistence that, since the human form was of divine origin, it was wrong to violate it. A strand in both Enlightenment thought and Protestantism of the 'Great Awakening' went on to advocate and disseminate new, more rational disciplines and punishments, in a search for a more civilized and effective system of constraints. Likewise, the subjective compulsion to work, and the propertyless labourers' need to put food on the table, would be far more effective than physical coercion. Paradoxically, the steady advance of this 'civilizing process' registered its main gains precisely in those kingdoms which played the most dynamic role in the plantation and slave trades – a paradox summed up in the life of John Newton, who composed the famous hymn 'Amazing Grace' at a time when he captained a slave-trading vessel. Only many years later did he discover his vocation as an eloquent and authoritative abolitionist.[20]

Many influential early protagonists of abolition were opponents of all types of political violence. Their rejection of slavery intensified in times of war, as if their virtue and courage in this cause would atone for their seeming absence of patriotism. Individual Quakers like John Woolman and Anthony Benezet pioneered the attack on slavery, and gradually persuaded local branches of the Society of Friends to make membership incompatible with owning slaves. John Wesley, the Methodist leader, in his *Thoughts on Slavery* of 1774 also sought to convince slave-holders to give up their slaves. But soon, notwithstanding patriot clamour, Quakers and Methodists added public agitation to personal witness. As we have seen, Quakers established the Society for the Relief of Free Negroes Unlawfully Held in Bondage in Philadelphia in 1775, and, in London in 1787, Quakers were behind the setting-up of the Society for Effecting the Abolition of the Slave Trade. Having played an important part in initiating organized abolitionism, Quaker resources and commitment continued thereafter to sustain anti-slavery movements in Britain, the United States and elsewhere. William Lloyd Garrison, who founded the *Liberator* in 1831 and led the turn towards 'immediatism' and radical abolition, was influenced by the Quakers in his espousal of non-violent agitation against slavery.

The revulsion against slavery manifested by the Quakers and Garrisonians was partly prompted by their sense of its inherently violent character. Pacifism and anti-slavery were thus connected both logically and emotionally.[21] Yet the overthrow of the major slave systems in the Americas was often framed by war and revolution, even though emancipation aimed at a pacification and normalization of social relations. The slave-holders saw themselves as champions of law and order, yet there was something lawless in the power they claimed over their slaves and something arbitrary in the demands that they placed on fellow

---

20   Rediker, *The Slave Ship*, pp.157–86.
21   Carleton Mabee, *Black Freedom: The Nonviolent Abolitionists from 1830 through the Civil War*, London 1970.

citizens and subjects. In principle slaves had no legal personality, and could not testify in courts of law against free persons. In the United States slave-holders were super-sensitive to criticism and demanded censorship of the public mails. The fugitive slave laws gave them the power to compel the assistance of free citizens in the recovery of their property. In Spanish Cuba up to 1865, and Imperial Brazil up to 1850, slave-traders and slave-owners brazenly flouted the treaties banning the slave traffic signed by their governments. In Cuba, defence of the slave order had led the dominant planter fraction to accept an arbitrary power – the *facultades omnímodas* of the captain general. Brazil had great difficulty elaborating a code that reconciled the traditional practices of slave-holding and the supposedly lawful institutions of the empire.[22] The abolitionist cause aimed to suppress the violence and arbitrariness of slave domination by an integral regime of law and order. The work of the world still had to be done, but employers would have to pay for it – and employees would be induced to accept wage labour by the absence of other ways of making a living. Economic compulsion was to replace brute force.

The succession of movements and emancipations, I would argue, had a cumulative character, each helping to bequeath hopes and fears to its successor. Chapters 8 and 9 plotted such connections in the case of the Haitian Revolution. British emancipation in 1833–8, French emancipation in 1848 and the ending of slavery in the Spanish American Republics in the early 1850s heightened the already acute tensions in the antebellum United States. The fact that British and French emancipation were achieved without great bloodshed increased the pressure on North American slave-holders to abandon their 'peculiar institution'. When it became definitive in 1865, the suppression of US slavery seemed to doom slavery everywhere else in the hemisphere. Spanish and Brazilian free -womb laws were enacted which both set a term on the institution and enabled these very profitable slave regimes to survive another generation. In Puerto Rico and Cuba emancipation was a by-product of war in the Caribbean and revolution in the metropolis; but in the Brazilian case the suppression of slavery and overthrow of the monarchy were both accomplished with little violence, though, in the case of emancipation, with considerable popular input.

Peaceful emancipation, when achieved, reflected both the broad appeal of anti-slavery and slave-holder fear that further resistance could backfire. The violence of the Haitian Revolution and the US Civil War made a contribution to more peaceable emancipation in other lands. The violence stemmed from the inherent antagonisms on which slavery was built, and the perceived threat to all

---

22   Keila Grinberg, 'Esclave, citoyenneté et élaboration du code civil au Brésil (1855–1917), *Cahiers du Brésil Contemporain* 53, 54 (2000), pp. 93–114. For the problems of the US legal order see James Oakes, *Freedom and Slavery*, New York 1985, and Thomas Moris, *Southern Slavery and the Law*, Chapel Hill 1996.

that the slave-holders and their followers held dear. It expressed the refusal of slave-holders to accept a new political power, and that power's refusal to countenance planter secession and independence. The abolition of the British and US slave trades in 1807 did not itself occasion violence, but it did take place against the backdrop of a momentous military struggle between Britain and Napoleonic France, and great tension between the US and Britain. David Brion Davis has observed that in an Age of Revolution Wilberforce was Britain's answer to Washington and Napoleon.[23] (Of course, Britain's rulers could elevate Wilberforce because they also had Nelson and Wellington.)

DYNAMIC CONTEXTS

There is, I would urge, something special about the sharp crises and deep social tensions associated with the passage of emancipation. These are true turning points for the whole social formation and polity (Jacobin France in 1794, Reform Act Britain in 1833, the embattled Union in 1862–3, being simply the most prominent). Moreover the social-revolutionary overturns are more important than the simple disruption associated with war. In fact, by itself, war in the plantation zone often had surprisingly little impact on slave relations, probably because it enhanced the military mobilization of the slave-owners and their allies or retainers. There were few slave outbreaks in North America in 1776–83, or in the Confederacy in 1861–4, or in Western Cuba in 1868–78, or in Brazil during its war with Paraguay. However, such events did allow for many more escapes. Great political crises, could bring emancipationism to a head, especially where slave desertions were compounding the crisis. As the characteristic songs and anthems of the age suggest, anti-slavery was a necessary ingredient of the new type of 'imagined community' then being born. But however striking a simple listing of dates may be, it does not explain which social forces and issues were at stake, nor trace a link between those forces and the moment of emancipation.

I have suggested some of the patterns in the social appeal of anti-slavery, but these only appear as the long-term consequence of shifting conjunctures and evolving social structures. The abolitionist movements were undoubtedly important to the constitution of anti-slavery, but they would have been nothing without the elemental anti-slavery of the slaves themselves and the diffuse popular prejudice against slavery, which considerably predated the rise of abolitionist movements. Abolitionism was in part provoked by, or informed by, black witness and the knowledge of slave revolt, just as it sought to chime in with popular hostility to servitude. Of course, abolitionism was sometimes animated by interests and motives which had little or nothing to do with the fate of slavery. Abolitionist themes linked up directly with that cult of freedom which,

---

23   Davis, *The Problem of Slavery in the Age of Revolution*, pp. 448–8.

as Orlando Patterson has argued, is central to the history of the West.[24] But the species of abolitionism which was most directly limited by ulterior motives – most 'ideological' in the pejorative sense of the term – was also prone to be weak or distorted in its emancipationist results. Progress towards emancipation invariably signals the presence of wider anti-slavery forces. Without an understanding of these 'non-ideological' anti-slavery impulses there can be no understanding of abolitionism and emancipation.

Anti-slavery could appeal to a wide variety of social groups, each of which contributed something to it at one time or other. Every social layer was caught in a dynamically evolving context of class struggle and national formation that might favour the slave-holders at one moment but expose their vulnerability the next. It is far from the case that each social category came ready-packaged with its own peculiar worldview. Rather, within each social layer there was typically a contest between rival notions of the social order and of the relationships between classes and status groups. Even inside the slave community itself there was not monolithic opposition to slavery. The slave elite – including slave-drivers, house slaves and privileged 'head people' – had to go through the motions of accepting the authority of the master and overseer on an almost daily basis. Among the mass of slaves there was often a justifiable caution about confronting a system that, with its patrols, bloodhounds and summary punishments, was very dangerous to defy. In normal times the yeomen and poor whites would seek the patronage of the planters, but if planter power was weakened they might abandon their slave-holding patrons. Patriotic or loyalist slave-owners themselves could – in extremity – contemplate emancipation if it served their wider purpose, though Puerto Rico in 1873 was the only real example where planters led a successful emancipation process.[25]

If anti-slavery breakthroughs required a profound crisis, anti-slavery ideas matured and sharpened over quite long periods, sometimes being driven underground for years before surfacing again when conditions were right. Whatever their compromises with the slave order, the maroons prepared the way for later action against the slave-holding power. Abolitionists made a critical contribution because, even when apparently isolated and marginal – as British abolitionism seemed in the later 1790s, or American abolitionism in the 1840s – their warnings as to the aggressive nature of the slave power seemed to predict such disturbing events as the fiasco of the British expedition to Saint-Domingue

---

24   Orlando Patterson, *Freedom*, vol. 1, *Freedom in the Making of Western Culture*, Boston 1991.

25   Luis A. Figueroa, *Sugar, Slavery, and Freedom in Nineteenth-Century Puerto Rico*, Chapel Hill 2005, pp. 105–20. By the time of emancipation in 1873 the planters of this island already faced a 'free-womb' law. Their plantations were more modest than those in Cuba. The relatively small size of Puerto Rico made it easier for the planters to construct a new labour regime, complete with a *libreta* for each freedman and a law against 'vagabonds'.

or the assertiveness of US slave-holders in the war against Mexico and in Kansas. Frances Fox Piven takes US abolitionism as a case study of a movement which was for long outside the channels of official politics, but reshaped the whole of political life.[26] Likewise Howard Zinn refers to abolitionists as a 'mixed crew of editors, orators, runaway slaves, free Negro militants, and gun-toting preachers.'[27] Slave-holder excesses in responding to abolitionist challenges and provocations ended up by isolating the supporters of the 'peculiar institution'.

I have noted that even Cuban and Brazilian slaveholders might admit that the institution was barbarous and unfortunate. Liberal and Enlightenment thinking was widely diffused among those who were literate, but the weight of slave-holding interests still prevailed in debates on policy. In the United States, especially in the North, public opinion was influenced by sermon-like essays on the dilemmas of a political order in hock to slavery, first published in magazines and then as books. Caleb Bingham's collection of speeches, sermons and dialogues, *The Columbian Orator*, is reputed to have sold 200,000 copies in the first half of the nineteenth century. Frederick Douglass found the book, with its dialogues on the rights and wrongs of slavery, an inspiration. The Unitarian minister William Channing delivered a withering critique of pro-slavery apologetics. Like other Unitarians he liked to judge issues in the light of reason and conscience, not by rummaging through the Bible for answers. Ralph Waldo Emerson and David Thoreau also enhanced the authority of the anti-slavery case.[28] Frederick Law Olmsted's account of his travels in the South and Harriet Beecher Stowe's *Uncle Tom's Cabin* further strengthened anti-slavery sentiment, both radicalizing it and helping it to become the 'common sense' of large portions of Northern and Western opinion. The South had its own intellectuals – and in *De Bow's Review* a sort of learned journal – but the circulation of their thought was, by comparison, very restricted.

The century of abolition – roughly from 1780 to 1888 – was marked by a speeding-up of communication and a proliferation of images. The printing press had already made a huge contribution to the Reformation, the English Civil War and the American Revolution, but slavery and the slave trade, slave revolt and abolition were issues that lent themselves to visual representation.

26   Frances Fox Piven, *Challenging Authority: How Ordinary People Change America*, New York 2006, pp. 55–80.

27   Howard Zinn, 'Abolitionism, Freedom-Riders and the Tactics of Agitation', in Martin Duberman, ed., *The Anti-Slavery Vanguard*, Princeton 1965, p. 417.

28   While he detested slavery, Emerson was sometimes an uncomfortable ally, since he was highly critical of any hint of abolitionist smugness. And as we will see later, his reverence for self-reliance was combined with a notion that 'races' ultimately had to justify themselves by their own efforts and – if necessary – ferocity. Despite this, Emerson's general endorsement of anti-slavery helped the cause. See Len Gougeon and Joel Myerson, eds, *Emerson's Antislavery Writings*, New Haven 1995.

Slave-holders commissioned artists to paint their estates, portraying the slaves either as devoted servants or, from a distance, as tiny sticks wielding an implement. This aestheticized, usually Palladian, view of New World slavery is still with us and drawn on even by such highly critical accounts as UNESCO's excellent film, *Les Routes des esclaves* (2009). The abolitionists responded with images of the crowded slave ship and of the slave-drivers' whips and instruments of torture. Apologists for slavery countered with awful depictions of slave revolt – one 1792 favourite showed a white baby skewered and held aloft on the pike of an insurgent. The popular culture of the mid-nineteenth century reworked images of slavery and resistance with cartoons, daguerreotypes or photographs of whipping, scarred backs and vulnerable females. The anti-slavery movement itself sponsored such images, but found them difficult to control. The anti-slavery message could easily be blunted or distorted by racial stereotypes. Thus the English edition of *Uncle Tom's Cabin*, exported in large numbers to the United States, was illustrated by Frederick Cruikshank – an illustrator weaned on the viciously reactionary visual idiom of Gillray and Newton.[29] While Cruikshank understood that the poor blacks should be rendered sympathetically, such figures as Tom and Topsy still came across as simple darkies. The messages of blackface minstrelsy were not easily overcome, though by the mid-1860s Unionist journals in the North had discovered the manly qualities of the enlisted African American. In Brazil it did not take a civil war to effect such a change, perhaps because many of the very striking cartoons and drawings to be found in the *Revista Illustrada* were contributed by coloured artists or used to accompany stories written by coloured journalists.

We are used to seeing 'race' as a trump card, but by the early nineteenth century labour was widely considered as the true source of value. Those who lived off the labour of others were increasingly suspect. Eric Foner has argued that 'free labour' ideology gave extraordinary appeal and reach to a certain type of anti-slavery sentiment, and allowed it to reshape political alignments in momentous ways.[30] First and foremost this ideology asserted the dignity of labour, something not generally acknowledged in the Europe of the *anciens régimes* or oligarchic bourgeois republics. Luther's notion of the 'vocation' had helped to nourish a Protestant 'work ethic' within the social layers which it attracted. In the Northern United States of the 1820s and after, the virtue of free labour became hegemonic. The word 'servant' disappeared from the classified advertisements, the term 'gentleman' was given wide application and a political list appeared calling itself the 'Workers Party'.[31] 'Free labour' ideology insisted

---

29   Marcus Wood, *Blind Memory: Visual Representations of Slavery in England and America, 1780–1865*, Manchester 2000, pp. 143–214.

30   Eric Foner, *Free Soil, Free Labor, Free Men: The Ideology of the Republican Party Before the Civil War*, New York 1970.

31   Robert Steinfeld, *The Invention of Free Labor*, Chapel Hill 1991.

that the labourer was worthy of his hire and that unrequited labour was an injustice. Racial distinctions did not disappear, of course, and black servants might take the place of white domestics, but the slave-holder living off the toil of others could not command respect, and his accomplice, the slave-trader, was odious.

On the eve of the Civil War the 'slave power' had become abominated in the North, in parts of the West and even in corners of the South. The consequence was a boost to the Republicans. Free labour was seen as inherently more productive than slave labour. The free man – whether farmer, artisan or wage worker – was someone whom the Republic should defend and cherish, and who should be able to provide for his family. The slave-holder and slave were a menace to this world. The racial and gender assumptions of free labour ideology varied in intensity according to period and region, but remained suspicious of the claims of the slave-holder. The US Republican 'free labour' philosophy drew on two apparently very different sources – abolitionism and Jacksonian 'Democracy'. But in the development of political anti-slavery, some important themes were owed to politicians who had been Democrats at the time of the clash over the banks.

While there were important differences between British and US abolitionism, both of them operated in societies experiencing the disruptions and class struggles of early industrialization. Leading abolitionists like Fowell Buxton and Joseph Sturge in Britain, William Lloyd Garrison and Wendell Phillips in the United States, or Victor Schoelcher in France, were intensely aware of the 'social question' and of the challenging new phenomenon of the 'working classes' or proletariat. Whether moderate or radical, abolitionism was not a doctrine of class struggle – in some ways it was the opposite – yet it was a doctrine which had a mass appeal in societies gripped by the onset of capitalist industrialization based on 'free labour'. Joseph Sturge, a Birmingham abolitionist, became a leader of the 'moral force' wing of Chartism in the 1840s. Confronting a stronger target and inhabiting a less hierarchical society, the US abolitionists tended to greater radicalism and to more emphatic assertions of the free labour doctrine.

The British parliament which outlawed the Atlantic slave trade had just been examining the implications of the 'factory system', while the parliamentary debates on slavery and 'apprenticeship' in the 1830s also brought up comparisons with the practice of apprenticeship and child labour.[32] In both its British and North American variant, abolitionism tended to construct an alliance between 'progressive' employers and responsible workers, offering the latter dignity and recognition. In contrast, abolitionism failed to mobilize large

---

32   Emma Rothschild, *Economic Sentiments: Adam Smith, Condorcet and the Enlightenment*, Cambridge, MA 2001, pp. 95–107.

numbers in societies where the pressures of class struggle were weaker or non-existent.

At first sight the Netherlands and Catalonia might appear to be counter-examples, since they were capitalist centres that failed to produce a mass anti-slavery. But while the Netherlands was a commercially developed nation, with manufactures and a strong Protestant tradition, it never produced a popular anti-slavery movement or a dynamic industrial capitalism. While it had been in the vanguard of bourgeois revolution in the late sixteenth and early seventeenth centuries it had subsequently relapsed into a sedate and prosperous oligarchy, missing out on industrialization and its strains in the eighteenth and nineteenth centuries. Nevertheless there were some anti-slavery impulses in Dutch culture, visible in the Germantown resolution of 1688 (most of the signatories were Dutch), the declarations of Anacharsis Cloots during the French Revolution, some (unsuccessful) proposals made by radical patriots in the era of the Batavian Republic, and a sort of abolitionist masterpiece – Eduard Dekker's extraordinary novel *Max Havelaar*, published under the pen-name 'Multatuli' in 1860.[33] Though there was no mass abolitionist movement, there was a public outcry in 1859–60 aimed at the 'cultivation system' in Java (a regime of forced tribute labour), which helped pave the way for the eventual act of slave emancipation in Surinam in 1863.[34]

The case of Catalonia is a more demanding exception. In the 1840s there was a questioning of slavery, but no sustained abolitionism. In the 1860s and 1870s Catalonia experienced the strains of industrialization – and US emancipation furnished encouragement. The overthrow of Isabella and the outbreak of the Cuban independence struggle (both in 1868) created a more favourable context. A Spanish Abolitionist Society became active, supported by leading Republicans. But it did not become a mass campaigning force. The Catalan bourgeoisie looked to colonial Cuba as a profitable and protected market, and it often defended the slave regime as essential to Cuban prosperity. This might well have disposed Catalan workers to oppose colonial slavery. However, in the 1870s Spain was torn apart by Republican revolution and Federal secession, offering no political centre as a target for abolitionism. In some ways Spain during the years 1868–74 – like the Batavian Republic of 1794–1805 – was too strife-torn and decentred to offer a focus for anti-slavery campaigning. At the level of popular sentiment in Catalonia and some other parts of Spain, these years saw the rapid growth of an anarchist movement which not only denounced slavery but looked forward to 'an end to the reign of

---

33 Multatuli [Eduard D. Dekker], *Max Havelaar, or the coffee trades of the Netherlands Trading Company*, [Amsterdam 1860], London 1983.

34 This paragraph is a partial response to Seymour Drescher's challenging argument that the Dutch case – with its feeble abolitionism – contradicts most accounts of anti-slavery, mine included. See Drescher, *From Slavery to Freedom*, pp. 196–234.

capital, of the state and the church'.[35] Barcelona did see meetings and demon-strations which attacked the war in Cuba and the persistence of slavery. A speaker at an anti-slavery gathering in the city in 1872 was quoted as declaring: 'If there is an insurrection in Cuba, it is because there is slavery. The slaveown-ers hide behind the farce of national integrity . . . If they demand soldiers it is to guard their slaves, not save their country. Catalans, you are the most liberal people in Spain. You cannot permit a few scoundrels to get rich from the blood of the unhappy blacks, our brothers. Catalans, down with slavery! Long live reforms in the Antilles!'[36]

This was the voice of an authentic abolitionism, but it was stronger in Madrid than Barcelona, and its main success was in Puerto Rico not Cuba. The Spanish Abolitionist Society, founded in the 1860s, received considerable support from Puerto Ricans who saw the survival of slavery in the Spanish Antilles as conducive to colonial oppression. The social landscape of this well-fortified island, with its Spanish garrison, was dominated by small planters and farmers who supplied the fleets and had long practised smuggling. Those who aspired to self-rule believed that the suppression of slavery would remove an obstacle to this. Julio de Vizcarrondo, assisted by his North American Protestant wife, Harriet Brewster de Vizcarrondo, joined with Spanish reformers to urge that colonial policy must cease to be determined by special interests and that Spain should join the mainstream of modern development, as exemplified by the ending of slavery in the United States and of Russian serfdom by Tsar Alexander. Christopher Schmidt-Nowara identifies the emergence of a new public sphere in Madrid as it bid for intellectual leadership in Spanish society. Its university had 5,000 students, and the Ateneo organized debates, enquiries and public campaigns. The Fomento de las Artes encouraged worker education and there was also an association for women's education. Most specifically linked to the Abolitionist Society was the Free Society for Political Economy, preoccupied with 'free association' and 'free labour'. The Spanish revolutions of 1854 and 1868 were both marked by labour agitation in Madrid.[37]

The Spanish Abolitionists had some success with the free-womb law (Ley Moret) in 1870 and Puerto Rican emancipation in 1873, but, in the face of fierce opposition from the Cuban slave-owners and the Spanish colonial trade lobby, they failed to secure emancipation in Cuba. The milieu of bourgeois and worker social reformers rallied to anti-slavery but simply did not have sufficient strength to prevail. The Republic led by Pi y Margall, a convinced abolitionist, fell before it could press through Cuban emancipation. The Republican govern-ment did not even control the Peninsula, let alone Cuba. Eventually slave

---

35   James Joll, *The Anarchists*, London 1964, p. 112.
36   Schmidt-Nowara, *Empire and Anti-Slavery*, p. 151.
37   Ibid., pp. 54–60, 73–88.

emancipation came to Cuba in 1878–86, via the conflict between colonial insurgents and the imperial strategists of a restored constitutional monarchy. The Cuban rebels enrolled and promoted large numbers of black and coloured soldiers. Senior figures in the army and government realized that they could not defeat this rebellion and would have to come to terms with it, if they were to rescue what could be saved from Spain's 'second empire'. The key figure here was a reforming Conservative, Arsenio Martínez Campos, a man tempered by his experience of revolution and counter-revolution (more on this in the next chapter).

Class interests can always be constructed or articulated in a number of different ways. The alliance between progressive bourgeois and 'free labour' was only one such axis. British Liberalism and US Republicanism both helped to end slavery and both momentarily embodied such an alignment. But this alignment was soon strained by the rise of Chartism in Britain and Radical Reconstruction in the US. Conflict over slavery itself helped to shape group identities. But the assertion of planter power, both in the plantation zone and in the wider society and polity, provoked an array of responses that over time, and in a context of challenges to planter power, encouraged a range of anti-slavery sentiments. In the next section I seek to identify the characteristic ideologies of resistance to planter power found in objectively defined social groups, albeit that there are overlapping categories, and emergent properties and affinities. The overall context and relationship of forces had much to do with the exact balance struck within and between the contending social forces. The 'radical democratic' pole attracted support in a crisis from several different classes and status groups. At its most consistent it opposed slavery and racial definitions of citizenship, but this was only after a vigorous struggle within this current, and the new understanding remained insecure. As we will see, there were Patriot planters willing to sacrifice slavery just as there were liberal merchants and lawyers who enjoyed good relations with slave-owners. Although there was no one-to-one match between classes or races and specific ideologies, nor was there complete randomness. In the end the institution of slave-holding became dispensable to most groups at one or another time as it was crushed between rival visions of modernity and morality.

THE SLAVES' ANTI-SLAVERY

Deciphering slave mentalities is not easy, due to the absence of good sources for many periods and places. Prior to the nineteenth century there are only a few first-hand accounts by former slaves. There are some reports of slave defiance and a mass of other documents – correspondence, diaries and legal records – which offer clues. For the antebellum United States there is a comparative abundance of direct testimony by slaves or former slaves. The unusual circumstances which produced this documentation certainly pose difficult issues of interpretation, but the volume of material is still impressive. For example there are over a hundred 'slave narratives', mostly written with abolitionist encouragement.[38] There are also several thousand interviews with former slaves, sponsored and recorded by the Federal Writers' Project in the 1930s. Most of the slave narratives are plausible and informative, but they certainly tend to stress the harshness of the slave condition. Some topics, such as sexual harassment, are treated euphemistically or indirectly.

None of the slave narratives, however powerfully written, should be seen as pure and transparent. Frederick Douglass wrote differing accounts of the same episode. While much of the testimony of Olaudah Equiano and Esteban Montejo can be verified, doubts have been raised about the exact dates and places of their birth. It may never be possible to confirm or rebut such doubts, but this does not reduce the great value of these texts. We know with certainty that Equiano was a former slave, that he lived and worked as a seaman and musician in the 1760s, '70s and '80s, and that he wrote and published an account of his life that checks out on most details and was accepted by most of his contemporaries.[39] Like the memoirs of statesmen, planters and merchants, or any other subjective historical document, slave narratives involve a presentation of self. They may contain errors or self-serving statements, or reflect the concerns of abolitionist editors. But they remain nevertheless a hugely valuable resource.

The Federal Writers' Project interviews were conducted long after the ending of slavery, and the interviewees were only children when slavery ended. The attitude and race of the interviewer also can be shown to elicit varying response patterns. Some recall festive Christmases and kind owners, but most confirm flogging and unremitting toil. Black slave-drivers were widely hated, but compromising black preachers viewed quite positively.[40] These accounts vividly evoke the

---

38   For a well-chosen selection, with an introduction discussing the entire corpus, see Yuval Taylor, ed., *I Was Born a Slave*, 2 vols, Edinburgh 1999.

39   Vincent Carretta, editor of the excellent Penguin Classics edition of *The Interesting Narrative of Olaudah Equiano, the African*, has unearthed two documents where Equiano earlier described himself as born in Virginia. An African origin certainly enhanced the impact of his story, but his associates never seem to have doubted his African birth, perhaps because he spoke with an African rather than Virginian accent. Esteban Montejo told his story to the Cuban anthropologist Miguel Barnet in *Runaway Slave*, also published as a Penguin Classic in 1970. Montejo claimed to be born in 1866, though a birth entry for someone with a similar name is recorded ten years later. I met Montejo in 1962 and found his stories vivid and fascinating – but he was clearly a practised *raconteur*. While details could have been embroidered or changed for effect, he is still an invaluable witness to the world of late-nineteenth-century Afro-Cubans.

40   Paul Escott, *Slavery Remembered*, Chapel Hill 1979; for resistance and the 'bases of black culture' see pp. 71–118. See also John Blassingame, *The Slave Community*, New York 1972, and George Rawick et al., eds, *The American Slave: A Composite Autobiography*, published in two series and thirty-one volumes in the 1970s.

sounds of the plantation – the bell or horn regulating the hours of work, the songs sung by the slaves as they toiled or tramped. Without the whip the slaves would not have worked, but that did not stop them from finding some satisfaction in songs, and call and response, that followed the rhythm of this work.[41] By the middle of the nineteenth century whites were increasingly aware of the black community's musical inventiveness and power, notably in the singing of 'Negro spirituals' by black congregations and choirs. Thomas Wentworth Higginson, a white Bostonian who commanded black troops in the Civil War, published a collection of as many Negro spirituals – their refrains and singing styles – as he could find. In an indication of white interest in this material, the *Atlantic Monthly* published his introduction to this in April 1867.

Notwithstanding inevitable problems of interpretation, historians of other periods and places would be grateful for the abundant archive of the last decades of slavery in the United States. Testimony relating to slavery in Cuba and Brazil is much scarcer, though some of it is of exceptional quality, illuminating issues not so vividly addressed by the North American material. For example, the Cuban poet Manzano produced a fragmented and fraught narrative of his ejection from his owner's household, and relegation to the field gang, which powerfully evokes disorientation and confusion. It helps us to guard against the assumption that all men and women, whatever their circumstances, enjoy some standard sense of self and identity.[42] Miguel Barnet's oral history of Esteban Montejo's memories also gives us insight into the milieu of slaves and ex-slaves in Cuba.[43] Brazilian historians have used interviews and oral tradition to reconstruct the world of the former slaves in a slave regime that persisted to almost the dawn of the twentieth century.[44] The final stages of slavery often witnessed attempts to regulate the slave condition and the transition from it – 'apprenticeship' in the British West Indies, the *patronato* in Cuba – and these could give slaves an opportunity to articulate their demands in ways that survive in the written record.

The slaves who reached a New World plantation after a traumatic journey are likely to have given value simply to survival. The slaves' oral culture stressed cunning, deception and other weapons of the weak. The stories linked to Brer Rabbit and Anancy the spider man celebrate a sly subversion rather than heroic insurgence. Any social order which persists across several centuries is likely to elicit accommodation and compliance. In well-invigilated societies where the slaves were a highly vulnerable minority, compliance was all but inescapable. Nevertheless the slaves tenaciously clung to African beliefs and customs,

41   Graham White and Shane White, *The Sounds of Slavery*, Boston 2006.
42   Ellen Willis, 'Crushed Geraniums', in Davis and Gates, *The Slave's Narrative*.
43   Esteban Montejo, *Runaway Slave*, Harmondsworth 1970.
44   Ana Lugão Rios and Hebe Mattos de Castro, *Memórias do cativeiro: Família, trabalho e cidadania no pós-abolição*, Rio de Janeiro 2005.

including, for example, widespread commemoration throughout the Americas of Ogun, the Yoruba war god. The rites associated with Ogun centred on metal implements, weapons and images – and on the furnaces required to make the metal.[45] Like all of us, slaves changed their outlook and held conflicting ideas. In an argument with a slave from another plantation they might praise their owner while still taking an interest in runaways. W. E. B. Du Bois was later to write of the 'twoness' of the African American, and we may suppose that the slave condition too gave rise to conflicting sentiments.[46] The deference that the more privileged slaves were obliged to act out when with their masters had a reality of its own, but its very exaggerations could betray hostility.

The slave-owners never felt really safe. They repressed any sign of resistance with great brutality and exhibitionism. Hilary Beckles argues that the spontaneous ideology of Caribbean slaves was what he calls 'an ethos of self-liberation'.[47] Beckles explores the wider meanings of slave resistance and of the rebel or revolutionary black contribution to anti-slavery, focusing on island societies where the existence of large black majorities offered scope for rebellion. However, he notes a 'proliferation of acts of "day to day" resistance' which were not designed 'to overthrow the slave system'. He observes that 'the more informed slaves saw their anti-slavery as articulated to those of metropolitan lobbyists'. He also makes the elementary but often neglected point that the actions and thought of slave rebels were marked by 'deep-rooted conceptual heterogeneity'. Fundamental to his argument is that slaves had minds of their own, and were well-informed as to their own oppression; by contrast, one might add, most white abolitionists had no direct experience of the workings of the system and often harboured stereotyped conceptions of the slave, and the slave condition.

Beckles holds that the evidence of slavery resistance shows that most slaves did not recognize the 'legitimacy' of their enslavement and sought to escape it when the opportunity presented itself. But in normal times slave society was successfully organized to divide, weaken and repress the slave community, making escape or resistance highly difficult and dangerous. Even in the Caribbean there were islands – such as Barbados or Martinique – whose size and terrain, and somewhat larger white population, made maroon activity or slave uprising far more difficult than in, say, Jamaica. On the other hand, after decades of relative calm the slaves of Barbados (1816) and Martinique (1848) mounted impressive demonstrations of their rejection of slavery.

The slave regimes on the mainland had greater opportunities to overawe the slaves, but planters still feared 'irrational' outbursts like that of Nat Turner

---

45   Sandra T. Barnes, *Africa's Ogun: Old World and New*, Bloomington 1989.
46   W. E. B. Du Bois, *The Souls of Black Folk*, New York 1996 (originally 1903).
47   Hilary Beckles, 'Caribbean Anti-Slavery: The Self-Liberation Ethos of Enslaved Blacks', *Journal of Caribbean History* 22/1–2 (1988), also available in Hilary Beckles and Verene Shepherd, eds, *Caribbean Slave Society: A Reader*, London 1992.

and his small band. Brazil's vast backlands were far more hospitable to runaway communities (*quilombos*) than most North America regions (Florida excepted). The ending of US slave imports in 1808 helped to impose stringent control over the slave minority. The small to medium size of cotton plantations created slave communities which were probably more permeated by the influence of white society than was the case in the Caribbean or Brazil. Nevertheless black Christianity – the 'invisible institution' – became important in the last decades of the eighteenth century and even more so in the nineteenth, offering both consolation and a space and moral framework within which the conduct of planters and overseers could be questioned.[48] Southern planters in the US disapproved of Negro preachers, but faced a difficult choice. Either they permitted black worship and recognized black preachers, or they sought to impose their own, tightly controlled religious observances, but with the nagging awareness that their slaves would repair to 'hush harbours' in nearby woods or ravines as night fell. Those who permitted black worship at least had the option of inviting 'plantation missions', which taught that true religion required obedience to planter authority and submission to earthly fate.

Frederick Douglass warned of the ignorance into which the slaves were plunged by the isolation of the plantations and by their tendency to idealize their own master.[49] Douglass knew how hard it was for the slave to gain knowledge of the outside world, but the point could be overstated – and by some strands of abolitionism, it was. The slaves possessed relevant local knowledge and, depending on the region, there were also networks of communication among slaves, though information about them is sparse.

The archaeological evidence found at the site of the slave cabins at Andrew Jackson's Hermitage plantation near Nashville contains some notable finds. These include five pairs of spectacles (perhaps implying literacy), an Egyptian coin with Arabic writing, about 90,000 beads, and scores of tiny brass or porcelain clenched fists – the latter probably of African provenance and a traditional good-luck token. They point to autonomy in the slave community.[50]

Larry McKee writes of the hidey-holes: 'Beneath their façades, the cabins hid evidence of less regimented lives, conducted in near secret. The most direct gateway to those secret lives was found under each cabin floor: small squared-off pits dug into the stiff clay soil . . . such pits served primarily as cool, dry root

48   Albert Raboteau, *Slave Religion: The 'Invisible Institution' in the Slave South*, 2nd edn 2005. For a fascinating account of slave religion in the Americas see also Eugene Genovese, *Roll, Jordan, Roll: The World the Slaves Made*, New York 1974, pp. 159–84.

49   *The Narrative of Frederick Douglass*, in Taylor, *I Was Born a Slave*.

50   Brian Thomas, 'Power and Community: The Archaeology of Slavery at the Hermitage Plantation', *American Antiquity* 63/4 (October 1998), pp. 531–51. Such objects are also found in abundance at other plantations – see, e.g., Andrew Cockburn, *Journey Through Hallowed Ground*, Washington, DC, 2007, pp. 95–8.

cellars . . . [They also included] coins, bone-handled cutlery and combs, a brass thermometer backing plate, glass beads in a wide variety of styles and colors.'[51]

The beads no doubt had decorative and ritual uses, helping the slaves to nourish their own sense of identity and belonging. Masters will sometimes have offered beads as the reward for good work. However, bearing in mind their large number and that there was a dearth of coins, and few opportunities for slaves to acquire them anyway, it is also quite possible that beads and other items served as currency inside and between the larger plantations. McKee writes: 'Some of the items may have made their way to Tennessee with new slaves from Florida or New Orleans. Given their diverse origins, however, many items probably arrived through surreptitious trade networks run by the slaves themselves. Passing from hand to hand, coat lining to coat lining, in a continual yet ephemeral system of barter and trade.'[52]

This trade was the natural outgrowth of other slave activities. It was also a by-product of the masters' decision to reduce slave maintenance costs by allowing slaves to supplement the basic rations which they received. Christopher Morris notes: 'Across the South, masters permitted their slaves to sell or barter garden vegetables, poultry, baskets, and firewood for sugar, tobacco, liquor, clothing, jewellery, cash, or credit. Slaveholders made rather half-hearted attempts to control the internal economy, to keep production and distribution of garden products and manufactured items within the borders of their plantations or neighborhoods or under their purview. Still, slaves did manage to trade with each other, peddlers, transient whites, and free blacks, although often illicitly and after dark.'[53]

As explained in Chapter 3, the self-provisioning activities of the slave communities were far more extensive in the Caribbean. Julius Scott not only gives many examples but also cites numerous expressions of official unease at the extent of communication among slave communities, facilitated by the markets and the activities of peddlers and higglers (with many of the latter being women).[54]

Slave funerals and burial grounds were a source of anxiety to planters and overseers. African attitudes to death were conspicuously different and, as it were, more highly charged. Fitful attempts were made to require that wakes be sober and restrained affairs, without drums and noisy instruments, and to prevent burial grounds from becoming unsupervised gathering points. Eugene Genovese observes: 'A slave funeral became a pageant, a major event, a

51   Larry McKee, 'The Earth Was Their Witness', *Sciences* (March/April 1995), pp. 35–41, 40.

52   Ibid.

53   C. Morris, 'The Articulation of Two Worlds: The Master–Slave Relationship Reconsidered', *Journal of American History* 8/3 (December 1998), pp. 983–1,008, 994.

54   Julius Scott, *The Common Wind: Currents of Afro-American Communication in the Era of the Haitian Revolution*, Duke University PhD thesis 1986.

community effort at once solemn and spirited.'[55] In Caracas Spanish officials reported in 1789 that officers of the *pardo* and *moreno* militia were demanding 'the same funeral observances and ceremonial garb as white officers'. [56]

While white Christians tended to see the departed as passively awaiting the Day of Judgment, Africans and their descendants saw them as still active in the affairs of the living. When Walt Whitman undertook a survey of Union bury-ing-places in the South he soon found that it was African Americans who could answer his questions, even when they concerned white burials: 'Most of the information obtained', he wrote, 'was from negroes, who, as I was told, paid more attention to such matters than the white people.'[57]

The funerals of both whites and blacks sometimes had a mixed character, but for the slaves this was just the beginning of a cult of the deceased. Burial grounds were seen as belonging to the slave community and were often deco-rated in African style, with shells and objects that had been used by the departed. Together with gardens and provision grounds they were a manifestation of the slave community, and were respected as such by overseers who wished to avoid trouble. Planters and overseers might seek to restrain the slaves' burial rites, regarded as heathenish and presumptive, but this was an area where they never-theless extended latitude to the slaves. Indeed New World masters, preoccupied by other considerations, were perhaps less concerned at their slaves' burial practices than would be an African master concerned to enforce obeisance to his own lineage.[58]

African captives knew that slavery was widespread in Africa, but this did not mean that they believed that it was right for them. Many new arrivals saw reason temporarily to accommodate to their new circumstances, hoping to find a way to ease or escape their condition. The soldier captured in an African war knew that his fate could be enslavement. In regions blighted by drought and famine, sale to a slave trafficker might spell survival. The journey from Old World to New was terrible, but brought some limited advantages to those who survived it, since food was more adequate and reliable. Land was more fertile in the New World, and the climate more benign. The American-born children of nineteenth-century Italian immigrants grew to be an inch or two taller than their parents, and American-born slaves were similarly taller than their African-born parents. On the other hand New World slavery was more rigid and

---

55   Genovese, *Roll, Jordan, Roll*, p. 197.

56   Scott, *The Common Wind*, p. 38.

57   Quoted in Drew Gilpin Faust, *The Republic of Suffering: Death and the American Civil War*, New York 2008, p. 227.

58   Vincent Brown, *The Reaper's Garden: Death and Power in the World of Atlantic Slavery*, Harvard 2008, pp. 60–91. See also Mechal Sobel, *The World They Made Together: Black and White Values in Eighteenth-Century Virginia*, Princeton 1987, pp. 214–25; David Barry Gaspar, *Bondsmen*, Baltimore 1985, pp. 144–5; David Barry Gaspar, 'And Die in Dixie: Funerals, Death, and Heaven in the Slave Community, 1700–1865', *Massachusetts Review* 22/1(Spring 1981), pp. 163–83.

demanding than African bondage, and more concentrated on menial labour. The New World masters extracted unrelenting toil, geared to the strong demand for their products. The arrangements of the plantation itself stressed the gulf between the free and the unfree in ways quite alien to African bondage. The African captive had a notion of freedom as well as of slavery.[59]

As we have seen, for the member of a particular African people the concept of freedom was usually quite specific. It meant the freedom to be a member of such a nation, people or tribe. The slave was someone who was not such a member, who was effectively kinless, though they might hope either to be restored to their own people or to be assimilated by their captors. The notion of slavery, on the other hand, had no absolute character since there were many subtle gradations of captivity and servitude. Being the direct slave of an important man could be an exalted status, and even the king could be a descendant of a slave mother.[60] The New World slave-owners cut off the possibility of return and denied that of assimilation. The racial character of New World slavery gave it an absolute and degraded character in the mind of the whites. The slave community, with its hierarchies, might qualify this within the space of a given plantation – but a black man walking along a road would usually need a ticket stating his business. By thus narrowing the slave's existence, the slave-holders of the Americas helped to intensify the slave's anti-slavery.

The African captives resisted enslavement at every point in their translation to the New World, but the carapace of slave-holder power, propped up by the colonial state and the mobilization of the free population, was strong enough to subjugate a mass of captives torn, as they had been, from many different African peoples. There was a continual process of negotiation between planters, overseers and slave-drivers, on the one hand, and the slaves on the other, but, as previously observed, in normal times the slave-holders had the whip hand, both literally and figuratively. They chose who did the most unpleasant and demanding tasks, and they could distribute petty incentives. While they might make a concession one day, they could withdraw it the next. They were armed and could call on help from patrols, militia and slave-catchers. Both the gang system and the task system could be used to pit slaves against one another. Awkward customers could be detailed to specially harsh work, or sold. The plantation itself represented a formidable productive ensemble, so the planter had ample means to hire help, offer small concessions to a slave elite and overawe the rest of the slave crew. While slaves grew much of their own food, they also often relied on the planter for key elements in their diet. African notions of servitude must have played some part in reconciling captives to their lot. But the systematic ferocity of the slave gangs and the brutality of the operations of full chattel

---

59   Suzanne Miers and Igor Kopytoff, eds, *Slavery in Africa*, London 1979.
60   Jean Bazin, 'War and Servitude in Segou', *Economy and Society* 3/2 (May 1974), pp. 107–44.

slavery clashed with many African conceptions of the status of the slave. In Africa slavery was often a transitional status; in the Americas it was usually permanent and hereditary.

Whatever the risks, many plantation slaves resisted their fate by flight or revolt. By the late eighteenth century there were, in consequence, well-established maroon communities in Brazil, New Granada, the Guyanas, many of the Caribbean islands, and the Floridas. Such communities sometimes retained some links with the slaves still on the plantations, but the price of survival was reaching a formal or informal *modus vivendi* with the colonial power and the slave-holders. As the price of their own freedom they might agree to return other fugitives to their owners. Maroon communities could act as a restraint on planters or overseers, but they did not raise the standard of a generalized emancipation. Eugene Genovese has described this phase of slave resistance as 'restorationist', in that he sees in it an attempt to return to remembered African forms.[61] In a similar vein, research has confirmed Roger Bastide's insistence on the fierce conservatism of the maroon communities.[62] Yet most maroon communities were more original than they may have wished. They generally spoke a creole language that brought together elements of different African, Amerindian and European idioms. It is likely that their culture and institutions were similarly syncretistic. The survival of these communities often depended on intercourse with native Americans, or with smugglers and buccaneers, or with the underside of plantation society. While traditional forms of servitude may have sometimes been present, the maroons clearly did not practice gang slavery or chattel slavery. Their presence in the slave-holder social formation, or at its margins, asserted a different Afro-American identity to that cultivated by the slave-owners and to that extent qualified the latter's power.

Slaves persistently sought to gain control over the reproduction of the slave community, and their resistance often stemmed from the attempts of slave-holders or overseers to obstruct or cancel such gains. The head people would assert control of the garden plots and slave burial grounds, while overseers or planters were often inclined to dispute this, especially if it reduced land needed for the cash crop. Market forces as much as slave-holder caprice were a menace to the slave family. The slave-holder's economic woes, or his death, regularly required the break-up of estates – and hence of slave families.

The female slave in Africa might become a concubine, and if she had children they would boost the lineage of her owner. While this was not the fate of all female slaves, nor was it unusual. In the New World slave systems, however,

---

61   Genovese, *From Rebellion to Revolution*.

62   Roger Bastide, *African Civilizations in the New World*, New York 1971. See also James Sweet, *Recreating Africa: Culture, Kinship and Religion in the African-Portuguese World, 1441–1770*, Chapel Hill 2003.

it was rare for female slaves to be openly accepted as concubines. (The few exceptions might include overseers on Caribbean plantations, but even then the union rarely had a formal character.) In all parts of the Americas slaves strove to form families, though not necessarily ones based on monogamy, with the evidence for slave families being particularly abundant in North America. The absence of the formal status of concubine or junior wife, combined with the lack of formal protection accorded to slave unions, exposed slave women to sexual abuse. Such abuse during the Atlantic or domestic slave trade was commonplace, and often continued on the plantation. But as it developed, the slave community – notwithstanding its own patriarchal features – cultivated the protection of slave women. Planters, overseers and drivers might offer payment for sex, or abstain from interfering with the partner of an influential slave. The white men's opportunities for abuse, and the resentment of this by the slave community, often supplied a motive for slave resistance.[63]

The pattern of slave revolt in the Americas partly reflects the opportunities furnished by terrain and the demographic balance between slave and free and – not the same thing – between white and coloured, or black. The extent of communication between plantations was an important variable and reflected the preparedness of different slave-holder classes to themselves take responsibility for the main subsistence needs of their slaves. Of course, in all parts of the Americas slave-holders furnished some items of slave consumption, just as slaves grew some of their own food just about everywhere, including in the gold-mining districts of Brazil and New Granada. As noted above, there is evidence that plantations in the US South were not heremetically sealed off from one another. Petty trading, religious observance and family links created a network between plantations that were typically smaller than those in the Caribbean. I have earlier stressed that North American slave-holders themselves organized collective work on the main subsistence crops, in contrast to the dominant Caribbean or Brazilian pattern, where slave-holders left the slaves to meet much of their own food needs from plots granted to them for the purpose. As the Caribbean slave colonies became established, so the proportion of locally grown produce supplied by the slaves increased, with local markets giving slaves the opportunity to diversify their diet by supplying others' needs. Masters or overseers found it made sense to give some of their slaves permission to trade on these local markets, since it promised to furnish their slave crews with a better diet at a lower cost. The slaves' rights to cultivation and trade tended to strengthen over time. North American slave-holders were able to keep such trends within much narrower limits. This North American pattern

---

63   It was not thought proper for slave narratives to go into details of sexual abuse, but it is often broadly hinted at. For persistent attempts to assert family life and resist sexual abuse in North America see Herbert Gutman, *The Black Family in Slavery and Freedom, 1750–1925*, New York 1976.

also probably reflected the presence of a much larger layer of free, non-slave-holding farmers. In Cuba and Brazil itinerant peddlers did business with both slaves and free smallholders and tenants. Planters acquiesced, as it allowed slaves to improve their diet. In the US South planters saw control of slave provisions as a useful curb on slave autonomy, but they still allowed some trading opportunities. In Brazil itinerant peddlers sometimes encouraged slaves to participate in local markets at the expense of their owners, since the goods traded by the slaves might be stolen, or at least were produced in time that could have been spent working for the planter. It also seems likely that the *vendeiros* brought news, including news that *fazendeiros* found unwelcome. Such rural trading networks were probably weaker in the Cuban plantation zone.[64]

The extensive slave involvement in autonomous subsistence cultivation and local markets in Saint-Domingue in the 1780s, or Jamaica in the 1820s, or in Guadeloupe and Martinique in the 1840s, created a vulnerable space in their slave systems and helps to explain the scope of slave conspiracy and revolt engulfing large regions. While most of the food eaten by Caribbean whites came from the local 'black market', in the US the planters themselves organized staple food production, for the slaves as well as themselves.

Thomas Haskell, as noted in the last chapter, has stressed the cognitive implications of market relations, and their capacity to stimulate perceptions over long distances.[65] Fear of untamed market forces often prevailed within the free population. The slaves' fear of the domestic slave trade was an extreme example. But the informal market in slave produce was another matter entirely, and offered the slaves possibilities for collective self-discovery and action. Under the right circumstances, the slaves could thus become subjects as well as objects of the new forms of social cognition fostered by market relations. The petty traders, peddlers and smugglers of the plantation zone would encourage slave autonomy by buying from them produce from their plots, or even stolen from their owners. In North America the planters saw the danger and were able to limit – though not extinguish – it. But in the Caribbean and Brazil, petty trading became a major breach in the slave system, developing its own information circuits and moral economy.[66]

While strategies of concession might work to the planters' advantage in normal times, they could furnish the slaves with a basis from which to contest planter power at times of crisis. We have seen that the great slave rebellion in Saint-Domingue in 1791 was made possible, in part, by the wide concessions

---

64   See Hebe Mattos de Castro, *Ao Sul da História*, São Paulo 1987. For Cuba see Scott, *Slave Emancipation in Cuba*, Pittsburgh, 2000, p. 150.

65   Thomas Haskell, 'The Origins of Humanitarianism', in Thomas Bender, ed., *The Anti-Slavery Debate*, Ithaca 1992.

66   See for example Castro, *Ao Sul da História*, pp. 108–13. Of course, as this account makes clear, the planters also had ways of bringing pressure to bear on the traders.

that had been made to those elite slaves who participated in the Bois Caïman conspiracy on 14 and 21 August.[67] The head people on the plantations in Saint-Domingue had participated in vigorous local markets and organized their own religious festivals. In the aftermath of the revolt, as we have seen, slaves who remained on the plantations often demanded *trois jours* – three free days a week – and larger garden plots, rather than a change in French colonial law. While the rebels certainly claimed 'liberty' for themselves and those close to them, amendments to national legislation may have seemed remote and abstract to many. At other times and places, such as the British colonies in the 1820s and 1830s, a weakened or contested slave system also prompted the slaves to demand quite specific concessions. Some rebels saw customary right, anchored in the resolve of their own communities, as a potent restraint on the planters. But rebel agitation also exploited the metropolitan or national controversies over slavery and colonialism. Slave unrest could stem from the belief that local officials were concealing laws and instructions favourable to emancipation. Partial demands were often stepping stones to a more general rejection of slavery, as in the French colonies in the 1790s and in the British colonies in the 1830s. But in both cases the slave rebels or former slaves rallied to a form of anti-slavery that embodied what Sidney Mintz has termed 'proto-peasant' aspirations – that is to say, their abolitionism was imbued by claims to property and land over which they had, or aspired to have, usufruct, while still slaves.[68]

Slaves resisted enslavement within the plantation, or, failing that, by fleeing to zones beyond the reach of the colonizers. The slaves' capacity to resist grew over time, but so usually did the slave-holders' capacity to contain such resistance and to marginalize or co-opt the maroons. Emancipation in the Americas was not achieved through the slow accumulation of concessions and customary rights but it was marked by revolutionary ruptures, involving both intervention from 'outside' the slave system and the action or reaction of the slaves themselves. Under slavery the slaves might develop real or surrogate families, or they might negotiate over the pace or extent of the working day, but any concessions could be revised or revoked. If physical coercion failed, then the slave-holder could sell the recalcitrant slave or slave crew. The mortality of slave-holders or market squalls often brought to an end the informal agreements they had allowed to develop. The legislation which attempted to regulate the physical punishment of slaves was impossible to enforce on the plantations. In the British West Indies after 1834, or in Brazil in the last days of slavery, the planters and overseers really did begin to find it impossible to

---

67   See the excellent account in Fick, *The Making of Haiti*.

68   Mintz, *Caribbean Transformations*, pp. 146–56. See also C. F. S. Cardoso, *Escravo ou camponês?*, São Paulo 1987. So far as Saint-Domingue is concerned, vital evidence concerning the forms of the decomposition of the slave regime there will be found in Geggus, *Slavery, War and Revolution*.

punish their slaves in the customary way, or failing that to sell them – but this was because slavery itself had failed, and the former slaves were able to refuse the old servitude.

At times of crisis the anti-slavery of the slaves became a significant force in all the slave systems and a factor in the emancipation process. In Saint-Domingue slave revolts spread like wildfire in the 1790s and put emancipation on the agenda. A third or more of the soldiers who fought for Spanish American independence were slaves or former slaves, persuaded to do so by promises of emancipation.[69] In the British West Indies slave unrest and revolt in the years 1823–32 helped to destabilize and discredit the colonial regimes, and reconcile émigré proprietors to emancipation. In Martinique in 1848, mass desertion of the plantations led to the collapse of slavery even before emancipation legislation had been received from Paris. In the United States, it seems that three quarters of the 180,000 black soldiers who fought for the Union army were former slaves. The political strategy of both Emancipation and Reconstruction required and received black support in the South. What might appear the 'spontaneous' anti-slavery of the African American bondmen and women of the 1860s should also be seen as the surfacing of a powerful undercurrent of resistance to the slaveholders, nourished by slave religion and the culture of the slave community.[70]

In Cuba in the 1870s the rebel army recruited large numbers from the ranks of former slaves; many officers, and about half the soldiers, were men of colour. Pressure from this quarter was a factor in persuading Madrid at last to sponsor emancipation in 1880. In Brazil the resistance of urban and rural slaves played a decisive part in the final collapse of slavery in 1886–8. This bald list is offered simply to show that it is absurd to disregard the slaves' anti-slavery. We may safely assume that the great majority of slaves in the Americas longed to be free, even if their conception of freedom varied greatly from period to period and region to region.

In the British and French Caribbean colonies, where slaves comprised the overwhelming majority of the population, the anti-slavery of the slaves, once released and concerted, could by itself overwhelm the slave regime. Framing the necessary alliance between free and enslaved blacks or people of colour, between creoles and Africans, between members of different cultural and religious groups, was still a challenge; but one in many ways facilitated by the extraordinary pressures created by the slave regime itself. We have seen that in the United States, Brazil and Cuba the slaves faced a greater problem in that they did not constitute the majority of the population. They also confronted states more heavily committed to slavery, and more directly responsive to

---

69   Nuria Sales, *Sobre Esclavos, Reclutas y Mercaderes de Quintos*, Barcelona 1975.

70   See Ira Berlin, Barbara J. Fields, Steven Miller, Joseph P. Reidy and Leslie Rowland, *Slaves No More: Three Essays on Emancipation and the Civil War*, Cambridge 1992.

slave-holders. If generalized emancipation always required broad alliances and a deep-going structural crisis, this was no less true of the antebellum United States, and of Cuba and Brazil. Despite major rebellions, slavery survived longest in these latter societies because of the difficulty of overcoming such obstacles.

While the relentless pace of toil and the oppression and vulnerability of the plantation slave community generated great social antagonism, the slaves were aware of spaces not so far away which planter power found it difficult to reach. The mangrove swamps, forests and mountain crags furnished a precarious physical shelter to a brave and lucky few. To survive at all, the refugee would often need good relations with native communities. Mangrove swamps in Florida, Louisiana, Puerto Rico, Cuba and Brazil offered good havens because they defeated the tracker dogs and offered many types of food (fish, fruit and game). The wooded hills of Jamaica's Blue Mountains and Cockpit Country were another such locale. Maroon communities sometimes specialized in bee-keeping and fostered petty trade with the slaves on the plantations. The importance of the wilderness as a space outside the plantation was important as a challenge to the psychological world of enslavement and planter hegemony, even though the numbers of refugees and runaways were always small.[71]

The slaves' anti-slavery was decisively confirmed at times when the slaveholders' apparatus of intimidation was weakened or paralysed by revolution, war or political crisis. At such times slaves defied orders and deserted the fields, as in Saint-Domingue in 1793, Martinique in 1848, and Brazil in 1888. The action of North American slaves in the last year or so of the Southern Confederacy has sometimes been called a strike, but it is perhaps more akin to the disintegration seen in these other cases. The collapse of 'apprenticeship' in the British West Indies in 1837–8 is also part of this pattern.[72]

'EITHER I'M NOBODY, OR I'M A NATION': THE FREE PEOPLE OF COLOUR AND RACIAL EQUALITY

The political stability of the slave colonies or slave states, and the vulnerability of slavery, was crucially affected by the presence and conduct of free people of colour. In most parts of the Americas free blacks could themselves own slaves.

---

71   The range of maroon experience is explored in Price, *Maroon Societies*.

72   For the Confederacy see Steven Hahn, 'Did We Miss the Greatest Rebellion in Modern History?', in *The Political Worlds of Slavery and Freedom*, Cambridge, MA, 2009, pp. 55–114; for Martinique see Edouard de Lepine, *Questions sur l'histoire antillaise*, Fort-de-France 1978, pp. 125–47; for Brazil, Robert Brent Toplin, *The Abolition of Slavery in Brazil*, New York 1971; for Jamaica, Thomas Holt, *The Problem of Freedom: Race, Labor and Politics in Jamaica and Britain, 1832–8*, Baltimore 1992.

They were capable of being mean masters and tenacious defenders of their slave property. But even when they owned slaves – and many, of course, did not – free people of colour also had reason to oppose the slave regimes. New World slavery bore down directly only on those of African descent. Free persons of colour, even if quite privileged, were an awkward, latently subversive component of the Atlantic social formation. They were constantly reminded that only people of African descent were enslaved, a fact that by association degraded them, too. In most parts of the Americas they suffered formal legal disabilities or a special status that ranked below that of whites. Free blacks were excluded from the US North-West territory and were barred from marrying a white spouse, even in Massachusetts. They might sometimes hide the fact, but an ideal of racial equality had great appeal for the free people of colour.

In addition to the freedmen or women and their descendants, there were also those slaves who were encouraged or permitted by their owners to behave more or less as if they were free, sometimes called *libres de savane* in the French colonies. In Spanish America, as noted in the first chapter, slave-holders found the offer of manumission or the payment of money incentives an effective way of motivating their household or artisanal slaves. Slaves would work hard for twenty years to free themselves, and then work some more to free still enslaved relatives. At the end the slave would be free, but the master would have enough resources to buy one or several new slaves. Slave-holders also freed slaves towards the end of their working lives as a reward for faithful service; in some parts of the Americas slave-holders freed their slave mistresses, or the children born to them.

The free Afro-American population formed in this and other ways constituted a major contingent of the 'picaresque proletariat' of the Atlantic world, as noted in Part III.[73] A large proportion of the port workers and sailors were former slaves or descendants of slaves. The conditions of shipboard life were apt to imbue the floating proletariat with common customs and a sense of solidarity. Free coloured communities were to be found in all the major Atlantic ports – in London and Liverpool as well as Fortaleza and Santos, in New York and Provincetown as well as Havana and Rio de Janeiro. This was a mixed, cosmopolitan and creative community which helped to invent the major creole languages. It was influenced by the traditions of the 'brethren of the coast' and pioneered a practical free-trade doctrine known as smuggling long before Adam Smith articulated it. This was a milieu influenced by Paineite democrats, Freemasonry, Jacobinism, Methodism and Afro-American cults – and where the latter were well established, in the Caribbean and Brazil, whites as well as blacks would take part.

---

73 The engaging term 'picaresque proletariat' was first used by Peter Linebaugh, and its implications are drawn out in a book he authored with Marcus Rediker, *The Many-Headed Hydra*. While these authors focus mainly on the Anglophone Atlantic their argument also illuminates events elsewhere in the New World, especially the impact of the Haitian Revolution.

The prosecution of 'freedom suits' required the courage of the reputed slave; it often received the support of free people of colour willing to endorse the claim of wrongful enslavement – usually the result of cheating by a slave-holder who had promised manumission. Such suits spilled over into challenges to slave-holder rights, as in the Somersett case in England in the 1770s. It was also this milieu of freedmen and women, or of slaves who had managed to escape the plantation zone for the larger metropolitan centres, which produced eloquent black testimony concerning the reality of the slave condition. The writings of Equiano, Cugoano, Mary Prince, David Walker, Frederick Douglass, James Pennington, Francisco Manzano and so many others were not only to express black resistance to slavery, but also played a large part in stimulating and informing abolitionist campaigns. Douglass and Prince were technically still slaves at the time their narratives were first published, a fact that heightened their reception. The abolitionist movement could be selective in its willingness to listen to the former slaves, but without them the anti-slavery movement would have had far less impact. They were invariably among the most popular speakers on abolitionist platforms.

The free people of colour were, of course, only a potential fault line in the structure of slave-holder power. In normal times, ways were found to ensure their integration and subordination. In Saint-Domingue there were coloured proprietors who defended slavery to the last. Yet whatever the conflicts between blacks and mulattoes in Saint-Domingue, at critical points they united in support of emancipation. In Brazil there was always a large free population of African or partly African descent. During long periods this posed no problems for slave-holders. But in the 1870s and 1880s, free people of colour played an important role in the final campaigns against slavery there; thus the *jangadeiros* (lightermen) of Fortaleza, mostly free people of colour, struck a blow against the internal slave trade when they declared the port closed to this traffic. The black and coloured abolitionists presumably acted out of both idealism and self-interest, seeing slavery as an oppression which dragged down all those of African descent – though they would also denounce it as an institution degrading any society which tolerated it. But while free people of colour had motives of their own, they often acted against slavery in concert with other free workers. The anti-slavery press in North America benefited from the many subscriptions they received from free African Americans.

The special contribution made by the free people of colour was their keen sense of equality. They knew that freedom without equality spelt misery and oppression. By 1860, the great majority of US Northern black males were excluded from the vote.[74] In the decades before the Civil War, the free people of

---

74   Out of eighteen Northern states in 1860 only six gave the vote on equal terms to white men and, with one exception (Massachusetts), these states had few blacks. A further three states, notably

colour in the US North supported a Convention movement which asserted the need for equality as well as emancipation. This embraced equality before the law, the right to vote, and respect for black organizations both religious and secular.[75] Apart from supporting the abolitionist press, the free blacks of the North produced a number of their own papers. In September 1862 Paul Trevigne's *L' Union* (New Orleans) declared: 'The hour has sounded for the fight for great humanitarian principles against a vile and sordid interest.'[76]

The antebellum US Constitution offered few footholds to arguments for racial equality.[77] The Declaration of Independence seemed far more promising but, in normal times, was decorative rather than functional. Free blacks were among the first to point out that the Thirteenth Amendment was not enough, before adopting at conventions in Syracuse and Charleston their own 'Declaration of Rights and Wrongs' that addressed the need for further amendments and proper enforcement. They were well aware that, even after further amendment, the Constitution would be interpreted by a judiciary wedded to racial exclusion; but they wanted, if possible, the law on their side.[78]

In Cuba free blacks pressed for equal consideration in the Cuban liberation army, and in Brazil free people of colour believed themselves entitled to an equality of civil and political rights. Indeed it has been suggested that in Brazil and Cuba the national idea made a special appeal to free people of colour, especially those of mixed race, because they lacked definite African or European ethnicity. The mulatto would not be accepted as Portuguese or Yoruba, even if their mother or father could be. As Assunção and Zeuske explain: 'Blacks and whites could often refer to their ancestry to define their identity. This was, of course, more complicated for members of a mixed population . . . The first expression of national consciousness is therefore generally attributed to the mestizos and mulattoes. According to Darcy Ribiero, "They were Brazilians or they were nothing". The mulatto poet Plácido was one of the first intellectuals to link the concept of homeland

New York, allowed a tiny number of black men to vote if they met tough residence and property qualifications. See James Oliver Horton and Lois E. Horton, *In Hope of Liberty: Culture, Community and Protest Among Northern Free Blacks, 1700–1860*, New York 1997, p. 169.

75   The lexical as well as political importance of the theme of equality is developed in interesting ways by Celeste Michelle Condit and John Louis Lucaites, *Crafting Equality: America's Anglo-African Word*, Chicago 1993.

76   An editorial published just after the announcement of the Emancipation Proclamation. See Charles Vincent, *Black Legislators in Louisiana During Reconstruction*, Baton Rouge 1976, p. 17.

77   There was one clause which might have been used, that which stipulated that 'the citizens of each State shall be entitled to all privileges and immunities of citizens in the several states.' Theoretically a free black who was a citizen in a 'free state' could claim the 'privileges and immunities' of a citizen in all other states. But so far as I know there were no cases of a free black from the North ever successfully claiming such 'privileges and immunities' in a Southern slave state.

78   Vincent, *Black Legislators*, p. 26.

with being Cuban.'[79] The coloured officer in Cuba and coloured man of letters in Brazil were certainly distinctive figures in the social landscape as the national idea developed. However, even the most ingenious analyst would not claim that free people of colour were the true inventors of US nationalism. Frederick Douglass or W. E. B. Du Bois would have been able to play this role but for the fact that they were not accepted as equals by most of their fellow citizens.

'FREE LABOUR': THE ANTI-SLAVERY OF WHITE WORKERS AND FARMERS

Britain and the United States were both experiencing the beginnings of industrialization when abolitionism acquired a broad character (roughly 1788–1838 in Britain and 1833–65 in the US). Both countries had growing numbers of wage workers in the early nineteenth century and both still had large numbers of artisans, small workshops and professional men. The anti-slavery agitation was focused on modernizing sectors, with much of it in or close to the main commercial and industrializing districts. The beginnings of popular abolitionism in France in 1847 also saw anti-slavery petitions obtain support from wage-earners in the Paris region. During the US Civil War, British trade unions and the International Workingmen's Association campaigned in favour of the Union and against diplomatic recognition for the Confederacy.

While sections of the new working classes in Britain and the US North undoubtedly inclined to anti-slavery, there were many complicating factors. The workers most attracted to anti-slavery and 'free labour' themes were not the most downtrodden and deprived, but rather the ranks of respectable artisans and craftsmen determined to improve their lot. Such people might aspire to become farmers and the owners of small workshops – and farmers and small employers often themselves responded to 'free labour' ideology and anti-slavery themes, whether they lived in William Wilberforce's constituency in Yorkshire or in upstate New York. A striking feature of the Republican watchword 'free labour, free soil, free men' is that it was open to two interpretations. One was a

---

79   Matthias Röhrig Assunção and Michael Zeuske, '"Race", Ethnicity and Social Structure in Nineteenth-Century Brazil and Cuba', *Ibero-Amerikanisches Archiv* 24 (1998), pp. 375–443, 424. Darcy Ribeiro's quoted remark may be compared to some lines in Derek Walcott's poem, 'Schooner':

> I'm just a red nigger who loved the sea,
> I had a sound colonial education,
> I have Dutch, nigger, and English in me,
> And either I'm nobody, or I'm a nation.

Derek Walcott, *Selected Poems, 1948–1984*, London 1992, p. 346.

generous 'stakeholder' concept of liberty that promised free homesteads carved from public land and available to all those willing to work them. But 'free soil' could more simply mean land which was barred to slave-owners. Likewise, some might believe that to be truly free the labourer needed to own tools, or a workshop or dwelling, while for others it simply meant the absence of legal compulsion.

In the early decades antagonisms between employer and employee were weak, because an apprentice would see himself as a future master. A man described as a 'shoe-maker' might own a shoe-making workshop or might simply work there. Many workers also retained a connection with the land or hoped to become farmers one day. The factory girls of the Massachusetts textile mills would work between the ages of twelve and twenty, but looked forward to becoming farmers' wives. The concept of 'free labour' embraced the wage worker, the artisan and self-employed craftsman, and the farmer. In itself it was an apparently descriptive rather than anti-slavery category. But by highlighting an implicit distinction between the condition of the slave and the rights of free labour, it carried latent anti-slavery implications. It was a term that made many slave-owners uncomfortable.

It is difficult to generalize about the conditions of the working classes in north western Europe or the US North, but the hours were long – at least twelve hours a day – and the pay was meagre. In the early industrial epoch employers hoarded currency and paid wages in kind, or in tokens that could only be redeemed at a company store. Physical punishment was far from unknown and the condition of the labourer thoroughly miserable, even if not resembling chattel slavery. US workers were fearful of being reduced to slaves, or replaced by slaves. Their first organizations soon sought limitations on the length of the working day, the banning of child labour, the promotion of schools, and the right to be paid in cash, not in kind or by bankers' notes.[80] This was the philosophy of free labour and the doctrine of 'Workeyism'.

The farmer, mechanic and artisan saw themselves as reliant on free labour. Proud of their way of life, they did not welcome slave-holder competition. The farmers of the US North and West, and the workers who aspired to become farmers, were keenly concerned with the availability of public land and hostile to the prospect of the lion's share being claimed by slave-owners. The Northern farmers had large families, and there were usually sons and daughters in search of new land. The 'free soilers' of the 1840s argued that Western land should be available on good terms to migrants from the East. Since at least the 1770s, John Millar and other philosophers and political economists had celebrated the

80   Charles Perrow, *Organizing America: Wealth, Power and the Origins of Corporate Capitalism*, Princeton 2002, pp. 53–95; Philip Foner, *History of the Labor Movement in the United States*, vol. 1, *From Colonial Times to the Founding of the American Federation of Labor*, New York 1947, pp. 123–7, 191–218, 266–96.

superiority of free labour over slavery. In the British or French context, such views reassured the colonial authorities that emancipation would not ruin the colonies. In the United States the concept of 'free labour' performed a different function: that of bringing farmers, artisans and wage workers under the same rubric in antagonism to the slave-holders.

In both Britain and the United States, the affirmation of free labour was in part a riposte to traditional notions that the wage worker was a pitiable and dependent being. England's intransigent Levellers of the 1640 and 1650s had not favoured giving the suffrage to servants, on the grounds that they would simply vote the way their employers wanted. The radical English writer William Cobbett likewise urged that men without their own independent means of live-lihood were little better than slaves. In the 1830s, Democratic labour organizers in the United States began to use the term 'wage slave' to characterize the new industrial working class and to stress its most wretched features. While it did draw attention to the fact that large numbers were now permanently dependent on wage labour, it failed to register that a still widespread abuse was failure to pay in good currency.

Nevertheless the term 'wage slave' saw slavery as a very negative pole of reference. In US antebellum political debate it could be twisted to suggest that, while it was wrong to treat white workers as slaves, it was acceptable to treat blacks that way. Some of those who used the term certainly meant to indict slav-ery, of both the open and harsh, or veiled and more subtle, varieties. But for others it fell into the trap prepared by Jeffersonian – and Jacksonian – doctrine, namely that freedom and democracy were only for white men. As it evolved, free labour ideology portrayed the slave-holders as enemies of the working man. The Jacksonians had extended the vote to all white males and had mobi-lized against the banks. The achievement of 'free labour' ideology was gradually to erode the supremacy of the Democrats by supplying a more attractive alter-native option than the Whigs. Eventually, some Northern Democrats broke with their party because it seemed subservient to the slave-holders, even allow-ing them to colonize the West.[81]

If consulted on the matter, free white workers in the United States usually objected to the rich having the added advantage of being able to deploy slave labour. Such workers had no wish to compete with slaves, and believed that all decently paid and dignified employment should be reserved for whites.[82] A racially tinged anti-slavery was to be of major significance in Northern America (with more universalist undercurrents to be considered below). In Cuba or Brazil there were no well-populated areas free of slavery, and the free population

---

81   Jonathan H. Earle, *Jacksonian Antislavery and the Politics of Free Soil, 1824–54*, Chapel Hill 2004.

82   This aspect of matters is powerfully conveyed in David Roediger, *The Wages of Whiteness*, London 1987.

was anyway racially mixed along a spectrum. When some agitation against slavery did eventually emerge in the later third of the nineteenth century, it embraced both white and coloured workers.

Many US labourers and artisans had experience of milder forms of personal dependence as apprentices, servants, or as teenage sons or daughters working unpaid for their father. They preferred to be able to choose their employer, to move from a job at will, and to receive a fair wage. They opposed masters having the power to inflict physical punishment. Slavery, as an extreme form of the dependence of the labourer on the master, was odious to them. Small masters employing artisans and labourers, or even slaves, seem often to have shared these sentiments. Their enterprises did not require gang labour, and the small manufacturers could often be brought to proclaim the 'free labour' ideology. As Seymour Drescher has shown, British artisans, journeymen, labourers and small manufacturers were drawn to support abolitionist agitation.[83] Indeed, the complicity of the British oligarchy in slave-trading and slave-holding had undermined its legitimacy: economic vulnerability could alienate propertyless whites from an established order in which slave-holders were prominent. Such moments were rare, but combined with a wider crisis they could be very threatening to the slave-owners.

The workers of the United States were, of course, even more assertive than those of the Old World in the early nineteenth century. It was in deference to the egalitarian spirit of the young Republic that those advertising a domestic vacancy now appealed for 'help', not for 'servants'. The 'free labour ideology' which animated 'free soil' Democrats and Republicans attracted the support of small employers as well as artisans, craftsmen, and those who were, or hoped to become, farmers. While skilled workers, professional men and small employers recognized themselves in the celebration of 'free labour', factory operatives and unskilled urban labourers were less likely to do so. Some of the latter were ground down by the long hours needed to earn a living. Unskilled or semi-skilled white workers might cherish racial privilege quite intensely, since it protected them from the competition of free blacks. In border states with a significant slave presence white workers could be very ambivalent at the prospect of emancipation, with some strongly opposed, and others quite receptive to the anti-slavery message, depending on differing constructions/perceptions of their interests and values. Gender, religion and ethnic allegiance interacted with class, and will be further considered below. But, according to free labour ideology, all who worked should be justly rewarded.

In the US North and West, 'free labour' values managed both to elevate the wage worker and to reflect the worker's aspiration to a social independence which would be enhanced by owning a farm, or a small workshop or business,

---

83   Drescher, *Capitalism and Antislavery*, pp. 67–72, 145–7.

of their own. Of course there remained those for whom the promise of 'free labour' was pie-in-the sky. 'Free labour' had greater appeal to workers who had a personal relationship with their employer and some hope of achieving the status of a craftsman or small master. The casual day-labourer, or the young female factory operative toiling fourteen hours a day for a pittance, were less likely to respond.

There were to be both Whiggish and Democratic currents contributing to the eventual rise of the Republican Party. The 'Free Soil' Democrats broke with their party in the 1840s and 1850s. While such men were hostile to the 'slave power' and its exorbitant demands, they took little interest in the rights of free blacks. With both Whigs and Democrats basically supporting slavery, Northern suspicion of slave-holders was to be found in both parties. Because Jackson's Democratic party was at least rhetorically opposed to plutocracy it attracted some anti-slavery currents. Jackson was a foe of soft money and the banks. He also opposed South Carolina's secessionist 'nullifiers', despite the fact that they were fellow slave-holders. This helps to explain why a Northern Democrat, David Wilmot, representing a rural county in the House of Representatives, secured the necessary support from his fellow Northerners in the House in 1846 to secure passage of his famous 'proviso' prohibiting the reintroduction of slavery into any land acquired from Mexico – the fact that Mexico had suppressed slavery in 1829 sharpened this argument. Together with eight Democratic colleagues, Wilmot was soon to leave the Democratic Party, dubbing it a 'tool of the slave-holders'. It is interesting to note that Wilmot was an opponent of protectionist tariffs, warning his constituents that he was no partisan of the industrial interest but took his stand in favour of 'the cause of labor against the sordid aims of capital'. On another occasion he put down an amendment that would tax all types of capital to pay for the Mexican War – manufacturers and planters would both pay at the same rate, assessed on the value of their enterprises. He used a fusion of class and race *ressentiment* to justify his proviso: 'Let us stop this mad career of human slavery. The negro race already occupy enough of this fair continent; let us keep what remains for ourselves, and our children – for the poor man that wealth shall oppress.'[84] Some of the Free Soilers were to be less hostile to African Americans. Frederick Douglass attended their 1848 Convention and was accorded a hearing. But the Wilmot mixture remained important – and the whole Free Soil defection hugely significant.

Eric Foner, Jonathan Earle and John Ashworth see class appeals as central to the emergence of the Free Soilers and the Republican Party, diverting support from both Whigs and Democrats to defeat the so-called Know-Nothings, with their nativist phobias.[85] Only about a quarter of Republican politicians were to

---

84   Quoted in Earle, *Jacksonian Antislavery*, pp. 134, 139.
85   See the essays by Eric Foner, John Ashworth and Sean Wilentz in Melvyn Stokes and

be former Democrats, but this was just enough to reach out to the Democrats' following. Robert Fogel argues that worker disaffection fed into the Republican advance in the 1850s. He shows that the 1850s were a particularly hard time for native-born manual workers in the US North, but that the Republicans, rather than Know-Nothings, managed to channel their discontent thanks to 'free soil', 'free labour' and a concern to improve conditions in Northern cities.[86] While some of the workers' anger was directed at their own immediate employers, most of it was directed against the 'slave power' and its Northern accomplices. Indeed some employers encouraged such a channelling of discontent.

How widespread was acceptance of the racist arguments for slavery? The new popular culture was saturated with racist sentiment. Such popular entertainments as blackface minstrelsy were suffused with racial notions, mainly of an 'aversive' description, and in normal times this could be mobilized by pro-slavery politicians. At the same time, the words put in the mouth of the cheeky 'Sambo' would include ribald speculations on the master or mistress, and disdain for demands of the workaday world. On the other hand there was no ambiguity in the vehemence with which the more insecure white workers sought to exclude free blacks from desirable jobs, and even to stop them from constituting themselves as a respected social group. They were, for example, prevented from forming their own fire-fighting organizations, as the Irish had done in New York or Philadelphia. They were also unwelcome in the state militia. Indeed, free people of colour were routinely subjected to intimidation in the 'free states' in ways which marginalized them economically and politically. Irish and Italian immigrants were invited to see themselves as white and to assert their new American identity by despising the black racial out-group.[87]

In normal times the white workers' sense of allegiance to the United States furnished a natural link between racial sentiment and pro-slavery. Nationalism and racism were allied. But at times of sectional conflict, racial prejudice could be neutralized by hostility to the designs of the Southern slave power. White

---

Stephen Conway, eds, *The Market Revolution in America*, Charlottesville and London 1996, pp. 99–148, 202–23. See also Foner, *Free Soil, Free Labor, Free Men*, and Foner, *Politics and Ideology in the Age of the Civil War* as well as John Ashworth, *Slavery, Capitalism and Politics in the Antebellum Republic*, vol. 2, *The Coming of the Civil War*.

86   Robert Fogel, *Without Consent or Contract*, New York 1989, pp. 320–87. John Ashworth's argument linking abolitionism to class formation is also relevant here, *AHR* (1987).

87   The thoroughgoing racialization of the class structure in the nineteenth-century United States is explored in three important studies: Roediger, *The Wages of Whiteness*; Alexander Saxton, *The Rise and Fall of the White Republic*, London 1989, and Noel Ignatiev, *How the Irish Became White*, New York 1992. For an interesting but over-polarized critical discussion see the special supplement on 'Whiteness and the Historians' Imagination' in *International Labor and Working Class History* 60 (Fall 2001), pp. 1–92. See also Peter Kolchin, 'Whiteness Studies: The New History of Race in America', *Journal of American History* 89/1 (2006). As Kolchin acknowledges these authors have raised important new questions, even if their concept of race embraces too much.

workers cherished their own freedom and, as noted above, believed that they should not be expected to compete with slave-owners or slaves for jobs or land. Slave-holders could thus easily be seen as oppressors, undercutting the aspirations of white labourers. The position of free workers in the South seemed unenviable to both Northern workers and newly arrived immigrants, who generally shunned the South. The racist but non-slave-holding whites in a largely white region could oppose the slave trade or slavery on the grounds that one or the other might produce an increase in the black population. This is a feeling that could be mobilized for anti-slavery ends in North American port towns of the eighteenth century, or among the American-born workers of the North, or Western settlers, in the 1850s. But despite the evidence for such views, there is also evidence that white workers were moved by feelings of solidarity and sympathy. Slave-catchers pursuing fugitives in the North found few willing helpers. While conceding that popular antagonism to slavery was rarely high-minded, it is worth noting that men and women of colour were accepted as equals by some working-class organizations. Equiano was a member of the London Corresponding Society; Wedderburn was a leader of the Spencean socialists. But asserting the rights of small numbers of black or coloured people in an imperial metropolis was a less difficult and demanding affair than vindicating the rights of sizeable black populations.

Though unskilled and semi-skilled white workers could be very susceptible to ethnocentric ideas and racial practices, it would be wrong to imply that they were more bigoted overall than the educated or the well-to-do. There were plenty of the latter in nineteenth-century Europe and America who valued slavery and had an investment in it, either financial or ideological. Racist ideas were widely entertained and quite respectable.

There was a potential, if elusive and highly unstable, axis of solidarity between free white workers, free black workers and plantation slaves. Signs of this potential can be detected in the earliest freedom suits, or in aspects of shipboard and popular culture. Childhood sometimes allowed for friendship between black and white, as noted by Frederick Douglass and as portrayed by Mark Twain in *Huckleberry Finn*. Although *Huckleberry Finn* was not published until 1883, it powerfully – if selectively – evokes antebellum South-Western life and culture. On the one hand there are anonymous 'niggers'; on the other hand Jim, the runaway, is portrayed in affectionate if often patronizing terms. Huck and Jim are not at all figments of some free labour ideology, but rather bearers of a picaresque romance, their brief idyll on the raft nevertheless taking them deeper into slave territory. Altogether Twain compellingly conveys the ambivalence of those who owned few or no slaves in the South-West and border regions. Albert Parsons, the future labour leader and Haymarket martyr, was raised by a black woman and – something he later apologized for – joined the Confederate army as a volunteer at the age of fifteen, later serving as an officer in the Reconstruction-era Republican militia in Texas, where he met his future wife, Lucy Parsons, a women of mixed race who was also to become an outstanding labour agitator.[88]

There were certainly long periods when any hint of interracial harmony was absent from public life, and pro-slavery politics was accepted by the great majority outside the plantation zone. The abolitionists caused a great stir but failed to attract more than a sliver of support when they ventured into electoral politics. It was not until the mid-1840s that some radical Democrats began to reject the tutelage of Southern plantocrats and to hearken to the free soil idea.

In certain conditions and contexts the hold of racial ideology could be undermined, or racial fears and sentiments allotted a secondary place. The slave-holder's racial stereotypes were weaker in the Revolutionary epoch, even in the South where there were many manumissions, but began to gather strength again in the 1790s. Abolitionism played an important role in challenging the racial ideologies supportive of racial slavery, but it was not until some wider crisis that their ideas, including their anti-racial beliefs, could acquire some wider following.

The *Liberator* did not seek to represent white workers, and in its early days frowned on strikes. But by the 1840s and 1850s it could be a magnet for those of radical temperament. Some working-class radicals easily identified abolitionism as a cause they should support. The following report of a meeting addressed by Frederick Douglass in Concord suggests that abolitionism could radicalize as it crystallized in the interstices of an already mobile social class system:

> In the evening, Douglass made a masterly and most impressive speech. The house was crowded, and with the best of our people – no clergy – and but a few of the bigots who are past hearing. He began by a calm, deliberate and very simple narrative of his life. After narrating his early life and briefly – his schooling, the beginning of the wife of his master's relative to teach him letters, and the stern forbidding of it by her husband, which Douglass overhead – how he caught a little teaching here and there from the children in the streets (a fact, he said, which accounted to him for his extraordinary attachment to children) – after getting through this, in a somewhat suppressed and hesitant way – interesting all the while for its facts but dullish in manner and giving, I suspect, no token to the audience of what was coming through though I discerned, at times, symptoms of a brewing storm – he closed his slave narrative, and gradually let out the outraged humanity that was labouring in him, in indignant and terrible speech. It was not what you could describe as oratory or eloquence. It was sterner, darker, deeper than these. It was the volcanic outbreak of human nature, long pent up in slavery and at last bursting its imprisonment. It was the storm of insurrection; and I could not but

---

88   For Albert and Lucy Parsons see James Green, *Death in the Haymarket*, New York 2006.

think, as he stalked to and fro on the platform, roused up like the Numidian lion, how that terrible voice of his would ring through the pine glades of the South, in the day of her visitation, calling the insurgents to battle, and striking terror to the hearts of the dismayed and despairing mastery. He reminded me of Toussaint among the plantations of Haiti. There was a great oratory in his speech, but more of dignity and earnestness than what we call eloquence. He was not up as a speaker performing. He was an insurgent slave, taking hold on the right of speech, and charging on his tyrants the bondage of his race . . . There is a prospect of having Douglass here again, and in other parts of New Hampshire. He is a surprising lecturer. I would not praise him, or describe him; but he is a coloured man, a slave, of the race who can't take care of themselves – our inferiors, and therefore to be kept in slavery – an abolitionist, and therefore to be despised . . . He is one of the most impressive and majestic speakers I have ever heard. The close of his address on Sunday was unrivalled . . . I have never seen a man leave the platform, or close a speech, with more real dignity, and eloquent majesty.[89]

FEMINIST EGALITARIANISM AND ANTI-SLAVERY WOMEN

Supposedly inhabiting the private sphere, women did not have a voice in the public sphere. But since slavery itself was a domestic institution, and women were viewed as custodians of the private sphere, there were opportunities to make their concerns known on this issue which some women were able and willing to take. Abigail Adams famously advised her husband to 'remember the ladies', and expressed her abhorrence of slavery to him, but these sentiments were conveyed in private letters. In Britain and the United States prominent women could sponsor charitable and philanthropic activity, and this seemed to legitimate speaking up for the slave. From almost the beginning women played a part in abolitionism, accounting for a tenth of the signatures to the first petitions against the slave trade. However, Wilberforce was uneasy at women playing any active role, whether in public meetings or in canvassing for signatures. In the first phase of British abolitionism, women could sign petitions or write against the slave trade but no female orator spoke from the platform. Quaker women were active in charitable work but not in the early stages of abolition where Quaker men took the lead, perhaps in emulation of their wives' philanthropy.[90] In France Olympe de Gouges, by her writing, and Madame de Staël, through her salons, found ways to express their hostility to slavery. Flora Tristan also espoused anti-slavery, both in France and during her sojourns in Peru.

---

89   Quoted in Marion Starling Wilson, *The Slave Narrative: Its Place in American History*, Washington, DC, 1981, pp. 250–1. For the redical milieu in Concord see Foner, *Ideology and Politics*, p. 68.

90   Claire Midgley, *Women Against Slavery: The British Campaigns 1780–1870*, London 1992.

In the last chapter we saw that the Birmingham Ladies Negroes' Friend Society pioneered the British demand for immediate, not gradual, emancipation in 1826. Mrs Elizabeth Heyricke declared: 'men may propose only *gradually* to abolish the worst of crimes, and only to *mitigate* the most evil bondage . . . I trust that no ladies' association will ever be found with such words attached to it.'[91] The British women's societies organized their own – sometimes huge – meetings, but women did not speak from the platform at mixed events, hence the controversy at the London World Anti-Slavery Convention in 1840 when American women sought full participation.

In the United States women became very active and prominent in the movement in the 1830s, though the more moderate male abolitionists, such as Lewis Tappan, thought this to be an unwise distraction from the cause. Unabashed, Lucretia Mott, Sarah Grimké and Elizabeth Cady Stanton spoke from the platform at many mixed anti-slavery events and their contribution was welcomed by the more radical abolitionists, notably William Lloyd Garrison, Wendell Phillips and Frederick Douglass. Garrison's *Liberator* had a 'Ladies Department'.[92] Following the exclusion of women delegates at the World Anti-Slavery Convention in 1840 there was a split in the US movement, with moderates quitting Garrison's American Anti-Slavery Society. The first public call for women to have the vote was made in 1848 at a women's convention in Seneca Falls, New York, organized by a group of female abolitionists. Their Declaration opened: 'We hold these truths to be self-evident: all men and women are created equal'.[93] Elizabeth Cady Stanton declared that she found abolitionism to be based on 'a great humanitarian idea', one that she found to be an essential corrective to 'the self-respect of one proud race' which had given birth to the Republic. It was also an idea that promised freedom and equality to women.[94]

The support given to anti-slavery by women of various classes reflected their opposition to arbitrary male power and the notion that they were their husband's property. They aspired to a redefinition of the female role. At this time the mistress of a middle-class household was likely to be managing a small team of domestic helpers. Female abolitionism was usually protective of the family, conceived as an integral sphere of personal fulfilment that should not be exposed to the gross intervention of the overseer or slave-holder. The abolitionist

91   Blackburn, *Overthrow of Colonial Slavery*, p. 423.

92   Bonnie Anderson, *Joyous Greetings: The First International Women's Movement, 1830–1860*, Oxford 2000, pp. 115–28. See also Louis Filler, *The Crusade Against Slavery: 1830–1860*, New York 1960, pp. 137–8, Seymour Drescher, *Abolition*, p. 307, and Vron Ware, *Beyond the Pale: White Women, Racism and History*, London 1992, pp. 47–116.

93   Anderson, *Joyous Greetings*, p. 168.

94   For Susan Cady Stanton's speech to the anniversary of the American Antislavery Society in 1860, see Elizabeth Cady Stanton and Susan B. Anthony, *Correspondence, Writings, Speeches*, edited by Ellen Dubois, New York 1981, pp. 79–85.

movements asserted the fundamental value of family ties at a time when they were threatened by economic or political dislocation. While there had been some resistance to women playing too public a role, important leaders of anti-slavery like William Lloyd Garrison and Victor Schoelcher were also to be early supporters of women's rights. Even many of the most conservative were aware that prevailing conceptions allowed women to be defenders of the integrity of hearth and home. The huge impact of Harriet Beecher Stowe's novel *Uncle Tom's Cabin* was to illustrate the power of the female voice. Likewise, in the early months of the US Civil War, one of the most prominent champions of an eman-cipationist policy was to be a young woman, Anne Dickenson.

In 1851 reports of a speech made by Sojourner Truth, a free black woman who had lived in slavery, made a great impact on abolitionist circles and beyond. She pitched her remarks in a quite different register from Frederick Douglass, with his command of classical oratory. Most of the reports sought to render her dialect in written form. I quote from the most widely diffused – though proba-bly not most accurate – version: 'Well, chillen, whar dar' so much racket dar must be som'ting out o'kilter. I tink dat, 'twixt the niggers of the South and de women at de Norf, all a-talking 'bout rights, de white men will be in a fix pretty soon. But what's all this here talking 'bout? Dat man over dar say dat woman needs to be helped into carriages and lifted over ditches and to have de best place eberywar. Nobody helps me into carriages or ober mud-puddles, or gives me any best place.' And raising herself to her full height and her voice to a pitch like rolling thunder she demanded, 'Ar'n't I a woman? Look at me, look at my arm' – and she bared her right arm to the shoulder, showing its tremendous muscular power. 'I have ploughed and planted and gathered into barns and no man could head me – and ar'n't I a woman? I could work as much and eat as much as any man (when I could get it), and bear de lash as well – and ar'n't I a woman? I have borne thirteen chillen, and see 'em mos' all sold off into slavery and when I cried out with a mother's grief none but Jesus heard.'[95] The evocation of the black woman's strength and toil – and the violation of her maternal role in slavery – extended and reinforced the abolitionist case.

In Britain and the US, women's contribution to abolitionism had allowed those involved to assert an autonomous political identity and to question gender subordination. But if female abolitionism could lead to feminism in peaceful civic campaigning, the onset of armed conflict brought a different dynamic. Republicans argued that the willingness of so many black men to fight for the Union meant that they had earned the right to vote. In the aftermath of the Civil War, the seemingly natural alliance of abolitionists and feminists was strained by the terms of the Fourteenth Amendment, which tried to extend the vote to

---

95   Nell Irvin Painter, *Sojourner Truth: A Life, a Symbol*, New York 1996, p. 167. There were several versions of the speech and Painter has an excellent discussion of how they differ.

black freedmen but not to women, whether black or white. Garrison's Antislavery Society had wound itself up by this time, but the relative importance of female and black male suffrage opened a rift, with a number of prominent abolitionist women, such as Elisabeth Cady Stanton and Susan B. Anthony, declining to support a measure that failed to accord equal rights to women. Indeed Stanton proposed an educational qualification that would have enfranchised the literate of both races and sexes, but excluded the mass of unlettered blacks (and many Southern rural whites).[96]

Wendell Phillips and Gerrit Smith were strong supporters of extending the franchise to women, but in the conditions of 1867–70 they urged that black manhood suffrage could be won first, largely because of the black soldier's contribution, and that it was needed by the black community as a whole for reasons of basic self-defence in the face of the violence of the Ku Klux Klan and kindred organizations. White women did not face the same imminent danger. Black women were the most vulnerable, yet few would qualify for the suffrage if the latter was based on a literacy test.[97] This dispute saw the emergence of a specifically feminist organization, the National Women's Suffrage Association, founded in 1869, which was formally dedicated to 'universal suffrage', male and female, black and white. But the aftermath of this dispute also spurred arguments as to what else, aside from the vote, needed to be changed if women and freedmen were really to enjoy an equality of rights and opportunities.

Some women joined the Brazilian campaigns against slavery in the 1870s and 1880s, but did so according to a script that portrayed women as defenders of household and family, notwithstanding the latter's very patriarchal features. In conformity with this script, only a few aristocratic women played any role in public anti-slavery events. The feelings of wives and mothers were invoked when abolitionists surrounded the homes of slaveholders, but they were kept away from direct confrontation. However, Princess Isabella, as regent, was destined to play a prominent part in the downfall of slavery. With her father the emperor absent abroad, it fell to her to sign both the Free Womb Law of 1871 and the Emancipation Law of 1888.[98]

---

96 Eric Foner, *Reconstruction: America's Unfinished Revolution, 1863–1877*, New York 1988, pp. 255–6.

97 Angela Davis, *Women, Race and Class*, New York 1981, pp. 30–69; see also Stanton and Anthony, *Correspondence, Writings, Speeches*, pp. 113–30, and the presentation by the editor, Ellen Dubois, pp. 88–112. For women's experience of the war see Drew Gilpin Faust, 'Ours as Well as That of the Men', in James McPherson and William Cooper, eds, *Writing the Civil War*, Charlottesville 1998, pp. 228–40. See also Louise M. Newman, *White Women's Rights: The Racial Origins of Feminism in the United States*, Oxford 1999, pp. 3–21.

98 Roger Kittleson, 'Women and Notions of Womanhood in Brazilian Abolitionism', in Pamela Scully and Diane Paton, eds, *Gender and Slave Emancipation in the Atlantic World*, Durham, NC, 2005, pp. 99–120. The editors' introduction to this collection helpfully charts the counterpoint of abolitionism and gender ideology in the nineteenth-century Atlantic world.

The peaceful character of Brazilian abolition allowed women to play a role, but, Isabella apart, not a truly public one. Feminist conclusions did not emerge in Brazil until the twentieth century.

PATRIOTIC ANTI-SLAVERY

A potential for anti-slavery derived not from social relations of production or reproduction but from the nexus of antagonism between metropolis and colony, or between an aristocratic state, with its exclusionary principles of operation, and the mass of commoners. To different degrees Freemasonry and Jacobinism helped to articulate hostility to aristocratic privilege and oligarchic power. While the Freemasons sometimes admitted free blacks to membership, they were far from being either consistent democrats or abolitionists. For their part the Jacobins were in principle devotees of the Rights of Man and of the Citizen, and some did indeed make common cause with rebel blacks. But there were also slave-holding and racist Jacobins in both the colonies and metropolis.

Opposition to the slave trade could receive support from patriots, including patriot slave-holders, who favoured a whitening of the national ethnic mix, a sentiment found in Virginia, Cuba, mainland Spanish America and Brazil. This type of thinking favoured bans on the slave trade, but had no necessary connection to emancipation. A more radical, usually minoritarian species of patriot abolitionism argued that the new nation should earn the gratitude of the blacks by freeing them – a high-minded view that was usually allied with the hope that the blacks might fight for, even die for, that nation. This species of anti-slavery played an important part in the enactment of emancipation in every Spanish American state, but it did not require a specifically anti-slavery organization. The leaders responsible for patriot emancipation will usually have judged that the new forces attracted or galvanized by an emancipationist programme would be more numerous than those alienated by it; in this way they themselves placed a wager on whether anti-slavery sentiment, including the anti-slavery of the blacks, was a stronger force than pro-slavery racism. Sonthonax in Saint-Domingue in 1793–4, Bolívar in Gran Colombia 1819–24 and Lincoln in 1862–4 each made such a wager. In so far as these patriot emancipators were on the winning side, their judgement was vindicated.

Several prominent critics of slavery had strong maritime connections – and perhaps a patriotic motivation. These include Fernão de Oliveira, who devoted a chapter of his book *Na arte da guerra do mar* (1555) to an attack on the slave trade, and Sir Charles Middleton, comptroller of the Royal Navy, who played an important role in spreading abolitionism in Britain. In France Admiral Truguet, colonial minister in the years 1796–8, backed the policy of revolutionary emancipation. Admiral Cockburn freed slaves in Virginia in the War of 1812, while Admiral Brion helped to put Simón Bolívar in touch with President Pétion of

Haiti. (However, Galbaud's attacks on Sonthonax were backed by those generically described as 'sailors', probably poor white *colons*.)

While patriotism could support anti-slavery, abolitionism itself challenged one of nationalism's blind spots concerning the 'bonds of dependence' discussed in Chapter 10. It is a merit of the main abolitionist movements that, on the whole, they challenged rather than exploited racism, albeit in terms that could be patronizing or double-edged. The original anti-slavery device – 'Am I not a Man and a Brother?' – helped to sum up the sometimes rather ethereal abolitionist theory of human unity. Whatever its defects by today's standards, it should be acknowledged that the mainstream of white abolitionism formed a key constituency for the slave narratives and the literature of black witness. Blacks spoke from the platform, though it took a long time before a few were invited to join the leading committees.[99] The French *Amis des Noirs* did much more to attack the exclusion of coloured proprietors, including slave-holders, from citizenship than to challenge slavery itself.

THE ROLE OF THE CHURCHES

Once the Quakers as a whole were won to anti-slavery in the 1780s, they made a crucial contribution to organized abolitionism. Not only did they help to launch abolitionist agitation in North America and Britain, but they continued to sustain the cause through its many ups and downs. Quakers also played a role in carrying anti-slavery ideas and tactics to France and, much later, Spain. They originated as a radical Protestant group during the English Civil War of the 1640s. Though several of their leaders had been militant soldiers of the Commonwealth, the Quakers converted to absolute pacifism by the time of the Restoration. Formally excluded from political life by the Test Act (which limited office-holding to those who took their communion with the Church of England), several leading Quaker families became enormously successful in trade, manufacture and banking. The Quakers placed greater value on the believer's 'inner light' than on a literal reading of Scripture. Quakers also took the lead in prison reform and, as noted in the last chapter, and bearing in mind their business success, served as a species of bourgeois vanguard.

The Methodists, an evangelical breakaway from the Anglican Church, gave support to moderate abolitionism. In Jamaica in the 1830s Methodist missionaries recruited hearers and worshippers among the slaves and were – not always fairly – deemed a radically subversive force by the planters. When these ministers were attacked and deported in 1832, sympathy for their plight greatly stimulated support for British emancipation. The Methodists and Baptists offered a lifeline of self-help and self-respect to many who had been buffeted by

---

99 Goodman, *Of One Blood*.

the new stresses and strains of an expanding market system. While they were scarcely anti-capitalist, they did express distrust of wealth. Many followers of these Nonconformist churches will also have had direct experience, as servants or apprentices, of dependence on the will and whim of a master or mistress.[100] The news of missionaries being set upon and chapels burnt by white colonists stimulated great indignation.

In Britain, Methodists and Baptists did not face the prospect of worshipping side by side with black members, or of accepting them into the governance of the Church. Instead they sent missions overseas with the idea that the missionaries would establish a benign tutelage over the natives. In the 1840s the Jamaican missions were to be disquieted by two trends: the survival of what the missionaries saw as superstition and African spirit worship, on the one hand, and a black aspiration to take on leading positions and to control resources, on the other.[101] Some found this very worrying, others believed that the former slaves had reason to be discontented. But at least British Baptists and Methodists did not have to contend with such issues at home. The US churches faced a stiffer test of their evangelical beliefs, and for a time seemed to meet it rather well. Black converts were generally welcome, and in the later decades of the eighteenth century the presence of blacks in these Churches was compatible with a rapidly growing white membership. But black members were expected to be modest, passive and unassuming. The 1780s and 1790s witnessed the growth of independent congregations of African Methodists and Baptists, with black preachers. Many blacks felt more comfortable in these congregations and with the styles of worship they offered.

The Methodists in the US South had never really challenged the slaveholders, but following the panics about slave revolt and the advent of radical abolitionism, they felt the need to reassert their support for social stability. The Northern Methodists and Baptists also rebuked the abolitionists at first, branding them as 'Jacobinical', 'revolutionary' and 'ultra'.[102] The US Churches refused to follow their British coreligionists in committing themselves to anti-slavery activism. But in the course of the 1840s the bonds between Northern and Southern branches of the same Church were first strained and then broken. Southern Protestants were drawn to a Biblical literalism which offered no challenge to the slave order. Their Northern counterparts, working in a context of

---

100   Mary Turner, *Slaves and Missionaries*, London 1987. In *Freedom* Orlando Patterson gives a persuasive account of Christianity as a freedperson's religion. Its etherealized, 'other-worldly' conception of spiritual emancipation could be quite consistent with tolerance for mundane slavery. Patterson does not pursue his story into the abolitionist age in this volume, but, especially in a context of secular challenge, this account would seem to suggest that Christianity did contain a latent emancipationism.

101   Hall, *Civilising Subjects*, pp. 140–264.

102   Richard J. Carwardine, *Evangelicals and Politics in Antebellum America*, New Haven 1993, pp. 133–74, 139.

headlong social transformations, stressed the need to adhere to the spirit of Christianity which they saw animating Scripture. The Presbyterians split in 1837, ostensibly because of differences over theology and church governance, though Garrison believed that attitudes to slavery had also played a part, since nearly all the supporters of the New School were in the North. The other two large US Protestant denominations – Methodists and Baptists – also split along sectional lines in the 1840s. Northern Protestants did not like to be intimately associated with Southern slavery, but most did not actively campaign against it. However, the majority of Protestant clergy declined to support political anti-slavery, which still seemed a threat to the Union and consequently irresponsible and anti-patriotic.

The anti-slavery cause was a major preoccupation for a small minority, such as those involved in the work of Oberlin College and the Lane Seminary, both of which received financial backing from Lewis Tappan, a New York businessman. Abolitionists attacked what they characterized as the ungodly practices of slave-holders: people who lived on the unrequited labour of others, neglected the spiritual needs of their slaves, committed grievous offences against them and broke up slave families. Their physical power encouraged pride and exposed them to temptation. Hostility to slavery sometimes had to compete for attention with temperance. The latter encompassed not only personal abstinence but legal bans on alcohol. Anti-slavery evangelicals had also campaigned for Sabbatarianism – in particular an end to postal deliveries on Sunday. These reform causes had a special appeal for evangelical women, but not for many new immigrants of either sex. Many abolitionist leaders were drawn from the ranks of the Unitarians and the relatively small, pro-Enlightenment wing of Protestant Christianity which was unenthusiastic about, or even hostile to, temperance and Sabbatarianism. Moderate Northern Protestants were more likely to be active in the temperance movement than in anti-slavery in the 1830s and 1840s, while supporters of the radical, Garrisonian wing of abolitionism supported immediate emancipation and equal rights for women.[103]

In the 1840s, most Northern Protestant clergy took a distance from the slave-holders but without endorsing anti-slavery. In the mid-1850s, as Southern slave-holders became more aggressive, Protestant clergy began cautiously to adopt moderate abolitionist themes. Following Southern secession the Northern Protestant churches and clergy rallied strongly to the Union, offering themselves as spokesmen of the Patriot cause and welcoming moves to strengthen the Federal power and to curtail or end slavery. George Fredrickson suggests that Protestant clergy saw a providential role for themselves as the custodians of the national spirit and destiny. Following the end of the war, a

---

103   The range of Protestant views is surveyed in John McKivigan and Mitchell Snay, eds, *Religion and the Antebellum Debate over Slavery*, Athens, GA, 1998.

number even canvassed for a new amendment that would enshrine a non-denominational Protestantism as a species of official religion. While this failed, the Protestant churches did set up schools in the South, and others expounded the need for a 'Social Gospel'.[104]

The Catholic Church at no point took an anti-slavery stance, though in 1889 it did beatify Pedro Claver, the Jesuit who, with Sandoval, had tirelessly baptized slaves arriving at Cartagena in the early seventeenth century. However, individual *curés* supported the black rebellion in Saint-Domingue and gave help to Toussaint Louverture, who was a seemingly devout believer – he would himself occasionally deliver sermons from the pulpit. The 'baroque' features of Catholicism often made for a milder and more flexible racial order, with Africans and those of African descent encouraged to form their own religious brotherhoods. In Cuba and Brazil people of colour might be buried in the same graveyard as whites, albeit that elite families would be commemorated in a grand and elaborate fashion while the poor would be tidied away in some marginal space or neglected altogether. In the last years of Brazilian slavery Antonio Bento and his followers used a baroque-tinged Christian imagery to campaign against slavery. For example, a black man would carry a huge cross labelled 'slavery' through the streets while being whipped. As the blood flowed, spectators would be asked to free their slaves immediately. In the United States, Catholics in the South fully accepted slavery but still catered to black worshippers. In the US North, Catholic immigrants were less likely to support abolitionism than Protestant immigrants.

IMMIGRANTS AND CIVIC REPUBLICANISM

From 1820 or a little earlier, the numbers of immigrants arriving annually in the New World began to overtake the number of captives arriving from Africa. While the immigrants went at first mainly to North America, tens of thousands of slaves were still brought to Cuba and Brazil each year until the 1850s. Catholic Irish and Italian immigrants were not attracted to abolitionism. These new arrivals already attracted nativist suspicion as Catholics, and wished to establish their credentials as patriotic Americans – abolitionism was either tepidly nationalist, or actively hostile to the Union. Immigrants also established their American, white identity by asserting racial superiority over the blacks.[105] These are, of course, gross generalizations. When the New York municipal authorities planned to clear Seneca Village in order to allow a generous Western boundary to Central Park, they explained that this was the sort of place where undesirable

---

104   George Frederickson, 'The Coming of the Lord: The Northern Protestant Clergy and the Civil War Crisis', in Miller, Stout and Wilson, eds, *Religion and the American Civil War*, pp. 110–130.

105   See for example Ignatiev, *How the Irish Became White*.

Irish and Negroes congregated to drink and dance. Such a place must have been an invaluable haven for the fugitive slave, but not necessarily a stronghold of anti-slavery agitation.

The Protestant or radical secular immigrants from England, Scotland, Ireland, Germany, Scandinavia and the Netherlands were attracted to the free labour doctrine and often supportive of anti-slavery. Those who left Britain during the conservative – and repressive – administrations of Pitt or Lord Liverpool (roughly 1792–1828), or who left continental Europe, especially Germany, after the 1848 revolution, brought with them a distinctive radical politics. The British included both disciples of Tom Paine and socialist utopians like the followers of Frances Wright. Many of these radicals supported the abolitionism of the later 1830s and 1840s. Following the failure of the 1848 revolution, large numbers of German revolutionaries sought refuge in the United States. Although only a minority of the mass of German immigrants, they were certainly a leavening influence. The Protestant British and Germans were often skilled artisans or professionals and, anyway, less beset by status anxieties than the Catholic migrants. If Republicanism attracted little support from Catholic immigrants, the Republican Party consolidated itself by defeating the crudely nativist 'Know-Nothing' party and insisting on a more broad-minded and secular civic identity, with a greater appeal to the immigrant, especially German American, vote. In many Northern states the male immigrant could vote after a year's residence.

The German newcomers contributed in two significant ways to the maturing of abolitionism as a political force. Firstly, they saw the struggle against slavery as a secular goal that needed to chime in with a broad reform agenda. Secondly, and linked to the foregoing, they did not favour making temperance a touchstone of reform politics. Indeed German migrants were strongly attached to their beer gardens, which were integral to democratic and radical politics. Anti-slavery was likely to make more headway if not invariably yoked to temperance.[106] Several German American leaders focused on labour organization, notably the *Amerikanische Arbeiterbund* – League of American Workers – founded in 1853, which declared itself open to 'all workers who live in the United States without distinctions of occupation, language, color or sex'.[107]

---

106   One study finds that about a third of the members of the US anti-slavery societies in the mid-1830s were British immigrants. See Leonard Richards, '*Gentlemen of Property and Standing': Anti-Abolition Mobs in Jacksonian America*, Ithaca 1971. The later contribution of the German refugees to US political life is the theme of Bruce Levine, *The Spirit of 1848*, New York 1992. Of course there were some British and German evangelicals too, but the rationalist and radical currents are worth noting. The British and German immigrations are often given little attention for the strange reason that they were so large and seemed to blend in with the 'American' so easily.

107   Levine, *Spirit of 1848*, p. 125.

Upon the outbreak of the Civil War, thousands of German Americans volunteered for the struggle against the slave power. Reviewing a collection of hundreds of letters written by these soldiers, Kenneth Barkin writes: 'the major reason for volunteering [for the Union army] was to bring slavery to an end'.[108] Eventually 200,000 German Americans fought in the Union ranks.

When larger numbers of European immigrants began arriving in Cuba and Brazil in the latter half of the nineteenth century, they made little contribution to abolitionism. In Cuba new immigrants from Spain were recruited to the so-called Volunteers, a militia force which in the 1870s protected Spanish privileges, the large planters and slavery. However, later migrants to Cuba and Brazil played an 'objectively' anti-slavery role, as they helped to persuade the large planters that there was an alternative to relying on slave labour. Subjectively many were influenced by anarchism and syndicalism, leading them to support a variety of subversive movements, including anti-slavery.

ELITE AND BOURGEOIS ANTI-SLAVERY: LIBERAL ABOLITIONISM

Most abolitionist organizations had a definitely bourgeois and middle-class character, even if they later proved able to attract a popular following. It should be noted however that British abolitionism received some aristocratic patronage at every phase of its history, a circumstance which contributed to its political effectiveness. Many titled personages subscribed to Olaudah Equiano's *Interesting Narrative*, their names being printed in the later editions. The French *Amis des Noirs* also attracted aristocratic patronage. Those wishing to be members of its successor during the Orleanist monarchy had to pay a substantial annual subscription.

British and American abolitionism in the 1830s developed a radical, immediatist strand that was willing to challenge slave-holder property head-on and disrupt public order. But prior to this British and North American abolitionism allowed abhorrence of slavery to be undermined by respect for property and the reigning order. The mainstream of French abolitionism in both the 1780s, and the 1830s and 1840s, was similarly inhibited.

Of course, several of the pioneers of anti-slavery, like Granville Sharp in England or John Woolman in Pennsylvania, should not be assimilated to the respectable abolitionism of the first national abolitionist organizations. These pioneers were moral radicals, whose challenge to slavery was not bounded by respect for property or social convention. Indeed a number of the earliest and most radical critics of slavery were also critics of private property – men such as George Wallace, Granville Sharp and Jean de Pechmeja. But the abolitionist

---

108   Kenneth Barkin, 'Ordinary Germans, Slavery and the US Civil War', *Journal of African American History* (March 2007), pp. 70–9.

organizations which were established in the United States, Britain and France in the 1790s shrank from any challenge to property or public order. As we saw in Chapters 8 and 9, the Haitian Revolution helped clear the way to the more moderate goal of ending the Atlantic slave traffic.

Christopher Brown's argument that 'moral capital' accrued to abolitionism was even registered within the financial domain. Wilberforce was widely admired by respectable opinion, and so whenever there was a run on the Bank of England or a royal scandal, the government of the day called on his services to help restore confidence in established institutions. The more radical abolitionists, such as Thomas Clarkson and Wendell Phillips, were not elevated to such a role. The Quaker businessmen who contributed so much to abolitionism also dedicated themselves to prison reform and to developing the trade of Africa. Valuing non-alcoholic beverages and personal cleanliness, the Cadburys and the Frys bought cacao from West Africa, while other Quaker businessmen purchased palm oil to use in soap-making. The New York abolitionist Lewis Tappan reflected a further mixture of morality and business when he established the first credit-rating agency, Dun and Bradstreet. The idea of this was that businessmen could police one another by reporting on how quickly those they traded with settled their bills. In this and other ways abolitionism overlapped with the attempts of a bourgeois vanguard to ameliorate bourgeois civilization. Samuel Chase was a prominent anti-slavery Republican who was deemed suitable to be treasury secretary, reorganizer of the banking system and eventually chief justice.

The anti-slavery vanguard was often strongly resisted by the mainstream, not least because of the latter's credulity and timidity. Racial ideas helped to limit their vision. The fortunes at stake in the plantations and plantation trades, and the ideological backlash against the Revolutionary age, make it unsurprising to find that large segments of bourgeois opinion were susceptible to racist ideas and inclined to believe that emancipation was a desperate and dangerous experiment. In the last chapter the racial fantasies associated with Agassiz, Gobineau and Knox were noted. Charles Darwin, in contrast, came from an abolitionist background, and his own anti-slavery views helped to inspire his research.[109] But he did not directly challenge the new racial theories, and sometimes urged that descent from apes was no more shocking than the kinship of the civilized and the savage. Many racial theorists believed that there were stronger and weaker races, with the latter doomed to extinction. Ralph Waldo Emerson attacked slavery, but sometimes in terms that seemed to give ground to racial 'Darwinism'. Writing on the results of emancipation in the British West Indies he allowed himself the following speculation:

---

109   Adrian Desmond and James Moore, *Darwin's Sacred Cause: How a Hatred of Slavery Shaped Darwin's View of Human Evolution*, London 2009.

If [racial groups] are rude and foolish, down they must go. When at last in a race a new principle appears, an idea – that conserves it, ideas only save races. If the black man is feeble and not important to the existing races, not on a parity with the best race, the black man must serve, and be exterminated. But if the black man carries in his bosom an indispensable element of a new and coming civilization; for the sake of that element, no wrong, nor strength nor circumstance can hurt him, he will survive and play his part . . . now let [the blacks] emerge, clothed and in their own form.[110]

Disturbing though it was, this line of thought at least regarded Afro-Americans as potential protagonists rather than simply victims. (For Native Americans, however, the conclusion was ominous.)

Bourgeois abolitionism became an effective emancipatory force only where it was prepared to reach a 'historic compromise' with broader social forces, including slaves, free people of colour, white artisans and labourers, immigrants and the native-born. Generally this meant countenancing inroads on already established property rights and extending the bounds of citizenship. In different ways the Jacobins in 1794, British immediatist anti-slavery in 1833–8, the *schoel-chéristes* in France and the French Caribbean in 1848, the radical Republicans in the US during the Civil War and Reconstruction, the Brazilian Anti-Slavery alliance in the 1880s, were prepared to make such a choice. The 'free labour' doctrine espoused by many abolitionists did not challenge the position of the 'fair-minded' employer, though it did usually envisage the use of public agencies and public resources to promote popular education and welfare. A significant layer of capitalists, not only those with interests in the plantations, abstained from supporting bourgeois abolitionism. On the other hand, a few idealistic bourgeois abolitionists declared support for socialism as they understood it (including Schoelcher in France, La Sagra in Spain, Lopes Trovão in Brazil; George Wallace and Granville Sharp both distrusted private property, while Horace Greeley was for a time a Fourierist).

The 'historic compromise' offered by emancipationism challenged power-ful ruling groups, resting on their own social alliances. It could prevail partly because it was based on the expansionary trends within Atlantic capitalism, partly because it offered slaves some form of freedom, and partly because it offered guarantees and promises to free workers and farmers. Anti-slavery did not deprive real capitalists of their property, though it might deny some merchants profitable opportunities. But many businessmen in Liverpool, New York and Barcelona opposed abolitionism. Not for the first time, a layer of

---

110 'Emancipation in the British West Indies', quoted in Henry Louis Gates, 'The Master's Pieces', in Dominick La Capra, ed., *The Bounds of Race: Perspectives on Hegemony and Resistance*, Ithaca 1991, pp. 17–38, 23.

capitalists opposed reforms that were not essentially anti-capitalist because they might empower the producers. The British Liberal Party and the US Republicans aimed to achieve a broader goal, for by reassuring their popular following, and sacrificing the detested institution of slavery, statesmen could usually gain a large political or military advantage. But the revolutions they planned from above had to meet answering social forces from below, which is why the 'historic compromise' of emancipation had socially revolutionary overtones.

CHAPTER THIRTEEN

The Keys to Emancipation

I have invoked the crises favourable to abolition on a number of occasions in the preceding chapters and offer here a sketch of what was needed to inflict decisive defeats on the slave-holders. Openings for anti-slavery arose when some combination of class struggle, war and a pressure for the recasting of the state had weakened or neutralized the claims of property, widened the conception of citizenship and redefined national interest. The great acts of emancipation coincided with decisive turning points in national life, with the onset of war, civil war, revolution or narrowly averted revolution. At such junctures the collectivity had to be defined in new ways and alliances forged around new political values. And such troubled times often brought economic hardship and a weakening of the belief that property was sacred. Wealthy planters and rich merchants could be represented as lacking in patriotism and ever willing to profit at others' expense. Attacks on slavery could rally public opinion, define the start of a new epoch and appeal to diverse constituencies.

Anti-slavery thrived on revolutionary crisis, beginning with the first steps taken in parts of North America at the time of the Revolution; in France and the French Caribbean, more intensively and extensively in the 1790s; in Britain, with a wave-like movement in 1788–91, 1804–7, 1814 and 1830–34, intensified by slave revolt in the years 1823–32 and culminating in the great Reform Bill crisis of 1832; in much of Spanish America in the years 1810–24, the period of the liberation wars, and sporadically thereafter; in France and the remaining French Caribbean, in 1848; in the United States, with a build-up from 1860–70, a period of crisis, Civil War and Reconstruction; in Spanish Cuba in the years after the Spanish Revolution of 1868 and the Cuban insurgency known as the Ten Years' War (1868–78); in Brazil in the 1880s in a period of awakening class struggle and incipient political crisis, with emancipation enacted eighteen months prior to the downfall of the monarchy. W. E. B Du Bois drew attention to the close connection between anti-slavery and democratic advance: 'One has but to notice the significant dates in the emancipation of Negro slaves and the enfranchisement of white workers to become aware of the close connection between these two series of events.'[1] (Du Bois would have had in mind Britain's second Reform Act of 1867, itself influenced by events in the United States, as well as the 1832 Reform Act.)

The emancipationist programme was reached only after many hesitations, false starts and procrastinations. Its adoption was usually a determined act of

---

1   W. E. B Du Bois, *Black Folk Then and Now*, New York 1939, p. 177.

leadership and hegemony. Conditions had to be mature and 'just right' for it to triumph. Thus military pressure was favourable, but those who issued emancipation proclamations did not wish such action to be mistaken for panic. Lincoln waited for a success on the battlefield before issuing the Emancipation Proclamation. Britain was isolated in 1807, but victory at Trafalgar had given it command of the oceans. The French Republic had repulsed the most threatening counter-revolutionary incursions by February 1794. On the other hand the Dutch Patriots of the 1780s and 1790s never enjoyed the maturity and real freedom of action that might have led them to endorse such a bid for hegemony. The radical Patriot leader Coert Lambertus van Beijma backed emancipation, but the Patriot leader Schimmelpenninck thought it an unjustified confiscation.[2] While the abolitionists eventually triumphed in France and Britain or the United States, it was only after periods of containment and stagnation. The foreshortened existence of the Batavian Republic gave no time for working out the dialectic of half-measures and radicalization in a crisis that so often permitted the advance of abolition.

Emancipation was not just a matter of decrees, laws and constitutional amendments, important though these were. Ultimately emancipation, if it was to be effective, came from below as well as from above, with slave de-subordination destroying plantation discipline while legislation denied the slave order the force of law within a given territory. The de-subordination of the slaves could be such a powerful factor that only emancipation allowed the government to get a lever on the situation. On the other hand, if slavery was to be truly ended, any action by slave rebels needed to be confirmed and consolidated by formal legislation anchored in a state that effectively controlled the territory in question. In some cases action from above prevailed with little or no contribution from below, but this was where the institution was anyway marginal or severely weakened. The major emancipation events – whether France in 1794 or 1848, Britain in 1823–38, or the United States in 1862–5 – are true turning points for this reason, as is the founding of Haiti in 1804. Emancipation in Brazil was preceded and accompanied by widespread resistance, but Cuban slavery was phased out in 1880–6 during a lull in the island's thirty-year struggle for independence, in which Afro-Cubans were a major force.

In the Atlantic world of this epoch there was intense pressure to approximate to the ideal of the nation-state, with its national spirit, legal statutes, bureaucracy and monopoly of organized violence. Those founding a new political and social order knew that a resounding act of emancipation helped to strengthen and symbolize its legitimacy. Such acts registered at the level of

---

2   Simon Schama, *Patriots and Liberators: Revolution in the Netherlands*, London 1992, pp. 249, 260–1.

national politics social impulses that had already gained ground within and between formal state structures. Atlantic and Caribbean cities and ports like Le Cap, Les Cayes, Port-au-Prince, Cartagena, Vera Cruz, Kingston, Trinidad, New Orleans, Charleston, El Salvador, Fortaleza and Santos were seedbeds of transnational anti-slavery impulses. The rural backlands and swampy coasts also harboured maroons, runaways and prophets. But such impulses could be defeated, dissipated or held at bay if they did not find expression in enforceable – and enforced – acts of emancipation. Likewise rural resistance or revolt, or mass desertions, could paralyse the plantation regime, but in prevailing Atlantic conditions the slave regime had to be formally wound up by national legislation – though, as we will see, even that might not be enough.

In the two previous chapters I have explored the essentially post-colonial slavery of the United States, Brazil and the Spanish Caribbean, together with the systemic conflicts and social forces which threatened or weakened it. In Parts II and III the movements making for an end to colonial slavery and the Atlantic slave trade were charted, and the gains there were eventually embodied in sovereign acts of legislation, sometimes buttressed by High Court judgments. These acts required the backing of states with a monopoly of legitimate and organized violence in a given territory. Often, I have suggested, the decreeing of emancipation itself contributed to defining the state, boosting its legitimacy and helping it (re)-establish its authority. In the circumstances of the time, abolition either furthered or hindered the spread of competing and legitimating nationalisms, with their notions of citizenship and 'imagined community'. In the nature of things the emancipatory process was uneven and might be more or less effective as a result of specific configurations of the state and nation.

No Atlantic state stood alone, or outside the ebb and flow of commerce. Each was profoundly marked by the spread of ideas, and the competition for resources and esteem, within the wider Atlantic space. But the state-form remained of critical importance. Each state served as a container of socio-economic forces and a place of resolution of the momentous battles over slavery. This means that emancipation was always worked out in national histories, even as it helped to shape the polity itself. Abolition in Vermont, Pennsylvania, Saint-Domingue and Spanish South America had been bound up with struggles for the independence of former colonies. British slave-trade abolition and emancipation had helped to boost the legitimacy of ruling institutions at a time when a critical situation demanded this. The French emancipations of 1794 and 1848 also helped to define momentous domestic and imperial turning points.

The emergence of the new American slavery, and the crises which eventually put it into question, also concerned the form and scope of the state. US slave-holders reached successive compromises with the leaders of the other sections in the Union, but everyone knew that the Union itself would be in question if the compromise did not stick. The Cuban elite had made a pact with the governments in Madrid and the Spanish monarchy, renouncing the ideal of independence in favour of the peaceful pursuit of plantation development. The latter was also a concern of the great landowners, slave-holders and merchants of Brazil who had compromised with the monarchy, and one another, to construct and defend a unified empire – an empire subjected to severe tests of foreign intervention and war in the 1860s. The undoing of slavery in the hemisphere was to be associated with attempts to reshape each state or territory, and with the disturbing force field of overlapping or competing nationalisms – Confederate or Unionist, Cuban or Spanish, imperial or republican. Any detailed narrative of this process will be impossible here – though I hope to attempt it at another time. As indicated in the Introduction, what follows is a preliminary reconnoitring of the terrain.

In Chapter 12 I identified different constituencies to which anti-slavery appealed, but abolitionism was more than the sum of its parts. Just as Atlantic commerce entailed a vigorous interflow between different regions and nations, overspilling all attempts to constrain it by tariffs and monopolies, so we may detect currents of political influence, and of action and reaction, crossing the oceans. Each emancipation process had its own particular dynamic and specific weight, but their rolling succession acquired a cumulative momentum. This contributed to a sense that the 'spirit of the times' demanded, and would ineluctably produce, emancipation. Both Howard Temperley and David Brion Davis have shown that mainstream abolitionists in Britain, France and the United States saw their cause as part of the wider movement of 'progress' and made anti-slavery one of its touchstones. Spanish, Cuban and Luso-Brazilian Liberals also subscribed to the ideals of progress. Progress was strongly linked to liberty, but not to social, still less racial, equality.[3] Progress can be read, at one level, as an ideology of an accumulation process that was flowering into the 'age of Capital'.[4] At another it expressed aspirations to a more representative and rational order, one harmonizing prosperity and freedom, and regulating the 'market revolution'. Some abolitionists, whether conservative like Wilberforce or radical like Garrison, saw in abolitionism an essential constraint on the regime of accumulation. The conservatives and radicals did not reject progress or the market revolution – to this extent they were liberals – but they wished to tame and regulate the latter by means of national legislation and international action.

Toussaint Louverture, Simón Bolívar and Vicente Guerrero were revolutionaries who sought to promote a militant yet orderly emancipation. In an 'age of revolution' reformers like Wilberforce and Thomas Macaulay, Benjamin Constant and Madame de Staël, saw abolitionism as a corrective to the excesses

---

3   Davis, *Slavery and Human Progress*; Howard Temperley, 'Capitalism, Slavery and Ideology', *Past and Present* 1 (1977), pp. 94–118.

4   Eric Hobsbawm, *The Age of Capital*, London 1983.

of 'patriotism' and slave insurrection. Paradoxically the revolutionaries and the reformers helped one another. Anti-slavery was carried forward both by quite moderate 'liberals' and by partisans of social revolution. Both the colonial slavery of the *anciens régimes* and the new American slavery of the United States and Brazilian Empire represented great concentrations of economic wealth and political power. Moderate measures could debilitate slavery, but its destruction generally required an emergency setting, a political crisis, with a willingness to extend citizenship to people of colour and a preparedness to challenge private property. Where moderate abolitionism failed to tackle slave-holder power, it could, by its half-measures and by discrediting itself, encourage radical and revolutionary currents.

The survival of Haiti impressed moderate abolitionists, especially when the tamer species of official anti-slavery were paralysed or blocked. The Haitain Revolution had freed half a million slaves and, as we have seen, encouraged the British and American slave trade bans. Haiti then lent valuable assistance to Bolívar. The Spanish American Revolutions closed vast regions to slavery by banning the trade and by enacting 'free-womb' laws. Mexico and Chile went further, and ended slavery outright. These gains were reported in Britain and France, and contrasted with the survival of large-scale slavery in their own colonies. British abolitionism in the 1820s and 1830s had its own dynamic, but anti-slavery activists certainly invoked advances elsewhere in their propaganda. British emancipation, albeit three decades after the foundation of Haiti, was of huge significance for the Atlantic world, freeing about 700,000 slaves.

In its turn British emancipation exercised direct pressure on the France of Louis Philippe (1830–48), since the July monarchy claimed to be inspired by abolitionism and the spirit of progress. The Liberal governments of Louis Philippe proclaimed abolitionist principles, but Guizot, de Tocqueville and other leading parliamentarians were paralysed by their respect for property and order. Nearly two decades of debates, enquiries, half-measures and compromises left slavery still in place in Martinique, Guadeloupe and La Réunion (in the Indian Ocean) as the Orleanist monarchy fell in February 1848. The Republic's first president – Lamartine, author of a tragic drama based on Toussaint Louverture – appointed the radical abolitionist and moderate socialist Victor Schoelcher as minister for the colonies. Schoelcher had helped to organize a petition in 1847 calling for immediate emancipation, attracting 11,000 signatures in the Paris region. Schoelcher moved quickly to issue a decree ending slavery in all French colonies, with details of implementation to follow. However, the slaves of Martinique deserted their plantations in droves in May, before the decree reached the Caribbean. The governors of Martinique and Guadeloupe found themselves obliged to anticipate the metropolitan decree and to declare the end of slavery. Thus action by the slaves in the Caribbean and a decree of immediate emancipation in the metropolis finally delivered the coup de grâce to an institution which had survived so tenaciously. One-hundred thousand slaves were freed. Many foreign observers – including Frederick Douglass – pointed to French republican emancipation as yet another sign that progress, whether reformist or revolutionary, was sweeping away slavery. And although the slaves had risen in rebellion, slavery had been ended without bloodshed, thus encouraging moderate as well as radical abolitionists. When Louis Napoleon seized power he gave compensation to the planters, helping them to modernize their estates.[5]

Slavery was also overturned in the Danish Virgin Islands in 1848, with slaves again taking an active role in ensuring this outcome and freeing the colony's few thousand slaves. The revolutionary impulses of the time also saw the winding up of slavery in Colombia, Argentina and Venezuela. However, the Caribbean colonies of the two European states that survived 1848 without either a revolution or a slave revolt – Spain and the Netherlands – saw the institution survive.

The new American slavery emerged unscathed, in its main territories, from the alarms and excursions of the 1840s. Avowed abolitionism was still a strictly minority current in the United States in the 1840s, and it was even weaker in Brazil, Spain and Cuba. A reformist approach would require compensation to the slave-holders, and this became an ever more impossible undertaking as slave wealth grew. The 4 million US slaves of 1860 were worth more than all the factories, banks and railroads of the North and West put together. The possibility of compensation was rendered implausible by the anti-tax reflex of voters in all sections. The prospects for a moderate, compensated emancipation in Cuba and Brazil were also remote because the Spanish and Brazilian treasuries were heavily burdened by debt. The impasse of moderate abolitionism in these states made it once again likely that anti-slavery would have to advance by the revolutionary road. Paradoxically, such a denouement was also encouraged by a new boldness among the slave-holders of the US South, who looked to the acquisition of Cuba and other lands suitable for plantation development. Some tens of thousands of young white Southerners mounted filibustering expeditions to

---

5   The complex events in France and the French Caribbean in the 1840s are well analysed by Lépine, *Questions sur l'histoire antillaise*, pp. 25–166. For the weakened state of French Caribbean slavery at this time see Tomich, *Prelude to Emancipation*. I gave an account in *Overthrow of Colonial Slavery*, pp. 473–516. Seymour Drescher suggests that I see the French emancipation of 1848 as a replay of the British emancipation of the previous decade. There were some similarities: the French abolitionists sometimes deliberately adopted tactics from the British, and the contexts of political reform and 'class struggle' have interesting points of contrast and comparison. But while revolution was averted in Britain, it was not so in France. British abolitionism was obviously far stronger than the French movement, but French anti-slavery, together with the direct action of slaves in Martinique, was just strong enough to secure Schoelcher's appointment and to confirm emancipation. Drescher, *From Slavery to Freedom*, pp. 158–96.

Cuba and Central America. For them 1848 was also a symbolic year. They identified with it as a year of challenge to European monarchy, but also because it brought huge territorial gains at Mexico's expense in the Treaty of Guadalupe Hidalgo.

SLAVERY AND THE NATIONAL COMPACT IN THE ANTEBELLUM REPUBLIC

The slavery of the US South was extensive and growing in the 1850s, but it was still overshadowed by the economic advance and demographic momentum of the North and West. The surging population and prosperity of the North was steadily undermining Southern leverage in Washington. The Northern contingent in the House of Representatives passed the two-thirds mark, and as the struggle over slavery in the territories was joined, Southerners saw their power to block undesirable laws, officials and amendments slip away.

Support for a pure politics of abolitionism remained marginal in the North, but nevertheless played a critical role in alarming the South and in challenging the dominant racial ideology. The abolitionist press was sustained by subscriptions from free people of colour as well as from the small bands of white abolitionists. The latter gave a platform to black anti-slavery activists, and circulated 'slave narratives'. The rise of the 'free soil' movement in the late 1840s, and resistance to Southern attempts to pursue runaway slaves and police the mails and the press, meant that a critique of Southern expansionism – and of Northern politicians who did the bidding of the slave-holders – reached a broader public in the North and West.

The storm of controversy provoked by the publication of Harriet Beecher Stowe's *Uncle Tom's Cabin* dramatized a clash of worldviews. The novel was serialized in newspapers in 1853, before selling hundreds of thousands of copies as a book and being adapted as a play for the stage. Stowe's novel was as much a political as a literary event. The story, which enthralled Northern readers, shocked and angered the South. The author's attempt to depict a good and kindly planter in contrast to other cruel and cynical slave-holders and dealers failed to appease Southern opinion. After all, even the kindly planter breaks up slave families when financial pressure recommends it. Some of the black characters make good their escape with the help of an abolitionist Northern senator, and one of the slave fugitives is prepared to defend himself weapon in hand. When the accuracy of the book was challenged, Stowe published a rejoinder in which she cited several slave narratives as sources for her account. White Southerners saw the book's popularity in the North as a sign that their fellow citizens held them in contempt – and that the Northern view of black slaves was hopelessly idealized. Such a cultural chasm rendered more menacing the rise of Republicanism in the North and West.[6] All Republicans were agreed that there should be no expansion of slavery, and regarded slave-holder claims on fellow citizens – expressed in fugitive slave laws, the memory of 'gag acts' and the like – as deeply regrettable at best, intolerable at worst. While 'moderate' Republicans, many of them former Whigs, were willing to accept compromises, the emergence of a radical wing of Republicanism was to prove highly significant. The radical wing gave secular and political expression to anti-slavery at the heart of government, and was consequently seen as a deadly threat by the slave-holders. When secession led to the withdrawal of Southern representatives from Congress, the radicals became even more important.

The Republican creed was defined by hostility to the 'slave power', but also by a set of positive measures summarized as follows by Senator John Sherman: 'to secure to free labor its just right to the Territories of the United States; to protect, as far as possible, by wise revenue laws, the labor of our people; to secure the public lands to actual settlers, instead of non-resident speculators; to develop the internal resources of the country by opening new means of communication between the Atlantic and the Pacific.'[7]

The 'free soil' component, and the Homestead Act (1862) which was to embody it, can be seen as an echo of 'agrarian' radicalism with its insistence on land distribution – ideas originally associated with utopian socialists like Frances Wright, but which spread to advocates of the working man like George Henry Evans, author of a pamphlet entitled '*Vote Yourself a Farm*', and to 'free soil' Jacksonian Democrats such as Representative David Wilmot.[8] Stakeholder ideas had no appeal to the leading Whigs who had patronized manumission societies and the milder anticipations of abolitionism. Instead they stemmed from Thomas Jefferson's and Andrew Jackson's regard for the yeoman farmer, and the idea that all citizens willing to work it should be entitled to a distribution of public land. Paradoxically it was these slave-holding political leaders who, together with tiny groups of socialists, helped to foster the Homestead idea within the political culture of the United States. Planter politicians were often quizzical of merchants and financiers, and in the case of Jefferson and Jackson they were also keen to appeal to the Northern worker and farmer. The idea sometimes voiced by Jefferson – that land should be made available to swell the ranks of the

---

6   Eric Foner, *Free Soil, Free Labor, Free Men* and *Politics and Ideology in the Age of the Civil War*.

7   Quoted in T. Harry Williams, *Lincoln and the Radicals*, 2nd edn, Madison 1965, p. 8. This rather hostile account of the radicals – referred to as 'Jacobins' by the author – nevertheless repeatedly acknowledges the tenacity of their anti-slavery views.

8   Earle, *Jacksonian Antislavery and the Politics of Free Soil, 1824–1854*, Chapel Hill 2004.

yeomanry and to populate the West – gained an autonomous momentum within the milieu of the North.

The 'free soil' Democrats saw no reason why wealthy Southerners should be able to steal a march on free white workers by settling the West with slaves. Republican ideology came to articulate and channel the aspirations of a generation of native-born workers and farmers in the North and West who were persuaded that the slave power intended to expand into the frontier territories. In this quarrel the defences of slavery were weakened, but the Homestead idea was not conveyed to poor white Southerners. The Southern press was controlled by the slave-holders, and literacy rates among the poor whites were anyway low. Both North and South had rapidly growing white populations and believed that they needed to expand westwards; the claims of displaced Native Americans and Mexicans were trampled upon by both sides.

The bonds uniting South, North and West, 'free' states and 'slave' states, were fraying but might yet hold. The United States was a huge success: its territory now spread from coast to coast, its economy was buoyant and it was attracting hundreds of thousands of immigrants each year. Even the most supercilious European statesman could not deny that the US was a rising power. Whatever their differences, the leaders of both sections honoured 1776, upheld the Protestant religion, spoke the same language, and had a similarly disdainful attitude to the rights of Indians, blacks and Mexicans. Nearly all had deep respect for the market and private property. Notwithstanding these shared traits, the elements of an amoeba-like splitting and separation were also at work as rival nationalisms – with their corresponding 'imagined communities' – took shape.[9]

The discrepant needs and values of Southern slave-holders and Northern and Western farmers, manufacturers and free labourers was a crucial fault line, underlying and exacerbating cultural and political conflicts. The dominant interests in each section needed a different type of state. Both saw the protection of property as central, but Southern and Northern property were different. Southern property could run away, while Northern could not. On the other hand Southern plantations, with their significant element of self-provision, were not wholly dependent on the market and could not be wiped out by a financial crash. Northern manufacturers needed the state to regulate finance, sponsor internal improvements and afford tariff protection. The slave plantation was economically more self-reliant but politically more vulnerable. As Benjamin Franklin had pointed out at the Constitutional Convention, Northern sheep and cattle were not going to rise in revolt – and, one might add, no 'gag act' was needed to prevent them reading incendiary appeals. South, North and West had shared responsibility for the Federal Mail and for the District of

---

9   Anderson, *Imagined Communities*.

Columbia but, far from bringing the sections together, such joint responsibilities created grounds of antagonism.

From the beginning, Southerners had insisted on their right to recover fugitive slaves. The North West Ordinance of 1787, which barred slaves from the territory, had also asserted such a slave-holder right. Indeed Southerners went further and insisted that every Northerner was obliged to give assistance to the slave-catchers, whether special marshals or bounty-hunters. The Fugitive Slave Act of 1850 had spelt out these unpleasant duties. But this had not stopped scores of runaways each year reaching the free states, some helped by the so-called underground railroad. The resulting pursuits and confrontations continually dramatized slave-holder insistence that courts and communities throughout the United States must uphold property in slaves. Each citizen was to be co-responsible with the slave-owners, which lent further substance to the notion of an expansive and intrusive 'slave power'. According to the new law, special Federal commissioners could settle the status of the supposed fugitive without a jury trial or the testimony of the accused. In the course of the 1850s about 300 alleged runaways were apprehended in the North, and more than half of them sent back to the South. Republicanism and abolitionism were able to channel Northern – and Western – reluctance to be forced into abetting the slave-catchers. (This is where *Uncle Tom's Cabin* touched a raw nerve, as well as illustrating how integral the 'chattel principle' was to the system.[10]) While the slave power encroached on the lives of citizens of 'free states' far from the plantation zone, it also – claimed the abolitionists and Free Soilers – set the United States on a course of expansion and aggression, with the lion's share of the consequent spoils claimed by slave-holders, as seemed to have happened with the territories seized from Mexico in 1848 and as would happen if the United States acquired Cuba, whether by conquest or purchase.

In 1857 sectional tension was aggravated by the pronouncements of Chief Justice Taney, speaking for a majority on the Supreme Court, in the case of Dred Scott, a coloured man held as a slave, who sued for his liberty on the grounds that his owner had taken him to a free state (Illinois) and free territory (Wisconsin). Taney ruled that Scott had no right to sue his owner, as he was still a slave, and that his status was unaltered by his residence in a free state or territory. The judgment went beyond a simple ruling on Dred Scott's status to argue that Congress had no constitutional right to limit slavery in the territories. The chief justice also declared that, at the time of the Declaration of Independence and Constitutional Convention, Negroes had been deemed 'so far inferior that they had no rights which the white man was obliged to respect'. He argued that the Constitution recognized slave-holding and that the 'unalienable rights' referred to in the Declaration of Independence were

---

10   See Johnson, *The Chattel Principle.*

implicitly reserved to the 'white race'. Any other view was untenable, since the Founders were 'incapable of asserting principles inconsistent with those upon which they were acting'.[11]

Meant to reassure slave-holders, the Taney judgment alarmed Northerners and challenged the ambiguities and compromises upon which the Union was based. In its turn the Northern reaction to Dred Scott exacerbated the split within the Democratic party. The planter elite knew that Kansas was unsuited for plantation development, but Taney's reasoning appealed to the pride of white Southerners. Southern Democrats regarded as treachery any hesitation or reservation on the part of Northern Democrats in endorsing the ruling. Yet Northern Democrats could not welcome slavery in the territories without alienating their own electorate. Stephen Douglas, the main Northern standard-bearer of the Democrats, devised a compromise formula leaving the matter to be decided by the assembly in each territory – but even without the appearance of two rival assemblies in Kansas, his stance did not impress many Southern Democrats. A further problem was Taney's argument that 'we, the people' referred essentially to the descendants of those represented in Philadelphia in 1787. While racial exclusion was acceptable to many Northerners it was best left implicit, and without the corollary that white natives were whiter than white foreign-born immigrants. The phrase 'no rights the white man is bound to respect' suggested that there was something lawless and excessive about racial domination in North America. As the obiter dictum of a chief justice of a nation based on laws, it was disturbing. Taney did not support the Confederate secession, and remained on the Court until his death in 1863. His specific conclusions immediately focused political debate, but his racial reasoning concerning the scope of citizenship was not to be settled even by three Constitutional amendments, and compromised the Court for a century to come.

In response to the Dred Scott judgment, Frederick Douglass observed that the slave power was both formidable and vulnerable:

[T]he slave-holders have a decided advantage over all opposition ... the advantage of complete organization. They are organized yet were not at the pain of creating their organizations. The State governments, where the system of slavery exists, are complete slavery organizations. The Church organizations in those states are equally at the service of slavery; while the Federal Government, with its army and navy, from the chief magistracy in Washington, to the Supreme

---

11   Roger B. Taney, 'Opinion on Dred Scott v. Sandford', in Manning Marable and Leither Mullings, eds, *Let Nobody Turn Us Around*, New York 2000, pp. 91–5. Taney had in his youth courageously opposed the extension of slavery and defended a Baptist minister indicted for attacking the 'sin' of slavery: see Timothy Huebner, 'Roger B. Taney and the Slavery Issue', *Journal of American History* (June 2010).

Court, and thence to the chief marshalship at New York, is pledged to support, defend and propagate the crying curse of human bondage.[12]

Yet Douglass saw the influence of anti-slavery ideas spreading inexorably in the free states, as demonstrated by growing support for the Republican party. In his Garrisonian days Douglass would have had to agree with Taney's claim that the Constitution endorsed slavery, but he now pointed to the fact that the document carefully avoided the word, and ridiculed Taney's interpretation of the Declaration of Independence. He also felt confident in the support of a higher law: 'Happily for the whole human race, their rights have been defined, declared and decided in a court higher than the Supreme Court. "There is a law", says Brougham, "above all the enactments of human codes, and by that law, unchangeable and eternal, man cannot hold property in man".'[13]

While Douglass went too far in denying that the Constitution countenanced slavery, he was right to draw attention to its ambivalence, and his sociological observations concerning the slave-holders' command of organization pointed to fundamental sources of political antagonism between the sections. Without control of the 'Washington magistracy' Southern leaders, unused to dealing with 'opposition', believed that slavery would be quite vulnerable. Loss of the postal service and the power of presidential patronage in the states would expose slave-holders to challenge at home. And loss of control in Washington was made very much more likely by the evident dynamism and expansionism of the 'free states'.

WHAT WAS THE IRREPRESSIBLE CONFLICT?

All were aware that industrialization and new means of communication were reshaping the Union. The railroads and canals of the North were far more extensive than those of the South, and brought the North-West and West increasingly within a Northern orbit. There were few genuinely national newspapers or magazines. There were syndicating pools whereby newspapers in different regions could share or exchange articles, but when sectional controversy ignited this could stoke the flames. Southern society might be less complex and more agrarian than the North, but there was some industry in the South and scores of newspapers in each region, usually selling a few thousand copies each. The leaders of society in both sections were Protestants but, as noted in the last chapter, the main Churches had split on sectional lines in the 1840s. Abolitionists were still a small minority but, from the Southern standpoint, the sectional splits

---

12   Frederick Douglass, 'On Dred Scott', Marable and Mullings, *Let Nobody Turn Us Around*, pp. 95–109, 96–7.

13   Ibid., p. 99.

suffered by Democrats and Whigs, and the resulting rise of the Republicans, removed a vital line of defence against anti-slavery. The burgeoning 'imagined community' of the North and West did not welcome slave-holders, slave-traders or slave bounty-hunters as fellow citizens. Likewise that of the South could not abide the presence of abolitionist subversives, black agitators, canting philanthropists and free-soil demagogues. As the secession crisis loomed, such considerations helped to align the North and West on the one hand, and the Upper and Lower South on the other. They also explain why Southern hotheads could prevail over moderates, and why those Northerners bent on crushing the rebellion by force prevailed over those who would have let the secession take place rather than descend into fratricide. Lincoln did well in the election of 1860, winning a majority in the Electoral College with his 40 per cent of the vote, but he would have had a harder time if Democrats had united behind a common candidate.

That the Civil War was an 'irrepressible conflict', that its roots lay in the different labour regimes of the two sections, and that it crystalized in opposing images of the good society, are not novel propositions. Different versions of them have been entertained by, among many others, such notable historians as David Potter, Don Fehrenbacker, Eric Foner, Eugene Genovese, and John Ashworth.[14] Yet why did the differences between the sections need to lead to war? Eric Hobsbawm, writing in 1975, stated the problem in this way:

> It can hardly be denied that slavery was the central institution of Southern society, or that it was the major cause of friction or rupture between the Northern and Southern states. The real question is why it should have led to secession and civil war rather than to some formula of co-existence. After all, though no doubt most people in the North detested slavery, militant abolitionism was never strong enough to determine the Union's policy. And Northern capitalism, whatever the private views of businessmen, might well have found it as possible and convenient to come to terms with and exploit a slave South as international business has with the 'apartheid' of South Africa.[15]

Part of the answer might lie in the title of the first chapter of the book that I have quoted: 'The Springtime of Peoples'. The ferment of 1848 in Europe witnessed a stirring of national sentiment which had echoes on both sides of the Atlantic. Another chapter heading of this book evoked the task of 'Nation-Building' that

---

14   David Potter, *The Impending Crisis*, edited by Don Fehrenbacker, New York 1976; Genovese, *The Political Economy of Slavery*; Foner, *Free Soil, Free Labor, Free Men*; John Ashworth, *Slavery, Capitalism and Politics in the Antebellum Republic*, 2 vols, Cambridge 1998 and 2007. Ashworth particularly stresses what he sees as the justified Southern fear of slave unrest.

15   Eric Hobsbawm, *The Age of Capital, 1848–75*, London 1975, p. 141.

gripped states old and new throughout the Atlantic world in the mid-nineteenth century.

Did rival nationalisms, rooted in different ways of life and expressing Atlantic rivalries, play the critical part in precipitating the conflict? Daniel Crofts takes seriously such an approach, but warns that

> it is tempting to project back onto the prewar months the fiercely-aroused nationalisms that appeared in mid-April [1861]. To do so would not be entirely in error, but it invites distortion. The irreconcilably antagonistic North and South described by historians such as Foner and Genovese were much easier to detect after April 15. Then and only then could Northerners start to think in terms of a conflict urged on behalf of 'the general interests of self-government' and the hopes of humanity and the interests of freedom among all peoples and for ages to come.[16]

But is this not to give too much weight to Unionist rhetoric? The Union's war aim was quite simply the preservation of the Union, not 'the interests of self-government', an idea to which the Confederacy also had a claim. Both rival nationalisms had a markedly expansive character, the Unionist being continental at this stage and the Confederacy craving new slave territories to the South (notably Cuba) and West. The clash was thus one of rival empires, as well as competing nationalisms.[17]

WHY DID THE SOUTH SECEDE?

The election of Abraham Lincoln in 1860 was bound to cause great consternation to the slave-holders. But why did it prompt such a hugely perilous experiment as secession? Elected president only by Northern votes, the candidate of a party with no Southern followers, Lincoln embodied the threat of a state power not under slave-holder control. As Southern slave-holders saw it, Lincoln's Republic was one in which they were losing both power and respect, and required to be perpetually apologetic. The sense of insult was exacerbated by the fear of injury. Slave prices started to drop. The president would be making thousands of appointments to Federal posts in the South. Many Southerners were convinced that Republicans were hand-in-glove with radical anti-slavery agitation and action. If the president himself declared that slavery was a wrong, was this not bound to unsettle the slaves? And if there was a slave outbreak, could the Federal power be relied upon? Even Southern moderates found Lincoln a very disturbing choice for president, as he had established his

---

16   Daniel Crofts, 'And the War Came', in Lacy Ford, ed., *A Companion to the Civil War and Reconstruction*, Oxford 2005, pp. 183–200, 197.

17   A theme well-explored in Richard Franklin Bensel, *Yankee Leviathan: The Origins of Central State Authority in America, 1859–1877*, Cambridge 1990.

reputation almost entirely by his indictment of the wrong of slavery and his absolute insistence that it must not spread.[18] Yet if it was not to spread, how could it restore leverage or esteem – let alone hegemony – in Washington?

Lincoln counted as a moderate Republican, since he repeatedly declared that he was willing to respect every slave-holder privilege enshrined in the Constitution and in existing legislation. But he still seemed an outrageous and alarming figure to slave-holders. His assurances that he had no designs whatsoever on slavery where it existed, and that he would not challenge even the Fugitive Slave Act, failed to persuade them that their property would be safe in his hands. By the late 1850s white Southerners did not even trust Northern Democrats like Stephen Douglas – and Lincoln had won prominence by warning that the Democratic leader was far too accommodating to the slave-holders. In his celebrated debates with Douglas in 1858 Lincoln sought to define what separated Republicans from Democrats. He declared that racial antagonism was so widespread and ingrained that he did not believe it was realistic to imagine that black and white could live together – which is why he supported schemes to resettle freed blacks in Africa or the Caribbean. These concessions might soothe the racial fears of Northern voters, but gave little comfort to Southern slave-holders. When he came to slavery itself, he berated Douglas for two major offences.

Firstly, he declared that Douglas's racial notions effectively denied the common humanity of blacks. This was to break with the Declaration of Independence, which held that all men were 'created equal' and had 'unalienable rights' to life, liberty and the pursuit of happiness. The Founders had compromised with slavery in the Constitution but still deplored the institution – avoiding its very name – while hoping, however vaguely, that it would be wound up at some future date. Lincoln was ready to respect all the Founders' compromises but not to abandon the ideals they had proclaimed.

Lincoln's second line of criticism of Douglas and the Democrats denounced slavery as an intolerable system of coercion based on unrequited labour. This was Lincoln's version of the free labour doctrine. With this argument he went further than the Founders, linking the rights of labour to the rights of man.[19]

In these exchanges with Douglas, Lincoln was careful to establish the limits of his concern for blacks and their rights. In a speech at Charleston on 18 September 1858, he insisted: 'I am not, nor have I ever been, in favour of making voters or jurors of negroes, nor of qualifying them to hold office, nor to

---

18   Lincoln's views developed over time but he publicly criticized the institution at all stages of his antebellum career – becoming more circumspect once elected president. See Eric Foner, *The Fiery Trial: Abraham Lincoln and American Slavery*, New York 2010, especially pp. 3–32, 132–65.

19   For a vivid account of the Lincoln–Douglas debates and for the influence of abolitionism on Lincoln, see James Oakes, *The Radical and the Republican*, New York 2007. (The 'radical' here is the outstanding black abolitionist Frederick Douglass.)

intermarry with white people.'[20] Commenting on this passage Richard Hofstadter remarks: 'How any man could be expected to defend his right to enjoy the fruits of his labour without having the power to defend it with his vote, Lincoln did not say.'[21] A ban on jury service and on intermarriage would also fix blacks as a lower caste. But Lincoln's real plan for African Americans was to persuade them to emigrate – to leave the land where they had been born and settle somewhere else, either in Africa or the Caribbean. Lincoln knew few African Americans personally, and it took a long time until he was persuaded to drop this idea.

The position staked out by Lincoln in the debates allowed him to appease the racial prejudice of many US voters and to sound a firmly patriotic note in his defence of the Founders. Lincoln's deference to racial feeling pointed to future problems. His stress on the common humanity of those of African descent rejected the most virulent strain of racial feeling while his tenacious support for colonization effectively treated them as native-born aliens. On the other hand Lincoln's characterization of the position of the Founders was generally plausible, though to be fully candid he would have had to ask why, since they deprecated slavery, they had devised a Constitution that made abolition so infernally difficult.

In the debates Lincoln at one point came up with a telling description of the black man's condition in the antebellum US that describes the fiendish imprisonment of the slave effected by the joint operation of the property system and the Constitution. Responding to the Dred Scott decision, he said of the North American slave:

> All the powers of the earth seem rapidly combining against him. Mammon is after him. They have him in his prison house; they have searched his person, and left no prying instrument with him. One after another they have closed the heavy iron doors upon him, and now they have him, as it were, bolted in with a lock of a hundred keys, which can never be unlocked without the concurrence of every key, the keys in the hands of a hundred different men, and they scattered to a hundred different and distant places; and they stand musing as to what invention, in all the dominions of mind and matter, can be produced to make the impossibility of his escape more complete than it is.[22]

---

20   Harold Holzer, *The Lincoln–Douglas Debates*, New York 1993, pp. 189–234, 189. This was not an off-hand remark but forms part of a careful introduction to his speech. He also repeated here his sally that 'Because I do not want a negro woman for a slave, [does not mean] I must necessarily want her for a wife.'

21   Richard Hofstadter, *The American Political Tradition*, New York 1968, p. 115, n. 11. White female workers and many workers in Europe faced the same kind of problem, even if to a lesser degree, but this also gave rise to the demand for the vote – so Hofstadter's point is well-taken.

22   Quoted in Oakes, *The Radical and the Republican*, pp. 78–9.

This remarkable passage summons up at once the distributed power of wealth in a market system and the multiple, mutually inhibiting distribution of power in the US Constitution, with its battery of checks and balances. Ending slavery within the normal workings of such a system and regime was going to be all but impossible, unless slave-holders themselves were fully in agreement.

In interpreting Lincoln's position, the context of the debates should be taken fully into account. The political culture of Illinois was influenced by an influx of poor white Southerners, but the main consequence of this was harsh laws against black immigration – and opposition to admitting slave-holders to the territories. Unlike Republicans from the northern part of the state, Lincoln had not himself opposed the legal disabilities placed on free blacks in Illinois, but he did powerfully articulate his state's hostility to slavery expansion. While Lincoln flatly opposed slavery in the territories, Douglas left the question to be decided by the 'popular sovereignty' of local assemblies. Douglas saw this as a convenient compromise but, as noted above, most Southerners distrusted it and preferred President Buchanan's support for the pro-slavery Lecompton Constitution.

Lincoln did not win this contest but, so far as the future was concerned, he strengthened his own position and weakened that of his opponent. Sentiment in the North and West was increasingly antagonistic to slavery expansion and impatient with politicians whose political formulae seemed designed to appease the South. By obliging Douglas to spell out his appeal to Northerners, he damaged his rapport with Southerners. Southern Democrats knew that many Northerners were racists, but that was not enough – the allies they wanted had to devoutly respect slavery as well. One of Douglas's ripostes sowed particular suspicion. In answer to Lincoln's question at Newport as to what could prevent slave-holders entering every US territory, and thus nullifying the 'state sovereignty' solution, Douglas's reply was that the slave-holder's right to enter any territory he wished, as asserted by the *Dred Scott* decision, would be 'barren and worthless . . . unless sustained, protected and enforced by appropriate police regulations and local legislation . . . These regulations must necessarily depend on the will and wishes of the people of the territory.'[23] To Southern ears such an observation both reminded them of their wider dependence on a supportive Federal authority, and suggested that no Northern politician was reliable when it came to slave-holder rights.

Lincoln might insist on his abiding respect for the compromises in the Constitution and established legislation, but such reassurance was thought to

---

23 Quoted in Potter, *Impending Crisis*, p. 337. See also George Fredrickson, *Big Enough to Be Inconsistent: Abraham Lincoln Confronts Slavery and Race*, Cambridge 2008, pp. 40–1.

be a sham when he went on to explain that 'a house divided cannot stand' and that one day the country would have to be either wholly free or wholly slave. Other Republicans, prior to secession, were already speaking of an 'irrepressible conflict'. For men of such views to hold the highest posts was a very disturbing prospect for many Southerners. It destroyed their confidence in the elaborate Constitutional defences of slavery. It also spoke to their fear of a Yankee behemoth so strong that it would crush slavery without even a fight. The 'common sense' of the North, articulated through countless publications, had already isolated the South, and the wavering of the border states suggested that one day it might even sap it from within. Most of the Northern press was quite muted between December 1860 and 12 April 1861, because they had no wish to provoke dis-union. But over the months and years prior to the secession crisis the Northern press and journals furnished frequent caustic or provocative commentary on the South.

There were clear white majorities for secession in the states that established or joined the Confederacy, with the matter decided by special conventions in ten cases and by the legislature in one other. Scrutiny of these decisions – and the contrary decisions taken by one special convention and three legislatures – shows that the delegates or representatives were considerably better off than the average free citizen. And the supporters of immediate secession were considerably richer than those who were lukewarm or opposed. Put another way, those with most slaves – the main form of wealth – were keenest on secession.[24] In the main plantation areas there was no active opposition to secession. (Of course blacks, even when free, did not have the vote in the rebel states, but neither did they in many Northern states.) Unilateral withdrawal by South Carolina forced the states of the Lower South to consider secession, just as the action of the Lower South put pressure on the Upper South. The leaders of the Southern states knew that their position in the Union would be undercut if even one slave state withdrew. The four 'border states' where slave numbers were limited, and ties to the North or North-West strongest, declined to join the Confederacy. But plenty of white citizens of these states agreed with the South on many issues and some, seduced by the romance of the new nation, flocked to the rebel standard.

The Confederacy's ability to maintain the rebellion offered its own proof that a majority of white men in the breakaway states had been won to secession, with many prepared to die for it. The rebels' own claimed justification heavily stressed continuity with the spirit of 1776 and states' rights, including the right of self-determination. Once the war had begun, allegiance to the new nation was powerfully supplemented by defence of the homeland, with the Confederacy disavowing expansionist aims.

---

24   Ralph Wooster, *The Secession Conventions of the South*, Princeton 1962, pp. 256–66.

Faced by imminent secession, Northerner leaders were prepared to go to great lengths to appease the South. Congressmen desperate to avoid a conflict introduced what they described as an 'unamendable' amendment to the Constitution stipulating that under no circumstances would the Federal authorities ever be able to suppress or tamper with slavery in any state where it was legal. This motion passed by a two-thirds majority on 28 February and was ratified by several Northern states. The president-elect endorsed the proposal.[25] But the momentum towards secession in the Lower South could not be stopped, and this particular Thirteenth Amendment proved stillborn. If slave-holders were to be reassured by paper promises, they had already had their fill. The Constitution already offered its 'hundred locks' protecting the institution. While these offered very real obstacles to abolitionist proposals of any sort, the planters remained convinced that they needed the unbounded goodwill and support of their fellow citizens to sustain their peculiar institution, and that these were lacking. They needed everyday support, not simply assurances that Southerners had a veto in Congress. The prospect of a president who so repeatedly deplored slavery was not only unsafe, it was insulting. As the *Atlanta Confederacy*, previously a Douglas-Democrat newspaper, put it: 'Let the consequences be what they may . . . the South will never submit to such humiliation and degradation as the inauguration of Abraham Lincoln.'[26]

If the Southern planters had emulated Bolívar – or anticipated Carlos Manuel de Céspedes, the Cuban independence leader, in 1868 – by freeing some slaves as part of their struggle for independence and introducing a 'free-womb' law, then the legitimacy of the secession would have been far more difficult to contest. But slave-holding was evidently central to their concept of the Confederate nation. In its last weeks the Confederate government did offer freedom to a few hundred slaves, if they agreed to serve in a special militia.[27] But this belated and farcical exercise was at odds with the strongly racialized character of Confederate nationalism – after defeat, nostalgia for Dixie was to become a powerful element in a new racial order and a new sectional compromise.

WHY DID THE NORTH ACCEPT WAR? . . . AND LATER FREE THE SLAVES?

Once the formalities of secession were complete, it was Lincoln who had to decide what to do. Lincoln wisely allowed the Confederacy to fire the first shot, but he still had a role to play in accepting the provocation and making war. In

25   William Freehling, *The South vs the South: How Anti-Confederate Southerners Shaped the Course of the Civil War*, Oxford 2001, p. 39; Richard Sewell, *A House Divided: Sectionalism and Civil War 1848–1865*, Baltimore 1991; Foner, *Fiery Trial*, p. 156.

26   Sewell, *A House Divided*, p. 76.

27   Bruce Levine, *Confederate Emancipation: Southern Plans to Free and Arm the Slaves during the Civil War*, New York 2005.

his First Inaugural he laid all the stress he could on the imperative of defending the Union and the precious inheritance of republican government. There can be no doubting the sincerity of these sentiments. As president he also had other concerns. Southern secession would diminish the Union in international standing as well as territory. It created a military threat and put in question free access to the Southern market and unfettered navigation on the Mississippi river. There were also rumours of Confederate moves to repudiate debts owed to Northerners.

As Washington raised 75,000 troops, Lincoln repeatedly insisted that they were to defend the Union, not to attack slavery. On slavery the two sections had divergent views – it was the only 'substantial difference' between them – but this should not and could not imperil the perpetual union established in 1787. The last words of his First Inaugural were an unabashed appeal, not to legal niceties but to national sentiment: 'We must not be enemies. Though passion may have strained, it must not break our bonds of affection. The mystic chords of memory, stretching from every battlefield and patriot grave, to every living heart and hearthstone, all over this broad land, will yet swell the chorus of Union, when again touched, as surely they will be, by the better angels of our nature.'[28]

Lincoln was intensely preoccupied with retaining the loyalty of the (slave-holding) border states. The defection of these states – especially Kentucky – would make it far more difficult to defeat the rebellion. Lincoln's consequent refusal to embrace Emancipation for its own sake was to endure beyond the Proclamation. The Gettysburg Address made no direct mention of slavery but used the word 'nation' five times, acting as a warmer term for Union. When Lincoln declared a 'new birth of freedom' it might refer to Emancipation, but slavery persisted in the Union as well as the Confederacy. The immediately following phrase in the Address could imply that the nation was being reborn through the revival of republican government.

It was not until his Second Inaugural in March 1865 that Lincoln described slavery as central to the conflict. 'To strengthen, perpetuate and extend this institution was the object for which the insurgents would rend the Union, even by war . . . Both parties deprecated war, but one of them would make war rather than let the nation survive; and the other would accept war rather than let it perish. And the war came.' While this attempt to brand the Confederacy as the warmonger is quite understandable, his own role had been much less passive and fatalistic than it implies. While still refusing to recognize the secession, he could have declined to make war upon it. The celebrated Republican editor Horace Greeley advocated exactly this in an editorial for the *Tribune* in December 1860. It was also, at first, the stance of William Lloyd Garrison, Wendell Phillips and Frederick Douglass. As late as the summer of 1864 a victory for George McClellan, the prospective Democratic candidate in the

---

28   Lincoln, First Inaugural, 4 March 1861, quoted in Foner, *Fiery Trial*, p. 160.

coming presidential election, might have led to a peace that accepted secession and allowed slavery to survive both in the border states and in rebel-held areas. The goal of many Southerners was more defensive than Lincoln would admit, even if it did indeed centre on the defence of slavery.

James McPherson argues that it was impossible for Northerners to 'let the erring sisters depart in peace'. However – the slave issue aside, and so long as there was a clear and deliberate majority for secession in the states that were leaving – that would be the response endorsed by modern liberal and democratic theory. When Belgium seceded from the Netherlands in 1830, or Norway from Sweden seven decades later, any attempt to prevent these moves by war would have been widely condemned by liberal and democratic opinion. McPherson explains the impossibility of accepting secession in the following terms: 'Lincoln and most of the Northern people were not willing to accept the nation's dismemberment. They feared that toleration of dis-union in 1861 would create a fatal precedent to be invoked by disaffected minorities in the future, perhaps by the losing side in another presidential election, until the United States dissolved into a dozen, petty, squabbling, hostile autocracies.'[29]

This is not a very plausible scenario. Could not a Yankee United States, despite the perhaps temporary loss of Southern territory, have remained sufficiently dynamic and attractive to have retained the voluntary allegiance of its remaining member states? In 1860 Lincoln had a plurality of the votes, not a majority, and many Democrats leaned towards the 'let the erring sisters depart in peace' approach. And why are notional further candidates for secession assumed to be 'autocracies'? The historian is here subscribing to the nationalism of one party to the conflict. This obscures something important about the response of Lincoln and his party. As I have suggested above, Lincoln and his supporters became aware that resisting secession by force relied on an argument from Great-Power nationalism that was, in crucial respects, inadequate and unsatisfying. The abolitionists – especially William Lloyd Garrison, Wendell Phillips, Anne Dickenson and Frederick Douglass, who commanded wide new audiences in 1861–2 – supplied an injection of ideas and ideals that remedied this deficiency in the ideological stance of Unionism, just as many Union soldiers felt better when they sang 'John Brown's Body'. The emancipationist policy was impressed on the president by the unrelenting pressure of the Radicals in Congress, by the growing influence of abolitionists, black and white, on Northern public opinion, and, last but not least, by the emergence of military abolitionism.

---

29   James McPherson, 'And the War Came', in *This Mighty Scourge: Perspectives on the Civil War*, Oxford 2007, pp. 3–20, 17. The phrase 'And the war came' has been adopted for many valuable accounts, but its implicit denial of Northern agency fails to acknowledge the emergence of a new nationalism or to pinpoint the Union's legitimacy deficit in 1861–2, and hence a vital factor impelling the president to remedy it. See e.g. Kenneth Stampp, *And The War Came*, Baton Rouge 1970; Crofts, 'And the War Came', pp. 183–200.

General Benjamin Butler tried his best to enforce the policy of upholding the property rights of loyal slave-holders while 'conscripting for the Union cause the labour of contrabands' – the refugee slave property of rebel masters. When stationed in Maryland he sought to uphold the rights of loyal slave-holders, while in Virginia he saw no problem in confiscating the slave property of rebels. The First Confiscation Act of July 1861 already allowed for such a policy. But the prospect of advance into rebel-held territory complicated matters and encouraged the emergence of a radical military abolitionism. As Union troops advanced, they were appealed to for support both by slave-holders proclaiming a new-found loyalty and by resistant slaves who hailed them as saviours and pleaded to be allowed to fight for the Union. When Butler was transferred to Louisiana he also encountered free men of colour eager to help crush the rebellion—but at first Butler spurned their offers, fearing that it would antagonize the slave-holders. Butler had particular difficulty with General John Phelps, a Vermont abolitionist and career officer, who issued his own anti-slavery proclamation in December 1861, offering to enrol all slaves who wished to join. Phelps's men, also from Vermont, prevented planters and overseers from using the whip or the stocks, and welcomed a stream of black volunteers without inquiring as to their master's opinions. Phelps proclaimed that 'the government should abolish slavery as the French had destroyed the ancien régime'.[30] Similar proposals came from General David Hunter, advancing along the South Carolina coast and islands. Both men were to be removed from their commands, but Phelps submitted a memorandum to the president setting out the necessity for a clear and consistent anti-slavery policy. Once aware of the way opinion was shifting in Washington, General Butler also came round to a more forward policy of forming black regiments, and freeing slaves to swell their ranks where necessary.

Lincoln eventually, as we know, struck out against Confederate slavery by invoking the war powers of the president. But for over a year he insisted that the war was to defend the Union, not challenge slavery. The provisional Emancipation Proclamation of September 1862 freed the slaves of rebel masters as a measure of military necessity. The slaves of slave-owners in the loyal border states and in Union-occupied areas were kept in slavery. Nevertheless, abolitionists celebrated the Proclamation as a great turning point. It allowed Union commanders not only to draw on the labour of 'contrabands' (slave refugees from rebel masters) but also to form black military units. The Proclamation helped to stiffen Northern opinion, draw on black support, punish the Confederacy, and head off any possibility that Britain or France would accord the rebels diplomatic

---

30 'The Destruction of Slavery', in Ira Berlin et al., *Slaves No More!*, Cambridge 1993, pp. 1–76, 36. The full text of Phelps's proclamation is given in Ira Berlin et al., *Freedom: A Documentary History of Emancipation*, Cambridge 1985.

recognition. Lincoln was pushed to act by the arrival of a few thousand black refugees from the South, and the disposition of some of his commanders to welcome them. The Emancipation policy greatly encouraged this movement. Eventually some 400,000 slaves fled the rebel-held areas. Some acted as scouts, others joined the new black regiments or toiled in a multitude of support roles. The Union Army included 180,000 black soldiers and 20,000 sailors; three-quarters of these fighters were former slaves. They proved very effective as a military force, even though, to begin with, they received lower pay than white troops. Only 120 black soldiers were to receive commissions, and those at junior rank as chaplains or doctors.[31]

Inside the Confederacy the authorities had to step up measures to contain and control an increasingly restive black population. As Union troops made deep incursions in Confederate territory slaves flocked to them, offering to help as guides and auxiliaries. The African American military contribution helped to ease a serious manpower shortage. Union generals believed that they had to accept heavy casualties if they were to prevail – Union losses numbered 360,000 men compared with 240,000 Confederate losses. Black enlistment allowed the Union leadership to fight with a largely volunteer army, and to spare both the border states and the well-off – who could buy exemption – the full rigour of the draft.

The success of the emancipation policy moved Republicans to propose a Thirteenth Amendment which would abolish slavery throughout the territory of the Union, and without any compensation to the planters. This was extensively debated in Congress in 1864 and eventually received its approval in January 1865. But it still needed to be endorsed by the states. Emancipation appealed to the Unionist desire to elevate their cause – and to punish the entirety of the Southern slave-holding elite – as much as to abolitionist principle. The Republican congressmen who pressed it through were thereby relativizing the claims of property. In a previous session the speaker of the house, Schuyler Colfax, had done likewise when he (successfully) proposed the introduction of a progressive income tax and (unsuccessfully) proposed that corporate stocks and shares should be no less subject to a property tax than his constituents' farms and dwellings.[32]

The Confederacy was not doomed to lose the war simply because of its inferior resources. Its aim of securing recognition as a separate state enabled it to adopt an essentially defensive posture, which required smaller forces. The Confederacy was not trying to subdue the North, but simply to obtain its agreement to secession. But it did have to sustain the sacrifices needed for a lengthy

---

31   Benjamin Quarles, *The Negro in the Civil War*, New York 1948.

32   Michael Vorenberg, *Final Freedom: The Civil War, the Abolition of Slavery, and the Thirteenth Amendment*, Cambridge 2001, pp. 206–7, and W. Elliot Brownlow, *Federal Taxation in America*, Cambridge 1996, p. 26.

war effort. The majority of white Southerners owned no slaves, yet many shared the nationalist yearnings expressed by secession and the setting-up of the Confederacy. The poorer, slave-less whites bore the brunt of the huge blood-shed entailed by the war, eventually eroding support for the rebellion and prompting high desertion rates. Once the first flush of enthusiasm was past, such strains showed that the holding of blacks as private slaves was not a solid basis upon which to construct a distinguishing nationalism.[33] There was the further problem that as more white men had to be sent to the front the slave order itself was sapped, and slave discipline and mobilization were undermined. In the hope of future sales the planters went on growing cotton, but failed to grow enough food. The planters also blocked taxes on their property or income, contributing to the chaos of Confederate finance. An act which exempted larger planters from the draft caused resentment. The slaves were still able to scale back their efforts, contributing to food shortages. The mere presence of the slaves, with their increasing partiality for the Union, also helped to rule out the adoption of guerrilla resistance to the Union armies, and, in doing so, to rule out a strategy that the Spanish had used effectively against Napoleon.

Emancipation had been undertaken first to weaken, and then to punish, those who had attempted to destroy the Union. Some abolitionists believed that they were simply using nationalism to gain their ends, but the reality was that Republican nationalists used abolitionism not only to defend the Union but to enhance the power of the Federal state. Paradoxically the rebellion enabled a constitutionally legitimate emancipation that would scarcely otherwise have been possible. It allowed Republicans to run Congress, unleashed the president's war powers and removed the veto power of the slave states. While the preliminary Emancipation Declaration said nothing about recruiting black soldiers, it was endorsed by the definitive version of the Proclamation issued in January 1863. However, it was to take many months before the Union high command really exploited the policy to disrupt the Confederacy. In denying compensation even to loyal slave-owners, the Thirteenth Amendment had accomplished a species of revolution from above. The protracted nature of the conflict radicalized even the Radical Republicans and allowed them, so long as there was some military momentum, to capture the popular mood.

My argument here is that a purely nationalist strategy failed to deliver a swift victory, as was hoped, and that as a consequence of this disappointment, abolitionism – civil and military, black and white – began to express the popular will of the North. I am not arguing that the abolitionists were responsible for the Unionist decision to fight the Confederacy. That decision, I maintain, was taken for nationalist reasons. A nationalist surge was already in flood by the time of the

---

33   Richard E. Beringer, Herman Hattaway, Archer Jones and William Still, *Why the South Lost the War*, Athens, GA 1986, pp. 424–42.

firing on Fort Sumter. Stephen Douglas and other Northern Democrats were swept along by it just as much as the still-small bands of abolitionists – Douglas visited Lincoln at the White House to assure him of Democratic support for the crushing of secession. The contribution of the anti-slavery radicals was not that they had influence on the option for war but rather that, once that war had begun, they influenced its course and objective. Patriotism, especially when confronted by a plausible rival, needs to reach outside itself, and new nationalisms need new sources of legitimacy. Around this time, and for the same reason, Cavour and Bismarck supplemented their military moves towards unification in Italy and Germany with proposals to set up elected national parliaments. The nation's citizens or subjects were invited to see themselves as participating in sovereignty.[34]

In the secession crisis, prominent Northern preachers offered themselves and the ideal of a Protestant nation as a supplementary source of motivation, and at stages in the war when Democratic support for it flagged, Lincoln was happy to receive support from this quarter. Protestant evangelical backing for abolitionism and Unionism was welcome, but not so claims for a privileged role for the Protestant Churches, since these would narrow the scope of the nation when the priority was to widen it. There was to be another powerful reason why abolitionism gained ground, namely that it explained the growing evidence that, as the conflict unfolded, Southern slaves themselves favoured the Union and would desert Confederate owners whenever this became practical.

As Benedict Anderson argues, nationalist sentiment relies on an 'imagined community' embracing large numbers of people who have never met one another but who are drawn together by what are thought of as natural and voluntary ties.[35] Newspapers, pamphlets, speeches and novels all helped to create this psychological space. The Emancipation Proclamation and the Thirteenth Amendment were framed at a time when the outcome of the war was still in doubt. They filled out the promise of a new US nationalism, freed from distasteful compromises with slave-holders and slave-traders. Lincoln had seen the necessity of capturing the moral high ground during the war. This is what had prompted the Proclamation, Gettysburg Address and Thirteenth Amendment.[36]

I have referred above to Lincoln's explanation for delaying the Emancipation Proclamation in the summer of 1862, namely that – following advice from Cabinet members – he decided to wait until there was good news from the battlefield so that the proclamation would not appear as a 'shriek on the retreat'. The bloody check to the Confederate forces at Antietam, and the rebels' orderly retreat across the Potomac, gave the Union a muted victory

---

34   Tom Nairn, *Faces of Nationalism*, London 1998.
35   Anderson, *Imagined Communities*.
36   Michael Lind registers the emergence of a new US nationalism after the Civil War, stressing its European and 'white' character. See Michael Lind, *The Next American Nation*, New York 1995, pp. 55–96.

which furnished the right signal. A sweeping Unionist victory would have made it implausible for Lincoln to propose emancipation solely on grounds of military necessity. If General McLellan had vigorously exploited his advantage, destroying the Confederacy's best army and capturing its capital, then a purely military, Union-defending argument for emancipation would have been strained and Lincoln's caution might have given the moderates and compromisers the chance to maintain slavery. The moralizing criticism of the abolitionists and the factionalism of the Radicals can appear to underestimate the president's long game, but by foregrounding the slavery issue, regardless of the shifting military conjuncture, the abolitionists and Radicals acquired real authority and educated the Northern public. This also allowed them to make the case for black citizenship, a topic Lincoln avoided mentioning until very near the end.[37]

Lincoln was taciturn by nature and inched forward cautiously step by step. When it came to justifying slave emancipation Lincoln was further bound by political and constitutional considerations. He was concerned to avoid a Supreme Court veto or to provoke the border states, where slavery remained legal, and to take only such actions as conformed to military necessity and his war powers as president. Hence the cautious phrasing of the Emancipation Proclamation and Gettysburg Address, even if both had an implicit anti-slavery message for those willing to hear it.

Lincoln's course from the Emancipation Proclamation to Gettysburg and beyond aimed not just to maintain and invigorate the Unionist coalition but also to appeal to public opinion in the wider Atlantic world, thwarting the conservative and meddling inclination of the governments in Paris or London. As the conflict dragged on, Lincoln's efforts to cultivate public support for the Union cause were to include a fleeting and formal – but not insignificant – exchange with representatives of the International Workingmen's Association (IWA), a body committed both to the 'self-emancipation' of labour and to a democratic revolution in the old continent. From the start of the conflict Europe's abolitionists and revolutionists had condemned the 'slave-holders' rebellion'. The 1848 refugees in the US North and North-West had flocked to join the Union army, swelling its German contingents until they comprised 200,000 men.[38] The IWA also counted on the support of many British and French trade unions, organizations which had undertaken public campaigns against any recognition of the Confederacy. The General Council of the IWA asked Karl Marx to draft a message of congratulation to Lincoln on the occasion of his re-election.

---

37   Once again the hostile account of the Radicals in Williams, *Lincoln and the Radicals*, is really a tribute to their contribution.

38   See Levine, *Spirit of 1848,*, pp. 257–72.

Marx complained to Engels that writing such a text was 'much harder [to draft] than a substantial work' since he was anxious that 'the phraseology to which this sort of scribbling is restricted should at least be distinguished from the democratic, vulgar phraseology'.[39] Nevertheless he allowed himself the following resonant, if complex, paragraph:

> When an oligarchy of 300,000 slave-holders dared to inscribe, for the first time in the annals of the world, 'slavery' on the banner of armed revolt; when on the very spots where the idea of one Great Democratic Republic, whence the first Declaration of the Rights of Man was issued, and the first impulse given to the European revolution of the eighteenth century . . . then the working classes of Europe understood at once, even before the fanatic partisanship of the upper classes for the Confederate gentry had given warning, that the slave-holders' rebellion was to sound the tocsin for a general holy crusade of property against labour . . .

Marx's Address also warned that so long as the republic was 'defiled by slavery', so long as the Negro was 'mastered and sold without his concurrence', and so long as it was 'the highest prerogative of the white-skinned labourer to sell himself and choose his own master', they would be 'unable to attain the true freedom of labour'.[40] The repeated invocation of the cause of labour in the Address thus gave its own more radical twist to the 'free labour' argument characteristic of Lincoln and other Republicans. The US ambassador to Britain, Charles Francis Adams, replied to the Address on behalf of the president a month later, declaring that 'the United States regard their cause in the present conflict with slavery-maintaining insurgents as the cause of human nature and that they derive new encouragement to persevere from the testimony of the working men of Europe'.[41] Thus both the Address and the reply embed the rights of labour in, respectively, the 'rights of man' and 'the cause of human nature'.

By the time of the Second Inaugural, in March 1865, Lincoln was less constrained than on earlier occasions and placed slavery as central to the conflict in a way that he had previously avoided. He gave vent to his sense of the heavy wrong which his nation had committed by permitting an extremity of human bondage. He declared that each side in the still unfinished conflict had looked for 'an easier triumph', but had not been able to contrive 'a result less fundamental and astounding'. He saw the carnage of the war as perhaps God's punishment for the nation's 'offences', and concluded that he could only hope and pray that 'this mighty scourge of war' would come to a speedy end. 'Yet if God wills that it continue, until

39 Karl Marx and Frederick Engels, *The Civil War in the United States*, New York 1937, p. 273. See also Robin Blackburn, *An Unfinished Revolution: Karl Marx and Abraham Lincoln*, London 2011.

40 'The Address', Marx and Engels, *Civil War in the United States*, pp. 260–1.

41 'The American Ambassador's Reply', ibid., pp. 262–3.

all the wealth piled up by the bondman's two hundred and fifty years of unrequited toil shall be sunk, and until every drop of blood drawn with the lash, shall be paid by another drawn with the sword, as was said three thousand years ago, so still it must be said, "the judgments of the Lord are true and righteous altogether".

This passage certainly put slavery at the centre, and strikingly memorialized its enormity as a system for the exploitation of labour (as Montesinos and Las Casas had done with reference to Indian slavery in the early sixteenth century, in equally Biblical terms). But the Inaugural did not mention the black soldiers, or the future fate of the emancipated slave. In the preceding months radical members of Congress had urged that the freedmen should be given the vote, as part of the Reconstruction of the rebel states. Lincoln had opposed this. One of his friends remembered him explaining: 'I am not in favour of unlimited social equality . . . The question of universal suffrage for the freedman in his unprepared state is one of doubtful propriety.'[42] On another occasion Lincoln wrote to the governor of Louisiana at a time when it was establishing franchise qualifications: 'I barely suggest for your private consideration, whether some of the colored people may not be let in – as for instance, the very intelligent, and especially those who have fought gallantly in our ranks.'[43] In this sort of communication a moderate tone was advisable. If Lincoln had lived it seems likely that, as the situation evolved, so would his views on this matter.

In the last year of the war Lincoln also gave up his long attachment to colonization. He found that colonization was rejected not only by black abolitionists and church leaders but also by the generality of African Americans. Prior to becoming president – and despite his preoccupation with slavery – Lincoln had scant contact with African Americans (he used a Haitian barber in Springfield, but whether they talked is unknown). However, from 1862 he did consult the views of a variety of black leaders, including journalists, clergymen and some 'contrabands'. Elizabeth Keckley, his wife's coloured seamstress and confidante, may well have played a part in arranging these encounters. Keckley was head of the Contraband Relief Association in Washington and thus well connected to black abolitionism.[44] The actions of African Americans had a double impact – firstly as contrabands, by obliging the Union authorities to take a stand on slavery, and secondly as free men, by helping to persuade Lincoln to give up colonization. African Americans had many reasons to reject 'colonization'. A point they often made may have had a special appeal to Lincoln, namely the argument from 'unrequited labour'. After all, the slaves' toil had built the seat of government in Washington, DC, and many fortunes in both South and North.[45]

---

42   Fredrickson, *Big Enough to Be Inconsistent*, p. 122.

43   Charles Vincent, *Black Legislators in Louisiana During Reconstruction*, Baton Rouge 1976, p. 22.

44   Foner, *Fiery Trial*, pp. 256–7.

45   Lincoln's long attachment to the colonization idea is documented by Eric Foner in

Frederick Douglass later wrote: 'Viewed from genuine abolition ground Mr Lincoln seemed tardy, cold, dull and indifferent but measuring him by the sentiment of his country, a sentiment he was bound as a statesman to consult, he was swift, zealous, radical and determined.'[46] This verdict doesn't directly refer to race, but we may assume that it is also covered by the term sentiment. Lincoln's attempts to reach out to Douglass in the last year of his life seem to signal the stirring of an awareness of the need for African American agency if freedom was really to be won.

It is often claimed that the ending of slavery vindicated the US Constitution. Yet in truth the outbreak of the Civil War represented its failure to furnish the institutional setting for a peaceful or swift resolution. Its 'hundred locks' had inhibited an earlier attempt to confront slavery. Constitutional procedures had failed peacefully to resolve the sectional conflict.[47] Lincoln found the keys in the president's war powers, but this required secession and a bloody and protracted war. The Emancipation Proclamation, when it came, lay quite outside the normal workings of the Constitution, presenting Congress with a fait accompli. The wartime measure did not, of course, ban slavery as such, requiring to be followed up by the Thirteenth Amendment. The Congress which approved the Amendment in January 1865 was a rump body lacking the Southern states.

Lincoln believed that the legitimacy of an amendment that had only been agreed by a majority of the loyal states would be challenged in the future. Many Republicans agreed. They consequently required the seceded states first to organize conventions that would repudiate secession, and then to elect administrations and legislatures comprising men who had not held Confederate office. There were just enough Southern Whigs or non-office-holding Democrats to make this a possibility. The reconstructed states were then to be required to adopt the Thirteenth Amendment as a precondition for admittance to the Union. This bristled with difficulties, since it required constitutional conventions somehow to guarantee the compliance of future state assemblies. Provisional governors appointed by the president superintended these proceedings in the occupied states.

With Lincoln's assassination the presidency passed to Andrew Johnson, who notoriously came to favour a rapprochement with the Southern planter

---

'Lincoln and Colonization', an essay in Eric Foner, ed., *Our Lincoln: New Perspectives on Lincoln and His World*, New York 2008, pp. 135–66. This volume also contains an essay by Manisha Sinha which explores the African American contribution to changing his mind on the question, 'Allies for Emancipation: Lincoln and Black Abolitionists', pp. 167–98. In this same volume James Oakes argues that the 'unrequited labour' strand in Lincoln's rejection of slavery became more marked in the late 1850s and the war years, 'Natural Rights, Citizenship Rights, States' Rights, and Black Rights: Another Look at Lincoln and Race', pp. 109–34.

46   Quoted in Fredrickson, *Big Enough to Be Inconsistent*, p. 126.

47   For critiques of the cult of the Constitution see Daniel Lazare, *The Frozen Republic*, New York 1995 and Anatol Lieven, *America Right or Wrong*, London 2004.

class. However, during his first weeks in office he brusquely insisted that endorsement of the Thirteenth Amendment was the essential precondition for Reconstruction and eventual readmission to the Union. While loyal border states might complain, the defeated had no alternative but to do as they were told. Johnson sometimes candidly explained to white Southerners that the sooner they accepted the inevitability of the Thirteenth Amendment, the quicker they could regain their old powers and be in a position to frustrate the radicals. Order and certainty had to be re-established even if it required dubious expedients and flagrant bullying. As Bruce Ackerman has explained, 'presidential Reconstruction', which saw the Thirteenth Amendment ratified by several 'reconstructed' states, involved many extra-Constitutional procedures and pressures, and probably could not have succeeded otherwise. In effect a reconstructed state's vote only counted if it voted for the Amendment.[48] Since several loyal states had voted against the Amendment, endorsement by at least some of the 'reconstructed' states was essential if it was to pass by the necessary qualified majority. These proceedings justify the claim that US emancipation was not only a gigantic act of expropriation but a 'revolution from above'. The elements of a 'revolution from below' emerged during 'Radical Reconstruction', but this was to be stifled. Many Radical and black Republicans sought to extend Lincoln's legacy by promising freedmen the vote and civil equality. Despite their success on paper – the passage of the Fourteenth and Fifteenth Amendments – they were to be defeated on substance.

Following the assassination Marx drew up another Address in which he praised Lincoln as a political leader who could not be 'browbeaten by adversity', nor 'intoxicated by success', but instead inflexibly pressed on, 'slowly maturing his steps, never retracing them'. Speedily disillusioned by President Johnson, Marx and Engels saw a great crisis looming. Engels wrote to Marx in July: 'His [Johnson's] hatred of Negroes comes out more and more violently . . . If things go on like this, in six months all the old villains of secession will be sitting in Congress at Washington. Without coloured suffrage nothing can be done there.'[49]

RECONSTRUCTION AND EQUAL RIGHTS: BATTLES WON AND LOST

Many Northerners believed that, with slavery ended, a free labour system would take its place without great difficulty. But the planters often lacked both the will and the means to play their part as regular employers. Many believed that their former chattels still owed them service, while the freedmen themselves often

---

48   Bruce Ackerman, *We the People: Transformations*, Cambridge, MA, 1998, pp. 136–59. Ackerman maintains that for the Constitution to work there must anyway be much presidential or congressional 'triggering' and 'consolidation', giving rise to what he terms *'amendment simulacra'* and *'amendment-analogues'* (his emphasis, p. 270).

49   Marx and Engels, *Civil War in America*, p. 277.

shunned contracts with their former masters. Most planters had little or no working capital, and the war had wiped out the former credit system, based on cotton factors dealing with large planters, who in turn lent to small-holders. Storekeepers struggled to fill the gap.[50] Unable to offer a living monetary wage, the planters instead offered accommodation, rations and the use of a garden plot – an arrangement reminiscent of the past. Union commanders were anxious to see cultivation resume, so pressured the freedmen to accept labour contracts for nominal or deferred wages. Officers of the occupying Union army supported the freedmen when they insisted that corporal punishment was no longer permissible, but their own practices as employers of black labour were both rigorous and economical.

The decision to set up the Bureau of Refugees, Freedmen and Abandoned Lands in March 1865 seemed to mark a recognition that the occupying power had to take responsibility for an extraordinary situation. But its activities were soon curbed. The freedmen's desire for land led many to enter into tenancy agreements with planters who continued to own the best land. The shortage of working capital, and the heritage of attitudes at variance with a wage regime, frustrated the 'free labour' ideology held by many Union commanders and Republican leaders. Senior commanders and some of those entrusted with running the Freedmen's Bureau believed that land must be made available to the former slaves. Tens of thousands of plots were distributed, but the experiment did not last long. Given their situation, the new small-holders or tenants prioritized subsistence cultivation, on the 'safety first' principle, rather than cultivating staple crops which might be difficult to sell. And long before this was clear, the mass of planters objected to land distributions on the grounds that they would simply dissuade the freedmen from accepting work for wages. A further problem was that the land already in public hands was either of poor quality or needed considerable investment (e.g. in communications) before it would be suitable for staple production. In the North and West, rail companies might strike a corrupt contract with politicians but at least they would have some commitment to building the infrastructure needed for agricultural development. Few were prepared to devote significant resources to Southern development, since the South could not offer much in the way of collateral, physical security, or buoyant markets. The freedmen were to prove very tenacious in their aspiration to become farmers, but the Federal government, which alone had the power to distribute land and resources to them, soon scaled back its very modest foray in that direction. A further problem was that properly substantial land distribution would depend on a willingness to expropriate disloyal planters.

---

50   Roger Ransom and Richard Sutch, *One Kind of Freedom: The Economic Consequences of Emancipation*, 2nd ed, Cambridge 2001, pp. 109–11.

With little land available, the freedpeople were pushed into a limited variety of sharecropping instead. The planter might allow black sharecroppers the use of a small garden, but they were labourers rather than tenants, working the planter's land under the direction of their employer or an overseer. They were 'share croppers' because they were paid a proportion of the value of the cotton they harvested. This locked the worker into a yearly cycle since they were kept waiting until the harvest was in, and sold, before receiving most of their pay. This system robbed the worker of the special leverage they would otherwise have at the height of the harvest season. It also placed the risk of bad harvests or poor prices on the labourer. Many Union commanders found such arrangements acceptable. Aware of the planters' lack of finance they were prepared to accept, as one Union officer put it, 'one cent a year' as a wage, so long as there were other benefits in kind.[51] Such expedients, adapted to the lack of currency or credit, actually perpetuated the problem –theyit also greatly limited the tax base available to the new governments that the occupying authority was seeking to form in the 'Reconstructed' states.

Many abolitionists and Radical Republicans believed that the suppression of slavery was not enough and that the freedmen required at least education, and preferably land and the vote as well. But the mainstream of Northern opinion was not, at first, persuaded of this – after all, most free blacks in the North did not have the vote – and Republicans were very cautious, fearing that the Democrats would be the beneficiaries if they attempted too much. In this situation it was important that some Union Leagues were responsive to abolitionist appeals, including those from black abolitionists. A convention of 150 black delegates from seventeen states met in Syracuse (New York state) in October 1864, comprising many veterans of black abolitionism and the antebellum black convention movement. The Syracuse convention, and subsequent gatherings in Charleston and New Orleans, framed a broad programme for equal civic and political rights. Most of the participants in these events were already free before the war. They articulated the aspirations of black communities in Louisiana, South Carolina and Tennessee – areas occupied by Unionist forces long before the final collapse. These leaders argued that black soldiers had earned citizenship by helping to save the Union. They also paid their taxes, and therefore deserved representation. At Syracuse, Charleston and elsewhere the call was not simply for rights in the abstract but for tangible expressions of a new status – the right to vote and serve on juries, and a Homestead Act for the South. A 'Declaration of Rights and Wrongs' adopted at both Syracuse and Charleston warned that measures favourable to the freedmen were being frustrated, and

---

51   Foner, *Reconstruction*, pp. 153–70. See also W. E. B. Du Bois, *Black Reconstruction in America*, New York 1935.

it would be a hollow mockery if planters were still free to intimidate and dragoon them.[52]

The Southern planters had lost their slaves but not their estates, or their control over much of the countryside. Confederate forces had been defeated on the battlefield, but former Confederate officials and military men still commanded the allegiance of many Southern whites. In some areas the patrols still operated, in others new white vigilante groups. They were able to exploit the very confused situation left by Confederate collapse, Republican divisions and Lincoln's replacement by an unstable and unsuitable deputy.

President Johnson set off alarm bells in the North with his outrageously indulgent attitude to the former rebels as he pursued his idea of 'presidential reconstruction'. So long as they approved the Thirteenth Amendment, he was prepared to recognize exclusively white Southern state assemblies as the basis for a new South. Unable to persuade Congress that this was the right approach, he acted on his own.

Johnson decided that, with slavery ended, the time had come to reach a generous settlement with the leaders of Southern society. He found a means to pursue this policy with no need to involve Congress. The US president has broad powers to pardon, and Johnson used these to lift the proscriptions on thousands of former Confederate officials or army officers. Johnson, himself a former 'poor white' Southerner, was flattered to receive the supplications of Southern gentlemen and ladies. He believed that, after the massive destruction visited on the South, clemency and reconciliation were in order. He was alarmed by reports of the movement of hundreds of thousands of black people through-out the South, as family members sought one another out and freedmen staked their claim to patches of land. Southern planters had always feared slave de-subordination and construed the new black mobility and visibility as a threat, even though black leaders insisted that there was no question of insurrection.[53]

Black freedom and mobility were enough to awaken white fears. The new incumbent of the White House shared these, and believed that discipline must be restored. Seeing himself as a peacemaker, President Johnson was will-ing to recognize assemblies entirely composed of whites in the supposedly 'reconstructed' states where many of the new office-holders were beneficiaries

52 Steven Hahn, *A Nation Under Our Feet: Black Political Struggles in the Rural South from Slavery to the Great Migration*, Cambridge, MA, 2003, pp. 103–5.

53 Hahn, *A Nation Under Our Feet*, pp. 116–59. See also Berlin, Fields, Miller, Reidy, and Rowland, *Slaves No More*, Peter Kolchin, 'Slavery and Freedom in the Civil War South', in McPherson and Cooper, eds, *Writing the Civil War*, pp. 241–60. While generally striking a balanced note this author, a distinguished comparativist, nevertheless inclines to exaggerate the gains made by former slaves and their descendants in the nineteenth- and early-twentieth-century US South. While such gains were real, white supremacy, as we will see, was quite quickly rebuilt in ways that had no counterpart in Cuba or Brazil. I return to this contrast in the next chapter.

of presidential pardons. Johnson was not disturbed when the assemblies enacted harsh new 'Black Codes', requiring freedmen to show proof of employment and to accept the terms they were offered by former masters. There was to be forced labour for those who declined. Enactment of the Codes was accompanied by violent attacks on the freedmen and women by white vigilante groups. Armed white vigilantes also sought to prevent the freedmen from hunting on the range. In previous times the landowners had been happy to allow their slaves some minor hunting rights on their own land, as this helped slaves to feed themselves. But planters now preferred to see the freedmen compelled to work for wages when they lacked adequate means of self-provision. Planters took to offering wages from which 'advances' had been deducted, and whose final value would be linked to the staple.[54] Others would offer 'checks' that could only be redeemed at stores where the goods were overpriced.

President Johnson's capitulation to the Southern gentry stimulated opposition in the North. Republicans sought to pass ever more radical legislation laying disabilities on former rebels, but they could not control the president and narrowly failed in an effort to impeach him. The presidential power which Lincoln had used to promote emancipation was now deployed to frustrate any measure favourable to the freedmen. To begin with, many Republicans had believed that the former slaves were not yet ready for the vote. In September 1866 a Loyalist Convention in Philadelphia split on freedmen's voting rights. With an election pending, even Radical Republican leaders feared that the issue would lose them support. Frederick Douglass and Anne Dickenson nevertheless pressed the case. The Congress did pass a Civil Rights Act in 1866, outlawing the many coercive features of the Black Codes. In the aftermath of an electoral victory and still confronted by a scheming and treacherous president, the Radical Republicans recovered their boldness. They were well aware that they needed freedmen's votes if they were to build Republican majorities in the Southern states.

Many of the Radicals believed that the freedmen should receive some land too – an equivalent of the Homestead Act of 1862 – but their hopes were blocked. The Freemen's Bureau's directive No 13. provided for parcels of public and confiscated land to be made available to the freedmen, and some Union commanders had already begun to distribute such land. But this directive was countermanded by President Johnson. Directive No. 15 declared the land distribution at an end. About 40,000 freedmen had already received some public land, but only those who had completed all legal formalities were allowed to keep it. A Southern Homestead Act was passed in 1867, making state land

---

54 Foner, *Reconstruction*, pp. 228–80; Peter Kolchin, *First Freedom: The Response of Alabama's Blacks to Emancipation and Reconstruction*, Westport 1972; Steven Hahn, *Roots of Southern Populism: Yeoman Farmers and the Transformation of the Georgia Upcountry, 1850–1890*, Oxford 1984, pp. 58–9, 241–3.

available to whites and blacks on equal terms, but it found few takers. The land was often marginal, and the cost of registering a claim and clearing the plot was beyond the reach of freedmen.

The Radicals gained support as the Northern public became aware of the new president's indulgence to the leaders of Southern society, and the latter's attempts to rebuild an unfree labour regime. Northern outrage at the presidential pardons for rebels and the brazen revanchism of Southern white assemblies swelled support for the 'Radical Reconstruction' imposed by determined Congressional majorities. In February 1867 the Republicans passed a Reconstruction Act which imposed military rule on the former rebel states and required them to adopt black male suffrage. A presidential veto was squashed. In the 1868 election Republicans eventually endorsed General Ulysses S. Grant, the Unionist commander, as the Republican candidate. The Radicals had leverage with Grant, though the corruption of his cronies was to compromise the party. The new president gave his backing to restoration of some of the sanctions on former Confederate officials. The Fourteenth Amendment (1868) gave Constitutional sanction to a rule that all born in the United States were to be citizens and to enjoy 'equal protection of the laws'. It forbade any abridgment of the rights of citizens except those guilty of rebellion. It further encouraged all states to award the vote to every male, whether black or white, by apportioning a state's weight in Federal arrangements in accord with the number of male voters. (The explicit gender discrimination embodied in this clause led to controversy in anti-slavery ranks, with some abolitionist women refusing to support it.) In many areas of the South, local authorities used literacy tests and other stratagems to exclude any black voter. The cumbersome wording and disappointing results of the Fourteenth Amendment led to the decision to formulate a Fifteenth Amendment (1870), which directly sought to outlaw vote suppression. The Reconstruction governments sought to enforce black male enfranchisement but only really succeeded in states like South Carolina and Louisiana, where there were Union troops and large and well-mobilized black populations.

Given the presence of Union occupation forces some white yeomen, especially those from outside the plantation zone, were prepared to vote Republican. Between a fifth and a third of the white electorate were willing, for a while, to defy the Southern white establishment. Many Confederate leaders were barred from holding office. The Reconstruction governments saw blacks elected to a string of posts, and there was intense black participation in Union Leagues and Republican Party branches. Mixed race meetings discussed the issues of the day, read and debated newspaper articles, and set out priorities for Republican elected officials. Over two hundred black delegates were elected to the constitutional conventions held in occupied states in

1867–8. The Reconstruction governments fostered a variety of social programmes: 'Public schools, hospitals, penitentiaries, and asylums for orphans and the insane were established for the first time or received increased funding. South Carolina funded medical care for poor citizens and Alabama funded free legal counsel for indigent defendants.'[55]

The Reconstruction governments, the Freedmen's Bureau and a number of Northern charitable or missionary organizations joined forces to extend education to the former slaves and their children. This had enduring consequences, laying the foundation for a racially-segregated educational system that comprised some black university colleges as well as high schools. While there were to be constraints on the curricula and attempts to confine the pupils to artisanal skills, they were not always successful. The antebellum Southern states had been grudging in their support for public services. But the higher taxes needed to cover the new public programmes were resented by white property-owners. Had the Northern Republicans extended greater economic help to the South, they would have improved the chances of the Reconstruction governments.

Several of the 'reconstructed' states adopted laws and constitutions that sought to make freedom and equality more tangible. In Louisiana, where attempts had been made to segregate public space and means of transport, the 1868 Constitutional Convention asserted the novel concept of 'public rights', which would give equal access to public space. The Constitution's Bill of Rights declared that all citizens of the state should enjoy 'the same civil, political and public rights and privileges, and be subject to the same pains and penalties'. The concept of public rights was clarified by a prohibition of racial discrimination on pubic transportation and in places of public resort or accommodations.[56] Rebecca Scott contrasts this clear requirement with the 'oblique language' of the Fourteenth Amendment.

During the heyday of Radical Reconstruction, white Northern working men also made important strides forward. The politics of Radical Reconstruction favoured public education and the first attempts to regulate the railroads. The stirrings of a new social radicalism and a very practical trade union movement were heightened by the polarizations around Radical Republicanism. Thaddeus Stevens, the Radical Republican leader first opposed, then endorsed, the agitation for an eight-hour day. At this time the average working day was over eleven hours. Wendell Phillips led prominent abolitionists and Radicals in supporting Eight Hour Leagues. In demanding the eight-hour day the 'labour reformers' were accepting 'clock time' and a degree of labour discipline as part

---

55   Foner, *Reconstruction*, p. 364.

56   Rebecca Scott, *Degrees of Freedom: Louisiana and Cuba after Slavery*, Cambridge, MA, 2005, pp. 43–5.

of a comprehensive scheme of improvement. Starting from free labour principles, Ira Steward argued that shorter hours meant higher pay, and that higher pay would combat unemployment. As he bluntly put it: 'new employments depend upon a more expensive style of living'.[57] Such a stimulus was badly needed in an economy where soldiers were returning home and slaves freed. Labour agitation increased in New York, Pennsylvania and Chicago. In 1867 a National Labor Union was formed to spread the demand for shorter hours. It declared: 'The National Labor Union knows no north, no south, no east, no west, neither color nor sex, on the question of the rights of labor.'[58] In response to the clamour, Congress established an eight-hour legal working day for Federal employees in 1868; by this time eight states had similar laws, though implementation was weak. The demand also had little leverage in the South, with its tenancy and sharecropping. The New *Orleans Tribune*, published by coloured journalists, supported the eight-hour movement while a State Labor Convention in South Carolina called for a nine-hour day. A Colored Workers' Convention in New York in 1869 sought to build a bridge between organized labour and the freedmen.

The International Working Men's Association, with fifty sections in a dozen urban areas, gained a wide and diverse following. In 1871 the IWA mustered 70,000 in New York to pay tribute to the martyrs of the Paris Commune. The march brought together banner-waving trade unionists, the Skidmore Guards (a black militia), supporters of the Cuban independence struggle, an Irish band, and Victoria Woodhull and the female leaders of Section 12. A heady brew of new ideas circulated. The International was adopted by *Woodhull & Claflin's Weekly*, which published lengthy extracts from the *Communist Manifesto* and Marx's writings on the Paris Commune. It declared in an editorial: 'This is the age of rights when, for the first time in human history, the rights of all living things are, in some way, recognized as existing. We are far yet from conceding to all their rights, but we talk about them, we see them and thought is busy to determine how best they might be secured.'[59] The enfranchisement of the freedmen helped to create this burgeoning extension of rights, and even their frequent difficulty in exercising them did not dampen expectations. The *Weekly* championed votes for women and ran a series of articles on the need to rethink the sexual division of labour, so that men could work in the home and women outside it.[60] The Equal Rights Association canvassed a proposal to offer as candidates in the forthcoming presidential election a ticket comprising Victoria

---

57   Quoted in David Roediger and Philip Foner, *Our Own Time: A History of American Labor and the Working Day*, London 1989, p. 85.

58   Ibid.

59   'The Rights of Children', *Woodhull & Claflin's Weekly*, 6 December 1870.

60   See 'Men's Rights: Or How Would You Like It', *Woodhull & Claflin's Weekly*, September 1870.

Woodhall and Frederick Douglass. For a brief moment an attempt was made to formulate a programme that would appeal broadly to workers, whether native or immigrant, black or white, male or female.[61] But as the 1872 presidential election approached, Reconstruction itself was threatened.

The years 1868–77 saw a brush fire of labour disputes, but no organization proved able to give them overall coherence and direction. Moreover, as Reconstruction ebbed, labour also encountered greater difficulty. The militancy of organized labour opened awkward divisions among Republicans. The eight-hour-day campaigns alienated some small employers as well as the large new corporations.

Giving the vote to former slaves in the South dramatized racial exclusion in many 'free' states, and prompted a questioning of racial barriers. Iowa was a case in point. In 1857 the state's voters had heavily defeated an attempt to extend the vote to free blacks. In what Robert Dykstra calls 'the egalitarian moment' the Iowa electorate reversed itself on this in 1868, strongly influenced by the African American contribution to the defence of the Union.[62] But while some measures favourable to free blacks in the North were endorsed, there was no strong political axis between white workers and the freedmen; the demand for female suffrage went unheeded, and troops were sent against the Native Americans.

Northern support for Reconstruction eroded in the 1870s, partly because of weariness with the lack of progress or security in the South, and partly because – short of raising a substantial force to occupy and police the whole territory – it was difficult to counter the mobilization of hundreds of thousands, even millions, of armed and angry Southern whites. The latter, unchecked, thrust freedmen and freedwomen into the condition of a new racial underclass, subjected to segregation, lacking freedom of movement and vulnerable to the lynch mob. They were no longer slaves but neither were they a 'picaresque proletariat'. Still paying off the costs of the war, Northern taxpayers begrudged the extra economic measures which could have helped revive the Southern economy and make a success of Reconstruction. Lurid accounts of 'carpet-bagger' corruption anyway made such assistance seem fruitless.

The abolitionists had overestimated the power of national legislation. Garrison stopped publishing his journal, the *Liberator*, in 1865 and helped to found the *Nation*, designed to be a more broad-based journal. Yet the *Nation*

---

61   Ellen Dubois, in her editorial presentation, argues that Stanton and Anthony were both in different ways adapting the women's movement to the need for wider alliances. While Anthony drew on 'free labour' ideology to criticize women's dependence, Stanton sketched the programmatic basis for an alliance between the women's and the labour movements. See Stanton and Anthony, *Correspondence, Writings, Speeches*, pp. 92–112, 166–9. The earlier disputes between some male and female abolitionists over whether black manhood suffrage should be given priority subsided after 1877, as it became clear that most black men were anyway cheated of the vote.

62   Robert Dykstra, *Bright Radical Star: Black Freedom and White Supremacy on the Hawkeye Frontier*, Cambridge, MA, 1993.

became a vociferous opponent of Radical Reconstruction and the threat it supposedly represented to 'good government'. One of the paper's writers – Garrison's son Wendell – urged that the violence of the Ku Klux Klan was a response to 'bad government become unendurable'. William Lloyd Garrison himself deplored the paper's 'lack of sympathy with and evident contempt for the colored race'.[63] The American Antislavery Society was wound up in 1870, and the National Reform League founded to take up the struggle for equality – but it failed to make its mark. Wendell Phillips and the elder Garrison continued to defend the rights of the freedmen and to denounce white terror, but, as the *New York Times* explained, 'Wendell Phillips and William Lloyd Garrison are not exactly extinct forces in American politics but they represent ideas with regard to the South which the great majority of the Republican Party have outgrown'.[64] McPherson estimates that three-quarters of the veterans of abolitionism defended Reconstruction and the freedmen, but many Republicans and some prominent abolitionists and radicals were to fall away in 1872 and 1876.

At some level white Northern opinion blamed the slaves and the abolitionists for having provoked such a fierce, fratricidal conflict, and the loss of 600,000 lives. The demoralizing effect of rampant corruption in Republican administrations – in the North as well as the South – undermined the legitimacy of Reconstruction. Grant failed to punish the outrages practised by Southern whites, while the Republican-dominated Congress failed to provide the economic assistance needed by the Southern Republicans if they were to retain white electoral support. Northern Republicans were embarrassed by the expedients resorted to by their Southern colleagues, and began to think that some modus vivendi with the Southern white majority must be reached. Republican governments found it difficult to protect their supporters from white vigilantes. The Republicans' mixed motives – more concerned to defend the Union than to free the slaves, more concerned to punish the Southern rebels than to elevate the freedmen and women – proved to be a weak basis for sustained Reconstruction.

White soldiers had returned home, but black troops could have been sent to uphold the authority of the Reconstruction governments. Since they were largely officered by whites, the 'provocation' to Southern whites would have scarcely been excessive. Instead thousands of these troops – the Twenty-Fourth and Twenty-Fifth Infantry regiments and the Ninth and Tenth Cavalry – were sent West to reinforce the last campaigns against the resistance of the Indian nations. A racially tinged Unionism was to justify both war against the Apache

---

63   James McPherson, *The Abolitionist Legacy: From Reconstruction to the NAACP*, Princeton 1975, p. 39.

64   Quoted in ibid., p. 49.

and leniency towards the Southern elite, as it constructed a post-emancipation racial order. In South Carolina there was a strong black response when the Reconstruction governor appealed for militia recruits in 1869, and for a while this militia – including some, if not many, whites – was a factor of stability.[65] However, in the mid-1870s Reconstruction governments everywhere became the target of 'white leagues', 'Redeemers' and 'rifle clubs'. Former Confederate soldiers were prominent in these movements, which had good training and weaponry. Grant did send in Union troops, in Louisiana in 1873 and on some other occasions. A permanent, bi-racial, locally recruited National Guard would have been a far more secure and permanent defence against intimidation. However, Republican governors like Kellogg in Louisiana and Chamberlain in South Carolina felt more comfortable with Federal troops, without sufficiently pondering the fact that they could be withdrawn.[66]

The closure of the Freedman's Bureau in 1870 and the abandonment of early initiatives to give land to former slaves also reduced the gains of emancipation. The generalized climate of racial intimidation, and the failure of many former abolitionists to prevent it, played a key role because it restricted mobility and association, and was by no means confined to the borders of the former Confederacy. While emancipation and the end of the war had prompted travel by freedmen and women seeking to unite with family, white vigilantism soon made this dangerous. There then began spasmodic attempts both within the South and on its borders to drive blacks even from land to which they had clear title. Such ethnic cleansing, as we now might call it, was little reported upon.[67]

Horace Greeley and the 'Liberal Republicans' mounted a challenge to the re-election of Grant in 1872, claiming to be supporters of clean government and sectional reconciliation.[68] Their defeat gave Reconstruction a few more years, but signalled the unwinding of the Republican coalition and waning support for the racial egalitarianism of the Reconstruction governments. Of course the real abolitionists had never been other than a tiny minority of Northern opinion, and even many former abolitionists became fatalistic or disillusioned in the 1870s.

North American capitalism was in the flood-tide of its continental development during these years. In 1862–8, abolitionist policy had helped to break the slave-holders' grip on the Federal state. But this left open some questions concerning the scope and character of Federal power. Businessmen wanted public contracts, but not regulation. The new working class wanted restraints

---

65   Hahn, *A Nation Under Our Feet*, pp. 302–13.

66   Ibid., pp. 163–411; C. Vann Woodward, *The Strange Career of Jim Crow*, 2nd ed, New York 1966, pp. 31–110.

67   Elliot Jaspin, *Buried in the Bitter Waters: The Hidden History of Ethnic Cleansing in the Americas*, New York 2007.

68   David W. Blight, *Race and Reunion: The American Civil War in American Memory*, Cambridge 2001, pp. 9–63.

on employers and good public services – resembling what a later age would call a welfare state. In the years that followed, an unleashed capitalism produced a disturbing spectacle of corruption and class strife. Following the denial of land to the freedmen, the railroad corporations somehow persuaded local and Federal authorities to give them millions of acres. The headlong growth of the years 1866–72 was brought to a shuddering halt by the panic of 1873. Rampant corruption and the spread of labour agitation together underlined the fact that Reconstruction and the Grant presidency had given capital continental scope, but failed to consolidate a well-ordered bourgeois regime. Following the dead-locked presidential election of 1876, the 1877 deal between Republicans and Democrats led to the withdrawal of remaining Federal troops from all the former Confederate states. In return, the Republican candidate entered the White House – even though he had won many less votes than the Democratic contender.

The deal between party leaders led not only to a new dispensation in the South but also to a new alignment in the North. Employers were determined to cut wages in an effort to recover profitability. They also hoped to inflict a salu-tary defeat on the trade unions. The resulting mighty battle between the rail workers and the railroad corporations – the Great Strike of 1877 – has been described as 'one of the bitterest explosions of class warfare in American history'.[69] Erupting three months after the end of Reconstruction, the Great Strike had a national character and attracted widespread urban support. The rail workers enjoyed considerable public sympathy. Some militia units refused to move against the strikers, and the employers had to engage an army of strike-breakers and special deputy marshals. The strike triggered urban protests at many points of the network. St Louis was closed down by a city-wide general strike instigated by the Workers Party, a successor to the IWA. The St Louis movement engaged many African Americans, and blacks were included in the strike leadership, a fact harped on by municipal authorities and the local press. In some areas the strikers kept public tramways running, but under their own control. Despite the eventual collapse of the strike the black population of St Louis remained a force to be reckoned with: in 1879, blacks fleeing Southern repression known as the 'Exodusters' were able to shelter in St Louis on the way to Kansas.[70]

In most parts of the South building trade unions was not feasible, partly because security was so lacking but also because the new social relations of

69   Foner, *Reconstruction*, p. 383. See also Robert Bruce, *1877: Year of Violence*, New York 1959, and John Lloyd, 'The Strike Wave of 1877', in Aaron Brenner, Benjamin Day and Immanuel Ness, eds, *The Encyclopedia of Strikes in American History*, Armonk 2009.

70   David Burbank, *Reign of the Rabble: The St Louis General Strike of 1877*, New York 1978. For the role of African Americans in the strike and later, see Bryan Jack, *The St Louis African American Community and the Exodusters*, Columbia 2007, especially pp. 142–50.

sharecropping and tenancy were individually negotiated. While the Northern and Western workers sought to regulate *time*, the freedmen and women were more concerned with *space* – access to land and equal access to public space. But labour agitation did occur in some Southern areas, where the political balance of forces permitted it. The most significant instance was in the rice plantations of coastal South Carolina in the 1870s. The freedmen on these large estates had considerable bargaining power, stemming from (1) the strong position of Radical Reconstruction in the state government, (2) black control of the county and its police in several localities and (3) the employer's heavy reliance on his workers at harvest time. In such conditions strikes could bring results, as they did for a decade or more after 1866.[71] Another area that later experienced labour battles was the coal mines of Tennessee, where black and white workers united in opposing the use of convict labour.[72]

The free labour doctrine of the Radical Republicans had been profoundly ambiguous. The employer might see its celebration of wage labour and the sanctity of contract as a message to their employees to consider how lucky they were not to be bondsmen. But the self-respecting working man and woman did not see it like that. They could easily believe that the dignity of the free worker meant that he or she should be free to combine to extract better terms and shorter hours – and that the worker should not be bound by long-term contracts, but could renegotiate at regular intervals. It is as if the hegemonic promise of one moment – that of the 1860s – was turning into the subversive nightmare of another – the 1870s. (The parallel is somewhat loose, but one can compare this sequence to that in Britain in the 1830s and 1840s as the triumph of slave emancipation and Reform in 1832–8 gave way to the rise – and fall – of Chartism, the first sustained British campaign for universal manhood suffrage and annual parliaments, in the 1840s.) The defeat of labour rounded out the end of Reconstruction and of the credibility of the Republican promise to the working man.

The Great Strike was crushed at the cost of one hundred lives and through recruiting thousands of 'special marshals' and Pinkerton men. Indeed, by 1878 the 30,000-strong Pinkerton organization actually outnumbered the Federal Army, now only 27,000 strong. Army numbers had been cut as an economy measure and also, perhaps, because army commanders did not always relish their strike-breaking role. The combined result of retreat from Reconstruction, withdrawal from the South, retrenchment in the North and lawlessness in the West was to undercut the 'modernization' of the Federal state which was part of the original Republican project. The resulting 'patchwork state' no longer aspired to check the South's brutal white supremacists.[73]

---

71   Foner, *Nothing But Freedom*, pp. 96–105.
72   Karen Shapiro, *A New South Rebellion, 1871–1896*, Chapel Hill 1998.
73   For the 'patchwork state' see Stephen Scowronek, *Building a New American State: The Expansion of National Administrative Capacities, 1877–1920*, Cambridge 1982, pp. 37–162.

JIM CROW AND THE ROBBER BARONS

The Federal government was not normally responsible for maintaining law and order within the states, and the latter, who did have this responsibility, were often prepared to outsource it to private bodies. This stemmed from both the desire for economy and a minimalist view of the state. While there were important differences between North, West and South, employers in each region had considerable latitude in dealing with their own workers, and could recruit their own security to deal with combinations and strikes. In the South this gave openings to vigilantism, in the North to 'Pinkerton's men' and company goons (though the corporations could also call on the National Guard). The level of violence in the North was far less than in the South, but still enough to make trade union organizing a hazardous undertaking.[74]

The violence against blacks began with the crumbling of the slave order in 1865 and surged in the 1870s as Reconstruction was driven back. It then remained as a ritual feature of the social order. Between 1884 and 1899 there were between 107 and 241 blacks murdered each year by lynch mobs, with the number of victims totalling over 3,000. The ostensible pretext for the lynchings was usually the rape of a white woman or some gesture that was deemed equivalent. A few thousand spectators would attend as the victim was exhibited, beaten and burned, with photographs taken to commemorate the event. The terrible spectacle of the lynchings aimed at cowing all blacks and deterring them from seeking their rights. It also implicated the generality of the white population in such practices. While lynchings were concentrated in the South and the great majority targeted blacks, they were not unknown elsewhere and sometimes targeted whites, Chinese and Mexicans. Along the Mexican border dozens of Hispanics were lynched during these years. And there were also lynchings of whites in other parts of the Union, especially the 'wild' West.[75] The intensification of Jim Crow in the South was accompanied by the spread of onerous, if less extreme, practices of racial exclusion in other sections, affecting residence, employment and education.[76]

Jim Crow did not prevail everywhere and at once in the Southern states. Emancipation and Reconstruction had brought real changes that were not so easily rolled back. In Virginia, the Readjusters – a coalition led by those who

---

74   For evidence that the level of repression helped to prevent the emergence of a US labour party in the 1890s see Robin Archer, *Why Is There No US Labor Party?*, London 2009.

75   Joel Williamson, *The Crucible of Race: Black–White Relations in the American South Since Emancipation*, Oxford 1984, pp. 117–18, 185–9; Ida B. Wells-Barnett, *On Lynchings*, with an introduction by Patricia Hill Collins, 2002 (1st ed. 1892), pp. 201–2.

76   Desmond King and Stephen Tuck, 'De-Centring the South: America's Nationwide White Supremacist Order After Reconstruction', *Past and Present* (February 2007), pp. 213–53.

wished to repudiate part of the state debt and supported by black voters – captured the legislature in 1879 and implemented some of their programme. But the Democratic party raised the cry of 'black domination' and unleashed a wave of political violence,[77] as Washington averted its gaze. Not all white Southerners immediately rallied to ultra-racism and segregation. But successive political battles involving conservatives and Populists led the more extreme racists to a position of hegemony in all parts of the South by the century's end. Cotton producers were squeezed by low prices and expensive credit. While some Populists favoured cross-racial alliances, the partisans of an ever more rampant white supremacy prevailed.[78]

The prevalence of lynch law underlined the limits of the gains represented by the ending of slavery and its suppression by a lawful state. George Washington had worried that slavery harmed the image of the United States as a civilized power. For many decades to come, and even in an Atlantic world where racism was respectable, lynchings persuaded many outside observers that the 'civilizing process' had not reached the US South and that the United States was not a fully modern state.

There was bitter irony when the Supreme Court allowed corporations to appropriate protections in the Fourteenth Amendment that had originally been framed to help the freedmen and women. The Court endorsed the idea that corporations were 'persons', and could therefore claim the latter's privileges and immunities, including the 'equal protection of the laws' as established in the Fourteenth. This Amendment also extended the 'due process' restraint from the Federal authority to the state authority, lending the corporations a powerful lever in their dealings with state regulation. And once they controlled state assemblies, the cartels and rings were able to control the Senate, since at this point senators were nominated by these assemblies. The same Supreme Court that had struck down civil rights protecting the freedpeople, endorsed the employer's right to claim a sanctity of 'contract' that outlawed much trade union activity.[79]

The lynchings were simply the most visible manifestation of a brutal and unabashed regime of racial supremacy. In 1883 the Supreme Court struck down the very moderate 1875 Civil Rights Law as unconstitutional. Public space and transport were segregated. Black prison inmates – toiling in chain gangs on former slave plantations or public works projects, or leased out to planters

---

77 William McKee Evans, *Open Wound: The Long View of Race in America*, Urbana 2009, pp. 177–8.

78 Lawrence Goodwyn, *The Populist Moment*, Oxford 1978. The rise and fall of the Populists in the decade after 1886 was marked by the adoption of an incipiently anti-capitalist programme—the Omaha platform—but became fixated on the monetisation of sliver and failed convincingly to bring together the aspirations of workers and farmers.

79 Kevin Phillips, *Wealth and Democracy: A Political History of the American Rich*, New York 2002, pp. 237–9. See also Matthew Josephson, *The Robber Barons: American Capitalists 1861–1901*, New York 1932.

– benefited state revenues as well as offering a warning to 'free' blacks of what would befall them if they stepped out of line.[80] Slavery's privatized form of domination had always been buttressed by the collective oppression of racial domination. In the post-emancipation era the latter predominated and the black person was free only within the narrow space that this permitted. The decisions of the Supreme Court enfeebled the Federal power, winked at lynch law and became the robber barons' charter.

The US Civil War had saved the Union and destroyed slavery. Some aspects of Reconstruction were genuinely impressive, but ultimately it was checked and abandoned. The regime of white supremacy in the former slave-holding states was rebuilt, and the legal integrity of the Union compromised. The conservative influence of Southern white supremacists was to be a significant factor in preventing the United States from developing a welfare state and the types of social inclusion found in other economically advanced countries in the late nineteenth century and after. The moment of Reconstruction had allowed glimpses of such a development, but the subsequent reconciliation and retreat debilitated the Federal authority and diminished its capacity to tame robber-baron capitalism.

The Southern counter-revolution placed a heavy burden on freedmen and women without securing prosperity even for most whites. The cotton planta-tion had withered and the planter had become a landlord, or been taken over by a merchant or creditor. Merchants and storekeepers offered credit against the main cash crop – basically cotton – and were uninterested in fostering diversi-fication. The result was an overproduction of cotton. This depressed cotton prices and led farmers into 'debt peonage', afflicting poor producers, whatever their colour. There was to be resistance from a Populist Farmers' Alliance that had some cross-racial support. But ultra-racists eventually prevailed and the Southern economy remained subdued. According to Ransom and Sutch, recorded per capita output of the major crops declined in five cotton states during the 1880s and 1890s, falling to below the levels reached in the days of slavery.[81] The Federal census sent officials into the field to quiz farmers on the crops they were producing, but they may have missed some of the subsistence cultivation by tenants and small-holders. Despite all obstacles, the former slaves made great efforts to work the land, as tenants if not owners. According to census returns for five cotton states in 1890, 31.7 per cent of coloured men and 5.9 per cent of coloured women were farm operators, while 41.9 per cent of men

---

80   Alex Lichtenstein, *Twice the Work of Free Labor: The Political Economy of Convict Labor in the New South*, New York 1996; Douglas A. Blackmon, *Slavery by Another Name*, New York 2006, and David Oshinsky, *'Worse Than Slavery': Parchman Farm and the Ordeal of Jim Crow Justice*, New York 1997.

81   Ransom and Sutch, *One Kind of Freedom*, pp. 244–53.

and 56.3 per cent of women were farm labourers.[82] These figures register a slow but steady advance in those working in some sense 'for themselves', compared with the days when all slaves worked for another. The quasi-autonomous Southern black rural community was also associated with the network of Southern black churches and the elements of a school system.

The position of Southern blacks was cramped by poverty as well as racism. I have drawn on the analysis of the reasons for this poverty put forward by Sutch and Ransom. They suggest a further conclusion. If credit had been available for the production of foodstuffs and a wider range of staples, then household income would have risen. Had a public cotton marketing board been established and a network of publicly supported rural banks been set up, this would have lent greater stability to the market, furnished better prices for producers and enabled Southern producers to climb out of poverty. But such ideas would quickly be denounced as anarchism or communism by the bankers and merchants. The Populists later reached for collectivist solutions to help the small-holder nevertheless, but were eventually overcome by the very same militant conservatism that defeated Radical Reconstruction, the Internationalists and the Workers' Party.[83]

Before considering the last emancipations in Cuba and Brazil, it will be relevant to relate a Caribbean attempt to enlarge the scope of black freedom, and its violent repression, since these events – taking place in the usually well-ordered British imperial space – were widely reported and remarked upon elsewhere in the Atlantic world.

THE MORANT BAY REBELLION

If the slaves and former slaves sought themselves to shape and interpret every act of emancipation, it is not surprising that the post-emancipation order represented a continuation of this struggle. Since British abolition and emancipation are often awarded a hinge role in the broader history of anti-slavery, it is fascinating to see how the impulse to freedom developed in the post-emancipation British West Indies and in particular Jamaica. Reference has already been made to the decline of plantation agriculture in the large British island, though British Guiana remained a buoyant sugar producer, thanks to its adaptation of a hydraulic cultivation system and to the importation of Asian contract labourers. In Barbados the planter class controlled all the land and was able to oblige many freedmen to work for wages on the plantations. However, in Jamaica the planters, try as they might, found it more difficult to prevent freedpeople from eking out a subsistence on former provision grounds, or to stop the emergence

82   Ibid., pp. 226–7.
83   Robert McMath, *American Populism: a Social History*, 1877–1898, New York 1993.

of a small but vociferous black and coloured middle class, including some peasant farmers and a few teachers, pastors and small merchants. The prospects of the black peasantry remained stunted by the absence of good roads and of the financial infrastructure they required if they were to become effective market suppliers. The large planters, themselves struggling to survive in a highly competitive environment, used their political and economic clout to ensure that roads were built to their estates but not to the areas of peasant production. In the early 1860s there was widespread controversy over the 'tramway swindle', whereby public money and land had been used to solve the transport problems of a few white planters. Mainly because of the property qualifications required of voters, the island's Assembly was responsible to an electorate of only 1,500. However, a handful of black and coloured men were among those elected, and there were conflicts between the Assembly and the governor and his council. At the level of local politics – the vestries – there were more black and coloured representatives, but the right to vote was qualified by property ownership and taxes.

While Jamaica did not yet have the elements of high culture seen in Haiti (e.g. the histories produced by Ardouin and Madiou), it did have a lively, radical press that attacked the island's authorities for corrupt practices and for neglecting the poverty of the great majority. Jamaica's economy was badly hit by the loss of all protection in the British market and the outbreak of the US Civil War. Radical political influences arrived from Haiti and elsewhere in 1848 and after, leading to demands that the colonial authorities support, or at least permit, the formation of collective or cooperative agencies for the marketing of peasant produce. This idea was sometimes advanced under the heading of a need for 'the association of labour', with groups of workers commanding their own means of employment. Among those who discussed such notions was George William Gordon, editor of the *Jamaica Watchman*, and a man with a following among the 'native Baptists', a growing network of black congregations. But the authorities believed that the island's serious problems had their root in the refusal of black Jamaicans to accept regular work at realistic (that is, very modest) wages. The agitation of the radicals was, in the eyes of the colonial authorities, simply a dangerous distraction from this basic fact of political economy.

In October 1865, as the Thirteenth Amendment was being ratified in the US, events in Jamaica gave warning of the strains and storms that could follow emancipation. Black Jamaicans were claiming a share of church governance and squatters appropriating land, on the grounds that 'outside land' – land not actually in cultivation by the planters – should be occupied by anyone willing to work it. This was anathema to planters, who liked to keep large reserves and oblige the rural population to accept waged work by constricting subsistence opportunities. Edward Underhill, the secretary of the British Missionary

Society, sent a memorandum to the Colonial Office which gave a detailed account of the wretched state of the rural population of Jamaica, blaming the planters and colonial authorities. When this document was referred to the governor he unwisely decided to circulate it among the leading men of the colony, including some coloured members of the Assembly. Knowledge of the memorandum soon spread beyond the educated elite and was discussed at tumultuous meetings in many parts of the island. The so-called Underhill movement acquired a momentum and demands of its own, going beyond the memorandum. Matters became more serious when a large crowd carrying a red flag marched on a vestry meeting at Morant Bay, surrounding the school and courthouse at a time when the vestry committee was in session. A hastily summoned militia unit fired on the crowd, killing six. The police station was seized by the rebels and the school and courthouse set alight. The column of rebels displayed some discipline, refraining from damaging any other buildings and following instructions not to attack anyone of their own colour. Eleven people, mainly whites, were killed by the crowd. The authorities brought up further militia forces and appealed to the Maroons to help restore order, which they did. Governor Eyre ordered the summary execution of those involved in the rebellion. The black-led Native Baptists were regarded as the organization behind the rebellion, and many were slaughtered. The village of Stony Gut, particularly suspected, was burnt down. Within a few days the forces of 'law and order' had killed over four hundred.[84]

At judicial proceedings taken against James MacLaren, one of the leaders, the following account of a speech delivered by MacLaren was given by an estate labourer. While this was prosecution evidence, it seems quite plausible and affords a glimpse into the motivations of the rebels:

> 'Why cause me to hold this meeting. Myself was born free, but my mother and father was slave; but now I am still a slave by working from days to days. I cannot get money to feed my family and I am working at Colley estate for 35 chains for 1s, and after five days working I get 2s 6d for my family. Is that able to sustain a house full of family?' And the people said, 'No'. Then he said, 'Well, the best we can do is come together, and send in a petition to the government; and if they will give up the outside land to we, we shall work the cane and cotton and coffee like the white. But the white people say we are lazy and won't work.' When he said that the people said, 'We have no land to work.' He said . . . 'if the outside land was given up to them to work, they should pay the taxes to the Queen . . . they did not want anything from the white people, they would

---

84 There is now an extensive literature on the Morant Bay Rebellion and its sequels. For a summary account highlighting the issues I am addressing here see Sheller, *Democracy After Slavery*, pp. 145–246. See also Gad Heuman, *'The Killing Time': The Morant Bay Rebellion in Jamaica*, London 1994, and Hall, *Civilising Subjects*.

try to make their own living themselves but they would not give them land to work, neither give them any money; how then were they to live?' And when he said that he said to the people without they come together and go down to Morant Bay in a lump, to let the white people to see that there was plenty black in the island, it was no use at all and cry out that they don't mean to pay any more ground rent again; and after twenty-seven years in freedom the outside land was given to them a long time, and the white people kept it to themselves, that is what I heard him say.[85]

When news of the rising and its suppression reached London, there was a demand for an investigation of the role played by Governor Eyre in the whole affair. The governor's critics were to include John Stuart Mill and other prominent supporters of anti-slavery and the Union cause. Eyre was recalled and never received another appointment, but no benefit came to the population of Jamaica. The local Assembly was wound up, a move accepted by most of its members, and Jamaica became a Crown colony. A black peasantry remained, but there was no redistribution of 'outside land' and no permission for cooperative organizations. And yet there is reason to believe that publicly sponsored cooperatives could have filled a vital need and helped to promote a prosperous peasantry (echoing the somewhat similar argument advanced in the previous section concerning marketing boards). In the more optimistic days of 1844, a mutually owned and multi-racial life insurance company had been established, and thrived – it was to outlive colonial rule.[86]

The events in Jamaica can be seen as part of a wider pattern in which the real conquests, and the even more ambitious hopes, of the emancipation period prompt subsequent attempts to extend the freedmen's control of land, time and other resources. In several cases this even led to attempts to build the associated power of the emancipated and their descendants in ways that went beyond 'free labour' ideology. Demands of this sort surfaced in the aftermath of the 'Liberal Revolution' in Haiti, and were articulated in the journal *Bien Public*. In Martinique and Guadeloupe the *schoelchéristes* also appealed in 1848 for government to endow cooperative 'association of labour' schemes. As we have seen, the Morant Bay rising was preceded and accompanied by the demand for such collective structures as a marketing organization and mutually owned agricultural bank. The Reconstruction order in the South Carolina rice country also included 'several large plantations operating under what a newspaper called "a sort of communism" with black laborers forming societies, electing officers, and

---

85 Quoted in Sheller, *Democracy After Slavery*, pp. 198–9.
86 Donald Lindo, *Time Tells Our Story: The History of Jamaica Mutual Life, 1844–1994*, Kingston 1994.

purchasing the estates collectively.'[87] In Cuba and Brazil, anarcho-syndicalist ideas also spread in the 1880s and 1890s and sometimes cross-fertilized with indigenous forms of utopianism and collectivism.

THE LAST EMANCIPATIONS

In 1865 there were still one and a half million slaves in Brazil and a third of a million in the Spanish Caribbean. The ending of slavery in the United States made a powerful impression on planters elsewhere in the hemisphere. The Dutch government introduced emancipation in 1863, freeing about 40,000 slaves. However, it was not until the Confederate surrender, and the passage of the Thirteenth Amendment, that the Spanish and Brazilian authorities concluded that they would have to act. Simply maintaining slavery was to invite unwelcome interference. The US administration had an interest in acquiring a Caribbean coaling station while Brazil, at war with Paraguay, needed Washington's goodwill. The Spanish government established a junta in 1866 to investigate what should be done about slavery, and the Brazilian Council of State began to scrutinize its options in 1868. The fluctuating fortunes of Reconstruction also had an impact on the course of Spanish and Brazilian policy. Eventually free-womb laws were passed in Spain in 1870 – the Moret Law – and in Brazil in 1871 – the Rio Branco Law. This approach to emancipation was far more moderate than the Thirteenth Amendment; it was designed to stave off a great national crisis, not to conclude a civil war. But for all their moderation, these measures meant the eventual winding-up of slavery in lands where it had existed for three-and-a-half centuries. The defeat of the Confederacy persuaded influential planters that the game was up. But they still schemed to extract as much labour as possible from their chattels while they had the power to do so. The stubborn rearguard action had its own logic, and was encouraged by the ebbing of Radical Reconstruction.

In Cuba the fate of slavery and the nature of the island's political institutions became closely intertwined. Cuba was not just the colony of a European monarchy, but one in which the great bulk of the free population was denied any representation. While the large sugar planters and merchants wielded influence in Madrid, the colony itself was subject to arbitrary colonial rule. The first stirrings of separatism in the 1840s saw members of the elite favour annexation to the United States. This social layer had failed to bid for independence in the 1820s, in part because Spanish power in the island was formidable. The annexationists looked to the US to come up with the military and economic arguments that might persuade Madrid to release the island from its grip, together with guarantees for the future of slavery. Annexation did not appeal to the mass of

---

87   Foner, *Nothing But Freedom*, p. 85.

free Cubans, and in the 1860s a more conventional nationalism appeared, led by landowners from the eastern province of Oriente and some former annexationists from the West. From the outset those hoping to build a new nation had to address the question of slavery, aware of how anomalous the institution had become and of their need for support from the people of colour, whether free or enslaved. The Cuban Republic proclaimed in 1868 declared an end to slavery, but in rhetorical terms that deferred implementation. Carlos Manuel de Céspedes, the leader of the revolt, freed his own slaves but also agreed to labour regulations which allowed the new Republican authorities to conscript former slaves for public works. Meanwhile Queen Isabella was overthrown in Madrid and a succession of increasingly Liberal and radical governments appeared, culminating in the Federal Republic of 1873–4. Several of these administrations adopted partial abolitionist measures – including full emancipation for Puerto Rico in 1873 – but none adopted a root-and-branch approach to Cuban slavery. Cuba's *sacarocracia* was still very much a force to be reckoned with, using its great wealth to intimidate Madrid, to suborn the Spanish military in Cuba, and to arm its own plantation militias and urban 'volunteers'.

The Brazilian Empire had long sought to convey the impression that it was a moderate and humane institution, committed to the eventual ending of slavery. The Emperor Pedro II had welcomed the ban on slave imports and urged that the Council of State should consider the situation of the 'servile element' in 1868. But he was cautious, since slave labour remained central to the growth of the coffee plantations, which in turn were critical to the imperial economy. The economic successes which allowed Brazil to bid for leadership in South America, and to present itself as a modern power, came from servile labour.

The delay to emancipation in Cuba and Brazil might be thought to reflect the comparative backwardness of capitalist development in Spain and Brazil. However, the interests centred on the most modern sectors in Spain, Cuba and Brazil – in Catalonia, Las Villas and São Paulo – failed to support the abolitionist cause.[88] Weak Spanish and Brazilian governments were bullied by Anglo-American diplomacy to accept free-womb laws in the late 1860s. Both territories depended on US and European markets, and looked to foreign investments to improve their infrastructure. The advances of Radical Reconstruction from 1868 to 1870 seemed to underline the passing of the old order. Madrid had promulgated the *Ley Moret* of 1870, well aware that the Cuban rebels had already gone further than this and were bidding for US recognition and belligerency

---

88   For Brazil see the essay by Seymour Drescher in Rebecca Scott, Seymour Drescher, Heve Maria Mattos de Castro, George Reid Andrews and Robert M. Levine, *The Abolition of Slavery and the Aftermath of Emancipation in Brazil*, Durham, NC 1988, pp. 23–54, especially p. 33. For Cuba see Rebecca Scott's essay in *Between Slavery and Free Labor: The Spanish-Speaking Caribbean in the Nineteenth Century*, edited by Manuel Moreno Fraginals, Frank Moya Pons and Stanley Engerman, Baltimore 1985, pp. 25–53.

rights. The Brazilian government, left in the invidious position of being the last to support slavery in the New World, followed suit with the Lei Rio Branco in 1871. In the Brazilian case, the experience of a long and difficult war against Paraguay (1865–70) had led to the recruitment of many thousands of slaves to the army and to an uneasy awareness among the Brazilian elite that the empire had been revealed as lumbering and backward in this exhausting military struggle. Though the size of the army was swiftly reduced, it now had a more professional character and was able to enhance the relative autonomy of the Brazilian state vis-à-vis the large slave-owners. Of course, many *fazendeiros* will have hoped to evade or thwart the provisions of the law. The Rio Branco administration, responding to a public clamour for change, also sought to reform the electoral system.

Moderate as it was, the Rio Branco Law was still a big step for Brazil's planter-dominated assembly. In the early 1860s the British ambassador, William Christie, had pressed for recognition that hundreds of thousands of Brazil's slaves had entered the country in clear violation of the Anglo-Brazilian Treaty of 1831, and that consequently they were wrongly held in slavery. Two Liberal senators came up with a plan to identify those who were held despite the Treaty's clear statement that no slave could be brought into the country. Over half a million could be freed if appropriate action was taken, including children born to mothers wrongly held in slavery.[89] These proposals enraged the *fazendeiros*. Given the presence of British warships and the fresh memory of the British role in 1850, there was also alarm. The extent of planter control of the countryside made the attempt to distinguish legal from illegal slaves impractical, besides the fact that it would still leave a slavery problem. However, it did open the way for a more realistic approach. Members of the Council of State saw the need for their own version of the Spanish deliberations that led to the *Ley Moret*. Nabuco de Araújo urged that the slave-holders should be given a guarantee of the integrity of their property, and a clear rejection of the attempt to identify 'illegal' slaves. This would pave the way for a more moderate but comprehensive proceeding – a free-womb law. Many coffee-planters still saw no reason to back this deal, but it was seized on by those looking for a compromise which would phase out slavery very gradually. The measure passed but exposed a regional rift between North-Easterners, who saw no long-term future for slavery, and Paulista coffee-planters who opposed any hasty abandonment of a still vigorous and profitable institution.[90] The standard-bearer of abolitionism was to be Joaquim Nabuco, a North-Easterner, son of Nabuco de Araújo and friend of the emperor.

---

89   Beatriz Mamigonian, 'O tráfico illegal e a inestabilidade da propriedade escrava no século XIX', paper presented to the conference 'Novas fronteiras da escravidão e da liberdade no XIX século', Rio de Janeiro 10–14 August 2009.

90   José Murilo de Carvalho, I, *A construção da ordem*, II, *Teatro de sombras* pp. 120, 285,

While the passage of a free-womb Law, if properly enforced, would eventually doom slavery, free people of colour and slaves still had a keen interest in bringing forward the institution's demise. The delay of emancipation in Cuba and Brazil reflected the continuing strength of their systems of plantation slavery and the political power of the large slave-holders.[91] The years 1850–75 were boom years; while searching for alternatives to slave labour – whether European immigrants or Asian contract labourers – the planters were reluctant to sacrifice a single year of extra labour from their slaves.

The context of the liberation war in Cuba put a premium on abolitionism. Cuban leaders needed to appeal to the free people of colour who made up nearly half the free population. The rebel Assembly adopted a gradual emancipation law which was less than radical – it required the supposed *libertos* to continue working for nominal wages. Male slaves of military age could acquire freedom by enlisting in the ranks of the liberation army; sometimes they could obtain the freedom of their partners too. But many *libertas* (former female slaves) were expected to continue working as domestics or field workers without pay.[92]

The Cuban rebellion was based in the Eastern part of the island, where slaves comprised less than a fifth of the population and where there were many free people of colour. The main sugar-producing regions remained under the at least nominal control of the Spanish authorities, though in practice the large *hacendados* were a law unto themselves. Sugar profits were so large that the *hacendados* could hire their own private militia and suborn the Spanish military.

The Moret Free Womb Law of 1870 had reflected a deire for abolition among some sectors of society in both metropolis and colony, as well as the desire to prevent Britain or the US from recognizing the rebels.[93] A modest abolitionist movement developed, supported by the Federal Republican leader Pi y Margall and making common cause with the Puerto Rican leaders. The representatives from Puerto Rico negotiated an emancipation law in 1873. There were 40,000 slaves in Puerto Rico compared with 340,000 in Cuba. The huge wealth of the Cuban slave-holders enabled them to prevent Madrid from running its supposed colony. The captain general and the military commanders were in the pocket of the *sacarocracia*. The Catalan business lobby also helped to defend both slavery and its own privileged trade with the colonies; this was the most modern and 'market-oriented' sector of the Spanish economy.

In Cuba itself the rebellion eventually won significant support from the people of colour. By the mid-1870s these made up at least a half of the effectives

---

91   Christopher Schmidt-Nowara, 'Empires Against Emancipation: Spain, Brazil and the Abolition of Slavery', *Review* 31/2 (2008), pp. 101–20.

92   Scott, *Slave Emancipation in Cuba*, pp. 48–9.

93   José Piqueras, *La revolución democrática (1868–1874). Cuestión social, colonialismo y grupos de presión*, Madrid 1992, pp. 315–52.

of the Cuban army. But throughout the fighting was largely confined to the eastern part of the island. In the west and centre, where most slaves were concentrated, the militarization of the plantations had ensured a successful defence of slavery. The Cuban Republic's two most effective generals were Máximo Gómez, born in Santo Domingo, and Antonio Maceo, a man of colour. Maceo advocated taking the war to the west, but failed to gain sufficient backing.

The Ten Years' War was brought to an end by the Pact of Zanjón in 1878. Spain's restored monarchy sent one of the country's most able generals, Arsenio Martínez Campos, to end a war that was exhausting both parties. He was given authority to seek a deal as well as make military dispositions. Martínez Campos offered the Cubans civil liberties and an elected assembly. The rebel generals could either retire to an honourable exile or, if willing to accept the new order, would be permitted to live peacefully in Cuba itself. Martínez Campos also realized that to persuade the rebels to stop fighting he would have to recognize the liberty of all slaves who had fought with the rebels or been freed by them. But since many saw Zanjón as simply a truce, this concession implied that slavery would have to be wound up – if not, it was an invitation for all slaves to desert their plantations at the first sign of a new insurgency. Antonio Maceo, the 'titan of bronze', rejected the peace because it did not free the slaves. The vulnerability of the truce was underscored when a new rebellion broke out in 1879, the *Guerra Chiquita*. There were reports of slaves deserting their plantations to join this rebellion. Though the military threat was soon contained, Martínez Campos exploited the sense of danger to press forward his emancipation plan.[94]

Martínez Campos had explained to the rebels that ending slavery exceeded his brief and that this would require legislation in the Madrid Cortes. In 1879 he was recalled to become prime minister. His government introduced emancipation in 1880.[95] The *hacendados* had been closely consulted over the provisions of the law, and neither Cuban nor Spanish abolitionism had much force at the time. The law offered the planters a further eight years of labour from their former slaves, under an apprenticeship scheme known as the *patronato*. The regulations of the *patronato* supposedly offered some limitations on the traditional powers of the slave-holder. Apprentices were to receive nominal wages and were not to be whipped (though until 1883 it was still permitted to subject

94   Richard Gott, *Cuba: A New History*, London 2004, pp. 82–3; Ada Ferrer, 'Social Aspects of Cuban Nationalism: Race, Slavery and the Guerra Chiquita, 1879–1880', *Cuban Studies* 21(1991).

95   The diplomatic pressures on Spain, the tenacious resistance of the Cuban slave-owners and the weakness or distraction of the Spanish and Cuban abolitionists are recounted in Arthur Corwin, *Spain and the Abolition of Slavery in Cuba*, Austin 1967. For the impact of the war see Scott, *Slave Emancipation in Cuba*, pp. 45–62, and for the overall context Christopher Schmidt-Nowara, *Empire and Anti-Slavery* and Piqueras, *La revolución democrática*. See also 'Cuba: Centenario de la abolición de la esclavitud (1886–1926)', *Anales del Caribe* 6 (1986).

them to the stocks or irons). A quasi-judicial body, the *Junta de Patronato*, was established to enforce these regulations. The former slaves, their relatives and well-wishers sought to use provisions of the legislation to end their bondage as rapidly as possible: 13,000 slaves paid their owners for immediate freedom. Between 1881 and 1886, when the *patronato* was prematurely wound up, a total of 113,900 *patrocinados* were freed by direct arrangement with their owners. The *Juntas* received complaints from *patrocinados* urging that they should be freed on grounds of cruel treatment, or non-payment of the nominal wages due to them, or because they were of an age at which it was no longer legal to hold them in slavery under the Ley Moret. Those who achieved freedom by mutual accord probably had their position strengthened by the existence of the *Juntas*, even though they did not appear before them. By 1886, when the *patronato* was brought to a premature end, there were only 25,000 *patrocinados* left.[96]

In Cuba in the 1880s, as in the British West Indies in the 1830s, a post-slavery bondage without the whip, but relying on a tradition of subjection, proved to be unsustainable – largely because of the pressure of the former slaves and their well-wishers.[97] The new colonial order sought to appeal to free people of colour by banning discrimination on the grounds of skin colour from all public places.[98] Antonio Maceo and other coloured commanders had some-times encountered rebuffs at the hands of white rebels, but the continuing reality of Spanish colonial oppression meant that white Cubans who wished to end Spanish rule needed the full support of their mulatto and black compatri-ots. The Cuban nationalism rekindled in the 1880s and 1890s appealed to black, brown and white.

Cuban tobacco workers in Florida and New Jersey, as well as those in the island, became strong supporters of the Cuban Revolutionary Party. The anar-chists were influential among the tobacco workers but were willing to commit to a struggle against the Spanish state,[99] which launched the liberation war in 1895. The Cuban Revolutionary Party was founded on the 'raceless' principle or 'myth' that race was of no importance within republican ranks. On the positive side this meant that men of colour could play leading roles, but coloured commanders still had to be careful to avoid appearing to favour coloured subor-dinates or to be preoccupied by issues specific to people of colour.[100] With black or coloured soldiers comprising over half of the soldiers of the Liberation Army,

96   Scott, *Slave Emancipation in Cuba*, pp. 148, 172–200, 279–93.

97   Scott, *Slave Emancipation in Cuba*. See also María del Carmen Barcia, *Burguesía esclavista y abolición*, Havana 1987, and Francisco de Solano, ed., *Esclavitud y derechos humanos*, Madrid 1986.

98   José A. Piqueras, 'Sociedad civil, política y dominio colonial en Cuba (1878–1895)', *Studia Historica. Historia Contemporánea* 15: (1997), pp. 95–114, 95.

99   Joan Casanova, *Bread or Bullets! Urban Labor and Spanish Colonialism in Cuba, 1850–1898*, Pittsburgh 1998; Gerald Payo, 'With All For the Good of All': *The Emergence of Popular Nationalism in the Cuban Communities in the United States, 1848–98*, Durham, NC, 1989.

100   Ada Ferrer, *Insurgent Cuba: Race, Nation and Revolution, 1868–98*, Chapel Hill 1999.

it is not so surprising that 40 per cent of the officers, and 22 of 140 generals, were also mulatto or black in 1898. José Martí, the leader of the Cuban Revolutionary Party, was not from an elite background (his father was a minor Spanish official) and made his living as a writer and journalist. The poem he wrote that supplies the words of the famous song 'Guantanamera' expressed a universalist ambition to improve the lot of the poor and downtrodden. The Cuban cause received vital support from the cigar workers of Florida. The nationalist movement had coloured leaders like General Antonio Maceo and the writer Juan Gualberto Gómez. The movement's multiracial leadership contrasts with the advances being made at the time by ultra-racism in the US South. This partly reflects a looser and less polarized Hispanic and Catholic approach to race, but also the pressures of a different political situation, where there was a premium on achieving the widest national unity, and where radical social ideas associated with anarchism, syndicalism and socialism had already made great inroads.[101]

The belated emancipation in Brazil is to be explained by both the long history of slavery in the country and the weakness of social forces not implicated in the slave economy.[102] The eventual triumph of emancipation was pressed by a coalition which included a dramatic mobilization of free blacks and rebellious slaves, together with new social forces in the cities, both North and South, with little stake in what had previously been a pervasive institution. The ending of the Atlantic slave trade in the early 1850s led to an increasing concentration of slave ownership in the hands of the richer planters in the new coffee regions of Western São Paulo. Urban slavery was in decline. Ricardo Salles sees a maturing of the social antagonisms generated by slavery in the epoch after 1865, as slaves became more concentrated in certain regions and occupations, the slave community became creolized and more homogeneous, the proportion of women in the slave population rose, and international developments isolated the Brazilian slave-holder.[103] As slaves were sold to the plantations, the 'increasing complexity of urban economic activities and the formation of a new urban working class' created a milieu favourable to abolitionist appeals.[104]

When the proportion of slaves in the total population in a state dropped below 10 or even 5 per cent, then the institution became vulnerable to abolitionist activism. The maritime trade from Fortaleza and other northern ports to

---

101   Jorge Ibarra Cuesta, *Ideología mambisa*, Havana 1968.

102   Emilia Viotti da Costa, *The Brazilian Empire*, Chicago 1985, pp. 125–71, and the same author's contribution to the *Cambridge History of Latin America* available in *Brazil: Empire and Republic*, edited by Leslie Bethell, Cambridge 1989, pp. 161–215, especially 169–70, 198–203.

103   Ricardo Salles, *E o vale era o escravo, Vassouras, século XIX. Senhores e escravos no coração do Império*, Rio de Janeiro 2008, p. 68.

104   Ricardo Salles, 'Abolição no Brasil', paper presented to the conference 'Novas fronteiras da escravidão e da liberdade no XIX século', Rio de Janeiro 10–14 August 2009.

Santos also became the target of agitation, with mulatto *jangadeiros* (lighter-men) refusing to handle human cargo. This success led to campaigns in Ceará, Goiás and Paraná in the early and mid-1880s which targeted domestic slaves. The owner's house would be surrounded by abolitionists who would then press him to manumit his slaves. The tactic was successful, leading to the former slave receiving a very modest wage and being able, if so inclined, to change employer. This type of emancipation allowed for a paternalist residue and certainly still left the *Paulista* bastions of Brazilian slavery intact.[105]

The workings of imperial institutions failed to reflect the enormous wealth of the *Paulista* coffee-planters. Scores basked in the title of baron, but *Paulista* planters were not well represented in the ministries that were formed in the 1870s and 1880s. The Rio Branco free-womb law had been imposed by Northern and North-Eastern votes against the *Paulista* majority. Joaquim Nabuco, the favoured imperial counsellor, was also, as noted above, a North-Easterner. His concern with the empire's good name abroad seemed to imply a sacrifice of tangible benefits from a prolongation of the tied labour of the slaves and *padronados*. The imperial authorities sought to foster immigration as an alternative labour supply, but the coffee barons resented being implicitly cast as greedy tyrants in abolitionist oratory.

According to Boris Fausto, 'The end of the [slave] trade liberated capital which gave rise to intense business activity and speculation. Banks, industries and steam-ship companies arose.'[106] The surge of the Brazilian economy in 1850–70 received much impetus from coffee, but led to a more diversified pattern outside the plantation zone. The 1870s were marked by the country's first labour struggles, and the 1880s opened with labour riots which toppled a government. Throughout the decade there was to be some overlap between abolitionist agitation and labour organization. In some cases abolitionist leaders, like Lopes Trovão, directly sought working-class support. The port of Santos was both a crucible of working-class organization and a place of refuge for escaped slaves. Anarcho-syndicalist currents, in Brazil as in Cuba, were the source of ideas which lumped together and vilified every type of exploiter. In São Paulo the Italian Workers Centre came out in support of abolition, while railway workers sometimes gave assistance to slaves fleeing their masters. Many of the slaves on the *Paulista* plantations had been brought there from Rio de Janeiro and the North-East. They left behind them family ties and claims over subsistence plots (*rocas*). Work regimes were invariably more intense and concessions to the slaves more limited in the newly developing regions. Conditions in the Paulista plantations were often more rigorous, with less land available for subsistence and, quite probably, longer working hours. This background may help to explain why the flight of slaves assumed such large proportions.

---

105   Robert Conrad, *Destruction of Brazilian Slavery*, Chapter 11.
106   Fausto, *A Concise History of Brazil*, p. 112.

It might seem that by the mid-1880s the Brazilian slave-holders and their representatives should have seen the writing on the wall, and been thoroughly prepared for emancipation. That this was not the case was made clear when the Dantas government met defeat in 1885. It proposed to free slaves once they reached the age of sixty. Given that Brazilian governments were rarely blocked on major legislation, this modest measure should have passed without difficulty. But the government suffered a humiliating rebuff. After two elections a Conservative administration eventually managed to pass a compromise bill which allowed slave-owners to keep their over-sixty slaves for an extra three years.[107] But by this time the disarray in the slave-holding centres and the mobilization of the abolitionists were such that parliamentary compromises were no longer relevant. Slaves were leaving the plantations, and soldiers refusing to act as slave-catchers.

The resistance of the slaves itself radicalized the abolitionists. Radical abolitionists like the *Caifazes* movement of Antonio Bento lent practical assistance to the fleeing slaves, though only after the phenomenon of slave flight was well established. Antonio Bento would later insist that the activist final phase of Brazilian anti-slavery was entirely the work of the poor: 'The republican papers discussed every question but abolition. The rich and powerful fled from any contact with the abolitionists. The cause ripened, the propaganda took shape, among the little people (*povo miúdo* or *menu peuple*) . . . Abolition was made by the poor with the greatest sacrifice you can imagine.'[108] Disappointed by the later behaviour of some middle-class abolitionists, Bento may have exaggerated this point, but certainly the thousands of activists who helped the plantation slaves to desert and find a haven were not the staid bourgeois who had so often been the public face of abolitionism.

With the emperor on a trip to Europe and the slave order visibly crumbling, Princess Regent Isabel supported a new administration committed to immediately ending slavery, without compensation. The *Lei Aurea* ('golden law') was publicly approved by the Princess Regent on 13 May 1888. Isabel made no secret of her sympathy for the cause. While the slave order was in grave difficulties the *Lei Aurea* headed off any danger of a general insurrection. It consisted of a single sentence and made no special provision for the former slaves. The coffee-planters found it much easier to attract immigrant workers with slavery ended.

In finally approving abolition the empire, which had been the target of anti-slavery pressures since its inception, came into line with the broad trend of modern developments. The Brazilian slave-owners had not been able to rally non-slave-holders to defend the institution, but many contrived to be passive or to sit on the fence. The Republicans – a party drawing for support on the most

107   Graham, *Patronage and Politics in Nineteenth-Century Brazil*, pp. 173–5.
108   *A Redempção*, 22 August 1897.

modern sections of the Brazilian elite and middle classes – avoided taking any stance on the *Lei Aurea*, although Liberals and Conservatives had overwhelmingly supported it. Imperial advisers who favoured emancipation hoped that it would consolidate the monarchy, but within eighteen months the empire had been overthrown. The ending of Brazilian slavery was scarcely impetuous but its air of improvisation, and its yielding in the face of popular tumult, had not impressed the business and military establishments. The overthrow of November 1889 was at bottom a military coup. Its leader, Marshal Deodoro, turned to the Republicans and to the Positivist thinker Benjamin Constant Botelho de Magalhães to supply an ideology for the new order. The project of modernizing the state apparently required, among other things, a doubling of the military budget.

The approach to abolitionism and emancipation which minimizes or ignores the role of free blacks and slaves usually concentrates on the British and North American cases. Such an approach is wrong in these cases, but would be even more perverse for Saint-Domingue/Haiti at the opening of the emancipationist cycle, and for Cuba or Brazil at its close. In the Anglo-American cases mainstream bourgeois abolitionism played a critical role, but only because of its insertion in exceptional political crises and by dint of its willingness to press through a new historic compromise that took account, albeit momentarily, of social forces hitherto excluded from political life. This was revolutionary conservatism, but undeniably a species of progress, for others besides the re-composed ruling groups.

In studies of anti-slavery, the British abolition of its Atlantic slave trade in 1808 and the eventual suppression of West Indian slavery in the 1830s are often seen as exemplary and normative. The fact that emancipation itself was achieved almost without bloodshed made an impression on contemporary opinion, and helped to recommend the cause wherever slavery survived. Plantation wealth was considerably less than 5 per cent of all British wealth at the time of slave-trade abolition, and much less subsequently. Slave-owners could be generously compensated for their loss of human property. In the United States, Cuba and Brazil – with slave property greatly more valuable – the state was unable to offer compensation. While the bloodshed of the Haitian Revolution has been widely deplored, and this has perhaps contributed to neglect of its true importance, the equally bloody road to emancipation in the United States – and the very disappointing restoration of a racially repressive order – is less often held to have dimmed the lustre of what had been achieved by Lincoln and the Republicans. The pressures of revolution and war in Spain and the Spanish Caribbean led the belligerents both to declare abolitionist ideals and to defer their implementation. Eventually the experience of war showed the Cuban Republic to be the more convincing vehicle for emancipation in the eyes of Cuban slaves and former slaves. Brazil achieved an emancipation that was largely peaceful, notwithstanding the continuing prominence of planters in the social order, but the authorities were under great pressure when they at last endorsed emancipation. In contrast to British and US abolitionism, and reflecting the strength of patriarchal values, women – with one notable exception, the Princess Regent – played no public role in Brazilian abolition, though their influence was often present in the private pressure for manumission.

The belated and largely peaceful process of emancipation in Cuba and Brazil in the 1880s made it less of a watershed than was emancipation and Reconstruction in the United States. There was no 'reconstruction' in Cuba and Brazil, and hence no backlash against it. The overthrow of the Brazilian Empire in 1889 and the outbreak of a new struggle for Cuban independence in 1895 somehow overshadowed the ending of slavery. The Brazilian Republic blazoned the Positivist motto 'Order and Progress' on the country's flag. Slavery was declared obsolete, but the disorderliness of the struggle for emancipation and Princess Isabel's impulsiveness in 1888 were deemed unfortunate and unbecoming. The Positivists had a small niche in which they honoured Toussaint Louverture, but the Republic's aim was to build a modern and more European nation with the aid of European immigration. Measures were enacted to encourage former slaves to become plantation workers, but planters preferred other sources of labour in the shape of immigrants.

Indeed the failure of successive imperial governments to attract European immigration as an alternative to slavery alienated the *Paulista* planters. The policy required expensive subsidies if it was to be successful, and the imperial treasuries lacked the needed resources. Few European migrants would come to Brazil unless their fare was paid. And if they were expected to work in the coffee groves, then provision had to be made for housing as well. The government of São Paulo stepped in to fill the gap. In 1888 São Paulo paid for the passage of over 80,000 immigrants, and in the next two decades 1.5 million European migrants were to follow. While the immigrants were encouraged to settle in the coffee districts, they were not obliged to sign long-term contracts. The planters believed that, given a steady and large influx of new workers, competitive pressures would prevent an escalation of wages. The motives of the Brazilian elite were not simply economic. The leaders of Brazilian society saw the 'whitening' of the country's population as an important goal in its own right.[109]

Cuban planters for their part were more willing to engage former slaves, but also looked to immigrants and to seasonal labourers to supply an extra labour force. Seasonal labourers from other Caribbean islands (Jamaica and Haiti) were themselves often descendants of slaves. While the coloured, especially black, people of Cuba and Brazil were to experience discrimination and

---

109   George Reid Andrew, 'Black and White Workers', in Scott et al., *The Abolition of Slavery and the Aftermath of Emancipation in Brazil*, pp. 85–118.

poverty, they did not suffer the extremities of racial segregation practised in the US South.[110]

In ending slavery, both Spanish and Brazilian authorities were displaying a wish to be modern. The Age of Empire had arrived, and political elites were anxious to shed unwanted baggage, to show that they could take care of themselves and to give no springboard to potential predators. Motivated by such ideas, the overthrow of the Brazilian Empire and the restoration of the Spanish monarchy had similar motives, summed up in the Positivist watchword: 'Order and Progress'.

My sketches of emancipation have identified the agency of Afro-American abolitionists and 'contrabands', the contribution of black soldiers in the US, Cuba and Brazil, and the readiness of the mass of slaves to exploit any weakness or division within the ranks of their oppressors. But were the slaveholders doomed to defeat simply because they were slaveholders? Was slavery brought down by its necessary consequences, or mainly by contingent error, poor judgment and bad luck? The planters of three major American territories had successfully navigated the Age of Revolution. But by the 1850s some planters grew to doubt the compromises they had made – the Southern pact with Northerners, the Cuban planters' pact with Spain and the Brazilian planters' pact with an imperial monarchy. In the new age of nationalism and 'progress', arrangements that had once served planter interests now rendered them vulnerable.

The defeat of the Confederacy was a crippling blow to the new American slavery. Was it the result of deep-laid structural flaws? I believe that it was. The slave regime provoked the enmity of the slaves themselves and of large numbers of non-slaveholding free persons. The slaveholders were rich and powerful yet the institutions they had promoted began to fail them after about 1850. The defeat of secession sealed the fate of New World slavery.

If the Confederate leadership had been possessed of greater consistency, skill and luck might it have imposed its defensive goal – Northern acquiescence in Southern independence. As late as the summer of 1864 the possibility that McClellan might win the presidency held the danger of a peace that would have condoned secession and left many enslaved. But inherent and characteristic features of the slave order – great inequality, the slaveholders' insistence on special protections and exemptions, and black enmity – sapped the Confederacy. The slaveholders resisted direct taxation and, to begin with, secured exemption from the draft for one adult male on estates with more than twenty slaves. The

---

110 The next (concluding) chapter has more on the post-emancipation social order, but proper coverage of this large topic goes beyond the scope of this book. However, see Frederick Cooper, Thomas Holt and Rebecca Scott, *Beyond Slavery: Explorations of Race, Labor and Citizenship in Post-Emancipation Societies*, Chapel Hill 2000, and Mary Turner, ed., *From Chattel Slaves to Wage Slaves: The Dynamics of Labour Bargaining in the Americas*, London 1995.

planters' hostility to taxation denied the Confederacy the revenue it needed to avoid debauching its currency. Just as damaging was the planters' insistence on continuing to cultivate and stockpile cotton for future sale when their fellow citizens were suffering privation and famine. Paul Escott stresses the failures of Confederate nationalism, as I have done above, and shows how Confederate morale was eventually broken by the inequality of sacrifice – 'Rich Man's War, Poor Man's Fight' – and by financial chaos, starvation, deteriorating security and slave desertions.[111] The plummeting value of the currency meant that planters and farmers had no incentive to produce food for sale. Transportation failures compounded the problem. The measures taken by the Union to mobilize its wealth were sub-optimal but greatly superior to those taken by the Confederate authorities. Whereas inflation ran at 80 per cent in the North in the years 1861–65 it reached 8,000 per cent in the Confederacy.[112]

Surprisingly enough, the South's industrial inferiority did not much weaken the logistics of the Confederate armies because the Richmond government and its Ordinance department proved highly effective at creating state-run war industries and keeping the rebel armies supplied with war materiel.[113] But as the war dragged on the failure of the Confederate economy to meet everyday needs demoralized the mass of poorer citizens, especially non-slaveholders, women, and city dwellers. The Confederate authorities belatedly sought to arm some blacks, as we know. They might have done better to allow the slaves to produce and sell – on their own account – badly needed foodstuffs. However, to have done this on any scale would have destroyed slavery almost as surely as would have large-scale arming of the slaves.

In the end the Confederacy collapsed because of defeats on the field of battle. Many of the poorer, slave-less whites went AWOL while leading planters could see that continuing resistance would provoke the Union forces to radicalize further. The Confederate military leadership negotiated an honourable surrender – retaining their side-arms and horses – rather than opt for a guerrilla resistance, which would have exposed the planters' homes and estates to reprisals. By making peace the ex-rebels probably anticipated that there would be other ways to defend or restore white domination and their special position.

---

111   Paul Escott, *After Secession: Jefferson Davis and the Failure of Confederate Nationalism*, Baton Rouge 1978, pp. 137–8. See also Mary DeCredico, 'The Confederate Home Front', in Ford, *A Companion to the Civil War and Reconstruction*, pp. 258–76 and David Williams, *Rich Man's War*, Athens GA 1998, pp. 98–103.

112   James Roark, 'Behind the Lines: Confederate Economy and Society', in McPherson and Cooper, *Writing the Civil War*, pp. 201–7, and James McPherson, *Battle Cry of Freedom: The Civil War Era*, New York 1988, pp. 442–50. The Union's effective financial expedients starkly contrast with Confederate failures while falling short of a modern or permanent public finance system, a problem very much compounded by postwar retreats and defeats. See Steven R. Weisman, *The Great Tax Wars*, New York 2003.

113   Raimondo Luraghi, *The Rise and Fall of the Plantation South*, New York 1978.

PATTERNS OF EMANCIPATION

Even when slave-holders had been defeated, and slavery declared at an end, its customs were tenacious. The ending of slavery in the United States, and the extension of formal citizenship to the freedmen, required three different Constitutional Amendments – the Thirteenth, Fourteenth and Fifteenth. Even then, the supposed beneficiaries were still not equal or free, testifying to the entrenchment of racial domination in social habits. As we have seen, the citizenship conferred on freedmen at the height of Radical Reconstruction was soon emptied of real content by the mobilization of white supremacist 'Redeemers', and the construction of Jim Crow. Sadly, other emancipations also proved difficult to enforce and sustain. France had to abolish slavery twice over, and the British parliament had to return to the topic when it ended 'apprenticeship' in 1838. Men of colour had subsequently been elected to Jamaica's Assembly, but following the 'Governor Eyre controversy' in the 1860s, the island's Assembly was suspended.[114] But the regression in the United States was to be more extensive and dramatic than anything seen elsewhere – essentially because the 'moral unity' of the white majority had not been broken.

The explicit, legal codification of white supremacy in the US South, which reflects the heritage of a slave society, contrasts with the absence of a formal racial order in Brazil and Cuba. While there was great racial inequality in these societies, they still maintained a civic ideal that claimed to be race-less, or even to embody 'racial democracy'. In a comparative study of the United States, Brazil and South Africa, Anthony Marx writes: 'Abolition and/or state consolidation in South Africa and the United States emerged out of the bloodiest conflicts in the history of these countries, while Brazil experienced nothing remotely comparable to the Boer War or [US] Civil War. It was the more liberal abolitionist British and Northerners who won, yet later policies towards blacks were closer to those advocated by the defeated Afrikaners and Southerners . . . because those defeated whites earned a reputation in the prior conflict as being capable of violent disruption.'[115] In the case of Cuba no such threat existed, because the colonial power – which had put up a last-ditch defence of slavery – had been forced to concede the loss of the island. The fierce racism of white US Southerners and South Africans itself reflected fear of blacks who had also displayed military potential and who had to be intimidated if they were to continue as a subject labour force. As will be seen in the next chapters, matters stood differently in Brazil and Cuba.

---

114   Hall, *Civilising Subjects*, p. 422.
115   Anthony Marx, *Making Race and Nation: A Comparison of South Africa, the United States and Brazil*, Cambridge 1998, pp. 11–12.

Mimi Sheller has suggested a schematic representation of nineteenth-century slave emancipation in the Americas which sharply distinguishes between the different paths it followed.

TABLE 14.1. TYPES OF ABOLITION OF SLAVERY

	State-Overturning	State-Contained
War-driven/immediate	Haiti	United States
Policy-driven/gradual	Cuba	Jamaica

SOURCE: Mimi Sheller, *Democracy After Slavery*, London 2000, p. 37.

This schema captures some contrasting aspects of emancipation while missing some common or overlapping features. If war is the continuation of policy by other means, then the distinction offered by the left-hand column is too neat. Likewise the 'state-contained' feature defining the right-hand column should be seen as the containment of 'state-overturning' challenges. The Brazilian emancipation – state-containing at one moment but triggering state-overturning at another – is difficult to capture using these categories. However, since I have myself often stressed certain common features marking the structural break of emancipation, this pattern of contrasts serves as an interesting foil. In the next chapter I will consider another of Sheller's typologies which tries to render the post-emancipation cycle – both the impetus to extend its democratic content, and its frustration or defeat.

CHAPTER FOURTEEN

Conclusion:
The Spiral Path

The slave plantations of the New World emerged, I have argued, as a by-product of European capitalism and colonialism. The growth of capitalism in north-western Europe stimulated the demand for exotic luxuries, and the New World slave plantations met the demand. Confronted with a labour shortage, planters resorted to buying captive Africans. The resulting systems of slave subjection reflected disparate proto-racist notions which became strongly focused and fixed as the systems grew stronger. In the subsequent 150 years the slave trade and slave plantations directly or indirectly furnished the early industrial entrepreneurs with credit, raw materials and markets. Just as the rise of slavery was ancillary to such momentous transformations, so, in a 'long century' of abolition, the great acts of emancipation also helped to give a new character and direction to the nineteenth-century surge of nation-making that emerged from the clash between Atlantic oligarchies, often slave-owning, and popular-democratic movements. The slave-holders occupied positions of great power and influence yet slave rebels and abolitionists, both coloured and white, eventually had the better of them, partly because new elites saw slavery an ideological liability and impediment. Hard-won gains for social equality often proved precarious. The power of the great slave-holders was broken, but almost everywhere it was replaced by the rule of landowners, merchants and banks.

Slavery would never return, but post-emancipation societies remained racially stratified and oppressive. The emancipatory impulse and process had worked through the contradictions of capitalism and modernization, Great Power rivalry and imperialism. But while the age of capital and empire was at its apex, abolition had signalled the presence of potential challenges and checks.

In the Introduction I cited Karl Polanyi's thesis that headlong market expansion periodically destroys its own conditions of existence and provokes a counter-movement of social protection.[1] The Atlantic boom in slaves and slave produce was, in its own way, a surge of market expansion, further encouraged by the retreat of mercantilism. This eventually stimulated a variety of efforts to contain the trade in human beings and to embed the plantation economy in social arrangements which were less reliant on physical coercion, and more reliant on economic incentives and imperatives – on the one hand bans on the

---

1 Karl Polanyi, *The Great Transformation*, London, 1944

Atlantic slave trade and acts of slave emancipation, and, on the other, acts of empire and missionary colonialism. In the Americas slavery and the slave trade were suppressed, but other social controls were elaborated and new supplies of constrained labour organized. The post-emancipation epoch was an Age of Empire: in the European colonial empires new varieties of colonial forced labour were invented, a trade in regulated contract labour was permitted, and even slavery itself survived.

EMANCIPATION, INNOVATION AND EMPIRE

Impulses to freedom and equality, regulation and protection, were intertwined in complex ways. Those impulses were embodied in declarations of rights that often soared above a reality that denied them. Great acts of resistance and rebellion were usually required where it was a question of overturning major slave systems. New universal principles helped to guide and stabilize the work of emancipation, but could not guarantee success. Emancipation in Saint-Domingue/Haiti and the US South came only at the price of much bloodshed. These were slave regimes at the height of their power and prosperity. The slave-holders and those they were able to manipulate put up a tenacious resistance. Emancipation in the British West Indies in 1831–8, the French Antilles in 1848, in Cuba in 1878–86 and Brazil in 1887–8 was hastened by the direct action of tens of thousands of slaves and free people of colour who were able to throw off their chains without great bloodshed, because the slave-holders were already weakened and demoralized – and ready to try alternative types of labour mobilization.

The emancipation process was instigated and nourished by prior acts of resistance, by exposés of cruelty and exploitation, and by the enunciation of new rights and principles. Highlights would include the late medieval and early modern 'free air' doctrine, the works of Bartolomé de las Casas and Inca Garcilaso de la Vega, the Germantown resolution of 1688, the Somersett judgment of 1772, the American Declaration of Independence, African American claims for 'unalienable rights', the pamphlets and speeches of the American and British abolitionists, the anti-slavery declarations of Sonthonax and Toussaint Louverture, the French Revolutionary Convention's decree of 16 Pluviôse An II, the founding documents of the Haitian Republic, Bolívar's speech at Cúcuta, David Walker's *Appeal*, the appearance of the *Liberator*, the doctrine of natural equality and freedom preached by Sam Sharpe, a black deacon, in Jamaica in 1831, the *History of Mary Prince*, Frederick Douglass's *Narrative*, the resolutions of the African American conventions, the 'free labour' doctrine, Lincoln's Gettysburg Address and Second Inaugural, the International Working Men's Address to Lincoln, the 1864 'Declaration of Rights and Wrongs' issued by the black convention in Syracuse, the Thirteenth, Fourteenth and Fifteenth

Amendments to the US Constitution, the equal 'public rights' asserted by the Louisiana state convention in 1868, the Cuban Republic's call to arms and emancipation declaration, the editorials of *A Redemção,* the Brazilian emancipation proclamation and the lyrics of 'Guantanamera'. Anti-slavery was articulated together with, and supported by, new conceptions of labour and association, popular sovereignty and national citizenship.

Just as there was pressure from below, so there were also forms of slave rebellion or resistance that sought to promote and shape a post-slavery order. When self-liberated blacks at Trois Rivières in Guadeloupe answered 'Amis et citoyens' when challenged by the guard, or when blacks in Saint-Domingue adopted the tricolour, they were sending such a signal (Chapter 8). So were the defenders of Crête à Pierrot in 1802, whose singing of French Revolutionary anthems demoralized the besiegers, and prompted one of them to ask himself: 'Are our barbaric enemies in the right? Are we really the only soldiers of the Republic? Have we become servile political instruments?'[2] Likewise the armed demonstrators in Barbados in 1816 or British Guiana in 1823 (discussed in Chapter 11). Likewise the 'contrabands' who joined the Union Army in 1861–2, or the fugitives who joined the Cuban liberation army (Chapter 13). These rebels, spotting the possibility of emancipation, pursued it rather than waiting for the opportunity to wreak personal revenge on a hated overseer or planter. Appealing to potential allies, and building the new, was the best way to destroy the old. It could even be thought of as an impulse to 'hegemony from below', though, sadly, as we will see, the former slaves were rarely in a position to retain leadership.

Abolitionism contributed to a discourse of freedom which colonialists and imperialists sought to appropriate. In the short run the appropriation might be successful in winning support at home for imperial projects, but in the longer run the practice of alien rule and the lust for commodities led to colonial pillage and oppression, belying the lofty objectives of the imperial mission. The record of 'abolition' and the 'civilizing mission' in Africa was particularly grim. The French, the Germans, the British, and King Leopold of the Belgians all invoked the sacred cause of slave-trade suppression when they carved up Africa at the Berlin Conference of 1884–5.

The British and US governments diplomatically endorsed Leopold's claims to the Congo, mainly because they did not want to see such a huge and valuable territory acquired by Germany or France. Leopold established the Congo Free State as a personal domain rather than as a Belgian colony, making it, as Jean Stengers and Jan Vansina have observed, a 'colony without a metropolis'.[3]

---

2   Pamphile de Lacroix, *Mémoires*, vol. 2, p. 164, quoted in Ott, *Haitian Revolution,*, p. 257.

3   Jean Stengers and Jan Vansina, 'King Leopold's Congo 1886–1908', in J. D. Fage and R. Oliver, eds, *The Cambridge History of Africa*, vol. 6, *1870 to 1905*, Cambridge 1985, pp. 315–58.

Leopold's agents declared that all uncultivated land – and the rubber and ivory that it yielded – belonged to the state. The Leopoldian state issued no currency, but its military arm – the *force publique*, black soldiers led by European officers – exacted food and labour from African villages. The state also licensed two companies – the Anversoise and the ABIR – to organize their own militias and levy tribute labour or 'taxes in kind' (foodstuffs, ivory or rubber) from the native villages of the territories allotted to them. By 1900 there were several hundred posts directly administering a million Africans, and having a devastating impact on the many millions they did not directly rule. Villagers fleeing the predatory militias disrupted the delicate balance of the vast river basin. Rail lines and steamers opened up the interior and broke the isolation of the inland peoples. The extraction companies dealt out grim punishment – such as ear-lopping – to those who failed to bring in their quota of rubber or ivory. Great loss of life resulted from the fact that the peoples of the interior had no immunity to many of the diseases which the colonists brought with them (eg. smallpox and sleeping sickness).

The ravages of the militias and *force publique* in the Congo during the 1890s and early 1900s, in the aftermath of the great emancipations of the Americas, resembled the horrendous impact of the Spanish conquistadors in the Americas in the early sixteenth century. The lust for commodities and the resort to forced labour was in both cases even more destructive than chattel slavery, because the workers had no value and were likely to die quite soon of disease or overwork. It is estimated that perhaps 5 to 10 million Africans lost their lives in the Congo Free State. The governments in London and Washington had set up this disaster, yet averted their gaze from the consequences until a neo-abolitionist movement led by Roger Casement exposed Leopold's rapacity and mounted an international campaign against him. The periodic mutinies of the *force publique* also sowed doubts. Eventually the Belgian government was persuaded to take over the Congo as a colony and to establish a more orderly and conventional regime of super-exploitation.[4] Neo-abolitionism sometimes compared Leopold's rule unfavourably with that of the leading colonial powers, and did not usually indict colonialism as such.

The European colonial empires all resorted to types of forced labour, but they also devised tax systems that encouraged Africans to work for wages or to practise commercial farming. The huge dimensions of the Atlantic slave trade had intensified Africa's indigenous slave-trading and slave-raiding complex, lending it a new scale and importance. After the extension of colonial rule in the 1870s and 1880s, the British and French themselves found great difficulty in suppressing slavery and the slave trade. Colonial administrators and commercial entrepreneurs

---

4 Adam Hochschild, *King Leopold's Ghost*, London 1998, and Catherine Coquery-Vidrovitch, *Le Congo au temps des grandes compagnies concessionaires*, Paris 1962.

discovered that African villagers were not willing to work for modest wages far from their homes. Indeed the notion of wages was itself problematic in the early decades, as a medley of currencies was in use – gold, beads, iron bars, notional iron bars (units of account), cowrie shells, government and company notes or coin, IOUs and 'good-fors', to name just a few. The colonial authorities stipulated that the hut tax would only be accepted in the form of their own notes, but matters were often complicated by rivalry between public and private employers. If they wanted something done, employers found that it made sense to hire bonded labourers from local traders to build roads and railways, to work in the mines or to tend plantation crops. Slave-traders were reborn as contractors supplying labour both for public works and for the cultivation of cash crops, such as cacao and palm oil. Slave numbers at first actually grew following the ending of the Atlantic trade in the 1860s and the subsequent extension of colonial rule. Vagrancy laws and taxation were used to shape the colonized populations in blatant, but not always successful efforts to coerce them into paid labour. Slavery remained legal in Nigeria until 1916 and was not effectively suppressed even after this date. In parts of West Africa and in the Portuguese colonies, forced labour remained important well into the second half of the twentieth century. And oppressive labour contracts lasted well into the independence period.[5]

The resort to tied labour in colonial Africa was matched elsewhere in the European colonial empires by a trade in Indian or Chinese contract labourers. Cooper, Holt and Scott point out that 'these semi-free systems developed within and at the very moment that the wage labor-driven capitalist system was maturing on a global scale. If this historical and systemic conjuncture was somewhat anomalous, it was clearly a "necessary anomaly" in situations where labor was not readily available in the right place, at the right time, or sufficiently detached from non-capitalist relations of production.'[6]

Most of the great abolitionist acts had a link to the fate of empires, with anti-slavery sometimes helping to symbolize a new imperial vision. Britain's long campaign against the slave trade in the Atlantic, Africa and parts of the Middle East – which persisted throughout the nineteenth century – went hand in hand with its 'empire of free trade' and its frequent practice of gunboat diplomacy. Christopher Brown has analysed the origins of British abolitionism as inspired by the quest for 'moral capital', and from 1808 onwards British

---

5   Paul Lovejoy and Jan Hogendorn, *Slow Death for Slavery*, Cambridge 1993; Frederick Cooper, 'Conditions Analogous to Slavery: Imperial and Free Labor Ideology in Africa', in Cooper, Holt and Scott, *Beyond Slavery*, pp. 107–56.

6   Cooper, Holt and Scott, 'Introduction', *Beyond Slavery*, pp. 22–3. The reference to a 'necessary anomaly' echoes the argument of Robert Miles, *Capitalism and Unfree Labour: Necessity or Anomaly?*, London 1987. See also Benot, *La Modernité de l'esclavage*, and Vergès, *Abolir l'esclavage*.

governments believed that the great credit due to them on this account endowed them with special power.[7] Lord Palmerston, the long-serving British foreign secretary and prime minister, pursued with equal fervour bilateral treaties against the slave trade and agreements to remove tariffs and quotas with Spain, Portugal, France, Brazil and other Atlantic states.[8] The British West African colony of Sierra Leone had been acquired as a place to settle former slaves who wished to return to Africa. Other West African territories were developed by Quaker merchants in the hope of fostering the production of cacao, palm oil and other alternatives to the slave trade.

The United States, described as an 'Empire of Liberty' by Jefferson, devoted itself to continental expansion in the nineteenth century; but its swift occupation of Spain's remaining colonies in the Spanish–American War of 1898 led to calls for the US to imitate the European powers and opt for full-blown overseas colonialism. This provoked the emergence of an Anti-Imperialist League, founded in Boston in the same year, which opposed the imposition of US rule on territories seized from Spain, especially the Philippines. The rhetoric of this movement directly evoked the anti-slavery cause.[9] While it failed to prevent the Philippines or Puerto Rico being retained as colonies, the Anti-Imperialist movement did contribute to a different outcome for Cuba. While the McKinley White House was bent on planning a full-blown US colonial mission, the US Congress had been influenced by a skilful and well-funded Cuban delegation and its US allies and supporters – notably including émigré Cuban tobacco workers – to press for a guarantee that Cuba's long struggle for independence would not be frustrated. An amendment of March 1898 declared that the purpose of the war with Spain was, *inter alia*, to ensure that Cuba, after so many sacrifices, obtained its longed-for independence. Many Puerto Ricans had shared in the Cuban Revolutionary party's civil agitation but, with less favourable terrain and slender resources, had not been able to sustain a military challenge.

But in 1901 the US authorities devised an onerous series of undertakings that the Cuban assembly was required to incorporate in the Republic's Constitution. If the Assembly failed to adopt these requirements, Cuban independence would be indefinitely delayed. The Platt Amendment set out the terms and conditions the Cubans had to endorse. They had to lease the US land for a naval base (Guantánamo), and to give the US government a right to intervene if it deemed that lives or property were in danger. The Cubans also had to undertake to maintain the sanitation systems in their cities and not to borrow

7   Brown, *Moral Capital*.
8   Jasper Ridley, *Lord Palmerston*, London 1978.
9   Robert Beisner, *Twelve Against Empire*, New York 1995; Leon Wolff, *Little Brown Brother*, New York 1972; Paul Kramer, *The Blood of Government*, Chapel Hill 2006. The 'anti-imperialists' sometimes used racial language to oppose the acquisition of colonies with non-white populations.

beyond their means. The Amendment was very unpopular, but the Cuban leadership eventually caved in as the price of US withdrawal.

In 1902 a Cuban Republic was established, and the US troops withdrew. The 'Cuban' variant of US empire, with its Platt Amendment and naval base, was later to be seen as a preferable alternative to territorial annexation. In the language of a later era this was the neocolonial solution, furnishing every opportunity for US business but sparing the US Treasury the cost of administration. The new Cuban government had accepted these arrangements in the belief it had no alternative. The liberation army had been disbanded and the war-devastated country was in no state for a new conflict. On one issue, however, the occupiers found Cuban opinion, and Cuban politicians, unbudgeable – they refused repeated requests to limit manhood suffrage by either a property or literacy qualification. Louisiana had just adopted, and the US Supreme Court would soon endorse, the disqualification of several hundred thousand coloured voters. Even Conservative Cuban leaders were not prepared openly to disenfranchise Afro-Cuban men, so many of whom had fought and suffered in the war of liberation.[10]

Cuba soon resumed its position as the world's main supplier of cane sugar, with output recovering to 1 million tons in 1900 and climbing to 3 million by 1910. Sugar companies, a half of them US-owned, bought up the best cane land; US corporations also came to own the railway, telephone and electric power companies. Spells of US occupation (1898–1902 and 1906–8) brought some gains for Cubans, chiefly in the provision of public health, but at the cost of losing control of their country.[11] So far as Afro-Cubans were concerned the influence of US racial concepts remained insidious, as Cubans visited the US, studied or worked there, and were exposed to North American racial notions. But such influences were not strong enough to neutralize the cross-racial motif in Cuban nationalism (on which more below).

Cuba's sugar expansion attracted an influx of immigrants from Spain and the Canary Islands, but much of the sugar cane was still cut by black or coloured Cubans, supplemented, when demand was strong, by large numbers of seasonal workers, also descendants of former slaves, brought in from Jamaica, Haiti and other parts of the Caribbean. The wider Caribbean and much of Central and South America now supplied bananas, coffee and other tropical products to the US market. Corporations like United Fruit owned and ran scores of plantations. US warships and marines were regularly deployed to tamp down popular unrest and ensure that foreign bond-holders were paid.[12]

---

10   Scott, *Degrees of Freedom*, pp. 189–252.

11   The sense of cultural alienation is well evoked in Louis Perez, *Becoming Cuban*, New York 1996.

12   For Cuba see Gott, *Cuba*. The economic and ecological dimensions of the US 'informal empire' are explored in Richard Tucker, *Insatiable Appetites: The United States and the Ecological*

THE AFTERMATH OF SLAVERY

In post-emancipation societies, labour was no longer a critical shortage as it had been in the seventeenth century. The owners of the plantations monopolized employment in many regions and were able to hire both a core and a seasonal labour force at quite modest pay. In the US South and in parts of Brazil former slave-owners still held much of the land, but in the wider Caribbean region planters often sold up – and the new owners were corporations rather than individuals.

In the Americas emancipation meant an extra margin of autonomy, narrow though it usually was, for the former slaves and their descendants. Freedmen and women were still constrained by racial hierarchy and a new imperial order, but, together with allies, they had seized the moment to establish some space of their own. The gains made by the coloured people of the Caribbean were facilitated by the fact that in many islands they comprised a majority. Though there were divisions between mulatto and black, or between those from different islands, these diminished as the people of colour entered a wider labour market and were sometimes able to combine against their employers.

The blacks of the US South gained least from the ending of slavery. I maintain this in the face of the apparently contrary claim of the noted US comparative historian Peter Kolchin, who contrasts US emancipation with the ending of serfdom in Russia, writing that 'the terms of emancipation were in most respects far more favourable in the [US] South than in Russia'.[13] But Kolchin is here referring only to the brief episode of Reconstruction, and he later concedes: 'Historians of the South have argued that virulent white racism prevented blacks from taking advantage of the new opportunities they theoretically enjoyed.'[14] He also stresses that 'other slave societies undergoing emancipation did not experience anything like Reconstruction'.[15] Though this is true, it is also the case that the other New World emancipations also did not exhibit anything as drastic, elaborate and long-lasting as the regime of racial segregation in the US South. Indeed, in the decades immediately succeeding emancipation the freedmen and women of Jamaica, Brazil, Cuba and Haiti experienced substantial material and spiritual benefits

---

Degradation of the Tropical World, Berkeley 2000. The military aspect is illuminated by Chalmers Johnson, *Sorrows of Empire*, London 2004. The non-territorial character of US empire was established by Gareth Stedman Jones, 'The History of US Imperialism', in Robin Blackburn, ed., *Ideology in Social Science*, London 1974, pp. 207–37.

13   Peter Kolchin, 'Some Controversial Questions Concerning Emancipation', in M. L. Bush, ed., *Serfdom and Slavery: Studies in Legal Bondage*, London 1996, pp. 42–68, 54.

14   Ibid., p. 59.

15   Ibid., p. 56.

from their new condition. Later they were willing to travel considerable distances in search of work, including to North America. But the US South was a destination they shunned.

The misery of blacks in the US South in the 1880s and 1890s, and the intensification of racist practices, must be seen against a backdrop of a depressed cotton economy, as Kolchin also rightly points out. Low cotton prices spelt difficulty for all and meant that, as argued by Ransom and Sutch, the visible living standards of freed people in the 1880s was worse than they had been under slavery, albeit that they worked fewer hours in the formal economy.[16] It is difficult to evaluate the gains made by cultivators who had garden plots and more time to tend them. In the Caribbean, black small-holding and an informal economy of barter and mutual help was widespread. On the other hand the newly liberated were constrained by laws against 'vagrancy', by the requirement to pay taxes and by the outlawing of combinations and strikes. The authorities hobbled the 'black economy' but could not suppress it. Instead, in areas of plantation development, they permitted labour contractors to bring in people from India and China who were bound to work for low wages for three or four years for whoever purchased their contract.[17] Between 1850 and 1914 about 2.5 million Asian contract workers were brought to European colonies. The US Congress banned Chinese 'coolie' labour in 1868 later seeking to exclude all Chinese workers.

In the US South, as in the British Caribbean, the ending of slavery gave room for the spread of black Churches and opened access to education, albeit that, in the US South, schools were segregated and there were continual attempts to confine black schooling to modest schemes of vocational training. However, even Jim Crow could not prevent people of colour, with some help from their churches, acquiring literacy and making good on their educational chances. Former abolitionists in the North helped to sponsor educational initiatives. Most deplored the racial violence in the South, but it was left to Ida Wells, an African American, to expose the horrific details of lynching – and, with Quaker help, to publicize and campaign against the 'lynch law' regime.[18]

It was not until the early twentieth century that a 'neo-abolitionist' campaigning organization, the National Association for the Advancement of Colored People (NAACP), was formed.[19] (To begin with the NAACP council included white members, many of whom had family connections to abolitionism.) It was also notable that the Southern blacks preferred black

16 Ransom and Sutch, *One Kind of Freedom*, pp. 225–6.
17 See Turner, *From Chattel Slaves to Wage Slaves*.
18 Wells-Barnett, *On Lynchings*.
19 Hahn, *A Nation Under Our Feet*, pp. 276–9; McPherson, *The Abolitionist Legacy*, pp. 143–223.

Churches with Southern roots to the missionaries sent by the Northern Churches.

In Haiti, slave-holding, colonialism and racism had suffered a momentous defeat and a small-holding black peasantry had emerged. But subsequently the black state was quarantined by the main Atlantic states, while domestically its citizenry became subject to a new military elite. French recognition was purchased at the price of a heavy debt. Long before the US occupation of 1916, Haiti was a target of debt-collecting expeditions and neocolonial pressure. The spread of minifundia, as tiny parcels of land were subdivided among numerous heirs, led to poverty and soil erosion.

In the greater Caribbean area the former slaves still cherished their new freedoms, even when marginalized and left in poverty. The memory of an emancipation secured with the help of metropolitan legislation was a factor in the survival of colonial rule far into the twentieth century, though it also fostered ideas which fed into labour and national struggles. In Jamaica, with its historic slave uprisings and maroon presence, there were both national and class mobilizations. Despite the fact that Haiti was bullied by debt-collecting expeditions and subject to US military occupation from 1916 to 1934, it retained a tenacious sense of national identity. In Haiti, as in Jamaica, formal political rights were bounded by property ownership. In this connection Mimi Sheller has observed: 'Former slaves were ready for democracy from before the first day of emancipation, but democracy was not ready for them.'[20]

However, Haitian anti-slavery was distinguished from the general run of abolitionism by its rejection of colonialism. This meant that Haiti's political culture was, in certain crucial respects, far ahead of that prevailing in Europe and North America. Rejecting colonialism, it also rejected racism. While tensions between black and mulatto sometimes belied the official doctrine, the latter was still of great importance. A sign of this was the publication of the classic study *Sur l'égalité des races humaines* (Port-au-Prince 1885) by the distinguished Haitian anthropologist, Anténor Firmin. This was the first thorough critique of the racial fantasies of such diverse writers as J. A. Gobineau and Immanuel Kant. There were, of course, outstanding critics of racism and imperialism – for example W. E. B DuBois and Erskine Childers – but it was a Haitian who most thoroughly debunked the poisonous delusion of the age.

Many have held that abolitionism had a powerful bourgeois impulse, both directly, by celebrating wage labour and fostering institutions that would help to reproduce the social relations of capitalism, and indirectly, by promoting bourgeois hegemony and increasing the 'moral capital' of those most conspicuously associated with abolition, including sections of the ruling class. I have no doubt that such effects existed, but they were accompanied by others, with a different

---

20   Sheller, *Democracy After Slavery*, p. 243.

logic. Thus we may ask, did abolitionism actually succeed in fostering a bourgeois order? In Britain, France and the United States abolitionism had been linked to capitalist forces, but with variable results. In the British case emancipation had been adopted by the liberal wing of the oligarchy, in part as a concession to a class bloc which included manufacturers, artisans, craftsmen and the new middle classes. On the other hand emancipation was associated with the appearance of a more assertive, but liberal state, and abolitionists were often also concerned with social improvements and reforms which helped to consolidate the bourgeois order: new prisons, educational projects, improved communication and the like.

While at some moments the great acts of emancipation served to channel and contain longings for a radical new order, where they were successful they often stimulated and encouraged them. French Revolutionary emancipation in 1794 was followed by the 'conspiracy of the equals' in 1795, British emancipation in the 1830s by the large-scale Chartist agitation of the 1840s, US emancipation in 1863–5 by the campaign for the eight-hour day and the militant labour organization of 1868 and after, Brazilian emancipation in 1888 by a 'rebellion in the backlands' in 1893–6 (on which more below). The boundaries of free labour ideology were unclear – it could lead on to syndicalist, anarchist or socialist goals. Such sequences suggest that 'free labour ideology' and the claim for equality and rights did not for long reconcile popular movements to bourgeois goals.

The legacy of British anti-slavery was a disputed one, with claimants including imperialists and missionaries, free traders and the 'moral force' wing of Chartism. But the concession made by post-Reform British governments to bourgeois economic interests encouraged the latter to take corporatist, not hegemonic, forms. Britain's industrial capitalists thought of themselves as 'middle-class' businessmen, and continued to defer to a political aristocracy and the wealthy bankers and merchants of the City of London. For a long time to come the state was by no means based upon, or always responsive to, industrial capital – hence the subsequent problems of British capitalist development.[21] British emancipation had paternalist and conservative features that belied the radical hopes of many abolitionists. The former slave-holders were fairly generously compensated, and there was no episode equivalent to Reconstruction. However, the presence of missionaries and 'stipendiary' magistrates furnished a

---

21   In the debate on David Brion Davis's *Problem of Slavery in the Age of Revolution*, considerable play was made of the Gramscian concept of hegemony. It also plays a role in the debate between Perry Anderson, Tom Nairn and Edward Thompson on which fraction and type of capital enjoyed hegemony in Britain in the eighteenth and nineteenth centuries. See Anderson, *English Questions*, and Thompson, 'The Peculiarities of the English'. For the link between 'gentlemanly capitalism' and the practive of empire see also Cain and Hopkins, *British Imperialism*, pp. 141–60.

context in which it was somewhat easier for the former slaves to press for higher wages and access to small parcels of land. The end of slavery was soon followed by the ending of tariff protection for West Indian sugar in the metropolitan market in 1846. Free trade leaders like Cobden and Bright had once been abolitionists, but they felt no duty to protect the free labour system in Britain's colonies. Cheaper Cuban and Brazilian sugar would reduce British labour costs, and any consequent encouragement to the slave regimes in those lands should be countered by British diplomats and warships (as, to a limited extent, they were).[22]

The possessing classes in mid-nineteenth-century Europe and the Americas were possessed of a nameless dread – that of a social explosion that one might call 'class struggle without classes'. Workers and peasants had not yet built substantial organizations, nor were they strongly attached to an ideology. But these circumstances were hardly reassuring to rulers who feared the sort of turmoil seen in 1848, or at the time of the Paris Commune (1871). Rumours of anarchist and socialist conspiracy, hard-fought industrial strikes, and the recalcitrance of former slaves merged into an imaginary but potent common threat. These inchoate fears could easily lead to a retreat to conservativism and a jettisoning of the more generous features of abolitionism.

The impact of abolition on Atlantic and global trade flows was also less than might have been expected. The challenges to slavery in the period 1780–1888 did not for long interrupt the rise of the trade in plantation products. Once a labour force was assembled, ways could usually be found to maintain output. And once the scope for staple cultivation had been proved, then new labour sources – immigrants, contract labourers, seasonal labour – could be developed. War sometimes disrupted commerce and accumulation, but the latter still had a strong upward trend. British colonial planters in the Caribbean and elsewhere acquired hundreds of thousands of Asian indentured labourers. The labourers had their passage paid and received a very modest wage in return for three or four years' labour.[23] The Cuban planters imported about 140,000 Chinese contract labourers in the years 1845–75, and their living conditions were sometimes little better than those of the slaves. But they were free to go home or to settle after a few years, and hence did not furnish the permanent labour force that the plantations required. In the decades following the 1860s the planters of the United States, Cuba and Brazil had to contend with stiffer competition and far-reaching political and economic transformations. The growing efficiency of steam-powered transport by ship and rail, the opening of the Suez Canal (1867) and the spread of European colonial rule in Asia and Africa made available new sources for tropical and subtropical goods. Cuba,

22   Temperley, *British Anti-Slavery*.
23   Hugh Tinker, *A New System of Slavery*, Oxford 1982.

Brazil and the US South remained the world's largest producers of their respective staples, with Cuban and Brazilian employers finding new sources of labour by attracting poor immigrants from Spain, the Canary Islands and Italy. Global competition led to lower prices, with planters and smallholders reliant on expensive mercantile credit. Some planters adjusted to the new demands of capitalism in Cuba, Brazil and the US South, but even the successful remained subordinate to the wider circuits of Atlantic and global capital in the new 'Age of Empire'.[24]

The export value of the main staples rose notwithstanding weak prices and political turmoil. Exports of US cotton rose from $211.5 million in 1880 to $241.9 million in 1900. Exports of Brazilian coffee rose from $60.0 million in 1880 to $116.4 million in the 1890s. Cuba produced just over 1 million tons of sugar, worth $64 million, in 1893. After declining to less than 300,000 tons in the war years and after, production swiftly rose to 3 million tons by 1910. There was much reorganization via bankruptcy and acquisition but, crudely put, emancipation cleared the way for expansion, whether this was the modest expansion allowed by sharecropping and small-holding in much of the US South, the robust growth of Brazil's coffee capitalists, or the rise of Cuba's sugar corporations. The relative decline of the British West Indies as sugar producers reflected, as we saw, the fact that the small island economies were not well-suited to the large-scale cultivation of sugar cane necessitated by the *centrales*, with their internal railways, steam-driven mill and vacuum pan.[25]

The recharged institutions of racial oppression in the United States noted in the last chapter pose the issue of whether slavery and Jim Crow, the lynch mob and the chain gang, the ghetto and the prison, were simply successive forms of an underlying impetus to racial domination, mutating down the centuries from the seventeenth to the twenty-first. Loïc Wacquant has drawn attention to the remarkable continuities to be observed in these successive and overlapping regimes: enslavement, Jim Crow, and sharply racialized forms of segregation and incarceration.[26] Wacquant is careful to insist that other outcomes were possible – for example, if Reconstruction had not been diverted and defeated. Certainly the progress made at this time was remarkable enough to allow for alternatives. The powerful elements of continuity are, nevertheless, sobering.

Radical popular demands in this epoch focused on individual landownership. There was a 'stakeholder' view, found among 'free soilers' in the antebellum United States, that the free labourer would be a mere 'wage slave' unless he (or more rarely she) owned a parcel of land and/or the tools of a trade. The proto-peasant impulse also focused on small-holdings. For a while the small-holders

---

24   Eric Hobsbawm, *The Age of Empire*, London 1984; Findlay and O'Rourke, *Power and Plenty*, pp. 387–414.

25   Fe Iglesias, *Del ingenio al central*, Havana 2000.

26   Loïc Wacquant, 'The First Prison Society', *New Left Review* 13 (January–February 2002).

were able to establish a niche.[27] However, small-holding farmers were not well-placed to block or tame the rampant capitalism of the Gilded Age. Black tenants were, of course, in an even more vulnerable and subordinate position. In the course of emancipation the former slaves everywhere asserted modest but significant new rights. But in most cases new patterns of capitalist plantation development, sometimes combined with planter revanchism, marginalized these gains and blocked the advance of black small-holders and landless labourers. In the 1880s and 1890s the miseries of white farmers and struggling planters led to the emergence of a radical Populist movement in the US South and West which sought to challenge dominant financial interests and commercial practices.[28]

Capitalism without American slavery had, to that extent, compromised with popular aspirations and struggles in the Atlantic world. But this was scarcely capitalism without racism. Indeed the spread of market society, while weakening the bonds of racial domination in some ways – by allowing freedpeople a space not controlled by their former masters – also permitted the construction of rivalrous identities which left former slaves and their descendants at a huge disadvantage. Charles Mills has drawn attention to the implicit 'racial contract' that was cemented by New World slavery in the first place.[29] The suppression of chattel slavery as a legal form did not prevent the reappearance of racial exclusion and oppression. In a more global perspective colonial labour, often subject to racially defined obligations and disabilities, supplied European markets with the tropical produce formerly produced by slaves. This helps to explain why white racism re-emerged in the aftermath of emancipation, becoming more respectable and widespread than ever before in the period 1880–1940.

I have contended that the radical abolitionists were, by the standards of their time, opponents of racism, albeit not always free of paternalism. Most urged the need for civic equality for blacks, including – in the US case – the vote for black men. Likewise most of the major acts of emancipation reflected the efforts and sacrifice of slaves and former slaves and free people of colour. The lily-white coloration sometimes given to abolitionism is ridiculous.

On the other hand, support for emancipation often stemmed from mixed motives. In February 1794, as we have seen, the French Convention was animated by hatred for treacherous planters as much as by sympathy with the slaves. Some influential British statesmen saw anti-slavery as a buttress to the Pax Britannica and as a powerful symbolic assertion of a new, reformed social order at home. During the US Civil War, Lincoln and the Radical Republicans

---

27   Mintz, *Caribbean Transformations*, especially pp. 4–11, 184–213, 133–5, 140–5.

28   *Robert McMath, American Populism: A Social History 1877–1898*, New York 1993. The failure of the Populists, to directly challenge racism is stressed by Ernesto Laclau, *On Populist Reason*, London 2005, pp. 200–08. See Michal Kazin, *The Populist Persuasion*, New York 1998.

29   Mills, *Racial Contract*.

often argued that their measures against slavery were undertaken for nationalist reasons, to save the Union and stamp out secession. The later Reconstruction measures favourable to the freedmen were designed to punish the rebels and consolidate Republicanism in the occupied states of the former Confederacy. If the presence of such ulterior motives – and conjunctural calculations and momentary passions – favoured the cause of the slave at one moment, they could easily dissipate as the situation changed. While emancipation could promote heightened national integrity during a crisis, in its aftermath, the plight of white planters and their families could attract the support and sympathy of respectable (white) public opinion. Thus emancipation undertaken for mixed motives was likely to have mixed results. Even so, the freedmen and women preferred this to any return to slavery.

At the high point of the emancipation struggles, black fighters and their radical anti-slavery allies won significant gains over and above the legal suppression of slavery. Men of colour were armed, and the coloured population gained some access to both land and political representation. But within a decade or two there were backlash movements seeking to undo these gains. Haiti's enduring significance is owed not simply to the fact that it was the first large-scale emancipation, but also to the fact that the subsequent attempt to reimpose white domination was defeated. In Jamaica, where coloured people had made significant gains, the wave of repression triggered by the Morant Bay rebellion in 1865 targeted all people of colour and set the scene for the cancellation or constriction of these gains. In the post–Civil War United States the upsurge of white 'redeemer' movements – of the Ku Klux Klan and Jim Crow – was to reverse the revolutionary implications of radical 'Reconstruction' in the US South, and to reconstruct white domination on a new basis.

Black and coloured insurgents and abolitionists played a key role in the eventual spread of emancipation throughout the entire hemisphere, but their gains were partial and precarious. White abolitionists sometimes became fixated on the legal trappings of slavery, and failed to identify and oppose forms of racial exclusion not based on property in persons. As we have seen, William Lloyd Garrison the *Liberator* in 1865 in the belief that its job was done. Likewise the American Anti-Slavery Society was wound up in 1870. The freedmen and women did not have the luxury of being unaware of what was happening, but they could be isolated and intimidated to varying degrees as many of their former white allies dropped away. Northern public opinion proved volatile. By the mid-1870s it was believed that respectable white Southerners had been punished enough, and that it was the responsibility of black Southerners themselves to make the best of their new freedom. Although abolitionists knew they were opposing a system of racial slavery, many of them underestimated the resilience of racial oppression and exaggerated the possibilities open to the freedmen and women.

CUBA AND THE DIALECTIC OF FREEDOM

The British and US governments, at last concerting their efforts, brought an end to the transatlantic slave trade in the mid-1860s and, by the same stroke, to the inter-American slave traffic. With only a trickle of new arrivals from Africa, the main Afro-American populations were now gathered in national containers. Music, beliefs and ideas crossed boundaries and streams of migration, from Africa to the New World, from Haiti to Cuba, from Guadeloupe to New York, or Jamaica to Chicago, or from Rio to Rhode Island, all of which gave enduring significance to the crucible of the Americas in shaping the African diaspora; but national settings and national struggles determined citizenship and legislation.

The Cuban liberation struggle launched in 1868 had forged a link between the fate of the nation and the fate of the slaves. When London and Washington refused to recognize the rebel Cuban government in 1869–73, they tacitly supported a Spanish government that was in hock to the Cuban slave-owners. The island's free people of colour and former slaves entered the ranks of the rebels in large numbers and became an important contingent of the liberation struggle. Ada Ferrer cautions that the notion of a 'raceless' nation held out by the philosophy of Cuban nationalism did not accord with the facts, as coloured commanders often encountered special problems – nevertheless it also furnished an ideological space for coloured soldiers to assert a claim for equal treatment.[30]

Following Spain's defeat in 1898, the US occupation authorities disarmed and disbanded the Cuban liberation army; but both the occupiers and the Cuban elite were disturbed to see veterans of the struggle, many of them men of colour, still enjoying great prestige. On occasion such veterans would take to the streets to protest their shabby treatment. At the end of his first term, the Cuban Republic's first president, Tomás Estrada Palma – a conservative concerned at the potential radicalism of the former members of the army of liberation – sought to secure his own re-election and the defeat of José Miguel Gómez, the Liberal Party candidate, by resorting to blatant electoral fraud. Gómez responded by calling on his supporters, many of them men of colour and veterans of the independence war, to mount an armed protest. Estrada Palma, lacking confidence in the Rural Guard and other forces at his disposal, requested US intervention. President Theodore Roosevelt duly sent in the Marines and another US occupation commenced. But the US authorities were not anxious to return to a full-blown occupation regime, and concentrated on building the Cuban army and arranging for new elections, which were won by

---

30   Ada Ferrer, *Insurgent Cuba: Race, Nation and Revolution 1868–1902*, Chapel Hill 1999.

Miguel Gómez. The Liberal president found room for several men of colour in his administration, but shunned the support of a radical group of coloured veteran officers led by Evaristo Estenoz and Pedro Ivonet (a former colonel). The latter issued a newspaper, *Previsión*, calling for enforcement of the equal rights promised by the Constitution, condemning the discrimination against people of colour practised by some – mainly Spanish – shopkeepers and employers. Describing themselves as the Partido Independiente de Color (PIC), they gained support in Santa Clara and Oriente. A prominent Liberal man of colour, Martín Morúa Delgado, introduced an Act banning the formation of parties with 'racist goals'.[31]

As the time approached for a new election in 1910–12, the PIC appealed for support to all Cubans and began to talk of the need for social reforms. However, their agitation was branded as racist by both liberal and conservative newspapers, and the appearance of armed supporters at their meetings finally led to the claim that the PIC was planning a black revolt. The Morúa Delgado law was adopted in an atmosphere of social fear and racial panic. Privately, senior members of the government were alarmed that the PIC's agitation was whipping up class war and that anarchists and syndicalists were exploiting the situation.[32] General Monteagudo of the recently reorganized Cuban army was ordered to suppress the PIC, which he proceeded to do with great brutality. PIC supporters offered some resistance, but there was no pitched battle and no attempt to mount the sort of guerrilla war with which the veterans would have been familiar. The PIC had intended an armed protest, like that convoked by the Liberals in 1906, not a military uprising. However, this was not a reassuring precedent for President Gómez, who had no wish to see himself ousted by a third US occupation. The army was invited to teach the rebels a lesson. Monteagudo's units slaughtered hundreds, perhaps thousands, of real or alleged PIC supporters. This repression destroyed the PIC and tarnished the Cuban army, but did not lead to an enduring racial fissure. The Liberal Party retained a coloured following. In Havana there were still bi-racial labour organizations, and in the countryside the cane cutters on the sugar estates were beginning to organize. During the closing stages of the Great War in Europe, sugar prices rose, and there were conditions in which increasingly militant labour and nationalist movements could contest the US-sponsored corporations and the strongmen with whom Washington preferred to do business.

The appearance of the Partido Independiente de Color and its bloody suppression remains an event that is difficult to interpret. The dominant role in the repression played by the army and Rural Guard makes it different from the

---

31 Scott, *Degrees of Freedom*, p. 233.
32 For the context and course of these events see ibid., pp. 216–53 and Gott, *Cuba*, pp. 110–29.

race riots in the US South, such as that in Colfax, Louisiana, in 1866, where white vigilantes hunted down and killed blacks. On the other hand the Cuban Liberal leaders were clearly out to destroy a potential rival and warn off what was seen as a dangerous underclass. The repression of the PIC in 1912 probably killed more people than the contemporaneous lynch mobs in the US South, but had little enduring impact. Cuba's racially mixed working class was not intimidated for long. Within a few years the cane workers – most of them descendants of slaves – mounted an impressive series of strikes and helped greatly to expand the scope of Cuba's very militant labour movement. This milieu proved hospitable to anarcho-syndicalism, socialism and various home-grown species of Caribbean radicalism.

BRAZIL: ORDER AND PROGRESS?

Events in Brazil in the 1890s and early 1900s were not identical, but showed the rulers of the recently declared Republic responding with ferocity to 'rebellion in the backlands'. The Brazilian Republicans had overthrown the monarchy in 1889 thanks to the action of Marshal Deodoro Fonseca, and remained deferential to military concerns. The discontent of the lower middle class was expressed in support for a grouping known as the 'Jacobinos', though they were not as subversive as the term might imply. The Republic's suffrage remained narrow and many, especially in the countryside where large landowners still held undisputed sway, were excluded from political life. This helps to explain the rise of the utopian movement led by Antonio 'Conselheiro' ('counsellor') in Canudos in North-Eastern Brazil. Antonio Vicente Mendes Maciel was a wandering preacher, a *moreno*, or man of colour, of good family but brought down by debt. Already in the 1870s he had attracted attention as a popular preacher who denounced slavery and the condition of the poor. In the years 1893–6 he attracted large numbers of followers to a remote new settlement in the hills at Belo Monte, in Canudos. Conselheiro denounced the government and predicted that it would soon collapse, along with the corrupt and wicked order of which it was a part. The settlement swelled to accommodate 15–20,000 people. The inhabitants of Belo Monte used a local scrip in preference to Brazilian currency. Conselheiro preached the need for hard work and a frugal lifestyle. The area had been severely afflicted by drought, and the regime at Belo Monte restored morale to those seeking refuge from distaster. Conselheiro's followers included many blacks and *caboclos*, those of mixed, partly African descent.

The fact that many of his followers were armed and that representatives of the government were unwelcome alarmed the authorities. A military detachment of 100 men was sent to establish control in 1895, but was easily repulsed. A second column of 1,200 troops met the same fate, and its commanding officer was killed. Finally, a third column was sent in 1896, numbering over 10,000 men, with machine guns and artillery. Antonio Conselheiro died, seemingly of natural causes, and many of his followers had fled by the time Belo Monte was taken. The progress of the second and third columns was closely followed by the press, and there was much anxiety that the 'rebellion in the backlands' exposed the hollowness of the Republic's pretension to be a modern state. Conselheiro, while rejecting the Republic and its currency, declared his respect for the laws of the monarchy. He also had some links to the local Conservative Party, though these were repudiated by the Conservative leader in the final phase. The saga of popular rebellion in Canudos was written up in a vivid, half-admiring, half-alarmed account, *Os Sertões* (1903) by Euclides da Cunha, one of the journalists who had covered the story.[33] This work, translated into English as *Rebellion in the Backlands*, became a best-seller in Brazil, helping to foster a myth of the country's untamed interior and of the strange cults which flourished among its populace. Though the Republican government obliged the Church to disown Antonio Conselheiro he was a doctrinally orthodox Catholic, albeit somewhat influenced, as were many others, by the millenarian cult of Sebastião, the Portuguese martyr king.

While the Cuban PIC had a clear connection to national traditions and republican values, the Canudos rebellion rejected the Republic, and drew on religious impulses and apocalyptic yearnings. But both tapped into class feeling, and both were suppressed by an arriviste bourgeoisie and by military men anxious to prove their worth as custodians of the established order. The watchword of Brazil's republican revolution of 1889 had been 'Order and Progress', expressing Auguste Comte's Positivist ideology. This religion of progress supposedly embraced moderate doses of reform. But the political structures of the Republic enshrined the power of the great landlords, bankers and merchants. Qualifications on the suffrage were so stringent that fewer had the vote than in the early days of the Empire. In practice the Republic did not have a strong enough state machine to entirely resubordinate the mass of Brazilians, especially in the often lawless backlands. Italian and German immigrants replaced blacks as labourers in the coffee groves, but Afro-Brazilians continued to lend a distinctive character to the country's great cities and to several major regions, including Bahia and the rest of the North-East, Rio de Janeiro, Minas Gerais and much of São Paulo. Though most of the descendants of slaves were economically marginalized, the Afro-Brazilian presence was not marginal to Brazilian life. There were many prominent people of colour – journalists, lawyers and proprietors. The mainstream of Brazilian culture had a dynamic African

---

33   Euclides da Cunha, *Rebellion in the Backlands*, New York 1957. For an excellent brief assessment of the meaning of the revolt see Robert Levine, '"Mud Hut Jerusalem": Canudos Revisited', in Rebecca Scott et al., *The Abolition of Slavery and Aftermath of Emancipation in Brazil*, pp. 199–266. For the broader context see also Fausto, *Concise History of Brazil*, pp. 141–55.

undercurrent, something recognized and explored in literature, anthropology and, more recently, film. Gilberto Freyre, Brazil's most famous social historian, writing evocatively about the great plantation houses, insisted that the country was pursuing its destiny as a 'racial democracy'. Fernando Ortiz, the Cuban anthropologist, had a different story to tell, as we will see, but he also emphasized the African contribution. Though there was, as we have seen, a large-scale European migration to Cuba, blacks and people of colour – some of them migrants from Jamaica or Haiti – remained integral to the plantation labour force in a way that ceased to be true of Brazil in the 1890s.

Mimi Sheller offers a striking schema of the dynamic of slave emancipation in the Americas which sees each process stimulating a distinctive claim to wider social equality and freedom. Her grid captures the audacity of this claim, its embodiment in 'peasant rebellion' and its ultimate containment or defeat. While the schema brings out some powerful underlying tendencies, it implies too great a uniformity of outcome. As I have already argued, the post-emancipation experience differed greatly in the various parts of the Americas because of the specific relation of forces, or the varying fortunes of war and peace, or differing positions in a temporal flow of events that constantly crossed borders so that national containers no longer quite applied. Indeed my own account itself remains schematic, incomplete and tentative. Sheller's grid – to which I have added Brazil – highlights key features of the processes of emancipation I have surveyed in this and preceding chapters.

TABLE 14.1. COMPARATIVE EMANCIPATION AND DE-DEMOCRATIZATION

Country	Context	Attempt to Expand Rights	Rebellion	Retreat
Haiti	Revolution/ Independence War	Liberal Revolution 1843	Piquet Rebellion 1844–5	Politique de doublure mulatto power
Jamaica	Apprenticeship 1830s	Underhill Movement 1864	Morant Bay 1865	Crown Colony martial law
USA	Civil War	Radical Reconstruction	n/a	'Redemption'
Cuba	Moret Law	Independence War	Guerra Chiquita	PIC massacre
Brazil	Rio Branco Law	Lei Aurea	Canudos	Belo Monte

Source: Based on Mimi Sheller, *Democracy After Slavery*, London 2000, p. 34, with the Brazil entry added to her grid.

CRUCIBLES AND STEWS

While the British and French colonial governments cherished an official account of abolition, using it to justify colonial rule, the governments of the United States, Cuba and Brazil had a more subdued and cautious approach to the memory of emancipation, reflecting an increasingly suspicious attitude to the freedmen and women, and friendly disposition to the planters. From the World Fair of 1876 onwards, the major theme in US public life was that of reconciliation between South and North, with emphatic repudiation of the 'excesses' of Reconstruction. White veterans in their blue and grey uniforms would meet to commemorate famous battles and to pick up the threads of brotherly respect, but black veterans were not invited. A tidy, moderate notion of emancipation was subsumed within a larger national narrative. Booker T. Washington, the African American leader, tried to swim against the current by stressing the new beginning represented by the striking-down of slavery. Unfortunately he combined this with a belittling of African influence and a tendency to downplay black resistance. Washington's approach was to be challenged by W. E. B. Du Bois, and overturned by the Harlem Renaissance of the 1920s and 1930s.[34]

In Cuba and Brazil the memory of slave emancipation was given only a modest role in the national story. The emancipation laws had been issued by, respectively, the Spanish colonial government and the imperial government, so the new Republican authorities had little to boast about. The ruling culture was willing to grant a folkloric position to their black and coloured population, but not to extend anything other than a purely formal civic equality. The social struggles of the 1940s and 1950s did bring some advances for the labouring poor, including many Afro-Cubans and Afro-Brazilians; but it was not until the 1960s and after that interest in slavery and abolition revived, leading to a flood of publications to mark the centennials in 1986 and 1988.

In most of the former slave zones, freedmen and women sought to become smallholders or tenants of tiny plots of land. In their fierce desire for personal independence they made great sacrifices to keep and tend these patches of soil. Certain rural and urban areas nurtured distinctive black communities that were to be the cradle of new cultures of survival and resistance.[35] Indeed the afterglow of the black saga of enslavement, survival and resistance was to become a major tributary to the counterculture of modernity.

---

34 David Blight, *Race and Reunion: The Civil War in the American Memory*, Cambridge 2002, pp. 362–4.

35 The classic modern study stresses survival as well as resistance. See Paul Gilroy, *The Black Atlantic*, London 1994.

The injuries of slavery and the often harsh conditions of racial subjection reassembled after emancipation meant that the working-through of the experience of bondage, and of the frustrations of emancipation, took several generations.[36] Black Christianity, gospel singing, the blues, soul and jazz can be seen as part of this work of recuperation and reconnection.[37] Sometimes a cultural influence specific to a particular African people was transplanted to a New World setting, but often there was intermixture and creolization. In other parts of the Americas, Cuban *santería*, Afro-Caribbean music and poetry or Brazilian *candomblé*, *capoeira* and carnival, Caribbean popular architecture, murals, kick-boxing and carnival, Haitian *meringue* music and vodou rites, are still further expressions of this diasporic ferment. In the early twentieth century the Jamaican Marcus Garvey focused some of the longings of Afro-American populations with his project of a return to Africa, something which was reworked by the Rastafarians in later decades.[38] In the Caribbean, nationalism plays a part, but it is typically imbued with social content and universalistic aspirations. Caribbean culture reflects this in the work of such outstanding writers and artists as C. L. R. James, Eric Williams, Frantz Fanon, Aimé Césaire, Wifredo Lam, Richard Wright, Nicolás Guillén and Derek Walcott. In North America the Harlem Renaissance recovered the inspiration of Afro-American history and, like the writing of Toni Morrison and many others, offered a profound reflection on slavery and emancipation. There is, of course, great diversity here and it would be wrong to imagine that history stopped with emancipation. Resistance to colonialism, labour struggles, the difficult conditions of an often flawed independence and a variety of achievements as well as sorrows also supply crucial themes.

Afro-American cultural traditions are imbued with historical resonance and answer at the same time to contemporary problems and impulses. They are part of the enduring legacy of the great bondage and the resistance to it. Indeed they – not the attempts of British, American or French statesmen to dress up their latest neocolonial venture in the rhetorical garb of abolitionism – are authentic expressions of this tradition.

I entitled this book 'American Crucible' because I believe that in the heat of these momentous clashes over slavery, a new notion of human freedom and human unity was proclaimed and sometimes precariously embodied. The Cuban anthropologist Fernando Ortiz urged that the American experience be seen as akin to a Cuban *ajiaco*, or stew, rather than a melting pot:

---

36   Du Bois registers this powerfully in *The Souls of Black Folk*. See also Ron Engerman, *Cultural Trauma: Slavery and the Formation of African American Identity*, Cambridge 2001.

37   White and White, *The Sounds of Slavery*.

38   For the variety of Caribbean radicalisms and their influence on North America see the superb account in Winston James, *Raising Aloft the Banner of Ethiopia*, London 1996.

It has repeatedly been said that Cuba is a melting pot of human elements. This comparison applies to our *patria* as it does to the other American nations. But perhaps there could be another metaphor, more precise, more comprehensive and more appropriate for a Cuban audience. For in Cuba there are no foundries and melting pots apart from the very modest ones of certain artisans. Let us rather turn to a Cuban simile, a metaphorical Cubanism, and we will understand each other better, more quickly and in detail. Cuba is an *ajiaco*. It is the stew most typical [of Cuba] and most complex, made from various species of legumes, which here we call *viandas*, and of pieces of diverse meats; all of which is boiled in water until it produces a succulent potage which is seasoned with the most Cuban [of ingredients], *ají* [a Cuban variety of capsicum], from which it takes its name . . . The characteristic thing about Cuba is that since it is an *ajiaco*, its people are not a finished dish, but a constant [process of] cooking. From the dawn of its history to the hours which are presently ticking away, there has always been a renewed entry of exogenous roots, fruit and meats into the Cuban pot, an incessant bubbling of heterogeneous substances. Hence the change in its composition, and [the fact] that *cubanidad* has a different flavour and consistency depending on what is at the bottom, the middle or the top, where the *viandas* are still raw, and the bubbling liquid still clear.[39]

The charming simile of the great anthropologist is apt in many ways, but some brief observations are in order. Firstly let us note the hint that the 'bottom' of the *ajiaco* is more tasty than the 'top', suggesting an interaction of class and nation. Secondly, that the history of slavery and race in the Americas constantly shows that the stewing and amalgamation does not just take place inside each pot but, as the meal is prepared and eaten, between the various national containers as well, so that the indigenous and the immigrant, the European and the African, the 'Hispanic' and 'Anglo' further intermingle in various ways. Thirdly, Cuba and other sugar-producing areas did have their own furnaces and bubbling coppers for making sugar from cane juice. Indeed the tradition of slave resistance and marronage that venerated Ogun also kept alive the idea of a smelting process that produced both tools and weapons.

EMANCIPATION AND 'HUMAN RIGHTS' FROM EMPIRE TO DECOLONIZATION

The struggle against slavery had demonstrated the power of the appeal to freedom, equality and common humanity, yet had failed to stem an increasingly brazen growth of racist sentiment in the leading states of the West. This racism

---

39 Fernando Ortiz, *Estudios etnosociológicos*, Havana 1991. This passage is quoted and its significance discussed in a most informative essay by Stephan Palmié, 'Fernando Ortiz and the Cooking of History', *Ibero-Amerikanisches Archiv* (1998), pp. 353–74. I am grateful to Mattias Assunção for bringing it to my attention.

helped to produce, and was intensified by, new structures of racial oppression as embodied in the regime of Jim Crow in the US South, the pact between US elites in different regions, the impetus to marginalize people of colour in Brazil and Spanish-speaking America, and the spread of European colonialism in Africa and Asia. In some cases the practices of racial segregation could seem more elaborate and demeaning than racial enslavement had been. The slave system had incarcerated the great bulk of the coloured population in plantations where they had limited and highly controlled contact with white people. The post-emancipation racial order made explicit a series of exclusions and prohibitions that, for many of the enslaved, had been merely latent under slavery.

Was there something in the core concept of emancipation that weakened the position of the freedmen and women? Moderate abolitionists celebrated the condition of the property-less free wage labourer without sufficiently insisting on 'public rights' of association and equal access. Some devoted themselves to missionary-style educational activity in ways that sought to sidestep questions of power. At its best the missionary approach might appeal to the doctrine of human rights and pave the way for later challenges to racism. But it still tended to present a positive image of the paternalist emancipator, dispensing liberation or guaranteeing rights. The sort of latterday abolitionism which believed in the rigours of the market, the superiority of Western civilization, and the benevolence of the state, adapted to racial subordination with few qualms.

In the period 1883–1914 each of the European colonial powers, no matter how extensive their resort to forced labour, claimed to be inspired by abolitionist principles. Rival commitments to shouldering 'the white man's burden' aggravated rather than removed the clash of national and imperial conceits and interests. Two non-European powers, Japan and the United States, used lightning military strikes – Japan's wars with China and Russia, and the Spanish–American War – to assert wider ambitions and explore new imperial formulas. The colonial powers often needed to deploy low-intensity military force to police their empires, but the slaughter of 10 million in the Great War of 1914–18 showed how deadly nations of white men could be towards one another, and how quick to drag their colonial subjects into their internecine quarrels. In late 1917–18 the US President Woodrow Wilson and the Russian Bolsheviks issued competing calls for a universal right of national liberation, but the victorious European powers remained committed to colonialism. The Western powers set up the League of Nations, making it both the repository of official abolitionism and the instrument for reapportioning German and Turkish territories. The League and its members made desultory, but not wholly ineffective, efforts to suppress slavery and the slave trade, though both traditional slavery and colonial forced labour regimes lingered obstinately in parts of Africa and the Middle East. The League also strove to prevent 'white slavery' – trafficking in females for the purposes of prostitution.

With the founding of the United Nations, the abolitionist legacy and the discourse of rights were once more affirmed by the victorious powers. They helped to inspire the 'Universal Declaration of Human Rights' adopted in 1948. The United States, Britain and the Soviet Union were initially reluctant to include any declaration of rights within the UN Charter. While the latter was an agreement between states, such a declaration would appear to give citizens and subjects a notional right of appeal against them. The victorious powers were each aware that they would be vulnerable. There was a blatant system of racial oppression in the US South, France and Britain had large colonial empires, and the Soviet Union ran a Gulag of prisons, just to mention the more obvious issues. However, China and the Latin American states, especially Cuba and Peru, not only held that a declaration of rights was needed but wished to see it encompass as well as political rights a commitment to the 'people's livelihood' (as Sun Yat-sen, leader of China's early-twentieth-century Revolution, called it), and similar aspirations expressed at gatherings of the Latin American states and embodied in the Havana Declaration of 1947. The Soviet delegation began to see that a broad statement, echoing some of the claims made by the Soviet Constitution of 1936, would enable them to pre-empt criticism and foreground their own concepts of social rights. The US administration also relented, so long as it was clear that the declaration would not have the force of law. Indeed the victorious powers were now the target of petitions and exposés of their own abusive practices and realized that a General Declaration would serve to deflect criticism and buy time. The US delegation was particularly concerned to parry attacks on the racial violence and oppression in the Southern states and to stress its commitment to humane values.[40]

Article 1 declared: 'All human beings are born free and equal in dignity and rights.' Article 2 stated that the rights it set forth were enjoyed by all 'without distinction of any kind, such as race, colour, language, religion, political or other opinion, national or social origin, property, birth or other status.' Article 3 guaranteed 'life, liberty and security of person', while Article 4 specified: 'No one shall be held in slavery or servitude; slavery and the slave trade shall be prohibited in all their forms.' Many of the remaining twenty-six articles laid out entitlement to a comprehensive list of civic freedoms and social rights, including to education and employment. The preamble made it clear that the Declaration was intended as a 'common standard of achievement for all . . . nations'. It defined aspirations and objectives, for none of its sponsors could remotely claim to have fulfilled its main tenets. However, in contrast to the bogus abolitionism of the League of Nations, the General Declaration did not anoint existing oppressions.

---

40   Hunt, *Inventing Human Rights,* pp. 176–229; Johannes Morsink, *The Universal Declaration of Human Rights,* Philadelphia 2004; Carol Anderson, *Eyes off the Prize: The United Nations and the African American Struggle for Human Rights,* Cambridge 2005, pp. 58–112.

Though intended as a 'standard', or norm, rather than as a statement of accomplished fact, the UN Declaration still faced problems of implementation, coverage and, beyond these, basic conceptualization. The fact that the US, the USSR, Britain and France had subscribed to the Declaration meant that a modest opening or advantage had been given to those resisting – or opposed to – racial oppression in the US South, colonial oppression in Africa and Asia, and the archipelago of Soviet penal colonies. Within roughly a decade these grotesque embodiments of oppression were deeply shaken from within and without. While not the principal factor, the UN Declaration had helped to undermine the legitimacy of such blatant violations of the ideals which had been so prominently and solemnly pronounced.

However, the received doctrine of 'human rights' can be faulted for its selectivity and for focusing on certain privileged spheres of social existence, while neglecting the real conditions of the impoverished, excluded and super-exploited who together comprise the majority of the world's population. Such diverse thinkers as Jeremy Bentham and Karl Marx questioned the arbitrary and metaphysical basis of the concept of natural rights. While a constitution or law can give rise to a clear and specific legal claim, an inflation of the notion of rights licenses a proliferation of claims and claimants – the right to life or the right to choice, the rights of labour or the sanctity of contract. In the course of the great battles and crises that led to the suppression of New World slavery, the focus was on specific acts of emancipation. Some urged this in the name of the 'rights of man', but many influential abolitionists, from William Wilberforce to Joaquim Nabuco, had no fondness for this term. The modern term 'human rights' was rarely used but anti-slavery advocates often denounced the institution in the name of 'common humanity' or some similar locution. Those who advanced a demand for 'general emancipation' in the name of 'the rights of man' or 'common humanity' were essentially making an appeal: they were seeking to awaken, shape and direct a new popular will. Sometimes this had an extraordinarily contagious effect, as with Saint-Domingue in the 1790s; one may try to pinpoint the origin of the demand, but in the end it had a collective character and authorship. True emancipation, ultimately, could only be self-emancipation; but it also had to reach out to the people or community as a whole, including those who could not be heroic actors because they were too young, or old, or sick. The language of rights and norms can help to energize and open up the sense of the collective.[41] Slavoj Žižek, in a text actually entitled 'Against Human Rights', develops an argument against rights that also registers that they may nevertheless have some value: 'the appearance of *éga-liberté* is more than a "mere appearance" but contains an efficacy of its own, which allows it to set in

---

41   See for example Göran Therborn, 'Back to Norms', *Current Sociology* 6 (2002), pp. 863–80, and the same author's *The Rights of Children in Modern Times*, Dartmouth 1994.

motion the re-articulation of actual social relations by way of their progressive "politicization". Why shouldn't women also be allowed to vote? Why shouldn't workplace concerns also be a matter of public concern as well? We might apply the old Lévi-Straussian term "symbolic efficiency": the appearance of *éga-liberté* is a symbolic fiction which as such possesses actual efficiency.'[42]

Régis Debray offers a more scathing verdict. In a work focused on the third term in the Revolutionary watchword, *Le Moment fraternité* (Paris 2009), Debray sees the cult of human rights as the 'perfect ideology of the videosphere'. His argument, in a nutshell, is that this ideology is a 'faux religion, that demands no responsibilities of its adherents, packaged with a fuzzy catch-all creed from which no one could reasonably dissent. This religion *manqué* works in melliflu- ous harmony with the reigning economic and political philosophies of the contemporary West to project the image of a serene global village, effectively camouflaging the interests of its principal players. Marx was only mistaken in describing the "ice-cold water of egotistical calculation", when in fact today "financial capital drips with tepid and sugary water, exudes compassion from every pore", while delocalizing the workforce between boom and slump. The rule of law, the *elementum* of the Religion of the Contemporary West, "tends to neutralize the inequalities of force, profit and influence" secured by the transat- lantic consensus. In contrast to religion proper this latter-day creed is bereft of historical memory. Its preferred sacred figure, the victim – the *harki*, the slave, the deportee – is interchangeable, non-specific, a testament to the videosphere's amnesiac, perpetual present.'[43]

The arrows of this critique certainly find plenty of targets, but this is not the whole story. As I have tried to show, 'human rights' have a history, and have been renewed and radicalized in succeeding generations. The abolitionists themselves had a notion of 'fraternity': 'Am I not a Man and a Brother?', 'Am I not a Woman and a Sister?' The notion of 'human rights' is clearly derived from a widening of the concept of the 'Rights of Man' central to Debray's own French republican outlook. The watchword of fraternity, like that of *éga-liberté*, can also be misused, especially Debray's accompanying stress on borders. C. L. R. James drew attention to the fact that it was the anonymous 'black masses' who were most faithful to the cause of freedom in Saint-Domingue in 1803 – but in the wider history of anti-slavery, names and bands of brothers and sisters are not at all lacking, some of them happy to cross borders. The comrades of emancipa- tion would include Toussaint Louverture, Pierrot, Pétion, Bolívar, Sam Sharpe, Garrison, Phillips, the Grimké sisters, Sojourner Truth, those gathered at Seneca Falls in 1848, Frederick Douglass, John Brown, the Maceos, Antonio

---

42   Slavoj Žižek, 'Against Human Rights', *New Left Review* 34 (July–August 2005), pp. 115–31, 130.

43   The quotations are from *Le Moment fraternité* and the summary is by Jacob Collins, 'Imagined Fraternities', *New Left Review* 64 (July–August 2010), pp. 131–8.

Conselheiro and Antonio Bento, just to name a few. Their anthems – 'John Brown's Body', 'Guantanamera', the songs sung by the 54th – are no less stirring than the Marseillaise.

The scorn expressed by Debray for this tepid religion seems, like that of Žižek, to be overdone and misplaced. The humanitarian doctrine does not really offer blanket endorsement to super-exploitation, militarism and obscene inequalities. It is secular rather than religious, and it infuriates so much because it has strong appeal, not because of its weakness. Those attacking the US or British governments for 'rendition' and the torture of suspects, or those claiming labour rights in China, find succour in this language even if they would also need to reach beyond it. In the end neither Žižek nor Debray can quite bring themselves fully to deny the 'human rights' perspective, and in this they are right, but by all means let us explore its real limits and inadequacy. One of these would be that many of the most damaging fissures in the world are to be found across and between rather than only within states. So that fraternity has to cross borders, as did the volunteers of the Lincoln Brigade, or the Cuban mission to Angola.

Notwithstanding the importance of setting a standard, and the recognition of social rights in the Universal Declaration of 1948, there remained a structural limitation that was already referred to in its Preamble, where the rights were said to extend both to 'the peoples of Member States themselves and among the peoples of territories under their jurisdiction'. Not only was colonialism extensive, and in some cases even rampant, in 1948 but so was ethnic cleansing and other types of oppression of 'stateless peoples'. The reference to the fact that Member States had other 'peoples' under their jurisdiction indicated the gap between rights and the structures needed to implement them. It was around this time that Hannah Arendt observed that human rights were of no use to those who lacked a state to enforce them, and that the postwar flood of stateless refugees made a mockery of the Declaration.[44] The problem was even more profound in a world of 'nation-states', since there were hundreds – if not thousands – of different 'peoples' and yet only a few score states, and endless problems of rival claims if each people was to have its own state. The setting up of the state of Israel in 1948 illustrated the problem. While giving persecuted Jews in Israel a state, it validated the ejection of Palestinians from their homes and lands.[45] It also made more likely the expulsion of long-settled Jewish communities from other parts of the Middle East, in violation of their human

---

44   Hannah Arendt, *The Origins of Totalitarianism*, new edn, New York 1973, pp. 267–305 (first published 1951).

45   Arendt wrote that 'the solution of the Jewish question merely produced a new category of refugee, the Arabs . . . And what happened in Palestine within the smallest territory and in terms of hundreds of thousands was then repeated in India on a large scale involving many millions of people.' Ibid., p. 290.

rights. By itself the state – especially the nation-state – is bound to be a flawed instrument of 'human rights' which will need global institutions to become properly entrenched. The admission of many former colonies to the United Nations itself somewhat mitigated – but by no means removed – this problem. Indeed the UN, with its Security Council, still reflects the world of 1945. The UN is a body that represents states, not peoples, and this weakens – indeed can wholly negate – its claim to represent 'human rights'. Until such time as there is a new cosmopolitan order, such rights will be as if suspended in mid-air. Their maintenance will depend on the emergence of international, intermediary and grass-roots institutions which deliberately foster democratic participation and socio-economic inclusion.

Gains for human rights and national self-determination may be compared with processes of slave emancipation in the way they combined the emergence of new social values within international settings and conjunctures. The vigorous survival of colonialism and racism in the aftermath of the First World War led prominent African Americans, West Indians and Africans to develop a 'Pan-African' perspective embracing 'Africa for the Africans' and a struggle for 'civil rights' in the Americas. Figures such as W. E. B. Du Bois, C. L. R. James, Eric Williams, Kwame Nkrumah and Paul Robeson championed this vision.[46] In the Francophone world and Portuguese Africa cognate efforts to challenge racism, colonialism and neocolonialism were made by Frantz Fanon, Aimé Césaire, Leopold Senghor and Amilcar Cabral. The emergence of new Asian, African and Caribbean states, the Bandung Conference of 1956, the Cuban Revolution and the emergence of the Non-Aligned Movement were historic gains for anti-imperialism. Moreover the context of Cold War rivalry in the 1950s and 1960s made it more difficult for US governments to continue to tolerate – and for the Democratic Party to support – racial segregation and voter suppression in the US South during the 1960s. However, white rule in South Africa and Portuguese colonial rule in Africa remained, with the acquiescence of Western governments, as defiant hold-outs.

Writing in 1970 on 'The Concept of Racism', Michael Banton commented that 'the word is a relatively new one' and that it was not 'neutral' with respect to the practices it referred to.[47] His observation is borne out by the fact that there was no entry for the terms 'racism' and 'racist' in the *Complete Oxford English Dictionary*, which appeared in 1971. By contrast the *Supplement* to the dictionary which appeared in 1987 had many references, some stemming from anti-fascist writing and others from anthropology, with Ruth Benedict's *Race and Racism* (1940) being perhaps the most substantial early contribution.

---

46   W. E. B. Du Bois, *Africa and the World*, New York 1948.
47   Michael Banton, 'The Concept of Racism', in *Race and Racialism*, London 1970, pp. 17–34, 17–18.

(Arendt used the concept of 'racism' in 1951.[48]) Prior to the gradual adoption of this term in the years 1940–70, the facts of racial exclusion, oppression and inequality were often discussed as consequences of racial 'prejudice' or 'bigotry'. Somehow the term racism referred to the way that attitudes were rooted in structures, and that racial exclusion could be no less baleful for being 'unconscious' or 'unthought'.[49] References to 'white supremacy' or the later coinage 'institutional racism' stress social practices as much as motivations. The new emphasis seems to coincide with decolonization, the breakthroughs in the US civil rights struggle and the appearance of 'political correctness' in the aftermath of the student movements of the late 1960s. The UN's Universal Declaration was vaguely supportive of the new approach, but not so pointed and specific.

The successes of the civil rights struggle in their turn helped to intensify pressure on ultra-colonialist and racist structures which were still part of the Western world, in the shape of Portuguese colonialism and South African apartheid. Portugal was a member of NATO, and South Africa leased a naval base at Simonstown to the alliance. The Portuguese Revolution of 1975 and 'Operation Carlota', the Cuban fraternal mission to Angola in 1976, consolidated Angola's independence and paved the way for the terminal crisis of the white regime in South Africa. It was fitting that the UN Conference which condemned the history of racism and slavery as a crime against humanity took place in South Africa in 2001. But in the late twentieth and early twenty-first centuries progressive principles did not prevail simply because of their moral and intellectual cogency. The struggle for a more democratic order in South Africa, South Korea, Poland and Brazil received key support from organized labour. International comparisons and transnational social movements helped to highlight racial oppression and inequality. The UN Universal Declaration offered a benchmark here, but ultimately one which was limited by its focus on the nation-state in a world where many of the most grotesque inequalities and deprivations occur, as it were, at the global level in the space between nations. In 2000 the gap between the rich and the poor was approximately fifty times greater than it was in 1800. Futhermore, around this time the International Labour Organization estimated the number of forced labourers at around 12 million, compared with 6 million slaves in the Americas in 1860. The new types of slavery target children and young people, reminding us that the majority of the victims of the Atlantic trade were just teenagers. However, in the modern world it is age and poverty as much as race which defines vulnerability to child labour.

---

48   Arendt, *Origins of Totalitarianism*, pp. 185–221.

49   In the late nineteenth and early twentieth centuries there was much talk of 'Anglo-Saxon' and 'Latin' 'races', but not a concept of racism. The term *racista* was used in Cuba in 1910–12 by those who attacked the Partido Independiente de Color, to protest a supposed coloured racism. However, this use was itself an expression of a racial panic. See Scott, *Degrees of Freedom*, p. 239.

The great sweep of decolonization in the aftermath of the Second World War had served to reveal the extent of the 'Great Divergence' that took place in the nineteenth and twentieth centuries. Of course colonialism impinged in different ways, and to a different extent, on the colonized in different parts of the world. Furthermore the variable experience of decolonization and the uneven advance of economic development, whether fully capitalist or otherwise, puts in a new perspective the formulation of human rights. The analysis of this situation in the work of, say, Amartya Sen, Thomas Pogge, Mike Davis, Göran Therborn or Nancy Fraser bears little or no direct relationship to the world of slaves and abolitionists, yet these authors employ the language of rights to which the anti-slavery movements contributed much – even if not all abolitionists subscribed to it.[50] Likewise David Harvey has written about the 'Right to the City', contrasting it with the social segregation promoted by the property speculators. While he evokes the Paris of Haussmann, a related point was being made by those who demanded 'public rights' in New Orleans in 1868.[51]

In the Introduction I cited Samuel Moyn's warning that the language of the 'rights of man' was the slogan of the rising nation-state and often presaged a violation of 'human rights' properly understood. I have noted many examples that could illustrate this contention. Yet I have also cited many cases of those arguing against slavery and racism appropriating the idea of rights, not infrequently improving it in the process. So there is a living tradition here that cannot be artificially arrested at some privileged moment that discloses its inner truth. Moyn urges that the UN General Declaration of Human Rights had only a modest immediate impact and that it was not until the 1970s that it suddenly acquired great resonance, in a wave of anti-Communism provoked by what seemed like dramatic Soviet gains. He shows that the term had often been used by the Catholic Church and had a distinctively conservative ring. But then, with the collapse of the Soviet Union, Moyn sees the cult of 'human rights' becoming 'the last utopia' championed by those whose God has failed. No doubt there is something to these various trackings of the itinerary of the concept, but they do not thereby discredit it. Abolitionism, as we have seen, was often evoked to obfuscate, and the same fate awaits all powerful ideas. The problem for me with Moyn's undoubtedly perceptive rereading is that he seems almost fearful of the increasingly ambitious agenda of rights. He intimates that it might harbour utopian excess. He believes that 'Instead of turning to history to

---

50   Amartya Sen, *Development as Freedom*, New York 1998; Thomas Pogge, *World Poverty and Human Rights*, New York 2003; Mike Davis, *Planet of Slums*, London 2005; Nancy Fraser, 'Reframing Justice in a Globalized World', *New Left Review*, 36 (November–December 2005): 69–88; Göran Therborn, *The Politics of Childhood: The Rights of Children in Modern Times*, Dartmouth 1993.

51   David Harvey, 'The Right to the City', *New Left Review* 53 (September-October 2008).

monumentalize human rights by rooting them deep in the past it is much better to acknowledge how recent and contingent they really are,'[52] and urges: 'it may not be too late to wonder whether the concept of human rights, and the movement around it, should restrict themselves to offering minimal constraints on representative politics, not a new form of maximal politics of their own.'[53] The history of abolition shows that a narrow approach to ending slavery usually proves misguided and unfortunate, allowing for the continuance or mutation of oppression and exploitation.

The history of slavery also poses an uncomfortable question. It required a horrendous destruction of indigenous peoples in the sixteenth century before some clerics, philosophers and administrators began to raise the alarm and enunciate some – very inadequate – protective principles inspired by the idea that the 'natives' were also human. Likewise it was not until many millions of Africans had been hauled to the New World, to experience one of the most exploitative regimes known to history, that there were stirrings of abolitionism in the metropolitan regions. Colonialism, militarism, war, racism and political persecution claimed at least 100 million victims in the first half of the twentieth century; the number would be much larger if account were taken of the millions more who died from famine and disease linked to war and civil strife.[54]

Does this grim record mean that it is only after terrible violation that basic human rights will be asserted? Are appalling disasters necessary to secure progress? The framers of the UN General Declaration were certainly aware of the terrible carnage that had wiped out some 70 million human beings, and they were seeking to offer a response to the widespread desire for a world without the terrible ravages that had just been experienced, and without the distempers and depression that had produced the war. Roosevelt's 'Four Freedoms' and the Soviet Constitution of 1936 – drafted by Bukharin not Stalin[55] – and the UN General Declaration reflected rather than created the longing for a very modest and attainable utopia, not the totalitarian vision and nightmare that seems still to transfix Samuel Moyn.

However, the reader of *The Last Utopia* can, by reading it against the grain as it were, discern that a current of African American racial egalitarianism

52   Samuel Moyn, *The Last Utopia: Human Rights in History*, Cambridge 2010, p. 225.

53   Moyn, *Last Utopia*, p. 227.

54   Millions of Africans died in the Congo of King Leopold in the 1890s and early 1900s. Some 10 million people died in the First World War, with maybe double that number dying from influenza in its aftermath. The Second World War brought 60 to 70 million deaths. The Nazi death squads and camps killed six million Jews. Large numbers of gypsies, communists, homosexuals and the disabled also perished. Russian losses totalled about 27 million. Chinese casualties from military action from the 1920s to 1945 ran to many millions, but were probably exceeded by the number of famine deaths. Some 2 million died as a result of the Bengal famine of 1942.

55   Stephen Cohen, *Bukharin and the Bolshevik Revolution: A Political Biography 1888–1938*, New York 1980, pp. 356–7. Gorbachev was later to claim Bukharin's legacy.

helped to shape a concept of human rights that cannot be reduced to the obfuscactions and cynicism of the Great Powers. Thus W. E. B. Du Bois helped to draft for the National Association for the Advancement of Colored People (NAACP) an 'Appeal to the World' which, as Moyn puts it, presented 'African American subordination as a human rights violation'.[56] Eleanor Roosevelt, a member of the council of the NAACP, was apprised of its content and worried that its well-documented accusations of racial oppression and violence would be exploited by Soviet propaganda. The document was formally submitted to the United Nations in October 1947 and was one of the impulses that led to the General Declaration. Du Bois saw the anti-colonial agenda and the demand for African American equality not as separate or rival enterprises but as compatible and mutually reinforcing. Without lessening his opposition to colonialism, he published an article arguing for 'Human Rights for All Minorities'. The strategy did not instantly succeed, but within little more than a decade it was helping to make possible an historic breakthrough. The alliance between anti-colonialism and human rights was an expansive formula that could be taken up in different ways by the South African Freedom Charter and Kwame Nkrumah, Martin Luther King and Malcolm X, the Student Non-violent Coordinating Committee (SNCC) and the Olympic Project for Human Rights.[57] Malcolm X explained: 'As long as it is civil rights this comes under the jurisdiction of Uncle Sam. But the United Nations has what's known as the charter of human rights . . . Civil rights means you're asking Uncle Sam to treat you right. Human rights are something that you were born with.' [58]

The history of slavery and abolition does not recommend either fatalistic or facile conclusions. At every point there were alternatives and eventually those alternatives were realized, albeit with many imperfections and much unfinished business. Atlantic capitalism gained global momentum partly by

---

56   Moyn, *Last Utopia*, p. 102.

57   The foregoing is all conceded by Moyn in a backhanded way that continually seeks to place anti-colonialism and anti-racism into separate universes, while still occasionally allowing some overlap, eg.: 'in a phenomenon as massive and complex as de-colonisation, the notion of human rights was not entirely absent' (p. 107). Carol Anderson, *Eyes Off the Prize* supplies a fascinating narrative of the African American contribution.

58   Quoted in Moyn, *Last Utopia*, p. 105. Moyn sees a gulf opening up between this African American take on human rights and the anti-totalitarian discourse of East European dissidents and Jimmy Carter. Obviously he has a point and rights talk – like any ideology – can serve different aims in different epochs. But the point can be exaggerated. I was present when Malcolm X met Nicholas Krasso, a Hungarian oppositionist, in London in 1964, and they managed to have a very interesting discussion on the differing, but not wholly discrepant, experiences of being black and a Muslim in the United States, a Jew in Nazi-aligned Hungary and a spokesman of the Budapest Workers Council as Stalinism reasserted itself. As for Jimmy Carter, his invocations of 'human rights' as president failed to prevent large-scale violations in Latin America and elsewhere. But his autobiography and later public career do qualify this picture; indeed *An Hour Before Daylight: Memories of a Rural Boyhood*, New York 2001, gives a very vivid account of the African American community in the pre–Second World War era and of its influence on him.

seizing young Africans and fertile acres in the New World. But the resulting slave systems proved highly vulnerable to the complex class struggles linking the plantation zone to the industrializing metropolitan regions. The broad legacy of anti-slavery struggles remains itself a resource in combating new oppressions and destructions. It should not be approached in the spirit of 'church history' as a search for saints or with the goal of monumentalizing the past. And the ambition must be neither maximalist nor minimalist, but rather adequate to the scope of the problems humanity faces.

Index

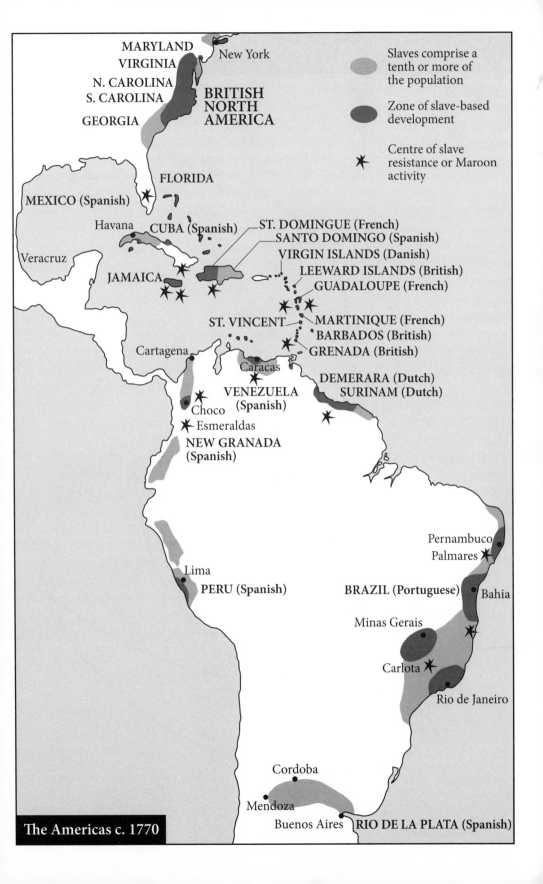

The Americas c. 1770

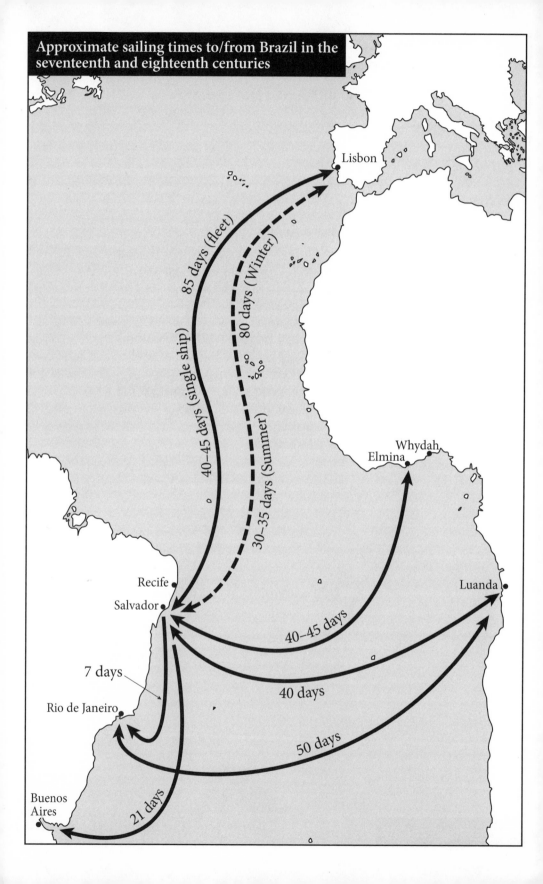

Approximate sailing times to/from Brazil in the
seventeenth and eighteenth centuries

Lisbon

85 days (fleet)

80 days (Winter)

40–45 days (single ship)

30–35 days (Summer)

Whydah
Elmina

Recife

Salvador

Luanda

40–45 days

7 days

40 days

Rio de Janeiro

50 days

Buenos
Aires

21 days

Latin America in 1830

MEXICO

Mexico
Veracruz

Atlantic
Ocean

SANTO DOMINGO
(occupied by Haiti 1822–44)

HAITI

CUBA
(Spanish)

PUERTO RICO (Spanish)

JAMAICA
(British)

TRINIDAD (British)

UNITED PROVINCES
OF CENTRAL AMERICA

Caracas
VENEZUELA

Bogotá
GRANADA

Quito
ECUADOR

EMPIRE
OF BRAZIL

Salvador
(Bahia)

Lima
PERU

La Paz
BOLIVIA
Sucre

Pacific
Ocean

PARAGUAY

Asunción

Rio de
Janeiro

CHILE

ARGENTINE
CONFEDERATION

Santiago

Buenos
Aires

URUGUAY
Montevideo

South
Atlantic
Ocean

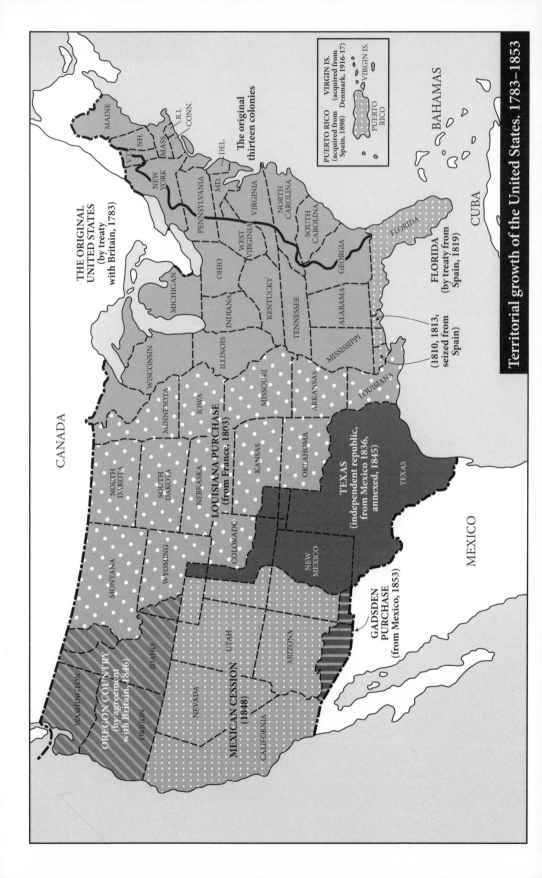

Territorial growth of the United States. 1783–1853